KOREA IN THE 21ST CENTURY

KOREA IN THE 21ST CENTURY

YANG TAEK LIM

Nova Science Publishers, Inc.
Huntington, New York

Editorial Production: Susan Boriotti
Office Manager: Annette Hellinger
Graphics: Frank Grucci and Jennifer Lucas
Information Editor: Tatiana Shohov
Book Production: Patrick Davin, Cathy DeGregory, Donna Dennis, Jennifer Kuenzig, and Lynette Van Helden
Circulation: Lisa DeGangi and Michael Pazy Mino

Library of Congress Cataloging-in-Publication Data
Lim, Yang-Taek
Korea in the 21st century / Yang Taek Lim.
p. cm.
Includes bibliographical references and index.
ISBN 1-56072-731-4
1. Korea--Economic conditions—1945- 2. Korea—Economic policy. 3. Korea—Politics and government.
I. Title. II. Title: Korea in the twenty-first century.
HC467.I448 1999 99-43353
338.95195—dc21 CIP

227 Main Street, Suite 100
Huntington, New York 11743
Tele. 631-424-6682Fax 631-424-4666
e-mail: Novascience@earthlink.net
e-mail: Novascil@aol.com
Web Site: http://www.nexusworld.com/nova

Printed in the United States of America

To my parents

CONTENTS

ACKNOWLEDGMENTS

The manuscript for this book has been developed in connection with many publications, papers and public speeches of mine for about twenty years of research and social activities since I came back, in 1979, to Korea from my doctoral study in the U.S.

In retrospect, one of the most valuable things to my academic life can be considered that I have been consecutively nominated as Outstanding Research Professor for 1997, 1998 and 1999 by Hangyang University. More happily, with this book I realized my long-cherished wish of mine to publish my book in English by such a well-known publisher as NOVA Science Publishers, Inc. I believe that this book be the most precious academic performance in my life, in many senses including the significance of the title of this book for Korea in the new century.

I would like to express my sincere appreciation to Mr. Frank Columbus, President and Editor-in-Chief of NOVA Science Publishers, Inc. for having provided me such a honorable opportunity to write this book. The preparation of this book required not only the author's endeavors but also the assistants' devotion and patience. My sincere thanks go to Mrs. Mi-jung Kim (Executive Officer of Economy & Investment Promotion Office, Kyonggi Provincial Government and also a doctoral student at the Department of Economics, Hanyang University) Ms. Joo-yeon Bae (Researcher at the Korea Institute of Socioeconomic Policy) and Mr. Kyeong Cheol Park (Graduate Student at the Department of Economics, Hanyang University) and Ms. Donna Dennis (Nova Science) for their unforgettable contributions to the preparatory and editorial work for this book.

January 2000
Yang-Taek Lim

PREFACE

Korea now stands at an important crossroads for national development and prosperity in the era of globalization. It is quite natural for a Korean to raise following questions:

> What trends will be evident in the global economic order of the 21st century? Will the US be able to maintain its economic dominance of the global economy? What will be the future choice of Japan in the on-going global trends? Will the international political and economic partner of Japan be the US or will it be China? Or will Japan opt for a more independent path? What will be the role of Japan in the 21st century?

The economic center of the world is moving from the Atlantic to the Pacific, from Europe and the US to Asia. Russia has already pronounced itself to be an 'Eurasia' and US has declared Asia to be a region of national interest. Japan has also returned to focussing on the region after attempting to break away from it.

What is a desirable direction for regional economic cooperation and joint prosperity in the region? Is the Mekong River an ideal economic cooperation zone? Or is the Tumen River a more optimal one? Why has progress for the TRADP (Tumen River Area Development Plan) been so slow despite the auspices of UNDP and the profound interest of ADB, the US, China, Japan, Russia, Mongolia, the two Koreas and European countries, not to mention various conferences which have already been held toward this end? What will be a more effective directive for the TRADP which will promote international industrial cooperation in the Northeast Asia region?

What political-military mechanisms will be required to support the sustained economic development of Asian countries? Even within the Asia-Pacific Rim, East Asia, particularly Northeast Asia is a key area in political, military and economic aspects. In particular, the national interests of four global powers (the US, China, Japan and Russia) collide in the Korean peninsula. What kind of collective security apparatus will be appropriate for this region in the coming era? What directives will ensure peace in the region while promoting industrial cooperation in a collaborative and complementary manner?

Which problem points out the economic development strategy of Asian countries have led to the recent financial crisis? If the crisis is indeed a product of erroneous development strategies, then which development model would be optimal one? What aspects of economic development, a primarily Western concept, contradict or complement to Asian traditions?

Japan, Korea, Taiwan and Thailand are all Asian nations. Why is Japan, the country with the largest trade surplus in the world, currently in the throes of an economic recession? Which factors was driven to the rapid downturn of Korea, which was often appraised as a successful model of economic development? How was Taiwan, with similarly scarce natural resources and a relatively weak domestic market, able to weather the financial crisis unscathed? Which factors had driven to the financial crisis in Thailand, which is one of the most open economies in the continent?

Korea had long been an envy of many developing countries, but was faced with the threat of a debt moratorium in November 1997. What are the causes of Korea's financial crisis? Is this crisis simply a contagion effect from the financial crisis in Southeast Asia? Was the crisis originated from the financial sector or the real sector? What is a more fundamental cause? Has the IMF Program for Korea's economic reform been successful so far? What are the complementary or counter-measures to it? What useful lessons, if any, can be drawn from Korea's economic policies and experiences over the past 40 years?

Now, what are the Korea's choice as it stands on the verge of the 21st century? What will be the governing values and objectives for the new century? What is the direction that it must take in order for its people not be regretful after 100 years? What will be its strategies towards this end?

It is at least fortunate that the Korean government has opted for capitalism and not socialism, democracy and not communism. The era of the ideologies has come to a close. In conjunction with the Korea's choice for the 21st century, the author proposes the four questions that need to be solved in the structural transition process as follows:

- First, how should Korea's future be shaped, *i.e.,* what will be its development strategy in the 21st century?
- Second, how should priorities be set in the distribution of resources to realize such a development strategy?
- Third, what are the practical roles of the government, enterprises and citizens to play pursue such a strategy efficiently?
- Last, how would a national consensus be democratically reached for such a strategy, setting of priorities and assignment of roles?

The author contends that there are three choices or objectives for Korea: first, domestically, a society that guarantees the greatest happiness for the greatest majority must be created based on humanitarian principles; second, a reunified nation must be constructed for Korean people; and lastly, Korea must take a leading role in the upcoming Asia-Pacific Age.

Will it be possible for Korea to achieve these aforementioned goals? The author foresees that other than national reunification, the other two goals of the greatest happiness for the greatest number and the assumption of a Korea's leading role in the Asia-Pacific Age are entirely possible through the efforts of the Korean people themselves.

The author shall attempt to answer about the previously-described issues, based on his many writings, especially *The People Perish Where There Is No Vision,*[1] *Prospects for Asian Economies in the 21st Century.*[2]

The main purpose of this study is to propose some strategies for Korea's survival and prosperity in the 21st century and draw possible lessons for the other developing countries, derived from the past economic development strategy and various reforms to solve the recent economic crisis.

Chapter II describes a historical perspective on the Korean economic development and derives some lessons from the Korean experience. Chapter III analyzes the development of the Korean economy with respect to its source of growth, development strategies, a new role for the government, and patterns of trade and industrial policy. Chapter IV describes weakening competitiveness, liberalization and downturn the Korean economy.

Chapter V analyzes the causes of Korea's financial crisis, evaluates the IMF bail-out and its program, and presents short and long-term prospects for the Korean economy. Chapter VI discusses financial sector reforms, monetary policy, foreign exchange policy, liberalization of capital account transactions, and corporate sector reforms. Chapter VII evaluates economic restructuring since the IMF bail-out and suggest some policy recommendations. Chapter VIII proposes a new economic development strategy for Korea in the 21st Century, in connection with structural problems of the Korean economy, a high technology-based economy, a new industrial policy, complementary relationship between big assembly enterprises and part manufacturing SMEs, a highly-efficient business organization and performance-based management, a flexible labor market, and liberalization for a higher competition and efficiency.

Chapter IX examines technological structure of Korea's manufacturing sector in connection with estimates of Schumpter and Schumpteterian hypotheses, the speed of technology diffusion and its determinants and technological gap between Korea and Japan: in case of the general machinery and electrical & electronic industries. Chapter X analyzes technology transfer to Korea with an emphasis on the role of foreign direct investment.

In the international context, Chapter XI suggests some industrial and technological cooperation of Korea with major countries: the US, Japan, China, and Russia in major industrial sectors including aerospace, maritime transportation, automobile, information, telecommunication and semiconductors.

In an attempt to discuss the national reunification issue, Chapter XII introduces South Korean Government's Policy on North Korea, especially in the Provision of Light Water Reactors to North Korea

---

[1] Yang-Taek Lim, *The People Perish Where There Is No Vision*, Seoul: Mail Economic Daily Press, Korea, September 1995.

[2] Yang-Taek Lim, *Prospect for Asian Economies in the 21st Century,* Seoul: Mail Economic Daily Press, January 1999.

and follows up the Four-Party Talks. Chapter XIII proposes a new model for Korean reunification based on a five-stage approach: 1) a preliminary normalization of relations, which then progressively moves on to 2) an with an emphasis on the proposed *Changdan* County Special Economic Zone, 3) social integration, 4) political integration and 5) military integration.

Chapter XIV discusses the current security status in Northeast Asia region including the US-Japan defense cooperation treaty, China's counter-measures, China and Russia's policics on North Korea and a new relationship between China and the two Koreas to maintain a multilateral security and cooperation system in the region, and proposes 'Northeast Asia Peace City' and its development plan in line with some historical examples of the world peace cities.

Chapter XV discusses globalization in Asia, particularly liberalization of tariffs, the prospects for APEC and the features of Northeast Asia, analyzes possibilities and obstacles for regional economic cooperation and suggests the future development directions with reference to TRADP (Tumen River Area Development Plan).

In an attempt to identify the role of Korea in the international society, Chapter XVI discusses multilateral cooperation in Asia with special reference to environment cooperation, energy cooperation and agricultural cooperation.

Finally, some concluding remarks shall be made in Chapter XVII.

Chapter I

OVERVIEW ON THE GLOBAL ECONOMIC ORDER IN THE 21ST CENTURY[3]

1. INTRODUCTION

Mankind now stands at the doorsteps of the 21st century. In retrospect, the 20th century has been filled with numerous conflicts among the nations and ethnic groups. For example, the First (1914~1918) and Second (1939~1945) World Wars were broken out in the 21st century and the world had divided into the Western and Eastern blocs, with the US-Japan-South Korea alliance in confrontation with the China-USSR-North Korea alliance in the East Asia region.

At the end of World War II (September 1939 ~ May 1945), the world was formed into a 'tight bipolar system' with the United States and the Soviet Union forming mutually exclusive and competitive military and political bipolars in the world order. However, the emergence of the non-allied 'Third World' in 1960s and America's defeat in the Vietnam War in the early 1970s transferred the international order into a 'loose bipolar system'. The Cold War system rapidly weakened in the middle of the 1980s as its turning point. This was mainly due to the fact that the national capacities of both the US and the Soviet Union had debilitated.

The structural recession and fall in productivity since the early 1970s in the Soviet Union propagated the dysfunction of the economy into the whole society, and acted as a centrifugal force on the Soviet political regime. In addition, the movement towards democratization in East Europe that started in the early 1980s became a challenge to the leadership of the Soviet Union. Since Gorbachev opted for reform and liberalization policies in the Vladivostok Declaration of the Pacific Doctrine in July 1986, the world has been again undergoing rapid changes, as the rationale for the Cold War that dominated the world history for the past half century has been replaced by a new world order. Gorbachev's *Perestroika* and *Glasnost* in 1988 were efforts to amend the internal contradictions and problems of the Soviet empire at such a time, and the 'New Thinking' diplomacy was an outwards extension of these internal reform policies.

Beginning with the dismantling of the Berlin Wall in 1989, Communist regimes of the Eastern Bloc crumbled one by one, and socialist planned economies were abandoned. In December of the same year, the US and the USSR held a summit meeting in Malta for a joint and official declaration of the end to the Cold War, which had lasted for 45 years since the Yalta Conference in 1945, between the same two principals. One of the symbols of the Cold War, the division between East and West Germany, ceased to exist with the reunification of the German people in October 1990, although the division between South and North Korea unfortunately survives as the lone remainder of ideological confrontation.

The global power structure is being transformed from a bipolar order centered around the US and the USSR to one based on diverse nations and blocs of power such as the US, China, Japan, the European Community and Russia under a single umbrella. By region, the world order in years to come is likely to be characterized by the formation of a European economic bloc as the COMECON is integrated with the EU, the emergence of an Asia-Pacific bloc with China and Russia and individual countries such as the US, China, Japan and Russia trying to secure leverage. This order will further diminish the importance of political ideology while intensifying hegemony in the form of economic interests of nations and blocs.

[3] This Chapter was heavily derived from the author's recent book: Yang-Taek Lim, *Prospect for Asian Economies in the 21st Century,* Seoul: Mail Economic Daily Press, January 1999.

What trends will be evident in the global economic order of the 21st century? This question is the main issue to be discussed in this Chapter.

2. New Round in the Era of WTO

The end of the Cold War has meant that 'military warfare' has been replaced by 'economic welfare', as the UR was at the end negotiated (December 1993) and officially signed (April 1994) as thus the new rule of the game under the leadership of the US and thus the WTO era was launched. Accordingly, unlimited competition under the auspices of the WTO has been gradually established as the standard for a new economic order to follow the one under GATT.

The so-called New Round is being pursued in the aftermath of successful negotiations with the UR. Whereas the UR negotiations sought to promote unlimited competition by tearing down trade barriers between nations, the New Round seeks to build a fair trade order by encouraging transparency in policies relating to such fields as the environment, labor, technology, competition and investment.

The five fields involved are still grey areas in the UR and are intimately inter-related. In other words, the manufacturer must produce without outside help (technological policy), employ laborers in a appropriate working environment (labor policy) and produce a commodity which is not harmful to the environment (environmental policy). Products to cross borders must be guaranteed conditions which allow for fair competition against local products (competition policy), while regulations inhibiting direct investment for production and distribution must be loosened (investment policy). Developing countries which are unable to reform existing corporate organization, industrial structure and governmental policies, customs and practices to level the playing field to the extent of advanced countries will be penalized.

In particular, the core of the environment round is the complementation of economic development with environmental conservation. Developing countries feel that it is unfair for advanced countries, who have exploited the earth's resources to their benefit in the past, to suddenly now recognize the importance of conservation. Such complaints, however, do not help in alleviating the environmental problems currently threatening the world. In looking at the trade deficit of the world's largest trading nation, the US, costs relating to the environment and pollution control can be seen to have had a tremendously adverse effect.

The technology round reflects this trend of advanced countries toward protecting of their technologies and intellectual property rights. Such a trend represents a big concern for Asian companies who have previously developed new products with the aid of imported technologies.

The labor round aims to establish guidelines for internationally accepted labor standards and allow for trade sanctions against products manufactured and exported by non-compliant countries. Due to the strong objections by developing countries, however, it is unclear whether it will be selected as an issue to be tackled by the WTO system. Still, Asian countries will have to implement systematic apparatuses to promote management-labor relations and enhance laborers' rights to keep pace with economic growth such as the social charters in European countries.

The rationale behind the competition round is that the customs and practices of an individual country's market structure and corporate organization can become causes for trade friction in an era of globalization, where products and capital should be allowed to move freely.

Another aim of the OECD is the liberalization of investments, which seeks to minimize and ultimately eliminate interference (laws, administrative regulations and practices) by governments imposed to direct investments. The greatest significance of OECD's multilateral agreement on investment is the formulation of rules which reflect recent trends in international investment. The present governing rules are grossly inadequate to cope with current changes. In particular, distorted measures and regulations remain as obstacles to progress despite significant liberalization. There is a need to do away with such regulations and improve the global environment for investment.

The OECD has also promoted the implementation of international rules to determine links in trade and investment with corruption. The rules are the result of recognizing the fact that bribery of foreign officials by multi-national corporations was the direct cause of not only corruption, but also unfair competition.

In 1977, the ICC issued a Report on Extortion and Bribery in business transactions. This broke new ground in calling for complementary and mutually supportive action by governments, intergovernmental bodies and the business community to combat extortion and bribery in international trade. The Report aroused interest in intergovernmental fora, such as the OECD and the UN Commission on Transnational Corporations. Moreover, corporations in a number of countries were prompted to establish or strengthen their internal rules of fair practices, taking as a model the Rules of Conduct for enterprises which were set forth in Part III of the 1977 Report.

The US in particular has enacted a Foreign Corrupt Practices Act (1977) to legislate bribery and is actively seeking the legislation of a similar, binding international agreement through the OECD so that American companies will not be at a competitive disadvantage. It is also seeking to institute principles of transparency, openness and due process as criteria for participation in bids in accordance with the WTO's agreement concerning government procurement (effective on January 1997). The EU is also in the process of enacting a corruption prevention legislation.

Today, the importance of effectively combating extortion and bribery is greater than ever. In the early 1990s, scandals involving extortion and bribery were a significant factor in toppling governments in many parts of the world. This situation, if allowed to continue, could undermine the most promising development of the post Cold-war era, *i.e.,* the spread of democratic governments and of market economies worldwide. It is all the more unacceptable in view of the liberalization of world trade in goods and services achieved through the UR: free trade must be matched by fair competition, failing which trading relations will be increasingly strained to the common detriment of governments and enterprises. In addition to being a crime, offering or giving bribes may constitute acts of unfair competition, which could give rise to actions for damages.

Against this background, the ICC, as the leading world business organization, decided in 1994 to review its 1977 Report and set up for this purpose an Ad Hoc Committee under the chairmanship of Mr. Francois Vincke (Belgium), Secretary General of Petrofina. The updated Report, which the ICC now presents, confirms the basic approach recommended initially, *i.e.,* the need for action by international organizations, governments and enterprises, both nationally and internationally, to meet the challenging goal of greater transparency in international trade.

Major responsibility in this area undoubtedly rests with governments, as has been recognised by the OECD, the Council of Europe, and UNCTAD. Part II of the Report accordingly urges all governments to demonstrate their political will to implement promptly the May 1994 OECD Recommendation on Bribery in International Business Transactions. The ICC considers it particularly important that the OECD Recommendation be implemented by all countries, including the developing countries.

To this end, the ICC recommends that the OECD establish close liaison with the WTO, in order to further understanding of problems associated with extortion and bribery and encourage acceptance of the principles of the 1994 OECD Recommendation by non-OECD member countries.

It is against this backdrop that Asian countries were attempting to adjust to the new world trade order (UR/WTO), as their efforts were reflected in the Bogor Declaration (November 1994) and the Osaka Action Directive (November 1995).

The writer believes that prospects for Asian economies are bright. The main reason is that Asia is a good market for the US and the EU. The collapse of the Asian economy would result in decrease in Asian demands for American and European products → accumulation of inventory in the US and the EU → rise in unemployment in the two continents → industrial collapse of the West. The grounds for such an optimistic prospect, in spite of the recent economic crisis situation, may be found in the concentration of direct and indirect investments by Great Britain, Germany, France and the US in the region, especially in the areas of aerospace, port and maritime transportation, automobiles and information-telecommunication.

Since the Asian financial crisis, investments by Western nations have shown the following tendencies. Investments into existing targets in the Southeast Asia have been reduced, and new target countries have been sought. Investments into China are making up a majority of investments into the region. Recent measures by the Korean government to induce direct investments have also attracted the interest of Western investors. In his economic report for 1997, President Clinton emphasized the need for expanded investments into Asia, and pointed to Asia as the optimal region for investments in the next 5 years.

Judging from the interest shown by European countries in the 1998 ASEM Conference, Asia has definitely become an important market for Europe. Great Britain, France and Germany have established policy to stimulate exports and have conducted active sales-diplomatic activities including visits to and from Asia while seeking to support entry into the region through the establishment of trade and investment organizations and hosting seminars and trade fairs.

In the case of Great Britain, the subject has become a priority since the establishment of a NICs bureau within the Department of Trade and Industry and the announcement of an export promotion policy (May 1993) titled 'The Future of British Manufacturing' which outlines directives for expanding exports to some 80 trade partners.

In the case of France, policy towards Asia has been stepped up with the announcement of "Directives for the Promotion of Exports to the Asia-Pacific" which followed President Miterrand's visits to Indochina and normalization of diplomatic relations with China. France then followed with export promotion policies with the goal of increasing the weight of Asia in its exports up to 10% within 5 years.

It is true that since the Asian financial crisis, the inflow from the West into Asia has slowed down. However, the inflow will not cease in the foreseeable future since Asia continues to be a growing market. The reason is that Asia has further demand for the construction of huge infrastructure and thus still keeps high investment potential. Moreover, positive conditions as production bases and consumption markets will be maintained based on its low wages, savings in production costs and market expansion owing to rapid growth.

At the same time, it is true that as human rights, labor and environmental issues remain as obstacles as Western nations attempt to advance into such countries as Indonesia, China and Myanmar. In spite of such obstacles, the trend toward more open and liberalized trade and investment in Asia and atmosphere of cooperation formed by ASEM will further strengthen prospects of this region.

3. The Current Status of Major Players

What will be the salient trends in the current status of major players in the region including the US, Japan, China and Russia?

A. The United States

First of all, the US is generally expected to continue as the dominant global power political, military and economic power. What factors did it enable to regain its competitiveness and what are the recent trends? While the US regained its economic power in the 1990s after a period of decline and restructuring in the 1980s, its recent trend of relative strength in the financial sector over the real sector gives rise to concerns that it is too susceptible to the perils of a bubble economy. Will the US be able to overcome the weaknesses of such an imbalance? Will the US be able to maintain its economic dominance in the global economy? If the worst case scenario materializes, would Asia be able to weather the current crisis on its own? Will a global depression recur?

The logical beginning point on the US's fall and rise should be back to the currency crisis of the US dollars in 1973. The crisis was triggered by the Nixon administration's emergency economic measure of abandoning the gold standard in 1971 and a transformation to a floating exchange rate system from a fixed one in 1973. The crisis led to the demise of the IMF-GATT system and a new global economic order based on the three major economic powers (the US, Japan and Western Europe).

The US economy, however, broke out of a sustained recession by late 1990 and has demonstrated a stable growth since then as the country re-established its dominance in the global economy. The current account deficit was greatly reduced while productivity and competitiveness of its manufacturing sector was considerably enhanced. According to recent reports by the IMD Research Institute of Switzerland, the US regained the top spot in the world in competitiveness between 1995 and 1997. Especially worth noting is the fact that the US outclasses rival countries in high-tech industries such as information technology, aerospace, data processing equipment and biotechnology.

What then, were the factors which enabled the US to regain its competitiveness so rapidly in the 1990s? Major factors include managerial reforms aimed at building corporate flexibility following the abandonment of government regulations, and the development of new technologies-industries based on entrepreneurship, creativity and innovation.

The US had in the 1970s and 1980s deteriorated into a second-class economy under the double strain of deficits in both trade and its current account and other major economic indicators. The American response was to focus efforts on enhancing competitiveness. In particular, efforts were directed at building an information society, as evidenced by the rising proportion of information-related investments (from 27% in 1980 to 34% in 1995) in total capital expenditures. As a result, the country came to possess the world's first super information highway and through the worldwide spread of the internet, it has become the center of production, storage and distribution of information. The US governmental organizations and private-sector enterprises are sharply enhancing efficiency by on-line sharing of information, which maximizes the benefits of a connected economy.

More recently, however, the US has shown signs of instability as the strength of the financial sector over the real economy (manufacturing and services sector) has become more pronounced. Indicators of such weakness include trade deficits, the slowing of industrial production, declines in labor productivity and deterioration of corporate profits. The trade deficit reached a record US$14.5 billion for the month of April 1998 and was attributable to the decrease in prices of imports and a corresponding rise in their consumption. This trend is expected to intensify with the Asian financial crisis.

While the US is geographically distanced from the East Asia, its impact on the region is huge. For example, Japan's economic boom in 1980s was ignited and fuelled by American aid. The US has a huge consumer market as the world's largest economy and a significant portion of its imports come from East Asia. Japan, Korea, Taiwan and other East Asian-countries ranked the US have as their main trading partner. The US has also provided these countries with capital and advanced technologies.

Therefore, the US must correct the weaknesses in the imbalance between its financial and manufacturing-services sector and oversee the restructuring of the global economy as its leader, for its own national interest as well as that of the world as a whole.

The primary role of the US in the resolution of the on-going Asian financial crisis will primarily lie in its private sector and the desirable path will be for its enterprises to seek expansion into Asia through mergers and investments. Asian governments have recently promoted favorable measures for the inducement of foreign investment and thus the timing is presently optimal.

Northeast Asia and the US are important partners in a variety of issues, with the US being both an important export market for Northeast Asia and a provider of capital and services. Trade volumes between the two have more than doubled over the past 10 years, and investment flows have greatly contributed to both Northeast Asian and American economies. *Levi Strauss, Coca Cola, Kodak,* and *IBM* already made investment into China, while American financial institutions such as the *Travellers' Group, Merrill Lynch,* and *GE Capital* have been actively seeking entry into the Japanese market through acquisitions.

B. Japan

What will be the future choice of Japan in the on-going global trends? Will the international political and economic partner of Japan be the US or will it be China? Or will Japan opt for a more independent path? What will be the role of Japan in the 21st century? What is the role of Japan in the resolution of the on-going Asian financial crisis and economic development in the region?

Japan was able to become a regional power through the Sino-Japanese War (August 1894~March 1895), then grow into a global power with the Russo-Japanese War (February 1904~September 1905), enter the Chinese market thanks to the effects of World War I (1914~1918), establish itself as a democracy after being defeated in World War II (1939~1945), revamp its industrial structure in response to the Oil Shock of the 1970s and adjust its economy to the high-Yen pressure of the 1980s. There had been active debates in the course of its economic development: in the 1950s as to whether the economic development strategy would be centered on the domestic or overseas markets; in the 1960s concerning liberalization; in the 1970s regarding limitations to growth; and in the 1980s as to what kind of contribution Japan should make to the international society. In this manner, Japan has seriously thought about national survival, external pressures and national development strategy and policy over the past 40 years or so.

The Japanese economy grew at a rapid rate during the 1950s and 1960s, thanks to the following main driving factors: while most of Japan's industrial machinery was destroyed after defeat in World War II, it maintained most of its human capital from the Meiji dynasty; economic policies such as agrarian reform, dismantling of large conglomerates and enactment of labor laws were implemented immediately after World War II; factors relating to labor included management-labor cooperation, high education level and skilled manpower, active management and technological innovation by entrepreneurs and superior government officials; intercomplementary market function and government planning; a high savings rate leading banks' credit support for corporate sector; and, domestic political and social stability, minimal defense expenditures and a peaceful international environment also contributed.

In the 1980s, Japan experienced a recession relating to a strengthening Yen and the background to which was as follows. US imports were rising sharply as a result of the *Reagan* administration's strong US dollar policy with the trade deficit reaching US$130 billion. Japan implemented voluntary programs to restrict exports and boost imports by expanding the domestic economy as part of efforts to curb the US trade deficit, but the need for exchange rate adjustments became clear as such efforts failed to yield results.

However, Japan was able to overcome these adverse effects through management rationalization and technological innovation. By 1987, the Japanese economy had returned to a boom period. Corporate managers shared an optimistic view for the economy and made capital investments actively. The thing to note here is that the expansion of the money supply, which was one of the policies implemented to counter the effects of the appreciating Yen, caused a bubble to rise, which became the thorn of the Japanese economy, dropping it into the current state of extended recession.

As shown by <Figure I-1>, the bubble phenomenon may be explained by the following chain of events. strong Yen → fall in import prices due to declines in imported raw material prices → fall of wholesale prices to post-World War → levels → decreases in corporate inventory levels → improved corporate cash flow → increasing investment in stocks and real estate → sharp rise in asset value → realization of "bubble" gains due to inflation → easing of corporate access to funds → active engagement in 'money games'

<Figure I - 1 >Causes of the Japanese Bubble Economy

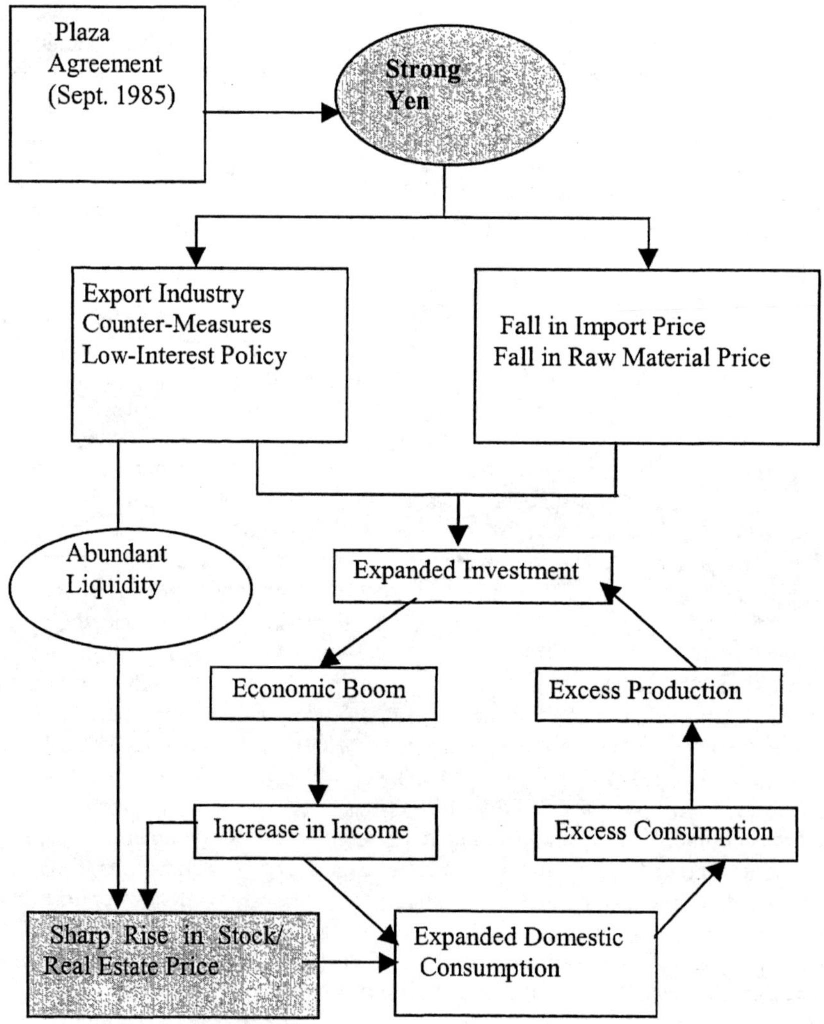

Japan's strategy to overcome the recession may be divided into short-term, medium-term and long-term for the sake of convenience. The main short-term strategy is cost reduction. The reduction of component parts, manufacture of smaller parts, development of light-weighted parts, shortening and improvement of processes, stimulation of demand and reduction of parts-raw material purchase prices are small examples. More broad examples include divestment- disposal of low-profit businesses, reduction of fixed costs through streamlining (personnel, inventory, plant and equipment) and strengthening of marketing activities to promote domestic demand.

The examples of medium-term strategy are strengthening of out-sourcing, expansion of offshore production activities, development of new products through active R&D, development of new businesses, endowment of high value-added to businesses and products, formation of strategic alliances, reforms in corporate culture and efforts to enhance technology.

The core of the long-term strategy is industrial restructuring. Japan had historically overcome recessions and fuelled growth by this strategy. Heavy and chemicals industries provided the base for high growth in the 1950s and 1960s. After the First Oil Shock in 1973, the country's energy-intensive industrial structure was transformed into an energy-saving one. After the Second Oil Shock of the late 1970s, the electronic revolution and movement towards the service sector was conducted simultaneously, as an industrial structure based on lightweight, miniature and energy-efficient products was established.

In this manner, the restructuring periods had helped the Japanese economy adjust successfully and swiftly to internal and external changes and strengthened competitiveness. Japan was thus able to sustain its economic growth and sizable trade surplus in spite of the strong Yen.

Japanese economy has been recently struggling with an extended recession *i.e.* a period of recession caused not only by cyclical recession due to excess investment but also by deflation mainly due to plummeting asset value. Since the burst of the bubble economy in 1993, corporate investment has been curbed by slowing activity, declines in profitability, sluggish investment and consumption due to losses in asset value and rises in non-performing loans at banks in line with the decline in asset and collateral value.

Economic crises of the past had been overcome with little difficulty with appropriate policies by the government, commitments by companies to raise competitiveness and improvements in the global economy. For the present recession caused by the strong Yen and the bursting of the bubble, however, there are various obstacles to overcome. The limitations of government policy, sluggish domestic demand and asset deflation have all resulted in an extended recession.

Table I-1 Japanese Corporate Strategies Against the Extended Recession

- Japanese companies are also implementing streamlining as a counter-measure against recession and for the future development.
- Restructuring has been evident. Efforts include the creation of new businesses through innovation of existing businesses and the development of new fields as a stepping stone into the 21st century.
- Re-engineering efforts are also noticeable.
- Strategic imitation or bench-marking is also being conducted.
- Efforts are being made to endow corporate flexibility and to imbue an active corporate culture.
- Companies and business divisions are being formed within companies to promote specialization.
- Domestic and overseas business sites are being integrated or re-organized.
- Management has returned to basics.
- Emphasis is being placed on product innovation, process innovation and mind innovation.
- The concept of collaboration has been introduced to corporate innovation.
- Focus is being placed on the establishment of a management system based on concepts.
- Marketing activities are being strengthened.
- Strategic alliances are being actively pursued.
- Personnel management systems based on ability, as opposed to seniority, are being implemented.
- There have been movements to exploit economies of network.

Source: Yang-Taek Lim, *Prospects for Asian Economies,* Seoul: Maeil Economic Daily Press, January 1999.

In the real economy, business fixed investment in November 1998, declined under increasingly severe conditions for fund-raising. Housing investment and private consumption have also declined further. With this weak demand, production has been reduced substantially. As a result, inventories are decreasing, but the recent recovery of the inventory / shipment is not expected to persist in the long run. The improvement of the inventory / shipment ratio mainly stems from the recovery in the automobile industry. However, domestic and other Asian countries' automobile demand is expected to weaken. This will in turn lead to the overall stagnation of shipments. With this decline in expenditures and production, corporate profits will continue to worsen, resulting in employees' income decreasing.

It is notable that the export promotion policy of the Japanese government described above aggravated the trade deficit of Southeast Asian countries and became a cause of the financial crisis in the region. Furthermore, instead of implementing fundamental solutions such as restructuring the financial sector, the government tried to survive the recession by injecting funds into financial institutions riddled with non-performing assets.

This was another cause of Southeast Asia's financial crisis. As their asset value declined, Japanese financial institutions refrained from making loans both at home and abroad, and added fuel to the fire by demanding early repayment of credit facilities which they had indiscriminately dispensed earlier. Japanese financial institutions had tried to make up for their losses at home by obtaining wide spreads on credit facilities extended in Southeast Asia. The MITI and the Bank of Japan were silent accomplices. In order to increase the lending limits of the financial institutions, they allowed for gains in book value on stocks and bonds to be counted towards equity.

Meanwhile, as the Yen weakened, Japanese companies reduced exports to the US via Southeast Asia, whereas increased the level of direct exports. At the same time, as companies in Southeast Asia became unprofitable due to inflation resulting from rises in wages and stock value such as happened in Thailand, the flight of Japanese capital from the region gained momentum.

The clearest example of Japan's responsibility in Southeast Asia is the concentration of short-term, speculative funds aimed at capital gains in the region. Japanese financial institutions were attracted to the region by liberalization in the stock and bond markets and the appreciating currencies, and became active in short-term investments such as stocks and bonds of local companies and financial institutions. It was logical for them to concentrate their investments in the region in 1994, when the Yen was strong, interest rates low and the stock market sluggish back home. At that time, such factors as market opening and an appreciating currency made such markets as Thailand attractive to foreign investors.

There was even competition among Japanese institutions to raise market shares in these countries and loan portfolios were increased in size as a means of obtaining a greater number of licenses for business sites. The number of branches of Japanese financial institutions in Asia as of June 1997 stood at 422, far exceeding the 244 branches in the North America region. The loan portfolio of these institutions in Southeast Asia also saw an exponential rise from US$ 40 billion in 1994 to over US$ 260 billion in 1996, which was over 4 times of the loan portfolio of American institutions to the region and by far the largest among advanced countries.

Japanese financial institutions also intensified investments into golf resorts, hotels and other real estate, made possible by connection with the privileged class. Even local entrepreneurs were encouraged by the inflow of Japanese money to speculate in real estate assets with short-term funds.

What then, is the role of Japan in the resolution of the on-going Asian economic crisis and future economic development in the region? Considering the interdependence of the Japanese and the other Asian economies (see <Figure I-2>), Japan has the most important role in the resolution of the on-going Asian economic crisis. Just as Japan is now once again emphasizing its return to Asia, it must conduct a role which befits its responsibility in the recent crisis, if only partly as compensation for its past aggressions. It must show a commitment to economic development in the region, similar to the role played by Germany within the EU, and it must show it in concrete form in the near future.

Japan must rid itself of the chronic misconception that 'exports are all good and domestic consumption all bad', reflect on the paradox of being the nation with the largest trade surplus in the world yet in the midst of an extended recession and realize that only a true partnership with the other countries of the region will bring about constructive development. In particular, Japan must recognize its responsibility in Southeast Asian financial crisis and direct the following efforts towards the recovery of the regional economy.

<Figure I-2> The Interdependence of the Japanese and the other Asian Economies

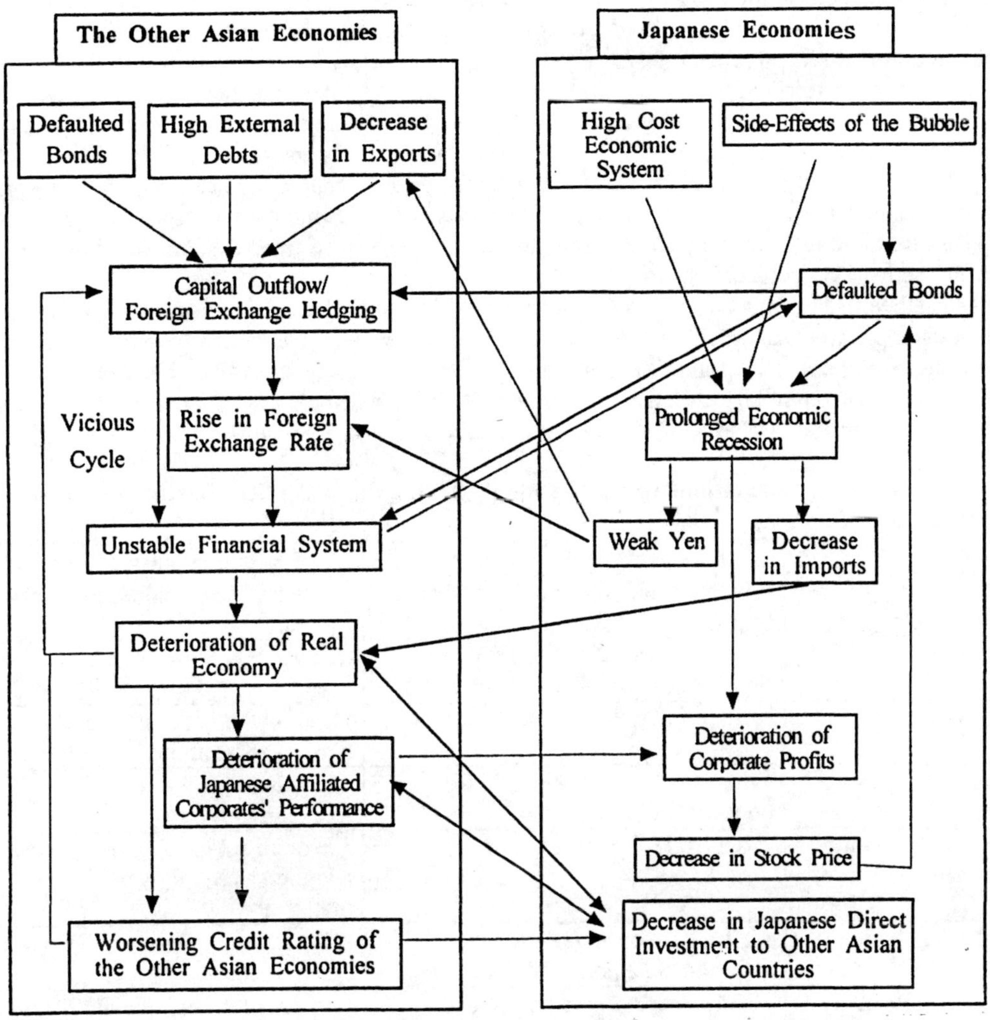

First, the country must realize the impact of its domestic consumption on the regional economy and pursue a policy of stimulating domestic demand rather than a contractionary policy aimed at budgetary balance. As of 1997, Asia remained as major trading partner of Japan, accounting for 42% of Japanese exports and 35% of its imports. Thus the effect of stimulating the domestic economy of Japan is expected to play a large role in the alleviation of the current crisis.

Second, Japanese companies must push ahead vigorous restructuring. In the past, Japanese companies countered the strong Yen by moving production base to offshore to cut costs and sustain the outward orientation of export-driven growth. While such measures helped secure competitiveness, they could not bring about fundamental changes in the internal financial structure of companies. Without responding to the factors of rising costs with fundamental changes, corporate competitiveness has been eroded through higher wages and costs as the widening of the trade surplus keeps the Yen strong. An escape from this vicious cycle must be attempted by restructuring in which unprofitable businesses are divested.

Third, Japan must pursue stability in its financial sector through fundamental policy changes. Financial instability may be alleviated by loosening regulations and reducing the taxpayers' burden to restore the market function of the sector.

Fourth, Japan must show greater commitment to the resolution of the on-going economic crisis, if only as compensation for the errors of its past. The huge trade surplus which it amassed prior to the crisis must be used for Asia, where Japan was able to secure raw materials and production bases at low costs. After all, they will be the ones to benefit the most from reciprocity.

C. China

China has emerged on the scene after many dormant years with Deng Xiaopeng's reform and open-door policies. It is expected for China to join the ranks of economic superpowers by 2020 after undergoing processes involving rural and urban reform, restructuring and a further round of reform and liberalization.

China's economic reform process may be divided into 4 stages: the first stage in 1978~1984, agrarian reform; the second stage in 1984~1988, reform of urban economy; the third stage in 1988~1991, restructuring; and the fourth stage after 1992, intensification of reforms and liberalization.

In 1979, China permitted trade business for manufacturing companies after reforming the previous monopolistic trade system. As a result, exports and imports have grown continuously at an annual average of 16%. Despite these reforms, however, there still remains a managed trade system, so China faces such requirements as market opening.

China has been discussing conditions for joining the WTO during the administrative conference since submitting its application to GATT in 1986. Since the UR agreement, China has been trying to enter the GATT by alleviating import restrictions, reforming its foreign exchange system and additional reductions in tariffs. It was not possible for China to enter the WTO, however, because it failed to join the UR agreement for service and discharge of obligations in intellectual property rights.

<Table I-2> Major Issues in China's joining the WTO Membership

Category	Requirements of Western Countries	Requirements of China
International trade company rights	- Endow trade rights to all companies by 1998	- Free trade accomplished by stages by year 2000
Tariff	- Each nations submit the list of Proposed low tariffs to China	- Under negotiation
Non-tariff barriers	- Abolition of the non-tariff barrier	- Submit the list of non-tariffs barriers to be abolished
Industrial policy	- Abolition of protectionism for domestic companies	- Regulations required for weakening industries.
Regulation on quantity of imported goods	- Removal of the regulations	- Require submission list and adoption as MFN by the United States
Special safeguards	- In the case of increasing imports, safeguards are permissible to impose	- Object to discriminative management against China
Obligatory performance period	- Time of opening to be decided by bilateral negotiations	- Negotiations on opening period to be postponed

Source: Yang-Taek Lim, *Prospects for Asian Economies,* Seoul: Maeil Economic Daily Press, January 1999.

<Table I-2> summarizes the major issues in China's WTO membership. The US has been serious about its deficit in trade balance with China, protection of intellectual property rights in China and its market opening. China could not give up the extension of its MFN (most favored nation) status and the US stuck to its policy that China should open its economy after joining the WTO. China promoted reduction in tariffs, alleviated non-tariff barriers and simplified the exchange rate. At the start of the WTO, China obtained an observer status under the assistance of Japan and the EU, and plans to reduce tariffs on 4,000 items to 23% by 2000. At the first WTO cabinet conference in 1996, a member of the WTO insisted that China, Taiwan and Russia expand markets and supported early entry on that condition.

China may not be able to achieve high growth as before[4], so there may not be any other than to devaluate the currency value of Yuan to solve the bottleneck of China's exports and a slowdown in foreign investment to China, in spite of the negative position of the Chinese government for the devaluation of Yuan.

[4] After 1992, Chinese growth was fell from the 10% level. 1996 growth was 9.7% as growth was suppressed for a soft landing. The growth rate fell to 8.8% in 1997, 7.0% in 1998, and the growth rate for 1999 is expected to show 3.8% by DRI or 8.1% according to WEFA. If the Chinese growth rate falls below 8%, a huge unemployed population (about 11~13 millions in urban cities) might cause a serious social problem.

<Figure I-3> Expected Effects of the Yuan Devaluation on the Chinese Economy

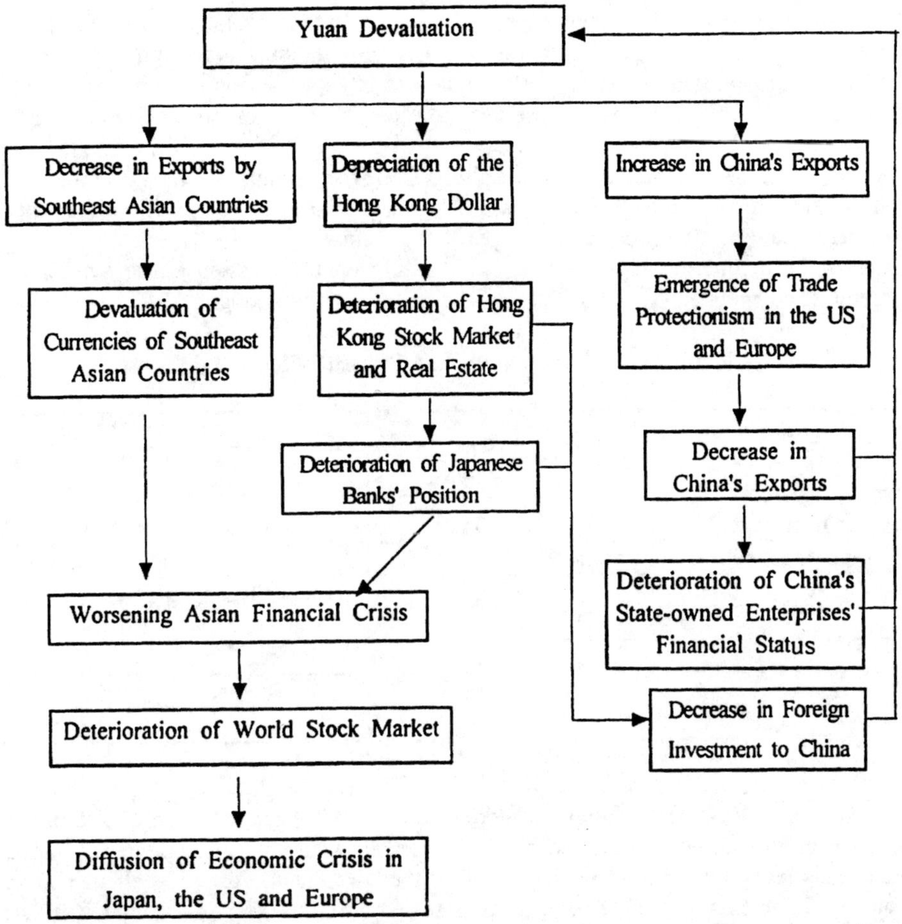

There is also a skepticism about the Chinese government's action for the Yuan devaluation, because it may neither help China to further execute its restructuring nor improve market conditions for foreign investments, although it may affect positively China's exports in the short run. At the same time, the Yuan devaluation may cause inflation and social instability and make the Chinese economy difficult to land softly. Externally, the Yuan devaluation may result in surpluses in trade balance with the US and consequently cause trade conflicts with the US.

Deng Xiaopeng has set forth three tasks for China: first, the fight against power hegemony; second, the national re-unification; and lastly, the modernization of the Chinese society. While China is earnestly pursuing reforms for its modernization, it must also address internal issues such as it loss of motivation by the system of private farming and enterprises which led economic growth after China's market opening, and the slow speed of the privatization of enterprises. It must also address external issues such as its increased influence threatening neighboring countries, frictions with the West concerning human rights issues and an increase of military expenditures, which often calls for a balance between the demand of the military and diplomatic desires for international peace.

D. Russia

The USSR and its socialist system experienced instability beginning the reform and liberalization policies of Gorbachev in 1986 until the Union of Soviet Socialist Republics were finally broken up in September 1991. President Yeltsin of Russia has followed in his predecessor's footsteps with greater intensity, but was forced to declare a moratorium on August 17, 1998 as the inefficiencies and side effects of 70 years of socialist rule could not be overcome. Since then the value of the Ruble currency has sharply decreased and prices of domestic commodities has swiftly increased. The Russian growth rate for 1998 is forecasted to be -5.0% and the rate for 1999 is also predicated to record -4.0%.

For the causes of Russia's moratorium, there are three factors to consider: one is the shortage of foreign exchange reserves (especially US dollar) compared its huge amounts of foreign debts. The total foreign debts of the Russian governmental sector in 1998 recorded US$143 billion including the short-term loan of US$60 billion. Russia's foreign exchange reserves, however, showed a mere US$16 billion as of February 1998.

The second is the heavy foreign debts resulting from the cumulative fiscal deficits of the Russian government, which is mainly due to the decrease of raw material price (especially oil) in the international market, the world financial crisis and the shortage of tax revenue.

The third is the degrading of foreigners' credit rating on the Russian economy. This is due to the retarded structural reform in Russia's tax system, foreign investment and land.

< Table I-3 > Russia's Foreign Debts (billion US dollars)

Governmental Sector		**Private Sector**	
The Soviet Union's Foreign Debts		Firms	15
Public Loan (Paris Club)	55		
Commercial Loan (London Club)	38	Banks	15
Russian Government's Foreign Debts			
Public Loan	24	Direct Investments	11
Euro Bond	16		
GKO/OFZ	10		
Subtotal	143	Subtotal	41
Total	**184**		

Source: IET. *Russian Economic Trends,* April 1998.

Recent reforms in Russia's economic systems have been concentrated on abolishing import-export tariffs which are good income sources. To protect domestic manufacturing, import regulations have been applied and a basic law set up to improve the investment environment. Foreign exchange business was also expanded and improvements in the foreign exchange system pursued. The basic purpose of these operations is to reduce the side effects of market opening to a minimum, to strengthen import regulations and to improve the investment environment and foreign exchange administration. However, because of the unstable domestic situation and conflicts between reform and anti-reform elements, these tasks may not be easily accomplished in a short period.

In 1998, international institutions like the IMF and IBRD, and developed economies like the US, Japan and the EU have strengthened economic cooperation through the extension of repayment periods and assistance in finance and technology. The IMF decided to provide US$62 billion in stages and has already disbursed US$5 billion while opening negotiations in the field of energy and agricultural sectors. The IBRD decided to grant US$6 billion in loans to support a free economic policy, providing for the abolition of import-export quota systems, license systems and tariffs.

Chapter II

A HISTORICAL PERSPECTIVE ON THE KOREAN ECONOMIC DEVELOPMENT

The modern economic development of the Republic of Korea has been rapid and sustained in the world. This is true despite its history, prior to 1962, of extreme turbulence in the form of oppression under the Japanese occupation (1910~1945) and overwhelming devastation caused by the Korean War (1950~1953), South Korea has shown a remarkable and sustained economic growth during the last four decades since the first overall economic development plan was launched in 1962 and Korea has been recognized as one of the most outstanding NIEs (newly industrialized economies).

The process of industrialization which took place between 1953 and 1997, prior to the recent economic crisis is analyzed in order to identify how Korea has been able to adapt itself to changing internal and external circumstances. Several lessons can be drawn from the Korea's experiences for other developing countries.

<Table II-1> shows the outlines of Korea's economic development plans (1962~ 1996) with respect to planned period, doctrine of plan and major objectives. How Korea managed to do so in spite of seemingly insurmountable obstacles in sustaining economic development is the focus of this Chapter.

<Table II-1> Outlines of the Economic Development Plans (1962~1996)

Planned Period	Doctrine of Plan	Major Objectives
1st Plan (1962~1966)	Growth, Self-Sufficiency	-Correction of social and economic vicious cycle -Construction of foundation for self-sufficient economy
2nd Plan (1967~1971)	Growth, Self-Sufficiency	-Modernization of industrial structure -Establishment of self-sufficient economy
3rd Plan (1972~1976)	Growth, Stability, Self-Sufficiency Equilibrium	-Development of agriculture and fishery -Epochal growth exports -Construction of heavy and chemical industries
4th Plan (1977~1981)	Growth, Equity, Efficiency	-Establishment of self-sufficient growth structure -Promotion of equity by social development -Technological innovation and improvement of efficiency
5th Plan (1982~1986)	Stability, Efficiency, Equity	-Construction of foundation for self-supporting growth and economic stability -Technological innovation -Improvement of standard of living -Transformation of government's function
6th Plan (1987~1991)	Autonomy, Stability, Welfare	-Enhancement of equity and fairness of economic management -Improvement of standard of living and balanced economic development -Liberalization and globalization of economy
7th Plan (1992~1996)	Competitiveness, Equity, Internationalization	-Liberalization and globalization of economy -Promotion of R&D and SOC investment -Improvement of social equity

1. Liberation to Civil War: 1945~1950

With the surrender of Japan to the US and Allied Forces of World War II, thirty six years of Japanese domination ended on August 15, 1945. The Republic of Korea came into being on the 15th of August 1948. The first President was Syngman Rhee, elected by a unicameral legislature for a period of four years and for not more than two consecutive terms. A parallel development led to the establishment of the Democratic People's Republic of Korea in the North on September 9, 1948. Both the North and the South are governed by different and hostile ideologies. A country that had been unified for thirteen centuries was divided along the 38th parallel. Even today this line becomes the root of continual dissension.

The North obtained the lion's share of industry and resources; 87.6% of nation's electric power generation facilities were located in the North and only 12.4% in the South. All facilities for light industries were destroyed during World War II. The South got less than half areas of total land with three-fifths of the population. This poor, hungry, ragged population was with time going to be the true capital and force for Korean economic development. But in 1945 millions of refugees were pouring into the South from the North seeking for freedom; unemployment was rife and poverty were rampant. Yet with the establishment of the First Republic in 1948, internal political squabbles seemed to subside. Considerable progress was made in a very short time. Special reference must be made of the land reform programme, which redistributed three-fourths of the cultivable land and benefited over half the rural households. Mention must also be made of the massive American and allied aid that was poured into the country. But peace and progress was long in coming.

A civil war burst out with the rash hope of a unified Korea: on June 25, 1950, North Korean troops suddenly crossed the 38th parallel and swept down upon a weak and unprepared South. Both China and the US intervened or as the Chinese themselves said: 'a sea of fire drowned by a sea of men.' It sounds lunatic but it was not. Intelligent Koreans saw this struggle merely as a struggle between two world powers competing for supremacy. After three years of bloody fighting, an armistice was finally reached on July 27, 1953. One-fourth of the population was rendered homeless and three-fourths of the land was laid waste. In the aftermath, the Neutral Nations Inspection Committee reported: 'The country is dead..., there is no activity..., the cities are completely destroyed.' The whole of the South had been truly devastated. For the South, from now on national security became a national obsession, economic development a dominant preoccupation and reunification a sacred goal.

2. Rebuilding & Import Substitution Strategy: 1953~1961

After the Armistice Agreement was signed in 1953, the Korean economy lay totally battered and torn. All the writers depict this period of the fifties as a dismal era for the Korean economy. Indeed, this was a period that was marked by spiraling prices, high inflation, economic stagnation and absolute dependence on foreign aid.

In fact, much of the economic progress that was to come in later years had laid foundation during these dismal years; it made possible the setting for the pre-conditions for take-off for the first five year plan and the success of their ventures to attract foreign aid. In December 1953 the Korea-US Joint Economic Committee for Economic Rehabilitation and Stability was set up.

Before 1962, Korean economy was largely a traditional, closed agrarian one with approximately two-thirds of the working population engaged in agriculture. What little industrial base there was had been destroyed during the Korean War (1950~1953). The economy of this period was characterized by a vicious circle of poverty involving a political instability, a rampant inflation and an inability to meet most of the basic needs of consumers. Additionally, because of a lack of planning experience, the government went though a long period of trial and error in its development projects. The rapid growth of population, accelerated urbanization, and unemployment further complicated the economic problems. The economic policy pursued during this period may be loosely characterized as one of import-substitution of non-durable consumer and intermediate goods. This import substitution development strategy, however, soon reached its limits in nature, especially due to the small size of the domestic market and large capital requirements. As a result, the annual average rate of growth of GNP during the nine years period following the Korean War (1950~1953) was only 3.7%, that of per capita GNP was a meager 0.7%.

The years 1954~1957 were difficult years of rehabilitation. This was indeed a very bitter stage of transition because of the economic and social reconstruction, but the bitterness was softened because of the backing of foreign aid, particularly from the US. During the years of 1954~1957, the average growth rate for the economy was as high as 5.5% per year, but the growth rate of income per head was only 2.6%. By 1957, Korea could have regained its pre-war economic level.

Another feature of this period was the attention paid to development. All Koreans know that Korea's greatest resource has always been its people, as a key building block for national development. The early 1950s proved to be a turning point in terms of rebuilding the human capital base. Korea's accomplishments in developing its human resources early, despite the low per capita income, constituted a very important foundation for subsequent economic development. During the 1950s, educational facilities were greatly expanded and school enrollment increased 265%, while the number of college students increased from about 8,000 to 100,000. One result was the illiteracy rate declined from 78% to 28% during the period.

The third major development in the 1950s was land reform. As the first step toward a more equitable distribution of income, the government established a limit on the possession of farmland, which was a major source of inequality in income, in promulgating the Land Reform Act in 1949. Consequently, the proportion of tenant farmers decreased from 42.1% in 1947 to 5.2% in 1964.

The most import source of inefficiency during the years 1954~1959 was the effects of over-valuation of exchange rates. The effects centered on the pattern of import substitution, stagnation of exports, competition for enormous profits accruing to those who got the imported goods; this profit was in excess of hundred percent and more over landed costs. In the early years, domestic industries which sprang up due to high levels of protection, displayed most of the characteristics of import substitution industries, *e.g.*, generally poor quality control, high levels of under utilized capacity, heavy dependence on imports of critical inputs, use of relatively capital-intensive techniques and relatively slow growth of employment in manufacturing. Nearly 20% of the industries could be said to be ill-advised import substitution ventures.

The years 1958~1961 were the period of stabilization; as a consequence of the grave imbalance in the political situation in the country, it was also a period of economic stagnation. There was constant bickering within the government, continual strifes among the political parties, endless demonstrations on the part of the young generations, particularly students. Economic problems came to a breaking point: uprooted farmers, galloping inflation, nearly three hundred thousand unemployed including 72,000 university graduates and 51,000 discharged soldiers. A series of protest from these citizens resulted in the forceful resignation of Syngman Rhee on April 27, 1960. This marked the end of the First Republic. The GNP growth rate fell to 4.1% the income per head to 1.2%. However, during this period there was a distinct change in the structural set-up. The production of the primary sector increased in absolute terms but fell in relative terms while those of industry and services increased.

In 1961 the economic situation in Korea was still 'typical' of any resource- poor, low income, agricultural country: per capita GNP in the same year was a meager US$82, the level of domestic savings was a negligible 3.9%, total exports amounted to only US$43 million; there was massive widespread unemployment touching one-fifth of the working population, while the annual growth rate of population had reached a very high peak of almost 3% per annum. The vicious circle of poverty, unemployment and high inflation was sought to be broken by the introduction of the economic policy of import substitution. Non-durable consumer and intermediate goods were being manufactured up behind a protective wall of high tariffs and stringent quotas. But this import substitution strategy soon reached its limits in nature because of the small size of the domestic market.

In the meantime the regime of Syngman Rhee became more and more autocratic; the students revolted in 1960 and toppled the government. Rhee was forced to resign on April 26, 1960. In July 1960 the Democratic Party was elected. But factional struggles continued and policy making became well nigh impossible. This paved the way for a military takeover by General Park Chung Hee on May 16, 1961.

3. Development Strategy for Export Promotion: 1962~1971

After many years of stagnation and efforts to reconstruct, a new (Park Chung Hee) government came into power in 1961. It was committed to economic development and initiated a series of Five-Years Economic Development Plans that have successfully transformed Korea into one of the fastest growing economies in the world. The period from 1962~1971 can be considered the most important one in the country's modern economic development, because of the significant progress made in strengthening the industrial base and implementing fundamental changes in the nation's development strategies through both policy reform and institutional change.

On the institutional front, the 1960s was a period of substantial changes. Key institutional measures included an active government involvement in economic planning, a revamping of tax administration, founding of the Export Promotion Council and, most noticeably, creation of the Five-Years Plans to be implemented by EPB (Economic Planning Board). Perhaps the most significant institutional development of this period was the rising influence of the EPB. Functioning as a 'superministry', it was the main actor behind the government's heavy intervention in orchestrating the Korean outward- looking development strategies. Through the Five-Years Plans and the institutional set-up whereby the Deputy Prime Minister concurrently held the position of Minister of Economic Planning, the EPB acted as the main force in directing country's economy in the 1960s and beyond. Unlike other developing countries with planning agencies, the EPB not only created all long and short-range development plans but was also directly involved in implementation and in controlling the output of government resources through its budgetary authority and regulatory function. Furthermore, the Deputy Prime Minister played a direct coordinating role with all the ministries, due to the EPB's budget function, in addition to chairing the weekly meetings of the Economic Ministers' Council.

The government adopted an outward-looking development strategy stressing the growth of exports[5], due to Korea's limited natural resources and small domestics increased from US$32 million in 1960 to US$3.3 billion by 1973; the ratio of exports to GNP increased from 2% in 1961 to 6.8% in 1966 to 12% in 1970 and 26.9% in 1973.

By effectively harnessing its abundant supply of skilled and cheap labor for production of manufactured exports, Korea in the 1960s overcame its acute shortage of natural resources and through successful marketing, swept aside the constraints which a small domestic market can impose on growth. Urbanization and employment grew at a very fast pace. Per capita GNP doubled more between 1962 and 1971 from US$87 to US$289 as shown in <Table II-2>.

<Table II-2> Major Indicators of the Korean Economy: 1962~1971

	1962	1971	Annual Change (1962~1971)
GNP (W 100 million)	3,555	34,191	-
GNP (US$ 100 million)	23	95	-
GDP (W 100 million)	3,524	34,234	-
GDP (US$ 100 million)	23	95	-
Per Capita GNP (US$)[1)]	87	289	-
Real GDP Growth Rate (%)	2.1	8.5	8.7
Real GNP Growth Rate (%)	2.2	8.0	8.9
Private Consumption (%)	6.4	8.0	7.6
Gross Fixed Capital Formation (%)	28.7	3.0	22.2
Exports (US$ 100 million)	0.55	10.68	4.0
(Exports/GNP ratio, %)	2.4	11.2	6.9
Imports(US$ 100 million)	4.22	23.94	11.2
(Imports/GNP ratio, %)	18.3	25.2	21.6
Trade Balance(US$ 100 million)	-3.35	-10.46	-6.0
Current Account Balance (US$ 100 million)	-0.56	-8.40	-3.0
Gross Domestic Investment Rate (%)[2)]	11.8	24.6	19.9
Gross Saving Rate (%)	11.0	16.1	15.8
WPI (1990=100)	10.6	8.9	12.3
CPI (1990=100)	-	12.2	12.5

Notes: 1) In current US dollars.
2) In current prices

Source: Ministry of Finance and Economy, Statistical Yearbooks (various issues).

[5] Broadly speaking, till 1962 the government took an active part in building the shattered economy. It did not advocate any 'free market' economy; every aspect of it was based on a rigid 'administrative guidance' with no encouragement to trade union activities. After 1962 Korea opted for two alternative approaches from 1962~1971, it was the outward-looking development strategy of promoting labor-intensive manufacturing exports in which Korea had a comparative advantage; from 1972 to 1979, it was more the inward-looking development strategy when emphasis was shifted to import substitution: heavy investments were made in the heavy and chemical industries.

At that time, countries which were rich in natural resource were expected to be forerunners in industrialization. But that expectation did not materialize. In 1964, among the developing nations of Asia, India had the largest merchandise exports of US$1.7 billion, followed by Malaysia (US$1.10 billion), Hong Kong (US$1.01 billion) and Korea(US$120 million). Ten years later in 1973 Korea's exports had increased to US$3.23 billion, Malaysia's to US$3.05 billion and India's only to US$2.92 billion.

At thc same time, there were significant growth rates in domestic savings and investment during 1964~1973 in Korea. Gross domestic investment rate of Korea increased from 15% to 23%. All this hclped Korea to withstand the First Oil Shock in 1973; the growth rate of Korea was around 9.4% in the year.

How could the outward-looking development strategy be a success in Korea as well as in several other NIEs? It was namely because when a country adopted the development strategy, market forces worked better in the export sector, and as a result, the efficiency of the whole economy could be enhanced.

Foreign capital inducement also took an important role due to insufficiency of domestic savings. Large amounts of investment were necessary for the Korean economy to get out of the so-called vicious cycle, so the government enacted a comprehensive Foreign Investment Promotion Act. This capital was channeled toward mainly light manufacturing industries, in which the depreciation rate of capital was much faster than that of other industries, such as agriculture. Heavy reliance on foreign capital, which made up over 50% of total investment during the 1962~1971 period, indeed was an unacceptable political risk to many.

The original comparative advantage of Korea was cheap, skilled and diligent labor; the strategy adopted was to move from dependence on light industry to the structure based on heavy and chemical industries. Only with the lapse of time and economic progress, with increase in capital accumulation and a rise in wages, did Korea move into the capital-intensive sector, namely, steel, petro- chemicals, ship-building, electronics. At this critical juncture, the government selected the 'strategic industries'; it started the first airline and the first automobile assembly plant, but eventually sold them to the private sector. There is little doubt that the exports proved to use Robertson's classic phrase, 'an engine of growth'. At the initial stage, exports were promoted to generate foreign exchange to pay for imports. This initial success promoted government to make systematic approach for 'export promotion'. As exports expanded production increased faster than projected; loans were now solicited from international agencies as also from foreign banks. The process of industrialization became marked again by the outward-looking development strategy.

The results of Korea's comprehensive changes in its development strategy and institutional structure were beyond anyone's expectations. As is shown in <Table II-2>, the average annual growth rate in real GNP for the 1962~1971 period was 8.7%. In short, Korea's success in the 1960s could be attributed not only to the outward-looking strategy but also to a well-educated population, dynamic entrepreneurs, inducement of foreign capital, a favorable international trade environment and finally institutional reforms.

A noticeable fact is that already in the First Five-Year Plan(1962~1966) the Korean government included in its goal of 'modernization' or restructuring of the traditional values and behavior as well as the more usual economic objectives. What is most unusual about this plan is the grim picture of earlier corruption and economic stagnation painted in its first chapter. In spite of large-scale aid, living standards were still very low. Arbitrary assessment by capricious tax officials made evasion prerequisite for staying in business many entrepreneurs went into unsavory league with politicians and bureaucrats. Virtually, all social evils were connected with greed and maladministration of government officials.[6]

4. EMPHASIZING MORE BALANCED GROWTH: 1972~1979

In accordance with an announcement made by Park Chung Hee in 1973, the government focused attention on heavy and chemical industry with an impressive arsenal of industrial, trade and financial policies. The reasons why the government decided on this risky venture were not far to seek; they were both economic and political. With better political relations between the US and China, there was a fear that the US would pull out the troops from Korea and so it was necessary to build an industrial base for an independent defense structure. From the economic point of view, the 'deepening of the industrial structure' was a necessary reasons to increase productivity in order to off-set rising Korean wages and to meet the global competitive challenges.

[6] Paul Kuznets, "Indicative Planning in Korea." *Journal of Comparative Economics,* Vol. XIV, No.4, December 1990, p.659.

The inward-looking development strategy was pursued in the context that Korea soon began to lose its comparative advantage edge in unskilled labor intensive industries such as plywood, footwear and textiles, and therefore needed to develop more sophisticated, high value-added industries.

The First Oil Shock in 1973~1974 which swept soon after the decision of the heavy and chemical industry drive, while exposing the volatility of the global market, also confirmed the need of import substitution. It was again import substitution with a vengeance; but the export drive continued unabated. However, the heavy and chemical industry drive substituted bureaucratic judgment for market tests and absorbed too much of the limited resources. All these excesses came home to roost with macroeconomic crisis of 1979 aggravated by the assassination of the President Park Chung Hee and the second oil shock in 1979~1980.[7]

Though the direction of the change from outward-looking development strategy to inward-looking one was correct, the speed of the change was too rapid in that the heavy and chemical industry projects not only needed quite a large amount of money per project but also had long gestation periods compared to light industries. Due to inflationary financing methods together with overly optimistic assumptions regarding world trade prospects, many projects turned out to be unwise and excessive.

Another important feature in this period was the export of construction services, mainly to the Middle East, which brought mixed effects on the Korean economy. The quadrupling of oil prices during 1973~1974 and the unprecedented pressure on the balance of payments position was eased by earnings from construction projects, which totaled US$15 billion by the end of 1978 in the Middle East Region alone. Despite the invaluable experience gained by Korean workers and firms from participating in large development projects, there were side effects. The departure of a large number of skilled workers to the Middle East Region pushed up domestic wages. This, coupled with the growing demand for skilled workers in heavy and chemical industries, widened the wage differential between skilled and unskilled workers, a development hardly desirable from the point of view of income distribution in the short run. In addition, the rather sudden improvement in the balance of payments due to the remittance of earnings from the Middle East expanded the domestic money supply, which aggravated inflation.

As can be seen in <Table II-3>, this active government intervention and aggressive policy measure led to remarkable economic growth according to the macro-economic indicators during the 1970s. On the surface, the economic improvements in 1970s looked good. The high growth rates, however, were also creating chronic structural problems and negative side-effects. The primary negative aspects of the hyper-growth were a significant inflation, a rapid rise in real wages in the expanding heavy and chemical industries and an over-expansion of government investment and low interest loans for the heavy and chemical industries. The results were threefold:

First, Korean industries experienced a deteriorating position in their international comparative advantage because of its rising labor costs.

Second, as a result of the high inflation rates and unbalanced regional and sectoral growth in the 1970s, Korea experienced a slight worsening in the distribution of income.

Finally, the nation began to experience increasing vulnerability to external shocks, complicated by the government's extensive financing and subsidy schemes for the agriculture and heavy & chemical industry sectors.

There is one peculiarity of Korea which does not have a parallel anywhere else except with the possible exception of Japan. Korea's economic expansion was sparked by the expansion of a broad group of companies headed by the most dynamic and aggressive entrepreneurs. These are the large business conglomerates, the family controlled business, the '*Chaebols*'. There are perhaps 50 groups worthy of this title. They grew out of small family owned retail sales operations or manufacturing enterprises and they are among the world's largest organizations as some companies have found their names among Fortune's List of the top hundred of the world. Promotion of large industrial houses seems to have proved beneficial for greater exports for encouraging large-scale enterprises and providing employment opportunities. For this reason, the government itself promoted their rapid expansion in the 1960s and 1970s, through licensing, subsidized bank loans, export financing. Undoubtedly, there is a danger of oligopoly and in the early years they co-operated closely with the authoritarian government. In 1990, the combined sales of these four business equaled half of the Korean GNP; four of these namely, *Samsung, Hyundai, Lucky-Goldstar* and *Daewoo* were largely responsible for the US$4.2 billion trade surplus in 1986~1987.

[7] World Bank Publication, *Korea: Managing the Industrial Transition,* March 1987, pp. 42~46.

<Table II-3> Major Indicators of the Korean Economy: 1972~1979

	1972	1979	Annual Change 1972~1979
GNP (W 100 million)	41,935	308,721	-
GNP (US$ 100 million)	107	616	-
GDP (W 100 million)	42,119	313,934	-
GDP (US$ 100 million)	107	627	-
Per Capita GNP (US$)[1)]	319	1,647	-
Real GDP Growth Rate (%)	4.8	7.1	8.9
Real GNP Growth Rate (%)	4.6	6.8	8.7
Private Consumption (%)	4.9	8.1	6.9
Gross Fixed Capital Formation (%)	1.3	9.7	16.2
Exports (US$ 100 million)	16.24	150.56	74.9
(Exports/GNP ratio, %)	15.2	24.4	23.8
Imports (US$ 100 million)	25.22	203.39	94.7
(Imports/GNP ratio, %)	23.6	33.0	31.0
Trade Balance (US$ 100 million)	-5.74	-43.96	-15.0
Current Account Balance (US$ 100 million)	-3.71	-41.51	-12.7
Gross Domestic Investment Rate (%)[2)]	20.9	35.8	26.7
Gross Saving Rate (%)	17.3	28.5	23.6
WPI (1990=100)	14.3	18.6	15.4
CPI (1990=100)	11.9	18.5	17.6

Notes: 1) In current US dollars.
2) In current prices

Source: Ministry of Finance and Economy, Korea, Statistical Yearbooks (various issues).

5. Stabilization-Cum-Selective Liberalization: 1980~1989

In April of 1979, the government announced a stabilization program that aimed at restructuring the whole economy so as to enable the nation to make full use of its potential for continued high growth. The stabilization program had three major components. To control excessive liquidity, the government set lower targets for the growth rate of the money supply and also proposed a fundamental reform of the banking sector. To deal with over-investment in the heavy and chemical industries and under investment in light industries, the government temporarily suspended all new projects in the heavy and chemical industries and realigned credit priorities in favor of light industries. To eliminate price distortions and to promote competition, the government decontrolled prices on many items and stepped up import liberalization efforts.

The slowest component of Korea's economic development strategy was the process of selective liberalization; liberalization played only a secondary role to export promotion. While Korean policy did offer protection to the domestic markets of industries producing importables, it offered little incentive for industries producing exportables to keep their output at home.[8] Since 1979, consistent with the liberalization process, the government intervention was focused on the three areas: restructuring of distressed industries, support for development of technology and finally promotion of competition. The government played an active role in these areas. Since the same year, the stabilization-cum-liberalization policy reforms have continued major external policy reforms eased non-tariff and tariff barriers. During the 1979~1988 period, the import liberalization ratio increased from less than 68% to 95% making virtually all industrial products free from non-tariff barriers, and dropping the average tariff rate from 25% to 17%. Korea has also been liberalizing FDI (foreign direct investment).

In detail, under the regime of Chun Doo Hwan (1980~1988) economic liberalization was pursued with vigour. Several domestic factors contributed to this sudden change in economic policies. International pressure, specially from the US gave the additional impetus to economic liberalization and more openness to FDI. Economic liberalization in Korea came as a result of the enormous success of the Korean economy. The '*chaebols*' and labor became vocal opponents of the state's heavy-handed intervention in the previous

[8] World Bank Publication, *Korea Managing Industrial Transition,* March 1987, pp.34~35.

decades. The pressure from the US was also the result of successful Korean exports which increased the trade deficit between the US and Korea. Thus, the primary push for Korean economic liberalization was the result of its own successful economic development and the success of its own economic policies.

The Monopoly and Fair Trade Law became operative on April 1, 1981. The basic purpose was to reduce monopolistic practices and promote competition in all industries. The number of industries to which the law applies has been steadily increasing, and the law has been vigorously enforced in all cases. Other internal policy reforms have included financial liberalization, reduction of deficits in government expenditure and restructuring of the industrial incentive system. Again, in 1981 the Ministry of Finance began to privatize many domestic banks, which had formerly belonged to the state.

Furthermore, the Korean economy was pressured mostly by the US to open its market to foreign investors and goods and hence the Foreign Investment Law was revised in 1987. Import liberalization and reduction of tariff rates were introduced; foreign banks were permitted to enter the capital market in 1981 and their share in the lending market increased from 4% in 1975 to 12.9% in 1984.

Also, beginning with the Fifth Five-Year Plan (1982~1986), the nomenclature of the plan was changed; it was now no longer just the Economic Development Plan, but it was renamed as 'the Five-Year Economic and Social Development Plan' to demonstrate the urgency of social transformation, so vital for economic progress. Social and welfare expenditure was now given a big boost, *e.g.* in 1990 this item accounted for nearly 40% of the government expenditure, 25% more than that in 1976. Economic ministries also underwent restructuring and industrial policies were changed from being developmental to regulatory and limited in scope.

<Table II-4> Major Indicators of the Korean Economy: 1980s

	1980	1987	1988	1989	Annual Change (1980~1989)
GNP (W 100 million)	368,570	1,097,265	1,313,713	1,479,416	-
GNP (US$ 100 million)	606	1,334	1,798	2,204	-
GDP (W 100 million)	381,484	1,121,303	1,331,342	1,491,647	-
GDP (US$ 100 million)	628	1,363	1,822	2,222	-
Per Capita GNP (US$)[1]	1,597	3,218	4,295	5,210	-
Real GDP Growth Rate (%)	-2.7	11.5	11.3	6.4	7.9
Real GNP Growth Rate (%)	-3.9	12.3	12.0	6.9	8.0
Private Consumption (%)	-0.4	8.1	9.0	10.8	7.0
Growth Fixed Capital Formation (%)	-10.7	17.0	13.7	15.9	8.5
Exports (US$ 100 million)	175.05	472.81	606.96	623.77	349.65
Export/GNP ratio, %)	28.9	35.4	33.8	28.3	31.8
Import(US$ 100 million)	222.92	410.20	518.11	614.65	346.51
(Import/GNP ratio, %)	36.8	30.7	28.8	27.9	32.9
Trade Balance (US$ 100 million)	-43.84	75.29	112.83	43.61	13.7
Current Account Balance (US$ 100 million)	-53.21	100.58	145.05	53.60	18.5
Gross Domestic Investment Rate (%)[2]	31.9	30.0	31.1	33.8	30.5
Gross Saving Rate (%)	23.2	37.3	39.3	36.2	30.4
WPI (1990=100)	38.9	0.4	2.7	1.5	6.9
CPI (1990=100)	28.7	3.1	7.1	5.7	8.4

Notes: 1) In current US dollars.
2) In current prices

Source: Ministry of Finance and Economy, Korea, Statistical Yearbooks (various issues).

On the other hand, the economic performance of the Sixth Five-Year Plan (1987~1991) far exceeded the original objectives as a result of underestimating the effects of exchange rates, the realignment of major currencies, falling oil prices and other favourable factors. Korea experienced a major economic boom. In 1987 the economy recorded a real GNP growth rate of 12.3% and a current account surplus of US$10 billion, as shown by <Table II-4>. Since the 1980s Korea's external debt position improved remarkably, declining from a peak of time, all debt ratios improved considerably. This is in sharp contrast to other developing countries in both Asia and Latin America where in the second half of the 1980s net financial inflows had been continuously negative. Non-debt financial flows were positive since 1983, partly due to expansion of portfolio investments (1983~1985) and FDI in Korea since 1985.[9]

From 1986 to 1988, the Korean economy grew at a remarkable annual rate of 12%. The nation also attained consecutive current account surpluses beginning with 1986, a welcome departure from its chronic deficits of the past. These achievements owed much to the favorable economic conditions of the mid-1980s known as the 'three lows' such as low international interest rates, low value of the US dollar and low oil prices.

In sum, during the mid-1980s Korea had pursued the structural reform throughout the economy. The upshot of all these efforts has been greater reliance on market mechanism than on government control in the allocation of resources. Although at this stage it may be too early to make a comprehensive evaluation, when Korea's economic performance in the mid-1980s is considered, the results have been quite favorable, as shown in <Table II-4>. Undergoing rapid transformation in its economic structure from a poor agricultural economy, Korea emerged in the mid-1980s as one of the leading NIEs.[10]

In 1988, per capita GNP reached US$4,040 while the country's total trade volume amounted to over US$111 billion, the thirteenth highest among the non-communist countries. The share of the manufacturing sector in GNP increased from 14.3% in 1962 to 31.6% in 1988, while that of the agricultural, forestry and fisheries sectors decreased from 36.6% to 10.8% during the same period. And the share of primary product exports declined from 78% of total exports to 5.2%, while that of manufactured goods increased from 22% to 94.8%.

Along with the disappearance of the three lows in late 1980s, many changes in the domestic environment came to pose as new challenges. With the historic June 29th Declaration for Democracy in 1987, which led to free and fair national elections, Korea entered a process of rapid democratization.

Despite these challenges, the economy continued to grow in 1987 and 1988 because of several factors. First, this period was marked by a thriving world economy. Concurrently, economic rivals such as Japan and Taiwan experienced greater currency appreciation than Korean Won. Second, entrepreneurs were able to absorb the shocks of wage increases and Won appreciation to a bearable degree by raising product prices. The 1988 Seoul Olympics also contributed as a special factor favoring Korean enterprises.

In retrospect, these factors have made the blows to the economy seemed less severe and the problems almost nonexistent in 1987 and 1988. Upon a close internal examination, however, the growth of economic maladies such as the dampening of investment spirit can be detected, foreboding the poorer economic performance in 1989. During the course of 1989, the real GNP growth rate dropped 6.9%, nearly half of the 12.0% growth rate of the previous years (1987 and 1988). Also a slump in the growth rate of manufacturing sector from 13.4% in 1988 to 3.7% in 1989 contributed largely to the declining GNP growth. The exports growth rate dropped form 28.4% in 1988 to 2.8% in 1989 nominal terms with little evidence of recovery in the early 1990s, while imports increased 18.6%. Reflecting this decrease, the 1989 current account surplus declined to US$5.36 billion, a significant drop from the 1988 surplus of US$14.51 billion.

In addition, price stability, which had been maintained until 1986, gave way to greater inflationary pressure. Consumer prices, which had risen on average by 2 to 3% between 1982 and 1986, rose by more than 5% between 1987 to 1989.

The immediate cause of the economy's slide into stagnation has been declining exports due to a decrease in international competitiveness of Korea's industries, which is largely attributable to sharp wage hikes brought about by labor disputes as well as to an appreciation of the Won. Moreover, under the booming economy between 1986 and 1988, marked by rising surpluses in the balance of payments, measures for increasing the potentiality for further development were neglected.

[9] Taka Fukuchi and Misuhiro Kagami ed., *Perspectives on the Pacific Basin Economy: A comparison of Asia and Latin America*. The Asian Club Foundation. Institute of Developing Economies. Japan, 1990, pp.33~39.

[10] But it was the foreign policy that received more attention, specially the re-unification of Korea and diplomatic relations with the former Soviet Union. The Summer Olympics held in Seoul in 1988 clearly showed that Korea had come to stay on the international arena.

6. 1990s Till the Eve of the Korea's Financial Crisis in November 1997

With the maturing of democracy, Korea held the relatively fair election in its modern history on December 18, 1992. Kim Young Sam was elected President for a term of five years with 42% of the votes, the largest proportion in the past. He has begun well in removing corruption from politics; the real named financial transactions decree made it difficult for politicians or businessmen to make illicit fortunes by hiding accounts under a pseudonym. All civil servants, had to report their assets. He had also made progress in dismantling the old authoritarian mechanism imposed by former, army-dominated regimes on the country.

Meanwhile, the economy continued to grow at a fairly high rate due to the expansion of domestic demand, despite the stagnation of export growth during 1990~1991. During the six-year period: 1985~1991, the economy grew 10.4% per annum on average, which far exceeded the growth potential of the Korean economy. The results were high inflation, reaching about 9% during 1990~1991, continued demand for wage hike and deterioration of current account balance.

These factors lead the government to increase its stabilization effort by reinforcing its management of aggregate demand from the second half of 1991. Tighter control was exercised over money supply and fiscal expenditure. It introduced restrictions on housing construction and consumer financing and phased out some measures geared to stimulate facility investment. And a wage guideline scheme was introduced in order to curb wage hikes. Under the impact of these various measures, domestic demand began to subside and consumer price inflation fell remarkably in 1992.

According to the 1992 statistics, Korea's GNP is the 13th highest in the world, while GNP per capita ranked the 38th. Korea ranks high in exports of textiles, iron and steel, automobiles, ships and electronics. Korea's energy consumption and car and telephone ownership rates have all risen. The average life span has been extended, while infant mortality rates have declined.

However, GNP growth rate fell very sharply in 1992 and 1993. Equipment investment decreased while bankruptcies among small business soared. The decrease in domestic demand stance 1992 contrasted with the steady growth of commodity exports. Inflation decelerated to slight 4.8% in 1993 as shown in <Table II-5>.

Meanwhile, its external economic environments improved with the strong Japanese yen, low international raw material price and low international interest rates. political uncertainties disappeared once the new administration came to power.

Helped by these factors, the Korean economy load already began a recovery track by the end of 1994. GNP growth rate increased to 8.8% in the first quarter of this year. The economy showed a strong recovery with GNP growth rates of 8.6% in 1994 and 8.9% in 1995.

President Kim Young Sam had synchronized the Seventh Five-Year Economic and Social Development plan (1993~1997) with his term of office. Interest rates have been liberalized, credit controls have been further eased; industrial restructuring is focused on technological innovation by increasing R&D (Research and Development) outlays to 3% and 4% of the GNP by 1998.

This stage of structural adjustment was more difficult as it involved cutting employment in inefficient and subsidized industry to permit new jobs in efficient industry and services. Besides, the structural adjustment was likely to create conflict in society as 'sunset' industries tend to fight to survive so as to maintain job tenure and benefits like pension, health welfare, subsidies etc. Korea seems to follow the pattern so aptly described by Michael Porter that 'competitiveness' was focused rather more on specific industries and on segments of industry rather than at the national level.[11]

Nevertheless, the Korean economy was marked by a puzzling dichotomy between a benign real economy and growing financial market tensions. The real economy appeared to be adjusting smoothly to the severe 1996 terms-of-trade shock and a cutback in business investment following a boom in the early 1990s.

---

[11] Michael Porter, *The Competitive Advantage of Nations,* Macmillan, 1990, pp.9, 17 and 475.

<Table II-5> Major Indicators of Korean Economy: 1990s

	1990	1991	1992	1993	1994	1995	1996	1997	1998 (e)	1999 (p)	Annual Change (1990~1997)
GNP (W 100 million)	1,782,621	2,142,399	2,387,046	2,655,179	3,037,726	3,489,793	3,864,382	4,160,179	4,431,270	-	-
GNP (US$ 100 million)	2,518	2,920	3,057	3,308	3,780	4,526	4,804	4,374	3,168	-	-
GDP (W 100 million)	1,795,390	2,157,344	2,403,922	2,671,460	3,059,702	3,519,747	3,898,134	4,209,867	4,495,088	-	4,665,901
GDP (US $ 100 million)	2,536	2,941	3,079	3,328	3,807	4,565	4,844	4,426	3,213	-	3,335
Per Capita GNP (US$)[1]	5,883	6,757	7,007	7,484	8,467	10,037	10,543	9,511	6,823	-	-
Real GDP Growth Rate (%)	9.5	9.1	5.1	5.8	8.6	8.9	7.1	5.5	-5.8	2.0	3.8
Real GNP Growth Rate (%)	9.6	9.1	5.0	5.8	8.4	8.7	6.9	4.9	-7.0	-	7.3
Private Consumption (%)	10.7	9.5	6.6	5.7	7.6	8.3	6.8	3.1	-9.6	2.7	7.3
Gross Fixed Capital Formation (%)	25.9	12.6	-0.8	5.2	11.8	11.7	7.1	-3.5	-21.1	-	8.8
Exports (US$ 100 million) (Exports/GNP ratio, %)	650.16 25.8	718.70 24.6	766.32 25.1	822.36 24.9	960.13 25.4	1,250.58 27.6	1,297.15 27.0	1,361.64	1,323	- -	978.38 26.44
Import (US$ 100 million) (Imports/GNP ratio, %)	698.44 27.7	815.25 27.9	817.75 26.8	838.00 25.3	1,023.48 27.1	351.19 29.9	1,503.39 31.3	1,446.16 33.1	933 -	- -	1,061.71 28.63
Trade Balance (US$ 100 million)	-24.50	-68.03	-17.55	23.19	-28.60	-44.44	-149.65	-31.79	390	-	42.67
Current Account Balance (US$ 100 million)	-20.03	-83.17	-39.43	9.90	-38.67	-85.08	-230.05	-81.67	400	200	71.03
Gross Domestic Investment Rate (%)[2]	37.1	39.1	36.8	35.2	36.2	37.4	38.8	35.3	20.9	-	37.0
Gross Saving Rate (%)	35.9	36.1	34.9	35.2	35.4	36.2	34.8	34.6	33.2	-	35.4
WPI (1990=100)	4.2	4.7	2.2	1.5	2.8	4.7	3.2	3.9	12.2	-	3.4
CPI (1990=100)	8.5	9.3	6.3	4.8	6.2	4.5	4.9	4.5	7.5	3	6.1

Notes: 1) In current US dollars.
2) In current prices

Source: Ministry of Finance and Economy, Statistical Yearbooks (various issues).

These factors had slowed GDP growth from an unsustainably high rate of 9% in 1994~1995 to 7% in 1996. The first quarter of 1997, when GDP growth fell to 5.5%, appeared to mark a successful 'soft-landing'. Indeed, notwithstanding sluggish domestic demand, GDP growth during the first three-quarters of 1997 still averaged over 6%, while industrial output growth was some 9% reflecting strong net exports.

Inflation, measured by the 4.3% rise in the private consumption deflator, was the lowest in a decade. Unemployment, albeit edging up to some 2.5% of the labour force, was very low by OECD standards. At the same time, the current account deficit, which had soared to US$23.7 billion in 1996 (almost 5% of GDP), had been halved by the third quarter of the year: and the capital account, although volatile, was recording small net inflows.

Moreover, the operations of Korea's 'floating' exchange rate system was in practice akin to an 'adjustable peg' system, and its monetary policy also proved to be inappropriate in a context of greater capital market openness. Indeed, from August 1997, almost to the eve of the crisis, the authorities vainly attempted to prop up the Korean won, while at the same time injecting substantial liquidity into the financial system in attempts to half the tidal wave of bankruptcies. At the onset, policy inertia, inappropriate exchange rate goals and capital flight quickly exhausted Korea's limited foreign exchange reserves. On November 17 1997, the government abandoned its attempts to support the Korean won and two days later announced an emergency program to stem the financial crisis.

A US$57 billion IMF (International Monetary Fund) stand-by agreement was announced on December 3, 1997. The centerpiece of the stand-by was stringent macroeconomic policy guidelines to choke off any second-round inflation effects from currency depreciation. An original aspect of this agreement was the detailed specification of microeconomic reforms aimed at opening up the Korean economy to greater domestic and world competition, reforming corporate governance structures and practices as well as improving transparency and reporting procedures. The central focus of these initiatives was to speed the pace of restructuring and reform of the financial system and the *chaebols*. These initiatives were supported by measures to increase labour market flexibility, change Korea's outdated bankruptcy procedures and to open up the market for corporate control to foreign capital.

The macroeconomy prior to the financial crisis gave few signs of imminent stress. In the past, high nominal GDP growth had masked many of Korea's financial problems and perhaps lulled regulators and foreign investors into complacency. However, the crucial pressure point between weak microeconomic structures and slower economic growth proved to be the corporate sector's weak balance sheet and cash flow positions. Insolvencies (especially among incorporated firms) were on the rise, while slowing economic growth exacerbated cash-flow problems. Insolvencies soared during the course of 1997 and reached dangerous levels in early 1998.

7. Lessons from the Korean Experience

What useful lessons, if any, can be drawn from Korea's economic policies and experiences over the past 40 years?

One of the most important lessons that can be learned has to do with the merit of an outward-looking development strategy. Without the adoption of such a strategy in the early 1960s, Korea's economic progress up to the recent IMF bailout would have been impossible. Some critics have argued that Korea's heavy dependence on trade has made its economy highly vulnerable to unfavorable external developments, supporting their argument by pointing out the painful adjustments that Korea had to make involving two rounds of oil shocks and the current wave of protectionism. In this regard, although an outward-looking development strategy is vulnerable to external shocks, it is still a better option than an inward-looking strategy. In general, an open economy has greater adaptability to external shocks than a closed economy for the simple reason that entrepreneurs in an open economy are more capable of exploiting new opportunities arising from changes in the external environment than businessmen or bureaucrats in a closed economy.

The second lesson seems to be the need to reaffirm the role of the market. In the 1960s, Korea successfully established a high-growth economy by following the basic principles of the market; more specifically, the idea that its scarce resources should be allocated on the basis of correct market price signals through the initiative of dynamic entrepreneurs operating in a competitive environment. In addition, a well-functioning market mechanism in an open economy is on the whole more efficient in processing information regarding external changes than the bureaucratic machinery one often found in a closed economy.

The third lesson has to do with the inflow of foreign capital. Korea's experience in this regard seems to indicate that at least in the early phase of development, when foreign confidence in the economy is weak, the biggest barrier to the international movement of capital is the uncertainty borne through investors or lenders. A government can reduce this uncertainty significantly through investors or repatriation of profits. One further institutional innovation that can be attempted in this area would be an international guarantee whereby all national governments are barred from any actions that could trap foreign capital.

The fourth lesson comes from the recent financial crisis. In November 1997, Korea, which had long been the envy of many developing countries, was faced with a threat of a debt moratorium.[12] But it would be a mistake to blame this debacle solely on the contagion from the financial crisis in Southeast Asia. There has been much debate about the various causes of the crisis, but in the end, it was mainly due to Korea's growing lack of international competitiveness with its high cost but low efficiency structure combined with its inability to properly adapt to the rapid changes and trends in the global economy. To be sure, by most criteria, Korea had sound macroeconomic fundamentals. However, owing to an excessively leveraged corporate sector and a weak financial system, they did not suffice to ride out the financial market firestorm sweeping through the rest of Asia.

Since the IMF bailout, Korea has worked closely with organizations such as the IMF and the World Bank and with advanced economies to get back on its feet and restore stability and confidence in the economy. By and large, their efforts have been successful. The immediate threat of the financial crisis has passed and the Korean Won has stabilized. Interest rates are dropping and the stock market is reviving. In addition, foreign investment in Korea appears to be picking up demonstrating that Korea is regaining the confidence of international markets.

In retrospect, though, Korea's response has been far from perfect. Perhaps the biggest criticism is that some policy measures have been geared toward short- term, immediate ends and lack credible long-term vision. The contractionary monetary policy adopted immediately after the IMF bailout and the resulting exorbitant interest rates may have been well intended, but in the end, they debilitated the real economy and weakened Korea's industrial foundation. Furthermore, the Korean government seems to lack a comprehensive master plan for boosting Korea's long-term growth potential and maintaining social cohesion in the midst of the ongoing restructuring process and growing unemployment.

For a country like Korea, which has scarce natural resources and is highly dependent on trade, the strengthening of competitive power is possible mainly through exports. In today's small world of increasing economic interdependence, strengthening competitiveness through exports seems to be desirable. Many countries today are committing themselves to increasing their exports. The United States government, for example, is strongly pursuing a policy to increase exports. A movement to boost workers' motivation is taking place in Germany. Yet, the export rate of Korea is decreasing, and it is necessary to study the present conditions and the underlying reasons and search for ways for improvement. It is estimated that if Korea's exports were to increase 10%, its economy would grow by 2%, and 150,000 jobs would be created. However, the growth rate of Korea's exports are continuing to fall.

The fifth lesson relates to the capacity to absorb new technology and manpower training. Korea's remarkable ability to absorb new technology from abroad for the 40 years under review, stemmed directly from the high level of education in the country. Various reform measures including accelerating technological innovation, fostering cooperative labor-management relations and providing adequate social infrastructure should have improved the overall efficiency of the economy, fostering competition and private initiatives. But these measures had not been introduced up to the IMF stand-by agreement.

Indeed, the country was fortunate in that in the early 1960s when the economy was taking off, it had an enormous reserve of well-trained manpower. Some believe, however, that Korea has now exhausted this reserve. Debatable as this judgment is, many policy-makers in Korea readily concede that in the future the government should devote more resources to education and manpower. Indeed, the crux of current policy efforts directed toward social development is the expansion of educational opportunities. For continued progress, the emphasis on education and training is not only a good economic policy but also a good social policy, because government investment in education and technical manpower training coupled with a policy providing for continued expansion of employment opportunities, serves as the most effective structural basis for an equitable distribution of income.

[12] Yang-Taek Lim, "The Role of Foreign Direct Investment for Korea's Economic Recovery and Future Directions in Foreign Investment Promotion Policy", paper presented at ACAES-Culalongkorn University International Conference, Bangkok, Thailand, December 16~18, 1998.

The final lesson goes beyond the scope of economic discussion. The critical precondition for economic development is social and political stability. The rapid growth in Korea which began in the early 1960s would not have been possible without the social stability provided by the new government that came into power at that time. As indicated earlier, political instability was responsible for the severe problems encountered by the Korean economy in 1980. In light of these experiences, the need for political stability cannot be overemphasized.

Chapter III

THE DEVELOPMENT OF THE KOREAN ECONOMY

The Korean economy has achieved rapid economic growth since 1963. GNP (Gross National Product) increased at an average annual rate of 9.0% in real terms during the three decades from 1963 to 1993. This outstanding economic performance is remarkable, considering the poor endowment of natural resources and the small domestic market. It is generally asserted that the acceleration of economic growth in Korea was made possible by a shift in industrialization strategy from import substitution to export promotion in the early 1960s and successful execution of this export-oriented strategy thereafter. For the above reasons, developing countries seem to acknowledge that the Korean experience as a model to emulate.

1. SOURCE OF GROWTH[13]

It is clear that a great number of factors influenced the economic growth and development of Korea. Kim and Park (1985) and Hong (1984) analyzed the economic factors that have directly contributed to Korea's economic growth. In their studies, they presented estimates of the source of growth from 1963 to 1992 by decomposing the growth into the supply of factor input which is directly required for growth and the factor productivity per unit of input. So they argued that sustained economic growth in Korea during last three decades was attained by increasing the supply of factor input and enhancing factor productivity. The increase in labor input accounts for 32% of growth rate of standardized national income in Korea. Comparing the contribution of major determinants to growth for three sub-periods, it was found that labor input made the largest contribution for all sub-periods. This reflects the fact that Korean growth during the past decades was largely attributable to increases in employment and average working hours.

The relative contribution of capital input to growth increased from 14% to 20% in 1960s and to 24% in later sub-periods, indicating that structural adjustment to heavy and chemical industries was achieved through capital investments. The contribution of advances in knowledge and miscellaneous determinants were significantly lower than those in Japan and the US. The overall size of this contribution is relatively small in Korea because the average quality of technology, business organization and management practices in Korea are believed to remain inferior to the average of the industrialized countries. The growth contribution by these factors may largely reflect the effect of domestic industry's efforts to catch up with the technological and managerial practices of advanced countries. This perspective leads to a plausible explanation of the decline in the contribution for the later sub-periods.

From the examination of the sources of growth it could be deduced that shifts in industrialization strategy from import substitution to labor-intensive export promotion was the major thrust for the sustained growth of the Korean economy.

There have been numerous attempts to unveil the forces which made it possible for the Korean economy to have been so successful during the past three decades. It is clear that a great number of factors have influenced Korean economic growth and development.

Yang-Taek Lim(1995 and 1996)[14] contends that the fundamental energy behind Korea's economic development from the 1960s to the 1980s came from the ability of the government to allocate resources,

---

[13] Yang-Taek Lim, "Export-led Development Strategy: the Korean Experience for India and South Asia", paper presented at the International Conference on *India's New Economic Policy* held by American Committee of Asian Economics at Jawaharlal Nehru University, New Delhi, March 11~14, 1996.

and the shift in industries from import substitution to labor-intensive export promotion. In addition, abundant and high quality domestic labor, cheap foreign capital, and readily available foreign technology were factors that made rapid growth possible.

Among the previously described sources of Korea's economic growth, particularly governmental influence in resource allocation shall be overviewed in this section, while the other sources shall be discussed later.

In 1961, as the military regime took power, a Five-Year Economic Development Plan was formed, and policies for the promotion of industries were implemented. In this period, the competitive power and foreign confidence in private corporations were low, and therefore the Korean government acted as a guardian for them. The Korean government intervened actively by forming low currency rates, lowering interest rates for loans for export purposes, changing authoritarian policies, and reducing taxes for export industries.

After 1970, as heavy and chemical industries grew rapidly, governmental market intervention, such as the appointment of industrialists in special areas and the restriction of free competition, became more intense. Due to the government's efforts, however, Korea achieved a GNP growth of 8.1% in the 1970s, and the industrial structure became highly developed as the weight of heavy and chemical industries rose from 11.9% in the 1970s to 26.3% in the 1980s.[15]

However, due to excessive government market intervention, side effects such as the inequity of the various industries, and the concentration of economic power in a few entities became more severe. In an attempt to reduce this, after 1980, the Korean government came to be more interested in policies that would promote competition in the market such as restriction of monopoly and the establishment of the Fair Trade Act.

In the 1980s, however, policies which were supposed to increase market efficiency did not do much for the promotion of competition, but focused more on new governmental market intervention plans that would correct past failures.[16] Also, in the 1980s, the Korean government increased market intervention under the pretext of investment adjustment in heavy and chemical industries, rationalization of industries, and organization of weak businesses. Therefore, a vicious cycle was formed, in which excessive government market intervention of the past presented new problems in industrial policies, only to be solved by more intervention.

The government regulations which were introduced and expanded in the course of rapid economic development are now encountering a new era of change. Economic expansion, internationalization, political and economic democratization, and self- regulation have made it very difficult for the Korean government to control private, economic, and social activities. Regulations have lost their purpose, and are causing more side-effects. It has became evident that the running of the Korean economy under the initiatives of the government as before, and its over-intervention in the market is no longer helpful for the nation's economy. They have become harmful factors that decrease economic vitality and weaken international competitiveness. On the foundation of these common understandings, the Korean government has been ambitiously promoting policies to ease regulations. However, it is generally believed that the deregulation policies of Korea are still in their initial stages.[17]

---

[14] Yang-Taek Lim, *The People Perish Where There Is No Vision,* Mail Economic Daily Press, Seoul, Korea, September 1995.
Yang-Taek Lim, "An Econometric Study on the Technological Characteristics of Korean Manufacturing Sector", paper presented at the 8th conference of Korea Technology, Economics & Management, January 30, 1996.

[15] However, there are evaluations that the industrial policies of the 1970s were not very effective. Exportation of heavy and chemical goods did not increase due to those policies. Rather, the phenomenon of the "three lows" (low interest rate, low oil price, and low exchange rate) and American commercial policies contributed to the economic success. "Effects of the Distribution of Capital by the Heavy and Chemical Industrial Policies of the 1970s", *Principles of the Korean Economy and Market* (Hanlim Economic Research Center, Hanlim Univ., July 1990), pp. 162~168.

[16] The KIET (Korea Institute of Economics and Technology), *Korea's Industrial Policies - Materials on Industrial Organization,* November 1988, p. 51.

[17] According to the *World Competitiveness Report* published yearly by Switzerland's Institute for Management Development, among the four economies of Korea, Hong Kong, Taiwan and Singapore, governmental market intervention is the highest in Korea and pointed out as serious compared to the other competing economies in regard to: the legal and institutional environment, currency and finance policies, efficiency and rationality of policies, flexibility of policies, and distribution of administrative power.

What must be done at this point is to decide which economic sectors need government regulations. It has to be made clear which factors cause market failures, and which provide a reason for market intervention and restriction by the government. Also, it must be made clear whether it is possible for the market to function properly without regulations by the government.

In the process of pursuing the alleviation of market intervention and restriction, various side effects and short term confusion can occur. When the purpose is pursued in steps, these side effects and short term problems can be misunderstood as being caused by the alleviation of such intervention and restriction, and there is a tendency to strengthen them. Therefore, it would be more appropriate to alleviate all cases of government market intervention and restriction in specific areas at once, in a bold and decisive way.

Some argue that Korea's historical situation as a divided nation is indeed a forceful motivating factor for Korea's successful economic performance. Faced with a security threat from the North, Korea has had to build a strong economy that alone can provide the necessary and sufficient base for security Kim(1992), Song(1990). Meanwhile, Hong(1990) contends that the economic success of Korea, has been due to the government's ability to identify most productive forms of economic activities for the nation's economy, institutionalize a system that maximizes the energy and effort of each individual member of the society and channels these mobilized energies into the identified productive activities, and maintain the new system with continuous improvement over a long period of time enough to bear tangible results.

For a resource-poor underdeveloped economy having one of the most dense population in the world, the most productive economic activity is obviously an international specialization in labor-intensive manufacturing.

For the sustained expansion of exports, the government had to develop an outward-looking mentality and the export promotion system which had been firmly incorporated into the national economy. By the mid-1960s, government leaders and associated technocrats had become fully convinced that expansion of manufactured commodity exports was the only means available for Korea to achieve a rapid industrialization by taking advantage of its most plentiful resource, labor. Though this course was chosen by the government, individual entrepreneurs were to be the vehicle for the actual execution of such industrialization efforts.

To encourage export-oriented manufacturing activities, the government utilized a fairly objective measurable performance test and various objective rewarding devices. Also, administrative support for export promotion were made available. Although it has been criticised for corruption and superficial efficiency, the Korean bureaucracy has indeed been an effective institution. Export targets were established at the beginning of each year. All the technocrats related with export administration worked to expedite the administrative process, to strengthen existing export support schemes and to innovate new subsidy measures.

An indispensable prerequisite for successful export-oriented growth is the actual implementation of the strategy to attain the intended effect. To ensure the actual implementation of intended policy measure the government established a monitoring system that could continually solve the implementation problem. The system included a continuous contact and feedback mechanism between the government's top decision-makers and the representative of private entrepreneurial decision-makers. Officials in ministries related to economic affairs supervised private entrepreneurs and helped them to acquire investment funds, import necessary plant facilities, raw materials and expand exports.

In sum, the government was wise enough to recognize immediately unexpected gains of massive employment opportunities created by labor-intensive export production activities. Then, it transformed these activities into enhanced national output based on improved overall allocative efficiency, economies of scale arising from mass production for the world market, and the tremendous learning effects arising from forced international competition in terms of quality, unit price and marketing.

2. Development Strategies

A. Export-Led Take-Off in 1960s

Until 1960, the situation of Korean economy was similar to that of any resource- poor, low income, agricultural country, despite massive inflows of foreign aid for nation's reconstruction and economic stabilization after the Korean War (1950 1953). With an annual population growth rate of nearly 3%, there was widespread unemployment touching a fifth of the working population. Domestic saving rate was very low and per capita income was a meager US$82. Preoccupied by the national reunification issue, the Korean government did not have much interest in economic development until it launched an ambitious Five-Year Economic Development Plan in 1962.

The vicious circle of poverty, unemployment, and high inflation was broken by the introduction of the economic policy of import substitution. Non-durable consumer and basic intermediate goods such as cement and fertilizer were begun to be manufactured under the umbrella of a protective wall of high tariffs and stringent quotas, but this import substitution strategy soon to be found out its natural limits because of the small size of the domestic market.

Therefore, the Korean government adopted an outward-looking development strategy to promote labor-intensive manufacturing exports such as textile and plywood in which Korea had a comparative advantage. This export-oriented development strategy was an ideal choice for a small open economy with limited natural resources but abundant labor, since cheap labor costs made it possible to generate comparative advantage in international markets and to absorb unemployed and underemployed human resources.

To implement this development strategy, the Economic Planning Board was set up in 1961 and institutional arrangements were established to mobilize available resources. The national tax administration was strengthened to reduce the fiscal deficit, and the official interest rates were dramatically raised to increase domestic savings in the banking system. Together with this, the Korean government took extensive export promotion measures to support export industries. Low interest-rate loans were granted to help export firms facing financial difficulties. Various forms of preferential tax treatment, such as tax exemptions and tariff rebates were given to export industries. Furthermore, the Korean government provided repayment guarantees to foreign banks to encourage foreign capital inflow.

The results of the outward-looking development strategy surpassed all expectations with the favorable international environment during the 1960s. Exports increased by almost 40% annually. Propelled by this rapid export growth, its GNP had begun to increase at an annual rate over 9%.

In the course of growth-oriented industrialization, a large amount of foreign capital had to be attracted because domestic savings were insufficient to finance the huge amount of investment demand, and money supply increased rapidly to finance various government projects. As a result, there was chronic inflation throughout the 1960s. On the whole, however, the Korean economy had successfully laid out the foundation for industrialization in the 1960s and was well prepared for a take-off in proceeding years.

B. Promotion of Heavy and Chemical Industries in 1970s

Entering the 1970s, the Korean economy suffered from serious internal and external challenges. Following the First Oil Shock during 1973~1974, industrialized countries raised protective barriers against the import of light manufactured goods produced by developing countries. Moreover, the emergence of China and other developing countries was seen as a serious potential threat to the continued export growth of Korea. In 1971, the United States had pulled out one-third of troops stationed in South Korea, which had to deal with the aggressive security threat from the North.

These circumstances forced the Korean economy to modify its strategic objectives. The government promoted the heavy and chemical industries aimed at building an indigenous defense industry and upgrading the export industrial structure. The overriding objective of tax, credit, interest rate and trade policies was to encourage investment in heavy and chemical industries such as shipbuilding, iron and steel, automobiles, machinery, petrochemicals and electronics.

At this critical juncture, the Korean government selected the "strategic industries". It started the first airline service and the first automobile assembly plant, but eventually sold them to the private sector. During the initial stage, exports were promoted to generate foreign exchange to pay for imports. This initial success prompted the Korean government to make a more systematic approach of 'export promotion'. As exports expanded, production increased faster than planned and loans could become to solicit from international agencies and foreign banks. The process of industrialization became marked again with an outward-looking character. So there is little doubt that the exports have proven to be, to use Robertson's classic phrase, "an engine of growth".

To make this export strategy work successfully, the Korean government guaranteed all credit institutions so as to induce confidence as well as to support such firms that were prepared to take up risky investments. Korea adjusted the exchange rate downwards and introduced essential legislation and policies. To promote exports, the multiple exchange rate was replaced in 1964 by a unified exchange rate system; the Korean Won was devalued by nearly a hundred percent.[18] In addition, a big arsenal of incentives were available: short term export financing, tariff rebates on raw materials imported for exports, simplification of customs procedures, and export insurance.

Providing tax incentives and limiting the import of competing foreign products played an important role in affecting the resource allocation among Korean industries. The Korean government also used credit allocation through the banking system as its most powerful means of supporting strategic industries. The banks were practically owned by the Korean government, and were directed toward making loans to strategic industries on a preferential basis. As a result, commodity exports increased from US$32 million in 1960 to US$3.3 billion by 1973; the ratio of exports to GNP increased from 2% in 1961 to 6.8% in 1966 to 13% in 1970 and 26.9% in 1973, respectively.

Urbanization and employment grew at a very fast pace. By effectively harnessing its abundant supply of skilled and cheap labor for production of manufactured exports, The GNP per capita more than doubled between 1963 and 1971 from US$100 to US$278. At the same time, there was a significant growth in domestic savings and investment during 1964~1973. The gross domestic investment rate increased from 5% to 23%. All these made the country possible withstand the First Oil Shock in 1973.

By virtue of successful transformation of heavy and chemical industries into new export industries, Korea was able to retain a strong pace of economic growth throughout 1970s. The share of heavy and chemical products in whole output of Korean manufacturing industry increased from 38% in 1970 to 52% in 1979. Exports increased rapidly at the rate of approximately 40% per annum. The Korean economy increased at an average rate of 9% per year and per capita GNP rose from US$252 in 1970 to US$1,644 in 1979. This remarkable progress allowed Korea to emerge as one of the NIEs (newly industrialized economies) in Asia.

However, in carrying out ambitious economic development plans with insufficient domestic savings, the Korean economy remained handicapped by the serious lack of funds. The investment-savings gap had been typically filled up either by inducing inflows of foreign capital or expanding domestic money supply. Consequently, foreign debt kept piling up and chronic inflation lingered. Also, disproportionate incentives given to heavy and chemical industries led to excessive investment in certain industries and, in turn, gave rise to serious sectoral imbalances.

There is one unparalleled peculiarity in the Korean economy that its economic expansion was sparked by the expansion of a broad group of companies headed by the most dynamic and aggressive entrepreneurs *i.e.* family controlled conglomerates or '*chaebols*'. There were perhaps 50 groups worthy of this title. They grew out of small family owned retail sales operations or manufacturing enterprises to become some of the world class businesses. Some of them have found their business names among *Fortune's* top listed companies in the world. Promotion of large business families seems to have proved beneficial for greater exports, for encouraging large scale enterprise and providing employment opportunities. For this reason, the Korean government itself promoted their rapid expansion in the 1960s and 1970s, through licensing, subsidized bank loans, and export financing. Undoubtedly, there was a danger of oligopoly and in the early years they collaborated closely with the authoritarian government. In 1990, the combined sales of the *Samsung, Hyundai, Lucky-Goldstar,* and *Daewoo* Groups equaled half of the nation's GNP.

---

[18] The reform of the exchange rate is a prerequisite for any outward-oriented growth policy. In the late 1950s the Korean Won was overvalued: there was almost full parity between the Dollar and the Korean Won. In 1961 and 1964 major devaluations gave a tremendous impetus to exports. The Korean Won was devalued by 25% in 1963, 65% in 1964 and 24% in 1965 respectively. As the real effects of the 1960 devaluation were neutralized by quick inflation, the 1964 devaluation introduced a sliding-scale system for adjustment. In May 1964, the devalued Korean Won was worth 256 to the Dollar, but with the floating exchange rates system introduced in June 1971, the Korean Won fell to 326. When real exchange rates were high, export rates were also high, meanwhile, when exchange rates were low, export rates were also low.

C. Structural Adjustment in 1980s

By the late 1970s, the side effects of the growth-oriented development strategy had become evident. They acted as major constraints on sustained economic growth by distorting the resources allocation and weakening the long-term growth potential. In addition, the Second Oil Crisis in 1979 hit hard on the Korean economy. In the 1980s, the Korean economy experienced its first-ever negative annual growth rate with a huge current account deficit.

Recognizing the fact that economic liberalization would increase the efficiency of the Korean economy by promoting competition and eliminating the ineffective allocation of resources, private initiative was encouraged and the opening-up the domestic market was accelerated. Coupled with these, there was also government-led rationalization through M&A (merger and acquisition) among enterprises which were in trouble due to excessively ambitious investment or poor management.

Under the regime of Doo-Hwan Chun (1980~1988), economic liberalization was pursued with vigor. Several domestic factors contributed to this sudden change in economic policies. International pressure, especially from the Unite States, gave the additional impetus to undertake economic liberalization, namely, changes in industrial policy priorities, which included changing industrial policies from developmental to regulatory, and opening more to FDI.

Beginning with the Fifth Five-Year Plan (1982~1986) the nomenclature of the plan was changed. To demonstrate the urgency of social transformation, so vital for economic progress, it was changed from the "Economic Development Plan" to the "Economic and Social Development Plan". Social security expenditures were now given a big boost, accounting for nearly 40% of the government expenditures in 1990.[19]

Economic ministries also underwent restructuring and industrial policies were changed from being developmental to regulatory. The Monopoly and Fair Trade Law became to enforce from April 1, 1981. Also in 1981 the Ministry of Finance and Economy began to privatize many domestic banks, which had formerly belonged to the state. The governmental support and protection of struggling companies was now limited to only three years, as compared to unlimited protection in the 1960s and 1970s, and licensing procedures were simplified.

Furthermore, the Korean economy was pressured, mostly by the Unite States, to open its market to foreign investors and goods, and hence the Foreign Investment Law was revised in 1987. Import liberalization and reduction of tariff rates were introduced; foreign banks were permitted to enter the capital market in 1981 and their share in the lending market increased from 4% in 1975 to 12.9% in 1984.

Strengthened economic fundamentals made it possible for the Korean economy to accelerate liberalization and globalization. With the considerable increase of the import liberalization ratio from 80% in 1983 to 95% in 1988, trade liberalization was accelerated. Together with the reduced quantitative import restrictions, the nominal tariff rate was gradually lowered from an average of 24% in 1983 to 13% in 1989. Some labor-intensive industries seemed to be seriously affected by these import-liberalization measures.

Financial liberalization was launched to promote competition and efficiency by relaxing restrictions on the financial market. The Korean government divested its equity share in banks, transferring ownership into private hands. Entry barriers into financial markets were eased, making possible the establishment of new nation-wide banks, commercial banks specializing in SMEs (small and medium-sized enterprises), and many non-bank financial institutions.

Recognizing the nature of the structural problem, the Korean government undertook a series of structural adjustment measures in order to enhance the efficiency of the economy. Top priority was given to fighting inflation. In line with this policy stance, a tight monetary policy and restrictive demand management were implemented in the early 1980s. Such policies included setting informal wage guidelines, stabilizing the government's purchase price of major grains, and controlling interest rates and dividend pay-outs. Indeed, these policies reforms worked. Consumer price inflation decreased from 25% in 1980 to 7% in 1982, and the Korean economy grew at 6% annually during the first half of the 1980s.

In the latter half of the 1980s, the Korean economy continued its strong performance recording a sizable surplus in trade balance for the first time in 1986. However, this was mainly due to favorable external-environmental factors such as the appreciation of the Japanese Yen, improved trade terms, low international interest rate, and falling oil prices. At the same time, domestic savings increased markedly.

---

[19] 25% more than that of 1976.

This not only enabled the economy to stand on its own feet but laid a sound foundation for reduction of the foreign debt burden.[20]

The rapid export growth and the large surplus in current account, however, turned out to be a mixed blessing. They brought rapid monetary expansion and generated inflationary pressure. At the same time, the large surplus in current account led to trade friction, intensified pressure to open its markets, and appreciation of the Korean won. During 1987~1989 the real effective exchange rate appreciated by nearly 27%. Hence, while Korean firms lost competitiveness in their traditional labor-intensive export items against countries like China, they were also unable to compete in more advanced export items with countries like Japan.

To worsen the situation, labor unions began to gain strength with the initiation of democratization process in the late 1980s. The results were frequent labor disputes, which led to huge losses in production and export, and a deterioration in both work ethic and productivity. As a result, the Korean commodity exports stagnated in 1989.

D. Liberalization and Globalization in 1990s

Despite the stagnation of export growth during 1990-1991, the Korean economy continued to grow at a fairly high rate thanks to the expansion of domestic demand. During the six-year period between 1985 and 1991, the Korean economy grew at an average annual ratc of 10.4%, which far exceeded its potential GNP growth rate, 7 7.5% per annum on average. The results were high inflation, reaching about 9% during 1990~1991, continued demand for wage hikes, and deterioration of the balance of payment in the current account. These factors led the Korean government to increase its stabilization effort by reinforcing its management of aggregate demand from the second half of 1991. Tighter control was exercised over money supply and fiscal expenditures. It introduced restrictions on housing construction and consumer financing, and phased out some measures geared to stimulate equipment investment. And a wage guideline scheme was introduced to curb wage hikes in 1992.

Under the impact of these various measures, domestic demand began to decrease and consumer price inflation fell remarkably in 1992. However, the GNP growth rate also decreased very sharply. Along with this, equipment investment decreased while bankruptcies among SMEs soared. However, inflation decelerated to 5% in 1993. Meanwhile, the external economic environment improved with the strong Japanese Yen, low international raw material prices, and low international interest rates. Helped by these factors, the Korean economy began to recover by the end of 1993[21] and exports have boomed until 1995. Korea did well in shipbuilding, electronics, and automobiles, but the light industrial base was shifting to China, Southeast Asia, and even Latin America because of high labor cost and government interference.

The newly elected government synchronized the Seventh Five-Year Economic and Social Development Plan (1993~1997) with its term of office. Interest rates were liberalized, and credit controls further eased. Korea still faced the tasks of increasing labor productivity, accelerating technological innovation, fostering cooperative labor management relations, and providing adequate social infrastructure. Needs for various reform issues called for the improvement of the overall efficiency of the Korean economy by promoting competition and private initiatives.

[20] In 1987 the Korean economy posted a growth of 13% and a current account surplus of US$ 9.9 billion. In 1988, the respective figures were 12.4% and $14.2 billion. Since the 1980s Korea's external debt position improved remarkably, declining from a peak of US$42.1 billion in December 1985 to US$35.7 billion in 1988 ; at the same time, all debt ratios improved considerably.

[21] The growth rate of GNP picked up to 8.8% in the first quarter of 1992. However, the economy showed the GNP growth rates 5.6% in 1993, 7.9% in 1994, 7.5% in 1995, with expectation of 7% in this year.

E. Privatization of Public Enterprises in 1980s and 1990s

Historically speaking, the privatization of public enterprises in Korea has steadily progressed since liberalization in 1945, but only began to show true progress since the 1980s. The most typical examples are the privatization of banking sector from 1981 to 1983, and in the latter half of the 1980s by the sale of public stocks.[22] The poor progress in privatization may be attributed to the protracted slump of the stock market, the strong influence of the related government authorities and their effort to maintain the privileges of entrepreneurs, and the opposition of interest groups including employees, labor unions, and management staff to protect their job security. On the other hand, privatization by the sale of stocks to the general public, which was first introduced at the selling of KEPCO (Korea Electricity and Power Corporation) and POSCO (Pohang Iron Steel Company), and came to reveal various problems. In the process of implementation, privatization by the sale of stock to the general public put emphasis on securing revenue and distributing income for the middle and lower classes, but neglected the efficiency of management. This made it difficult to establish a system of responsible management of businesses, which was largely due to the difficulty of creating owner-managed undertakings by the diffusion of the stock.

The announcement to privatize high-grade public enterprises such as KEPCO, Korea Telecom, and Kookmin (formerly Citizens' National Bank) Bank in 1987 invoked great interest of the Korean people. Since 1987, however, the implementation of the plan for privatization has been delayed except for the cases of the Korea Stock Exchange (February 1987) and POSCO (June 1988).

Efforts for privatization commenced with the organization of "the Commission for the Privatization of Public Enterprises" in 1987. Eleven public enterprises, including KEPCO, were chosen as the targets, and the scale of sales reached 5 trillion Won on the basis of internal liquid assets. The program appeared to be ambitious, as it included such plans as the partial sales of POSCO and KEPCO through public subscription, complete sales of the Korea Stock Exchanges, Korea Exchange Bank, Korea Appraisal Board, and functional readjustment of Korea Housing Bank among other undertakings. However, the plan did not make great progress due to the various political and social restrictions. In 1990, the implementation of the plan came to a complete standstill.

In December 1993, the administration made an announcement of the 'Privatization of Public Enterprises and Plans for Functional Readjustment'. One-hundred two government - invested corporations and the sixty one government-invested companies were submitted for privatization. The privatization plan announced by Kim Yong-sam government may be assessed as a positive policy toward privatization in that it aimed at a wider transfer of public enterprises to the civilian sector, and tried to raise management efficiency through privatization. However, the plan is still in its drafting stages, and actual implementation of the plan as originally planned, and commissioned to the related ministries, is likely to be delayed.

The major problems in public enterprises are the lack of entrepreneurship, bureaucratic management, and inefficient business caused by political intervention in decision-making. While the average labor productivity of all Korean industries in 1992 was 10.2%, that of public enterprises was mere 6.2%. This is a significant loss for the country as a whole since public enterprises were run by a budget of 76.42 trillion Korean wons in 1994, which amounts to a little less than twice that of the total government budget of 43.25 trillion Korean wons.

Kim Yong-sam administration, taking this as a serious problem, had made an announcement that it would launch a campaign for the improvement of public enterprises in a spirit of reform. However, faced with opposition from labor unions, the Korean government has retreated from this plan, and ended up announcing that existing practices in personnel management and labor systems would not be changed. In order to enhance the national competitiveness and to become a developed country, large-scale improvements in public enterprises are indispensable.

[22] In 1981, privatization of Hanil Bank was soon followed by that of Korea First Bank, Seoul Trust Bank, and Choheung Bank. The privatization of the four banks was achieved by selling stocks under competitive bids. In order to prevent the financial monopoly of large stock holders, corporations and private persons were restricted to holdings of less than 5%, and 5,000 stocks respectively, and after being listed on the Stock Exchange, shares were limited to less than 8%.

4. A New Role for the Government

The traditional role of the Korean government in the economy during the last four decades could be described as in <Table III-1>.

< Table III-1 > Traditional Government Role in the Korean Economy

Areas of Active Government Involvement	Areas of Inactive Government Involvement
• Resource Allocation	• Income Distribution
• Entry and Exit Regulation	• Social Welfare
• Direct Ownership of Enterprises	• Anti-trust Regulation
• Price and Wage Controls	• Pollution Control

Many of the targeted industries in the so-called heavy and chemical industries reveal economies of scale. As a result, the government had a licensing system whereby it allowed only a small number of companies to enter an industry and prevented other firms from doing so. The government also channeled funds to the targeted industry by allocating its own funds and also by directing commercial banks under the direct control of the government to do so. These funds were made available to private firms in the form of loans. Therefore, the ultimate responsibility for utilizing and paying back those loans was laid in the hands of private business firms. When some private companies with the heavy government borrowing became insolvent due to mismanagement, the government or a bank became directly involved in finding a new company which can take over the insolvent one.

The resource allocation and the entry-exit regulation by the government have been closely linked, and since the government has been directly involved from the initial stage of the industry development to the mature stage, it is natural that the government bureaucrats feel that they are guiding and supervising the industry. Even today, MOCIE (the Ministry of Commerce, Industry & Energy) announces specific production and export targets for not only an industry but also for particular companies in the industry. This may seem very strange to an observer from a Western market economy In any case, the Korean way of developing a certain target industry through the cooperation of the government and business firms is very interesting in that it is a mixture of the state and market economies. It is neither a free market economy nor a centrally planned economy; it is a regulated market economy.

Has this peculiar type of a regulated market economy been efficient compared to alternatives? Theoretical literature on the subject deals with the incidents of market failure and government failure. But the Korean case is a mixture of the two, so theories dealing with pure markets and pure governments are of limited value here. It seems clear that a regulated market economy is superior to a centrally planned economy. But is a regulated market economy more efficient than a free market economy? The answer to the preceding question seems to be affirmative at the early stage of industrialization when there are not enough resources for the industry development. All the ingredients for the successful industry development - technology, capital, management, human resources and even raw materials - are lacking. The government mobilizes the resources inside and outside the country and channels them to successful and trustworthy entrepreneurs. The latter, in turn, work hard in order to realize profits and build their own empires.

Under these circumstances, the government regulation of an industry has two major potential problems: a misjudgment of the demand size either way and/or an inefficient operation of the enterprise due to lack of competition. Several factors may have worked to prevent these problems from occurring in the Korean context.

First, at the early stage of industrialization, the supply tends to create its own demand, and the shortage of resources tends to limit the size of a plant to the minimum economic scale. There are exceptions to this when a particular government is more interested in the demonstrative effects of an industry rather than its efficiency. In the Korean case, since private companies were eventually responsible for making the venture profitable, they may have been keen to avoid overcapacity. The lack of competition and the resulting inefficiency has been partially covered with the protection of the domestic industry from foreign competition. In the export industries, international competition forced the private companies to be efficient in order to survive.

As the economy moved to a more mature stage toward the end of the 1970s, the regulated market economy started to show some failures. Overcapacity and underutilization of the plant became serious problems in some heavy and chemical industries, especially the defense-related industries. The lack of competition in some industries may have made the management in those industries rather lax and inefficient. As the economy began to be open to foreign competition, these inefficient industries suddenly became vulnerable.

There were several cases of government failures since the late 1970s. The first and foremost would be the excessive investment is the heavy machinery industry, especially related to the defense industry. The overcapacity and the resulting losses have persisted even until today in the form of Korea Heavy Industry Corporation.

Second, there was the case of the shipping industry. The government provided various incentives to private firms in order to increase the total capacity of the national flag carriers, but the companies who followed the government policy later found themselves in serious financial trouble. Eventually, the industry as a whole had to go through a major reorganization because many companies became bankrupt. The shipbuilding industry is another case of investing in overcapacity at the prodding of the government and found itself in deep financial trouble. Another case would be the restructuring of the automobile industry in the early 1980s. Because of the recession, the domestic automobile industry ran into serious problems in terms of the overcapacity and mounting losses. The government intervened to restructure the industry, forcing the companies to be specialized into the production of passenger cars, trucks and buses. In retrospect, one can raise a question about the efficacy of the restructuring policy.

Over-regulation of the industry still persists to the present day. Despite the announced policy of liberalizing barriers to entry to major industries the government is still involved in entry and exit. Taking again the case of the automobile industry the government had blocked some companies from entering the industry, and also played more than a bystander's role in its on-going restructuring. There are strong arguments for the government intervention and there are many believers of the argument. They believe that, if a free entry is allowed in the industry, this will result in the excessive investment and cut-throat competition. This will then result in the waste of the 'national resources'. The automobile industry has many natural entry barriers such as a large production plant, technology, a presence of the loyal suppliers and a distribution channel. These natural entry barriers are more than enough to prevent many potential entrants from entering the industry. The government regulation is a redundant barrier which hinders effective competition. If there are some companies who still enter the industry, this may be an indication that either the current competitors are not very efficient or potential entrants are miscalculating the industry potential. Samsung Motors was a good example of the latter. The issue boils down to the question of who is in a better position to forecast the future potential of the automobile industry, the government or a private business firm.

It is also possible that a new entrant might possess a new technology which the existing companies either do not have or are reluctant to utilize due to their committed position. It is worth pointing out that a breakthrough innovation for an industry is sometimes introduced from outside the industry. The quartz technology for the watch industry is an example, it is possible that the industry could suffer from the overcapacity and excessive competition after free entry into the industry is allowed. The choice is between a free competition with the possibility of over- investment or a regulated industry with the possibility of inefficiency and under- innovation The choice is not between a perfect market and a perfect government, but between an imperfect market and an imperfect government. As the economy becomes more mature, however, an imperfect market tends to perform better than an imperfect government. First, there are not as many new industries as in the early industrialization stage when the country has to mobilize limited resources to build new industries As a result, the waste of resources argument is less convincing. Second, private companies now have enough experience to make their own judgement about the industry and enough resources to enter into a new industry.

Third, in the age of global competition, only the companies that have been seasoned in the fierce domestic competition could survive in the global market. In addition, when a government has to allow foreign competitors to enter the domestic market, how can it not allow domestic companies to enter a certain industry? A stronger argument of the government failure can be made about the direct ownership of key enterprises by the government. There are dozens of state-owned enterprises in Korea and many of them operate in the monopolistic market. Some of them are very large even compared to the private big business groups. Since many of these state enterprises also operate the highly regulated industry, their profits do not represent the performance of the companies. As a result, these companies are not operating like business firms but more like government offices. In many cases, retired government officials or generals are appointed to the top posts. In state enterprises, there is little geese of "urgency" that is often found in private companies and little incentive to innovate. The situation is not very different from the state enterprises in socialist countries.

All in all, the Korean government should change its role in the coming decade. It has to dramatically reduce its role in the areas where it has been very active before. They are the areas of direct fund allocation, entry and exit barriers, direct ownership of the enterprises and price and wage controls. On the other hand, it has to increase its role in the areas where it has been rather inactive. They include more active income distribution policy through taxation, increase of the social welfare programs, regulation of the pollution, and more active environmental programs. This kind of shift requires a major restructuring of the government organization and retraining of government officials.

5. Patterns of Trade and Industrial Policy

Trade is the most practical way of exchanges between nations. While there may be some distortions in the process of economic development for purposes of protecting industries, it is a realm where the discipline of competition applies strictly and market shares are eventually lost if price and quality lag behind. This principle has become more pronounced with the advent of the WTO.

The comparative advantage theory of David Ricardo (1815) was the first to explain such phenomena, the factor endowment theory of Heckscher-Ohlin followed, and theories started diverging into different directions in the 1960s and 1970s with emphases on key factors such as technological development, human capital, and product life cycle. However, in the more complicated trade environment of the modern world, it is quite unrealistic to explain trade simply in terms of a few restricted factors.

A. Changes in the Composition of Exports and Imports

1) Exports

The export volume of Korea, which merely amounted to US$54.8 million at the start of the initial Five-Years Economic Development Plan in 1962, has grown over 2,000 times to reach US$130 billion as of end 1996. When the country achieved exports volume US$100 million in 1964, Syria, Iceland, and Tunisia were at similar levels, but currently their exports stand at the level of US$3.5~4.5 billion. When exports reached US$1 billion in 1971, Indonesia, the Philippines, Chile, and Israel were at similar levels, but they have only grown into the US$12~40 billion range. Meanwhile, the growth of imports also kept pace as the dependence on trade stood at 54% of GNP as of end 1996; Korea without trade would be unthinkable.

Product diversification has also been pronounced, with only 142 items in 1964 when exports reached US$100 million, but an increase to 983 in 1971 (US$1 billion), 5,558 in 1977 (US$10 billion), and 8,100, or a 55-fold increase since 1964, at the end of 1997 when exports amounted to US$130 billion. In terms of market diversification, Korea exported to 41 countries in 1964, but that number had grown to 108 in 1971, to 154 in 1977, and to 227 in 1996 respectively.

A look at the ten major export items over the years is also useful to understand Korea's export pattern. In 1961, minerals such as metals, stones, and coal, and agricultural and marine products occupied nine out of the top ten spots while processed wood was the only industrial item to make the list. By the 1970s, textiles accounted for over 40% of total exports and ranked at the top until the mid-1980s. Since then, however, items within the heavy and chemical sector such as electronic products, steel, ship, synthetic materials, and metal products started to emerge rapidly. By 1990, electric and electronic products ranked at the top with automobiles and general machinery advancing into the top 10 export items. With the semiconductor boom, electric and electronic products accounted for over 30% of exports in 1993 as the weight of previous main export items such as textiles and shoes declined sharply.

2) Imports

Among industrial products, Korea could not but depend on importation of the heavy and chemical sector until the early of 1970s in order to make up its weak areas. The policy of promoting heavy and chemical industries, started in 1973 with a view to import substitution and export market diversification, was still not significantly effective by the end of the decade. At the same time, imports of primary products encompassing raw materials such as crude oil and agricultural and dairy products continued to increase due to the lack of natural resources.

According to the Ministry of Trade, Industry and Energy, imports of primary product grew by an average of 47% until 1982 and 37% until 1985, and the rate started to decline to the 25~30% level after 1986. On the flip side, the percentage of imports of industrial products remained low at 53~58% until 1982~1983, but the figure grew to 70% in 1986, and stood at 74%, 72%, and 76% in 1990, 1993, and 1995, respectively. The obvious difference between the compositions of imports and exports is that the weight of primary products is relatively large in those of imports.

Since natural resources are scarce domestically, it might be more relevant to analyze imports by use. In 1987, 44% of all imports were related to exports, but this figure has fallen to 32% in 1996 as imports for local consumption had grown in proportion. Consumers' tastes are changing toward imported products in line with rises in income and as a result of market opening. A look at the percentages, however, reveals very little change as import of raw materials made up 55% of the total in 1987 but still a relatively high 50% in 1996.

One thing to note here is the increasing dependence on petroleum as the import of crude oil have risen steeply since 1989. In the case of capital products, their weight among imports was 35% in 1987, but the figure rose to 39% in 1996, pointing to a weakness in technology within the machinery industry.

B. Patterns of Trade

1) Theoretical Background

While Ricardo's theory is extremely simplistic in that it considers only production variables, the factor endowment theory put forth by Heckscher and Ohlin, which incorporated the various production factors of each nation, was a more novel approach. If the production coefficient between two products is identical, their relative prices vary with the relative prices of production variables. For countries with ample labor supply, labor-intensive products entail a relatively low price, while the same may be said for capital-intensive products in countries with abundant capital.

The technology gap theory explains the trade phenomenon in terms of the gaps in technological levels between countries and thus has a decisive focus on technology. A country which develops a new product or a new production technology in a given field will attain technological edge, and thus relative advantage in trade, until other countries imitate that product or technology. This theory thus explains international trade in terms of an ever-changing factor. The theory has been supported by such theorists as Posner (1961), Gruber, Mehta, and Vernon (1967), Hufbauer (1970). However, this theory views technological imitation and acquisition in an excessively simplistic manner, and thus fails to explain the direction, time required, and determinants of comparative advantage.

Leontief (1956) classified labor skill acquisition into five stages and studied their effects on export industries and import substitution, claiming that the Heckscher-Ohlin theory does not apply to the United States. As a result, he explained that the reason behind the labor-intensiveness of the US exports was attributable to the outstanding skill level of its labor force relative to other countries. However, his explanation of this paradox in terms of the quality of labor was decidedly inadequate, and thereafter Kenen (1965) tried to estimate the human capital invested in the U.S. export industries and industries competing with imports. Human capital is realized through education and training, which requires extended periods of time but stays with laborers throughout their lives and thus contributes to a big jump in productivity.

Baldwin (1971) argued that the export industries in the United States utilized skilled labor more than import substitution industries by estimating human capital in terms of the actual and opportunity costs of education. Keesing (1966) calculated human capital in terms of the weight of skilled labor, and also concluded that a large portion of skilled labor was being used by export industries by finding out the correlation between absolute export volume and skilled labor invested.

2) Survey of Literature

In Korea, representative research on the determinants of trade includes Bon-Young Ku (1989), Soo-Yong Kim (1982), Heun-Hoon Lee (1990), and Sang-Ryul Kim (1993). Kim (1982) classified 28 industries and analyzed them over 4 years (1966, 1970, 1975, and 1979), and ran a cross-sectional regression of pure export volume on labor, capital, and human capital. In the factor endowment model, labor was found to be the most significant determinant of comparative advantage while, R&D (research and development) and human capital were relatively insignificant. In the regression analysis with various factors as dependent variables, per capita human capital showed comparative disadvantage, while, in the analysis by industry, those industries with capital concentration displayed comparative advantage. Furthermore, a high level of correlation was discovered between capital and labor, and also between human capital and labor.

In Kim (1993), the manufacturing sector was divided into 8 categories over the 1979~1990 period and the determinants of international competitiveness were analyzed. The results showed that abundance of labor enhanced competitiveness. In particular, technology was shown to have a decisive effect on the strengthening of international competitiveness. Estimated coefficients of capital and human capital did not indicate statistical significance and were thus deemed inadequate. However, in studies from 1984 on, human capital was found to have a positive effect on strengthening competitiveness, and technology levels also heightened comparative advantage.

As for similar studies abroad, Dosi, Pavitt and Soete (1990) analyze how technology affects trade patterns. 40 three-digit code industries were designated and analyzed over 15 years between 1963 and 1977 in 22 OECD countries to see the correlation between technology and trade, and the effect of the former on the latter. The number of patents registered was designated as the best technological variable. Gruber, Mehta, and Vernon (1967) analyzed the relationship between exports and technological development based on 1962 data. accounted for a high portion of costs and personnel in 5 sectors including transportation, electronic, chemical, and machinery, and exports accounted for a large proportion of sales. In particular, the weight of R&D was by far the highest in the aircraft industry, and exports also accounted for a much higher percentage of sales.

3) Empirical Analysis

From the regression results, the following can be concluded regarding the determinants of Koreas exports and imports for the period of 1976 to 1995.

First, the coefficient of the labor variable is of the same sign as that of the capital variable. In existing research, the two have generally been treated as a single variable exerting adverse influence. In the case of exports and imports, however, the two have the same sign and thus may be assumed as having a complementary rather than offsetting effect. In terms of the labor coefficient, both the export and import coefficients are of similar magnitude. The coefficient of the capital variable for exports is 0.1251 and that of imports is -0.0421, so that capital has had the effect of increasing exports and reducing imports, although the impact on the former is more pronounced than the impact on the latter.

Second, the values of substitute variables of dynamic theories of trade such as those relating to human capital and technological development also show positive effects (values) on export growth. The coefficient of the labor variable, which combines the work experience and education level of the worker as an index of his/her ability, shows a positive sign for exports and a negative sign for imports. In existing research, human capital displays a negative sign as opposed to capital and labor variables, so that the role of human capital on export competitiveness is smaller in Korea than it is for other countries. However, the positive sign of this coefficient in this study shows that over the past 20 years, human capital also has had competitiveness relative to competing nations. In other words, the competitiveness of exports is partly attributable to superior personnel with high levels of education and continued training and skill improvement on the job. The sophisticated workforce with higher education and longer working experiences has thus more than offset rises in wages and contributed to the growth of exports. The negative value for imports implies import substitution (reduction) effect. In comparing exports and imports, it may be considered that the effect (magnitude) on exports has been greater than that on imports. The role of human capital in Korea over the past 20 years has thus had a bigger impact on export growth than on import substitution.

Third, the coefficient value of the technology gap variable shows a positive sign for exports and a negative sign for imports. This indicates that improvements in technology have had a positive effect on both export growth and import substitution, thus contributing to an improvement in the balance of trade. Over the period under review, Korea has promoted industrial competitiveness through R&D investments, increases in research personnel, and active introduction of technology. In comparing exports and imports, the coefficient value for imports was -0.0255 while that of exports was 0.0147, which implies that while technology-intensive industries have contributed to export growth, they generally had a greater import substitution effect.

Fourth, in regard to excess expenditure on advertising and marketing costs according to the product life cycle theory, both the coefficients for exports and imports show negative signs, which implies that they have been concentrated domestically. In other words, if advertising costs as a percentage of sales is taken to represent the product life cycle in Korea, it is inappropriate in explaining export competitiveness in overseas markets.

4) Summary

The findings of the empirical analysis can be summarized as follows:

First, the variables relating to capital, labor, human capital, and technological development are significant at the 1% level and thus are reliable in explaining the dependent variables. This means that these variables have all contributed to raising the relative competitiveness of Koreas exports while having a substitution effect on imports. The advertising costs/sales variable which was selected for the life cycle theory displayed negative coefficient values for both exports and imports and was thus inadequate in explaining trade patterns.

From a Heckscher-Ohlin point of view, previous analyses of Koreas trade may have assumed that the country had attained export competitiveness through the use of its relatively abundant labor, but the data analysis reveals that over the past 20 years, capital, human capital, and technological development have been at least as valuable as labor. The coefficient for capital has increased after 1986, signifying that capital- intensive goods have been attaining competitiveness in overseas markets.

Second, in the case of the labor variable, while it did have a positive effect on exports, the coefficient declined after 1986, and thus it was not contributing to an enhancement in export competitiveness as effectively. The import coefficient also rose to positive levels from negative, so that the competitiveness of labor-intensive products was decreasing to the point of economic rationale dictating either imported goods or imported labor.

Third, human capital was shown to have competitiveness in both export and import arenas, with a positive coefficient for exports and a negative coefficient for imports. Dividing the past 20 years into two periods, export competitiveness was high in the earlier period but the coefficient fell to negative levels during the latter period, pointing to an actual drop in competitiveness. Since rises in productivity could not keep pace with the rises in wages, skilled labor actually contributed to an increase in imports rather than exports. Changes in the human capital index also indicate a considerable drop-off in growth after 1986, and a negative effect on export competitiveness.

Fourth, the coefficient relating to technological development continued to be positive in sign, and thus it may be assumed that technology-intensive products maintain their competitiveness. Again, however, the coefficient for this variable fell after 1986. The reason for the decline, which signifies a decline in competitiveness in more recent years, may be explained by inadequate investments in technological development and/or training of technical personnel.

These findings have the following implications for future policy-making.

First, the comparative advantage of the capital factor is becoming increasingly pronounced in its contribution to exports while the human capital factor of skilled workforce and the technological factor are on a relative downward trend so that policies to induce investments in workplace education and training, research and development, and trained personnel should be sought.

Second, the desirable method of alleviating the deepening trade deficit is not short-term solutions such as currency depreciation, wage raise constraints, and restriction on excessive imports, but long-term directives for maintaining competitiveness in overseas markets by successfully completing the transformation from industries involving simple labor to higher value-added industries which are intensive in technological and human capital elements.

Third, the capital factor has sustained an increase in its comparative advantage over the labor factor from the late 1980s and on, thus investments in fixed assets should continue as this factor is likely to become even more important in the future. Accordingly, policies to promote capital-intensive industries and the localization of materials should continue to be strengthened.

C. Industrial Policy

Until the early 1980s, trade and industrial policy In Korea was designed to achieve pre-designated export targets set by the consecutive Five-Year Development Plans. The quantitative export targets were scheduled on the basis of orthodox comparative advantage. As some incentives, such as policy loans, which are not classified into the category of export incentives, actually have an indirect subsidy effect on exports activities, it is necessary to fully take into accounts both direct and indirect subsidy effects in estimating subsidy magnitude. The exports incentive measures comprise tariff reductions and exemptions, quantitative import restrictions; export-import link system; ex-factory price controls; tax exemptions and reductions; and a preferential credit scheme. The main policy instruments deployed for promoting import substituting activities are quantitative import restrictions and tariffs on imports.

The priorities of trade and industrial policy of Korea may be divided into three different stages over the period 1965~1994. From 1965 to 1974, there was a minor trade bias for exports aimed at protecting or subsidizing the export industries. As the government launched the promotion of heavy and chemical industries, with an aim of upgrading the industrial structure, the industry bias for exports increased significantly for the cases of heavy and chemical industries during the period 1975~1984. This industry bias culminated over between 1975~1979 in order to accelerate the capital formation for the developments of heavy and chemical industries, to increase the value-added content of the manufacturing sector and to increase defense capability by promoting the developments of the machinery industry. Although the government adopted the "Comprehensive Programme for Economic Stabilization" in 1979, this bias was maintained until 1984 in order to achieve a cornerstone for the development of heavy and chemical industries. The overall policy since 1985 has been characterized by the shift towards liberalization. One good example is the removal of restrictions on entry to the petrochemical industries in the mid-1980s, in comparison with the entry restrictions placed on the machinery industries in the late 1970s. Korea has also joined Article 8 of IMF in 1988 and the Article 11 of the GATT in 1989 implying that its readiness to lift the foreign exchange controls, which has fully liberalized in 1999 and trade restrictions, Korea has maintained a positive stance of promoting multilateral trade as well as deep integration movements in the 1990s. As a member of the WTO (World Trade Organization) and the OECD, Korea has been trying to align her market liberalization programme and competition policy with the industrialized countries.

The revisionistic approach puts an emphasis on the important role of technology capability of the Korean economy since the launch of the export-oriented policy. According to this approach, technology capability is the ability to make effective use of technological knowledge. It is divided into production, investment and innovation capability. It seems that two points are missing in this argument.

First, some industries in Korea, such as textiles, shipbuilding, cement, mining and fertilizer industries, have made considerable technology advances in production engineering before Korea launched the export-oriented policy.

Second, emphasis is placed mainly on production or investment capability and does not systematically analyse the disembodied technology developments of related industries. Disembodied technology refers to the technology related to the design arid implicit know-how, *e.g.,* the design and production of capital goods and core components by its own capability. Revisionists explain that the human resources educated in domestic or foreign academic institutions have contributed to the diffusion of technology in a disembodied form. Their argument may be correct for the 1960s when Korea promoted exports of light industrial products. Expensive education or institutional arrangements may be less helpful for the promotion of sophisticated heavy and chemical industries which require, not only intensive education in specified areas but also the indigenous technology base and market outlets. A certain level of indigenous technology base may be required to absorb disembodied technology related to the basic design in capital goods and core components.

As pointed out by Westphal (1982) and Enos and Park(1988), "learning by doing" in process and production technology has contributed to an increase in GNP and exports. Amsden and Hikino (1994) posit the positive role of microeconomic agents of conglomerates by highlighting their organizational know-how of expanding corporate growth through diversification. The organizational know-how of conglomerates, however, can be acquired by the effective tactics of procuring credit from the formal financial institutions instead of increasing their technology capability. A significant concentration of economic power by conglomerates has been shaped by the availability of low cost financial resources in the 1970s.[23] Another reason may be the elimination of new entrants by allowing entries into a new business realm to a limited number of firms. Such a measure is taken as a means of preventing overlapping investment. Whether or not conglomerates have moved to diversification after achieving specialization through the use of imported technology is an open question.

A mastery of production technology may be a necessary, but it is not a sufficient condition for upgrading the industrial structure. This is because such an industrial adjustment requires a diffusion of

[23] See Corbo and Suh(1992), pp.207~212 for details.

disembodied technology and/or an equipment- embodied diffusion from upstream industries which act as suppliers of new technology through knowledge dissemination or sales of technology-intensive parts to downstream industries. For instance, most NIEs (newly industrializing economies) may encounter constraints in shifting their industrial structure towards more sophisticated manufactures unless they procure relevant product technology. They can produce a certain range of sophisticated products by importing process or production technology, but sooner or later they are bound to be caught up by the fierce competition from other developing economies.[24] The reason for such a phenomenon is very simple: given a similar range of embodied technology the competitive edge is mainly determined by wage rates and the financial stamina to modernize production facilities. Before the capital goods are augmented with the codified control technology, the NIEs have enjoyed reaping the gains of productivity increase by stretching the process technology and by modifying production technology. But the introduction and adoption of capital goods, augmented by codified control technology, have reduced the barriers to entry for potential entrants amongst LDCs (Less Developed Countries) into the production of unsophisticated manufactures. This implies that the competitive advantage of NIEs has been eroded in parallel with the development of codified technology in capital goods sector. The industrialized countries can influence the allocation of production activities by keeping their competitive edge in the disembodied technology of capital goods and the core components sector. A more plausible criteria for evaluating evolving competitive advantage might be extent to which Korean firms have reduced the gap of non-price competition with industrialized countries in terms of disembodied technology.

Amsden (1989) suggests that Korea can be the next economic giant in Asia. She analyses the changes in technology capability in large firms, but misses the link between technology capability and industrial adjustment capability. The latter refers to the capability of integrating technology with the production and marketing activities at the industry level. The underdeveloped condition of disembodied technology may have been a major impediment in the reduction of flexible adjustment at both firm and public-policy level. If there is a poor link between the technology base and imported disembodied technology, the path of technology developments will become discrete. A discrete technology base may reduce the maneuvering power of firms by limiting their capability to applying generic technology to the production activities. Without achieving considerable progress in disembodied technology, the implementation of flexible production may be infeasible because of the technological constraints in upgrading and diversifying product range. By the same token, a public policy designed to facilitate a flexible adjustment of industry may be less effective due to the limited options in microeconomic policy.[25]

D. Policy Implications

Bhagwatl and Krueger (1973) assume that a neutral incentive system is equivalent to an export oriented policy. However, the empirical evidence of export-oriented policy in Korea highlights the fact that a move from import substitution policy to one of neutrality is one step, and that a positive bias towards exports is a second, non-neutral step. The orthodox approach emphasizes the role of the market whereas the revisionist approach stresses the role of institutional factors, but trade policy in Korea cannot be classified exclusively as market based or as being driven by the invisible hand.

It has been operated on a two-tier system in which a substantial portion of trade policy is based on the free trade argument while some of it is based on the protectionist stance developed to foster several strategic export industries. The trade and industrial policy exhibited a mild export bias over the period of 1965~1974. It showed a bias for heavy industry during 1975~1979 which then declined between 1980~1984. The improvement of external balance and high growth rates in the 1980s, helped by the low interest rates, low material costs and the depreciated domestic currency, gave the Korean government room to adopt a more neutral trade and industrial policy. Although some interventionist measures are found to set off the capital market imperfections and foreign distortions, the overall balance of trade policy of Korea has been shifted towards freer trade since the mid-1980s.

---

[24] A good example may be the Korean textile industry which is squeezed by the price competition from developing countries and the non-price competition from industrialized countries.

[25] This pattern of adjustment is explained by tracing out the constraints on the industrial adjustment policy in section four and six of the authors paper(forthcoming).

The classification of trade policy in the orthodox approach is based on the price distortion between export and import substitution activities, as well as among difference industrial sectors. It can be used as a 'rough' gauge to make a judgement about a trade policy regime. It may, however, be misleading to use the degree of bias as a measure for evaluating the allocative efficiency of trade policy because it does not reflect a transformation process of the economy in terms of disembodied technology.

Besides, it does not explain the prerequisite of import substitution activity in the capital goods sector as a means of upgrading the industrial structure and diversifying product range. The revisionist approach stresses the institutional factors and selective promotion of infant industries, but it makes light of the dynamic role of market forces and entrepreneurs in transforming the industrial structure. Any plausible exposition of trade and industrial policy has to take into account the changes in technology development and industrial transformation.[26]

The evaluation of selective intervention on the 'learning process' may be inconclusive at the aggregate level due to difficulties of segregating the accumulation of disembodied technology with respect to the transformation process from other elements. The positive role of large firms and the flexible adjustment capability may also be inconclusive. A sector-specific study is required to evaluate trade and industrial policy in terms of economies of scale, technology catch-up and vertical collaboration via an inter-industry linkage effect.

[26] The export-led growth can be achieved at the initial stage of industrialization, but a sustained exports may not be realized without accomplishing an industrial transformation of growth-led exports. For a similar lines of argument, see Bradford (1994).

Chapter IV

WEAKENING COMPETITIVENESS, LIBERALIZATION AND DOWNTURN OF THE KOREAN ECONOMY

The Korean economy having enjoyed an unprecedented boom in the late 1980s has slide into stagnation in 1990s mainly due to the weakening international competitiveness by worsening its structural problems and adopting itself to the rapid globalization.

Without properly responding to the deterioration of its international competitiveness, the Korean economy had taken a path toward a globalization as launching of the WTO system in 1995 and joining the OECD in 1996. In this boardless world, the Korean government could not but push ahead opening and liberalization policies.

The purpose of this chapter is to provide an overall picture of the Korean economy in 1990s prior to the IMF bail-out in 1997, what had made the international competitiveness of the Korean economy weakened, especially with respect to its export competitiveness, and further how the situation had been deteriorated to make it inevitable for the Korean government to seek for an official request for an emergency liquidity which finalized the Stand-by Arrangement with the IMF in December 1997.

1. WEAKENING KOREA'S INTERNATIONAL COMPETITIVENESS

As changes have taken place in international economies since 1990, economic stagnation, especially in developed countries, has continued and demands for imports have decreased. Moreover, protectionist measures as well as restrictions on the environment were proliferating in international trade and conditions for Korea's export activities were getting worse. Korea's export growth rates to its major trading partners were much lower than the rates of the decrease in imports from them. Korea's exports had a weakness of being price-elastic during the periods of recovery and price-inelastic during the periods of recession.

In 1990s, the primary cost of production rose drastically, while the amount of production stagnated and price competitiveness fell. Efforts for improvement in such areas of product quality, technology development, marketing and so forth were also inadequate and general interest in exports slackened.

The performance of the Korean economy in the late 1980s and the early 1990s did not appear too bad, at least in terms of macro-variables. The economic situation, however, was considered to be unsound. The price competitiveness of Korean exports has been sharply decreased. Moreover, the content of economic growth was very far from being sound. Growth was supported by consumption, rather than exports and investment. And more serious effects resulted from economic behavioral changes of key economic agents including businessmen, workers and government. <Figure IV-1> shows the factors in weakening competitiveness of export and its derivative impact. <Figure IV-2> describes the relationship between declining exports and economic recession.

<Figure IV-1> Factors for Weakening Competitiveness of Export and its Derivative Impact[27]

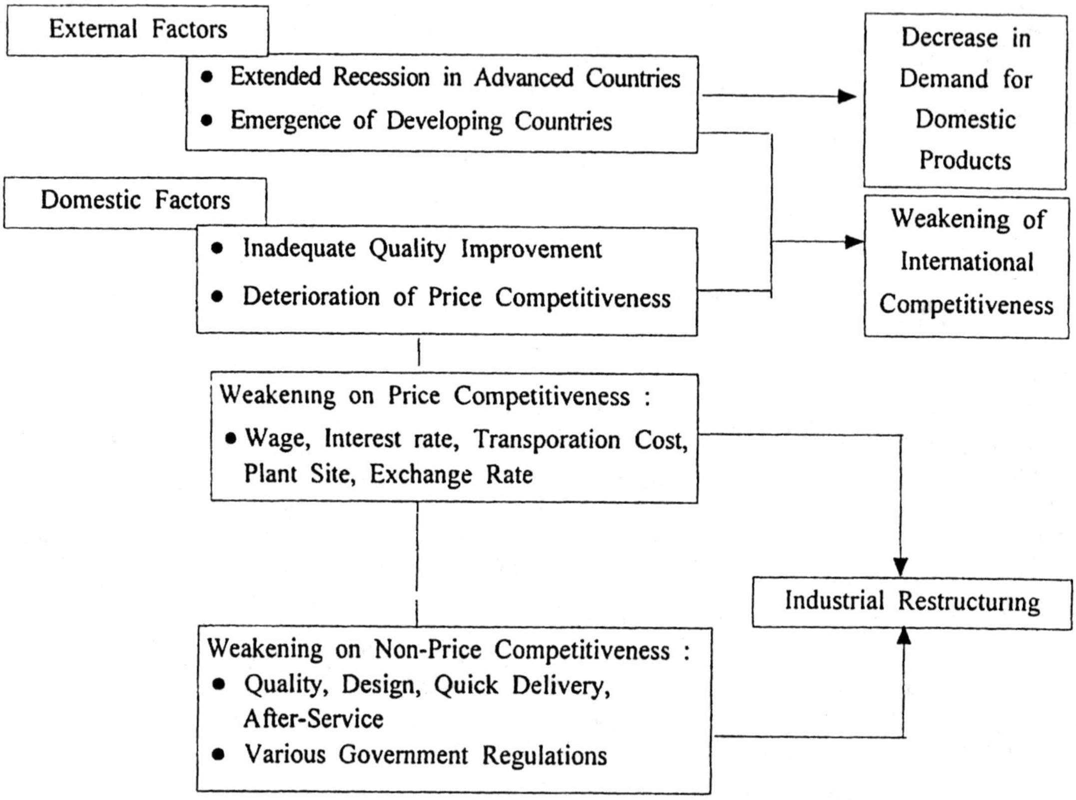

<Figure IV-2> Relationship between Exports Declining and Economic Recession

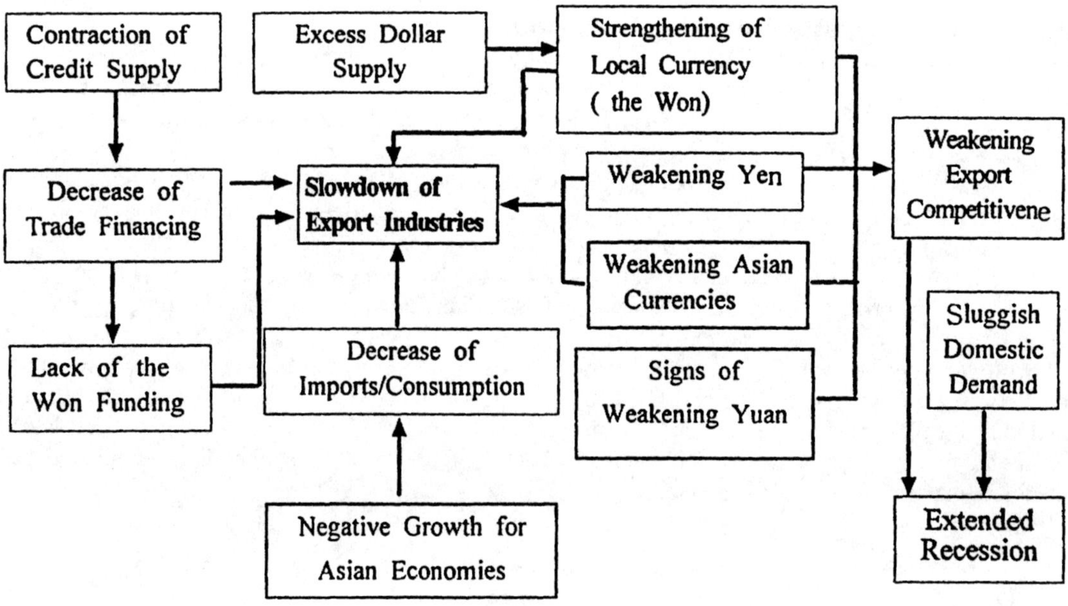

[27] Yang-Taek Lim, "Korea's Liberalization Policy Directions and Korea's Weakening Competitiveness", *Journal of Asian Economies,* Vol 7, No 4, 1996, pp 603~634

A. Deterioration of Structural Problems in Early 1990s

Since the implementation of the 5-year Plan for Economic Development in 1962, the Korea's oriented development strategy with a dependency on imitating technologies to meet the changing market demands, had heightened Korea's capital dependency on Japan, and as a result Korea was unable to raise the value added export industries. Moreover, the import dependency of heavy and chemical products, which had high export growth rates, had been increasing. Although superficially the amount of exports in heavy and chemical goods seemed to be rising, labor-intensive goods, which use relatively more labor input than capital input, had a higher rate of exportation. This is the result of an artificially assembled structure of exportation which utilizes cheap labor.

Differences in the time to meet market demand is a central factor in determining international competitiveness. Korea has been experiencing decreases in exports in home appliances and automobiles due to slow response time. Moreover, the 'Third Industrial Revolution', which the developed countries are trying to lead by reforming production systems, has raised concerns about Korea's economic power. Korea's exports still depend on the OEM (Original Equipment Method) to the great extent, which does not has raised value-added in the marketing process or bring about a long-term dominance in the markets. In particular, securing a stable market dominance has lowered the price elasticity of demand, thus preventing the decrease of exports due to a rise in exchange rates.

As the technology protectionism prevails in the world, Korean firms had been suffering from bottlenecks in technology upgrading, which was brought about by the slow domestic technology development and reluctance of advanced countries to transfer technology. Hence, while Korean firms lost competitiveness in traditional labour-intensive export items to the countries like China, they could not compete in more advanced export items with countries like Japan.

In particular, the content of economic growth was very far from being sound in the early of 1990s. Growth was supported by consumption, rather than exports and investment and it has become apparent that growth potential is diminishing. Further analysis of the content of growth reveals the following characteristics.

First, exports decreased over 6% in absolute terms in 1997. Such a decrease was the greatest ever in the development history of Korea. One of the major underlying causes was the failure of Korean firms to effectively adapt themselves to rapid environmental changes, such as sharp appreciation of the Korean Won, high wage hikes and increasing trade frictions.

Second, private consumption increased more than 10% in absolute terms over the period of 1997. We labeled it overconsumption. This spending behavior was supported by large windfall profits from real estate speculation and from the securities markets, and by substantial wage increases. Increased consumption might have help boost the economy in the short-run but it ultimately undermined the growth potential in the long-run.

Third, investment in plants and equipment was very poor in the manufacturing sector but very active in service sectors such as the leisure industry. This fact further implies that resources were not effectively used to expand growth potential. The underlying reason for low investment for plants and equipment in the manufacturing sector was the unfavorable business environment, both internally and externally.

In terms of the behavioral factors of economic agents, the situation was even more serious. On the business side, the entrepreneurial spirit to do business was substantially dampened. Businessmen conducted large-scale strikes for the first time in 1987 and could not yet adjust themselves to the new environment. In the past, the authoritarian government enforced industrial peace, which might be impossible today. As a result of this environment, firm owners became more interested in real estate speculation and short-term financial assets investment.

Meanwhile, on the worker's side, the work ethic seemed to have deteriorated greatly. In the past, workers worked hard for considerably low wages. Korean workers were reputed for their quality of work, diligence and self-discipline, but these merits had largely dissipated. Newcomers to the labor market were very reluctant to work overtime unlike in the past but demand higher wage rates. Strikes occurred more often in fields with higher wages and better working conditions such as research institutes, subways, hospital and financial institutions. Subsequently, the defects ratio had increased in the midst of wage hikes.

B. Weakening Price Competitiveness

Since 1989, international price competitiveness of Korean goods has fallen drastically, leading to economic recession. The competitiveness of export prices is divided into price competitiveness and non-price competitiveness. Price competitiveness means the unit cost of exports compared to other competing countries, while non-price competitiveness concerns such elements as quality, design, marketing, and after-service. Price competitiveness affects exports directly and quickly.

A random sample by the Conference of Korean Trade and Industry of six hundred foreign agencies specializing in imports of six types products - home appliances, automobile components, general machinery, industrial electronic goods, precision instruments - revealed that domestic goods lag behind those from the less developed countries in price competitiveness, and behind those from less developed countries in non-price aspects such as quality. The price competitiveness of Korean goods is greatly behind other competing countries such as Taiwan, China and the Southeast Asian countries.

The author would like to describe the status of production costs such as labor, financial, raw material and transportation and industrial site costs in 1990s.

(1) Rise in Labor Costs

In 1996, the wage level of general workers in Korean manufacturing sector is higher second to that of Japan among major Asian countries (see table IV-1), whereas the labor productivity (value added per worker) is very low (see table IV-2).

Moreover, the numbers of public holiday (including Sunday) in a year and the paid annual leave are 69 days and 22~32 days, respectively, for Korea, in contrast to 68 days and 7~30 days for Taiwan, and 117 days and 10~20 days for Japan.

<Table IV-1> Major Asian Countries' Wage level (as of Dec. 1996) (unit: US$)

Country (City)	Korea (Seoul)	China (Shanhai)	Taiwan (Taipei)	Malaysia (Kuala Lumpur)	Indonesia (Djakarta)	Japan (Yokohama)	Singapore
Monthly Wages	1,100 ~ 1,580	82 ~ 186	960 ~ 1,400	210 ~ 360	96 ~ 160	2,960	620 ~ 1,090

Source: JETRO, April 1997.

<Table IV-2> The International Comparison of Labor Productivity (unit: US$)

Country	Korea	US	UK	Japan	Taiwan	Malaysia	China
Hourly Labor Productivity Per Worker	10.28	31.64	22.65	39.42	13.55	5.67	1.21

Source: IMD, *The World Competitiveness Report for 1997*, 1997.

(2) High Financial Costs

Korea's interest rates have started to rise since 1988. Comparing the general loan interest rates, which reflect the trend of market interest rates. Korea's interest rates were 11.4% in 1996, while those of the other competing countries' rates were only 2 to 8% (see Table IV-3). In particular, the yield on company bonds was five times that of Japan.

Also, the share of equity capital in Korea's manufacturing industries was 23.8% in 1992, which was extremely low compared to 54.5% of Taiwan, and 31.2% of Japan. This shows that the businesses' financial structure is quite weaker than that of the competing nations, Such a poor financial structure and facing high interest rates, the ratio of sales to financial burdens in Korea's manufacturing industries is inevitably rising, weakening the price competitiveness of export goods. In 1992, the ratio of sales to financial burdens was at a high level - at least three times Japan's 2.2% and Taiwan's 2.5%.

<Table IV-3> The International Comparison of Nominal Interest Rates (unit: %)

	Korea[1]	US[2]	Japan[3]	Taiwan[4]
The Annual Average Interest Rate (1996)	11.4	5.2	2.1	8.1
The Debt Ratio of the Manufacturing Sector (1996)	303 (1995)	87.2	287	209

Note: 1) The yield on company bonds
2) The yield on Treasury bonds
3) and 4) The yield on government bonds.

<Table IV-4> The Comparison of Financial Costs to Sales in Manufacturing Sector (unit: %)

	1990	1991	1992	1993	1994	1995
Korea	5.1	5.7	6.3	5.9	5.6	5.6
Japan	2.1	2.2	2.0	1.8	1.6	-
Taiwan	2.5	2.4	2.3	2.2	1.7	-

Source: Bank of Korea, internal data, 1996.

<Table IV-5> The Comparison of Average Profit Ratio in Manufacturing Sector (unit: %)

Ratio to Sales	Korea		Japan	Taiwan	The US
	(1996)	(1997)	(1996)	(1995)	(1996)
Business Profit	6.5	8.3	3.6	7.3	7.4
Financial Cost	5.8	6.4	1.0	2.2	-
Current Profit	1.0	-0.3	3.4	5.1	8.3

Source: Bank of Korea, May 1998.

Why is the ratio of financial costs to sales so high in case of Korea compared to major competitors? This ratio can be defined as :

$$\frac{financial\ costs}{sales} = \frac{financial\ costs}{total\ debts} \times \frac{total\ debts}{total\ capital} \times \frac{total\ capital}{sales}$$

$$= the\ average\ interest\ rates\ on\ the\ external\ followings \times \frac{the\ portion\ of\ external\ debts}{the\ turnover\ rate\ of\ total\ capital}$$

Therefore, it can be concluded that the ratio of financial burden is related positively with the portion of external debts, but inversely with the turnover rate of total asset.

In case of Korea, the major cause of high interest rate is the heavy reliance on external debts. The average ratio of corporate internal procurement for the period of 1986 to 1990 was 31.8% for Korea, in contrast to the 73.2% of US and 70.3% of Germany where the profit rates and the capital consumption ratios are relatively high.

<Table IV-6> The Corporate Internal Capital Procurement Ratio (1986~1990) (unit: %)

Country	Korea	US	Japan	Germany	Taiwan
Ratio	31.8	73.2	40.0	70.3	29.0

Source: Bank of Korea, *Capital Circulation Statistics of Korea*, 1992.

(3) Quasi-Tax Burden[28]

There are 28 kinds of quasi-tax burdens imposed on Korean firms, of which amount being 5 trillion wons equivalent to 8% of tax revenues in 1997 and having been increased by 22.6%. If firms' sharing of financial burden for some public purposes is added, the total burden of quasi-tax is estimated to be 9 trillions wons in the same year.

(4) High Transportation Costs

Due to inadequate social overhead facilities, the portion of transportation cost in total sales took up 14.3% in Korea, 5.8% in Europe, 8.8% in Japan and 7.7% in the US in 1995. (see Table IV-7)

<Table IV-7> The Ratio of Transportation Costs to Sales in 1995 (unit: %)

Korea	Europe	US	Japan
14.3%	5.8%	7.7%	8.8%

Source: Korea Institute of Transportation Development, *An Analysis of National Transportation Costs,* 1996.

<Table IV-8> The Ratio of Total Transportation Costs to GNP (1994) (unit: %)

Korea	The US	Japan
15.7%	10.5%	8.8%

Source: Korea Trade Association, internal data, 1996.

Korea Trade Association estimated that the transportation costs of Korea's exporting companies increased from US$ 13.2 billion in 1993 to US$ 20.6 billion in 1995 and the ratio of transportation costs to export volumes was raised from 16.1% in 1993 to 16.5% in 1995 in contrast to 7% for the US and 11% for Japan in the same year.[29]

It is generally known that the transportation costs from Pittsburgh in the US to Kwanyang in Korea is 22,000won/ton, whereas those from Kwanyang to Incheon port in the same country costs 23,000 won/ton. And it takes 14 hours (or 10,000 km) by airplane from Seoul to Los Angeles, whereas it takes 13 hours (or 430 km) by freight train from Seoul to Pusan in the same country.

(5) High Costs of Industrial Parks

The cost of industrial sites of Korea is about 1.5~9 times as high as those of US, UK, China, and Malaysia, as shown in <Table IV-9>. For this reason, indirect costs in manufacturing have risen and become a factor in raising production costs, discouraging foreign and domestic investment.

<Table IV-9> The International Comparison of Lotting-out Prices of Industrial Parks (unit: thousand won/pyung)

Korea		US	UK	Japan	China	Malaysia
Foreign Exclusive Industrial Park (Kwang-ju)	*Myong ji – Nogsan* Industrial Park (Pusan)	(average of top 10 Industrial Parks)	(average of top 7 Industrial Parks)	(average of top 10 Industrial Parks)	(average of top 63 Industrial Parks)	(average of top 8 Industrial Parks)
375	656	95	203	1,109	78	149

Source: KOTRA, *Directory of Major Countries' Industrial Parks for the selection of Best Investment Destination,* October 1996.

---

[28] The author originally coined the word, 'quasi-tax' burden implying 'enforced' payments or contributions of various kinds to public authorities. For details, see Yang-Taek Lim, *A Study on the Quasi-Tax Burden of Corporates in Korea* Seoul: Korea Economic Research Institute, No, 18, September 1983.

[29] Korea Trade Association, The Analysis of Transportation Costs in 1995, April 1996.

2. Determinants of International Competitiveness

The international competitiveness of the Korean manufacturing industry can be determined by many factors: the factor endowments (K and L) according to Hecksher-Ohlin's neo-classical trade theory; the technological gap (T) between countries and industries that technology-emphasizing theories support, such as R. Vernon's product life cycle model or the technology-gap model of W. Gruber and G. C. Hufbauer; or human capital (H) as claimed by O. B Keesing's human-skill theory. Examining which factor holds true would not only be very interesting, but it would also serve as a very important basis for finding a strategy for the survival and growth of the Korean economy in the age of globalization.

Eight manufacturing industry sectors were analyzed based on the KSIC (Korean Standard Industry Classification) standard: Industry 32 (textiles, clothing and leathery), Industry 35 (chemical compounds, oil, coal, rubber and plastic), Industry 36 (non-metal mineral products), Industry 381 (assembled metal products), Industry 382 (machinery), Industry 383 (electric and electronic equipment), Industry 384 (transportation equipment), Industry 385 (medical, optical, scientific, measuring and controlling equipment). The period of analysis was from 1979 to 1990. The general results of the analysis are as follows.

A. Analysis of the Determinants

1) The Model

B. Balassa (1963) suggested a RCAI (revealed comparative advantage index), which can be formulated as below.

$$RCAIit = \frac{KEXit / TKETt}{WEXit / TWEXt} \qquad \text{(IV-1)}$$

where

$RCAI_{it}$ = RCAI for the Korean industry i at time t
KEX_{it} = The amount of exports for the Korean industry i at time t
WEX_{it} = Total amount of world exports for the concerned industry i at time t
$TKEX_t$ = Total amount of Korea's exports at time t
$TWEX_t$ = Total amount of world exports at time t

S. Y. Kim (1993) set a model, as written in equation (IV-2), in which capital, labor, human capital and technological capability are chosen as explanatory variables to be used to calculate RCAI.

$$RCAI_{it} = F(K_{it}, L_{it}, H_{it}, T_{it}) \qquad \text{(IV-2)}$$

where

i = industry
t = time
$RCAI_{it}$ = RCAI for an industry i at time t
K_{it} = Capital stock for an industry i at time t
L_{it} = Labor force for an industry i at time t
H_{it} = Human capital for an industry i at time t
T_{it} = Index of technology capability for an industry i at time t

With the model above, an empirical analysis was conducted on whether a country's international competitiveness is determined by the theory of Hecksher-Ohlin, the traditional theory of factor endowment, the technological gap model by Gruber and Hufbauer, the product life-cycle model by Vernon, or the human capital hypothesis of Keesing.

In order to mitigate the effects of business cycle on the relative trade performance and to overcome the negative effect caused by using labor input as a scale variable, we divide capital stock (K), labor (L) and human capital stock (H) by sales (S) representing a scale variable. The adjusted model of equation (IV-2) is as follows.

$$RCAI_{it} = F\left[\frac{K_{it}}{S_{it}}, \frac{L_{it}}{S_{it}}, \frac{H_{it}}{S_{it}}, T_{it}\right] \tag{IV-3}$$

where

S_{it} = sales for an industry i at time t

Equation (IV-3) could be transformed into the linear regression model below.

$$RCAI_{it} = \beta_1 + \beta_K \frac{K_{it}}{S_{it}} + \beta_L \frac{L_{it}}{S_{it}} + \beta_H \frac{H_{it}}{S_{it}} + \beta_T T_{it} + u_{it} \tag{IV-4}$$

i) Human Capital Stock

$$H_{it} = \frac{W_{it}^{*} - W_{it}^{1}}{S_{it}} L_{it} \tag{IV-5}$$

where

H_{it} = Human capital stock for an industry i at time t

L_{it} = The number of employees for an industry i at time t

W_{it}^{*} = The average annual income for an industry i at time t

W_{it}^{1} = The average annual income of workers with the education background of not higher than middle school for the whole industry at time t

D = The discounted wage differential between unskilled labor and skilled worker (as a discount rate, D = 0.10)

ii) Index of technology level

Index of technology level has been generated by the factor analysis method by Yang-Taek Lim (1987).

<Table IV-10> Selection of Variables to derive Technology Index

	Technology Capability	Performance of Technological Development
The Degree of Technology Embodiment in the Aspect of Production Process	-Ratio of R&D to GNP -Number of R&D Researchers per 10,000 Population -R&D Expenditures per R&D Expenditures -The Intensity of R&D Expenditures -The Intensity of R&D Researchers	-Number of Technology Trades -The Volume of Technology Trade
The Degree of Technology Embodiment in the Aspect of Product	Number of Patents	Value Added GNP

<Table IV-11> Classification of Technology Index-related Variables

Classification	Variables
Social Technology Index-related Variables	GNP (T_1)
	Ratio of R&D Expenditures to GNP(T_2)
	Ratio of Number of R&D Researchers to 10,000 Population(T_3)
	R&D Expenditures per R&D Researchers (T_4)
	Number of Patents (T_5)[1)]
Industrial Technology Index related Variables	Value Added (T_6)
	Number of Technology Trades (T_7)[2)]
	The Volume of Technology Trades (T_8)[3)]
	The Intensity of R&D Expenditures (T_9)[4)]
	The Intensity of R&D Researchers (T_{10})[5)]

Notes: 1) Number of Patent Registrations
2) Number Technology Import Cases plus Number of Technology Export Cases
3) Technology Import Cases plus Technology Export Cases
4) R&D Expenditures / Sales
5) Number of Researchers / Number of Employees

The factor score to be calculated by weight is the technology index for the analysis. The formula for the indices of variables is described as follows.

Technology index of each variable = Σ(weights of each technology-related variable) x (statistic of standard normal distribution of each technology-related variable) (IV-6)

2) Correlation Analysis of Explanatory Variables

<Table IV-12> summarizes the annual growth rate of index of comparative advantage, capital, labor, technology index and human capital for the analysis of the determinants of international competitiveness.

<Table IV-12> Annual Growth Rate (1979-1990) (Unit: %)

Industry Variable	32	35	36	381	382	383	384	385	Total
Index of Comparative Advantage	-3.1	-0.43	-4.34	-2.81	9.90	1.14	3.95	-4.21	0.011
Capital	19.36	19.98	24.98	20.34	24.93	27.14	22.60	25.47	23.10
Labor	0.44	4.99	2.20	5.88	7.80	6.22	6.79	4.60	4.87
Human Capital	-14.2	23.15	18.23	25.89	24.61	26.14	24.77	74.33	25.37
Technology Index	4.32	6.18	4.33	4.34	5.29	7.58	5.10	4.73	5.23

Notes: 1) RCAI was quoted from the Ph.D. dissertation of S.Y. Kim (1993).
2) Capital stock statistic of H. K. Pyo was used for the capital factor.
3) The numbers of employees in *Report of Industry Census and Statistic Report of Mining and Manufacturing* released by Economic Planning Board were used for the labor factor.
4) Yang-Taek Lim (1986 and 1987)'s methodology was used for the technology index.
5) Human capital (H) represents qualitative differential in labor, which causes wage gap. It was estimated by the formula of Branson and Monoyios (1977) by using the wage gap between each industry derived from *Statistics Year book of Labor and Report of Wage in Each Profession* issued by Ministry of Labor.

On the other hand, <Table IV-13> shows the Spearmann RCC (rank correlation coefficient) for each variable.

<Table IV-13> Rank Correlation Coefficient (RCC)

Year	RCC for Capital	RCC for Labor	RCC for Human Capital	RCC for Technology Index
1979-1983	-0.0714	0.5476	-0.14285	0.0476
1980-1984	-0.0476	0.7380**	-0.10914	0.5000
1981-1985	-0.1428	0.8095**	-0.67857	0.4761
1982-1986	0.2857	0.4285	-0.14285	0.4523
1983-1987	0.4285	0.7380	0.28571	0.5714
1984-1988	0.2142	0.3333	0.53571	0.6829**
1985-1989	0.5952	0.5238	0.03571	0.3380
1986-1990	0.7571**	0.4047	0.28571	0.3809

Note: Those marked with two asterisks (**) identify coefficients that are significantly different from zero at the 5% significance level.

3) Econometric Results

From the estimation by the Seemingly Unrelated Regression Model shown by equation (IV-7), it can be known that the coefficients of labor factor (L/S) and technology index (T) were statistically significant but those of capital factor (K/S) and human capital (H/S) were not at the 1% level. This result is almost identical with the result of the rank correlation coefficient analysis.

$$RCAI_{it} = -0.033488 + 0.458301\frac{K_{it}}{S_{it}} - 1.149E-10\frac{H_{it}}{S_{it}} + 0.007124\frac{L_{it}}{S_{it}} + 0.107521T_{it} \qquad \text{(IV-7)}$$

(-0.58) (0.96) (-0.19) (2.73)*** (4.93)***

where

$R2 = 0.5659$

The values indicated in parenthesis are t-values

*** indicates significance at least at the 1% level

i) Analysis of Structural Change in Time Series Determinants

For the analysis of structural change in time series determinants, time series dummy variable were used.

$$RCAI_{it} = 10.9432 + 4.82963\frac{K_{it}}{S_{it}} - 0.00772\frac{L_{it}}{S_{it}} + 8.732E-0.9\frac{H_{it}}{S_{it}} - 1.0965T_{it}$$

(4.33)*** (5.14)*** (-1.21) (-7.57)*** (-3.93)***

$$-9.9814D_{it} - 2.93941D_{Kt}\frac{K_{it}}{S_{it}} - 0.02604D_{Lt}\frac{L_{it}}{S_{it}} + 3.408E-0.9D_{Ht}\frac{H_{it}}{S_{it}} + 1.14816D_{Ti}T_{it} \qquad \text{(IV-8)}$$

(3.62)*** (-2.72)*** (2-10)** (2.49)** (4.00)***

where

$R2 = 0.6544$

** and *** indicates the significance at least at the 5% and 10% levels, respectively

$D_t = 1: t \geq 1984, D_t = 0: t < 1984$

ii) Analysis of Structural Change in the Determinants by Industry

$$RCAI_{it} = 2.7829 + 3.3548\frac{K_{it}}{S_{it}} + 0.0074\frac{L_{it}}{S_{it}} + 8.053E-0.9\frac{H_{it}}{S_{it}} - 0.1268T_{it}$$

(3.38)*** (7.53)*** (1.67)* (-10.89)*** (-1.97)*

$$-4.5292D_{Ki}\frac{K_{it}}{S_{it}}-0.0055D_{Li}\frac{L_{it}}{S_{it}}+5.567E-0.9D_{Hi}\frac{H_{it}}{S_{it}}+0.1555D_{Ti}T_{it} \qquad \text{(IV-9)}$$

(-3.38)*** (-0.71) (3.79)*** (4.06)***

where

$R^2 = 0.6743$

$D_i = 1$ (Industries : 382, 383, 384)

$D_i = 0$ (Other industries)

*, **, and *** indicates significance at least at the 10%, 5%, and 1% levels, respectively.

B. Policy Implications

(1) The composition of trade and exports of the Korean manufacturing industry is undergoing change. Industries traditionally at comparative advantage were lagging behind in this period, while industries that were at comparative disadvantage in the past were gaining comparative advantage.

The RCAI (Revealed Comparative Advantage Index)'s of industries 32 (textiles, clothes, and leather), 36 (non-metal mineral products), 381 (assembled metal products) and 383 (electric and electronic equipment) were greater than 1 during almost the entire period. This signifies that these industries had comparative advantage in the international trade market. In particular, industry 32 yielded the greatest RCAI, which is in line with the fact that, in the case of the Korean manufacturing industry, textiles and shoes had a very high comparative advantage in the international trade market.

However, among these four manufacturing sectors, industries 32, 36 and 381 each had a negative rate of change of RCAI during most of the period. One can see that their comparative advantage in the international market was decreasing, meaning they were falling behind in price competition.

Industries 383 (electric and electronic equipment) and 384 (transportation equipment) each showed a negative rate of change in RCAI for several years during the period, while retaining a positive rate during other years. This suggests that the two manufacturing industry sectors were being confronted with severe international competition.

For example, in the case of Industry 384 (transportation equipment), the RCAI had a value greater than 1 until the mid 1980s, but fell below 1 thereafter, showing industry 384's regression in trade from comparative advantage to comparative disadvantage.

On the other hand, industries 35 (chemical compounds, oil, coal, rubber and plastic), 382 (machinery), and 385 (medical, optical, scientific, measuring and controlling equipment) displayed RCAI's below 1 for most of the period. Therefore, one can see that these three sectors still had comparative disadvantage in the international trade market. The fact that the RCAI of industry 35 (chemical compounds, oil, coal, rubber and plastic) showed an average annual rate of increase of -0.43% despite intense investment and research in the petrochemical industry, signifies that the petrochemical industry could not retain international competitiveness in the international trade market. However one can see that during the late 1980s the comparative disadvantage of industries 35 and 382 were decreasing, in other words, they were gaining comparative advantage.

(2) As the comparative advantage of the manufacturing industries mentioned above vividly fluctuated, the industrial sector had a small overall annual 0.011% increase in their RCAI's. An important reason that the rate of growth in comparative advantage was low despite much progress in exports during the analyzed period (1979-1990) was because there were switch-overs between industries: those that previously had comparative advantage fell back, while those that were formerly at comparative disadvantage gained comparative advantage.

Such reasoning is backed by the yearly average rate of change in the RCAI of each industry. In the case of industry 32 (textiles, clothes and leather), the industry's comparative advantage was weakened as its RCAI showed an average annual rate of increase of -3.0%. On the other hand, industries 382, 383 and 384 showed an average annual rate of increase of RCAI of 9.90%, 1.14% and 3.69%, respectively, indicating a strengthening comparative advantage.

(3) As a result of an analysis on the determinants of international competitiveness based on actual data, both physical capital variable (K/S) and human capital variable (H/S) showed little significance, while

estimated labor factor (L/S) and technology index (T) showed significance at the 1% level, both with positive values.

Thus, the international competitiveness of the Korean manufacturing industry during 1979-1990, although it does not support the human-skill hypothesis of O. B Keesing, it supports Hecksher-Ohlin's traditional trade theory and agrees with R. Vernon's product life cycle model, which emphasizes the importance of trade, and W. Gruber and G. C. Hufbauer's technology-gap model.

Due to Korea's reputation of having, in comparison to other countries, more abundant labor (L) than capital stock (K), one can see that, according to Heckshe-Ohlin's theory, a relatively abundant factor endowment, labor resources (L) was a determinant of international competitiveness in Korea's case. It is also evident that technology (T) was another determinant of international competitiveness of the Korean manufacturing industry. Industries 382 (machines), 383 (electric and electronic equipment), and 384 (transportation equipment), having further increased their technologies by technical development and introduction of technology, yielded a relatively higher rate of increase of RCAI. From this, we can see that technology raises international competitiveness.

(4) The average annual rate of increase of capital input (K), which is one of the factors that explain international competitiveness, was 23.10%, showing the highest rate of increase after human capital (H). The change in RCAI and the change in capital input (K) from 1986 to 1990 displayed a positive significant relationship at the 5% level. Therefore it can be inferred that the international competitiveness of capital-intensive goods improved through continuous input of capital (K).

As for time-related structural change in the determinants of international competitiveness, the capital factor (K/S) was estimated at 4.82963 with significance at the 1% level before 1984 and dropped to 0.89022 after 1984. This indicates that the positive influence of capital on international competitiveness was gradually decreasing as time passed. Following such a structural change, it is essential for Korea's priorities, which were investment in the heavy and chemical industries until the early 1980s, to shift to the development of advanced technology and innovation.

In the case of the lower industries, 32 (textiles, clothes and leather), 35 (chemical compounds, oil, coal, rubber and plastic), 36 (non-metal mineral products), 381 (assembled metal products), and 385 (medical, optical, scientific, measuring and controlling equipment), each of which had an average annual rate of increase of RCAI less than 0, the estimated capital factor (K/S) was 3.3548 with significance at the 1% level. In contrast, in the case of the three top industries, 382 (machinery), 383 (electric and electronic equipment), and 384 (transportation equipment), that had an average annual rate of increase (1979-1990) of the index greater than 0, the estimated capital factor (K/S) was -1.1743 with significance at the 1% level.

This implies that, in the five industries (32, 35, 36, 381 and 385) with relatively weak international competitiveness, comparative advantage from capital input (K) was increasing. Within the three industries (382, 383 and 384) with relatively high international competitiveness, comparative advantage was decreasing. Hence, it is evident that these may also be regarded as technology and knowledge- intensive industries, with the causes found from factors other than simply capital input (K).

(5) The average annual rate of increase of labor (L) stands at 4.87%, the lowest of all factors. This means that there was more capital input than labor input in the production process of the manufacturing industrial sector. Especially in the case of industries 381 (assembled metal products), 382 (machinery), 383 (electric and electronic equipment), 384 (transportation equipment) and 385 (medical, optical, measuring and controlling equipment), capital input (K) shows a rate of increase of 20.35%, 24.93%, 27.15%, 22.61% and 25.48%, respectively.

However, the change in RCAI and the change in labor (L) showed a relationship of positive significance during the period from 1980 to 1987. This indicates that during this period only, labor (L) played an important role in determining international competitiveness.

According to analysis on the structural change of the manufacturing industry, the estimated labor factor (L/S) was 0.0074 with significance at the 10% level for the five lower industries, while insignificant with a value of 0.0019 for the top three industries. This means that the international competitiveness of the technology and knowledge-intensive top industries is no longer simply determined by labor input (L). In agreement, traditionally labor-intensive manufacturing industry 32(textiles, clothes, and leather) had an average annual rate of increase of labor input of a mere 0.44%, and the labor factor of each manufacturing industrial sector displayed a common decrease in the average annual rate of increase after the mid 1980s.

On the other hand, the analysis of the time related structural change in the determinants of international competitiveness reveals a labor factor (L/S) estimated as positive and significant at the 5% level. This deduction coincides with the study on the determinants of international competitiveness and Spearmann's rank correlation analysis of its explanatory variables.

(6) Human capital stock (H) showed the highest average annual rate of increase of 25.37% among the four factors of international competitiveness during the period of analysis (1979-1990). In spite of this, human capital stock (H) and the change in RCAI did not show a significant relationship during the entire period.

According to analysis on the structural changes of manufacturing industry, the estimated human capital factor (H/S) was negative, with a significance at the 1% level in the five lower industries, while it showed no significance in the case of the three top industries. This indicates that human capital (H), although a determinant of the international competitiveness of major countries, had little influence on growth in productivity in the case of the Korea's manufacturing sector, whether the industrial sector was weak or strong in international competitiveness. This concurs with the above analysis on time-related structural change, and is a matter of how much education and training contribute to the qualitative improvement of skilled labor.

Industry 32 (textiles, clothes and leather) displayed an especially low average annual rate of increase of human capital stock (H) in comparison to other manufacturing industrial sectors. This shows that entrepreneurs of the particular industry did not invest enough on the training and education of their labor forces, conscious of the fact that the industry was in decline. It could also indicate that less workers were being committed to '3D' (dangerous, difficult and dirty) businesses including those that manufacture textiles and shoes, and more were being committed to service sectors or other industrial sectors.

In contrast, industries 382 (machines), 383 (electric and electronic equipment) and 384 (transportation equipment), that showed high rates of increase of RCAI, yielded high rates of increase in human capital stock (H); 24.01%, 26.14% and 24.77%, respectively. This implies that, in the case of these top industries, future (not present) human capital stock could be a factor of the increase of comparative advantage.

However, if the time-related structural change in the determinants of international competitiveness is analyzed, the estimated values of the human capital factor (H/S) were all significant and negative before and after 1984. Not only does the result of this analysis conflict with the hypothesis, it also shows contrast with the earlier analysis of the Spearmann's rank correlation among the explanatory variables of international competitiveness and its determinants. It also disagrees with O. B. Keesing's human-skill theory and the empirical studies of Sang-sup Lee (1983) and Hyun-Hoon Lee (1990).

The author's own interpretation of this is that although Korea's human capital is being formed by investment on training and education out of a strong emphasis on education, the increase of skilled labor is not having much effect on the productivity of the manufacturing industry. This raises the question of how much training and education is actually contributing to the quality of skilled labor. The recently proposed reforms on the Korean education system should start from this perspective, and should also target its objectives on this matter.

(7) The technology index (T) was revealed as having increased at an annual rate of 5.23%. The fact that the technology index (T) increased at an annual rate (5.23%) lower than that of capital input (23.10%) suggests that the Korean manufacturing industry concentrated more on capital input (K) than technological development or adoption.

However, according to Spearmann's rank correlation analysis of explanatory variables of international competitiveness, the change in the RCAI and the change in the technology index (T) showed a relationship significant at the 5% level during the short period of 1984 ~ 1988.

According to the analysis of the structural change in the Korean manufacturing industry, the estimated technology coefficient (T) of the five lower industries was, contrary to the hypothesis, -0.1268 with significance at the 10% level. However, in the case of the top three industries it was 0.0287 with high significance at the level of 1%. This indicates that the contribution of the technology index (T) to international competitiveness was increasing for the top three technology- and knowledge-intensive industries.

In addition, the industries with a relatively high rate of increase in the technology index (T) also showed a rapidly increasing RCAI. Thus, it can be seen that technology does not only determine but also increases the Korean manufacturing industry's international competitiveness, as claimed by W. Gruber and G. C. Hufbauer's technology-emphasizing trade theories. The technology-gap model of W. Gruber and G. C. Hufbauer implies that much time is consumed for nations to assimilate and absorb new technologies that a certain country has technologically developed. Korea can be seen as having specialized in certain products that can have international competitiveness with only intermediate technology, thus increasing the amount that technology contributes to international competitiveness.

On examining the time-related structural change of the determinants of international competitiveness, the technology coefficient (T) before 1984 was estimated at -1.0965 with significance at the level of 1%, contrary to the hypothesis. However, later it increased to a 0.05162, holding a positive value with significance at the 1% level, agreeing with the hypothesis. This implies that technology was becoming a more and more important determinant of international competitiveness.

The results, from the perspective of the theory of technological economics, can be associated with M. V. Posner (1961)'s dynamic economies of scale and R. Vernon (1966)'s theory of product life cycle.[30] According to Posner, when a technological advance takes place the pertinent industry and the nation-wide unit production costs drop, and the corresponding economies of scale that result by this make comparative advantage possible. When a certain enterprise of a nation, through technological innovation, develops and produces new products and effectively replaces the older products that were in demand, other enterprises in the same industry feel that the markets for their own products are threatened.

In particular, the more competitive the companies of the industry (the various products of the industry were of similar quality before the innovation), and the closer the ties between the enterprises of the industry (the production equipment of certain enterprises were likely to be used for products of another enterprise), the greater the tendency for other enterprises to imitate new products.

In such a situation, the time needed to imitate the products includes not only a learning period but also a reaction lag. Posner called the learning period and reaction lag collectively as domestic imitation lag, and domestic imitation lag and foreign reaction lag collectively as total imitation lag. He defined foreign reaction lag as the time from when the technological innovation devised by an enterprise of a foreign country is successfully put to use until when a similar new product that can compete with this is produced by a domestic producer. Also, he asserted that during this total imitation lag, the industry and nation that developed the new product through innovation obtains comparative advantage. He also explained that in the case of a demand lag, the total imitation lag would change because the new foreign product would not be considered a complete substitute for domestic products until a certain amount of time has lapsed.

R. Vernon stated that comparative advantage in trade is determined by the active change from maturity to atrophy in new products, that is, the active change in technology described by development, diffusion and degeneration. He asserted that as newly developed products undergo the phases of rebirth, maturation and standardization, the international distribution of their centers of production changes, and this in turn changes the trade pattern of the product. This change is accelerated by foreign direct investment. He said that a product goes through a life cycle of three phases such as new product, maturing product, and standardized product.

Therefore while the elasticity of demand is relatively low during the early phase of a new product due to its monopolistic property, no problem exists even when production costs are high due to high elasticity of demand. However, as the product matures, domestic and foreign demand for the new product highly increases. Thus, competition due to the emergence of competitive enterprises and efforts to reduce production costs are enhanced. In turn, domestic enterprises of the nation, which developed the new product, launch foreign direct investment to increase production and cut production costs.

During the phase of standardization of a new product, under-developed countries that have larger low-cost unskilled labor forces become the producers. Thus, not only the enterprises of the country that developed the new product, but other foreign enterprise hasten direct investment on these under-developed countries. When standardization has ripened, it is even possible for the developing nations to become the exporters, shipping their products to the nation which formerly developed the new product, and to the other advanced countries.

As discussed above, the two technology-emphasizing trade theories imply that the international competitiveness of technologically-less-developed countries is determined by their technological gaps with technologically-advanced nations, and that such technological gap can be estimated by the length of the life-cycle-related technological lag. Moreover, one method of decreasing this technological gap is to domestically develop new technologies.

---

[30] This theory indicates that technology had started to contribute to the international competitiveness of the Korean manufacturing industry while the products were passing through the maturation and standardization stages due to the entrance of new products.

3. Markets Opening and Liberalization under the WTO System

The markets opening and liberalization of Korea has been in progress since 1980s and, in particular, Korea came to face with the international and external pressures of full liberalization in trade and opening its capital, service and agricultural markets at the same time in the 1990s with the joining of the WTO and the OECD.

A. Trade Liberalization

Since 1990, Korea has pursued trade liberalization as a member of the 11th group of the General Agreement on Tariffs and Trade. Korea has complied with the obligation to liberalize her import system to the level of an advanced nation since qualifying as a member of the 11th group of GATT in January 1990. The main obligations of a nation pertaining to this group are the elimination of all kinds of restrictive measures on imports and exports, such as quotas and tariffs, and preferably the achievement of facto import liberalization. Upon carrying out such obligations, Korea is now showing an extremely high level of import liberalization of 97.3% in 1991. This is an upward movement from 87% in 1985, and a level similar to most advanced nations. The Korean government is also planning additional reductions in the tariff rate. The average tariff rate on industrial products was 20.3% in 1985, 11.2% in 1989, and 8.4% in 1991. Again, this is as low a level as that of the advanced nations.

B. Opening of Capital Markets, Prior to the IMF Bail-out

Another step that has sped up the opening of the Korean economy is the opening of the capital markets, which began in 1992. The advancement of foreign securities companies into the nation increased in 1992 due to the opening of capital markets. Standards for the establishment of domestic branches by foreign stock companies, and for the establishment of joint venture companies were set in November 1990; specific standards for qualifications for membership of the stock exchange market were set in June 1991, so that domestic branches of foreign stock companies could make commissions and sales. Following this, in late December 1993, nine branches of securities companies, including those of the US and Britain, and 26 offices entered the country.

They must gain operation licenses on the basis of the stock exchange laws, according to the type of securities business, such as undertaking, consignment selling of securities, and direct sales. Also, the extent of areas permitted for business is being discriminated according to the size of business funds. Foreign securities companies are concentrating more on the consignment sale of securities to institutional investors, such as foreign pension funds and insurance companies, and leading the issuing of stock of domestic companies abroad. However, the basis for operation is still quite weak. Therefore, in the fiscal year of 1993, the operational share of foreign securities companies in the domestic market reached only at 1.1%.

Among the measures dictated by the UR financial negotiations, the effects of the national treatment of foreigners residing in the country is as follows. As foreign residents have gained national treatment from 1994, stock investment restrictions on foreigners have been eliminated, and trust grants, related to stock purchases and sales, have been authorized. Considering those who are residents according to foreign currency control laws and income tax laws, the number of home residents who are citizens of developed countries, such as Japan and the US, is rather low. Therefore, even since resident foreigners began being treated as locals in 1994, the stock market has not been greatly affected.

Still, such measures would have the following effects on Korean stock market. After permission was given for foreigners to invest in securities, for two years from early 1992 to 1993, the limit of foreigners' attainment of stock in each area was 10%, and 3% per person. With the extent of foreign investment widened in 1994 as planned, it was estimated that in 1994, the amount of increase of the real inflow of foreigners' stock investment funds reached around US$5 billion (about the size of the real inflow of funds in 1993), and investment demand of this amount would be created, which activate the stock market. The supply of companies' own capital had increase would and contributed to the reliability of the financial structure. In addition, the increase of the supply of companies' own capital had generally absorbed the demand for the issuance of corporate bonds, which would contribute to the stability of the interest rate in financial markets.

Strategies for coping with the change of environment in stock markets, resulting from UR financial agreements, are the following:

1. If the limitations on foreign stock investment is loosened, demand for stock will increase, and domestic stock prices will rise. From this there will be positive effects such as opportunities for the opening of businesses, and the increase of capital as the issuance of new stocks increases. However, due to the increase of foreign loans to companies, partial opening of the bond market, and loosening of limitations on foreign stock investment, currency management problems will occur if foreign currency of at least US$ 10 billion flows into the country as expected. Therefore, to cope with the rise of the Won value, and the pressure of the increased issue of currency, restrictions on the outflow of capital should be alleviated by allowing more investment abroad and weakening the system of concentrating foreign currency.
2. When domestic residents, who are foreigners according to stock exchange laws, are permitted to be treated as locals when investing in stock, foreign investment capital will increase slightly. A plan of loosening restrictions step-by-step according to the demand and supply of the stock market, and after a certain period of time to limited, selected areas can be considered.
3. Extension of stock investment and restriction of commercial loans can restrict the inflow of capital. However, to maintain a balance, the outflow of capital by the extension of direct foreign investment should be promoted. The promotion of customer service abilities by the maintenance of transfer and credit functions of foreign stock companies will raise the possibility of not only foreign investors, but some domestic investors, in utilizing foreign securities companies.
4. The government should abolish discriminatory restrictions on securities companies, grant restrictive permission to work in foreign currency and exchange foreign capital, and extend self-management of property. Also, irrational stock-related rules, such as unrealistic limitations in trust funds, interest rates on customers' deposits, irrational price limitations and fees should be corrected in order to help domestic securities companies gain competitive power.
5. Before proper opening of markets, adjustment of working areas among investment management businesses cooperation and sharing of information with foreign investment consultation offices, and computerization of international operations are necessary, and specialization, including that of manpower, should be attained.

C. Early Stage of Opening Distribution Markets

The distribution sector links supply with demand through provision of information and services related to retail-wholesale, delivery, storage and packaging.

The Korean distribution industry has taken up an important position in the national economy, making up 14.4% of the GNP in 1992 and 27.8% of aggregate employment. Nevertheless, a large part of the Korean retail industry has kept at the family or personal business level, with 91% of total enterprises employing 2 or less persons, and 78% located in factory areas of less than 10 *pyong* (approximately 33 square meters). A dual structure existed within the economy between large-scale retail stores such as department stores and supermarkets and other retailers in terms of size.

A look at the progress made in the early stage of opening distribution industry showed that there were 55 cases of foreign investment in the retail and wholesale industries in December 1993 with a net worth of US$0.129 billion. However, the weight of such an investment size over aggregate foreigners' investment was a mere 16.0% in the number of investments and a 10.1% of the amount invested. The background of such poor results was the distribution environment in Korea, which were characterized by restrictions in the number of stores and land acquisition for foreigners as well as diversification of import routes. The government, under the notion that it is now inevitable to open up the distribution market, has been pursuing a gradual opening policy.

Looking at the expansion of items available for foreign investment, it might be seen that it had been carried out in steps, accompanied by a transition from a positive system of restrictions to a negative system. By January 1994, 77 of 89 wholesale items and 57 of 68 retail items had been freed from restrictions. Those items (12 wholesale and 11 retail) which remained placed under restrictions would be allowed to be opened under the enactment of the Five-Year Plan for Opening to Foreign Investment. Restrictions on the number of stores held and the area occupied had also been largely mitigated.

It could be expected that as complete abolition of restrictions on opening stores was carried out, more foreign enterprises would run their own retail/wholesale shops or use existing domestic sales networks by taking over domestic companies through stock purchases.

4. Downturn of Korean Economy in 1997

As discussed above, the Korean economy has slid into stagnation in 1990s with its weakening international competitiveness and deteriorating structural problems. It will be meaningful to review how the accumulations of those factors had inter-played to have driven the Korean economy to the IMF bail-out in late 1997, analyzing macroeconomic indicators of the year 1996 and 1997.

A. Industrial Sector

Looking at each economic sector in comparison with its performance in 1996 and 1997, it is clear that the slowdown affected most of the industries. The growth rate of manufacturing fell from 7.4% in 1996 to 6.2% in 1997. The production of the light industrial sector continued its negative growth trend, which had become evident in 1996, with most sub-sectors including textiles, apparel, and footwear maintaining a downward trend. The production of the heavy industrial and chemical sector slowed its upward pace from that of 1996. Its deceleration, which occurred despite an export driven boost in electrics and electronics and petrochemicals, was largely attributable to reduced production in the industrial machinery and transportation equipment by the sluggish facilities investment.

The pace of growth in construction industry dropped sharply from 6.6% in 1996 to 2.8% in 1997. Government construction showed brisk activity centered on infrastructure projects, whereas private construction slumped, reflecting the slackness of residential construction business, the contraction of facilities investment, and an increase in the number of insolvent contractors.

The growth rate of the service sector eased to 6.5% from its pace of 7.9% of 1996. The wholesale and retail trade displayed a growth rate lower than that of 1996 as a result of the slow pace of transactions involving domestic industrial and imported goods alike amid sluggish domestic demand.

Financial businesses witnessed slower growth, due to the increase of non- performing loans arising from the string of large corporate bankruptcies, and the growth rate of the business services sector also declined largely owing to lackluster advertising business. However, the communication sector maintained its strong growth pace thanks to the continuing massive expansion in mobile communications and information communications services.

Agriculture, forestry and fishing production maintained a growth rate of 2.5% owing to the lackluster production of vegetables and animal husbandry, the effects of which dulled the favorable increases in the rice harvest and fish catches.

<Table IV-14> Major Indicators of Korean Economy (Unit, % 1990 Constant Price)

	Real GDP Growth Rate	Private Consumption Expenditure	Equipment Investment	Construction Investment
1Q 97	5.7	4.2	-0.2	0.8
2Q	6.6	4.8	-1.8	1.8
3Q	6.1	4.8	-12.7	3.8
4Q	3.9	-1.0	-28.2	3.7
Yearly	**5.5**	**3.1**	**-11.3**	**2.7**
1Q 98	-3.9	-10.6	-40.7	-7.7
2Q	-6.8	-13.0	-52.4	-13.2
3Q	-6.8	-12.0	-46.3	-15.8

Source: Ministry of Finance and Economy, Korea, February 1999.

B. Labor Market

During 1997, the economically active population increased by 2.0%, similar to its rise in 1996. However, the total number of persons employed grew by only 1.4%, less than that of in 1996, reflecting the decrease in job opportunities and the downsizing efforts of enterprises in response to the economic slowdown. In consequence, the unemployment rate rose to 2.6%in 1997 from 2.0% in 1996. Most significant, in December 1997 it climbed over 3%. Meanwhile, during 1997 as a whole, the total number of the unemployed increased by 556,000 persons, the significant increase compared with 425,000 persons in 1996. Also, employment security deteriorated, as the share of daily and temporary workers rose at the expense of permanent and full-time workers.

Viewing the pattern of employment by industry, manufacturing employment decreased by a broader margin than in 1996, affected by the contraction of production and increasing insolvencies in the labor-intensive light industrial sector. Construction employment also slackened greatly in response to the slowdown in the construction business. In contrast, employment in the services sector maintained its brisk pace of increase with a parallel to the year of 1996.

The rate of increase in nominal wages in all industries dropped sharply from 11.9% in 1996 to 7.0% in 1997, reflecting the deepening worries over job security, the fewer hours worked, and the deterioration in firms' financial status. Most notably, in the case of the manufacturing sector, the rate of increase in nominal wages fell to less than half of 1996. Moreover, in December 1997 the absolute level of wages in manufacturing was far below that of the same month in 1996.

C. Prices

The pace of price increases accelerated greatly from 1996, with consumer prices and producer prices rising by 6.6% and 10.9% respectively. In December 1997, however, they shifted to a steep upward trajectory due to the rapid depreciation of the Korean Won. Consumer prices in December 1997 rose by 2.5% over the previous month while producer prices climbed to 8.2%. By commodity, the prices of agricultural and marine products temporarily showed unstable movements earlier in 1997 centering on fruit and grain, but they gradually stabilized from the second quarter as demand-supply imbalances cleared. The prices of manufactured goods continued to move within a stable range until November 1997 owing to lackluster demand amid dull business conditions together with the stability of international prices of raw materials including crude petroleum. The higher cost of imported raw materials due to the massive depreciation of the Korean won, though, quickly fed through to the prices of manufactured goods, which rose steeply from early December 1997. Charges for services maintained stable movements from the second quarter onwards, thanks to the stability of charges for personal services and housing rents, which largely offset the inflationary pressures caused by the upward adjustment of charges for public utilities.

Among real estate prices, land prices maintained a stable range of movements throughout 1997, thanks both to the large area of land put on the market by several large corporations facing insolvency and to the choking of demand by the persistent economic slowdown. Housing prices showed a somewhat steeper upward trend earlier in 1997, centered around apartments in the Greater Seoul area, particularly in the satellite cities, but from the second quarter onwards, they shifted back to their stable pace affected by subdued demand.

D. Monetary Sector

1) Monetary Supply

From the beginning of the year, the emphasis of monetary and credit policies was placed on maintaining stability in the supply of liquidity in order to narrow the current account deficit and moderate inflationary pressures. Parallel efforts were also directed toward ensuring financial market stability so as to accommodate the enlarged portfolio shifts among financial business sectors and financial products arising from the reorganization of the financial system.

The target ranges for the growth rate of the money supply were set at 14~19% for M2, on a December daily-average basis, and 15~20% for MCT, which adds negotiable CDs (certificates of deposit) and money-in-trust to M2. The BOK(Bank of Korea)'s adoption of this type of double monetary target system was guided by the strong possibility that M2, long employed as the main intermediate target, would continued to show unstable movements, affected by realignment of the trust account system in 1996.

In 1997 under review, the growth rate of M2, a relatively narrow monetary indicator, increased sharply, while that of MCT declined steadily during 1997; and that of M3, the broadest monetary indicator, also continued its downward trend during 1997. The growth rate of M2 rose from the 17.8% of 1996 to 21.1%, on the December daily-average basis, due to the large shift of funds from non-bank financial institutions into commercial banks as a result of the introduction of MMDAs (money market deposit accounts).

However, the growth rate of MCT eased to 14.7% from the 18.6% of 1996, on the December daily-average basis. This was mainly due to the contraction of firms' demands for funds amid the protracted economic downturn, and to portfolio shifts into cover bills and sales of bond RAs (repurchase agreements) rather than CDs, upon which reserve requirements were newly imposed.

The growth rate of M3, upon which the effects of shifts of funds following the realignment of the system related to deposit products were broadly neutral, also declined on a December daily-average basis, from the 17.1% of the previous year to 15.9%. Its deceleration reflected the slowdown of firms' demands for funds and the tightening of liquidity supply.

From early December 1997 onwards, the monetary authorities, acting in line with their agreement reached with the IMF strengthened their existing tight monetary policy stance, lowering the growth rate of money and inducing sharp rises in market interest rates. Their objective in doing so was to stabilize the exchange rate and price movements.

During the same month, the monetary management system was also changed, with M3, which is more neutral to changes in the financial structure, being adopted as the monitoring variable in place of the previous dual system involving M2 and MCT. Once the appropriate growth of M3 has been determined, the corresponding growth rate of the indicative limit on reserve money is derived. The BOK (Bank of Korea) fixes the floor of NIR (net international reserves) and the ceiling of NDA (net domestic assets) as performance criteria, and concentrates its efforts on achieving them.

Partly as a result of these efforts, growth rates of reserve money and M3 as of the end of December were below the indicative limits set under the IMF program, and the balances of NIR and NDA also satisfied the performance criteria. Meanwhile, market interest rates rose to about twice their level before the recourse to the IMF as the BOK's market intervention interest rate was operated at a very much higher level in the process of tight monetary policy.

The BOK also lowered reserve requirement ratios on commercial banks' deposit liabilities, bringing them down from 5.5% to 3.3% on average. This represented a further step, following 1996s reduction, toward increasing commercial banks' discretion in operation of funds. In order to pave the way for the establishment of an indirect monetary management system and improvement of the effectiveness of open market operations, the BOK expanded the scope of its counterparts for RP transactions, previously restricted to commercial banks, to include merchant banking corporations, securities companies, and investment trust companies.

2) Money Market

In 1997 under review, as the economic downturn became protracted corporate insolvencies increased drastically and the percentage of dishonored bills rose markedly. There were bankruptcy of Hanbo Group on January 23, bankruptcy of Sammi Group on March 19 and Jinro Group filed for bankruptcy suspension accord on April 21, 1997. The number of corporate insolvencies increased rapidly to 17,168 from the 11,589 for 1996. Among them were many large corporations belonging to large interlinked business groups such as *Hanbo* and *Kia*. Accordingly, the nationwide percentage of cheques and bills dishonored in clearing houses nationwide increased considerably to 0.40% from the 0.14% in 1996. Particularly in December 1997, when the financial and currency crises were at their height, the percentage rose steeply to 1.49%.

The magnitude of financial institutions' non-performing assets increased steeply with the effects of the widespread corporate bankruptcies. The figure for NPLs (non-performing loans), which is the sum of substandard credits, doubtful credits and estimated loss credits, in all banks including specialized banks, doubled from 15.2 trillion wons in 1996 to 32.3 trillion wons, on an end-of-year basis. In the case of merchant banking corporations, bad loans approximately tripled from 1.3 trillion wons at the end of 1996 to 3.9 trillion wons at the end of October 1997.

Market interest rates showed stable movements on the whole during the first half of 1997, despite the increase in corporate bankruptcies, but shifted to a pronounced upward trend from the second half of 1997.

The yield on (three-year) corporate bonds rose narrowly at the beginning of 1997, reflecting financial market apprehensions caused by the insolvencies of several large corporations, notably *Hanbo Iron and Steel*. Thereafter, it turned to a downward trend owing to the government's announcement of an accelerated opening plan for the capital market. Early in June 1997, it dropped to 11.4%. However, in July 1997, it shifted back to an upward trend again, climbing to 13~14% in mid-November 1997, as market fears deepened and financial institutions experienced difficulty in borrowing abroad amid the repercussions from the insolvency arrangements for *KIA Motors*.

From late November 1997, when the Korean government applied for IMF emergency financing, the benchmark yield continued its sharp upward trend, driven by the preemptive demand for funds in anticipation of a fast-approaching tightening in money markets, and apprehensions of a further wave of corporate failures. Following the strengthening of the austere monetary policy stance upon the conclusion of the arrangement with the IMF, it fluctuated around the high level of 30% toward the end of December 1997.

Call market rates, which had been fluctuating within a range of 12~14% since the beginning of 1997, showed a steep upward trend from early December 1997, rising to 26% by the end of 1997. Yields on CP (commercial paper), which was perceived as carrying a generally higher insolvency risk, soared to 41%.

3) Financial Market

The Korean government and the BOK undertook a number of measures from the beginning of 1997 in response to deepening financial market instability aroused by the succession of large corporate insolvencies. Amid the deterioration of liquidity conditions during the first half of 1997 for some types of non-banking financial institutions, particularly merchant banking corporations, the Korean government cancelled its plan to enforce a system permitting call brokerage on a limited scale, which had initially been scheduled to come into effect from May 1, 1997, and also abolished the system regulating the volume of corporate bonds that might be issued.

In the face of the substantial deterioration in the financial status caused by the series of corporate insolvencies, the BOK supplied, from early in the third quarter onwards, one trillion Won in the form of special loans to Korea First Bank, and another one trillion Won to 16 merchant banking corporations. For its part, the government decided to set up a Non-Performing Asset Resolution Fund, initially capitalized at 3.5 trillion wons, under the aegis of the Korea Asset Management Corporation.

In early November 1997, when panic mounted in the financial and foreign exchange markets, the government took measures to increase this Fund to 10 trillion wons so as to clear off the bad loans from financial institutions' books as fast as possible. It was also decided that the assets and liabilities of banks and merchant banking corporations should be examined at their market value with a view to encouraging internal structural adjustment on the part of financial institutions.

E. External Sector

1) Current Account

Exports, on a customs-clearance basis, registered a growth rate of 5.0%, a little higher than in 1996, as the volume of exports rose rapidly, offsetting the effects of the drop in the unit value of exports due to the fall in the international prices of major export items. Viewed by commodity group, exports of heavy industrial and chemical products showed an upward trend, higher than in 1996, thanks to the favorable performance of exports of both petrochemical, and iron and steel products. However, the growth of exports of light industrial products decelerated from 1996's performance, held back by lower exports of footwear, tires and tubes. By region, exports to developed countries picked up again, thanks to the briskness of EU-bound exports which served to offset the protracted decrease in those to Japan. In contrast, exports to developing countries, notably the Southeast Asian and Latin American countries, slowed their growth rate, compared with 1996.

Imports, on a customs-clearance basis, decreased by 3.8% in response to the sluggishness of import demand, which reflected the dullness of domestic business activities and the depreciation of the Korean Won, and also to lower international raw material prices including for crude oil and grain. By commodity group, imports of capital goods and consumer goods both decreased in response to the contraction of domestic demand, while imports of raw materials maintained only a slow growth rate. By region, imports from developed countries decreased sharply, led downward by those from the US, Japan and the EU,

Meanwhile, those from the developing countries showed only modest growth at a lower level than in 1996, held back by the downturn in those from the Southeast Asian and the Central and South American countries.

During 1997, the current account deficit narrowed greatly from the US$23.0 billion in 1996 to US$8.6 billion. Most significantly, the fourth quarter figures showed a shift into surplus on the current account, the first quarterly surplus in four years. Contributions to this improved performance came mostly from the large surplus on the goods account arising from the sharp decrease in imports induced by the slowdown of domestic demand.

Other factors included a shift into surplus on the services and transfers balance as a result both of declines in overseas travel and in payments for other services, and the rapid improvement in the current transfers account, due to increased personal remittances from expatriate Koreans. The deficit on goods narrowed to US$3.9 billion from US$15.0 billion in 1996 due to the steady increase in exports together with the sustained deceleration of import growth. Measured by the difference between exports and imports on a customs- clearance basis, the trade balance with developing countries maintained a surplus similar to that of 1996, and the deficit on trade with the developed countries narrowed to about US$12.0 billion.

The deficit on services lessened from US$6.2 billion in 1996 to US$2.9 billion in 1997. This was attributable both to sharply increased inflows for transportation services, reflecting the increase in the volume of freight transportation, and to a rapid decline in overseas travel in response to the abrupt depreciation of the Korean Won from early November 1997.

The deficit on the income account widened to US$2.7 billion from US$1.8 billion in 1996, as interest payments increased in response to the heightened external debt and the increased cost of borrowing funds abroad owing to the country's loss of international credibility. The current transfers account shifted into surplus to the tune of US$0.86 billion from the small deficit of 1996. The transition occurred in December 1997 when inward remittances from expatriate Koreans increased greatly while personal remittances overseas declined.

Meanwhile, the capital account surplus decreased to post a net inflow of US$ 5.4 billion, a figure substantially less than the US$23.3 billion in 1996, despite the inflow of bailout funds for Korea from international financial institutions. Its contraction was attributable to the decline in both the issue of foreign currency securities and the induction of trade credits, along with large-scale repayments of financial institutions' short-term borrowings. These developments came in addition to the large net outflow of foreign portfolio capital from the stock market from August onwards as doubts spread about the credit standing of the Korean economy.

2) Foreign Exchange Markets

From the beginning of 1997, when signs of a demand-supply mismatch in the exchange market began to appear, the government took measures to promote inflow of foreign capital, such as raising the overall ceiling on foreigners' stock investment. During the fourth quarter of the year, as the foreign exchange situation worsened acutely, Korean government struggled to soothe the unrest in the foreign exchange market by widening capital market liberalization and shifting to a freely floating exchange rate system. Notably in December 1997, in line with its agreement with the IMF, Korean government greatly liberalized capital transactions through the complete opening to foreign investment of all listed bonds, and the raising of the ceilings on foreign investment in a company's stocks to 55% for aggregate foreign holdings and 50% for individual foreign holdings. Also, it allowed Korean corporations for a limited time period to raise overseas commercial and cash loans with maturities of at least 3 years and to issue foreign securities.

In early November 1997, the foreign exchange market was paralyzed by the spread of expectations of an early and massive depreciation of the Korean won. The government responded by widening the daily fluctuation band from ± 2.22% to ± 10% of the previous business day's market average rate. Soon after, the exchange regime was effectively converted to a free floating exchange rate system with the complete elimination of the band on December 16, 1997.

<Table IV-15> Usable Foreign Currency Reserve and Foreign Exchange Rates (US100 million)

Classification	'97. 12	'98. 1	'98. 3	'98. 6	'98. 9	'98. 12	'99. 2.
@Won/Dollar	1,484	1,705	1,505	1,385	1,373	1,207	1,175
Foreign Reserves	39.4	123.6	241.5	343.5	433.7	490.0	522.2

Source: Economic Policy Bureau, Ministry of Finance and Economy, Korea, March 1999.

F. Government Spending

The government conducted public finance with an emphasis on strengthening support for the improvement of national competitiveness and of the quality of life for the general public. These objectives were pursued subject to the dual constraints of maintaining a tight fiscal stance for price stabilization and the improvement of the current account position.

Fiscal expenditure increased by 10.5%, on an overall account(net) basis, much less than in the previous year. Nevertheless, the ratio of fiscal expenditure to GNP at current prices rose from 21.7% in 1996 to 22.2% in 1997, as the rate of expenditure increases outpaced that of GNP.

By account, the general account expanded by 9.4%, lower than its 13.6% growth of 1996. Its deceleration was helped by rigid expenditures such as those on defense and personnel, whose effects were only partially offset by the expansion of the fiscal spending on public works and on social welfare. Special accounts, meanwhile, were also held to a 6.9% increase, much lower than 14.2% in 1996, due to the slowdown in the expansion of all major special accounts other than the National Railroad Enterprise Special Account and the Communications Service Enterprises Special Account.

The growth rate of total tax revenues slowed from the 13.9% of 1996 to 9.4%, due to the sharp slowdown in collections of direct taxes such as income tax, and corporate tax in response to the economic stagnation. The ratio of tax revenues, including local tax, to nominal GNP registered 21.2%, similar to that of 1996.

Chapter V

The Korean Financial Crisis: Its Causes, Progress and Prospects

1. Causes of the Korean Financial Crisis[31]

In November 1997 Korea, which had long been the envy of many developing countries, was faced with the threat of a debt moratorium. It would, however, be a mistake to blame this debacle solely on a contagion effect from the financial crisis in Southeast Asia.

To be sure, by most criteria, Korea had sound macroeconomic fundamentals. However, as shown by <Figure V-1>, owing to an excessively leveraged corporate sector and a weak financial system, they could not ride out the financial storm sweeping through the rest of Asia. Above all, the operations of Korea's "floating" exchange rate system was in practice akin to an "adjustable peg" system, and monetary policy also proved to be inappropriate in the context of greater capital market openness.

From August 1997, to the eve of the crisis, the authorities vainly attempted to prop up the Korean Won, while at the same time injecting substantial liquidity into the financial system to check the wave of bankruptcies. Still, policy inertia, inappropriate exchange rate goals, and capital flight quickly exhausted Korea's limited foreign exchange reserves.

Prior to the financial crisis, the Korean economy was marked by a puzzling dichotomy between a strong real economy and growing financial market tensions. Up to late October, 1997, the real economy appeared to be adjusting smoothly to the severe 1996 terms-of-trade shock and a cutback in business investment following a boom in the early 1990s.

These factors had slowed GDP growth from an unsustainably high rate of 9% in 1994~1995 to 7% in 1996. The first quarter of 1997, when GDP growth fell to 5.7%, appeared to mark a successful 'soft-landing'. Notwithstanding sluggish domestic demand, GDP growth during the first three quarters of 1997 still averaged over 6%, while industrial output growth was some 9% reflecting strong net exports.

Inflation, measured by the 4.3% rise in the private consumption deflator, was the lowest in a decade. Unemployment, albeit edging up to some 2.5% of the labour force, was very low by OECD standards. At the same time, the current account deficit, which had soared to US$23.7 billion in 1996 (almost 5% of GDP), had been halved by the third quarter of the year, and the capital account, although volatile, was recording small net inflows.

As in the past, the economy was firmly underpinned by cautious monetary and fiscal policies with the budget oriented towards a balanced current position and a small surplus on the social security accounts. The macro-economy prior to the financial crisis gave few signs of imminent stress. In the past, high nominal GDP growth had masked many of Korea's financial problems and perhaps lulled regulators and foreign investors into complacency.

However, the crucial pressure point between weak microeconomic structures and slower economic growth proved to be the corporate sector's weak balance sheet and cash-flow positions. Insolvencies especially among incorporated firms were on the rise, as increasing gearing resulted in higher business break-even points, while slowing economic growth exacerbated cash-flow problems. Insolvencies soared during the course of 1997 and reached dangerous levels in early 1998.

---

[31] Yang-Taek Lim, "The Role of Foreign Direct Investment for Korea's Economic Recovery and Future Directions in Foreign Investment Promotion Policy", paper presented at ACAES-Culalongkorn University International Conference, Bangkok, Thailand, December 16-18, 1998.

< **Figure V-1** > **Inter-Function of Each Entities Driven to the IMF Bail-out**

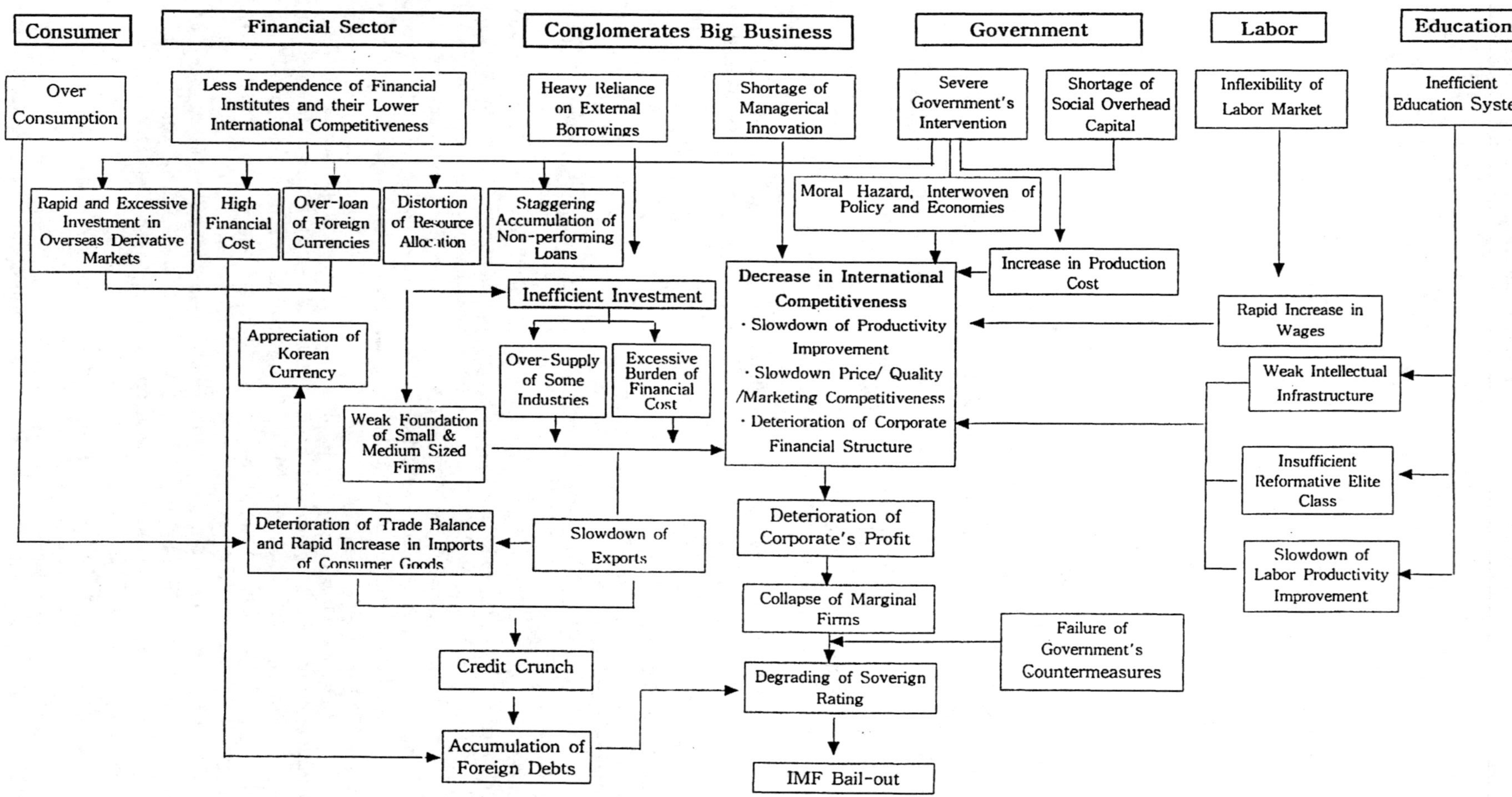

A. The Monetary Side

The crisis *per se* started in early July 1997 with Thailand's 'surprise' decision to float its currency. This was followed a few weeks later by KIA Motor's request for a 'debt work out' programme with its major creditors, (involving some US$8 billion), to avoid bankruptcy.[32] These events increased the sensitivity of investors to financial sector problems. Soon after, major international credit rating agencies which had failed to foresee the Thai situation began to reassess countries with similar characteristics.

The first critical fault line was inconsistent monetary policy during the second half of 1997. Monetary policy has limited independence in globalized financial markets and the authorities must choose to target either domestic monetary conditions (interest rates or money growth) or the exchange rate. Policy can address different policy goals at any moment in time, but credibility and consistency require concentrating on a single overarching objective, such as low inflation or a fixed exchange rate. This basic principle was ignored in Korea.

Monetary policy in 1997, as in the past, was oriented towards achieving neutral conditions by supplying sufficient monetary growth (M2 and MCT) to underpin output growth at around its potential, while allowing 'unavoidable' inflation and trend income velocity. This proved to be difficult. Although money growth was well sustained through 1997, this was misleading as it masked significant shifts and distortions in the allocation of credit. Bank loans to the 30 largest *Chaebols* actually rose by 43% in December 1997, and indeed some 40% of the growth in bank credit over the second half of 1997 might have been emergency loans to distressed firms at rates below market. Such non-market lending practices continued into 1998, resulting in an acute liquidity shortage for some healthy SMEs.

On 25 August 1997, a high-risk decision was taken to "implicitly" guarantee the foreign liabilities of the merchant banks to facilitate their overseas borrowing needs even though some of these institutions may have been close to insolvency. This guarantee foiled because in the wake of the *KIA* failure, domestic and foreign financial institutions refused to increase their exposure to shaky merchant banks. More importantly, the decision to underwrite the foreign liabilities of the banks meant that the Bank of Korea was trying to play the role of lender of last resort in US dollars (similar in nature to Mexico's Tesobonos problem).

This high-risk strategy was compounded by the decision to prop up the Won. From August to end-November 1997, the Bank of Korea lost at least US$8 to 10 billion in foreign reserves through exchange market intervention, even though the Won was theoretically floating within a predetermined band.

In short, through the latter part of 1997 monetary policy was being run in a fixed-exchange rate mode. This approach to policy may have reflected an illusion that the cautious dismantling of capital controls served to protect the economy from sharp swings in capital.

In fact, Korea's foreign liabilities had tripled since 1994, and its usable foreign reserves were less than a third of its short-term external liabilities prior to the crisis though the authorities may have been ignorant of the scale of external debt, owing to a chronic lack of transparency. With the benefit of foresight, the quick adoption of a freely floating exchange rate (even as late as July 1997) might have avoided some of the worst excesses of the crisis. To be sure, a severe financial crisis and a loss of international confidence would still have been inevitable. Though it is impossible to say whether the attack on the won would have been tempered or not. the Bank of Korea would at least have been able to play the role of lender of last resort in domestic currency.

A final action, which added fuel to the flames, was an ill-judged decision to bail out *KIA Motors* in late October 1997 (after repealed public statements that the government would not do so). But by this time, foreign banks had already sharply reduced their credit lines and foreign investors were quitting Korea in large numbers.

[32] Financial market confidence was particularly shaken in January 1997 by the first such insolvency, that of Hanbo Steel (Korea's 14th-largest conglomerate). The scale of the ensuing bribes-for-loans scandal was stunning, even for a Korean Public long hardened to 'cosy' arrangements: and foreign investors' confidence appealed to have been irrevocably shaken. This fragile situation calmed in Spring 1997, in part because Korean banks entered into a voluntary 'Bankruptcy Avoidance Agreement' in April to avoid driving 'solvent' firms into receivership (albeit at the costs of weakening their own balance sheets). But this respite proved short-lived.

B. The Real Side

The second critical fault line on the path to crisis was the rapid build-up of short-term domestic and foreign debt to finance the investment boom of the large conglomerates, known as *chaebols*, in the 1990s. By the end of 1997, Korea's 30 largest *chaebols'* average debt to equity ratio had soared to over 500%, 100 points higher than in 1996. Such traditionally high leveraging reflected *inter alia* the *chaebols'* pursuit of rapid growth on a global scale by diversifying into capital-intensive industries, as part of an ambitious strategy to 'leap frog' quickly up the value-added chain into higher technology products.

This strategy had been successful in the 1970s and 1980s, when Korean companies were small and achieving economies of scale and establishing extensive distribution channels were critical to increasing productivity and shareholder value. But by the late 1980s, global competitive conditions had changed radically, and past strategies of debt financed growth became increasingly risky in the face of falling profitability.

Chaebols' management structures were slow to internalize these basic changes in international competitive conditions and shareholder value was systematically being destroyed from the late 1980s onwards. Indeed, rapid expansion in the late 1980s into a number of 'prestige' capital-intensive, high-risk industries where Korean industry had weak technical or management comparative advantage, probably laid the seeds of the corporate sector's current dire situation. Worse, given the simultaneous entry of a number of *chaebols* into similar industries (for example, semiconductors, steel, consumer durables and especially automobiles), rates of return were quickly depressed by the rapid build-up of capacity and fierce competition. Given the limited size of domestic bond and equity markets and preferential access to credit from a docile banking sector, this industrial strategy left the *chaebols* with a legacy of 'too big to fail' but with excessively- leveraged balance sheets and ill-prepared for the rigors of global competition.

Korea's non-financial corporate sector as a whole exhibits balance sheet characteristics similar to those of the *chaebols,* albeit with a debt - to - equity ratio of just under 400% (excluding the *chaebols*). Nonetheless, by the end of 1997 total corporate debt had risen to 26.8%, 810.6 trillion wons (around US$600 billion) or 167% of GDP. A key feature in 1997 was the marked rise (from 9 to 28%) in financing coming from non-bank financial institutions (especially shaky 'merchant banks'), reflecting weak bond and equity markets, as well as reluctance of banks to increase their lending activities.

Heavy debt service is a quiet essential feature of fragile firms. Combined with rigid lay-off laws, weak cash-flow and cross-debt guarantees, a recipe for serial bankruptcies and high systematic risk was in place. Warning signs first appeared in the mid of 1996, when over-capacity emerged in key export sectors following an investment boom concentrated in semiconductors, cars, steel and petrochemicals. Export prices softened with semiconductor prices plummeting some 80%.

Notwithstanding a modest recovery in profit margins, a critical point was reached around the mid of 1997 when financial costs exceeded profits, and corporate cash-flow was caught in a savage squeeze. Given the highly leveraged position of the corporate sector and resulting balance-sheet problems, the slowdown in growth in 1997 triggered a 50% jump in the number of insolvencies. Although large-scale bankruptcies in Korea have been quite rare, 8 of the 30 largest *chaebols* representing around 4% of the assets of non-agricultural, non-financial business failed in 1997.

2. Negotiations of the Stand-by Credit Arrangement with the IMF

A. An Official Request for an Emergency Liquidity Arrangement

From the beginning of 1997, as a mismatch between foreign exchange supply and demand emerged, the government undertook a series of policy initiatives to stabilize the foreign exchange market and to restore the foreign credibility of the Korean economy.

On March 31, 1997, it announced plans for the acceleration of the capital market opening. These involved removing restrictions on foreigners' investment in the domestic equity and bond markets, and encouraging overseas financing by Korean financial institutions and corporations. On August 25, 1997, the government unveiled measures designed to stabilize the domestic financial markets and shore up the credit standing of domestic financial institutions in the international financial markets. The package included a government guarantee of repayment of all overseas debt liabilities by Korean financial institutions, and the provision by the Bank of Korea of short-term foreign currency liquidity to financial institutions.

On October 29 and 31, 1997, the government again acted to stabilize the securities market and the foreign exchange market. This time the package included the wider opening of the corporate bond market, the encouragement for the inducement of cash loans, the placing of temporary restraints on purchases of foreign currency to place on deposit, and the adjustment of the limits on banks' spot over-bought position.

A further financial market stabilization package followed in November 1997, its initiatives included arrangement for the early resolution of bad loans through the Non-Performing Asset Management Fund of the Korea Asset Management Corporation for the promotion of the structural adjustment of the financial industry, and the widening of the Korean won's daily fluctuation band from ±2.25% to ±10%.

These policy responses, however, failed to calm market fears. Korea's foreign currency liquidity status had deteriorated sharply in late October following the sharp fall in the Hang Seng index (Hong Kong) on October 23, 1997 and the downgrading of Korea sovereign rating by international credit rating agencies. Facing almost insurmountable difficulties in external financing, the government turned to the IMF for financial assistance on November 21, 1997. It engaged in full and frank negotiations with the IMF's working-level delegation on the amount and conditions of the financial assistance including policy programs from November 25, 1997. An agreement was reached on December 4, 1997 over a Letter of Intent containing the economic and financial programs with Korean the government should implement in conjunction with the financial assistance from the IMF.

In spite of the conclusion of this agreement, foreign currency liquidity continue to worsen and instability mounted in the domestic foreign exchange market. Therefore, on December 24, 1997, the government and the IMF agreed on a Second Letter of Intent, whereby Korea undertook to speed up its economic reforms, including the full opening of the bond market, the setting of a timetable for the opening of the domestic money market and the abolition of the Interest Limitation Act. In recognition of this, it was agreed that disbursement of the support previously committed to Korea by the IMF and major advanced countries would be brought forward and accelerated.

B. Details of the IMF Stand-by Arrangement

The total scale of the emergency credit package put together by multilateral financial institutions, including the IMF, the IBRD, the ADB and a number of industrialized countries, which was announced on December 4, amounted to US$57 billion. This was increased to US$58.35 billion when additional supplementary financial commitments were made by other participant countries on December 24, 1997.

The IMF granted a stand-by credit of 15.5 billion SDRs (approximately US$ 21 billion), the conditions being repayment in installments over two years after a three-year grace period and an interest rate of about 4.7% per annum. Later, the Korean government and the IMF agreed that the disbursement equivalent to 10 billion SDRs would be completed between December 18, 1997 and December 17, 1998 and should be handled under the SRF (Supplemental Reserve Facility). This enabled the accelerated provision of financial support subject to the condition that repayment of each tranche be made within one to one and a half years of the date it was drawn down. The interest rate during the first year was set at 300 basis points above the rate carried by the IMF loans (4.7% per annum), and it is to be increased by 50 basis points at the end of that year and subsequently every six months until it reaches 500 basis points. Under these arrangements, the Korean government drew 4.1 billion SDRs (US$5.56 billion) on December 5 and 8, 1997, 2.6 billion SDRs (US$3.53 billion) between December 19 and 22, 1997, and 1.5 billion SDRs (US$2.02 billion) on December 30 and 31, 1997, respectively.

In addition to the financial assistance from the IMF, the Korean government took up financial assistance equivalent to US$10 billion from the IBRD. On this facility the period of repayment was set at five years following a five-year grace period, the interest rate was set at Libor+1.0% per annum, and it was to be used in support of specific structural reform programs. The Korean government drew down US$3 billion on December 23, 1997, in the first tranche according to the agreement with the IBRD. Similarly, Korea was granted US$4 billion by the ADB in support of policy and institutional reforms, the conditions being repayment in full after a seven-year grace period and an interest rate of Libor+0.4% per annum. Under this arrangement, the Korean government initially drew down US$2 billion on December 24, 1997.

A number of countries, including members of the G7 countries also participated in the emergency credit package put together by the IMF. They made supplemental financial commitments totalling US$22 billion (Japan US$10 billion; the United States US$5 billion; Germany, the United Kingdom, France, and Italy US$1.25 billion each; and Australia and Canada US$1 billion each). This second line of defense would be made available through bilateral negotiations in the event of unanticipated adverse external circumstances creating a need for additional resources to supplement Korea's reserves and the resources provided by the IMF and other multilateral institutions.

<Table V-1> The Summary of the IMF Stand-By Arrangement

(1) Objectives

The program is intended to narrow the external current account deficit to below 1% of GDP in 1998 and 1999, contain inflation at or below 5%, and (hoping for an early return of confidence), limit the deceleration in real GDP growth to about 3% in 1998, followed by a recovery toward potential in 1999.

(2) Monetary Policy and Exchange Rate Policy

To demonstrate to markets the authorities resolve to confront the present crisis, monetary policy will be tightened immediately to restore and sustain calm in the markets and contain the impact of the recent won depreciation on inflation.

Money growth during 1998 was limited to a rate consistent with containing inflation at 5% or less. A flexible exchange rate policy was maintained, with intervention limited to smoothing operations.

(3) Fiscal Policy

A tight fiscal policy was maintained in 1998 to alleviate the burden on monetary policy and to provide for the still uncertain costs of restructuring the financial sector.

The cyclical slowdown was projected to worsen the 1998 budget balance of the consolidated central government by about 0.8% of GDP. The present estimates of the interest costs of financial sector restructuring is 0.8% of GDP. Offsetting measures amounting to about 1.5% of GDP was taken to achieve at a minimum budget balance and, preferably, a small surplus. This was achieved by both revenue and expenditure measures to be determined shortly. These measures include, among others:

- Increasing VAT coverage and removing exemptions;
- Widening the corporate tax base by reducing exemptions and certain tax incentives;
- Widening the income tax base by reducing exemptions and deductions;
- Increasing excises, luxury taxes, and transportation tax;
- Reducing current expenditures particularly support to the corporate sector; and
- Reducing low priority capital expenditures.

On December 24, 1997, four more countries agreed to participate in the second line of defense. Belgium, the Netherlands, Sweden and Switzerland volunteered to make a total of US$1.25 billion available, and New Zealand made a supplemental financial commitment of US$100 million. This brought the total amount committed to the second line of defense to a total of US$23.35 billion. Upon the IMF's formal declaration that it would accelerate the provision of financial support to Korea, the countries participating in the second line of defense also agreed to make available earlier than scheduled almost one third (US$8 billion) of the total committed, as well as accelerating the provision of other agreed financial commitments.

C. The IMF Programs and the Agony of the 'Four Highs'

1) The IMF Program in Action

The economic program negotiated with the IMF as a condition of the stand-by arrangements included a macroeconomic stabilization and structural reform program, financial sector restructuring, trade and capital account liberalization, the reform of corporate governance and corporate management and labor market reform.

At first, the macroeconomic objectives of the program included: narrowing the external current account deficit to below 1% of GDP in 1998 and 1999, containing inflation at or below 5% and limiting real GDP growth to about 3% in 1998, followed by a recovery toward the potential growth rate in 1999.

Monetary policy was to be tightened immediately to restore calm in the markets and contain the inflationary impact of the recent Won depreciation. A flexible exchange rate policy was to be maintained with intervention limited to smoothing operations. In line with these policies, the fiscal stance was to remain tight throughout 1998 to achieve equilibrium or a small surplus through measures affecting both revenue and expenditure.

The centerpiece of the economic program was a comprehensive restructuring and strengthening of the financial system to make it sound, transparent and efficient. Concerning financial sector restructuring, the strategy was to comprise three broad elements: a clear and firm exit policy, strong market and supervisory discipline and increased competition. The exit policy would seek to ensure the rapid resolution of troubled financial institutions in a manner that minimized systemic distress and avoided moral hazard.

The government's policy would involve the restructuring and recapitalization of all banks that failed to meet the BIS ratio requirement. In order to improve transparency in the financial sector, large financial institutions were to be required to upgrade their accounting and disclosure standards toward best international practice. To strengthen financial sector supervision, the government urgently requested passage of 13 financial reform bills including the revised 'Bank of Korea Act' in December 1997. This would provide for the central bank's independence with price stability as its overriding mandate in a bill to set up an agency that would integrate the supervisory functions distributed among various agencies, a bill requiring that corporate financial statements be prepared on a consolidated basis and be certified by external auditors. To promote competition and efficiency in the financial sector, the government would allow foreigners to establish banking and securities subsidiaries by the mid of 1998.

Regarding trade liberalization, a timetable would be set in line with the commitments to the WTO to eliminate trade-related subsidies, restrictive import licensings, and the import diversification program. Steps would also be taken to streamline and improve the transparency of import declaration procedures.

The Korean government would substantially accelerate the ongoing capital account liberalization program. The ceiling on aggregate foreign ownership was to be increased from 26% to 50% by the end of 1997 and to 55% during 1998. By the end of February 1998, steps were to be taken to liberalize other capital account transactions, including those restricting foreigners' access to domestic money market instruments and the corporate bond markets, and these would be a further reduction of restrictions on foreign direct investment by the simplification of approval procedures. A timetable was set by the end of February 1998 to eliminate restrictions on foreign borrowings by corporations.

Concerning corporate governance and corporate structure, the government was to take measures to improve the transparency of corporate balance sheets, to change the system of cross-debt guarantees among inter-linked business groups to reduce the risks involved, and to reduce the restrictions on the take-over of corporations by foreigners.

The Korean government undertook to strengthen the employment insurance scheme to facilitate the re-deployment of labor and to remove labor market rigidities so as to make the rationalization of employment easier for structural adjustment or a merger and acquisition.

Moreover, the government would review the Bank of Korea's international reserves management with the intention of bringing it more closely into line with international standards and regularly publish data on foreign exchange reserves, including their composition and net forward position. The government also undertook to release twice a year data on financial institutions, including their non-performing loans, capital adequacy, ownership structure and affiliations.

2) The Agony of 'Four Highs'

The IMF Programs on Korea's recent foreign financial crisis has been to pursue financial reform, open money markets, restructure of the conglomerates, and reform the labor market under policies of low economic growth, reduced budget and high interest rates.[33] The purpose of this program has been to attract foreign capital → improve trade deficit → stabilize exchange rate and market prices. In reality, however, it is true that the IMF Programs caused unstable exchange rates and soaring market prices, inactive inflow of foreign capital and an increase of corporate bankruptcies and industrial collapse due to super-high interest rates. Thus, the impact of the original IMF Programs is now being questioned in retrospect.

<Figure V-2> Vicious Cycle of 'Four Highs'

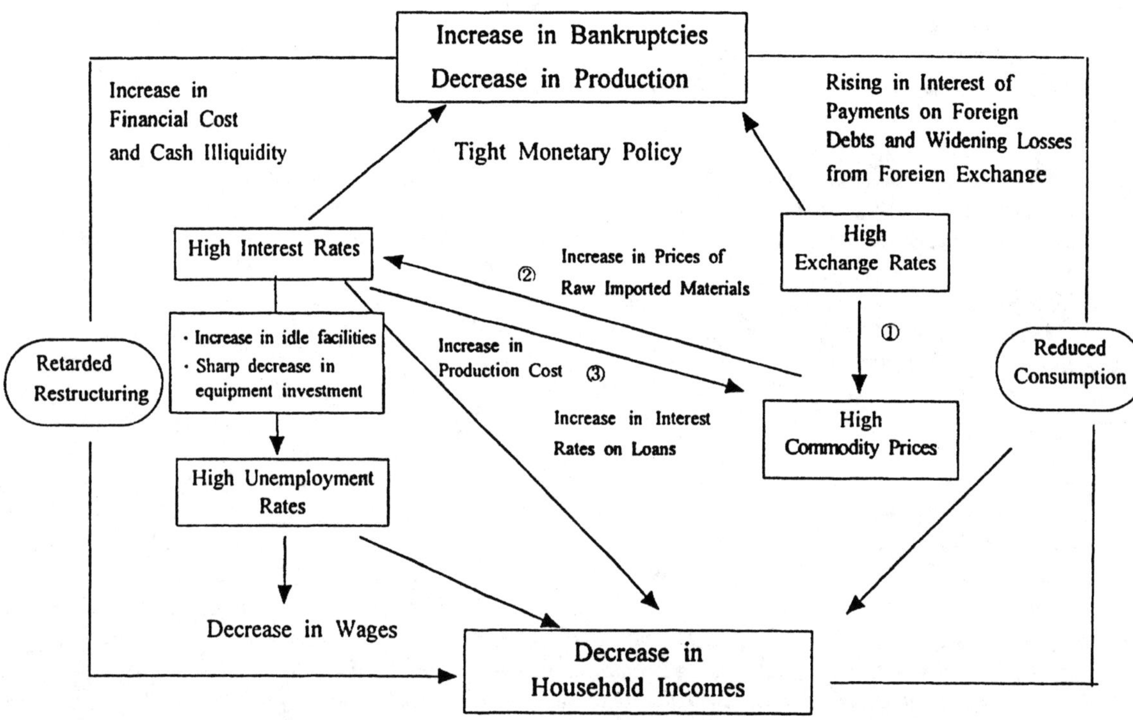

The first problem was the 'high interest rate'. At interest rates over 20% which the IMF required, strong companies which could yield profits under normal interest rates had no choice but to have gone bankrupt, not to mention those already in critical condition. That is to say, the high interest rate policy of the IMF beyond its original intention to control excessive investment, almost destroyed the industrial foundation and the potential export capability. This super-high interest rate caused a vicious circle of a decline in the manufacturing industry → prevalence of capital rearrangement → capital stringency → chain bankruptcy of companies → weakening foundation of manufacturing industry.

Another negative impact of the IMF policy has been 'high unemployment'. Once the industrial structure reform got started full-scale, there was a series of bankruptcies of conglomerates as well as small and medium-sized companies. The number of unemployed people soared to well over 2 million by the end of 1998. Unemployment is expected to get even worse in 1999 with the economic recession and low growth.

[33] The IMF claims that the countries in crisis like Thailand, Indonesia and Korea should maintain temporarily tight financial and monetary policies and also high interest rates. They say keeping the interest rate high is inevitable in order to deal with the insolvent companies and financial institutions whose financial structure is not solid enough to attract the foreign capital. It was a requisite that interest rates be kept at over 20% temporarily.

< Figure V-3> The Relationship between Devaluation of Foreign Exchange Rate and the Foreign Exchange Crisis

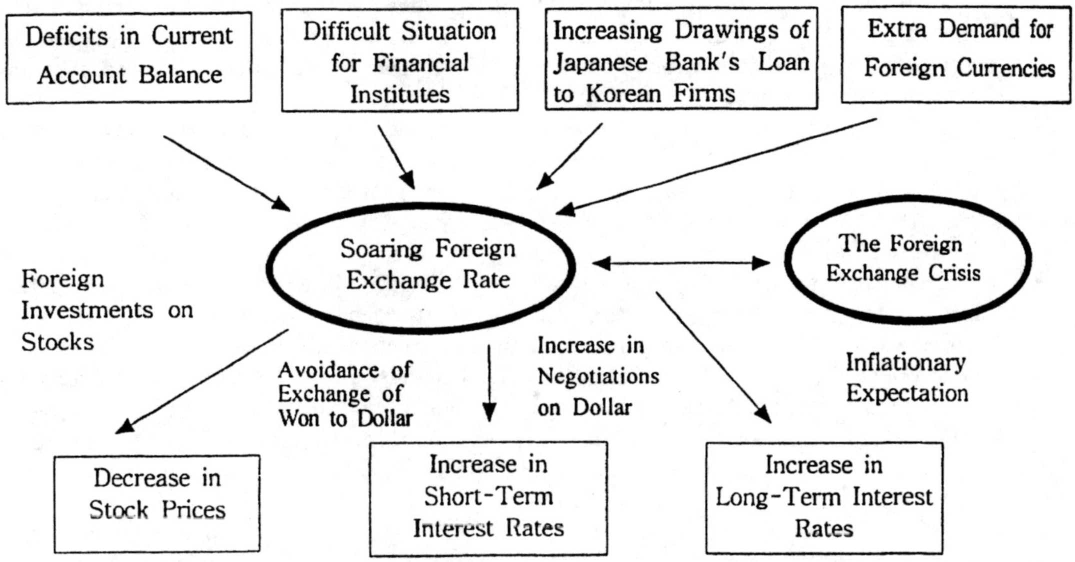

The third high that the IMF Programs brought about is 'high market prices'. The original intention of the IMF to stabilize market prices by a reduced budget actually got reverse results. The reason is that the excessively reduced budget shrank market demand, which created another vicious circle of bankruptcies of domestic industries → increase of bad loans at financial institutions → lowering of international confidence → more difficulties in introducing foreign capital → additional rises of exchange rates → higher market prices.

This complicated loop of the vicious circle could be stopped only by stabilizing the exchange rate. In order to stabilize the exchange rate, promotion for the inflow of the dollar into the domestic market was strongly needed. This can be accomplished by foreign investment and export growth. Under the present structure of exports in which price competitiveness is swayed by the relative devaluation of the Won against the Yen, the reflective profits under a low Yen, which used to be in the past, could not be expected.

Korea thus needs to focus on non-price competitiveness through development of technology, introduction of new products, and quality improvement instead of price competitiveness based on the fluctuations of exchange rates. Unfortunately advances in technology and quality cannot be achieved in a short period of time. Thus, the Korean government has focused on attracting foreign investment to draw dollars into the country.

D. Cases of Other Recipients of IMF's Liquidity Arrangement

It has been roughly a year since Thailand and then Indonesia, and finally Korea were forced to approach the IMF for financial aids in the face of worsening the foreign exchange crisis. Since that time, the IMF Programs for these countries have come under increasing criticism by many for being partially or even wholly inappropriate. Thus, at this point in time, it would seem appropriate to examine how the three recipients of IMF's financial aid have fared over the past year.

In spite of some positive signs, the short-term outlooks for these countries were hardly bright. After growth of 5.5% in 1997, Korea's economy was expected to contract by -7.0% in 1998, according to the IMF's recent World Economic Outlook. Thailand's GDP growth rate fell from 5.5% in 1996 to -0.4% in 1997, and fell further to an estimated -8.0% in 1998. And Indonesia's situation was even worse: the IMF predicted Indonesia's growth rate could fall from 4.0% in 1997 to an astonishing -15% in 1998.

These growth rate predictions have been revised downward sharply from initial predictions: for example, Korea's original Letter of Intent assumed a 1998 growth rate of 2.5%. In its recent report, the IMF basically admitted that it misjudged the impact and depth of the Asian crisis. Equity markets and asset values fell more than expected, and the mounting problems in financial and corporate sectors were worse than originally thought. Furthermore, each country's problems have worsened one another's, resulting in sharp contraction of regional trade.

Regarding the financial crisis itself, the exchange rates of the three countries above have been overvalued considerably. In Korea, the Won/Dollar exchange rate had been stabilized in the 1200 range in the early 1999 after hitting almost 2000 at one point. The Thai Baht seemed steady at around 40 Baht/Dollar after climbing to around 55, and the Indonesian Rupiah had overvalued to under 8000 Rupiah/Dollar from the all-time low of 17,000 in mid-May of 1997.

Korea and Thailand are generally considered to be the stars of the IMF program. IMF officials readily conceded that the two have made significant progress in macroeconomic stabilization and structural reforms,[34] and felt that if the reform program was steadily implemented, the two economies could turn around in 1999. Policy-determined interest rates have already come down to pre-crisis levels, but monetary policy must still remain cautious to ensure exchange rate stability and to prevent inflation. Lending rates have been falling slowly and should continue to fall in the future. Meanwhile, the IMF has allowed fiscal deficits to widen to deal with the worsening recessions, to strengthen the social safety net and to finance financial restructuring.

Indonesia's course has been rougher. Indonesia has more recently begun to re-establish financial stability after the collapse of its currency, its financial system and its distribution network in May and early June of 1997. Real GDP fell to a seasonally adjusted 2% between the second and third quarters, much less of decline than in the previous two quarters. Interest rates and inflation are also showing signs of dropping. According to the IMF, the tasks ahead for the Indonesian government include rehabilitation of the financial system, restoring confidence to reverse capital flight, restructuring the corporate sector, and repairing the distribution system and market mechanisms. All in all, the IMF thinks the economic situation remains fragile, but if current programs succeed, output may bottom out during 1999.

It would be hard to fully blame the IMF for misjudging the severity of the Asian financial crisis. Few, if any, accurately predicted how the Asian financial crisis would spread to all emerging markets and then to developed markets as well, precipitating fears of a global recession. The IMF's predictions of an early recovery for Korea were predicated based on a huge current account surplus more due to relatively increased exports than a drop in imports.

It is probably true that the IMF-mandated high interest rates and tight monetary policy killed growth more than necessary. Thus, criticism of the IMF's 'one-size-fits-all' policy prescriptions were deserving to a degree. It should also be remembered, however, that particularly in the initial stages, the IMF's primary duty was to restore stability. Even though the Asian financial crisis was still not over and overall global economic conditions are bleak, the situations in Korea, Thailand, and Indonesia appear to be stabilizing.

---

[34] In an exclusive interview with the Korea Herald-Naeway Economic Daily on January 5, 1999, IMF Managing Director Michel Camdessus said that Korea would soon overcome its current recession and resume economic growth in 1999 thanks to substantial progress in its ongoing restructuring efforts. The IMF chief believes that the worst is over for Korea and that the nation is moving in the right direction. Mr. Camdessus said,

> "A powerful sign that the economic typhoon has passed Korea is the government's recent decision to pay back US$2.8 billion to the IMF." "Among the IMF-rescued countries, Korea and Thailand have made particularly good progress in achieving stabilization and implementing structural reforms".

He cautioned against being overly optimistic at this stage because Korea's recovery depends on how quickly domestic consumption can increase and structural reforms in various sectors progress. He said, "There is no room for complacency. Most critically, the government must further accelerate structural reforms to return to the path of sustained economic growth."

3. The IMF Bail-out - One Year Later

Since Korea was forced to go the IMF for a bail-out, there has been much debate about the various causes of the crisis. In the end, it was mainly due to Korea's growing lack of international competitiveness with its high cost-low efficiency structure combined with its inability to properly adapt to the rapid changes and trends in the global economy.

Since the IMF bail-out, Korea has worked closely with international institutions such as the IMF and the World Bank and with the advanced economies to get back on its feet and restore stability and confidence in the economy. By large, efforts have been successful. The immediate threat of a currency crisis has passed, and the Won has stabilized back under 1,200 wons to the Dollar. Interest rates are dropping, and the stock market is reviving. In addition, foreign investment in Korea appears to be picking up, showing that Korea is regaining the confidence of international markets.

In retrospect, though, Korea's response has been far from perfect. Perhaps the biggest criticism is that some policy measures have been geared toward short-term, immediate ends and lack credible long-term vision. The contractionary monetary policy adopted immediately after the IMF bail-out and the resulting exorbitant interest rates may have been well intended, but in the end, they debilitated the real economy and weakened Korea's industrial foundation. At the same time, a detailed program for monitoring external debt, a key cause of the currency crisis, still has not been announced, much less implemented. Furthermore, the Korean government seems to lack a comprehensive master plan for boosting Korea's long-term growth potential and maintaining social cohesion in the midst of the ongoing restructuring process and growing unemployment.

Lately, two main themes have emerged concerning the current business cycle of the Korean economy. One is the debate over how much the business cycle has truly entered into a recovery phase; in other words, even though most major economic indicators have apparently rebounded, the perceivable economic situation has not really improved. The other major issue is identifying the main constraints or hindrances preventing a full-fledged economic recovery. In fact, the two themes are closely related to each other. If we can properly identify or address these potential shortfalls, then we can abridge the gap between the movements of the 'indicator' business cycle and the 'perceived' business cycle.

Looking at the actual economic indicators, we find that consumption expenditures and (facility and construction) investment remain sluggish. Many people are pointing to these components as the main culprits for the delay in the real recovery, but in truth they are merely reflecting other constraints or underlying problems.

The first constraint is the falling value of the yen. The lower yen has not had an immediate impact on Korea's exports yet, but it will definitely discourage the investment attitude in the business sector unless the won/dollar rate adjusts accordingly such that Korean products continue to have price competitiveness over Japanese products.

The second constraint is the cost of the banking sector restructuring and the resulting budget burden. The total amount of non-performing loans is estimated to be 150 trillion won, and the Korean government has already spent or is planning to spend 64 trillion wons in order to clear them out, most of which is being financed by the issuance of new bonds. The repayment of the principal and interest will be a significant burden and a major constraint on government spending to boost the Korean economy.

The last constraint is the official withdrawal of the two major labor umbrella groups, the KCTU (Korean Confederation of Trade Unions) and the FKTU (Federation of Korean Trade Unions), from the Tripartite Comminute to protest the unbalanced nature of the restructuring process and the inadequate social safety net. If they stay out of the agreement for an extended period of time, the Korean economy will undoubtedly see its credibility fall once again and present a dismal picture to foreign investors.

The main factors which will determine the future outlook of the Korean economy are how smoothly the current restructuring process will be completed and also how favorable the outside circumstances are to Korea. In light of this reality, it is much more critical to resolve the above constraints since they are the main components determining Korea's restructuring process and the favorableness of the outside conditions. The challenges for the Korean economy should be whether it possesses the willingness and capability to regain the momentum for a real recovery in every sector, not just for a technical rebound in mere numbers.

4. Korea's Repayment of International Borrowings and Prospects on Economic Recovery

According to the BOK (Bank of Korea), the balance of Korea's borrowings from international financial institutions stood at US $24.9 billion as of January 8, 1999. Originally, Korea had made an agreement on a total of US $35 billion worth of borrowings with the IMF, World Bank and ADB while the actual amount borrowed by December 31 1998 totaled US $28.7 billion: US $19 billion from the IMF, US $6 billion from the World Bank and US $3.7 billion from the ADB. However, Korea could begin to repay US $2.8 billion[35] and US$1 billion in the borrowings from the IMF in December 1998 and on January 8, 1999, respectively, and the balance decreased to US$24.9 billion.

<Table V-2> Korea's Borrowings and Repayments (unit: US$ billion, as of January 8, 1999)

Institutions	Total Agreed	Borrowed	*Future Borrowings (1999-2000)*	repaid	Balance
IMF	21	19	2	3.8	15.2
World Bank	10	6	4	0	
ADB	4	3.7	0.3	0	3.7
Total	35	28.7	6.3	3.8	4.9

Source: Ministry of Finance and Economy, Korea, February 1999.

The BOK said that Korea's usable foreign exchange reserves totaled US$48.5 billion in 1998, surpassing the US$41 billion level projected by Korea and the IMF. Overall foreign exchange reserves (usable foreign exchange reserves plus foreign currency deposits at overseas bank branches) rose to US$52.0 billion. This marks an increase of US$31.6 billion from 1997, the BOK said.

The central bank cited financial institutions'repayment of emergency foreign loans to the BOK and an inflow of funds from the IMF and other international financial institutions as well as a rise in the current account surplus and an increase in FDIs in Korea, as a key factor for the rise in foreign exchange reserves. Korea's goal is to increase the total of its usable foreign exchange reserves to US$55 billion in 1999.

The Korean government has announced that the preliminary figure for Korea's total external liabilities aggregated by the Bank of Korea reached US$152.5 billion as of the end of November 1998. The figure showed a decrease of US$5.6 billion and US$1.1 billion during the year and November 1998, respectively. This was mainly due to the redemption of loans on schedule by financial institutions.

The total external assets corresponding to the total external liabilities were compiled at US$132.5 billion for the same month showing a slight increase. As a result, the net external liabilities, at US$20.0 billion, were reduced by US$32.7 billion and US$1.2 billion during the year and November 1998, respectively. It is expected that the net external liabilities will continue to decrease as the current account surplus and foreign direct investment sustain.

[35] The Korean government decided to make repurchases of the IMF's SRF (Supplemental Reserve Facility: a short-term emergency loan) worth US$2.8 billion maturing in December 1998. The government's repurchase decision was mainly based on the substantial improvement in the usable foreign currency exchange reserve condition and positive outlook for the Korean economy in 1999. As of November 30, 1998, Korea's usable foreign exchange reserves recorded US$46.5 billion, surpassing the government's target of US$41 billion set for the year's end. The decision to repurchase SRF proved that the Korean economy was on the right track to economic recovery. In addition, the repayment had shown a favorable signal to the international financial community, soon resulting in upgrade of Korea's credit rating.

<Table V -3> Total External Liabilities of Korea (hundred millions US dollars)

	Dec. 1996	Dec. 1997	Oct. 1998	Nov. 1998	Change (%) In Nov. '98	Change (%) Up to Nov. '98
Long-term Liabilities (I+II+III)	713.6	948.4	1,225.2	1,214.8	Δ10.4	266.4
I. Public sector	60.6	222.6	373.8	370.3	Δ3.5	147.7
II. Financial institutions (A+B)	435.2	472.4	558.4	550.1	Δ8.3	77.7
A. Domestic financial Institutions	400.2	428.9	499.5	492.2	Δ7.3	63.3
Resident domestic Financial institutions	229.9	266.3	303.8	300.6	Δ3.2	34.3
Off-shore banking of Domestic financial Institutions	117.3	110.0	109.4	107.7	Δ1.7	Δ2.3
Foreign branches of Domestic financial Institutions	53.0	52.6	86.3	83.9	Δ2.4	31.3
B. Branches of Foreign banks	35.0	43.5	58.9	57.9	Δ1.0	14.4
III. Domestic corporations	217.8	253.4	293.0	294.4	1.4	41.0
Short-term Liabilities (I+II)	929.8	632.2	310.1	309.7	Δ0.4	Δ322.5
I. Financial institutions (A+B)	730.1	423.6	179.1	173.7	Δ5.4	Δ249.9
A. Domestic financial Institutions	599.9	271.5	106.0	101.7	Δ4.3	Δ169.8
Resident domestic Financial institutions	261.4	121.6	61.1	60.3	Δ0.8	Δ61.3
Off-shore banking of Domestic financial Institutions	74.5	55.7	19.0	16.4	Δ2.6	Δ39.3
Foreign branches of Domestic financial Institutions	264.0	94.2	25.9	25.0	Δ0.9	Δ69.2
B. Branches of foreign Banks	130.2	152.1	73.1	72.0	Δ1.1	Δ80.1
II. Domestic corporations	199.7	208.6	131.0	136.0	5.0	Δ72.6
Total External Liabilities	1,643.4	1,580.6	1,535.3	1,524.5	Δ10.8	Δ56.1

Source: Foreign Capital Management Division, Minister of Finance and Economy, Korea, February, 1999.

Recent developments in Korea's financial situation suggest that things may be turning around. It should be noted however, that the speed of improvement in the financial markets is much faster than in the real economy. While it seems that the bottom of the Korean business cycle is around the corner, however, when economic recovery will begin is still uncertain. If economic recovery is delayed, the recent developments in the financial sector might turn out to be mere bubbles.

Many of Korea's economic indicators have recently begun to improve, leading a growing number of domestic and foreign analysts to believe that the Korean economy may bottom out soon. For instance, industrial output rose 0.3% in September 1998 from the same month of 1997, a sharp improvement over August 1998 11.8% decline. The capacity utilization rate also rose up 70% for the same month, from August 1998's dismal of 62.9%. In addition, the rates of decline in consumption and investment are slowing down; whole and retail sales fell 11.9% in September 1998, as compared with August 1998's 16.7% fall.

Even exports, which declined 12.8% in October 1998, compared to the same month of 1997, are showing some positive aspects. The monthly export volume actually increased over the previous month, and the average daily export volume in fact rose even higher. Furthermore, when considerations are made on the export performances of Korea's competitors and the state of the world economy, Korean exports are actually showing a comparatively strong trend.

There are two different opinions concerning when the Korean economy will turn around. The optimists point to the positive economic indicators such as the turn-around in industrial production and the slowing decline of consumption and investment and argue that the economy will bottom out in the near future.

Others, however, are being more cautious. They contend that the recent improvement in indicators were largely the result of temporary or seasonal factors. For example, the production figures for September 1998, were boosted by production carried over from the previous month due to the strike in automobile industry, the heavy rains and more work days. These analysts feel that the economic trends bear watching for the next few months before safely declaring that the worst is over.

<Table V-4> Total External Assets of Korea (hundred millions US dollars)

	Dec. 1996	Dec. 1997	Oct. 1998	Nov. 1998	Change (%) In Nov. '98	Change (%) Up to Nov. '98
Long-term Assets(I+II+II)	344.7	324.1	321.2	317.7	Δ3.6	Δ6.5
I. Public sector	4.6	5.0	5.2	5.1	Δ0.1	0.1
II. Financial Institutions(A+B)	305.8	273.0	254.4	249.7	Δ4.7	Δ23.3
A. Domestic financial institutions	301.7	271.3	250.7	246.4	Δ4.3	Δ24.9
Resident domestic financial institutions	81.7	72.2	87.5	86.4	Δ1.1	14.2
Off-shore banking of domestic financial institutions	113.4	114.6	94.9	93.8	Δ1.1	Δ20.8
Foreign branches of domestic financial institutions	106.6	84.5	68.3	66.2	Δ2.1	Δ18.3
B. Branches of foreign banks	4.1	1.7	3.7	3.3	Δ0.4	1.6
III. Domestic corporations	34.3	46.1	61.6	62.8	1.2	16.7
Short-term Assets (I+II+III)	769.8	729.7	1,003.0	1,007.4	4.4	277.7
I. Public sector	341.0	211.9	492.9	505.3	12.4	293.4
II. Financial Institutions (A+B)	365.6	447.4	436.3	431.2	Δ5.1	Δ16.2
A. Domestic financial institutions	340.4	414.5	405.1	395.7	Δ9.4	Δ18.8
Resident domestic financial institutions	261.0	353.4	335.5	333.5	Δ2.0	Δ19.9
Off-shore banking of domestic financial institutions	42.8	37.6	22.8	20.5	Δ2.3	Δ17.1
Foreign branches of domestic financial institutions	36.6	23.5	46.8	41.7	Δ5.1	18.2
B. Branches of foreign banks	25.2	32.9	31.2	35.5	4.3	2.6
III. Domestic corporations	63.2	70.4	73.8	70.9	Δ2.9	0.5
Total External Assets	1,114.5	1,053.8	1,324.2	1,325.0	0.8	271.2

Source: Foreign Capital Management Division, Ministry of Finance and Economy, Korea, February 1999.

Looking at the CI (composite indexes) of business indicators, even though the economy continues to decline, the pace of decline is slowing down. The cyclical component of the coincident CI actually rose 1.2% in September 1998, but again this was attributed to seasonal factors. Nonetheless, the rapid decline in this index since June 1998 has turned out or at least stopped. The leading CI index also dropped much less in September 1998, than in previous months, indicating that the economy may turn-around 7 or 8 months later.

The production, consumption, and investment indexes also suggest that the economy may soon bottom out. How much the economy recovers, however, will largely depend on the trends in domestic demand and exports. If domestic demand stops declining and external conditions are favorable (current vitality of US economies' to be continued, partial recovery of Asian economies, low material prices and interest rates, etc.) the Korean economy could turn around and recover in the near future. If domestic demand continues to contract, however, and the world economy does not break out of the current malaise, even when the Korean economy bottoms out, it might also remain in a prolonged recession.

The expectation that the Korean economy will hit bottom soon does not necessarily mean that it will be on the upturn soon after. The recent improvement of production indexes is mainly based on the production surge in the automobile and semiconductor industries, driven by growing exports. But the problem is that while exports are showing signs of recovery, domestic demand is still severely contracted. For example, consumption dropped sharply by 11.8% in the third quarter of 1998, with household spending plummeting by 12.1% in the aftermath of corporate and financial sectors restructuring. Facility investment plunged by 46.3%, the eighth consecutive quarterly decline since the first quarter of 1997.

In other words the key point is that domestic demand does not seem likely to recover in the near future. Wage reductions and increasing unemployment are expected to continue in 1999, so consumption is not expected to increase greatly. Since most firms are compelled to reduce debts and improve their short-term cash flows, facility investment is likely to be strongly restrained.

The recent recovery of exports was supported by the improvement of abroad factors, in particular, so called new 'three lows': low dollar, low interest rates, and low oil prices. These 'three lows', however, were not expected to last for a long time.

5. PROSPECTS FOR THE KOREAN ECONOMY

A. Short-term Economic Prospects After the Crisis

Signs of more normal financial market conditions began to appear in late January 1998. By March 1998, corporate bond yields had dropped from their peak of almost 30% to 18%, and the Won had stabilized at around 1,400 wons to the dollar and 1,200 wons later on. With interest rates stuck at such punitive levels, the economy was on a razor's edge and pessimism in Korea (and Southeast Asia) deepened. The short-term economic prospects are thus unusually clouded and will depend crucially on how this interest rate conundrum is resolved.

Beyond that, economic performance will depend on how quickly economic agents adapt to the "new economic paradigm" in three areas: first, the corporate sector's adjustment to an era of interest rate fluctuations and intense competition; second, households' adaptation to uncertainty concerning job security and compensation; and thirdly foreign investors' reaction to investment opportunities following the unprecedented opening up of Korca's capital markets.

Survival of Korea's industrial base will thus require large-scale restructuring, wage cuts and labor streamlining. Assuming that a 15% reduction in the wage bill is realized, a break-even point could be attained by late 1998, even though full year results will probably show a loss. But by 1999, quite large operating surpluses could emerge. Even so, the scope for quickly reducing corporate debt-to-equity ratios under this central scenario is modest. If 1997 figures for new share issues and foreign direct investment (mostly in the form of joint ventures and M&As) are simply extrapolated, corporate gearing might drop to 400 or 350% between 1997 and 1999, and this figure might drop further to the 300 to 325% range when recent tax changes which encourage land and asset revaluation are included.

Nonetheless, these estimates underline the difficulty of bringing down debt- to-equity ratios to the government's suggested 200% target level quickly. Indeed, reaching this figure would require combined asset sales and foreign direct capital inflows of US$90 to 100 billion over the next two years. Investment banking reports suggest a surge in foreign interest in buying parts of or entire Korean enterprises. *Chaebols* have already sold some of their overseas subsidiaries and real estate (for roughly US$2 to 3 billion), and a few of their domestic operations (for some US$4 to 5 billion). For some of the five largest *Chaebols,* attaining the 200% debt-to-equity target by 1999 might be possible though very difficult.

The Korean economy will be driven by the two powerful equilibrating forces over the next two years: first, nominal wage cuts which will restore corporate profitability and damp job losses; and second, a drop in business investment which will produce large on-going current account surpluses.

During the first few months of its mandate, the Korean government has introduced a wide range of policy measures, touching virtually every aspect of the economy, to create a 'new economic paradigm'. The goal of these reforms is to fundamentally transform a guided economy into a modern, free market- oriented economy. Although many of the details are yet to be spelled out, the core feature of the new paradigm is to create the legal and institutional framework necessary for rational incentive structures to govern economic behaviour in the direction of exposing the economy more fully to world competition, and introducing effective management structures into banks and businesses.

To be sure, other components of reform such as measures to enhance labor market flexibility[36] and more effective bankruptcy laws are also critical elements of reforms, but without these core measures, their impact would be significantly less positive.

---

[36] The financial crisis has had a surprisingly quick and severe impact on labor markets, more so as large scale restructuring of the *Chaebols* has yet to begin. Total employment plummeted by some 1.5 million from July 1997 to April 1998, while the unemployment rate rocketed from 2.2 to 6.7%, even to 8% in January 1999, despite a sharp drop in labour force participation. The Korean government has introduced pay cuts of 10 to 20% according to grade, and the vast majority of business has implemented plans to slash their payrolls and investment outlays. Wages and overtime/bonus payments will thus be under intense pressure to save jobs. However, this assumes that management and labor will share the burden of adjustment, and that sharply rising unemployment will be shouldered by society as a whole through social transfers to the jobless.

B. Long-term Economic Prospects

Although the government has made an impressive start in putting a promising legislative framework in place, the challenge will be to implement these measures and change the attitudes of economic agents during a period of severe recession. The initial effects of the financial crisis have been a collapse in business investment, industrial restructuring and large-scale labor streamlining. These shocks might lower potential output growth from 6 to 7% prior to the crisis to between 3 and 4% per annum or lower in 1998~1999 (consistent with scrapping 10 to 15% of business capital stock).

If microeconomic reform is not implemented promptly, the economy risks stagnation with low growth as Korea's structural weaknesses steadily sap potential output growth, and investors' confidence is undermined. However, the OECD's MTB (medium-term baseline)[37] assumes that reform is carried out quickly and that social cohesion is maintained. Nevertheless, the rate of potential output growth from 2000 to 2003 is projected at between 5 and 6%, somewhat below the pre-crisis rate (6 to 7%), reflecting the three following factors.

First, labor input will slow as the expansion of the working-age population decelerates from 2% in the first half of the 1990s to only 0.5% in the first year of the next decade.

Second, national investment rate may fall by as much as 6 percentage points from its average of 35% during the first half of the 1990s as firms surviving the crisis become sensitive to profitability in expanding operations.

Third, structural reforms are unlikely to have a significant impact on TFP (total factor productivity growth) immediately.[38] Judging by the experiences of other OECD countries (such as New Zealand and the United Kingdom), this will take at least 5 years.

Thus, supply side factors suggest growths in the range of 5 to 6%, a rate that is assumed to be achieved by the end of the OECD's MTB (Medium-Term Baseline) scenario (1998~2003) as private consumption and fixed investment recover. Inflation is projected to be low and stable during the next five years. By 2003, the unemployment rate might be back to 4%, even though discouraged workers re-enter the labor market. Nevertheless, unemployment would be higher than in the past, reflecting greater frictional unemployment in a more flexible labour market.

The Korean government will face significant spending pressures to finance higher unemployment and social welfare benefits and to rehabilitate the financial system, which alone may cost as much as 1% of GDP a year from 1998 to 2003. Nonetheless, the budget surplus could be back in the 3% range by 2003. However, a small surplus in the social security accounts would not be sufficient to deal with the fiscal consequences of a rapidly aging population.[39]

At the same time, a current account surplus of 1% of GDP is projected for 2003. This would imply cumulative current account surpluses of over US$100 billion from 1998~2003 which would allow quick repayment of borrowings of some US$35 billion from international institutions, and a build-up of official reserves to US$80 to 90 billion equivalent to 6 to 7 months of imports. However, the desirability of such a large build-up of foreign reserves is questionable, given their high opportunity costs. Beyond 2003, the

---

[37] The MTB assumes that the Won will correct for overshooting and reattain the 1,200 wons level by 2000. Beyond 2000, the exchange rate has been assumed to remain constant in real terms.

[38] TFP has contributed around 3 percentage points to growth since 1979, according to Yang-Taek Lim (1996) and Kim and Hong (1997). If the TFP contribution remains in that range, potential growth, taking account of labor and capital inputs, would be between 5 and 6% during the period 2000 to 2003, as the OECD's medium-term baseline projected.

[39] Although the government plans to increase the contribution rate by 3% points every five years from its current level of 9%, the Social Security Fund will cease to accumulate assets in 2008 and will move into deficit before 2030. To put the system on an actuarially-sound basis, fundamental reform, including some combination of a higher retirement age, less generous benefits, and a rapid increase in contributions, will be required.

productivity gains resulting from the new market-oriented paradigm and more efficient resource allocation might allow Korea to match its pre-crisis potential growth rate of 6 to 7% despite a one-third decline in inputs, as TFP (Total Factor Productivity) in Korea continues to converge to the level of other OECD members.

Chapter VI

ECONOMIC REFORM AND RESTRUCTURING FOR OVERCOMING THE CRISIS

1. FINANCIAL SYSTEM REFORM

A. Basic Principle of Financial Sector Reform

The most immediate challenge facing the Korean government was to address the sharp decline in balance sheet quality of the banking system in 1997 and the likelihood of additional losses in the several years thereafter. In general, financial reforms aims to improve the performance of financial institutions that is restore solvency and profitability, improve the capacity of banking system to provide financial intermediation between depositors and borrowers and restore public confidence. For this end, three important improvements are required.

First, financial institutions must improve their balance sheets. This can be done by raising additional capital, receiving cash from existing or new owners or from the government, by reducing liabilities, or by boosting the value of assets.

Second, they should enhance their profitability. Measures can include renewed attention to business strategy, improved management and accounting systems, and better credit assessment and approval techniques. In addition, eliminating unnecessary branches and staffs may cut operation costs.

Thirdly, improving supervision and prudential regulation is required. In other words, the resolution of widespread banking problems usually requires the adoption of a carefully designed financial sector restructuring strategy to restore confidence in the banking system and to set it on a path that will return it to soundness and profitability.

The basic contents of the government's financial sector restructuring are summarized by <Table VI-1> and the restructuring system is shown in <Figure VI-1>

<Table VI-1> The Basic Contents of Financial Sector Restructuring

Early normalization of financial market through prompt and determined reform
Full-scale restructuring using competitive market nature
Promotion of voluntary restructuring by connecting public aid with self-help
Prevention of a recurrence of the financial crisis by establishing accountability principle of executives, staffs, and stockholders
Compliance to the rule of market economy based on international standards established in advanced countries

Source: Economic Policy Bureau, Ministry of Finance and Economy, Korea, 1999.

<Figure VI-1> Financial Sector Restructuring System

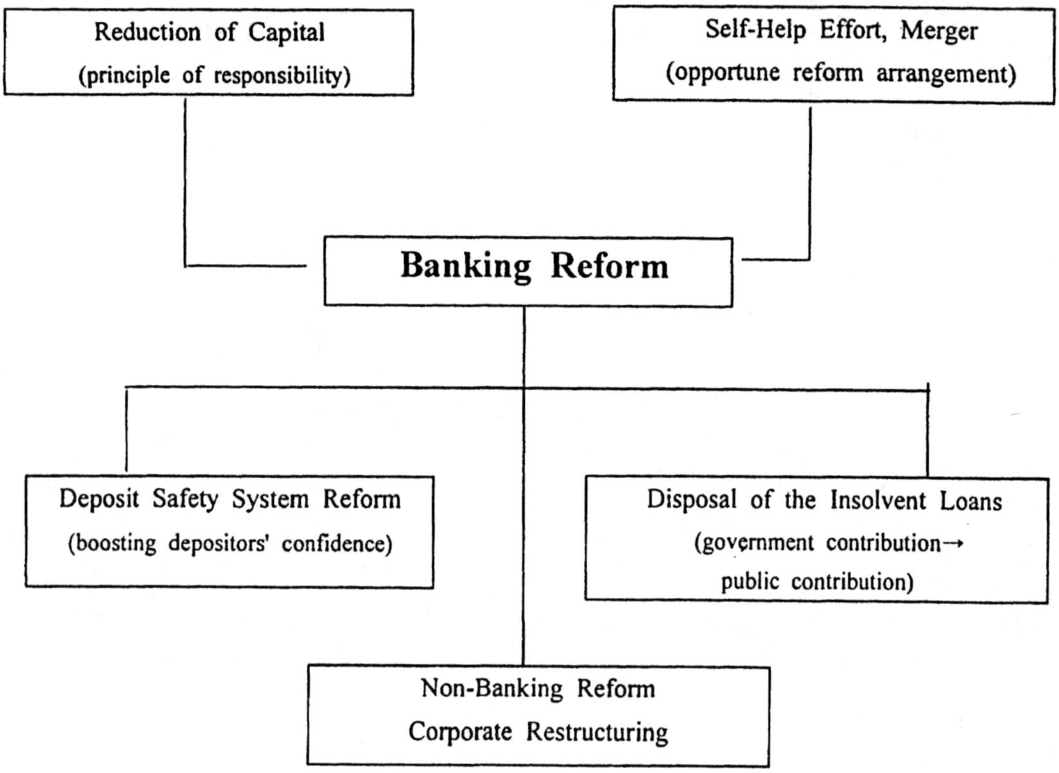

In line with this, the Korean government has designated the goals and principles of the restructuring process, whereby troubled financial institutions will be restructured and recapitalized within a specified time table. A credible and clearly defined exit strategy will involve requiring troubled institutions to present a viable rehabilitation plan and closing insolvent financial institutions which are failing to carry out their rehabilitation plan within the specified periods.

Restructuring could also involve M&As (mergers and acquisitions) by domestic and foreign institutions, provided the viability of the new groupings is assured. The disposal of non-performing loans will be accelerated. All forms of assistance to banks, including through the KAMCO (Korean Asset Management Corporation) and the Deposit Insurance funds, should be provided as part of viable rehabilitation plans. All support to financial institutions, other than Bank of Korea liquidity credits, is expected to record transparently in the fiscal accounts. Market-oriented terms and conditions is also expected to establish for any support to financial institutions.

The government prepared a comprehensive action program to strengthen financial supervision and regulation in accordance with international standards. It was convinced of the need not only to address the immediate problems of the financial system, but more fundamentally to set the basis for a strong domestic financial system. To do this, efforts must be made to increase market discipline.

B. Policy Measures to Improve Solvency

The most crucial decisions will involve measures to rehabilitate the commercial banking system. The problem of the merchant banks or the investment trust companies may be serious and costly, but at worst, the situation ultimately can be resolved by closing these institutions and settling their liabilities. On the other hand, market-driven banks that are capable of participating actively in resource allocation are indispensable to a modern market economy. Banking rehabilitation is best seen as part of a reform process, of which the ultimate goal is the emergence of a number of viable banks that can play an active role in credit allocation and exercise discipline over the corporate sector. To accomplish this, the management systems of banks must be transformed so that banks are given direction to achieve high levels of profitability and to introduce strong risk management systems. Strong governance usually emerges in response to predictable pressures from shareholders, supervisors and rating agencies and competitive markets.

Financial market supervisors will play an indispensable role in instilling a market-oriented culture in all participants. From the outset it will be essential for the FSC which is in charge of bank rehabilitation to convince the main participants, *i.e.,* bank management, corporate borrowers and prospective foreign and domestic investors, that the rules of the game have permanently changed and that the transition towards a competitive soundly regulated banking system is proceeding under a tight schedule. Supervisors will also have to demonstrate that they have the required independence to pursue their task and that they are enforcing transparency.

Until now, the programme has maintained broad support because the authorities have communicated their determination to restructure the financial system. It is important that this support be maintained. Half-hearted attempts to rescue banks, tolerance of poor disclosure practices and regulatory forbearance, will increase the costs of the eventual rescue and delay the emergence of a well functioning banking system while undermining the confidence of investors whose support is vital to any rehabilitation plan. Furthermore, if the plan is not pursued with sufficient vigor and credibility, popular support for the reform can wither.

Transparency is one key to success. Transparency must be reflected in the banks accounting and disclosure policies and must also guide the reports that the supervisors present to the government, investors and the public. From the outset, the supervisors must make it clear that higher standards of disclosure will be strictly enforced.

The rehabilitation plans should be structured so as to reward banks that report their financial situation accurately and that take credible action to restore credit worthiness. If banks are convinced that the authorities are tacitly willing to overlook under-reporting in order to buy time and lessen political resistance, they will act accordingly. Most of the actions taken to date have been encouraging in that the authorities are pressing for full disclosure of the extent of the impaired loan situation. An additional positive development was the admission at a relatively early time that large amounts of public money will be needed to resolve the problems. It is essential to continue this approach as the restructuring effort progresses.

C. Legal and Institutional Framework

The crisis in the financial system came at a time when the authorities had been moving toward reform of the financial system. In January 1997, a Presidential Commission for Financial Reform was formed. In June 1997, the Commission issued a report calling for a general acceleration in the process of reform and liberalization that had begun in the early 1990s. While little progress was made in the months immediately following the release of the report, the new administration elected in December 1997 placed itself squarely behind the policy of de-regulating and opening up the economy to foreign competition. Moreover, agreements reached with the IMF and World Bank in late 1997 were aimed at accelerating the transition toward a market-oriented system being integrated into the world economy.

Recent legislation to restructure the financial sector has been well-considered and sweeping. In December 1997, 15 major financial reform bills were passed eventually aiming at transforming the institutional and regulatory basis of the financial system. The aim has been to move decisively toward an efficient market- based financial service industry, in line with accepted international practices. The General Banking Law and the Financial Industry Restructuring Act of 1997 were amended to allow the formation of financial service firms offering a wide range of services, thus breaking down many functional and institutional rigidities. These firms will be linked through transparent ownership and control relationships. Moreover, markets which had previously been highly segmented will be open to greater competition. Commercial banks, investment trust companies and merchant banks will be allowed to discount commercial paper, an activity previously reserved for the merchant banks. Prudential regulations applied to merchant banks will be aligned with those applied to commercial banks. In the long run, the difference between commercial banks and merchant banks is expected to narrow.

A radically overhauled regime for supervision of financial markets and institutions was initiated in December 1997. The ousting agencies to supervise banks, merchant banks, capital market institutions and insurance companies were consolidated into a single agency, the FSC (Financial Supervisory Commission) which began operating under the Prime Minister's office in April 1998. A Financial Supervisory Board now presides over the Commission. To assure independence of financial supervisors, the President issued a decree on prudential standards that is expected to reaffirm the primary task of supervision and guarantee the independence of supervisors. One determinant of the success of the new regime is to assure that the individuals and institutions assigned roles in financial supervision acquire the needed technical skills to perform their tasks with sufficient independence.

The decision to consolidate financial supervision in a single agency follows similar decisions made by other OECD countries. It reflects the reality that differences between the financial products have already narrowed and are likely to narrow further with deregulation. Since many multi-purpose financial institutions are likely to be formed, they can be best supervised by a single regulator which will provide for comparable regulation for similar products and can assess the risk position of the institution. Efforts will be intensified to assure that no financial institutions, including merchant banks, securities firms and investment companies, are subject to lax supervisory regimes. Additionally, individuals seeking to lodge complaints can deal with a single regulator. A significant part of the responsibility for the oversight of securities markets will be delegated to self-regulatory organizations.

D. The Directions of Financial System Reform

1) The Role of Rationalization

An overriding goal of the reform is to have a banking system with a viable cost structure. The optimal number of banks is almost certainly smaller than the current number, although 8 banks have been absorbed (Daedong, Donghwa, Dongnam, Kyungki and Chungchong) or merged (Boram, Korea Long Term Credit Bank, Hanil and Commercial Bank of Korea) since the IMF bail-out package has been put in place. Transformation of the banking system has resulted in the decrease in the number of institutions and large-scale cuts in the number of workers in the sector.

Prospects for the resolution of the banking crisis through purely domestic consolidation of existing banks are limited. M&As can remedy some problems; where duplication is found in branch networks, back office operations or staff, cost savings can be made. However, most countries have found that, both in the banking sector and elsewhere, mergers between poorly managed institutions cannot lead to an enduring improvement in performance.

In most OECD countries, mergers tend to be of two kinds: mergers of equals which almost always lead to strife between the management and staff of the two institutions; and outright acquisitions which lead to the stronger bank imposing its management culture on the acquired bank. In the case of Korea, the latter pattern of merger is preferable. Few Korean banks have sound balance sheets and advanced management skills. These banks could be induced to acquire parts of weaker institutions. However, such a strategy would probably require injection of public funds and it also runs the risk of distracting the management of the stronger banks from their urgent task of restructuring.

Reportedly, the authorities are thinking in terms of identifying a small number of well-managed domestic institutions with the potential to emerge as market leaders and to encourage these banks to take control of other banks and perhaps in some cases to reach agreements with strategic foreign investors. Part of the process of restructuring will be to encourage the regional banks to cease dealing with the large industrial conglomerates and focus on lending to SMEs.

A critical source of stronger bank supervision and capitalization is increased foreign presence. In addition to injections of capital, foreign banks and investors can provide monitoring and managerial skills and will apply international profitability standards. In fact, Commerz Bank and Bank of America have already invested in Korea Exchange Bank and Boram Bank, and several other banks have also announced plans for links with foreign institutions and a large number of such alliances are under active consideration. The attraction for foreign institutions is that Korea offers the potential gains of a 'turnaround situation'.

Dynamic banks in OECD countries are able to achieve returns on equity in excess of 15% annually by aggressive cost control, strong credit and risk management systems and a commitment to shareholder value. If gains of this kind are achievable in mature markets, then the relatively backward Korean market, on the threshold of major consolidation should have far greater potential provided that management serves the interests of investors. Currently, Korean bank shares are selling at very low prices. Traditionally, great opportunities for investors arise when an industry passes through a period of restructuring and consolidation. However, portfolio investors and strategic investors will shun the Korean banking sector until they believe that thorough and credible reform is taking place.

2) Deepening Capital Markets

Although the reform of the banking system is the most urgent task facing the authorities, there is need for reform in the capital markets as well.

Until the recent collapse of equity prices, the stock market was moderately advanced in some respects. The share of market capitalization in national income was in the middle range of OECD countries and share ownership was fairly diversified among individual and institutional owners. The technical infrastructure of the market including trading, clearing and settlements systems were adequate and a market in equity futures and options had been introduced. Thus, the equity market had no basic technical deficiencies and a solid foundation for future development was present.

On the other hand, official market regulation was not unequivocally committed to investor protection and systemic soundness, but continued to support the existing pattern of industrial promotion or to stabilize the market more generally. A major shortcoming is that the market was relatively ineffective in monitoring corporate performance. Securities market regulations as well as the network of formal and informal linkages have effectively isolated corporate management from financial market monitoring and discipline. Independent institutional investors that provide corporate monitoring in many OECD counties were absent. Major domestic institutional investors such as the investment trust companies, have little inclination to provide monitoring of the corporate sector.

Past severe restrictions on participation by foreign investors also deprived Korea of the increasingly effective influence of international institutional investors on corporate performance, while the limited possibility for M&A activity, including hostile take-overs as a device or sanctioning poor performance and facilitating corporate restructuring, were also absent. Now that many firms are faced with urgent needs to increase their equity base, the equity market will have to assume a more active role in corporate finance and monitoring.

The debt market also had serious shortcomings. Government debt which is usually the foundation of any fixed income market, lacks depth and maturities tend to be short. A number of government and government-guaranteed issues are traded but amounts are uneven and hence liquidity is lacking. No instrument has established the status of a 'benchmark' bond. Due to obligatory purchases of new issues, primary distribution techniques still do not result in market-based prices and there is still a wide spread between primary and secondary market interest rates. No derivatives to hedge interest rate or currency risk existed and foreign participation in the fixed income market was limited. Thus, the fixed income market lacked the vitality that characterizes most OECD sovereign debt markets. Current plans seek to rectify many of these shortcomings in the government securities market.

The Korean government will encourage the development of well-capitalized primary dealers as well as adequate hedging and liquidity facilities. Mortgage bonds and mortgage-backed securities will be developed. Additionally, stronger disclosure requirements on bond issues and a stronger set of rating agencies would help create a deeper market in non-government paper. Until now a considerable amount of bonds have carried bank guarantees which has increased the banks' off-balance sheet risks. Since a period of financial innovation, with relatively slow growth of balance sheets and banks seeking to engage in more off-balance sheet activity, may well be in prospect, the deepening of a fixed income market should be a high priority.

It is also advisable to reconsider the current structure of institutional investment. As of now Korea does not have a collective investment industry *per se* mutual funds, unit trusts etc. These are becoming increasingly important means of holding wealth in all OECD countries and major world financial institutions see institutional investment and portfolio management as one of the best potential areas for expansion in coming years.

In Korea, investment trust companies have some characteristics of collective investment but in general the range of investment options offered to the public is narrower. Additionally, these institutions often carry guarantees from investment trust companies which means that additional risks must be borne by these companies, and ultimately by the authorities. Furthermore, these institutions have not been effective as active monitors of debt and equity markets. Until a set of independent collective investment institutions emerges, the asset management industry may not develop in line with world standards. For all these reasons, it might be advisable to introduce a system of collective investments comparable to those found in most OECD countries. Legislation to permit mutual funds was in August 1998.

E. Major Policy Measures to Bolster Financial System Reform

1) Exit Strategy, Recapitalization & Deposit Insurance System

Troubled financial institutions shall be closed or, if they are deemed viable, restructured and/or recapitalized. The Korean government has already suspended 9 insolvent merchant banks (on December 2, 1997). These banks have been placed under the control of MOFE (Ministry of Finance and Economy) and required to submit a rehabilitation plan within 30 days.

A credible and clearly defined exit strategy will include closures as well as M&As (mergers and acquisitions) by domestic and foreign institutions, provided the viability of the new groupings is assured. Clear principles on the sharing of losses among equity holders and creditors will be established.

Meanwhile, the financial sector restructuring agreement with enterprises only emphasized the supervision role of banks. The credit mediating function should also be reconsidered, in the case of the small and medium-sized companies are facing a chain bankruptcy due to falling credit.

To bolster Korea's financial sector, the government has injected 40.9 trillion won in public funds since last November 1997. As part of the nation's financial restructuring efforts, it has allocated 19.9 trillion won of public funds to purchase NPLs (non-performing loans) from weak but financially viable financial institutions.

< Table VI - 2 > Public Funds Injected to Bolster Financial Sector (Unit: trillion wons)

Classification	Amount Injected Nov. 1997-Dec. 1998	Amount to be Injected By 1999	Total
Purchase of NPLs	19.9	12.6	32.5
Recapitalization & Loss Coverage	13.2	4.3	17.5
Deposit Payment	7.8	6.2	14.0
Total	40.9	23.1	64.0

KAMCO (Korea Asset Management Corporation) has purchased NPLs totaling 44.1 billion won in book value from financial institutions such as banks, merchant banks, insurance companies, and securities firms. Purchase and payment amounts are as follows:

< Table VI - 3 > KAMCO's Purchase of NPLs(as end of 1998) (Unit: billion wons)

Category	Purchased Amount (A)	Payment (B)	Ratio (B/A in %)
Banks	35,376	16,724	47.3
Merchant Banks	2,699	1,756	65.1
Surety Insurance Co.	5,863	1,366	23.3
Securities Co.	115	56	48.7
Life Insurance Co.	23	5	21.7
Total	44,076	19,907	45.2

Source: Ministry of Finance and Economy, Korea, February 1999.

KDIC (Korea Deposit Insurance Corporation) has injected funds into bank and life insurance companies for recapitalization and loss coverage purposes. The affected institutions are seeking to conduct merger or P&A (purchases and acquisitions) transactions.

Deposit insurance for commercial banks was only introduced in 1996, although it was always generally assumed that the government would never allow bank depositors to lose money. The KNDIC (Korea Non-Bank Deposit Insurance Corporation) has provided deposit insurance since 1981. In exchange for fees, the KNDIC provides insurance on deposits at investment and finance companies, merchant banks and mutual savings banks up to 20 million wons per depositor).[40] As a measure to prevent a collapse of confidence and a run on deposits, an ad hoc regime under which the government has guaranteed all deposits will be maintained until 2001 when the system will return to a partial deposit insurance system.

[40] Due to the magnitude of losses of NBFIs and the low level of the NBFIs capital and the insurance fund, the government may well have considerable liability for losses in the NBFI sector.

The new consolidated Deposit Insurance Corporation will increase its resources from 900 billion won at the end of 1997 to 8.4 trillion wons in 1998; funding for the agency will be obtained through bond issues.

The five non-viable banks were liquidated through P&A in July 1998 and their assets were transferred to acquiring banks selected on the basis of financial soundness (BIS ratio of 10% or higher), long-term business strategies and comparative advantages.

< Table VI - 4 > KDIC's Fund Injection by December 1998 (Unit: trillion wons)

Classification	Capital-Injected Institutions	Injected Amount
Recapitalization	Merged Banks: (Commercial & Hanil) (Hana & Boram)	3.6 (3.3) (0.3)
	Banks in P&A Transactions (5 acquiring banks)	1.2 (1.2)
	2 Troubled Banks (Korea First) (Seoul)	1.5 (0.75) (0.75)
Loss Coverage	5 Acquiring Banks	5.8
	4 Acquiring Insurance Companies	1.1
	Total	13.2

Source: Ministry of Finance and Economy, Korea, February 1999.

2) Strengthening Corporate Governance and Foreign Participation

In November and December 1997, KAMCO (Korea Asset Management Corporation) bought some 3 trillion wons in NPLs from the merchant banks and the Deposit Insurance Corporation reimbursed depositors for 5.5 trillion wons. In December 1997, the operations of fourteen merchant banks were suspended and all inadequately capitalized merchant banks were ordered to submit restructuring plans, These plans would have to specify how these banks would reach BIS capitalization ratios (4% by the end of March 1998, 6% by the end of June 1998, and 8% by June 30, 1999). Merchant banks are encouraged to increase their capital adequacy ratios beyond the 8% minimum after June 1999.

If the rehabilitation plan is accepted, banks would be obliged to sign a managerial contract with the government, which would include an explicit commitment to meet these deadlines as well as to achieve other performance indicators. In the event that the plan was not judged acceptable, the bank would be closed. Similarly, if the merchant bank does not meet the performance criteria in its agreement, stronger corrective measures would be applied, including closures. A bridge merchant bank, which was formed on December 3, 1997, assumes the responsibility of paying depositors and disposing of the institution's assets.

The rehabilitation process is apparently being applied in a very stringent way to the merchant banks, with the government seemingly willing to close insolvent institutions. At the end of March 1998, the NPL ratio of the sixteen merchant banks which remained in operation (*i.e.*, less the fourteen whose operations were suspended) had risen to 5.9%. More ominously, when provisions for securities trading losses were included, only two merchant banks had capital adequacy ratios of 8% or more and only three had shown positive net income during the year ending March 1998. With stricter auditing procedures and more difficult financial conditions, the entire merchant banking sector may move closer to insolvency. In view of the sharp decline in the financial strength of merchant banks through 1998, it appears inevitable that many, if not most, merchant banks will have to be closed.

Rules governing ownership of banks will be eased, with both foreign and domestic interests permitted to acquire strategic stakes in Korean institutions. Foreign ownership of up to 100% will be possible. As foreign owners reach the thresholds of 10%, 25% and 33% of total equity, they will be subject to increasingly strong review by the Financial Supervisory Commission. Similar rules will be imposed on domestic investors seeking strategic positions in banks and parallel rules concerning ownership of securities firms will be introduced. However, the authorities will reserve the right to determine whether prospective acquirers of strategic stakes are 'fit and proper', partly to prevent undesirable corporate and relationships from emerging.

Increased foreign participation and the resulting increase in competition are seen as keys to raising managerial skills of Korean institutions for building capital in the system. Foreign banks and securities firms will be authorized to establish both branches and subsidiaries (previously foreign institutions were restricted to set up branches).

Laws were also enacted to strengthen the powers of boards of directors of banks and to require greater transparency on the part of management in dealings with shareholders and boards. Foreigners are allowed permitted to be directors of boards. The Korean government announced a policy of ending direct interference in the management of banks. The Securities and Exchange Act was amended to facilitate hostile take-overs in the financial sector and relevant laws amended to allow for the reduction of excess personnel.

3) Enhancing the Supervision of Bank and Risk Management

On April 1, 1998, Office of Bank Supervision of the Bank of Korea was transformed into the BSA (Banking Supervisory Authority) operating under the FSC[41]). The BSA published proposals to bring banking supervisory closer to international standards as expressed in the Basel Committee's 'Core Principles for Effective Bank Supervision'. The regulations encompass: the deduction from tier 2 capital of all sub-standard assets; the introduction of market-to-market accounting for all traded securities positions other than those hedging assets valued at a historical cost; and full disclosure to trust beneficiaries of any agreements by managing banks to offset or guarantee losses to market participants. All trust accounts with guarantees will be considered on-balance sheet and weighted at 50% by January 2000. Rules requiring the segregation of trust accounts will be made more explicit.

Loan classification and provisioning regulations have been toughened. In January 1999, classification standards were made more rigorous, meaning that decisions will reflect the actual ability and not past history of borrowers to repay. As of August 15, 1998, all loans in arrears by 90 days were classified as 'substandard'. Provisioning requirements were increased from 1 to 2% for precautionary loans and from 0.5 to 1% for normal loans.

Disclosure, auditing and accounting practices have also been upgraded to assure that published accounts, including off-balance-sheet positions, are reported in line with international standards. Regulations ensure that accounting standards for financial institutions meet those standards specified in the IAS 30 (International Accounting Standard 30), which covers disclosure in the Financial Statements of Banks and Similar Financial Institutions.[42] Groups under the effective control of particular interests are obliged to file combined statements. Rules covering large exposures for all financial institutions have been made clearer with the aim of ultimately reducing such limits. As a temporary measure, however, limits on exposures to individual companies were raised from 10% of bank capital to 15% in the expectation that part of the resolution of the credit problems in the corporate sector may involve debt to equity swaps.

The BSA is seeking to move beyond simple inspection of loan portfolios and develop the capability to evaluate the quality of bank management as well as in-house credit evaluation procedures and risk management systems. Additionally, the authorities have adopted a regulatory approach under which banks with higher ratios of capitalization and adequate risk management systems will be permitted to assume increased risk while bands that cannot meet those standards will be limited in activities and subjected to progressively rigorous procedures to produce corrective action. At very low levels of capitalization, banks have been obliged to close or merge. Efforts will be made to assure that banks' risk management systems are robust enough to detect the full range of contingent liabilities, whether the assets appear on the balance sheet of the parent company or of some affiliated entities, including foreign branches and subsidiaries.

In November 1998 regulations governing global spot and forward foreign exchange positions were implemented. Similar regulations for merchant banks are expected to be phased in by the end of 1999. Banks and merchant banks are required to demonstrate that they have implemented strong in-house systems to track and manage market risk. Both categories of institution are required to disclose publicly their

[41] The responsibility for rehabilitation of the banking system was originally assigned to the OBS (Office of Banking Supervision). With the consolidation of regulatory functions in April 1998, the FSC assumed responsibility. During the early months of 1997, the OBS originally adopted a rather lenient policy with the view of allowing the banks to extend credit while allowing the banks time to bring the problem of impaired credit under control gradually. However, as the crisis appeared increasingly threatening and as the government's attitude hardened, the banks were held to more rigorous standards for taking action to improve credit quality. In June 1997, the OBS issued rules requiring banks to set aside full provisions for losses by June 1999. In December 1997, policy was made yet more exacting with full provisioning required at the end of 1998.

[42] Among the items covered by the IAS 30 are guidelines on the treatment of contingent commitments, losses on loans and advances, assets pledged as security, roust activities and related party activities.

foreign currency positions on a monthly basis. Prudential requirements are extended to specialized and development banks as well as commercial and merchant banks.

The new agency intends to take a prudent but positive attitude toward product innovation. In order to implement the transformation to a modernized system of financial supervision, Korea will make considerable use of expertise from advanced market economies and international organizations to train its personnel in the latest techniques of market supervision.

2. MONETARY POLICY TO SOOTHE MARKET INSTABILITY

A. Monetary Target Ranges

In view of the disruptive impact of the realignment of the trust account system on its chosen monetary aggregate, the Bank of Korea adopted a system of dual monetary intermediate targets for 1998: namely, the growth rate of M2 and that of MCT (M2+CDs+Money-in-Trust). The target range for the growth of M2 was set within a range of 14~19% and that for MCT at 15~20% on a December daily-average basis.

The emphasis of monetary and credit policies was placed on flexibility in the supply of money with a view to regaining stability in the financial markets, which were unsettled by the managerial difficulties of some financial institutions and the credit crunch arising from the increased number of large corporate insolvencies. In particular, when financial institutions and firms alike experienced an acute shortage of liquidity owing to the financial and currency crises, the Bank of Korea purchased bonds issued by the Non-Performing Asset Resolution Fund, extended special loans to some troubled financial institutions and raised the aggregate credit ceiling. However, it subsequently acted to minimize the inflationary pressures on aggregate demand by absorbing the excess liquidity through open market operations.

Under the terms of Korea's agreement with the IMF, the Bank changed its method of monetary policy operation in December 1997, from a focus on the dual intermediate targets to the management of reserve money itself determined in consideration of M3 which serves as an informative indicator. Reserve money is classified into NIR (Net International Reserves), which are the BOK's net external assets and the NDA (Net Domestic Assets). Reserve money is managed by setting a floor for NIR and a ceiling for NDA.

The BOK in concert with the IMF set the indicative limits of M3 and reserve money as of the end of December 1997 at 15.4% and -9.5% respectively and established the floor for NIR at US$ -3 billion and the ceiling for NDA at 26,570 billion wons as the performance criteria. In response to the conduct of monetary policy, the growth rate of reserve money stood at -12.5% at the end of 1997 and that of M3 at 13.9%. Meanwhile, the NIR and NDA met their performance criteria by registering US$ -3 billion and 25,819 billion wons, respectively.

<Table VI-5> Monetary Policy under the IMF Programs
(Unit: billion wons, as of the end of December 1997)

	IMF Program(A)	Performance(B)	B-A
Reserve Money (%)	23,270.0 (-9.5)	22,519.3 (-12.5)	-750.7
NIR <billion US$> NDA	-3,300.0 <-3> 26,570.0	-3,300.0 <-3> 25,819.3	0 <0> -750.7

Note: Figures in parentheses represent percentage changes compared with the same period of the previous year.
Source: Ministry of Finance and Economy, Korea, 1999.

B. Rediscount Policy

1) Special Facilities and Market Stabilization Measures

On February 24, 1998, the BOK improved its marginal lending facility (B2 funds), which is a system of loans to banks suffering from temporary shortages of reserve requirements or settlement funds. Because the determination and scale of B2 lending had been at the discretion of the Bank, call rates had risen steeply and call market transactions had shrunk dramatically whenever there was a shortage of reserves. Thus, it was decided to allow banks to borrow B2 funds at their discretion in order to heighten the predictability of their fund management and inhibit excessive volatility in short term interest rates. Ceilings for each bank's B2 borrowings were set at 50% of the daily average reserve requirement for one day and at 100% of the average reserve requirement for each half-month reserve period. However, in the case of requests for borrowings of B2 funds over and above these, the Bank decides whether or not to lend and the scale of the accommodation on a case-by-case basis.

The BOK also lowered the ceiling on its aggregate credit by 2.8 trillion wons, reducing the amount available from 6.4 trillion wons to 3.6 trillion wons in order to absorb the excess liquidity induced by that month's reduction in reserve requirements. In addition, the BOK changed its method of allocating credit quotas to individual banks as a means of inducing their support for SMEs and high-tech industries. The method of quota calculation was changed from an item-by-item basis, for example, commercial bill discounts and foreign trade financing, to the sum of such items. In calculating eligible commercial bill discounts, the weighting of local branch lending and the ban on those to non-manufacturers were abolished. On April 1, 1998, banks' loan to information and telecommunication industries were included in calculating the aggregate ceiling allocated by provincial branches. On May 1, 1998, in order to induce banks to expand their credit-based lending, the BOK raised the weighting of such lending from 5 to 15% in calculating their quotas under the aggregate credit ceiling.

On September 8, 1998, the Bank provided a special loan of one trillion won with a one-year maturity to the KFB (Korea First Bank), which was acutely short of liquidity owing to its accumulation of bad loans. The interest rate on this special loan was set at 8%, the average cost of funds for commercial banks. In an attached memorandum, KFB agreed to carry out faithfully the self-rescue scheme it had submitted to the BOK.

On October 16, 1998, the BOK also extended special loans to the sixteen merchant banking corporations whose loans to firms falling under the "Bankruptcy-Prevention Accord" exceeded 50% of their equity capital. The terms of the loans were identical to that provided to the KFB. It imposed a condition that failure to carry out self-rescue schemes sincerely might result in the loans being called in before maturity or having their interest rate raised.

On November 28, 1998, through purchasing in full a two-trillion won bond issue by the Non-Performing Asset Resolution Fund, the BOK gave its support to banks in clearing bad loans, thus backing financial market stabilization and financial industry restructuring. The discount rate on the bonds was 5%. The BOK made payment to the Fund in the form of Monetary Stabilization Bonds (MSBs) of which redemption was permitted if necessary.

2) Financial Support for SMEs and Export Firms

The BOK extended emergency funds to SMEs in order to prevent chain bankruptcies in response to their acute shortage of funds owing to the large corporate insolvencies and tight financial conditions. On February 14, 1998, the Bank channelled 182.6 billion wons to banks by redeeming MSBs to the same value as their loans to SMEs shrank as an after-shock of the failure of *Hanbo Iron and Steel*. On October 1, 1998, it furnished support to sub-contractors and other firms associated with *Kia Group* which had fallen into managerial difficulties and been brought under the Bankruptcy Prevention Accord. The support took the form of an increase in banks' individual quotas under the aggregate credit ceiling system equivalent to half of their loans extended to the affected firms, subject to an overall limit of 350 billion wons.

In relation to the foreign trade financing system on February 15, 1998, the BOK linked the basis for calculation of the unit loanable amount to the average exchange rate. So SMEs and independent large firms were allowed to borrow up to 90 and 60% respectively, of the required funds. Raw materials purchase funds and raw material import funds were unified as Raw Material Funds. On April 23, 1998, the BOK expanded the range of instruments eligible for foreign trade financing from letters of credit and advance bills of export to other instruments including export factoring contract documents.

Moreover, as banks were reluctant to discount export bills owing to the tight foreign exchange market following the standby loan accord with the IMF, the BOK from December 4, 1998 supplied liquidity to banks by redeeming MSBs to an amount equivalent to their lending performance against export bills.

C. Reserve Requirement Policy

The BOK reduced the average reserve requirement ratio by 2.1 percentage points on February 23, 1998 with a view to improving commercial banks' autonomy in their asset management and providing 'a level playing field' between banks and non-banks. Previously the level of reserve requirements had been differentiated by type of deposit but this system failed to reflect their varying degrees of liquidity. The BOK thus realigned the reserve requirement system by grouping deposits into either demand deposits or time deposits including special purpose deposits and imposing reserve requirement on the basis of the degree of liquidity.

<Table VI-6> Reduction of the Reserve Requirement Ratios of Banks (unit: %)

<table>
<tr><th colspan="2">Type of Deposit</th><th>Previous</th><th>Feb. 23, 1998 Onwards</th></tr>
<tr><td>Deposits for Special Purpose</td><td>- Workmen's property formation saving deposits
- Workmen's long-term saving deposits
- Workmen's saving deposits for housing.
- Household long-term savings deposits
- Long-term savings deposits for housing
- Mutual installments deposits and
- Housing installments deposits</td><td>2.0</td><td>1.0</td></tr>
<tr><td rowspan="3">Time Deposits</td><td>- Time & savings deposits with a maturity of less than two years</td><td>4.0</td><td rowspan="2">2.0</td></tr>
<tr><td>- Time & savings deposits with a maturity of at least two years</td><td>7.0</td></tr>
<tr><td>- Demand deposits and other time and savings deposits</td><td>7.0</td><td>5.0</td></tr>
<tr><td colspan="2">Average(excluding CDs)</td><td>5.5</td><td>3.3</td></tr>
<tr><td>Time & Savings Deposits</td><td>CD</td><td>-</td><td>2.0</td></tr>
<tr><td colspan="2">Average (including CDs)</td><td>4.6</td><td>3.1</td></tr>
</table>

Source: Ministry of Finance and Economy, Korea, 1999.

The BOK also imposed reserve requirement on negotiable CDs (certificates of deposit), setting the ratio at 2%. However, inter-bank CDs remain exempt from reserve requirements. In a matching move, the BOK absorbed the approximately 2,800 billion wons in surplus liquidity released through its lowering of reserve requirements by the reduction of its aggregate credit ceiling.

D. Banking Institution Deposits

1) Easing Regulations of Banks' Fund-Raising

The BOK continued to ease regulations concerning banks' fund-raising both to enlarge their autonomy and to promote competition in the financial market. On February 10, 1998, it abolished restrictions on the maximum maturities (10 years) of bank deposits in a move corresponding to the abolition of regulations on those (10 years) of bank loans under the Revised General Banking Act. Its regulations on the minimum maturities (one year) of deposits with fixed maturity on which floating rates could be applied were also eliminated.

The BOK, however, kept in place the regulations on the maximum maturities of special-purpose deposits such as long-term savings for households, which were stipulated under relevant legislations, notably the Regulation of Tax Reduction and Exemption Act.

On February 17, 1988, the BOK eliminated ceilings on banks' issuance of CDs, the need for which had disappeared with the imposition of reserve requirement on CDs. It also removed those on banks' issuance of cover bills to enlarge their fund-raising capacity for the discount of firms' commercial bills. The ban on banks' acceptance of their own CDs as collateral, which had been imposed to prevent their abuses as a form of compensating balance, were abolished as lending rules were deregulated.

As of July 7, 1998, saving-type products were consolidated with the integration of savings deposits and preferential savings deposits, which allow 'free deposit and withdrawal' at any time and all restrictions abolished except those concerning depositor eligibility (individual persons only) on interest rate, ceilings on the amount of deposit and the method of calculating the interest. For corporate savings deposits, although the Bank freed up interest rates, it decided not to permit the payment of interest on deposits of less than seven days in order to maintain the effectiveness of regulations concerning interest rates on passbook deposits and checking deposits. As a result, banks were able to launch market-interest-bearing MMDAs (money market deposit accounts), products which combine the features of demand deposits with the high yields of time and savings deposits.

Regulations were lifted on the interest rate payable after the maturity of deposits with fixed maturity whose effectiveness had disappeared with the liberalization of those interest rates in November 1995 and the abolition of restrictions on maximum maturities in July 1998. Individual banks were allowed to set interest rate for the mid-term cancellation at their discretion for deposits with fixed maturity held for at least one month, the minimum contract period.

<Table VI-7> Deregulations Interest Rate Per Time and Saving Deposits

<table>
<tr><th></th><th>Before July 6, 1998</th><th>After July 7, 1998</th><th>Remarks</th></tr>
<tr><td>Saving Deposits</td><td>3.0% per annum</td><td>liberalized</td><td rowspan="2">Integrated</td></tr>
<tr><td>Preferential Savings Deposits</td><td>- 3 months or more: liberalized
- less than 3 months: 3.0% per annum</td><td>Liberalized</td></tr>
<tr><td rowspan="2">Company Savings Deposits</td><td rowspan="2">- 3 months or more: liberalized
- less than 3 months: 2.0% per annum
- less than 7 days: non-accrued</td><td>7 days or more: liberalized</td><td rowspan="2"></td></tr>
<tr><td>less than 7 days: non-accrued</td></tr>
</table>

Source: Ministry of Finance and Economy, Korea.

<Table VI-8> Broadening Deregulation of Financial Instruments

<table>
<tr><th rowspan="2"></th><th rowspan="2">Dealing Institutions</th><th colspan="2">Maturity</th><th colspan="2">Minimum Denomination (million wons)</th></tr>
<tr><th>Before July 1998</th><th>After July 1998</th><th>Before July 1998</th><th>After July 1998</th></tr>
<tr><td>CD</td><td>banks</td><td>30~270 days</td><td>30 days or more</td><td>10</td><td></td></tr>
<tr><td rowspan="3">Cover Bills</td><td>banks</td><td>30~180 days</td><td>30 days or more</td><td rowspan="3">5</td><td rowspan="7">liberalized</td></tr>
<tr><td>merchant banks</td><td>1~180 days</td><td>less than 1 year</td></tr>
<tr><td>community credit cooperatives</td><td>30~180 days</td><td>liberalized</td></tr>
<tr><td rowspan="2">Large-Value RPs</td><td>banks</td><td>30 days~1year</td><td>30 days or more</td><td rowspan="2">10</td></tr>
<tr><td>securities firms</td><td>30 days~1year</td><td>liberalized</td></tr>
<tr><td>Large-Value Commercial Bills</td><td>banks</td><td>30 days or more</td><td>liberalized</td><td>10</td></tr>
<tr><td>Sale of Government & Public Bonds</td><td>banks, securities firms</td><td>one day or more</td><td>one day or more</td><td>10</td></tr>
<tr><td>Small-Value Commercial Bills and Trade Bills</td><td>banks</td><td colspan="4">liberalized within 7.0% per annum</td></tr>
<tr><td>Low-Value RPs</td><td>banks</td><td colspan="4">: 91 days~1 year: within 8.0% a year
30 days or more: liberalized</td></tr>
<tr><td></td><td>securities firms</td><td colspan="3">less than 7 days: non-accrued
7 days~1 year: within 8.0% per annum</td><td>liberalized</td></tr>
</table>

Source: Ministry of Finance and Economy, Korea, 1999.

In addition, the Bank removed restrictions on the minimum issuance of CDs, cover bills and high-value RPs, and deregulated interest rates on low-value financial products. It also scrapped most requirements on the issue of short-term marketable financial products such as those on the maturities of commercial bills, trade bills, and RPs. However, the thirty-day minimum maturity on CDs, cover bills and RPs remained in place.

2) Other Deregulations

In keeping with the trend toward financial liberalization, commercial banks were allowed to issue financial debentures from July 7, 1998 with a view to encouraging the development of long-term financial business. Banks were allowed to determine the types of financial debentures, the method of issuance and the use of the funds raised, at their discretion, but the minimum maturity was set at three years to minimize side effects arising from the direct competition with banks' deposit products and the existing financial debentures offered by specialized banks and development institutions. Repurchase by the bank prior to maturity was also prohibited.

Meanwhile, the issuance ceiling on financial debentures was set at 50% of a bank's equity capital with a proviso added that it be set at 25% thereof for one year from the date of enforcement. But the Bank abolished this proviso on December 22, 1998 so that banks could improve their BIS capital adequacy ratios through the issue of subordinated notes. In addition, Korea Development Bank and Korea Long Term Credit Bank, which had long issued financial debentures as a source of funds, were allowed to issue CDs and cover bills to keep 'a level playing field' with commercial banks.

Seeking to stabilize financial market and increase institutional investors' purchase of stocks, the Korean government on November 26, 1998 raised, by two trillion wons, the ceiling on development money in trust which had been frozen since January 1998. Banks were instructed to use more than 30% of amounts newly raised through development money in trust for the purchase of stocks. On December 15, 1998, the Korean government shortened the minimum maturities of banks' trust account products (one year and six months) to one year and reduced the penalties for mid-term cancellation to a fixed rate of one of the amount cancelled where the period held in trust was less than six months and allowed banks to set penalties for mid-term cancellation at their discretion within a maximum of 0.5% where that period held in trust was at least six months.

This paved the way for the launch of new type installment trusts whose effective maturity was 6 months. These moves represented back-up measures following the suspension of the operations of some merchant banks and were taken in the light of the need to strengthen banks' fund-raising capacity so as to facilitate their trust accounts discount and purchase of CP, an activity previously carried out by merchant banks.

On August 30, 1998, the Korean government introduced interest-income tax-exempted Workmen-preferential savings with maturities from three to five years to support worker's accumulation of financial assets. On September 18, 1998, the BOK set the reserve requirement ratio on these products at one percent in view of their characteristics as long-term saving products with a low possibility of mid-term cancellation.

E. Loan System of Banking Institutions

1) Easing of Regulations on Credit Extension

The BOK continued to ease regulations on the credit extension of commercial banks with a view to establishing the loan management of banks on the bases of market principles and the strengthening competitiveness of firms. With effect from February 10, 1998, to increase infrastructure investment, the BOK allowed banks to lend funds for purchase of land needed for road construction by local governments and for primary facilities including roads, railways, ports, airports, multipurpose dams, water supply, sewage disposal and telecommunications among the private-initiative facilities selected by the government. The BOK eased remaining prohibitions on credit extension except for business which threaten to provoke a recurrence of real estate speculation.

The BOK on July 4, 1998 lowered the mandatory ratio for lending to SMEs by regional banks and Industrial Bank of Korea. The ratio applied to regional banks was reduced from 70% to 60% in view of their comparative disadvantage in attracting funds from households because of the limitation imposed by the higher ratios than those on with nationwide commercial banks (45%). The Enforcement Decree of

Industrial Bank of Korea Act was also amended to bring down its mandatory ratio for lending to SMEs from 90% to 80% with effect from November 29, 1998.

On August 1, 1998, the BOK abolished regulations imposed on the main banks of the ten largest conglomerates in connection with the latter's acquisition of real estate. It was considered that the effectiveness of such restrictions had declined since an institutional frameworks had already been put in place and the interlinked business groups were themselves pressing ahead with sale of own real estate in the course of corporate restructuring.

2) Realignment of the Credit Management System

With effect from August 1, 1997, credit ceilings on *chaebols* were introduced, the main objectives being to enhance the effectiveness of the credit concentration management of banks and to avoid joint failures on the part of the *chaebols* and banks. The legal foundation for this system, which prohibits an individual bank's credit extension to a *chaebol* from exceeding a certain ratio of its equity capital, had already been laid under the 1982 Revision of the General Banking Act. However, since the size of banks' equity capital had been too small and information about individual firms and banks' credit statistics had not been computerized, introduction of the system had been deferred. However, these obstacles having been resolved in the course of time, it was decided to put the system in operation.

Loans including loans from banks' trust accounts, acceptances and guarantees in won fall within the scope of the system. The ceiling on such credit to a single *chaebol* is set at 45% of an equity capital of bank. An interim period of 3 years until July 31, 2000 was allowed so that banks could call in credit in excess of the ceiling as of the enforcement date, August 1, 1997. A bank unable to handle the problem within this time frame must obtain the consent of the Superintendent of Banks or his successor, the Financial Services Commissioner.

Meanwhile, the BOK decided to retain the existing system of credit ceilings on *chaebols* as a whole until July 31, 2000 when the interim period set for withdrawal of credit in excess of the ceiling expires. This decision was motivated by worries that if it were to be abolished, smaller *chaebols* or SMEs in relatively poor credit standing would find themselves in a more difficult position as a handful of the leading *chaebols* might borrow up to the limit of the ceiling from several banks at the same time.

3) Single Obligor Limits on Trust Accounts and Handling of Commercial Paper

With effect from August 1, 1997 the Korean government introduced single obligor limits on banks' trust accounts restricting loans to single individuals or corporations to 5% of the outstanding balance of a bank's total trust account loans as of the end of 1996. The system was introduced to prevent the possibility of loans from banks' trust accounts being used to circumvent the ceilings on bank account credit to single borrowers. Banks were required to withdraw that portion of their credit from their total account in excess of the new single-lender ceiling within three years. But, when approval is obtained from the Minister of Finance and Economy, a bank may exceptionally be allowed to continue extending credit from its trust account in excess of the new ceiling.

Alert to the likelihood of a further contraction in firms' short-term fund raising due to the suspension of nine merchant banks' operations on December 2, 1997, the Korean government allowed seven local banks to handle the discount of bills between December 16, 1997 and March 31, 1998. On December 10, 1997, it allowed banks' trust accounts to purchase CP up until the end of 1998. Meanwhile, securities companies received permission to engage in the underwriting, dealing and brokerage of CP without any limit on the amount as of August 1, 1997.

F. Open Market Operations Policy

In the year of 1997, the BOK took several measures to enhance the efficiency of its open market operations.

First, it moved to a completely competitive bidding system for all its offers of RP transactions and the issuance of MSBs without exception. However, in spite of this measure, the competitive bidding ratio for the BOK's MSBs issuance (the proportion of the total offered through competitive bidding) decreased from 89% in 1996 to 60% in 1997. This was due, on the one hand, to a big increase in unsuccessful bids owing to the large gap between market interest rates and the Bank's market intervention rate from November onwards and, on the other hand, to branch operation of foreign banks for their funds in the form of MSBs.

Second, on July 23, 1997, the BOK changed its method of conducting open market operations from receiving written bids to screen-based offers and bids through BOK-wire. As the complete procedure from announcement of bidding to the reporting of the result went on-line, the BOK's counterparts could reduce their bidding-costs and the Bank was able to heighten the efficiency of its open market operations.

<Table VI-9> Competitive Bidding for the BOK's RPs and Issuance of MSBs

	1994	1995	1996	1997
RP Transactions	49.6	75.7	99.1	100.0
Issuance of MSBs	31.5	33.0	89.1[1]	59.5

Note: 1) Excludes the issuance of MSBs in connection with the reduction of banks' reserve requirements on April 23, 1996.
Source: Ministry of Finance and Economy, Korea, 1999.

In a further move, the BOK extended its counterparts for repurchase transactions which had been limited to banks, to include merchant banking corporations (September 1, 1997), securities companies (October 2, 1997) and investment trust companies (December 19, 1997). Thereby, it opened up a channel for the direct supply of liquidity to merchant banking corporations and securities companies through its use of reverse repurchase transactions, which should be helpful in relieving temporary shortage of funds on the part of these non-bank financial institutions.

The BOK made active use of repurchase agreements involving government and public bonds during 1997 in order to maintain money supply at an appropriate level. During 1997, the overall value of the BOK's RP operations amounted to some 104 trillion wons in a total of 122 transactions, figures respectively 1.8 and 1.5 times for those from 1996. Apart from the second quarter when the market showed relatively stable range of movements, purchases of government and public bonds under resale agreements, or reverse RPs, exceeded sales. Particularly in the second half of 1997, the BOK greatly enlarged the scale of its offers of reverse RPs to the market as banks were experiencing acute liquidity shortages owing to the failure to resolve the problems of the *KIA Group* and the foreign exchange crisis.

As the BOK provided liquidity by way of MSB redemption to alleviate the very tight conditions in financial markets throughout much of the year, net redemption of MSBs totaled 1,559 billion wons during 1997. Thus, their outstanding balance eased from 25 trillion wons to 23.5 trillion wons at the end of 1997 and the ratio of the outstanding balance of MSBs to M2, correspondingly, dropped from 14% to 12%.

<Table VI-10> Transactions under Repurchase Agreements Involving Government and Public Bonds

	1995	1996	1997				
			Year	I	II	III	IV
Purchases	12,424 (15)	38,902 (31)	72,786 (80)	8,650 (10)	5,375 (9)	26,088 (31)	32,673 (30)
Sales	38,838 (61)	32,350 (37)	30,784 (42)	3,646 (7)	13,338 (18)	4,700 (6)	9,100 (11)
Total	51,262 (76)	71,252 (68)	103,570 (122)	12,296 (17)	18,713 (27)	30,788 (37)	41,773 (41)

Note: Figures in parentheses represent the number of RP transactions.
Source: Ministry of Finance and Economy, Korea, 1999

The net redemption of MSBs increased in the first quarter as the BOK eased its monetary management to soothe market unrest. However, the second quarter saw a net issuance when the BOK needed both to sterilize inflows and to absorb excess liquidity released during the first quarter of 1997.

<Table VI-11> Issuance and Redemption of MSBs (Unit: billion wons)

	1995	1996	1997
Net issuance	485	-795	-1,559
Issuance	39,458	30,725	31,224
Competitive tender	12,243	23,705	18,577
Direct sale	27,215	7,019	12,647
Redemption	38,972	31,520	32,783
Outstanding balance	25,825	25,030	23,471

Source: Ministry of Finance and Economy, Korea, 1999.

In the third quarter, MSBs shifted back to a slight net redemption position, because the BOK provided liquidity in accordance with an enlarged short-term capital account deficit and the deepening financial market turmoil. Moreover, in the fourth quarter, the scale of the net redemption was greatly enlarged as the Bank strove to ease the shortage of liquidity arising from its large-scale intervention in the foreign exchange market in support of the Korean Won.

3. FOREIGN EXCHANGE POLICY & LIBERALIZATION

A. The Foreign Exchange Market

1) Introduction of the Free-Floating Exchange Rate System

In accordance with the government's agreement with the IMF, the daily exchange rate fluctuation band was eliminated as of December 16, 1997. Korea thereby could effectively switch to a free-floating exchange rate system. This decision was dictated by the need to restore the price function of the exchange rate after the won had collapsed against the dollar repeatedly hitting its daily lower limit shortly after market opening and paralyzing the domestic FX (foreign exchange) market.

This pattern had continued even after a massive widening of the band from ±2.5% to ± 10% on November 20, 1997. It was agreed, however, that the basic rate, which is the weighted average of the previous business day's transactions in the inter-bank FX market, would continue to be used when commercial banks set their own FX selling-buying rates or when the BOK conducted FX transactions.

2) Improvements in Foreign Exchange Position Management System

To dampen the excess demand for foreign exchange and promote capital inflows, the government carried out a number of measures on October 31, 1997. The limit on a bank's spot over-bought position was set at the higher of 5% of its equity capital or US$8 million, and the amount of spot FX sold, where it resulted from swaps involving selling spot and buying forwards, was excluded from the calculation of the spot FX position. Furthermore, the limit on the spot over-sold position was increased on November 1 from the higher of 3% of equity capital or US$5 million to the higher of 5% of equity capital or US$8 million.

Starting from October 31, 1997, in order to constrain the excess FX demand, the government imposed temporary restrictions on purchases of foreign currency for Korean won until the market recovered its stability. Accordingly the purchase of foreign exchange for holding purposes, which was previously allowed up to US$20 thousand annually per person and its purchase to make FX deposits, were both prohibited. Even in the case of real demand transactions, the purchase of foreign exchange was allowed only within the five days before the actual payment.

Previously, foreign exchange banks had to file FX transaction records with the National Tax Administration when receiving or purchasing foreign currency from a single person to the value of more than US$20 thousand per year. But with effect from December 12, 1997, this requirement was suspended in order to promote the inflow of foreign exchange held by overseas residents into the domestic market.

3) Expansion of FX Business

Approval from the Minister of Finance and Economy had previously been required for a securities firm to set up an overseas branch, however, from the April 1, 1998, only a simple notification was necessary. From September 11, 1997, leasing companies were allowed to engage in the extension of loans to local subsidiaries of financial institutions and to take on medium and long-term borrowings of foreign capital for this purpose.

The Korean government as of November 1, 1997, allowed sales of foreign-currency denominated assets abroad through the off-shore marketing of banks' loan receivables and the issue of asset-backed securities. As of that same date, a new system was introduced for granting authorization for participation in the capital of overseas financial institutions whereby preliminary authorization would first be given after which full institutional authorization had to be obtained.

On December 31, 1997, the Korean government allowed domestic securities firms to engage in currency exchange business and short-term FX forward transactions related to investment in bonds, stock index futures and stock index options. Also, seven investment trust companies were allowed to conduct a similar range of FX business to that allowed for securities firms except for the borrowing of foreign capital for the purchase of foreign securities. Restrictions on the Export-Import Bank of Korea's operations were eased to allow it to engage in foreign exchange business on the same basis as commercial banks.

B. Improvement for Current Account Transactions

1) Liberalization of Deferred Payment Period

In order to ease exporters' difficulties in raising foreign capital when they import raw materials for export use from neighboring countries, the period for deferred payment was lengthened from 150 days to 180 days in the case of SMEs on April 14, 1998, and from 120 days to 150 days in the case of large enterprises on August 29, 1998. For imports intended for domestic use by SMEs, the settlement periods for deferred payments were, as of October 31, 1998, all lengthened to 180 days, the same as for imports for export use.

On December 12, 1997, after the currency crisis had erupted, for the settlement periods for deferred payments, imports were standardized at 180 days, regardless of use, source and size of the importing firm. However, where the credit is supplied by the US Commodity Credit Corporation, the maximum period of settlement could be extended to 36 months. In a related move, which came into effect from November 28, 1997, it was provided that for imports of crude oil against shipper's credit or ex-post payment that portion of the eligible deferred payments period exceeding the duration of the credit offered might be financed by borrowings of short-term foreign funds or the issue of commercial paper.

2) Abolition of Receipt Limit on Export Advances and Deposits

As a measure to improve the current account balance, the Korean government raised the ceiling on large enterprises' receipt of advances on exports from 20% of the previous year's exports to 25% on February 10, 1998 and increased the ceiling on deposits against contracted exports during the manufacturing period from 30% of the total contract amount to 40% thereof. On August 29, 1998, the former ceiling was abolished and the latter ceiling was raised from 50 to 60%. From November 1, 1998, exporters were allowed to receive advances against exports from other companies' local subsidiaries or overseas branches. Effective from December 12, 1998, the period for the performance of the exports corresponding to the export advances was lengthened from 120 days to 180 days and limits on deposits against exports made at the time of entering into a contract were liberalized to help ease exporters' financial woes.

The Korean government relaxed restraints on some types of invisible payments on November 1, 1998. First of all, the remittance of interest accrued from non-residents' won-denominated accounts to another country would require only a declaration to the head of FX bank rather than the previous approval by the Governor of the BOK. When Korean residents abroad wished to take their financial assets out of Korea, they might do so up to a limit of US$1 million per year through an emigration account with no limit on the number of withdrawals after declaring their intention to their prime foreign exchange bank.

C. Liberalization of Capital Account Transactions

1) Opening of the Korean Stock Market

During 1998 under review, the Korean government greatly widened the opening of the Korean equity market, easing restrictions on both direct and indirect investment in domestic stocks by foreigners and liberalizing stock index futures and options markets. In order to promote inflows of foreign capital, the aggregate ceiling within which foreign investors could purchase domestic stocks listed on the KSE (Korea Stock Exchange) was raised on May 1, 1998 from 20% to 23% of the outstanding stocks issued by a listed firm and from 15% to 18% of those issued by a public corporation. The ceiling on holdings by an individual foreign investor was also raised from 5% to 6% of a firm's outstanding stocks. On November 3, 1998, the aggregate ceiling was further raised to 26% for a firm and to 20% for a public corporation. The individual ceiling was at the same time increased to 7%. On December 11, 1998, the aggregate and individual ceilings on the purchase of stocks in a listed company were both raised to 50% in line with the agreement with the IMF, the ceilings for a public corporation remaining at the same level as before. The aggregate ceiling was further raised to 55% on December 30, 1998.

As for indirect investment in the domestic equity market, on January 3, 1998, foreigners were allowed to invest in equity-type beneficial certificates subject to a maximum limit of 20% of each new issue. On February 26, 1998, equity-type mutual funds were allowed to acquire stocks in the primary or issue market. And on May 2, 1998, a capital increase of US$140 million by the Korea Fund was authorized.

The Korean government substantially raised the ceiling on foreign investment in the stock index futures market from 30% of the average daily open interest for the last three months to 100% with effect from July 7, 1998. In addition, it set the ceiling on foreign investment in stock index options at the same level as that in stock index futures. On September 1, 1998, a foreigner-exclusive funds whose capital was gathered through the sale of beneficial certificates were allowed to invest in KOSDAQ-listed stocks without limit and also in stock index futures and options.

The Korean government announced that taxes on capital gains from stocks, which were imposed on nationals of countries such as Japan that did not have bilateral taxation agreements with Korea, would be scrapped beginning from October 25, 1998. On November 15, 1998, foreigners were allowed to invest in companies listed on the KOSDAQ market, subject to aggregate and individual foreign investment ceilings of 15% and 5% respectively.

2) Widening of External Liberalization

On January 3, 1998, the Korean government raised the ceilings on foreign investment in non-guaranteed CBs (convertible bonds) issued by SMEs. The aggregate ceiling was increased from 30% to 50% of each issue and the individual ceiling from 5% to 10%. From June 2, foreigners were allowed to invest in the non-guaranteed CBs of large listed companies and in the non-guaranteed bonds of SMEs with a maturity of more than three years. Aggregate and individual limits for non-guaranteed CBs of large listed companies were set, respectively, at 30% and 6% of the volume of any issue listed. The aggregate limit for foreign investment in SMEs' non-guaranteed long-term bonds was set at 50% of the volume of the issue listed but no individual limit was set.

On December 12, 1997, immediately following the currency crisis, foreigners were given *carte blanche* to invest in the non-guaranteed CBs of large enterprises and in the guaranteed bonds and non-guaranteed bonds of large enterprises, both with maturities of at least three years. The aggregate and individual investment ceilings for large enterprises' non-guaranteed CBs were set at 50% and 10% respectively and for their guaranteed bonds and non-guaranteed bonds at 30% and 10%, respectively. Meanwhile, foreign investment ceilings on non-guaranteed long-term bonds and SMEs' non-guaranteed CBs were abolished.

Furthermore, the Korean government removed the individual foreign investment ceiling on corporate bonds on December 23, 1997. Also national and municipal bonds, specific-law bonds including financial debentures and corporate bonds with maturities of less than three years were opened up to foreign investment. The aggregate foreign investment ceiling on such bonds as set at 30% of those of each issuer and the individual ceiling at 10% thereof.

On December 30, 1997, all restrictions on foreigners' investment in corporate bonds were removed completely liberalizing the domestic bond market. This had originally been scheduled only for such time as stable macroeconomic conditions were maintained or the differential between Korean and international interest rates fell below two percentage points.

Regarding the issuance of bonds in the domestic market by non-residents, the government on March 17, 1998, permitted international financial institutions, including the IBRD (International Bank for Reconstruction and Development) and the EBRD (European Bank for Reconstruction and Development) to issue Won-denominated bonds and list them on the KSE. In accordance with this measure, the IBRD listed bonds to the value of approximately US$100 million on April 23, 1998 and the EBRD floated a similar amount on May 2, 1998.

3) Lifting of Restrictions on Inward Foreign Direct Investment

The revision of the previous Foreign Capital Inducement Act came into force being renamed the Foreign Investment and Foreign Capital Inducement Act and Foreign Investment Promotion Act. Under the revision, foreign enterprises were allowed to receive loans from affiliated companies within a limit of the amount of foreign investment committed. The loan had to be used for the import of capital goods and have a maturity of more than five years. Also friendly mergers and acquisitions engineered by a foreign company were permitted if approved by the board of directors of the targeted enterprise. An exception, however, was made for enterprises having assets of at least two trillion Korean won in view of the potential impact on the national economy. In these cases, the permission of the Minister of Finance and Economy had to be obtained.

With effect from July 14, 1998, the Korean government dismantled most restrictions on the use of long-term cash loans with maturities of more than five years by foreigner-owned manufacturing firms, allowing them to borrow working capital abroad subject to a ceiling of the lower of 50% of the total investment committed or US$10 million.

The system for receiving authorization to set up an office in Korea for a foreign securities-related institution such as a securities firm, an investment trust company or an investment consulting firm was changed as of January 1, 1998 from approval by the Minister of Finance and Economy to a notification, with conditional acceptance upon its examination. On November 1, 1998, foreigners and foreign-invested companies were allowed to operate currency exchange business. To open a registered currency exchange business or altering its type of operation, simple notification to the Governor of the BOK was required instead of a declaration whose acceptance had been conditional upon its examination.

The Korean government on December 31, 1998 designated ten branches of foreign securities firms in Korea as institutions for the conduct of FX transactions enabling them to engage in currency exchange business and short-term FX forward transactions related to securities investment.

4) Easing of Restrictions on Foreign Borrowings by Residents

Starting from January 1, 1998, both large enterprises and foreign-invested companies were allowed to receive commercial loans for the import of capital goods. For infrastructure projects of over 500 billion wons conducted in line with the Private Capital Inducement Act, the Korean government allowed foreign borrowings of up to 20% of the annual net cost per project in order to finance the domestic part of the infrastructure project. This was subject to a ceiling of US$50 million, but for those projects with a net construction cost of over 1 trillion Korean won, the ceiling on such foreign borrowings was set at US$ 100 million.

The Korean government also permitted firms the ratio of whose domestic-made machinery use for plant investment was at least 50% and also fifteen local governments to raise overseas funds through commercial loans or the issue of foreign currency securities. The annual limit on long-term foreign borrowings by domestic banks was abolished on March 15, 1998 and that on domestic firms' issue of stock-related securities on April 1, 1998. The previous ceiling on individual firms' issue of equity-related securities of 50% of total stocks issued was eliminated on April 14, 1998 along with the requirement of at least a BBB rating from an international credit rating agency for the issue of debt securities overseas.

On November 1, 1998, the Korean government liberalized residents' use of foreign borrowings raised via local financing for all purposes other than overseas portfolio investment, overseas real estate purchases and funds for the establishment and operation of overseas branches. Similarly, the ex-post management of local financing was loosened so that a declaration to the Governor of the BOK was needed only when the debt outstanding was over US$30 million and the increment during the year exceeded 30% of the balance outstanding at the end of 1997. The Korean government liberalized both the use of funds raised through the issue of depository receipts by foreign exchange banks and the borrowing terms for commercial loans, which had previously been set at no more than Libor + 2% for SMEs or Libor + 1% for other companies.

Following the currency crisis, foreign borrowings in the form of commercial loans of cash with at least a three-year maturity or the issue of foreign currency denominated bonds by private firms were allowed for an interim period from December 16, 1997 until the end of 1998. In addition, the government improved the system for the raising of foreign currency funds by firms and this was scheduled to be put into practice from January 1, 1998. Under the new arrangement, the various uses of firms' fund-raising were integrated and the limit on commercial loans intended for the import of capital goods abolished.

The Korean government also permitted firms operating in a technological frontier industry to receive commercial loans for the purchase of domestic-made capital goods even if the ratio of domestic-made machinery of the relevant enterprise was less than 50%. Furthermore, the ratio of the required funds that might be borrowed when large enterprises purchase capital goods using commercial loans was raised to the same level as that when the purchase was financed through the issue of foreign currency securities; namely up to 80% of the cost incurred.

5) Liberalization of Overseas Direct and Portfolio Investment

The Korean government eased or abolished many restrictions on overseas direct investment to allow enterprises to carry through their own investment strategies in pursuit of profit at their own initiative and risk. On August 1, 1998, the system of a notification to the BOK and its acceptance for overseas direct investments exceeding US$10 million was replaced by a simple notification to a commercial bank. Regarding routine overseas direct investment, the examination by the Overseas Direct Investment Examination Committee and the requirement that a certain ratio of equity capital be met were abolished.

In order to allow interested parties such as small stockholders to obtain a better grasp of intended overseas investments, the list of items subject to public disclosure by the firm involved was expanded to include the total projected scale of the operation and the method of raising the required funds in addition to the amount and ratio of invested capital and the name of the local subsidiary. Also the responsibility for the compilation of statistics related to overseas direct investment which had been handled by the BOK, was transferred to the National Federation of Banks.

Regarding overseas portfolio investment, having liberalized institutional investors' investment in unlisted foreign stocks on March 20, 1995, the Korean government allowed private investors to invest in such stocks as of March 11. The aggregate ceiling on Korean residents' investment in each issue was limited to 10% of the total outstanding of any foreign-currency denominated unlisted issue and the individual ceiling was set at less than 10% of the value of individual's outstanding investment in foreign-currency denominated securities.

4. THE DIRECTIONS OF CORPORATE SECTOR REFORMS

The Korean government took steps in 1996 to address some of the weaknesses in the practice of corporate governance. In the wake of the crisis, corporate reform has become one of its top priorities, leading to a wide range of new initiatives in late 1997 and early 1998. Reforms were focused on four areas: strengthening the rights of shareholders, particularly those with minority holdings in a company; abolishing 'incestuous' relationships between *chaebol* affiliates and encouraging independent behaviour; promoting transparency through enhanced disclosure rules; and improving exit mechanisms for non-viable firms through a more open market for corporate control and better insolvency and asset disposal procedures.

An important element of the new government's policy is its declared intention to establish a new policy paradigm in addressing corporate issues based on enhancing competition and establishing rational incentive structures. Rather than imposing changes on the business sector by direct or indirect flat, it will put in place a framework to facilitate change including an orderly exit procedure for those failing to adapt. The direction and sequencing of change will be left to the decision of the companies themselves. Notwithstanding the government's good intentions, it is not yet clear whether this new paradigm has filtered down to the civil servants actually implementing policies on a day-to-day basis. Indeed, it might take some time for lower level officials as well as company managers to realize that the government's 'priorities' are no longer binding orders and that if their strategies fail, they will be taken over or forced out of business.

A. Strengthening Shareholder Protection

Korean law provides protection for shareholders[43]. They are given adequate rights of preemption when new stock is issued and of appraisal when their situation fundamentally worsens. Listed companies cannot restrict the mobility of shares through their articles of association and the system of "one share, one vote" guarantees a level playing field among common stockholders. In addition, the so-called "shadow voting" regulation - the obligation for financial intermediaries to vote with the management on all issues - is to be abolished. However, the voting rules for listed companies should be further upgraded. Proxy mechanisms are expensive and therefore rarely used. A postal ballot could spread equity market manipulation by insiders including major shareholders and affiliates. These rules must be strengthened along with their enforcement, which is now the responsibility of the unified Financial Supervisory Commissions[44] that was created in April 1998.

Changes in the Securities and Exchange Act in 1996 have simplified access to redress mechanisms by minority shareholders in listed companies. In particular, derivative suits[45] in the most important cases now only require 0.05% of common stock. The current six-month deadline for derivative suits is adequate, provided that the time limit is measured from the point when the relevant facts have been disclosed to shareholders. Joint shareholders' suits against the company, however, are still not possible in Korea. Allowing such suits could further lower the cost of judicial protection for small shareholders.

The responsibility of company directors is one of the weak points of the Korean corporate governance system. Corporate law does not adequately reflect the fact that the main decisions in *chaebol*-affiliated companies are taken by the planning and coordinating office directed by the founder or major owner of the *chaebol*. The `authority of directors of such companies is fictitious and proper accountability is thus absent. Fiduciary duties, especially the duty of loyalty to the company, have until now been fairly vague. They need to be defined more clearly in the law and more vigorously enforced. The existing criminal law provisions regarding the willful breach of fiduciary duty to the company by directors have rarely been enforced by prosecutors. In addition, there is no limitation on the number of board seats that one person might hold. Inter-locking directorates appear to be another element of *chaebol* management which deprives minority shareholders of their rights. A rule limiting interlocking directorates, as is the case in France and Italy, would be beneficial.

Another area of major concern is the provisions in laws related to conflicts of interest between a company and its directors and management that arise from the major transactions of the company, especially those with important shareholders. Most of these transactions, including the disposal of major assets, loans, collateral and other guarantees, are under the responsibility of the board of directors with minimum information to shareholders. Transparency should be considerably increased by requiring specific prior disclosure of such transactions, in addition to reporting them in company accounts. Shareholders, as well as creditors in certain cases, should be given the power, within reasonable time limits to stop these transactions before they become irreversible.

One of the most important changes announced in the wake of the crisis is the requirement that all company boards include external directors. Beginning in 1999, at least a fourth of the members of the board of a listed company must be independent external directors[46]. In contrast to 'normal' directors, external directors cannot sit on more than three corporate boards. However, there is no special procedure for nominating or appointing outside directors. Furthermore, these directors have not been assigned special tasks such as heading the remuneration and audit committees or ensuring an arm's length relationship between the corporation and its management. Such functions should be assigned to external directors to

---

[43] The most important legal provisions concerning shareholder protection in larger companies can be found in the Korean Commercial Code (the Company Law), Securities and Exchange Law and the listing requirements of the Korean Stock Exchange.

[44] The Financial Supervisory Commission combines the functions of the Office of Bank Supervision, Securities Supervisory Board and the Insurance Supervisory Board.

[45] A derivative suit is an action brought by shareholders against one or more directors of a company in the name and eventually, at the cost of the company.

[46] It should be noted that some of the *chaebols* already have outsiders sitting on the boards of their major listed companies. In many OECD countries, including the United States, the United Kingdom and the Netherlands, this requirement is part of a voluntary code. In the case of Korea, however, it seems appropriate that the Korean Stock Exchange has made it part of its listing requirements, given the urgent need for increasing transparency in the market.

allow them to influence effectively the way companies are run. Moreover, external directors have very little independence in practice unless their power base lies with outside shareholders. If they have to rely on the nomination and/or vote by the 'inside' group, they will hardly ever be independent. Introducing a cumulative voting system, which stipulates that a minority of directors can be elected by a minority of shareholders, would help ensure the presence of such directors and their real independence.

Executive remuneration is not transparent in Korea. Increased transparency in this area would improve managerial accountability and enhance shareholder value. As regards incentives, stock options became available in 1997 but are still not very popular. More widespread and transparent use of this and other incentive-based compensation schemes might enhance corporate profitability. In any event. both the amount and the structure of executive compensation, as well as major changes affecting it, should be visible to investors in listed companies.

B. Prohibition of Cross-debt Guarantees & Arrangement on Allowing Holding Company Structure

One of the most radical steps taken by the Korean government in the wake of the crisis was the prohibition of new intra-group debt guarantees and the obligation to eliminate existing guarantees by the end of 1999[47]. These guarantees had a domino effect leading to a string of *chaebol* bankruptcies in unrelated sectors in 1996 and 1997. The outright prohibition of cross-debt guarantees will require a fundamental shift in the operation of banks, which have relied on these rather than developing the necessary credit risk skills. Such a change in bank behaviour will not be easy and may lead to a further weakening in the quality of loan portfolios in the short term. Moreover, it may create difficulties for the *chaebols* in ensuring adequate financing as banks apply stricter credit standards. In the medium term, though, the efficiency gains from this reform should far outweigh these adjustment costs.[48] Once greater transparency is established, such guarantees could be allowed as in other OECD countries.

In the process of restructuring, it might be helpful to allow legal consolidation between companies belonging to the same *chaebol* by permitting 'going private' transactions. It is now possible for *chaebol*-affiliated companies to acquire other firms at a level superior to the 25% of their net assets previously allowed. Many of the business groups argue that another positive reform in this regard would be to allow a holding company structure. The Korean government has recently announced that holding companies will, in fact, be allowed but only under very restrictive conditions which will in practice rule out this option for virtually all *chaebols* in the short run. Moreover, the ownership structure of the *chaebols* is so complicated that a rapid transformation into holding companies does not look feasible in the short term. Consequently, increasing transparency and strengthening the concepts of a director's duty to the corporation are still the most effective tools to encourage restructuring.

C. Enhancing Transparency of Corporate Accounts

Increased transparency is the most important tool for reform and restructuring in the corporate sector. Although the accounting practices of Korea are generally consistent with GAAP (Generally-Accepted Accounting Practices), important loopholes remain in the accuracy, timeliness, depth and veracity of reported information.

A number of improvements were introduced in the second half of 1997, including: business-line accounting; a requirement that management comment on financial results and operations, gives more detail on internal audit and control systems and provide forward-looking information; a strengthening of reporting off-balance-sheet transactions such as derivatives, intangible assets and debt guarantees. In particular, listed companies are required to report details of collateral or debt guarantees when their total amount exceeds 10% of outstanding equity. Disclosure must be immediate if transactions exceed 10% of equity *vis-a-vis* a major shareholder.

---

[47] Since most loans have relatively short maturities, the rapid phasing-out of debt guarantees will be too disruptive.

[48] It could be argued that improving corporate governance and increasing transparency would cause this practice to disappear gradually. However, given the deeply-entrenched nature of debt guarantees and the likelihood that changes in corporate governance will be more evolutionary than revolutionary, an outright prohibition seems preferable.

The most important accounting reform is the requirement for the *chaebols* to produce CFSs (combined financial statements) beginning from fiscal year 1999[49]. In the absence of CFSs, the extremely complicated web of intra-group loans, guarantees and other transactions has remained closed to most investors[50]. The new system is based on a broad definition of what constitutes an affiliated company, which will in principle make the statement very comprehensive. They will include the combined balance sheet, income and cash flow statements, as well as footnotes reporting intra-group loans, loan guarantees and other major transactions. It is important that information related to these transactions be complete, adequately explained and put in a proper historical context for investors to evaluate.

Another area where standards need to be tightened is accounting of asset values, especially securities. Since book values are often unrealistic, market-to-market accounting needs to be introduced to allow investors to assess the market value of a company's assets.

The Korean government has also moved to enhance the independence of external auditors responsible for verifying company accounts. Three changes were introduced at the end of 1996: first, the minimum contract for auditors was extended to two years; second, shareholders representing 3% of common stock can stop the appointment of auditors; and thirdly, the Korean government may appoint the auditors for companies deemed to be controlled by a majority shareholder.[51]

In 1998, the requirement that the board approve the audit report was abolished. The government is now considering the introduction of an auditor selection committee which includes outside directors, which would be an important step. Finally, further reform is needed in the regulation of the accounting or audit profession in order to guarantee the fairness and veracity of accounts. Institutions in this area need to be strengthened and tighter sanctions for failure of auditors to adequately perform their duties should be introduced.

D. Improving Exit Mechanisms for Non-Viable Firms

1) Market Mechanism for Corporate Take-Overs

In a broader sense, a market for corporate take-overs is the most powerful mechanism by which inefficient management can be disciplined. In Korea, hostile M&As (mergers and acquisitions) were not allowed, and even friendly M&As were limited to cases where the total assets of the companies involved did not exceed 2 trillion wons in the past. One of the main ways to activate a market for corporate take-overs and to promote widespread corporate restructuring is to either portfolio or direct foreign investment.

The Korean government has decided to allow FDI in almost half of the 48 business lines in which it has been prohibited, including several related to financial markets and defense industries. Moreover, the ceiling on total foreign share holdings in individual companies was abolished in May 1998. In addition, the market for corporate control has also been considerably opened up to foreigners by relaxing the rule which limited holdings acquired without the approval of the board of directors to only 10%. It is now possible to acquire up to a third of a company in the market and the approval requirement is to be abolished. Finally, the government provides an 'one-stop service' for foreign investors, who were once bogged down by excessive red tapes, by re-inventing the KOTRA (Korea Trade and Investment Promotion Agency).

Tax and labor legislation has also been streamlined in recent months to facilitate mergers although more remains to be done in the area of taxes. Another important measure to be implemented this year will allow corporate spin-offs, which will make it easier for companies to break themselves up and thus become more digestible by prospective buyers.

However, in its desire to open the market for corporate control, the government recently abolished two important stock market rules. First, it abolished the rule requiring statutory tender offers in the case of a purchase of 25% or more. Second, disclosure of incremental acquisitions of stakes larger than 5% is no longer required. Although this may facilitate take-overs in the short run, in the longer term, the market may

[49] Some of the *chaebols* have already produced CFSs on a voluntary basis. For example, LG adopted this practice in fiscal 1995. A closer look at these accounts, however, reveals that a considerable degree of obscurity still remains as regards intra-group transactions. Moreover, large parts of the group, most notably its financial businesses, remain at arms-length accounting. The government's plan to require CFSs should effectively address these issues.

[50] Individual companies have been required to mention in their footnotes such dealings with affiliated companies since 1996. However, without the duty to combine financial statements, intra-group obligations have remained concealed.

[51] In the case of a listed company, this means that at least 30% is owned by one shareholder; the threshold is 50% for a non-listed company. These rules with have very little impact on *chaebols,* given their ownership structure.

become less transparent, as portfolio investors, especially foreigners who face higher information costs, might decide to stay away from Korean equities. Many OECD countries, such as the United Kingdom, France, Italy and Germany, still consider such restrictions to be useful.

2) The Legal Framework and Procedures to Deal with Corporate Insolvency

The legal framework and procedures that deal with insolvency are inadequate. While more than 17,000 cases of insolvency were reported in 1997 by the Bank of Korea, only 490 were filed before the court. Nationwide, only 41 judges handle bankruptcy cases and, with the exception of Seoul, they are not specialists in commercial law, lengthy proceedings often lasting several years, invite strategic and opportunistic behavior by the debtor, thus making insolvency an unattractive course of action to creditors.

The government took a first step in addressing these issues by amending the bankruptcy law in February 1998. From a procedural point of view, the legal changes make it easier for a court to accept and to hear cases, even when the file is not complete, and it facilitates the consolidation of related cases under the same court, such as when a case concerns different companies belonging to the same *chaebol.* In addition, it shortened the deadlines for the approval and submission of re-organization plans to between 12 and 18 months. Another welcome change concerns the possibility of switching from the composition or re-organization options (see Table VI-12) to bankruptcy proceedings.

Much, however, remains to be done if Korea is to have a modern insolvency framework on which domestic and foreign investors can rely with sufficient confidence. First, the time limits should be further shortened. Second, the replacement of the three options presently available by a unitary procedure[52] might alleviate a lot of the remaining procedural hurdles and further streamline the process to a considerable extent. Third, the trigger mechanism for initiating insolvency proceedings should be addressed. Although the 1998 amendment has made it easier to file a petition for voluntary composition or re-organization when insolvency is imminent, debtors are not required to file, under civil and/or penal sanctions, until cash-flow insolvency reaches certain thresholds. Requiring debtors to initiate composition or re-organization proceedings before reaching insolvency might be helpful in imposing tighter financial discipline and in encouraging debtors to restructure rapidly.

<Table VI-12> The Framework for Bankruptcy Proceedings

- Bankruptcy, a procedure involving straightforward liquidation of the debtor's assets by an independent court-appointed liquidator. Only 38 bankruptcy petitions were filed in 1997.
- Composition, a settlement procedure between the debtor and creditors in which the court plays a rather minor role while the debtor stays in possession of its estate. This is the most popular method with 322 cases in 1997. It is, however, available Only to enterprises that owe less than 250 billion wons. This option is limited to smaller enterprises on the grounds that it offers very few guarantees to the creditors.
- - Corporate re-organization, a procedure close to Chapter 11 of the US Bankruptcy Code, in which the court directs the creditors to make a deal with the debtor. Under this debt work-out procedure the debtor's estate is administered by an External administrator, who, however, is usually under the influence of the debtor. Two-thirds of the creditors have to approve the re-organization plan, whose Implementation period can last up to 10 years. The creditors and the debtor may initiate any of the procedures provided there is Evidence of cash flow insolvency, *i.e.,* when debts are not paid as they become due. The debtor, though, is under no obligation to file. In all three procedures, the court can (and usually does) order a moratorium on individual claim satisfaction outside the insolvency framework, which, as noted, may last for a long period of time. Setting off claims against the debtor is possible, unless there was bad faith involved.

Source: Ministry of Finance and Economy, 1999.

[52] A unitary procedure does not distinguish between re-organizing and liquidating assets. Instead, it allows the administrator of the debtor's estate (whether the debtor or a third party) and the creditors to proceed to the restructuring and/or liquidation of assets as they see it in order to preserve value for the creditors.

Overall, the current system gives weak incentives to both debtors and creditors to initiate insolvency proceedings. In the re-organization procedure, it gives the courts the possibility to choose an independent administrator or the debtor's management or both.[53] This makes it less attractive for large debtors, who cannot file for composition to file for protection since they run the risk of losing control. As for creditors, they are never happy to open bankruptcy proceedings, which trigger a moratorium on their claims and, in the case of banks, increase their provision requirements by imposing re-classification of the loans[54]. For these reasons, it might be worth allowing a straightforward debtor-in-possession system in re-organization proceedings in conjunction with a mandatory trigger for the debtor. This should be accompanied by a substantial shortening of deadlines and a streamlining of procedures, unless the creditors are strongly opposed.

3) Asset Disposal

Unsatisfied claims including those that are non-performing, might not result in insolvency but instead lead to individual collection proceedings, including foreclosure and sale of collateral. In Korea, this is a streamlined process involving the courts, which takes place within reasonable time limits. If the auction fails to raise the amount of the claim, the title to the underlying security is transferred to the creditor. Collection of NPLs in the financial sector is managed by a statutory monopoly, the KAMCO (Korean Asset Management Corporation). In the past, KAMCO operated on a commission basis. However in November 1997, KAMCO was entrusted with a fundamental role in financial sector restructuring - the management of the bail-out fund and the purchase of non-performing assets from the banks at an unprecedented scale, scope and speed.

5. *CHAEBOLS'* STREAMLING, A CORE ISSUE OF CORPORATE SECTOR REFORMS

The rapid expansion of debt-financed investment by the *chaebols* resulted in excess capacity, declining profits and a squeeze on balance-sheet positions. These problems have placed Korea in its current dire predicament despite its fundamental structural strengths, such as high savings and investment rates and a well-trained work force. The difficulties in the corporate sector, in turn, have seriously weakened the banking system. In the wake of the crisis, firms will have to restructure to survive.

A. The Significance of *Chaebols* in the Korean Economy

Chaebols are multi-company business groups operating in a wide range of markets under common entrepreneurial and financial control. Although holding companies are prohibited and each company is legally independent, *chaebols* are, nonetheless, characterized by centralized planning and co-ordination. These business groups have been a driving force behind Korea's successful export-led growth and rapid industralization. Given the scarcity of entrepreneurial talent in the early stages of development, economic resources became concentrated around the founders of these groups. The success of the *chaebols* also reflects their ability to overcome the imperfections of factor markets such as those for capital, labour and technology, and to benefit from the synergies and economies of scope that are possible in large organizations.

Moreover, the groups profited from their close links to the government in a period when nearly all economic activities were regulated, a factor that has led many to question the legitimacy of the *chaebols'* strong position in the economy. In particular, the industrial policies adopted in the 1970s to accelerate the

[53] The attitude of the courts seems to be shifting significantly towards a more rigorous application of existing norms. In March 1998 two major cases involving *KIA Motors* and *New Core Group*, judges refused to appoint incumbent management as administrators or receivers. This is a hopeful sign that insolvency proceedings will be used in the future as the important financial discipline and asset re-allocation tool they we intended to be in a market economy.

[54] This also argues for a change in classification requirements. Loans should have been fully provisioned simply on the fact of delinquency, *i.e.* independent of the legal fling. Moreover, classification and provisioning requirements should not vary according to the type of the procedure chosen, *i.e.* composition instead of bankruptcy, as is currently the case.

development of heavy and chemical industries encouraged the growth of the *chaebols*. It should be noted that Chinese Taipei, an economy whose situation was broadly comparable with that of Korea, has achieved similarly rapid growth with small and medium-sized firms playing a much larger role.

The Fair Trade Commission is required by law to identify each year the 30-largest business groups, which are subject to special regulations. In 1996, this group accounted for about two-fifths of the capital stock in the mining and manufacturing sector and almost a fifth of employment. In terms of shipments, the *chaebols'* share has fluctuated between 35% and 40% since the late 1970s. In general, their share declined during periods of rapid expansion, as new firms entered the markets and increased during periods of slower growth. There is a considerable gap, though, between the largest *chaebols* and the other business groups. In particular, the top five have steadily increased their share of shipments over the past twenty years and, at present, account for about a quarter of the total in the mining and manufacturing sector. The business groups, however, are less important in the service sector. Consequently, the shares of GDP accounted for by the 30 and the five-largest *chaebols* were estimated at 16% and 9% respectively in 1995.

Another measure of economic concentration, the share of manufacturing output by the 100 largest firms has declined during the past fifteen years. From a peak of 46% in 1980, their share of shipments fell to 37% in 1994, while their share of employment also decreased. In an international context, the Korean level of concentration might be expected to be higher than in other OECD countries, given the relatively small size of the Korean economy and the economies of scale necessary to achieve international competitiveness in such industries as steel, shipbuilding, cars and semiconductors, all areas where Korea has achieved success. In terms of sales, *Hyundai Motors*, the biggest Korean car manufacturer, is only about 7% as large as *General Motors,* while *Samsung Electronics* is 14% the size *of Matsushita* in Japan.[55]

The business groups tend to focus on large manufacturing industries that require big investments. In 1996, 26 industries with shipments of more than 2 trillion wons accounted for almost half of the manufacturing sector. The 30-largest *chaebols* participated in all but one of these industries and had a combined market share of 63%. Moreover, the five-largest *chaebols* alone, which include such groups as Hyundai, Samsung and Daewoo, had a 43% market share in these large-scale industries, including fast-growing sectors such as cars, electronics and machinery. In contrast, the smaller *chaebols* tend to be more focused on chemicals and metal products. The business groups were under- represented in small-scale industries, some of which are legally reserved for small and medium-sized companies. For example, the *chaebols* had only a 5% share in industries with shipments of less than 100 billion wons.

Chaebols have diversified into a wide range of industries. The number of affiliates of the 30-largest business groups increased from an average of 4 companies in 1970 to 22 companies operating in almost 19 different industries[56] in 1996. The 5-largest *chaebols* were even more diversified with an average of more than 40 companies competing in almost 30 industries. The large number of affiliates has been criticised as symptomatic of the founders' preoccupation with market share and 'empire-building'. However, admittedly there have been several factors to suggest that diversification may be a logical response to changing economic conditions and government controls.

First, diversification in a well-designed portfolio of business lines helps to reduce risk when firms and/or their shareholders do not have access to efficient capital markets, as was the case in Korea. Many of the specialized *chaebols* of the 1960s and 1970s have disappeared, while today's most successful groups are highly diversified. Moreover, the six major business groups that filed for bankruptcy protection in 1997 were all relatively specialized with an average of fewer than 16 companies operating in 11 industries.[57]

Second, in a rapidly-growing economy undergoing substantial structural change, there are many profitable business opportunities, particularly given the protection from foreign competition.

Third, government intervention to ensure that failing companies were taken over by other firms rather than allowed to go bankrupt also contributed to the diversification of the *chaebols*, which were the only forms large enough to handle such take-overs. Companies that agreed to acquire failing firms were compensated with debt relief, tax reductions and other benefits.

---

[55] However, the share of the 100-largest firms in Korea is comparable to the 48% in the United States and 40% in Germany, though higher than the 27% in Japan. This reflects the fact that individual Korean companies are not large by international standards.

[56] This refers to three-digit industries in the KSIC system of classification. In total, there are around 100 such industries.

[57] The number of affiliates of the six were; *Hanbo* (21), *New Core* (18), *Hall* (17), *Kia* (16), *Jinro* (14) and *Sammi* (8). *Hanbo* and *New Core* operated in 13 industries, while *Kia* and *Jinro* were in 11, *Hall* in 12 and *Sammi* in 9.

B. The Direction of *Chaebol* Reforms

Chaebols are characterized by a relatively high level of internal ownership - the sum of holdings of the founding family and relatives (*i.e.* individuals) - and affiliated firms (non-financial corporations). This reflects the desire of owner-managers to maintain control and their reliance on debt finance[58]. Similar ownership patterns are also found in other Asian countries that are still in the first generation of capitalism. Internal ownership in Korea tends to be centralized in one or more of the core companies near the top of the pyramid of ownership. The chairman, often the founder of the *chaebol*, tightly controls group policy through an informal but powerful centralized management team called the 'office of planning and co-ordination',[59] which directs the individual companies in the group. The important role of this office appears to impinge on the authority of the directors of the individual companies which, in theory, are independent. The rate of internal ownership is highest for the five-largest *chaebols*.

The concentration of corporate ownership and the strong influence of the founder's family and the central management team on the affiliated companies in the *chaebols* is a key issue in Korea. In theory, such a structure can have advantages, including reduced agency costs and the ability of companies to react rapidly to changes in the business environment. During the past year, however, business groups with high levels of family ownership have experienced the greatest difficulties. In 1996, there were only four *chaebols* in which the shares of the founding family and relatives exceeded 20%: *Kia, Hall,* New Core and *Hanbo*. By the mid of 1997, all four were insolvent. The other two *chaebols* that went bankrupt in 1997, *Sammi* and *Jinro* had family ownership shares well above the average of 9.5% for the top thirty business groups. This suggests that in Korea, where monitoring of management decisions by financial institutions is weak, the advantages of the owner-management model is more than offset by the risk of an abuse of power which often results in unwise business decisions.

The ratio of internal ownership has fallen from 57% in 1983 to 43% in 1997. The fall in the share held by affiliates reflects the introduction of regulations in 1987 on equity investments by companies in the same business groups. The decline in the family and relatives' share from 17 to 8.5% over the past 15 years is due to the development of capital markets and the *chaebols*' increased reliance on the stock market to finance their rapid expansion. Still, only about a quarter of the 669 firms affiliated with the top 30 *chaebols* in 1995 were listed on the stock market. But since larger firms are more likely to be listed, the share of listed equities in the total capitalization of the 30-largest *chaebols* amounted to 62%, up from 57% in 1993. Although *chaebol*-affiliated firms represented less than a quarter of all listed firms, the increased reliance of the large groups on equity finance has been a factor boosting the importance of the stock market. By 1994, its capitalization was equivalent to almost 50% of GDP, a figure near the OECD mean. However, four years of steady decline in stock prices have reduced its value to only 16% of GDP, one of the lowest figures, along with Austria and Spain, in the OECD area.

Given the controls on loans to the business groups, the 30-largest *chaebols* accounted for only 14% of total commercial bank loans at the end of 1995, while their share of credit from non-bank financial institutions was significantly higher at 36%. Consequently, the *chaebols* accounted for about a fifth of all loans. In 1997, concessionary loans to large finns in distress boosted the *chaebols'* share to a fourth. However, the significance of loans to *chaebols* is greater than this figure implies. Given the cross-debt guarantees between companies in the same group, a practice imposed by banks, the bankruptcy of a single firm could lead to a chain reaction, resulting in a collapse of a business group or requiring large bail-out loans from financial institutions. Credit financing has been supplemented by bond issuance: the Korean bond market has grown steadily since the deregulation of issue rates in the early 1980s. In 1997, corporate bonds were equivalent to more than 20% of GDP, although maturities are typically limited to three years.

Despite the limits on bank loans and the development of capital markets, debt-equity ratios are exceptionally high in Korea. For the 30-largest *chaebols,* they reached more than 500% in 1997. The high level of debt is due, in part, to the reluctance of the founders of *chaebols* to rely on equity finance, which would reduce their control. Moreover, the willingness to accept such high leveraging may reflect, in pin, the legacy of government-business relations, which is sometimes described as 'Korea, Inc.'. The

[58] The high concentration of ownership is not unique to *chaebol*-linked firms; it is also found in independent companies as well.

[59] For example, the *de facto* holding companies of the leading *chaebols* are *Hyundai Heavy Industries, Samsung Life Insurance* and *Samsung Electronics, LG Chemicals* and *LG Electronics,* and *Daewoo Heavy Industries* and *Daewoo Corporation.*

government's role as insurer or underwriter of large investment projects created a moral hazard, which encouraged the *chaebols* to expand their businesses faster and in a riskier manner than otherwise. Given their important role in the economy, the government was reluctant to allow large business groups to go bankrupt. This 'too-big-to-fail' argument led it to continue its implicit insurance role and provide bailout loans on an ad hoc basis to *chaebols* on the brink of bankruptcy. From the perspective of the corporate sector, the tight control of the government made it essential to be large enough to exercise influence and exert pressure on bureaucrats and politicians. Sheer size has thus tended to become an objective in itself.

Debt burdens, combined with the financial crisis, has led to widespread insolvency in the corporate sector. By early 1998, nine of the top thirty business groups were insolvent, while close to 30% of the listed companies on the stock exchange were reported to be close to insolvency. The failure of large *chaebols* is producing a ripple effect on smaller enterprises. The conglomerates are already notoriously slow in settling their accounts with their suppliers, taking up to six months. This loose payments discipline might deteriorate significantly due to the financial crisis. Unless strict insolvency rules are introduced, a generalized payments crisis might follow on the heels of the credit crunch. with devastating effects on otherwise healthy smaller firms.

C. Reforms on Chaebols' Streamlining

A key issue of the corporate restructuring involves business swaps between top five *chaebols* to streamline over-investment and enhance efficiency in such key industries as semiconductors, petrochemicals, aerospace, rolling stock, power plant equipment vessel engines and refining. In December 1998, the top five reached agreement on much of the deals and are currently working on closing the rest of the deals.

Following the December 7th agreement (1998), the 'Big Five' signed financial pacts with their creditor banks that called for dramatically reducing the number of their subsidiaries from 272 at the end of 1998 to 136 by the end of 2000. In addition, the top five *chaebols* pledged to slash their debt-to-equity ratios and improve their financial structure by asset sales, recapitalization and US$28.8 billion foreign capital inducement.

<Table VI-13> Business Swap Agreements Between Top Five *Chaebols* (as of Dec. 7, 1998)

Industry Category	Agreements
1. Semiconductors	*LG* and *Hyundai* to make a single corporation and decide on the majority control pursuant to the assessment of an outside professional agency
2. Rolling Stock 3. Petrochemicals 4. Aerospace	Domestic firms to shares 50% of the equities on a net-asset basis, and foreign investors to take the rest
5. Power Plant Equipment 6. Vassel Engine	*Samsung* and *Hyundai* to transfer their power plant equipment and vessel engine to Korea Heavy Industry
7. Oil Refining	*Hyundai* to take over *Hanhwa's* oil refining section

Source: Ministry of Finance and Economy, Korea, February 1999

<Table VI-14> Financial Pacts between Top Five *Chaebols* and Creditor Banks

	Hyundai	Samsung	Daewoo	LG	SK
Core Competence	Automobiles Electronics Heavy Industries Chemicals Construction Financial Services	Electronics Finance Trade Services	Trade Construction Automobiles Heavy industries Financial Services	Chemicals Energy Electronics Telecommunicati on Financial Services	Chemicals Energy Finance Info. Telecom. Construction Distribution
Debt-to-Equity Ratio	332.6% at end-1998→177.6% by end-2000	253% at end-1998→100% by end-2002	306% at end-1998→147% by end-2002	364% at end-1998 →186.4% by end-2000	377% at end-1998→163% by end-2002
Number of Affiliates	63 at end-1998 → approximately 30 by end-1999	65 at end-1998→40 by end-1999	41 at end-1998 →10 by end-1999	53 at end-1998→ 32 by end-2000	49 at end-1998→22 by end-2002
Elimination of Cross-debt Guarantees	By early 2000	By end-1999	By end-1999	By end-1999	By end-1999
Foreign Capital Inducement	US$10.4 billion total by end-1999 (US$5.9 billion)*	US$5 billion by end-1999 (US$2.83 billion)*	US&4.9 billion by end-2002 (US$2.8 billion)*	US$6.5 billion by end-1999 (US$1.78 billion)*	US$2 billion under way

Note: The figures in the parentheses denote the amount of foreign capital induced in 1998.
Source: Ministry of Finance and Economy, Korea, February 1999.

D. Government Policies prior to the Economic Crisis

Reducing the concentration of economic power has been a major government objective since the mid-1980s. In particular, the *chaebols* have been accused of 'reckless diversification' and over-investment, which has reduced their economic efficiency. This goal of reducing the role of the business groups has influenced a wide range of policies, including the privatization of state-owned enterprises, measures to induce private investment in social infrastructure and the deregulation of entry and ownership of certain industries. However, these regulations also tend to protect incumbent firms from new competitors. For example, entry regulations intended to prohibit 'excessive competition' and 'duplicative investments' in some industries may reduce diversification by *chaebols* but also limit competition. In addition. restricting certain industries to small and medium-sized companies may be inefficient.

Four specific policies to limit the influence of the *chaebols* can be identified: first, there have been controls on the quantity of bank lending to the business groups since 1984; second, the Monopoly Regulation and Fair Trade Act was revised in 1987 to prohibit direct cross-holdings between any two companies within a *chaebol*. Total equity investments in other companies (both within the same conglomerate or outside) were limited to 40% of net assets[60] of the investing company. In 1994, this ceiling was lowered to 25%; third, trade between affiliates is regulated to prevent *chaebols* from assisting weak companies in the group, thereby injuring independent firms competing in the same market; and fourth, cross-debt guarantees between companies in the same group were limited to a maximum of 200% of the equity capital of a firm in 1992 and lowered to 100% in 1996.

The Korean government introduced a 'specialization policy' in 1991 to limit the diversification of the *chaebols* by inducing them to concentrate on core activities. The conglomerates were encouraged to pick core businesses - three in the case of the 5-largest *chaebols* and two for the smaller groups. In these areas, the *chaebols* were exempted from regulations such as credit controls and limits on investment. This policy, though, was generally ignored by the groups, who viewed it as interference in their activities and continued to increase the number of their affiliated firms.

---

[60] Net assets are defined as total assets minus the sum of liabilities, equity investments made by other affiliates and any government subsidies.

The Korean government has also attempted to accelerate the dispersion of ownership of the business groups by promoting the development of capital markets and by using inheritance and gift taxes to prevent wealth from remaining in the families of the founders of the *chaebols.* Such policies, though, are likely to be effective only in the long run. To accelerate the dispersion of ownership, the Fair Trade Commission has exempted the *chaebols* judged to have made rapid progress in reducing internal ownership from the restrictions on capital investment and ownership in other firms.

As noted above, the government has intervened frequently on an ad hoc basis to provide assistance to *chaebols* on the verge of bankruptcy. The lack of a well- functioning exit market has created a serious moral hazard problem. To correct this problem, the government adopted a policy of not interfering in the series of bankruptcies of *chaebols* in the first half of 1997. This new approach, however, was undermined by the government's decision to assume temporary control of *Kia Motors* in October, three months after it applied for protection from its creditors.

Overall, the regulations imposed on *chaebols* to limit their size in order to improve their efficiency appear to have been misguided. First, the capacity of *chaebols* to develop and compete in new markets has been amply demonstrated in the past[61]. Their problems appear to stem, in part, from the fact that they have had to design their corporate development, finance and structure as a reaction to government policies. Consequently, they were responding to bureaucratic, as well as market incentives. Second, these regulations have foiled to achieve their objective of limiting the number of companies in the business groups while, at the same time, seriously impinging on corporate management and the functioning of the market. By restricting competition, such controls probably have had an important effect on the determination of winners and losers. Such interference strengthens the links between politics and business, thus widening the scope for corruption.

---

[61] However, the rising market shares of *chaebols* are due, at least in pan, to their easier access to finance and technology. To determine the efficiency of the large business groups, it would be necessary to compare the total factor productivity of independent firms to that of *chaebol* affiliates in the same industry.

Chapter VII

EVALUATION OF ECONOMIC RESTRUCTURING AND POLICY RECOMMENDATIONS

1. EVALUATION OF ECONOMIC RESTRUCTURING

A. The Year 1998 in Retrospect

Korea has made great strides toward recovery since the onset of financial crisis in 1997. The foremost step for recovery was to stabilize the foreign exchange market by securing reserves. A comprehensive strategy was then set for restructuring almost every sector of the economy, with priority placed first on swift and prudent reform of financial and corporate sectors. Economic measures were put into place to ease the credit crunch and to cope with rising unemployment.

These measures have dramatically altered Korea's economic landscape, and financial and foreign exchange markets have stabilized; as of December 15, 1998, usable foreign exchange reserves grew to a record high of US$48.8 billion and the Won/Dollar exchange rate has stabilized around 1,200 level. Three-year corporate bond yields, a benchmark for long-term interest rates have dropped below 10%, lower than the pre-crisis level. Aided by stable foreign exchange and financial markets, Korea has already began repaying its rescue loans, when it repaid US$2.8 billion of the IMF's SRF (Supplementary Reserve Facility) in December 1998.

In the course of unprecedented financial sector restructuring, 5 ailing banks and 16 merchant banks have been closed. With the injection of fiscal resources, the capital adequacy ratio of all banks surpassed the BIS 8% minimum requirement as of the end of September 1998.

With respect to the corporate sector restructuring, transparency in corporate governance has substantially improved, and mergers and business swaps aimed at raising core competence and resolving the excess capacity problem has expedited. On the labor front, labor market flexibility has significantly improved, while the social safety net has been considerably expanded.

These efforts are currently paying off, as seen by the moderate recovery in economic indicators. Year-to-year growth of industrial output moved out of red in November 1998. The ratio of dishonored bills dropped to 0.12% during December 1998 below the pre-crisis level.

B. Financial Sector Restructuring for Further Progress

Given that Korea's economic crisis originally started from financial market turmoil, it seems only natural that full-scale restructuring and enforcement measures have been implemented most strongly in the financial sector. Since the outbreak of the crisis 92 financial institutions were forced to close by September 1998. Even those who survived underwent severe downsizing programs. Despite these pains, the difficulties are not yet over. Though the Korean government often claims reform in the banking sector is over, what has happened in this sector is just the beginning of financial restructuring.

In the course of financial restructuring many hardships and burdens have been thrust upon Korean businesses and Korean taxpayers as well. The amount of bad loans is expected to be even more than 100 trillion wons and cannot be resolved by the financial institutions themselves. The KAMCO (Korea Asset Management Corporation) which is a government-held company, is shouldering a major portion of this debt. And the KDIC (Korea Deposit Insurance Corporation) is injecting public funds for a recapitalization program with 64 trillion wons to be financed for this operation.

<Table VII-1> Suspension and Closure of Financial Institutions (as of January 20, 1999)

Classification (Total No.)	License Revoked	Suspended	Subtotal
Banks(33)	5	-	5
Merchant Banks(30)	16	-	16
Securities Companies(37)	3	3	6
Insurance Companies(50)	4	-	4
Investment Trust Companies(6)	1	1	2
Mutual Savings and Finance Companies (230)	18	12	30
Credit Unions(1,666)	1	22	23
Leasing Companies(25)	-	-	-
Total(2,077)	48	38	86

Source: Ministry of Finance and Economy, Korea, February 1999

As a result of this first stage of financial restructuring, the soundness of banks has improved significantly. The average BIS ratio is currently higher than 10%. A series of mergers in banking sector including Commercial-Hanil, Hana-Boram and Kookmin-Korea Long Term Credit, has created world class banks at least in terms of asset size.

Compared a year ago(1998), the financial market is dominated by apparently new rules which conform to principles such as openness, competition and self-responsibility. Many regulations were liberalized not only for domestic institutions but also for foreign ones. As the business categories of banking industry are being integrated with each other, financial institutions are going to be exposed to more and more competition.

While there have been these improvements, there have also been some shortcomings especially in the process of implementation. Even though it is true that Korea has made some significant steps in terms of financial restructuring, one year is too short a period to practice policies to their full extent. Also, it is hard to expect an improvement in the banking sector immediately after some of the "soundness" measures were imposed. But being anxious about the apparent outcome, in many cases, the FSC (Financial Supervisory Commission) directly forced private institutions to follow its own intentions. Instead, it should have focused on 'supervising' financial transactions. Some of the reform policies were executed based on ambiguous standards without a full consensus among the policy-makers, thereby evoking unnecessary confusion in the market. Some were lacking clear vision or action plans to follow. In addition, while many bad banks were forced to close or to be merged with other good banks, in some cases, some banks were heavily recapitalized by the government. This kind of government-led restructuring is in contrast to the ultimate goal of restructuring itself; the establishment of a free and competitive financial system.

While the government has finished just the banking sector restructuring, other sub-areas of the financial sector have not yet been sufficiently restructured. With the corporate sector still being under the burden of tremendous debt, restructuring in these areas could cause another wave of a credit crunch, a previous one which already severely damaged Korea's real economy in the first half of 1998.

The first year of financial restructuring has generally been recognized as having been successful. Korea tided over the financial crisis such that the credit crunch was significantly relieved. What should be done now is focusing on improving the competitiveness and efficiency of the financial industry. For this job, financial restructuring must be conducted in a way that conforms to the market principle. In order to avoid another possible credit crunch and to relieve the negative repercussions felt by businesses, future restructuring in other sub-areas of the financial sector should also be accompanied by the supplementary flexible monetary policy or by relevant tax policy measures.

C. Corporate Sector Restructuring for Further Progress

Corporate restructuring efforts in Korea have been focused on three main areas of improving firms financial structures, improving their governance structures and improving their business structures. Toward this end, the Korean government has revised and expanded upon various laws and institutions to facilitate restructuring, while firms have been spontaneously trying to attract foreign capital, pursue M&As and eliminate unprofitable business lines. Progress has certainly been made in all three areas.

First, various institutional measures and systems have been adopted or strengthened to provide enhanced management transparency and improved governance structures. These include the introduction of the outside-director system, the strengthening of the rights of minority shareholders and the mandatory provision of combined financial statements.

Secondly, firms are in the process of improving their financial structures through efforts including the gradual elimination of cross-subsidiary debt guarantees and the reduction of their debt-equity ratios.

Thirdly, the big business groups are readjusting their business structures to focus on their respective core industries including the elimination of failing companies or business lines, work-outs with creditor banks and business swaps with other companies.

In spite of this progress in corporate restructuring, however, there are still several problems with the current economic policies.

First, there are negative side-effects stemming from the excessive intervention of Korean government's. Many markets to be affected by restructuring are not functioning properly, and some markets are totally unprepared. In that sense, government intervention is needed. But if the government does not limit its efforts to fostering markets to function more efficiently, then firms will lose their incentive to restructure spontaneously and take a passive response to the government's policies, which in turn will cause the restructuring actually needed to restore competitiveness to be delayed.

Secondly, because of hasty policies shooting for short-term results, the original objective of corporate restructuring has been lost and restructuring is now only focusing on downscaling and downsizing. Restructuring should be aimed at eliminating inefficient areas and finding new competitive advantages in order to enhance a firm's overall competitiveness. The Korean government policies, however, have been overly focused on eliminating bad sectors. Not only is it unclear when this will translate into stronger competitiveness, but it could eventually lead to weakened growth potential.

Thirdly, the Korean government has not been able to provide a suitable environment or proper incentives for firms to restructure themselves autonomously. For example, allowing the establishment of holding companies would be a useful and practical means of facilitating restructuring, but their establishment is still banned. In addition, the government has done little to promote the restructuring of the market in terms of expanding the buyer side or the brokerage functions instead concentrating only on the supply side or business divestitures. This has, of course, caused asset values to fall and weakened any chances of real progress being made.

To sum up, the government has provided or improved various legal and institutional measures to promote the corporate restructuring process, and there have been some visible results. However, in order to truly stimulate corporate restructuring and have this translate into strengthened competitiveness, many additional steps are still needed.

Of these, the first and foremost should be clearly delineating between the role of the government and the role of firms. The government should focus its efforts on implementing and putting into full effect the existing or planned restructuring measures, thereby providing firms with the requisite environment for pursuing restructuring autonomously.

Toward this end, in the short term, the government should quickly adopt systems such as the holding company system which can catalyze restructuring, while quickly eliminating from the market companies which have been judged to be failing.

In the long run, the government should focus its attention on setting up institutional measures to ensure better corporate governance and management transparency, while refraining from directly intervening in firms business portfolios or their ownership of management structures.

D. Labor Market Reform

Issues regarding labor and employment are often not just an economic problem but more frequently social and sometimes political ones as well. In Korea where most households are dependent on labor income and where most people have not experienced unemployment or lay-offs during the last 30 years, the situation is far more complicated. A flexible labor market where a firm can freely hire and fire depending on its business situation is an indispensable component in the reform of the Korean economy. Naturally, policy makers in this field would surely face an intrinsic dilemma. Therefore, the restructuring process in the labor sector should be one that is based on the principle of consensus and fairness as well as providing unemployed workers with a minimum level of living. Toward this end, in February 1998, the Korean government, labor and businesses reached the Tripartite Agreement (Korean version of a social pact) for the first time in history. Among the issues that they discussed and reached an agreement upon were the social security net, basic rights of labor and general conditions for lay-offs among others.

These efforts have achieved many important steps for a more flexible labor market. Layoffs for managerial reasons and the worker dispatch system were finally legalized. In fact, layoffs were first legally supported by law starting in March 1997, but it was practically impossible to lay off workers since the law defined many complicated pre-conditions. By eliminating or simplifying most of the pre-conditions (except for the obligations of sincere efforts of avoidance of lay-offs) and priority in rehiring, it became a more effective legal system with the February 1998 amendment.

While this progress based on the tripartite agreement among the three parties is very encouraging, there are still some shortcomings.

First, though simplified, many pre-conditions are still ambiguous in their interpretation and as a result, many parts are subject to arguments from both labor and businesses. The definitions of making an effort of avoidance of lay-offs or the effort of rehiring are examples.

Secondly, the flexibility of the labor market must be more extended. The current legal system just focuses on 'quantitative' flexibility. Labor market flexibility is not just a matter of the number of the employed; it should include qualitative concepts such as expected income level, proper placement and positioning. In fact, the Korean labor market is far from being qualitatively flexible. Complicated regulations related to employment, wages, working hours and other issues still remain as obstacles against enhancing labor market flexibility.

Labor market restructuring policy should focus on eliminating complicated regulations to effectively guarantee labor market flexibility. Also it should comprise of provisions to infrastructure which will enhance the efficiency of the labor market not only from the viewpoint of employers (demand side) but from that of workers (supply side). The vocational training system and employment security network are typical topics that we should be worked on more. In addition, labor policy, in a larger sense, has to concentrate more on creating jobs. The ultimate goal of labor market flexibility is not only downsizing the workforce but also improving the labor market environment by providing new kinds of jobs.

E. Public Sector Reform

Public sector reform is an extremely critical issue for the Korean economy. Over the past year under the IMF program, restructuring efforts have been concentrated on the corporate and financial sectors for various reasons. Not only were there clear calls for reform in these areas from the start of negotiations with the IMF, but it was also pointed out by many that the direct causes for the currency crisis lay in these two sectors. Accordingly, public sector restructuring seems to have taken a back seat to corporate and financial restructuring.

If more profound examination is conducted, it is clear that public sector reform is the most critical and urgent task for the Korean economy's revitalization. The fundamental reason why Korea's enterprises and banks lack competitiveness is the government's habitual interference in financial and industrial policy. Especially in Korea, the public sector has had the tradition of controlling and regulating the private sector. Therefore, for restructuring in the corporate and financial sectors to be truly effective and meaningful, public sector reform must be carried out in connection with corporate and financial reforms.

Public sector restructuring over the last year can be divided into 3 parts: reorganization of the government's structure, privatization of state-owned enterprises, and deregulation. Initial efforts centered around structural reorganization, resulting in a general reduction in personnel and size and also a redefinition of functions. For example, the Deputy Prime Minister system was abolished, trade-related responsibilities were transferred to the Ministry of Foreign Affairs and Trade, and the Office of the National Budget was newly established.

The highlight of public sector reform has been the privatization of state-owned enterprises. Firms like the POSCO (Pohang Iron and Steel Company), Korea Tobacco & Ginseng Corporation, the KEPCO (Korea Electric Power Corporation) and the KT (Korea Telecom), are to be sold off to private hands, including foreign investors. It is expected that privatization will provide various benefits, including the inducement of foreign capital, introduction of competition to the current monopoly or oligopoly system and enhanced managerial efficiency.

Regarding the privatization and restructuring plans for public organizations, even though the government has announced the general plan and direction, some of the announced plans have been infeasible from the start, while others have been delayed or postponed due to resistances from related businesses or government organizations. And as for deregulation, reform has been a piecemeal and centered around the number of regulations scrapped as opposed to their effectiveness with administrative practices remaining virtually the same.

To make the privatization of public corporations truly effective, it is essential that privatization is pursued in harmony with the overall industrial policy as well as the fair trade policy. Concrete plans should be developed to ensure that competition is fostered in conjunction with privatization.

In the case of deregulation, a Deregulation Commission under the direct control of the President was established in the early 1998, with the goal of eliminating 50% of all regulations at the ministry level within the year. To effectively conduct deregulation, entry barriers and price regulations hindering private economic activities must be abolished. Also, deregulation should be undertaken from a qualitative aspect focusing on end-user satisfaction rather than a quantitative aspect focusing on the number of regulations which are eliminated, regardless of their relevance. In addition, a regulation evaluation system should be quickly implemented and applied to all regulations so that deregulation can be pursued more efficiently.

Progress in public sector restructuring to date has been somewhat lacking in terms of visible results. Regarding the reorganization of the government structure, the biggest problem has been policy confusion among the ministries and/or special commissions which have been established since the new administration stepped in. For example, there is confusion and overlap on trade-policy-related duties and functions among the Ministry of Finance and Economy, the Ministry of Foreign Affairs and Trade, and the Ministry of Commerce, Industry and Energy. A similar situation exists among the Ministry of Finance and Economy, the Bank of Korea and the Financial Supervisory Commission. There is also the overlapping of the budget function between the Planning and Budget Commission, which is an independent office and the Office of National Budget under the control of the MOFE (Ministry of Finance and Economy). The policy confusion and overlap among the government authorities makes the private sector even more uncertain about the future direction of the economy.

To effectively pursue the downsizing of government personnel, an obstacle to government restructuring, measures allowing greater labor flexibility need to be implemented. Just as in the private sector, the government should introduce a restructuring layoff system, job sharing programs, temporary on-demand employment and other flexible measures.

2. Policy Measures for Acceleration of Reforms and Restructuring

A. Basic Economic Policy Directions for 1999

Against this background, the major goal of 1999 economic policies is expected to center around improving Korea's credit rating and inducing economic recovery. In line with this, basic economic policy directions are contained in following agendas:

First, an emphasis is expected to be placed on the expedited implementation of structural reforms. Early completion of economic restructuring can be considered as a precondition for bolstering Korea's competitiveness. During 1998, the hardware for economic restructuring has been set through structural reforms. Based on this, the 1999 reform will center on the improvement of software such as the empowerment of the financial sector and improvement in corporate management and transparency. To this end, practices in credit assessment and risk management by financial institutions will be strengthened and corporate governance will be upgraded to international standards.

Second, supportive macroeconomic policies is expected to aim at speeding up the pace of economic recovery. Fiscal outlays in the first half of 1999 is expected to complement the contracted domestic demand in the private sector, followed by revamping the real sector by normalizing intermediary functions of the financial sector in the second half. In considerations of uncertainties looming in the international financial market, stabilization of the foreign exchange market and securing the investor confidence is also expected to be emphasized.

Third, the effectiveness of counter measures against unemployment is expected to be enhanced, and a new cooperative relationship between management and labor will be fostered. Since unemployment will continue to rise despite a modest growth, effective counter-measures and cooperative labor-management relationships is expected to become the catalyst for a sustainable economic recovery.

Fourth, a foundation is expected to be laid for nurturing the knowledge-based economy of the 21st century, as such base is expected to constitute the engine of medium and long-term growth of the Korean economy.

B. Financial Sector Restructuring for Further Progress

Productivity, profitability of financial institutions and overall stabilization of the financial system is expected to be pursued. To this end, financial institutions is expected to be encouraged to adopt an advanced risk management system based on proper credit analysis. The ownership and management structures of the financial institutions is expected to be improved through facilitating the re-engineering of the financial sector. Furthermore, in order to prevent further loss or deterioration of the financial institutions, prompt corrective actions is expected to be strictly implemented with the strengthening of financial supervision.

Another measure is expected to be the continued purchase of non-performing loans by the KAMCO (Korea Asset Management Corporation). Self-rescue efforts is expected to be made by financial institutions. Also included are measures to recollect already injected fiscal resources for the financial restructuring. The government is expected to exert its efforts to recoup the fiscal resources over time by sales of collateralized assets, the divestment of acquired equity shares of financial institutions and by liquidation of insolvent financial institutions. For the proper management of injected fiscal resources, a monitoring system within the government is expected to be operated.

<Table VII-2> Planned KAMCO Sales of Purchased NPLs (unit: billion won)

Classification	1999	2000	2001	2002	2003	Total
Sales of Securities	7,863	9,900	10,275	7,514	6,241	41,793
Sales of Assets	8,077	6,722	3,398	3,159	2,498	23,854
Sales of Worked Out NPLs	100	290	300	300	300	1,290
Total	16,040	16,912	13,973	10,973	9,038	66,937

Source: Ministry of Finance and Economy, Korea, February 1999

In order to improve the financial structure of corporations, capital market development will be essential. To this end, first of all, corporate pension funds is expected to be encouraged and entry barriers to the securities industry is also expected to be eased so that the role of institutional investors will be bolstered. As for the debt market, disclosure of a company and listing in the stock market is expected to be separated, with the easing of listing requirements. Dealership specializing government bond trading is also expected to be launched.

The present timetable for capital account liberalization and financial restructuring is to be implemented by taking steps as follows:

The question to be raised here is what can be expected to be the potential role of FDIs for Korea's economic recovery from its financial crisis. To derive the potential role of FDIs, the process of Korea's financial crisis needs to be reviewed.

From the early November 1997, Korea, which had long been the envy of many developing countries, found itself in financial crisis, lacking sufficient foreign currency liquidity to meet its maturing liabilities following a sharp decline in its foreign exchange reserves and was faced with a threat of a debt moratorium.

From early 1997, the relation between receipts and payments of foreign exchange showed unstable movements. The large amount of deficit in the current account and the slowdown of foreign capital inflows combined to bring about a sharp decrease in the country's foreign exchange reserves and in the exchange value of the Korean Won. In April 1997, however, the Korean Won strengthened temporarily against the US dollar, thanks to the announcement of an early capital market opening schedule by the government and the narrowing deficit in the trade balance.

<Table VII-3> Timetable for Selected Measures Implemented in Financial Sector

Type of Measure	Measures	Date Implemented
Capital Account Liberalization	▪Eliminate the ceiling on foreign acquisition of Korea equities	May 25, 1998
	▪Allow foreigners to participate in hostile mergers and acquisitions of domestic financial institutions	May 25, 1998
	▪Submit legislation bill to abolish three additional trade-related subsides (pledged to WTO by end-1998)	Feb. 1998
	▪Lift US$2million borrowing cap on venture companies	Feb. 6, 1998
	▪Full liberalization of money market instruments issued by financial institutions	May 25, 1998
Financial Restructuring	▪Complete second round assessment of rehabilitation plans submitted by merchant banks	Feb. 22, 1998
	▪Assume government control of Korea First Bank and Seoul Bank and remove the management responsible for losses. Amend relevant legislations to empower the supervisory body to write down equity of current owners to absorb existing losses	Jan. 13, 1998
	▪Submit legislation bill to authorize the supervisory authority to close insolvent institutions	Dec. 29, 1997
	▪Commercial banks to report capital adequacy ratios as of end 1997 based on full provisioning	Feb. 25, 1998
	▪Commercial banks to satisfy BIS ratio requirement of 8%	Sept, 1, 1998
	▪Submit legislation bill to abolish regulations that prohibit foreigners from becoming bank managers	May 5, 1998
	▪Submit legislation bill to authorize the relevant authorities to issue necessary quantities of bonds to meet the 100% deposit guarantee	Dec. 29, 1997
Monetary Policy	▪Abolish daily exchange rate band	Dec. 16, 1997
	▪Eliminate interest rate ceiling	Dec. 29, 1997

Source: Ministry of Finance and Economy, Korea, February 1999.

But from the beginning of the third quarter of 1997, foreign investors' misgivings about the health of the Korean economy deepened, owing to the delay in the handling of *KIA*'s financial difficulties, financial institutions' accumulation of bad loans and the contagion effect of the Southeast Asian crisis.

Accordingly, there was a large net outflow of foreign portfolio, new external borrowings became almost impossible, and Korean financial institutions faced substantial difficulty in rolling over their existing short-term debts in the international financial markets. In this way, Korea had entered into the state of the financial crisis.

What brought about this large mismatch between demand and supply in the foreign exchange market was mainly the heavier foreign debt taken on to finance, the deficit in current account and the difficulty in coping with a flood of repayment demands because of the heavy reliance on short-term external borrowings.

Besides these factors, the building of expectations of a massive depreciation of the Korean Won due to the persistent widening of the deficit in the current account also played a large part in the further worsening of the foreign exchange situation.

The country's foreign exchange reserves, which had stood steady at around US$30 billion until October 1997, declined sharply to the near-depletion level at the end of November 1997.

The reason foreign exchange reserves dwindled so rapidly was because the Bank of Korea was forced, as the lender of last resort, to provide support for the settlement of foreign claims on domestic financial institutions when demands for the redemption rather than the customary roll over of their maturing short-term foreign liabilities mounted from early November of 1997.

Most seriously, usable foreign exchange reserves, which are official foreign exchange reserves less the BOK's deposits at overseas branches of domestic banks, decreased to just US$7.3 billion as of the end of November and US$3.9 billion in mid December against US$22.3 billion as of the end of October 1997.

Consequently, the Korean government had to turn to the IMF to request a stand-by credit on November 21, 1997. An agreement was reached with the IMF on December 4, 1997 for the provision US$21 billion.

In addition, major international financial institutions such as the IBRD, the ADB, and a number of developed countries including the United States and Japan indicated their readiness to provide an additional US$36 billion upon the conclusion of the agreement with the IMF. This meant that Korea was to receive in stages a total amount of US$57 billion by way of the emergency rescue package.

With domestic demand imploding, the current account surplus reached US$ 10.6 billion or some 14% of GDP in the first quarter of 1998. Much of this resulted from a precipitous drop in imports of machinery and equipment and consumer durables.

To date, the rise in export prices has exceeded that of import prices and the usual 'J' curve following devaluation has been absent. This development largely reflects comparatively 'weak' increases in import prices, owing to depressed world oil and commodity prices.

In addition, the collapse in imports of investment goods may have induced foreign suppliers to offer their prices to the market. By contrast, export prices have risen sharply in local currency terms, as exporters boosted their profit margins to compensate for depressed domestic demand.

Customs data suggest that export volumes increased by some 10 to 12% in the first quarter of 1998, though these figures included the one-time effects of the extraordinary nation-wide campaign to collect some US$2.2 billion in gold to help pay off the nation's foreign debt. Nonetheless, it appears that the current account to date reflects the depressed state of the Korean economy.

In effect, Korean capital markets have been fully open to foreign investors as of July 1998. The desirability of large-scale foreign investment to help restructure Korean industry as well as to upgrade managerial skills and technological standards to world class levels, is now indisputable.

Foreign investors, however, are still wary to see how legislative changes are implemented in practice. All in all, although a significant rise in FDIs is possible following full capital market liberalization, the amounts will be minor compared with total corporate assets. As in early 1998, much of these inflows in the beginning is likely to take the form of portfolio investment, M&As (Mergers and Acquisitions) and joint ventures. Hence, the catalytic role of FDIs needs to be complemented by vigorous domestic corporate restructuring.

C. Corporate Sector Restructuring for Further Progress

The major reforms of corporate sector further to be accelerated can be outlined as an enhancement of corporate governance, *chaebol* restructuring, non-viable firm exit and corporate workout programs.

1) Enhancing Corporate Governances

For the improvement of corporate financial structure, agreements made between corporations and creditor banks are expected to be strictly implemented as scheduled. The average debt-equity ratio is expected to be lowered to about 200% by the end of 1999 and corporate business structures is also expected to be streamlined to focus on core competence.

As for the transparency in corporate governance, a newly established independent body is expected to formulate new corporate accounting practices in line with international standards. Improved accounting standards and practices are expected to contribute to the improvement of corporate governance. Roles of the board of directors and shareholders are expected to be enhanced in order to increase management accountability.

2) Correction of the Bipolar Economic System and Restructuring of Industrial Organization

The drive for the high growth policy in the past has caused monopolies, accumulation of wealth in big companies and relative vulnerability of SMEs, which are the fundamental weakness of the Korean economy. In order to recover from current economic difficulty and to cope with rapid changes in the internal and external environment, the following three conditions should be achieved.

First, efficient industrial organization should be ensured, for which policy must focus on market liberalization.

Second, reinforcement of equal opportunity must be provided through relief and demolishment of barriers to entry.

Thirdly, smooth flow of information and efficient industrial organization means specialization between enterprises of different sizes.

Active SMEs enable balanced development of a national economy. The recent economic crisis of Korea has resulted from a weakened competitive edge. In Korea, the number of SMEs make up one-third of the total, which is marginal compared with the numbers in the US, Japan and Taiwan. The reason for the comparatively low number of SMEs is due to the dependence of factors and commodities markets upon the conglomerates or *chaebol*. In other words, the primary reason for the decline of SMEs is the development of conglomerates.

Another important dimension of the corporate sector restructuring is expected to be facilitated through prompt exiting of non-viable firms and revamping of viable ones. To this end, revisions of such laws as the Corporate Liquidation Act and the Court Reconciliation Act are in the works.

With respect to fair competition, policy measures are expected to be set in order to extend the coverage of the Fair Trade Act and to strengthen monitoring activities within *chaebols'* subsidiaries.

3) Reforms on Chaebol*-based Economic Structure*

Kim Dae-jung administration announced *chaebols* reforms (Tables VII-4 and VII-5) in 1998, whereby the administration removed several obstacles to restructuring and at the same time provided *chaebols* financial and tax incentives for restructuring.[62]

<Table VII-4> Agenda for *Chaebol* Reform

- Adoption of combined financial statements from the fiscal year 1999 - Compliance with international standards of accounting - Reinforcement of voting rights of minority shareholders - Mandatory appointment of outside directors - Establishment of external auditors committee - Prohibition of cross-subsidiary debt guarantees from April 1998 - Resolution of all existing cross-debt guarantees by 2000

Source: Ministry of Finance and Economy, Korea, February 1999.

[62] Until August 1993 when the real-name transaction system was implemented, President Kim Young-sam's policy toward business groups was more harsh than any other previous administrations, including ownership decentralization, specialization in core businesses, and the establishment of professional management systems. But in late 1993, in the mood of strengthening national competitiveness, regulatory policies toward business groups were replaced by the logic that they should lead economic recovery by strengthening competitiveness. From 1994, *chaebol*-centered policies were aggressively implemented. The FKI (Federation of the Korean Industries) was given the right to decide on a second mobile telecommunication company. Before privatizing major government corporations, the administration argued that only *chaebols* were able to take over corporations due to management ability and capital. While policies toward *chaebol* before 1994 were characterized by simple concepts based on the negative public opinion about the extensive growth of *chaebols*, Kim's policy after 1994 was extremely *chaebol*-centered based on opinions about improving their management efficiency.

<Table VII-5> The Korean Government's Reforms on *Chaebol*-based Economic Structure

Classification	Contents
The Foreign Capital Inducement Law	- The increased upper limit of foreign shareholders` obtaining stock by the approval of the relevant company is from more than 10% to more than 1/3. - Abolition of approval from the Minister of Finance and Economy in case of acquisitions by companies with over 2 trillion wons in assets
Fair Trade Act	- Abolition of limits on total amount of investment (25%). - Reservation on establishment of pure property companies
Securities Exchange Law	- Obligation of nominating external directors - Limitation on acquisition of owner's share from 10% to 1/3 - Litigation right of minority shareholders from 1% to 0.05%, a right of claim over displacement of directors and a right to demand compensation from 1% to 0.5% (0.25% over 100 billion wons' capital), right of call for investigation of books and plenary sessions of shareholders from 3% to 1% (0.5% over 100 billion wons' capital) - Abolition of obligatory public buying system (25%~40%+1)
External Auditor Law	- Practice of consolidated financial statements from fiscal year of 1999 - External auditor's participation in accounting
The Banking Law	- Limitation on possession of other companies' shares by financial institutions from 10% to 15%
Composition and Bankruptcy Act	- At the time of applying for re-organization, large stockholders are offered mortgage shares. - 50% of shares destroyed in case of legal management due to excess debts
Corporation Tax Law	- Non-recognition of loss due to interest expenses for companies with debt ratio over 500% (2,000), 450% (2001) and 300% (2003)
Regulation Law on Tax Exemption	- In case of restructuring, transfer income tax, corporate tax, acquisition tax and registration tax will be reduced or exempted.

Source: Yang-Taek Lim, *Prospects for Asian Economies,* Maeil Economic Daily Press, January 1999, Seoul, Korea.

(1) The Suppression of Control of Financial Institutions by Chaebols

Financial institutions conduct the role of mediation in capital economic sectors. If their screening function is preserved to some extents, funds would be able to be injected into competitive corporations and consequently, strengthen the competitiveness of the national economy. On the other hand, Korea's financial institutions usually lend a large portion of their money regardless of its technology and managerial ability. The concentration of credits on *chaebols* has used to give rise to serious economic inefficiency.

There are two reasons why *chaebols* can mobilize funds readily from financial institutions. One is that *chaebols* have financial institutions as their direct subsidiary companies. Another is that *chaebols* maintain a peculiar structure of guarantees of among affiliates. It is the same as a guarantee on a discharge of liabilities. To prohibit excessive concentration of credit, *chaebols'* participation in local banks and secondary financial institutions as well as their possession of financial institutions should be restricted.

The government decided to maintain a total investment limit (25% of net property) regulated under the Fair Trade Law. The main requirements on authorizing the establishment of a holding company for restructuring purposes are as follows: the debt ratio must be within 100% and restrictions on ownership of financial subsidiaries.

A core issue of *chaebol* reforming which was designed to improve transparency of companies was the limitation of intra-group payment guarantees and investment. The mutual payment guarantees are expected to be 100% of equity by March 1998.

The preparation of consolidated financial statements is also a core issue of *chaebol* reform and is the crucial for strengthening transparency of corporate management. Joint financial statements combine the statements of affiliated companies under a flagship company. Under this system, bad practices such as bilateral investment in bonds and cross-debt guarantees between affiliates could be eliminated.

<Table VII-6> Regulations & Restrictions on the Control of Financial Institutions by Conglomerates

Classification	America	Japan	Germany	Korea
Banks	Prohibition of possessing shares (prior to approval of FRB):	Downward trend of limitation on possession of a corporation's shares from 10% to 5% after 1998	No general restrictions except a few	Limitation on possession of same corporations' shares by 10% and ownership capital and subsidiary companies.
Life Insurances	Allowed possession of other companies' shares by 2% of owned capital: New York Insurance Act	Allowed possession of other company shares by 10%: Antitrust Act	Allowed possession of shares by 20% of owned capital: Insurance Act	Restriction on the possession of the same corporation's shares by 10% and owned capital by 30%: Insurance Act
The Rest Insurance Companies	Prohibition of restrictions on non-insurance companies: New York Insurance Act		No restrictions	
Mutual Funds	Excess possession of other companies' shares by 10%: heavy imposition of taxes	No restrictions	No restrictions	Limitation on a single corporation's shares by 5% (a trust account 20%)
Annuity Funds	Requisite decentralized investment	Strict restrictions on shares investment	No restrictions	Strict restriction on shares investment
General Provisions	SEC's report provision of 5% possession: Restriction on active possession of shares by Internal Transaction Act	No restrictions	Report regulations over 25% of shares possession	Report regulations about over 5% of shares possession over 25%

Source: Yang-Taek Lim, *Prospects for Asian Economies*, Maeil Economic Daily Press, January, 1999, Seoul, Korea

(2) The Separation of Management from Ownership

Eventually *chaebols* have to separate management from ownership, as most large companies of advanced countries already do so. This is a pre-condition for Korea to become an advanced country. Large businesses in Korea are mostly owned by *chaebol* and they do not have much room for professional management skills due to the supreme leader who always has an absolute power.

Currently, upper management is able to practice the right of management only within the authority given by the supreme leader. The separation of ownership and management means that managers have authority to control over companies even though they have no shares. The supremacy of the corporation means that the power is vested in a board of directors. So to be a company that separates management and ownership, a chief executive must have authority to appoint a successor.

In Korea, however, the supreme leader who has the most shares not only appoints a representative director but also intervenes in management. Consequently, the structure of Korean corporations is a far cry from the principle of separation of management and ownership. An international comparison of business management structure is summarized in <Table VII-7>

<Table VII-7> International Comparison of Business Management Structures

Classification	U.S.A.	Japan	Germany	Korea
Authority of the Board of Directors	inadequate	fragile	strong	fragile
External Director	numerous	almost non-exist	a board of directors for supervisor: 50% a board of directors for management: nil	almost nil
CEO	generally hold two positions concurrently	generally hold two positions concurrently	separated positions	generally holds two positions
Participation of Banks in the Board of Directors	minimal	average	high	minimal
Supervisory Function	a committee of supervision under a board of directors	a committee of inspection	a board of directors for supervision	inspection
Incentive Managers	high	low	low	low
Supervisory Function of Banks	strong	strong	strong	weak
Major Form of Finance	securities	bank advances	bank advances	bank advances
The Form of Possession	decentralization (individuals/ institutions)	centralization (banks/ interrelated corporations)	centralization (corporations/ banks/family)	centralization (family/ interrelated corporations
Capital Markets	very fluent	somewhat fluent	not fluent	somewhat fluent
Bank System	decentralized business	centralized business	collective	centralized business
Supervisory Function of Minority Shareholders	strong	strong	strong	strong
Supervisory Function Of Corporate Management	strong	almost nil	almost nil	strong
Transparency of Management	transparent	translucent	translucent	obscure
Separation of Ownership From Management	complete separation	separation	separation	imperfect separation
Major Characteristics of Corporate Management Structure	market machinism	relationship of interrelated enterprise/informal practices	development of corporate management related corporations	mighty authority of owner-manager

Source: Yang-Taek Lim, *Prospects for Asian Economies*, Seoul: Maeil Economic Daily Press, January 1999.

It seems to be a waste of human resources that professional managers do not exist within companies. On a national level, there are plenty of men of ability who cannot get promoted into virtual top manager sin Korean *chaebols*. They are always under the command of the supreme leader, even though it is not guaranteed that the latter's managerial ability is superior to the former's since they have no opportunity to demonstrate it.

In order to pursue rational management and prevent 'dictatorship' by major stockholders, a representative authority under the Securities Exchange Law is expected to be reduced to 0.01% and the general meeting summary requirement is also expected to be reduced to 0.5% from 3%. Individual stockholders, however, claim that only one share should be enough to meet requirements. The appointment of external directors in listed firms is expected to be mandatory and the system to apply legal responsibility for poor management is expected to be established to hold dominant stockholders such as the chairman's family.

The supreme head of *chaebols* appoints presidents of group companies who have no responsibility for management and no legal grounds, then command all by way of a chairman's office or an office of planning and coordination.

A general meeting of stockholders is nothing but a ratifying institution as directors are arbitrarily appointed by supreme leader himself. The situation means that a family of only 25% effective shares could run a company arbitrarily and exclusively although the other shareholders have remaining the 75%. To prevent arbitrary management, delegates groups who have interests in the company including employees, minority stockholders, creditors and consumers should be able to participate in the management process, which should be supported by an institutional apparatus. For example, by transferring some part of the shares sub-contractors and employees can make it possible for employees to take part in a board of directors. And it is also recommendable that external directors involving in financial institutions or public corporations apply strict inspection and supervision on management.

Also, illegal inheritance of ownership and management to direct relatives is one of most negative factors of Koran *chaebols* because gaping loopholes exist in inheritance tax and donation tax. In spite of the real-name financial system, borrowed names are still generally used to conceal their assets. The ultimate resolution to this problem is a drastic reduction of equity shares of owner families.

Global competition and the information revolution makes it clear that only innovative enterprises adjusting to the changing environment can survive and maintain competitiveness. Therefore, new paradigms including new management methods, shareholders' rights and the relationship between parties with interests are required. Attention should be paid to the fact that most global companies are specialized in one business and their scale having been expanded by means of exports.

D. Public Sector Reform for Further Progress

On the basis of ongoing management diagnosis of the public sector, government organizations are expected to be reshuffled according to core functions of each government body. Emphasis is also expected to be given to the operating systems, as well as the prevailing culture of the public sector.

Downsizing of the government is also an important feature of the public sector reform to raise efficiency. The government streamlined its organizational structure in February 1998. It plans to reduce its employees by 11% or approximately 18,000 out of 162,000 employees by the end of 2000. As many as 9,084 jobs were eliminated in 1998. 6,400 more will be cut in 1999 and 3,400 more in 2000.

Local autonomies have also streamlined their organizations. By September 1998, 35,070 jobs or 12% of the total, have been eliminated. In conjunction with the government reform, the quasi-government sector, including public institutions and various government-affiliated associations, has also been streamlined.

In addition, the Korean government is expected to formulate a medium-term public finance plan for the soundness and transparency in the fiscal sector. This plan encompasses the introduction of a performance-based budgeting system, the streamlining of fiscal resource allocation between special accounts and public funds, and the informatization of budget management system. Also in store is reforming the tax administration. Tax organization currently based on respective taxes is expected to be reorganized *vis-a-vis* its functions such as notification, survey and information management.

Furthermore, the government is expected to expedite the privatization of public enterprises, and outsourcing is expected to be encouraged. State-owned enterprises (SOEs), in particular, require drastic overhaul by means of privatization and/or management reform is necessary. Twenty public institutions of the 109 SOEs have already been privatized in 1998. More such actions are planned ahead.

The 89 subsidiaries of the 30 parent SOEs are also subject to privatization or management reform: future status of the 21 subsidiaries of those SOEs for immediate privatization in 1999 will be determined by the new acquiring private management. Of the remaining 68 subsidiaries, 31 will be privatized either immediately or in time, while 37 will be restructured or consolidated.

<Table VII-8> Reform Plan for State-Owned Enterprises

Reform Stages	Deadline	Targeted SOEs
Full/Immediate Privatization	By end-1999	Five parent companies (including POSCO, Korea Heavy Industry & Construction and Korea Technology Financing Corporation), and 21 subsidiaries
Gradual Privatization	By end-1999	Six parent companies (including Korea Telecom, Korea Tobacco & Ginseng Corporation, Korea Electric Power Corporation), and 31 subsidiaries
Management Reform and Restructuring	Ongoing	13 parent companies (including Korea Securities Printing & Minting Corporation, Korea Trade-Investment Promotion Agency, Korea National Tourism Corporation, and Korea Coal Corporation), and 37 subsidiaries

Source: Ministry of Finance and Economy, Korea, February 1999.

Another important element is the improvement of fiscal soundness of local governments. For this purpose, national and local taxes are expected to be re-allocated, and a comprehensive resource allocation system, including a new system for issuing local government bonds, is to be introduced.

3. Policy Recommendations for Revitalizing the Economy

A. Supportive Macroeconomic Policies

As for monetary policies, a flexible monetary policy is expected to be maintained. In order to revamp domestic demand, money supply is expected to continue to be increased with an emphasis on open market operation.

Expansionary fiscal policies is also expected to be maintained. In order to boost sagging domestic demand, the fiscal deficits for 1999 is expected to remain at 5% of GDP. For maximizing expansionary effects, 70% of total fiscal resources for government projects are expected to be allocated during the first half, and efforts are also expected to be made in order to realize 50% of fiscal deficits during the same period.

Also, policy mix in the field of macroeconomic variables including money supply, interest rates, fiscal policy and foreign exchange are expected to be implemented to support the real sector.

For the SMEs severely affected by the credit crunch, the Korean government is expected to expand credit guarantee facilities through the injection of 1.3 trillion wons from the IBRD and 1.2 trillion wons from the 1999 national budget.

The credit crunch has dealt a particularly severe blow to housing and construction industries. Economic policies in this field are to center on the normalization and facilitation of real estate transactions. To this end, various regulations or institutional barriers, which have discouraged transactions, are expected to be lifted in 1999. These measures include expanded tax exemption for new housing transactions. Furthermore, loans for new housing are expected to be channeled more readily to consumers. Institutional support is also expected to be given to encourage the early development of the MSB (mortgage-backed securities market). Companies specializing in the MBS is allowed to set up in the first half of 1999.

In addition, various measures are expected to be taken in order to stimulate consumption and investment. They include the activation of consumer financing through interest rate cut, provision of tax incentives and the encouragement of investment in knowledge-based venture businesses. Various regulations restricting the opportunities of employment and business are also to be eliminated through massive deregulation efforts.

B. Improving Credit Worthiness in External Sector

Against uncertainties in the international financial market, the Korean government is expected to increase its usable foreign exchange reserves to more than US$55 billion in 1999. Associated efforts are expected to be made to improve its external debt structure.

As for financing measures, an emphasis shall be given to the equity financing and ABS (asset-backed securities). Also the development of foreign exchange markets in Korea is included. For this purpose, a launch of the Won/Euro market is envisaged and the Won/Dollar market is expected to be activated.

In addition, complementary measures to prevent negative effects arising from the free flow of capital are expected to be implemented in line with the new Foreign Exchange Transaction Act, effective from April 1999 allowing further liberalization of capital and foreign exchange transactions. They include the development of early warning systems and the introduction of an ALM (asset-liability management) system in the public sector.

The Korean government is expected to make utmost efforts to increase exports. To this end, restructuring in export industries is expected to be expedited in order to strengthen Korea's export competitiveness with the priority re-oriented to high value-added businesses and capital goods industries. In addition, export financing is expected to be expanded within the context of international norms and standards. Niche markets are also expected to be developed through implementing a cross export guaranteeing system with major trading partners.

As for FDI, concentrated efforts are expected to be made toward a goal of attaining US$15 billion in 1999. For this purpose, about 10 large investment projects are expected to be designated and local governments along with the KORTA (Korea Trade and Investment Promotion Agency) are expected to play a major role by providing an one-stop service for foreign investors.

C. A New FDI Policy, 'Promotion and Support'

Unlike loans, FDIs has been considered the most effective way to induce foreign capital and technology through the recent economic crisis situation. The basic direction of the Korean government policy of FDIs is to foster further economic development by upgrading domestic industrial structure through attracting FDIs into high-tech manufacturing and service industries, thus raising international competitiveness through the absorption of the state-of-the -art technologies.

The Korean government must recognize the importance of the improvement in the business environment for foreign investors. Korea's foreign investment climate was relatively less attractive than those of Southeast Asian countries which had greatly improved their investment climates after the second half of the 1980s.

FDIs in Korea have been done on a much smaller scale than Taiwan and ASEAN countries, not to mention China since its. FDIs in Korea rose by 180% during the three years of 1989~1992 compared to the five years of 1984~1988: FDIs in Taiwan recorded an 250% increase, and FDIs in Malaysia, Indonesia and Thailand recorded an 400%~500% increase during the same period. FDI in Korea accounted for 0.3% of GDP during 1984~1992, a very low figure compared to the other Asian countries.

High wages negatively affect FDIs. Stabilization of wages therefore can be considered as one of the surest way of attracting FDIs to Korea. The traditional type of FDI attempting to take advantage of low wages in assembly work will continue to decline.

Korea has already been losing international competitiveness to China, Thailand, and other low-wage countries for simple labor-intensive assembly work. Thus it is being forced to shift to high-tech industries for joint ventures with foreign investment partners. It needs to have both trained scientists and technicians. The Korean government should support the expansion for institutes of higher learning. It should also offer a variety of intense support for re-training and re-education for technical staff in the private sector.

The OECD's medium-term reference scenario illustrates the large potential benefits of rapid economic reform and transforming Korea to a more market-oriented economy. From this perspective, Korea's financial crisis can be seen as a catalyst to structural reform which might have taken decades to implement under 'business as usual' circumstances.

The new legislation of Action Foreign Investment Promotion sets Korea's of FDIs liberalization and deal with comprehensive incentives for and protection of FDIs in Korea. To fulfill these goals, the government has carried out various reform packages in the legislation.

1) A Historical Perspective of Korea's FDI Policy

FDIs are thought to have much different effects on long-term economic development than does borrowing from international capital markets. The way in which industrialization has been financed in East Asian countries has taken different forms. Korea relied on foreign borrowings, whereas Singapore and Hong Kong did on FDIs.[63] Until the mid-1980s, most long-term capital inflows needed for economic development was channeled through official loans, hence the role of FDIs was not significant. The lack of attention given by the Korean government to FDIs can be explained as follows: First, FDIs are essentially intrusive of territorial sovereignty of a state and the Korean government has been fearful that the economy would become dominated by foreign interests.

Second, the Korean government would like to channel limited amounts of capital resources to some strategic industries vital to long-term growth. With this strategy in mind, the Korean government preferred foreign borrowings to FDIs in which foreigners kept control of foreign resources. Over the period 1985~1995, Korea attracted only US$8.8 billion in FDIs, less than one-tenth the amount received by China.

Since the mid-1980s, Korea has been repaying its foreign debt and FDIs in long-term capital inflows have gradually increased its importance. Moreover, the Korean economy began to experience serious difficulties as a result of the side-effects of the economic plan to build up heavy and chemical industries in the 1970s. The new industrial strategy was designed to upgrade Korea's industrial structure as a whole by moving into more technology and skill-intensive industries.

An important policy instrument of this technological upgrading was to liberalize the regulation on FDIs. The Korean government implemented the automatic approval system which exempted certain categories of FDI projects from government screening before approval in 1984. In other words, there was a structural change in Korea's FDI policy from the positive system (1960~1983) to the negative system (1984~1992).

In 1992, business categories subject to notification were expanded to yield a notification-oriented system with approval as exceptions. In 1993 the Korean government began an active investment liberalization policy of FDIs by expanding liberalization measures and also started introducing deregulation programs to promote FDIs and provide a more hospital environment.

In 1994, the processing period for notification was greatly shortened from 20~30 days to no more than 3 hours. The processing period for amplifications subject to approval was also reduced from 30 days to 5 days (15 days, if consultation with related ministries is required).

In April 1995, the Korean government established a comprehensive service system for FDIs by introducing an 'One-Stop Service System' in Seoul and local provinces. This system is now able to resolve grievances of foreign - controlled firms, arrange linkages to joint partners and provide comprehensive information and administrative services. In March 1998, initiatives to reform the 'Foreign Direct Investment and Foreign Exchange & Capital Transaction Systems' were announced and at the end 'Act on Foreign Investment Promotion' has been enforced in November the same year.

2) The Current Regime

The basic law governing FDIs in Korea is the Act on Foreign Investment Promotion and working rules specifying matters under the Act and its enforcement measures. The conclusion of the UR (Uruguay Round) negotiations in 1993 has led to great changes in the international economic climate. Since then, the need for the Korean economy to upgrade its industrial structure to enhance its international competitiveness has been greater than ever.

In February 1995, foreign investment procedures for trading firms with the exception of Japanese trading firms, were also simplified from the previous approval system to the notification system. The Korean government continues to pursue further liberalization of FDIs by conforming to international standards of investment protection such as WTO/TRIMs, OECD Code and NTI (National Treatment Instrument).

In March 1998, initiatives to reform the 'Foreign Direct Investment and Foreign Exchange & Capital Transaction Systems' were announced. In April 1998, a public hearing to discuss a proposed draft of the 'Foreign Investment Promotion Act' was held. After the approval by the Cabinet, the draft of the 'Foreign Investment Promotion Act' was submitted to the National Assembly on July 24, 1998 for approval and

[63] Yang-Taek Lim, "The Role of Foreign Direct Investment for Korea's Economic Recovery and Future Directions in Foreign Investment Promotion Policy", paper presented at ACAES-Culalongkorn University International Conference, Bangkok, December. 16~18, 1998.

enforced from November 17, 1998. The major points of the Act are summarized as the simplification of the notification and registration procedures, the abolition of the report on customs clearance of foreign capital and the resident agent notification requirement, the establishment of the foreign investment promotion center and the central government support for local government activities to induce FDI.

First, the Acceptance of FDI Notification System will be changed to a simple Notification System. The Foreign Investment Company Registration System will be maintained in order to provide tax reduction or exemption incentives and other supports for foreign investors. Notification and applications for registration can be submitted to the branches and headquarters of the Foreign Exchange Bank and the overseas offices, local offices and the headquarters of KOTRA's Investment Promotion Center. Previously, applications could only be submitted to the headquarters of the Foreign Exchange Banks.

Second, the law requiring notification to the Minister of Finance and Economy within one month of the customs clearance of induced foreign capital will be abolished. The law requiring a non-resident to appoint a resident as an agent to submit notifications, applications or reports regarding FDI transactions will be abolished too.

Third, within KOTRA, the Investment Promotion Center will be established to serve as the central institution in inducing FDIs. This Center shall deal with all matters of assistance for foreign investors and foreign invested enterprises. The Center shall provide one-stop service, a substitute settlement[64] and direct settlement[65] of approval or authorization applications for foreign investors and foreign invested enterprises, guidance and support in all matters relating to FDI, and other assistances in the promotion of FDI and execution of investment surveys. The head of KOTRA shall hold the Right of Request to dispatch public officials from related ministries and cooperation in matters related to FDI. Related ministries and related institutions shall dispatch experienced officials to work under the Head of KOTRA.

Forth, central government will support local government activities by supplying funds for designating foreign investment zones (FIZ). Rental fees of public land will be reduced or exempted for foreign investors and foreign invested enterprises. Public subsidies for various purposes such as job training, will be provided as same as local companies.

Under the previously-mentioned background, the recent changes from 'regulations and control' to 'promotion and support' in FDIs policy have resulted from several factors as follows.

First, prior to IMF bail-out, Korea's restrictive economic policy had been facing increasing pressure from the international community, including international trade-related norms stipulated by the WTO. There were intensified pressures for market liberalization from Washington, Brussels and Geneva while the UR trade negotiations was in progress. These pressures increased even further with the completion of the UR negotiations.

Secondly, confronting challenges of the economic crisis, Korean government has undergone overall reforms and restructuring of the economy with emphasis on the principles of market economy.

Korea's xenophobic fear of its economy is determined by foreign interests could not be no longer existed in a market mechanism. Any preferential treatment or protection for local firms against foreign firms is no longer efficient and desirable in such a dynamic economy.

Thirdly, facing with its usable foreign exchange reserves plunged into the near depletion level, Korean government could not but desperately seek for a way to secure certain level of foreign liquidity other than borrow emergency liquidity arrangement from international institution. Coupling with its economic reforms and liberalization policies, foreign businesses have begun to see potential has made a complete turnabout on FDI policy from 'regulations and control' to 'promotion and support'.

[64] Substitute settlement: upon submitting the appropriate application forms to KOTRA, it will settle applications with other related administrative institutions for foreign investors and foreign invested enterprises.

[65] Direct settlement: upon submitting the appropriate application forms to KOTRA, it will directly settle applications through dispatched public officials from related ministries at KOTRA, the Investment Promotion Center for foreign investors and foreign invested enterprise.

<Figure VII-1> The Comprehensive Process and the Automatic Approval System for FDI

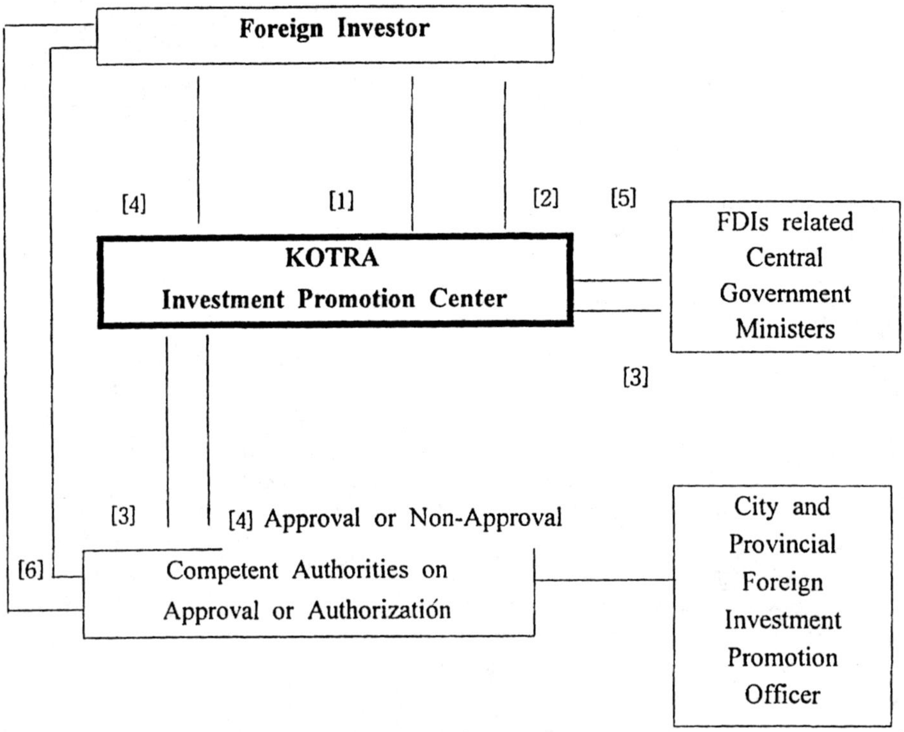

[1] Approval and authorization (*e.g.* the comprehensive process packages)
[2] Immediate settlement of directly settled civil affairs
[3] Substitute settlement of approval or authorization applications
[4] Settlement of approval or authorization (automatic approval upon lapse of time period determined by law)
[5] Report of the decision
[6] Monitoring settlement procedures related to FDIs

The major points of current Korean government policy on FDIs are summarized as follows :

(1) National Treatment

Unless otherwise specified by laws foreign investors and foreign-controlled firms are treated equally as Korean nationals and firms. Tax exemption and deduction pertaining to Korean firms are equally applied to foreign-controlled firms. The notification requirement for foreign invested enterprises, when wishing to engage in a additional businesses beyond those notified to the Ministry of Finance and Economy, is abolished by the Foreign Investment Promotion Act.

(2) Guarantee of Transfer and Property Rights

The overseas remittance of dividends from the stock or shares acquired by a foreign investor and of the sales of proceeds of stocks or shares is guaranteed in accordance with the contents of approval, the acceptance of the notification or the agreement at the time of the remittance. The property rights of a foreign investor and a foreign-invested enterprise are guaranteed in accordance with the provisions of the laws.

(3) Taxation and Incentives

The Korean government provides tax incentives and support for foreign- controlled firms which bring in advanced technology that is deemed necessary in achieving an advanced industrial structure. The basic framework for advanced technology eligible for financial and tax benefits was established in 1984. Since then, however, the industrial structure has changed and more advanced technology has emerged, necessitating the readjustment Korea's industrial development policy.

Under the Foreign Investment Promotion Act (November 1998), the FDI incentive system shall be mainly augmented as follows:

- **Tax Reduction or Exemption**

Tax reduction or exemption on corporate and income tax on dividends for 10 years for FDIs in Korea shall be augmented. Also, the tax reduction or exemption of local tax will apply to acquisition tax, property tax, aggregate land tax and registration tax. Previously, registration tax was not included. Concerning the tax reduction or exemption period, local governments have the autonomous power to grant tax reduction or exemption period from anywhere between 8 to 15 years. However, the tax reduction or exemption period and ratio will be higher than that of the previous law (5 years at 100%, the remaining 3 years at 50%).

A foreign investor may check potential tax reduction or exemption incentives prior to deciding to invest. Presently, foreign investors may apply for tax reduction or exemption only after giving notification of their investment. In case of a foreign invested enterprise seeks to convert a farm or forestry land into a factory site, conversion fee shall be reduced or exempted.

<Table VII-9> Tax Incentives for Foreign Invested Enterprises

Type of Tax	Past	Present
• Corporate tax • Income tax	• Full exemption for the first 5 years • 50% reduction for 3 years thereafter	• Full exemption for the first 7 years • 50% reduction for 3 years thereafter
• Corporate tax on dividends • Income tax on dividends	• Full exemption for the first 5 years • 50% reduction for 3 years thereafter	• Full exemption for the first 7 years • 50% reduction for 3 years thereafter
Local taxes • Acquisition tax • Property tax • Aggregate land tax • Registration tax	• Full exemption for the first 5 years • 50% reduction for 3 years thereafter ♣ Registration tax was not reduced/exempted	• Local tax incentives can be granted from 8 to 15 years • The minimum required by law is: - Full exemption for the first 5 years - 50% reduction for the first 3 years thereafter ♣ Registration tax is newly included
• Customs duty • Special excise tax • Value added tax	• Full exemption on imported capital goods	• Full exemption on imported capital goods

Source: Ministry of Finance and Economy, Korea, October 1998.

- **Renting National and Public Land**

Under the Foreign Investment Promotion Act, national and local government properties can be rented on the basis of private contracts. Previously, this was not allowed. Installment payments and delayed payments for the lease of national and local government properties are permitted. Rent reduction or exemption is possible for national government properties in Foreign Exclusive Industrial Parks, National Industrial Parks and Foreign Investment Zones. As in the case of national government properties, the rental period of local government properties is expanded to 50 years and extension for another 50 years is allowed. Businesses eligible for rent reduction or exemption, as well as the rates to be applied, will be autonomously determined by local governments.

(4) Mergers & Acquisitions

FDIs through M&A was previously not permitted in Korea. Only portfolio investment of shares listed on the Korean Stock Exchange was allowed with limitation of ceilings on foreigner's purchases of listed shares set by Korean Government. Under the current legislation, however, M&A even hostile one, having the characteristics of FDIs has been completely liberalized. However, with further progress in liberalization and with the gradual elimination of ceilings on stock market purchase, M&A in the form of stock market transactions will be more widely open to foreign investors.

(5) Acquisition of Real Estate

High population density has been the reason behind strict government regulations of the real estate market in Korea. Moreover, the land price bubble that occurred in the late 1980s further strengthened the restrictions by creating such measures as tax disincentives or zoning regulations. These regulations are equally applied to foreign and domestic investors, but foreign investors, including those enterprises whose ownership exceeds 50% of total share capital, are subject to additional restrictions in purchasing real estate properties in Korea.

Rules on land purchases by foreigners differ from those on purchases of other types of real estate. Non-residents are required to have authorization from the Ministry of Finance and Economy before purchasing real estate properties other than land pursuant to the Regulation on Foreign Exchange Management. According to a new act under the jurisdiction of the Ministry of Construction and Transportation, however, foreign-controlled firms are easily able to purchase land, as long as they do so for legitimate business purposes.

For foreign-controlled firms belonging to the manufacturing sector, only notification of purchases of factory sites are required for legitimate business operations. The title of ownership shall then be issued within fifteen days upon the notification. However, different rules apply to foreign-controlled firms in the service sector. Notification is the only requirement for purchases that do not exceed specified ceilings. These measures are all part of efforts made by the Korean government to reduce the soaring land prices and should not be viewed as discriminatory given Korea's real estate situation.

(6) Loans over Five Years

Under the current foreign investment law, loans of maturities more than three years are treated as commercial loans rather than FDIs. Commercial loans are allowed only for imports of facilities and equipment by foreign-controlled firms in high-tech industries, SMEs in manufacturing industries, firms engaged in the construction of infrastructure and firms that have already repaid existing loans.

Loans with maturities of more than three years are subject to approval by the Korean government, considering that various liberalization measures on capital movements may induce excessive capital inflows from abroad. Under the new regime of Foreign Investment Promotion Act loans with purpose of direct investment and maturities of five years or more is classified as being tantamount to FDIs.

3) Further Liberalization of Foreign Business Categories

The Korean government has also expanded the business categories of FDIs. By January of 2000, the number of restricted businesses are scheduled to be brought down to 21, while 1,078 categories are also scheduled to be fully open and another 47 partially open to foreign investment.

Meanwhile, the Korean government has an authority to reject the foreign investment application only for reasons related to maintenance of public order, the protection of public health, moral and safety purpose, the protection of its essential security interests or the fulfillment of its obligations relating to international peace and security.

The Korean government firmly believes that further liberalization in currently restricted business categories is necessary. In the near future, the Korean government plans to speed up to the ongoing process of liberalization and establish a timetable for business categories not yet scheduled to be liberalized by 2000.

D. New Labour Policies Facing Rising Unemployment

1) The Rise of Contingent Employment

Recently, the term 'contingent employee' has come into fashion to describe various types of workers. They are different from 'regular' full-time employees. While the term has not been precisely defined by law, the contingent workforce includes temporary help workers, independent contractors, workers hired on a part-time or project basis and workers from firms which provide sub-contracted services to large firms.

The standard employment relationship in economic development since the 1970s for the majority of Korean workers had three fundamental characteristics: full-time employment with a single employer, life-time employment, and certain legal protection against unfair dismissal. Employees, in fact, have been almost free from worries about serious job insecurity.

The situation has been rapidly changing, however, since Korea's economic slump. Firms have cut back on workers as part of their business restructuring programs. As the effects of restructuring hit the nation, unemployment has soared to a 20-year high of 7% in June 1998, leaving almost 1.53 million people out of work. As a result, for an increasing number of workers, this standard employment relationship is starting to be replaced by various forms of contingent employment.

In 1997, contingent employment accounted for 7% of all employments in the country. The proportion has increased from the beginning of the 1990s, although its still lags behind the 30% in America, 20% in Japan and 30% in Europe. In what has now become an international trend, corporations are shrinking the size of their core workforce and are increasingly hiring people on a contingent basis. This rise has been cited as a key factor in recovering corporate competitiveness via gaining labor flexibility.

2) Counter-measures against Unemployment

One of the major problems is the massive unemployment created in the process of restructuring. The basic solution is to deal with the fundamental causes and raise job-creating capability. The measures of the Korean government to counter the unemployment problem are summed up in <Table VII-11>.

<Table VII-10> Counter-measures of the Korean Government against Unemployment

- Create jobs in the private sector by activating corporate business
- Increase public-funded projects up to the proper level
- Increase the efficiency of the job training and job recommendation
- Increase the efficiency of government assistance in stabilizing employment
- Expand gradually the social welfare measure for the unemployed and the poor
- Prevention of social hazards such as broken families

Source: Ministry of Finance and Economy, Korea, 1999.

The debate over flexibility in the labor markets has been under way in Korea since the early 1980s. The focus was on government controls on layoffs and unemployment benefits.

Some argue that government programs to stabilize employment should be eased altogether. They contend that government regulation of the labor market has been a major cause of the market's rigidity and that employment stabilization programs have made a smooth transition of the labor force impossible while serving to increase labor costs. Its rigidity is working as an obstacle for firms seeking to enter or exit local markets through the process of M&As (mergers and acquisitions). Although easing the regulations will lead to massive layoffs and increased unemployment, this is necessary for production efficiency to rise, investment to increase, new technology to be introduced and production expansion to proceed, thus creating new jobs and reducing unemployment in the long run.

The reason behind the rise in contingent employment is that it provides firms with increased flexibility in a world of changing business demands. The 'just-in-time' concept is being introduced not only in inventories but also in staffing. The use of a flexible work force has become a notable trend in the world. Firms that have beefed up their payrolls during the 1980s and the early 1990s were hurt when recession occurred in the late 1990s. Contingent workers who can be easily laid off are now seen as a hedge against other unforeseen changes in the economic climate. In addition, firms relish the ability to respond rapidly to business conditions and borrow skilled employees who can be on the job very quickly, which is often faster and cheaper than recruiting permanent employees.

3) Legislation of the Temporary-Help Agency System

It has been recognized that the rigidity of the labor market has served as an impediment to the nation's economic restructuring efforts, and many are insisting that enhanced flexibility in the labor market must be the first priority in economic reform. There have been several studies presenting programs, such as introducing a temporary-help agency system; hiring part-time workers; improving compensation flexibility;

and reducing retirement benefits, annual vacations and paid leave. This push to make the labor market more flexible has gained momentum with the onset of the current economic crisis.

Agreements on the early introduction of the layoff and temporary-help agency systems were reached at the tripartite negotiations among labor, management and the government. The system was presented at the session of the National Assembly based on the proceedings from the committee for labor-relations reform in January 1998. The government legalized the temporary-help agency system in order to accommodate flexible employment practices in the labor market in February 1988.

Hiring temporary help is still highly regulated, however, with legislation primarily geared towards ensuring that temporary work complements stable employment. Regulations are geared towards: governing conditions for the use of temporary workers, ensuring that temporary workers are not used to replace permanent employees, limiting the duration of temporary assignments, and limiting the maximum number of jobs that can be filled by temporary workers. A summary is as follows: first, a firm cannot hire temporary workers within 2 years after the firm cuts back on workers due to restructuring; second, there are only 26 kinds of jobs where workers can be hired on a temporary basis, including secretaries, interpreters and telephone operators; third, contracts for temporary employees are limited to 24 months (after which point employees must be converted to a permanent status).

4) Expanding Social Safety Net

The Korean government plans to expand its social safety net by increasing funds for the unemployment from 5.7 trillion wons in 1998 to 7.7 trillion wons in 1999. Important policy measures for the social safety net in 1999 are those for the improvement in its effectiveness. They are the prompt compiling of database for the unemployed and a monitoring and feedback system. In addition, new public projects having more productivity are expected to be created with the participation of non-governmental organizations. A voucher system for job training is also expected to be strengthened.

Government's support to the unemployed and low-income classes is expected to be strengthened. Eligibility for those supports shall be clearly defined and expanded.

Chapter VIII

A NEW ECONOMIC DEVELOPMENT STRATEGY FOR KOREA IN THE 21ST CENTURY

Since resorting to the IMF in November 1997, Korea is pushing ahead vigorous financial, corporate and public sectors restructuring as a means of survival. The problem here is that such restructuring has not been able to bring about sufficient synergy effects, and the speed of reform is being slowed down by the conflicts between restructuring and rising unemployment; there is thus the risk that the effect of reform may become diluted.

The connection between corporate and financial restructuring is an example. The very reason of corporate restructuring is that companies have become insolvent due to the loss of competitiveness, coupled with excessive level of non-performing loans at financial institutions, which in turn leads to the insolvency of financial institutions and becomes the cause for financial restructuring. Therefore, an environment in which corporate insolvencies is minimized only can be created by strengthening competitiveness.

In preparation for the 21st century, the Korean economy should redirect its development strategy to a technology-based economy. For this purpose, economic policy directions for 1999 is to be focused on fostering an environment nurturing technology-intensive industries.

Technological weakness has been playing a significant role in undermining the overall competitiveness of the Korean economy. Therefore, the process of overcoming the current economic crisis in its true sense should be based on addressing technological weakness and on establishing a new industrial structure in the Korean economy. Moreover, domestic industries need to adjust rapidly to the abrupt changes in the external economic environment, with turning to the 21st century.

1. STRUCTURAL PROBLEMS OF THE KOREAN ECONOMY

In conjunction with the forthcoming possibility of Korea's economic crisis in the near future, Yang-Taek Lim (1991 a and b, 1995 and 1996)[66] had consistently pointed out that the structural problems of the Korean economy as a result of the preceding high-growth policy. These structural problems stem from the six major imbalances as follows.

First, the imbalance between industry and agriculture has intensified as industrial development has been achieved at the cost of the agricultural sector, not through the latter's development. A prevailing sense of helplessness in the face of the pressure to open up the agricultural market in the aftermath of the Uruguay Round is a reality.

Second, because the savings rates are lower than investment rates, the driving force of industrialization was provided not by domestic capital, but by foreign capital.

---

[66] Yang-Taek Lim, "Vision for the Korean Economy in the 21st Century and the Counter-measures against the possible Economic Crisis", Seoul: The FKI (Federation of the Korean Industries), January 17, 1991a.

Yang-Taek Lim, "The Causes of Korea's Economic Crisis and Its Counter-measures", Seoul: Korea Economic Daily Press, September 10, 1991b.

Yang-Taek Lim, *Vision and Challenges for Korea in the 21st Century: Toward the Construction of a Reunited Korea*, Seoul: Mail Economic Daily Press, September 1995.

Yang-Taek Lim, "Korea's Liberalization Policy Directions and Korea's Weakening Competitiveness", *Journal of Asian Economies,* Vol. 7, No. 4, 1996, pp. 603~634.

Third, the policy emphasizing conglomerates business, export-oriented industries, and finished goods industries has resulted in the relative decline of small businesses, domestic consumption-oriented industries, and parts industries. As a result, the imbalance between business conglomerates and small businesses, export-oriented industries and domestic consumption-oriented industries, heavy and chemical industries and light industries have been intensified, and an extreme distortion of the market structure by the monopoly of conglomerates business and an excessive concentration of economic power has been created in the way of rapid economic development.

During the period 1986~1989, business conglomerates pursued quick growth relying on bank loans without accumulating their own capital despite a surplus in their balance of payments. Extra capital from the surplus in balance of payments went into investment in real estate and stock, causing a raise in interest rates and in stock prices. As a result, a strange phenomenon occurred under the appreciation of the Korean won; domestic interest rates were higher than foreign interest rates, stock prices were high, and domestic prices rose. At the same time, the extra capital of corporations in the stock market were diverted into the real estate market.

As the conglomerates used up all of the financial resources, bankruptcies of small businesses cropped up one after another as they found themselves unable to obtain necessary loans. Meanwhile, during the period that the conglomerates had extra capital from a surplus in the balance of payments, they speculated in real estate, which had a high rate of profit expectancy, instead of paying back bank debt. Government forced the secondary financial sector to undertake the currency regulation bond to absorb foreign currency, raising premium rates of distribution for company bonds and currency stabilization bonds, which in turn influenced the real interest rates of the market and caused them to rise.

Fourth, the export-oriented policy built on quantitative growth weakened international competitiveness. Export-oriented industrialization based on cheap labor debilitates when the relative cost of wages rise. Price-subsidy measures such as public loans with low interest rate, exemptions or reduction of local taxes and tariffs and exchange rate manipulation have caused businesses to be preoccupied with achieving quantitative growth goals, while neglecting improvement in quality and technological development. For these reasons, businesses pressured the government to lower interest rates, raise exchange rates, and reduce tariffs instead of trying to increase their own productivity or reorganize management when they faced with hardships in exports.

In addition, the export-oriented industrialization strategy without technological development inevitably intensifies dependency on other countries for technology through imports. Particularly, the heavy reliance on Japan for parts, materials and machinery has lowered foreign currency earnings and value added ratios, thus becoming the direct cause of the chronic deficit in the international balance of payments. The trade deficit with Japan is the cause for a reversal in the overall balance of trade to deficit levels, and internally, it represents a handicap against the realization of a developed welfare state with equitable income distribution, sustained economic growth and price stabilization.

Fifth, the financial sector has not been developed to match the growth of the real sector. Because the financial sector has been a monopolistic stepping stone for the growth of the real sector, the former is relatively lacking, and as the intermediary function of finance has decreased, a dualistic alienation has intensified between the real sector and the financial sector. Even with the release of much money, improvements in productivity in the real sector and its function of increasing employment are not realized.

Sixth, the 'growth first, distribution later' policy was pursued in the hopes that it would naturally solve the standard of living problems and improve welfare through what is called the 'trickle-down effect' of economic growth. Social development has been put aside or foregone for accelerated economic development. This policy has aggravated the disparity of income distribution between high and low-income classes and caused friction between employer and employees. In addition, the astronomical rise of capital gains through real estate speculation and the likes have brought about a sense of incongruity among the classes and weakened the will of civilians to save, the will of laborers to work, and the will of businessmen to invest.

Therefore, the structural problems of Korea have emerged from not being able to cope with the externally-manifested internal pressure of the dualistic structural imbalances between industry and agriculture, between government and market, between business conglomerates and small businesses, between enterprises and workers, and between growth and distribution.

Rather, the structural problems that Korea is facing internally were caused by excessive emphasis on the quantitative expansion through an extensive-growth policy, thus failing to accomplish a qualitative reform through an intensive- development strategy. The problem lies in the fact that each sector and the status quo have not recognized and endured what Joseph Schumpeter (1934 and 1942)[67] has called 'the creative destruction process' as an active opportunity for development. The whole nation should be ready to share the burden of such structural changes[68].

2. A New Strategy for Economic Development

A. Introduction

In the past, there was a clear development model for economic growth. In the early 1960s the government chose a growth strategy that concentrated investment of limited resources in export-oriented manufacturing industries. The economy underwent rapid growth as human resources from agriculture and unofficial service sectors in the cities, both areas suffering from low productivity, shifted into the high productivity area of the manufacturing sector.

The world economy is being transformed from a resource-based economy to a knowledge-based economy. According to the OECD, a "knowledge-based economy" means an economy which has more direct dependency on the use of knowledge than before. In other words, a knowledge-based economy is an economy in which knowledge is the most important factor in the determination of competitiveness.

The fundamental background of this change is technological innovation in the fields of information and telecommunications. The revolutionary development of information and telecommunication technologies has made it possible to transform complex knowledge into simple electronic information (digital revolution) and to produce, distribute it and use massive amounts of knowledge easily and quickly. The massiveness and speed of this knowledge production shorten the life cycles of products by a great deal. To survive in this increasingly competitive environment, one must acquire new knowledge faster than others and generate higher value-added.

The technology needed in the course of such rapid growth could easily be introduced from abroad by importing capital resources, foreign direct investment, and license agreements on technology introduction. Unfortunately, the present international environment does not readily permit the government-led industrial development strategy. The main characteristics of the new international technology environment are strategic technological ties among advanced nations, greater dual-technology development, a set of new 'rules of the game', stronger protection for intellectual property rights, and stronger enforcement of international environmental regulations.

As Korean firms have become major competitors in many fields, foreign companies have reportedly become less willing to sell them technology, making R&D programmes in Korea more important. Investment in R&D has increased at a 20% real rate since the early 1980s, rising from 1.2% of GDP in 1984 to 2.7% in 1996, the third-highest among OECD countries. Korea thus appeared to be close to its target, established in 1993, of boosting such expenditures to between 3 and 4% of GNP by 1998.[69]

The business sector had played the major role in increasing its share of R&D spending from 40% in the early 1980s to 73% in 1996. The four largest *chaebols* have accounted for a major share of business R&D, with about four-fifths of this investment concentrated in electric machinery and electronics. R&D is facilitated by the availability of trained personnel; the share of the population with graduate degrees in science and engineering is higher in Korea than in Japan.

However, three-fourths of Korean scientists and engineers with Ph.D. degrees are employed by universities, which accounted for less than 10% of total R&D investment, compared to the OECD average of 18%. The relatively limited role of universities has hindered basic research, which is considered to be essential for building longer-term innovative capacity. Although the government has sought to strengthen R&D activities in universities by expanding budgetary resources, the gap between university research and industry remains large.

---

[67] Joseph Schumpeter, *The Theory of Economic Development*, Cambridge, MA: Harvard University Press, 1934 (reprinted by Oxford University Press in 1994). Joseph Schumpeter, *Capitalism, Socialism, and Democracy*, New York: Harper, 1942.

[68] This is also a fact proven by the historical experience of South American countries. Although they had an abundance of natural resources, they collapsed right at the gateway of becoming developed countries due to the result of not having skillfully endured the process of structural change.

[69] This target, though, is unlikely to be met as surveys report that firms are planning to cut R&D expenditures by 10 to 30% in 1998 in the wake of the economic crisis.

The government has promoted private-sector R&D through preferential tax and credit policies. The most important measure is the Technology Development Reserve Fund, which allows companies to set aside 20 to 30% of pre-tax profits in any given year for R&D activities during the following four years. The government has also increased its spending on R&D. Boosting its share from 16% of activity has been the ten-year Han project, initiated in 1992 to develop product technology in ten areas and to develop fundamental core technologies in eight areas considered essential to the economy. [70]In addition, there are sector-specific R&D programmes focused on information and communications, bio-technology and aerospace.

The five-year plan for scientific and technological innovation seeks to increase government expenditures in this area from the current 3% of the total budget to 5% by 2002. The plan is designed to modernize Korea's science system and enhance the innovation potential of the economy by supporting key technologies and nurturing new technology-based firms. The increased emphasis on R&D is to be accompanied by educational reform based on the principles established by a presidential commission.[71] The commission stressed the importance of making lifelong educational opportunities available to those who have finished their formal schooling. In addition, school curricula should be broadened by focusing less on entrance exams and more on promoting creativity and the international dimensions of education. Finally, the report calls for more diversity in the education system in order to offer more choice to students.

Yang-Taek Lim (1996)[72] analyzed the success of Korea in achieving economies of scale following massive investment in human capital and export-oriented economic growth. Due to insufficient technological development, however, the total factor productivity has been declining. In addition, he also concluded that economies of scale within the Korean economy have reached a limit because of inadequate investment in R&D (research and development) and SOC (social overhead capital). Furthermore, the rate of increase of labor cost per unit was much too fast compared with other countries. Thus, the factor cost advantage has been disappearing and there has been a real possibility of massive unemployment unless a technology innovation- oriented national competitiveness emerges.[73]

The globalization of economic activities stemming from the end of the Cold-War era and the start of the WTO has made such competition fiercer. As technological innovations are to be accelerated in the 21st century, a technology- based economy in which technology is the most important determining factor for competitiveness will become even more important and widespread.

Therefore, a comprehensive plan for the development of a technology-based economy has to be made. This plan shall emphasize institutional buildings for technology- intensive industries, such as standardization, intellectual property rights protections, informatizations and R&D investment.

In spite of the outstanding economic performance in the past three decades, the Korean economy is rapidly losing its price competitiveness. Factors include high rate of increase in wages that had been around 20% per year till before the IMF bail-out, an interest rate burden of more than 10%, costs for establishing factory sites that are 3~5 times higher than competing nations.

Korea is lacking in natural resources, so the only strategy for national survival has been an export-oriented policy. Though attempts to enhance its quality-based competitiveness rather than the price one have been carried out to confront the changing international economic order and the changes in global industrial structure, its international competitiveness continues to weaken as a result of neglect of technological development.

There is the need for industrial policies which concentrate on the development of technology. Technological development is the most essential factor in the restructuring of industry and strengthening of

---

[70] The Han project, which absorbs about 13% of government spending on technology, includes 256 megabits semiconductor chips, high-definition television and high-speed railways. The government requires the private sector to fund four-fifths of the programme.

[71] The original report, Educational Reform: Proposals for the Establishment of a New System of Education for an Age of Globalization and Information, was released in May 1995 and followed by series of reports in February 1996, August 1996 and June 1997.

[72] Yang-Taek Lim, "The Effects of Technical Progress on Growth, Employment and Distribution: the Korean Manufacturing (1972~1990)", paper presented at the Korean Economic Association, Seoul, Korea, January 1996a.
Yang-Taek Lim, "An Econometric Study of Technological Progress, Innovation, Diffusion, Transfer and Their Impacts on International Competitiveness: with respect to the Korean Manufacturing (1972~1996)", paper presented at the 8th Academic Conference of Korean Society for Technology, Management & Economics, January 30, 1996b.

[73] Sweden is lately becoming a good example of unemployment rising due to ineffective response to high labor cost per unit over the last five years, resulting in the industrial devastation.

competitiveness. In particular, under the present international situation in which technology protectionism has taken root, it is impossible for a country that lacks technology to achieve industrial development, export growth, or environmental improvement, much less survive the fierce competition from other countries.

Under the aforementioned internal and external environments, it is necessary for Korea to choose technological innovation as its foremost priority in industrial policies and pursue both the development of high technology and technology needed in the workplace for all sectors of the industry as well as strategic sector-specific technology.

B. New Techno-Economic Development Strategy

Technological innovation can be divided into process innovation[74] and product innovation. In the context of the product life cycle, the dynamic process of product innovation consists of the following three stages such as the initial stage (where a new product is created as a result of product innovation), the middle stage (where the product innovation goes hand in hand with process), and the finishing stage (where standardization of the technology is achieved).

At the last stage, the product innovation comes to an end and the focus shifts to process innovation in order to reduce its production cost. Thus, innovations in product and process support each other in an orderly manner during the process of industrial development. From the point of view of international division of technology, advanced nations usually possess competitive advantage in the initial stages in which product technology is important, whereas semi-advanced and less developed nations specialize in the finishing stage, which emphasizes process innovation. This creates a pattern of international trade, which is well described by the product cycle hypothesis of R. Vernon (1966 and 1979).[75]

Korea has remained in the finishing stages until now. Korea's main export industries, such as automobile, electronics, and textiles, have all drawn their competitive advantage from the reduction of production cost through process innovation rather than introduction of new products. Nevertheless, it is now time to move beyond the limits of a less developed nation's model of manufacturing structure and technological innovation. It is time to shift the core of Korea's technology from process innovation to product innovation.

Yang-Taek Lim (1995 and 1996)[76] presents shows a model for building a nation on the basis of technology. In this model, the nucleus of S&T (science and technology) policies consists of three pillars; independent R&D (research and development), introduction of advanced technology and international technological cooperation. The synergy effect between independent R&D and introduction of advanced technology creates an elevated interaction through assimilation, absorption and improvement. This effect will then spreads to dynamic developments through inter- industrial and inter-corporate diffusion technology.

Private and public sectors should cooperate together to develop creative technologies. The public sector should put more emphasis on various fundamental and basic scientific research and national defenses, while the private sector focuses on commercial technologies. The National Science and Technology Committee should determine the priority of national research projects, and universities and research institutes are encouraged to compete with each other. Goals of research projects should be clearly defined when selecting the projects, and the principle of 'free to fail' should be applied to alleviate the burden of failures. Associated efforts are financial and tax incentives for the investment in technology-

---

[74] The oldest and the most classic example of technological innovation of manufacturing process can be found in the invention of the conveyor belt in late 18th century. With the development of precision electronics, applying electronics-related technology to the manufacturing process is being widely pursued these days. Examples include FMS (Flexible Manufacturing System), CIM (Computer Integrated Manufacturing), and CAD (Computer-Aided Design).

[75] R. Vernon, "International Investment and International Trade in the Product Cycle", Quarterly Journal of Economics, Vol. 80, 1966, pp. 190~207. R. Vernon, "The Product Cycle Hypothesis in a New International Environment", Oxford Bulletin of Economics and Statistics, Vol. 41, 1979, pp. 255~267.

[76] Yang-Taek Lim, *The People Perish Where There Is No Vision,* Seoul: Mail Economic Daily Press, September 1995. Yang-Taek Lim and Chung-Hwan Song, "An International Comparative Study of Basic Scientific Research Capacity: with Reference to the OECD Countries, Taiwan and Korea", *Technological Forecasting and Social Change,* Vol. 52, No. 1, May 1996, pp.75~94.

intensive projects. Technologies should be able to become collateral for loans, and various tax incentives should be provided.

In line with the division of roles between the government and the civilian sector, the civilian sector should take the lead in developing mid-term and long-term core technology in high-tech industries and energy sectors. The government in turn must design S&T policies which give specific priorities to technology, similar to the export promotion policies of the past, in order to achieve the national goal of entering the ranks of first-class S&T nations in the 21st century.[77]

<Figure VIII-1> A New Technology Development Strategy for Korea

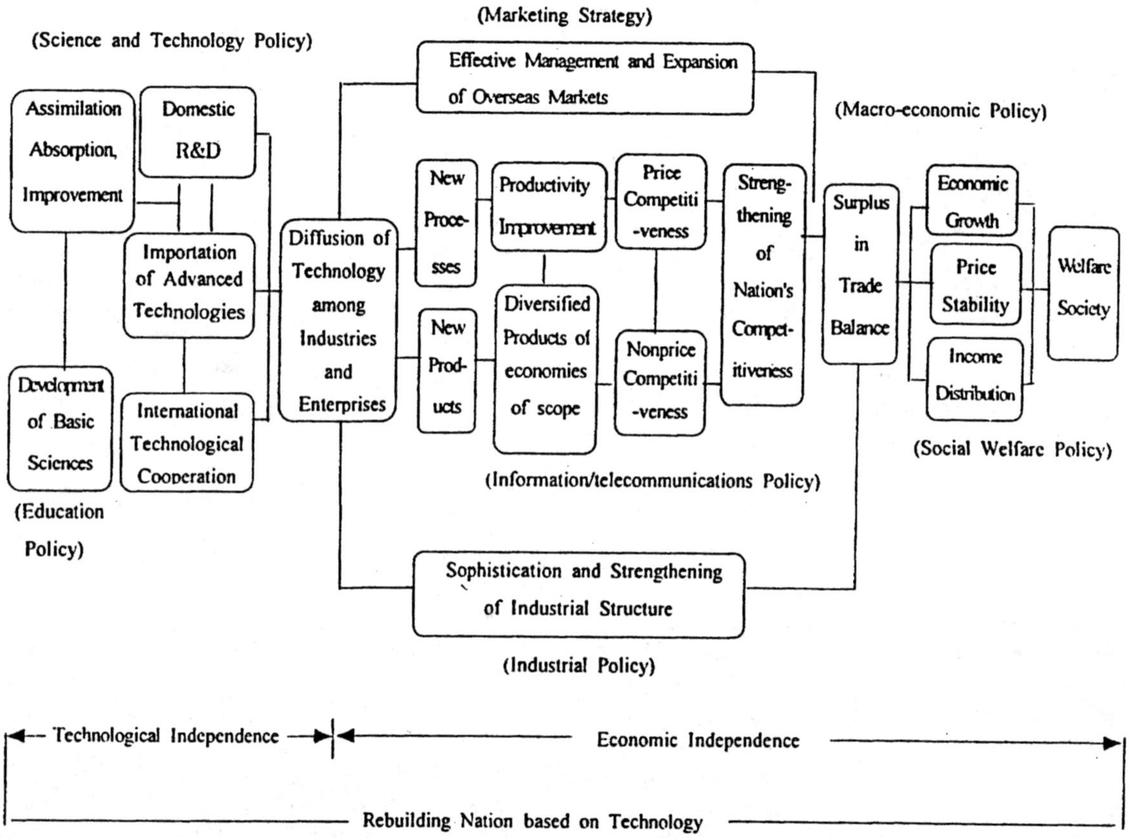

---

[77] Looking at Korea's strategy for technological development, the government has drawn up a "Five-Year Plan for The New Economy". The basic concept of this plan is to establish "the public's participation and creativity" as a new force for economic development in response to declining government control. This force, to be accumulated over the next few years, is to become the basis of Korea's continuous economic development. The fundamental strategy of the Plan is to have private sectors play leading roles in technological development. The government has announced in the Meeting for the Promotion of the New Economy in February 1994 that the top priority task of the new economy was technological development.
The "strategy for technological development" within the Five-Year Plan includes (1) establishment of a private sector-led system of technological innovation; (2) specialization of funding according to function, and support for building a joint research system involving the industrial, academic, and research communities; (3) expansion of R&D investment to 3-4% of GNP by 1998.

As R&D becomes more complicated, the exchange of new ideas between government-funded research institutes and universities is required to support R&D for businesses. Therefore, cooperation in R&D among businesses, universities, and research institutes should be strengthened[78] and supported by the government.[79] The parties involved should be encouraged to take part in the processes of planning, management and evaluation of government-funded R&D projects. Also, businesses should be induced to invest in related industrial technical research conducted at research institutes and universities.

There must be also an atmosphere of technical cooperation among domestic firms themselves, and several firms have participated in national R&D policy projects, but because the projects have been divided up closer to divisions of the work load among participants, they cannot be regarded as true technological cooperation.[80]

Meanwhile, the main characteristics of the new international technology environment are strategic technological ties among advanced countries, greater dual-technology development, a set of new 'rules of the game', stronger protection for intellectual property rights, and stronger enforcement of international environmental regulations.

The Korean government must mold supportive policies, enhance the technology infrastructure, and pursue a strategy of 'competition and cooperation' with other countries to survive in the world 'economic war'. The core of this strategy should be international technological cooperation.[81] The country must move from friction to cooperation with the United States and Japan, from political considerations to economic reasoning, and toward mutually beneficial scientific and technological development with China and Russia.

C. A Desirable Governmental S&T Policy

As state-sponsored S&T development projects have been restricted by the conclusion of UR agreements,[82] the government's S&T policy should now focus on inducing private firms to develop their own technologies through inter-corporate and industry-university cooperative efforts. The Korean government must muster the greatest possible institutional support within the boundaries set by international norms under the UR so that the industrial, academic and research communities can devote all their energies to technological development.

The current government support systems for technological development can be divided into financial and taxation support systems.[83] The financial support system for R&D investment has been classified into authorized support funds, offset support funds, and prohibited support funds. Thus government-supported programs must be operated within the boundaries of international rules.

The following paragraphs outline the author's proposal for a new strategy of government support for technological development, as follows:

---

78 In Korea, there are 14 SRC (Science Research Centers) and 16 ERC (Engineering Research Centers) in Korea to support cooperative research between industry and universities. These 30 research centers conducted 137 industry-commissioned studies and 12 industry-university joint studies in 1991, and set up 8 consortia (67 corporate members). However the share of joint research is very low. Thus, creating an appropriate atmosphere for joint R&D has become an impending task.

79 The Korean government is trying to expedite the practical application of the results of research by encouraging substantial cooperation among universities, industry, and research institutes in government R&D projects (essential intermediate technology, essential guiding technology) and basic scientific research, eliminating the waste factor in R&D "model projects" among universities and businesses, universities and government-funded research institutes, and universities, businesses, and government funded research institutes are to be supported.

80 An exception and an exemplary case of technical cooperation between rivaling domestic firms is the contract over a joint permit drawn between Goldstar Inc. and Samsung in July of 1993. The fact that most Japanese firms within the same sectors draw such contracts with each other has much to show us.

81 There have been a few cases for international technological cooperation of a strategic nature, such as the technological ties between *GoldStar Inc.* and the micro-chip producers of United States and Japan, but the number of Korean firms involved in technological cooperations is very small due to the fact that few domestic firms have reached the standards set by advanced nations.

82 Korea Institute for International Economic Policy, *Comprehensive Review of the Uruguay Rounds*, December 1993.

83 For a detail discussion about them, see Yang-Taek Lim, *A Study on the Effective Tax Incentives for Stimulating Research and Development in Korea,* (with the co-author Yong-Hoon Known), Asian Social Welfare Foundation, Seoul, Korea, 1996.

First, a reorganization of the industrial support system based on the authorized support funds is needed. Those funds or support systems which are prohibited by international norms at present must be changed into forms of authorized support or offset support. A gradual reduction is recommendable. Offset support systems targeted for particular industries must also be transformed into authorized support systems which are not specific and have no trade effects.

Second, all sector-specificities should be eliminated, at the same time objectivity should be improved. Objective standards, conditions for qualification, and the amount of supporting funds must be established in order to reduce any problems regarding sector-specificity. Special attention should be paid to the use of supporting funds and financial incentives which obviously raise questions of particularity.

Third, reducing the size of policy financing and improving its efficiency is needed. The financial policy funds, which set concessional interest rates, must be absorbed into currency policy funds, which set market interest rates. Those funds whose origin and uses are in question must be eliminated or integrated into fewer systems under a unique authority in order to improve efficiency and cohesiveness.

Fourth, the financial support system for R&D investment must be revised. The governmental R&D support which influences the competitiveness of individual firms may classify as authorized support, but this could cause friction if it injures trading partners. Thus, a strict management of funds and compliance with the maximum allowable amount of grants and loans is necessary. In particular, a comprehensive review of government-led R&D investment plans in specific areas is urgently needed.

Finally, it is important to emphasize the following: a national consensus to accomplish economic self-support through the means of technological self-support, consistency in the government's technology policy, and government support for the research activities of universities in the basic science.

D. The Importance of the Basic Science

In connection with the importance of the basic science, Yang-Taek Lim and Chung-Hwan Song (1996)[84] recently estimated the basic scientific research capacity (hereafter BSRC) of Korea. Korea's BSRC ranked 17th out of 21 countries in 1992. The forecasted value for the year 2000 will be 15th place out of the 21 countries, and 7th by the year 2010. However, the above estimation includes the possibility of overestimating Korea's BSRC by using the R&D expenditures instead of the R&D stock, due to data limitation. Also, it should not be overlooked that there are many countries excluded from the analysis, of which BSRC exceeds that of Korea.

Moreover, the perspective for the year 2000 is a relative analysis based on the 1981~1992 period. Hence, if the other countries continue to strive for scientific and technological development, Korea's rank might not be much improved. In spite of the perspective that Korea will rank 7th by the year 2010, the gap with developed countries remains large. It would take 68 years for Korea to reach the US's level of 1992, 41 years to reach Japan's, and 16 years to reach Germany's. Consequently, consolidation of investment in basic science is urgent to establish a basis for the promotion of science and technology the (S&T) through the 2000s. Without the support of basic science, development of Korean industry would soon reach its limit. The government must seek to maximize BSRC by supporting more positively the research activities of universities in basic science.

The emphasis on education in Korean society has brought a sharp increase in enrollment rates during the past thirty years that appears to be unmatchable by any other countries. The rapid expansion of education does not appear to have been at the expense of quality. According to standardized tests in mathematics and science given to students in 17 OECD countries, Korean fourth-graders scored the highest in both subjects, while eighth-graders in Korea were first in math and third in science. These excellent results were achieved despite a relatively low level of expenditure. In 1994, public expenditure on education amounted to 3.6% of GDP, well below the OECD mean of 5.1% despite the fact that school-age children account for a relatively large share of Korea's population.[85] Korea has economized by having

[84] Yang-Taek Lim and Chung-Hwan Song, "An International Comparative Study of Basic Scientific Research Capacity: with Reference to the OECD Countries, Taiwan and Korea", *Technological Forecasting and Social Change,* Vol. 52, No. 1, May 1996, pp.75~94.

[85] The 5 to 14 age population accounted for 16.4% of Korea's population compared to an OECD average of 13.7%.

relatively large class sizes. The ratio of students to teachers in Korea in 1995 was the highest in the OECD countries for both primary and secondary schools.[86]

Public expenditures on education in Korea have been supplemented by a high level of private spending reflecting the important role of private schools and universities.[87] In 1994, such spending accounted for 2.5% of GDP, the highest in the OECD countries. Combining private and public expenditures, Korea's spending on education is near OECD norms, given the country's level of development: expenditure per student relative to GDP per capita in 1994 was almost identical to the OECD average. This does not include spending on private tutoring. Such expenditures, which accounted for an additional 2~7% of GDP in Korea in 1995, played a significant role in Korea's successful results in education.

Despite the favourable performance on international tests, there is concern about the quality of education in Korea. In particular, a presidential commission in 1995 noted that the emphasis on *rote* teaming is poorly-suited to a globalized economy that will require creativity and individual initiative. The current system tends to focus narrowly on preparing students for the all-important university entrance exams. A second concern is the absence of life-long educational opportunities for people who have finished their formal schooling.

Therefore, the principles for educational reform proposed by the presidential commission should be put into practice. Increased emphasis on lifelong learning and curricula that focus less on entrance examinations and more on creativity would be beneficial.

Once again, creative personnel should be emphasized as be one of the most important driving forces towards knowledge-based economy. A lifetime education system should be secured for this purpose through the introduction of various measures such as education accounts. In the public sector, competition should be put into force in the management of public job training centers. In addition, entry barriers to universities or colleges should be eased to enhance competition among educational institutions and various policy measures should be made for the improvement in their capital structures.

3. A NEW INDUSTRIAL POLICY

A. Introduction

In retrospect, the current economic crisis was, to some extent, the result of inadequacies of the existing industrial structure. While it is true that the current crisis directly stemmed from the financial sector, the banks were enfeebled by too many non-performing loans to a weak corporate sector. The corporate sector in turn was weak because there were too many companies in industries where they were not competitive.

The focus of on-going overall restructuring of economies should be on the strengthening Korean industries so as to enable companies to regain competitive edge and resume growth while maintaining an adequate level of employment, which will in turn boost exports and assist in the repayment of debt. In other words, the focus should be on eliminating the critical weaknesses of economy, *i.e.* monopolization of industries, concentration of economic power to large corporations and the collapse of the small and medium-sized industrial base to name but a few.

In order to overcome the current economic crisis and capably response to internal or external changes, emphasis must be placed on heightening the effectiveness of industrial structure, loosening and/or elimination of barriers to entry to ensure the fairness of opportunity and free flow of information, all of which will enable the economy to respond more positively to market opening. Professor Michael E. Porter[88] has pointed out that under such a reorganization of the international order, there are many barriers to remove before moving from a factor-based advantage of the past which relied on abundant manpower and low wages to an innovation-based advantage.

---

[86] At the primary school level, the ratio was 32 in Korea compared to a mean of 19 in the OECD countries. The ratio for secondary schools was 25 in Korea compared to an OECD mean of 15.

[87] In 1992, enrollment in private schools accounted for 27% of students in lower secondary schools, 63% In upper secondary schools and 66% in four-year universities and colleges. Consequently, private spending was particularly important for tertiary education, where it accounted for more than four-fifths of spending, reflecting the major role of private universities.

[88] Michael E, Porter, *The Competitive Advantages of Nations,* The Free Press, New York, 1990.

At the same time, Korea must transform its low-value-added industrial structure into a high-value-added one in order to enhance international competitiveness. Korea now faces the critical task of building or developing a new industrial structure. The fundamental direction towards reform of the industrial structure itself is to achieve a transition of labor and capital-intensive industries into knowledge and technology- intensive industries that create high value-added. At the same time basic materials industries in machine parts should be supported to transform the current industrial structure, which relies on imports from Japan, into a self-sufficient one. This will raise the inflow of foreign reserves and the rate of value-added. To successfully achieve the structural transformation of Korean industry, it needs industrial policies which concentrate on the development of technology.

B. Existing Problems in the Korean Industrial Structure[89]

A country with a high dependence on foreign trade can only be successful when its balance of trade is sustainable and it can maintain a continuous trade surplus by exporting successfully. However, at present Korea is suffering from a weak competitive position in exports due to various factors, both domestic and external. It is important to improve price competitiveness, but what is most important in heightening Korea's international competitiveness is improving product quality through technological innovation.

Korea possesses an industrial structure in which it is impossible to manufacture major products without importing essential components and parts and high-tech production facilities from advanced countries. Such a structure is based on what is called technological dependence on advanced nations, and this is the reason for the failure to resolve structural trade deficits. Self-efforts to design and manufacture essential components & parts and high-tech production facilities are most likely to meet with technology barriers set up by the advanced nations.

The existing problems in the Korean industrial structure can be summarized as follows; There is an imbalance between heavy and light industries. The component ratio of light industries to the total value added in Korea as of 1996 stood at 23.8%, which is much lower than that of Japan (36.0%) or Taiwan (30.9%). In the case of Japan, the component ratio has remained at the 36% level for the past 30 years due to their efforts of sophistication and diversification.

Exports are concentrated around a small number of heavy industry items. The component ratio of heavy industries in exports rose sharply from 56.5% in 1990 to 71.7% in 1996, whereas the component ratio of light industries to the total exports fell from 38.7% to 24.3% over the same period. In particular, the component ratio of the six major export industries, *i.e.* petrochemicals, steel, machinery, electronics, automobiles and shipbuilding, rose from 45.2% in 1985 to 55.0% in 1995. Reliance on the five major export items, *i.e.* semiconductors, steel, petrochemicals, electronic appliances and automobiles almost doubled from 20.5% in 1980 to 40.7% in 1995, while their component ratio declined from 38.6% to 29.8% over the same period.

These major export items are capital-intensive or assembled products whose export volume and price are susceptible to changes in overseas supply and the business environment. The result is increased instability in the export structure. In other words, a jolt in international markets will have large side-effects for the country's macro- economy.

The desirable counter-measures are expected to develop strategic export items which have stable markets and to diversify export items and structure. Excessive reliance on trade is a problem but excessive reliance on a few items is an even greater problem. For example, Japan has been able to maintain the component ratio of its light industries in the 30% range through sophistication and diversification efforts. In the case of Taiwan, export of light industry items remains active and exports of heavy industry items have been diversified and centered around machinery items, resulting in a relative high degree of export stability.

The relative under-development of capital industries, *i.e.,* intermediate products such as parts and materials, machinery etc. has caused imports to rise in line with expanded production and investment. About 17% of intermediate products required by the manufacturing sector is currently imported (6% from Japan). Imports of US$30 million are required to generate US$100 million in exports (the comparative figure is about US 10 million for Japan). Due to such dependence in trade structure, a large portion of

[89] This section is the summary of the author's paper and book listed as follows: Yang-Taek Lim, "An Analysis of Korean Industrial Structure", Korea Economic Association, February 1985. Yang-Taek Lim, *A Study on the Development Direction of the Korean Capital Industry,* the Korean Chamber Commerce and Industry, June 1997.

profits generated from exports are lost to overseas suppliers. The export profitability of the manufacturing sector has naturally declined.

Accordingly, the industrial competitiveness of capital industries which form the industrial foundation must be strengthened. Korea's industrial structure, however, was not developed on the foundation of basic technologies and parts industries. As a result, the foundation industries are relatively weak compared to final product industries, resulting in an inverted pyramid structure.

The industrialization of final product industries being inevitable, reliance on external sources for parts and materials, particularly Japan, has resulted in increasing dependence on imports. In the early 1990s, the trade deficit with Japan for parts and materials has constantly exceeded the overall deficit by US$1~3 billion. In contrast, Japan has continued to maintain a current account surplus despite the contraction of domestic demand and strong Yen. This is exactly the opposite case of Korea.

Unlike other items, the component ratio of machinery in Japanese exports rose from 13.9% to 24.2% during the 1980's. This points out the fact that the demand for machinery in world markets has become quite stable. Machinery is a typical capital industry and requires basic technologies and parts competitiveness along with long-term investments and accumulation of know-how.

A recent report by the Nomura Economic Research Institute *The Revival of Japanese Companies' International Competitiveness* shows that capital industries maintain a high level of international competitiveness despite fluctuations in exchange rate and economic activity. For example, exports of tooling machinery actually grew in 1995 despite the record strength of the Yen against the Dollar. It is evident that to enhance the present industrial structure centered around assembly industries which are reliant on imports, the internalization of core parts and materials, which will bring about both import replacement and export growth effects, must be actively pursued.

The Korean industry is mostly made up of low-value-added assembly industries due to inferior technological level. In terms of industrial development, its industry is limited to simple assembly or those which utilize widespread technologies. Technology and information-intensive industries still remain at levels which require imports or import replacement.

While the value-added coefficient of exports has risen steadily from 0.618 in 1980 to 0.72 in 1993, it still lags far behind advanced nations (Japan's coefficient approached 0.9 in 1990). Moreover, while the coefficient of light industries is 0.76, that of heavy industries remains at a relatively low 0.69. It is estimated that the technology level of Korean industries is generally 5 years behind those of advanced nations.

Energy-intensive basic industries occupy a sizable component ratio of 38% within the entire manufacturing sector. About 70% of the energy utilized by the sector is utilized by such industries as steel, petrochemicals and cement. Even within identical industries, the use of energy is much more inefficient than in advanced countries. [90]

Therefore, the focus of the industrial structure must be shifted from large, energy-intensive industries to light, environment-friendly, energy-saving industries. For example, Japan transformed the core of its industrial structure to energy- saving assembly industries after suffering from the two oil crises.

C. Learning from the Japanese Experience

Korea must solidify its industrial structure by remedying its structural weaknesses. In this connection, Korea can learn the following lessons from the example of Japan;

First, Japan has achieved an active growth based on leading industries. After World War II, light industries centered around textile industries led industrial growth and petrochemicals also played a leading

[90] A look at the strengthening energy-saving policies of advanced countries shows that the US, Japan and European countries have, after the signing of the December 1997 agreement in Kyoto, intensified their technological development goals in line with the trend of using energy more efficiently, reducing the greenhouse effect and increasing environment-related government budgets. More specifically, goals have been set for all sectors including all industries ranging from heavy industries to home appliances, transportation and households. As a result, while the energy consumption and CO_2 production of the OECD stands at 57.4% and 54.6% of the world's total (for 18.1% of the total population), its level of energy-efficiency was three times higher than that of non-OECD countries (1994). With the recent conclusion of the discussions on climate change (effective March 1994) and the accompanying agreement (December 1997), there has been a trend towards the strengthening of technology related to the reduction of energy consumption and energy-related technologies in general.

role. Thereafter, steel and shipbuilding were the leading industries in the 1970s, electronics and automobiles played the role in the 1980s, and semiconductors and software industries have emerged in the 1990s.

Second, Japan was a successful in coordinating technological development and promoting SMEs. Industrial development has been helped along by the import of advanced technology, which was used not just for the transfer of technology but also for adaptation and application to existing industries. The application of electronics technology for the computerization of the industries is a prime example of such application. The development of SMEs also contributed greatly to cost reductions for larger companies and they also acted as shock absorbers in time of domestic and external economic shocks.

Third, Japanese enterprises kept up R&D investment even in times of recession, which in turn was a major factor in the recovery of competitiveness. They have maintained their comparative advantage in global markets through technology and information-intensive investments and products.

Fourth, after World War II, Japan conquered overseas market by volume business, whose goal was to sell 'good things cheaper' through the achievement of economies of scale. The information-telecommunication revolution, however, has made economies of speed rather than economies of scale the determinant factor of comparative advantage. That is, the ideal corporate structure in the age of information has been decidedly different from that of large Japanese companies of the past. In information industries, companies which lack the flexibility to respond fall behind. An optimal corporate size must be maintained while financial structure is constantly strengthened.

Japan is presently concentrating its efforts on expanding and establishing an information infrastructure as one of the means of overcoming the extended recession. In 1995, the information and telecommunication industries, grew by 13.5%, and this growth in turn fuelled growth in other industries including a sharp rise in PC-related literature and rises in the production quantity of semiconductor and communication equipment. Japanese companies have also utilized CALS (Computer-aided Acquisition and Logistics Support) to effectively manage such business aspects as production, process, sales and inventory, while information networks have enhanced the productivity of white-collar laborers.

Fifth, throughout its restructuring period, Japan has seen a rise in intra-industry trade rather than inter-industry trade. The increase in such trade is attributable to the two kinds of specialization, *i.e.* process specialization and product differentiation. In the electronics industry for example, important parts requiring a high level of technology are produced domestically while other parts are imported from NIEs. Likewise, cheap and mass- produced products are thus replaced with imports while high value-added items or special products are made at home.

Sixth, Japanese companies undertook active overseas investment in order to avoid external trade friction and counter the internal effects of rising costs and the stronger Yen. As a result, trade between offshore subsidiaries and their parent companies in Japan or intra-group trade, became active. Investments into advanced countries are aimed at market entry into high-tech industries while investments into developing countries are aimed at increasing demand. In this manner, the composition of Japan's trade shifted from the inter-industry trade of the past to intra-industry trade and intra-group trade.

Another point worth noting is that the direction of FDIs by Japan has shifted from vertical integration based on aid and supply of parts to horizontal integration between products with a corresponding rise in the incidence of M&As. Under vertical integration, simple and labor-intensive processes were deferred to developing countries with only the complicated and technology-intensive processes being undertaken in Japan, the two being combined to eventually put out a final product. In contrast, under horizontal integration, an entire product is manufactured overseas and cooperation is more mutual. By technological level, high-tech products are generally produced in Japan, while products requiring intermediate levels of technology are produced abroad. By item, high value-added and high-quality products are made in Japan, while generic products are made offshore. In this manner, sophistication of industrial output can be achieved and responsiveness to local demand can be heightened.

FDIs into advanced countries are shifting from investments to active M&As for the purpose of avoiding trade barriers. During the first half of 1996, there were 67 cases of M&As in the US, which represented over 90% of all M&A cases. They generally took place in the form of acquisition or equity participation and the average equity injection was greater than the global average. By industry, M&As involving the internet and non-memory semiconductor firms occurred most frequently. Even in the Asian region, cases of M&As have become more frequent, led by equity participation or assignment to third parties of automobile parts manufacturers.

D. A New Industrial Structure to Emerge

High-technology industries have grown rapidly in Korea in recent years. In the manufacturing sector, their share of output rose from 18 to 30% between 1990 and 1995, while their share of employment increased from 14 to 24%.[91]

Technology from abroad has played an important role in Korea's rapid growth. The most important sources have been the technology embodied in imports of capital goods and licensing arrangements. Following the liberalization of licensing arrangements in 1978)[92], royalty payments rose from an annual average of less than US$100 million to US$1 billion by 1990 and to almost US$2 billion by 1995.[93] In addition, Korean businesses have participated in joint ventures with multinational companies and acquired foreign firms to gain access to technology.[94] In contrast, the inflow of foreign direct investment, a major source of technology for many countries, has been very low in Korea, reflecting high barriers in the past.

Since 1980, due to the rise of domestic costs, developed countries have occupied a larger share of Korea's business. In light of the conventional technology sector, the catch-up phenomenon has been accelerated, in such developing countries as China, and other ASEAN countries. Also, the Korean economy is basically pegged to the Yen with the Korean economy's structure being similar to that of Japan and being many products competing with each other.

Many problems of the Korean economy have exposed. It is lack of elasticity to environmental changes and a high rate of dependence on imports in major mechanic parts that has hampered the generation of value-added. More developed countries seek to organize frontier industries, so the Asian economies are stressing international division of labor in the industrial sector. Korea must rearrange its strategy of industrial structure to adapt quickly to globalization of the world economy.

Once restructuring is completed, a new industrial structure needs to emerge based on new practices and new businesses. Of course, some new practices are now being adopted and implemented in the course of restructuring. For example, the accounting system is being revised to conform with international standards and corporate governance and accountability are taking on much greater importance in the Korean business culture. In addition, the financial sector is being restructured to foster stronger, more independent institutions which are better able to analyze risk and allocate credit in a more efficient manner. Still, more needs to be done. Businesses need to become more flexible and adaptable, perhaps by more actively utilizing processes such as out sourcing or strategic networking.

At the same time, Korea's industrial composition must change. Looking at the larger picture, the new industrial structure must evolve around new and future- oriented business areas. Given Korea's scant resources, it is essential that the industrial structure move away from traditional heavy industries and toward knowledge-intensive industries that produce higher value-added. Centering the new industrial structure around high-tech industries such as semiconductors and information technologies should help boost Korea into the ranks of advanced economies and ensure that the Korean economy maintains a competitive edge in the constantly changing world economy.

In a similar vein, Korea needs to promote the other main types of knowledge- intensive industries such as engineering, design and other kinds of service industries. In many ways, this has been one of the biggest weaknesses of the Korean economy so far and is a sector which holds great potential for Korea. Enhancing Korea's proficiency in these areas will help firms be more productive and close the gap with the world market.

Of course, this kind of new, ideal industrial structure will not simply emerge overnight. Developing such a structure will be a long and complicated process which must be in line with short-term imperatives.

---

[91] The government defines high-tech industries as electronics, information, advanced machinery, chemical, aircraft and advanced automobiles.

[92] The licensing system was liberalized by abolishing the requirement for prior government approval and replacing it with a reporting system. The Korean government can still block licensing agreements, however, since it could refuse to accept the report. For example. the government had blocked *Samsung's* entry into the car market by refusing for two years to accept its technology licensing agreement with a Japanese company. See Kim and Seong (1997), "Science and Technology: Public Policy and Private Strategy", in *The Korean Economy* 1945~1995, edited by Cha, Kim and Perkins, Korea Development Institute.

[93] The major sources of technology have been the United States, which has accounted for about half of royalty payments and Japan, which received another third. By industry, the major purchasers of technology have been electronics, accounting for almost half, followed by machinery and chemicals.

[94] For example, *Hyundai* acquired AT&T's G15 micro-electronics division and *Samsung* purchased AST Research.

Therefore, industrial restructuring should be pursued firmly, but gradually, trying to ensure that the gains are applied and build upon each other. For example, better design, engineering and technology can be combined and applied to existing industries to produce newer, more advanced products with higher value-added. Only in this way will Korean industries be able to keep ahead of late comers to economic development such as China or other Southeast Asian countries maintaining their competitive edge.

E. Strengthening the Industrial Structure

1) The Previous Industrial Policy

Until the early 1980s, trade and industrial policy in Korea was designed to achieve pre-designated export targets set by the consecutive Five-Year Development Plans. The quantitative export targets were scheduled on the basis of orthodox comparative advantage. As some incentives, such as policy loans, which are not classified into the category of export incentives, actually have an indirect subsidy effect on exports activities, it is necessary to fully take into accounts both direct and indirect subsidy effects in estimating subsidy magnitude. The exports incentive measures comprise tariff reductions and exemptions, quantitative import restrictions; export-import link system; ex-factory price controls; tax exemptions and reductions; and a preferential credit scheme. The main policy instruments deployed for promoting import substituting activities are quantitative import restrictions and tariffs on imports.

The priorities of trade and industrial policy of Korea may be divided into three different stages over the period 1965~1994. From 1965 to 1974, there was a minor trade bias for exports aimed at protecting or subsidizing the export industries. As the government launched the promotion of heavy and chemical industries for the purpose upgrading the industrial structure, the industry bias for exports increased significantly for the heavy and chemical industries during the period 1975~1984. This industry bias culminated over between 1975~1979 to accelerate the capital formation for the developments of heavy and chemical industries, to increase the value-added content of the manufacturing sector and to increase defense capability by developing the machinery industry. Although the government adopted the 'Comprehensive Programme for Economic Stabilization' in 1979, this bias was maintained until 1984 in order to achieve a cornerstone for the development of heavy and chemical industries.

The overall policy since 1985 has been characterized by the shift towards liberalization. One good example is the removal of restrictions on entry to the petrochemical industries in the mid-1980s, in comparison with the entry restrictions placed on the machinery industries in the late 1970s. Korea has also joined Article 8 of IMF in 1988 and the Article 11 of the GATT in 1989 implying that its readiness to lift the foreign exchange controls, and trade restrictions, which has fully liberalized in 1999. Korea has maintained a positive stance of promoting multilateral trade as well as deep integration movements in the 1990s. As a member of the WTO (World Trade Organization) and the OECD, Korea has been trying to its her market liberalization programme and competition policy with the industrialized countries.

2) The Weaknesses of Korean Industrial Structure

The Korean economy under the IMF program has been showing signs of recovery towards the end of 1998. The complete recovery of the Korean economy, however, is possible only if the weaknesses of Korean industries are overcome fundamentally. The problems or weaknesses can be identified as follows;

First, Korea has developed a very rigid industrial structure centering around a handful of top-notch export items and a mass production system which puts emphasis on large-scale investment. Industries such as steel and petrochemicals are among the examples. Naturally, it became impossible for these industries to flexibly respond to changes in the demand and supply situations of the international markets.

Second, an import-inducing structure has become deeply rooted. With shortages of endowed resources and the underdevelopment of capital goods industries like general machinery, an increase in exports of final goods often brings about a larger increase in imports of capital goods from Japan.

Third, price or cost competitiveness of production factors such as capital, land and labor has weakened drastically since the end of 1980s. Rising wage rates, high interest rates and rent hindered the Korean industrial structure from transforming into a more efficient and higher value-added one.

Fourth, there has been a widening disparity between the manufacturing sector and the service sector. These two sectors could not develop a harmonious relationship in which advances in one sector complements and leads the other's development. For example, certain parts of the manufacturing sector were approaching world class levels, while many sub-areas in the service sector possessed only second class competitiveness. Also, the production-led effects on the service industry stemming from the development of the manufacturing industry are very low.

Lastly, light industries, which were conventionally the powerhouse of the Korean economy in the 1960s and 1970s have deteriorated considerably. The industrial foundation of light industries has been weakened by the industrial policies focused on heavy or chemical industries and several high tech industries such as semiconductors. The SMEs mostly in the light industries did not have the opportunities to grow and foster their core competencies as they did in the past.

3) The Focus of New Industrial Policy

New industrial policy should focus on overcoming the weaknesses of the domestic industrial structure and on nurturing the growth of a knowledge-based economy. Primarily in the short run, emphasis should be put on strengthening the currently weak industrial structure.

First, self-managed restructuring of industries should be pursued. For this, an environment where industries can restructure themselves through activities such as M&As should be fostered. Also, we should pursue the higher value-added of the domestic basic industries through the implementation of advanced technologies into traditional industries should be pursued.

Second, the industries of parts and intermediate capital goods need to be further developed. For this, more support in terms of human resources and technologies to SMEs should be provided.

Thirdly, the connection between manufacturing and service firms should be strengthened. For example, the function and the competitiveness of service industries such as finance, advertising, transportation and communications and strengthen the support from these sectors toward the manufacturing sector should be enhanced.

In the medium and long run, industrial policies which will help to establish a mature knowledge-based economy should be pursued.

First, the basis of knowledge within the economy has to be strengthened. For this, the distribution system of flexible technological innovations and knowledge must be improved. An example is the 'technology park' which combines industry and academia. The innovation of educational system and the construction of information highways are other examples.

Second, the related administrative systems of the government have to be innovative. And an increase of the budgetary support of government agencies for education and enhancement of science and technology need to be strengthened. This will help to build a solid intellectual infrastructure for the production, capital accumulation and use of knowledge.

Thirdly, in order to promote the commercialization of new technologies, stronger measures are needed to guarantee the property rights. More active support for venture capital firms is another condition toward this end. The government has adopted a wide range of policies to promote SMEs (defined as firms with fewer than 300 workers) in order to counterbalance the large role of the *chaebols*.

4) The Direction of Industrial Structuring

Based on the previous discussion, the basic direction of Korea's industrial restructuring recommended should be emphasized on fostering qualitative sophistication of industries. In details, it includes the qualitative export sophistication of leading industries, establishment of a foundation for the development of high-tech industries, promotion of the use of information and software and the fostering technology, information- intensive SMEs and re-activation of traditional industries as discussed further.

First, in export-oriented central businesses, preparing the qualitative export sophistication of leading industries, the stress should not be put on quantitative expansion of ordinary goods but on the quality to become world-class. That is to say, through innovation of productive technology and development of new products which suit consumers' tastes, initiative must be taken in the world-market.

Second, it is recommended to establish a foundation for the development of high- tech industries. The Korean industry is now facing a transformation period and it is now that promotion of quality internally and globalization externally should be sought.

For this end, it is necessary for the Korean industry to be restructured in the directions as follows:

First, strategic industries should be proficient at accommodating cycles. As strong export-driven policy was applied in the 1970s, active technology- driven policy must be promoted now in the form of direct intervention methods such as policies nurturing specific industries and indirect support policies involving for support for R&D projects and expansion of infrastructure. The Korean industry is familiar to boom, so it is naturally very vulnerable to depression.

Second, Strategic industries should have a powerful ability for accommodating of internal-external disturbance factors. The semiconductor, petrochemical and steel- industries are representative products which compete with Japan in foreign markets. As it is generally known, recently supply of these three items are in excess world- wide and prices have fallen. In particular, semiconductor prices have fallen rapidly. The Korean economy is more vulnerable to international market structure compared with Japan. Korea now has to abolish its industrial structural based on economies of scale and adopt a high value-added one based on economies of efficiency.

Third, it is the promotion of the use of information and software. The necessary information service functions such as database buildup and knowledge networks can affect international competitiveness and thus industries needs to keep up with up-to-date information and software.

Lastly, the fostering of technology and information-Intensive SMEs and re-activation of Traditional Industries need to be encouraged. Venture SMEs have more significant employment creation effects and more quickly adapt to changes in foreign demand than big businesses do.

Nowadays conventional and light industries are considered 'sunset industries'. Some of these industries, however, which are expected to produce high value- added, should be fostered. A good example is high value-added fiber and clothing products in Italy and Germany.

4. Complementary Relationship between Big Assembly Enterprises and Parts Manufacturing SMEs

<Table VIII-1> shows an international comparison of the relation between big assembly enterprises and parts manufacturing SMEs. In case of Japan, assembly enterprises intensely invest in R&D in the area of basic parts or materials but, rely on SMEs in other technical areas. The assembly enterprises (mother companies) are minority shareholders of the parts enterprises (sub-contractor companies). Sub-contractor companies obtain technologies suitable for its usage, and contribute to not only consistent quality innovation and stable market but also a higher quality product or processing technology. Such serialization in Japan has contributed to the growth of sub-contractor enterprises and international competitiveness, distinguished from the case of Korea.

<Table VIII-1> International Comparison between Large Assembly Enterprises and Parts Producing SMEs

	Relationship between Large Enterprises and SMEs
Korea	• Korean large enterprises do not have good relationship with local part producing SMEs, rather rely on imports from Japan. • As a result, there is an instability of such SMEs in markets and the competitiveness of large assembly enterprises is weakened accordingly.
Japan	• SMEs are independent from large enterprises and supply parts to them. • Large assembly enterprises support SMEs' development of technology, labor and funds as minority shareholders. • As a result, such SMEs of parts can secure development of goods and stability in markets
US	• Large assembly enterprises such are self-reliant for their parts • As a result, efficiency is lowered on the grounds that the scale of large enterprises becomes excessive and the competitiveness of SMEs are weakened.

Source: Yang-Taek Lim, *The People Perish Where There Is No Vision,* Seoul: Mail Economic Daily Press, September 1995, p. 415.

In the case of Japan, specialization of technology has been pursued and large assembly enterprises and parts producing SMEs maintain complementary relationships according to technological characteristics. Larger companies invest heavily in R&D for main parts and components, but rely on SMEs for peripheral technologies. They are also often the assemblers of products and often participate in the equity of SMEs who are sub-contractors for parts and components and also support them in terms of technology development, personnel and financing. The sub-contracting SMEs obtain information on processes and technology from the parent company or sometimes send technicians for in-house training. As a result, SME sub-contractors are able to achieve steady improvements in quality and secure a stable buyer while attaining optimal levels of expertise or production technology. Such arrangements have strengthened the horizontal relationship between the parent and sub-contractor and contributed to the heightening the competitiveness of Japan in international markets.

One of the main factors in the strength of Taiwanese economy is that the overall economy has maintained flexibility and competitiveness because of the well-developed SMEs. Government policy can also be flexible since economic power is not concentrated and the SMEs serve as a shock absorber when economic activity is slow or there is an external shock.

Taiwan's promotion of venture capital industries is also a characteristic of its policy. Guidelines for the management of venture capital businesses were already established in 1983 and venture capital companies were established in the early of 1984 with the foundation of the first private venture capital firm. A 20% of tax break was extended for companies' equity participation in such firms, and further breaks were provided by staggering income tax rates. The industrial policy of Taiwan is thus noticeably different from that of Korea, and has produced positive results based on stronger capability to respond to the Southeast Asian crisis. Therefore, the Taiwanese experience is valuable indeed in applying 'Asian Values' to economic development.

In the case of Korea, one of the obstacles to the development of SMEs is the concentration of production elements and market shares by a few *chaebols*. In other words, the development of *chaebols* and the decline of SMEs are two sides of the same coin. Excessive borrowings by the larger business group through intra-group cross-debt guarantees substantially reduce available funds for SMEs and reduce the motivation appetite for investment. Moreover, unfair trade practices by *chaebols* often cause SMEs with superior technology and management capabilities to lose ground in the market. Thus, the Korean government must implement stronger regulations against unfair trade practices and cross-debt guarantees while expanding support for SMEs from a policy standpoint.

The Korean government has taken measures to promote the emergence of technology-based firms. Since 1986, thirty venture capital firms, all jointly- invested by the state and the private sector, have been created. There are numerous special financing programmes that provide funds at below-market interest rates.[95] In addition, nationwide commercial banks have been required to allocate 35% of their total loans to SMEs, while the guidelines for such lending were set at 80% in the case of regional banks. The government provides tax incentives to encourage investment and restructuring by SMEs. Some lines of business have been reserved exclusively for SMEs. At the end of 1994, large companies and their affiliates were prohibited from 237 areas. In general, though, these policies have tended to make SMEs dependent on government support while protecting them from competition.

A look at the SME Promotion Act enacted in 1975 reveals that the goal of the policy is to effectively stimulate specialization and division of the production process but there is an urgent need to provide a cooperative environment between larger companies and SMEs, policies to encourage the fairness in their relationships, including prohibition of delayed payment terms. Article 5 of the Act provides for mandatory production of certain items by sub-contractors for industries to be considered as being vital for the promotion of SMEs and strengthening the international competitiveness and industrial structure of the country. There are also provisions which allow the establishment of joint business plans by the parent and sub-contractor and support for their implementations.

While the scope of industries and items falling under this article is very wide, *de facto* joint business plans are generally limited to fix the quantity to be supplied with virtually non-existent of tie-ups. Moreover, the designation of items for sub-contracting have been centered around those which already exhibit a high rate of sub-contracting. Therefore, the integration between large companies and SMEs in Korea have had a minimal effect on the alleviation of reliance on foreign technology in the development of the parts industry by technological development and innovation. Korea's future policy in this regard should be re-directed toward support for technological development through cooperation.

According to the promotion of systematization of SMEs, mother companies can settle the range of commodities belonging to the type of business and impose duties to produce contractual production of the item designated, although the item of systemization and designation accomplishes mass production.

[95] These programmes include Banks' Investment Fund, Equipment Financing Fund, Foreign Currency Loan, Small and Medium Industry Fund for Equipment, Main Equipment Fund and Lease Fund (Ministry of Finance and Economy, *Economic Bulletin*, May 1996).

Likewise, Korean policy of promoting systematization has to be changed for the development of the component industry and technical advancement. For this end, institutional devices like the following have to be established;

First, items with a high dependency on imports should be designated for import substitution of the mother company using the same production process. On the blueprint for common business, capacity, quality and technical situation of the pertinent product must be considered.

Second, to promote the common business, the mother company should prepare funds for meeting the facilities and operating fund. By setting up a systematic loan system focused on systematization, financial support has to be magnified for the development of new products and techniques. This financial support should be accomplished over the long-term and its conditions should be also simplified.

Third, stable funds for contractual dealings should be established as a means to support SMEs. The funds should be used to supply a change in equipment, the rationalization of management, and the supply of operating funds. The systematic reorganization fund for SMEs required a special fund for the effective magnification of contractual dealings.

5. TOWARD A HIGHLY-EFFICIENT BUSINESS ORGANIZATION AND PERFORMANCE-BASED MANAGEMENT

A flexible and small organization is better to respond to a new business environment than a rigid and large one. A large corporation with rigid organization structure tends to be bureaucratic and vulnerable to mis-communication and mis-judgement on business opportunity. Thus, facing a rapidly changing environment, a business organization ought to be simplified, divided, and loosely interconnected by a network.

A network organization is a structure that endows unit organizations with independent authority. In other words, it means establishing a responsible management system and constructing a vital and active network among small-size unit organizations. In order to make such a successful network organization, three core practices are needed, which are summarized as follows;

First, an organization should develop a system which guarantees and enhances the independence of unit organizations. In this system, with an independent budget system, each unit organization has independent business authority and practices autonomous management. The firm must evaluate each unit's performance and further determine its destiny - whether to develop it or eliminate it.

Second, it is naturally necessary to reduce headquarters' authority. Instead of directly controlling each unit's practices, the headquarters ought to support and coordinate its activities. The headquarters should focus on overall strategic planning and evaluating functions as well.

Third, a firm should be able to construct an outside network to respond to a rapidly changing environment. Using outsiders of core competencies, a firm can enhance its competitiveness.[96]

In order to improve a firm's overall productivity and flexibility of employment, human resource management using various forms of employment should prevail more than before. A 'diverse employment form system' uses regular and non-regular workers. By doing so, a firm can develop an optimal human resource portfolio. A sensible human resource management system, however, must be accompanied by packages of various management practices that match each employment form. A 'diverse employment form system' has three core practices as follows:

First, a firm may classify all jobs into a 'core' group and a 'peripheral' group by criteria composed of revenue contribution. IBM Korea classifies regular and non- regular workers where the latter consists of 'temporary' workers who perform temporary jobs in shorter periods of time (3~11 months) and 'contracting' workers who make labor contracts via agencies and work only for a period specified in the contract.

Second, a firm must arrange a human resource system not only for the regular workers but also for the non-regular workers. This system should comprise of a recruitment timing, a reward system, and a recall program.

---

[96] In Korea, strategic alliances are being made as the first stage of networking. For example, *LG Telecom,* by using handsets and beepers supplied by *Appeal Telecom,* has been able to increase the number of subscriptions. Meanwhile, as a sole supplier to *LG Telecom, Appeal Telecom* could triple its turnover. Another example is the cooperation between *Dong-A Pharmaceuticals* and *Yuhan* for developing a new type of pharmaceuticals.

Third, a firm should eventually establish human resource infrastructures such as a HRDB (Human Resource Data Base) and a HRIS (Human Resource Information System). Using these Human resource infrastructures, a firm can link necessary human resources to available positions in the most effective way.

The current management environment of Korea is rapidly changing, restructuring thus toward an efficient business organization in this manner is much more needed than ever. After the IMF era began, the volume-focused and growth-driven management revealed its limit while performance-based management which puts top priority on a firm's revenue and profit has become more important in Korea.

Also, it has become increasingly important to reward every employee according to ability and performance. In a recession, or in a crisis, a firm should pursue strategies for enhancing efficiency and reducing cost in order to survive. This performance- based management should include various sub-categories such as ability-based reward system, horizontal organization network organization, and diverse employment form.

Many firms try to promote individual's and organizational competitiveness by introducing a wage system that properly rewards capable and hard working employees. Thus, an ability-based reward system such as an 'Annual Salary System' which determines an employee's rewards by appraising the individual's ability and performance is proliferating. An ability-based reward system has three core practices.

First, a firm should set up an objective criteria. An employee's salary should be determined by a well-specified job analysis and evaluation system.

Second, it is necessary to set up and disseminate an objective and fair appraisal system. A firm needs to educate its personnel to objectively evaluate the ability and performance of junior employees. The education should help the members of an organization to understand that the evaluation system is a good means to enhance competitiveness of each individual.

Third, it is important to expand the ability-based reward system step-wise. For example, the new system should be applied to the upper & middle class of a hierarchy or to special staff first.

It is possible to implement speedy decision making, efficient performance, effective communication, and a cooperative culture by cutting down the decision making line and eliminating organizational boundaries. To establish a horizontal organization, first of all, the number of decision-making positions should be cut down and effective empowerment should be firmly implemented. This could be accomplished by clearly defining both job characteristics and competency qualifications.

At the same time, a firm should devise mechanisms which will help prevent employees from losing their motivation. An ability-based reward system is another necessary condition. A business organization must reward its employees based on ability and performance appraisal not on seniority standards. Recently, many Korean big businesses have tried to simplify their internal organizations by improving the hierarchical system. These changes, however, still remain in the incipient stage.

6. A Flexible Labor Market

Since the economic crisis at the end of 1997, the Korean labour market has faced perhaps its most difficult challenge ever Korean firms struggling to survive are implementing drastic measures to reduce labour costs by adjusting both the price and volume of labour. Nominal wages are being cut by as much as 10 to 20%, reflecting sharp reductions in bonus payments. Even so, the number of unemployed has almost tripled from about half a million in the third quarter of 1997 to 1.4 million in April 1998, primarily as a result of bankruptcies and the difficulty of new graduates in finding jobs. Consequently, the unemployment rate has risen from around 2 to 6.7%, even prior to the layoffs that are under consideration by large firms.

Ensuring sufficient labour market flexibility is essential in the short run, as the highly-indebted corporate sector restructures in the wake of the crisis, and in the longer term, as changes in corporate governance practices and financial sector reform increase the emphasis on creating value for shareholders. One important element is to maintain the flexibility of wages. The large nominal wage cuts announced by troubled firms during the past few months suggests a high degree of social cohesiveness, with workers and management prepared to make sacrifices to limit declines in employment. However, wage flexibility needs to be accompanied by greater freedom for firms to shed surplus employees. In this regard, the impact of the new layoff provisions passed at the end of February 1998 is still uncertain, given the required 60-day notification period.[97]

While the new layoff provisions are a step in the right direction, Korea's employment protection legislation still appears to be more stringent in some respects than in other OECO countries. In particular, the newly-added preconditions for layoffs that have been imposed on management, including the 60-day advance notification to labour unions and proof of their efforts to avoid dismissals, resemble provisions in high-protection countries, such as Portugal. Spain and Austria.

Moreover, the requirement that collective dismissals be reported to the Ministry of Labour corresponds to regulations found in many European countries. The commitment by the Ministry to 'strictly control reckless layoffs' suggests that this could act as a constraint on the freedom of firms to shed surplus workers. It is important that the new layoff provisions be implemented in a way that allows firms a sufficient scope to reduce their work forces. Meanwhile, the severance pay regulation remains extremely generous, reflecting its origin as a substitute for both pensions and unemployment insurance. However, as the social welfare system develops, there would appear to be room to ease the legal severance pay requirements.

To address the social costs of the economic crisis, a number of changes in the unemployment insurance system have been announced in recent months, including expanded firm coverage, relaxed worker eligibility conditions and extended benefit periods.

First, the coverage, which was initially limited to firms with 30 or more employees, was extended to firms with at least 10 employees in February 1998 and to those with at least five employees beginning in July 1998. At that point, the scheme will cover more than two-thirds of employees. The government is to extend coverage to temporary and part-time workers during the latter half of 1998 and to all employees, regardless of company size, during 1999.

Second, the minimum contribution period needed to qualify for benefits was temporarily reduced from 12 to 6 months until July 1999.

Third, the minimum duration of benefits was lengthened from 30 to 60 days. These reforms should slightly boost the proportion of the unemployed receiving benefits, which at one-fourth is one of the lowest in the OECD countries.

It is important that the social safety net be expanded to reduce the hardship resulting from the sharp rise in unemployment. The expansion of unemployment insurance is beneficial in this regard. However, other policies are needed for job losers who do not qualify for benefits or who have been cut off after a short period, as well as for former employees of bankrupt firms who have not received severance payments. In particular, the eligibility requirements under the Livelihood Protection Programme, which provides payments to about 3% of the population, could be eased to mitigate poverty. In addition, the payments provided under this programme should be boosted to a subsistence level of income during the next few years. However, in expanding the social safety net, it is important that the generosity of the system does not expand to a point which undermines the incentives to work and save in the longer term.

Several issues related to labour union rights remain under discussion within the Tripartite Commission. Among the most important is whether public servants will be allowed to form proper labour unions

---

[97] Comparatively greater flexibility in allowing layoffs was accompanied by increased rights for labour unions. The reforms introduced in March 1997 and February 1998 addressed a number of the concerns that have been expressed by OECD member governments and the ILO.

First, the March 1997 reform has paved the way for labour union pluralism at the sectoral and national levels. Nevertheless, the KCTU (Korean Council of Trade Union) has not been granted recognition at the national level, mainly because it includes the illegal teachers union (*Chunkyojo*). This problem should be resolved by legislation, which is to be submitted to the National Assembly later in 1997, allowing teachers the right to organize. In contrast, labour union pluralism at the enterprise level, where most bargaining occurs, will only be allowed from 2002. The delay reflects government concerns about conflicts within the labour union movement. In particular, the government is concerned about possible rivalry between FKTU and KCTU affiliated enterprise unions within firms, which could undermine industrial peace. To reduce this risk, the government has proposed establishing "a single bargaining channel" at the enterprise level. The ILO has asked Korea "to speed up the process of legalizing labour union pluralism at the enterprise level" (309th Report of the Committee on Freedom of Association, March 1998). Ideas discussed in labour union circles in Korea include a merger of the FKTU and KCW and a shift of bargaining to the industrial level, which would reduce the importance of enterprise unions.

Second, the 1997 and 1998 reform allowed third-party participation in labour negotiations and granted unions the right to engage in political activities. Third, the requirement that companies establish workplace councils was strengthened and the role of these councils was enlarged. Fourth, lower-level public employees will have the right to form consultative associations beginning in 1999.

endowed with collective bargaining rights. Most other OECD countries have recognised the right of civil servants to organize unions or other types of employee associations, although important restrictions remain as to the nature and scope of bargaining and the right to reach collective agreements.

A second issue is the scope of public services defined as 'essential' and therefore subject to compulsory arbitration in the case of industrial action. Many other OECD countries, though, restrict the right of public service employees to strike without constraining their right to organize.

A third issue is how to organize bargaining once multiple unions are allowed at the company level beginning in 2002. Other issues include the ban on the payment of wages by firms to full-time union officers, a matter left to collective bargaining agreements in other OECD countries, and the law stipulating that dismissed workers may not remain members of a union. In other member countries, unions are allowed to set the qualifications for membership.

7. Liberalization and Deregulation

In the longer term, deregulation is a key to enhancing competition increasing the knowledge base, efficiency and innovative capacity and the growth of sustaining output and employment. In particular, a transparent, rule-based regulatory regime would help attract foreign investors by assuring them of non-discriminatory treatment. Reducing entry barriers, which remain pervasive, should promote job creation. In addition, it is essential to reduce red tapes, which discourages entrepreneurship. Competition should also be increased by removing formal trade barriers and aspects of the domestic regulatory system that limit imports.

Since joining the OECD in December 1996, the Korean government has increased its commitment to reforming economic and administrative regulations. The Economic Regulatory Reform Committee, which is chaired by the Fair Trade Commission, was established in April 1997 to take the lead in this area.

This was followed by a law in August 1997 requiring that new regulations go through a screening process and that existing regulations be reviewed. The Committee has established six general principles for regulatory reform as follows: first, entry barriers in specific business sectors, including those aimed at preventing 'excessive competition', should be removed; second, social regulations in such areas as consumer protection, safety and public health should be made more transparent and based on objective criteria; third, competition should be introduced into monopolistic industries in the public sector; fourth, regulations on price, business location and other commercial practices should be eliminated in principle; fifth, regulations by business associations should be minimized; and sixth, exit barriers need to be reduced. Specific deregulation measures are planned, particularly in telecommunications[98] and the energy sector.[99]

Korea has also agreed to take steps to reduce trade barriers. Most importantly, the abolition of the import diversification programme, which had been planned for the end of 1999, has been accelerated to June of that year. At the end of 1997, twenty five products were removed from the list of items that could not be imported from Japan, with the remaining eighty eight to be liberalized in three steps.

Korea has reduced import barriers over the past two decades. The simple average tariff declined from 24% in 1982 to 10% in 1992 (WTO, 1996). The average, though, has fallen only slightly since then for the two reasons as follows:

First, the tariff cuts that the government agreed to in the UR will be phased in gradually over ten years since Korea claimed developing country status.

Second, quantitative restrictions on sixty seven agricultural products were replaced in 1997 with tariffs, which were very high in most cases.[100]

The nine remaining quotas will be phased out in 2001, with the exception of that on rice. Rice imports, which were allowed for the first time in 1995, were initially set at 1% of domestic consumption, rising to 4% by 2004. The agricultural sector, with average tariffs of almost 20%, is more highly protected than the manufacturing sector, where the average is 7.5%. Although rising imports of wheat, corn and soybeans

---

[98] The approval system for the tariffs on long distance and international telephone calls was changed to a notification system in January 1998. Charges for mobile phones and local telephone service will also be liberalized within three years. Later 1997, entry barriers in the voice resale, internet telephone, and international call-back service markets are to be removed and the new entrants will be allowed to compete with conventional service providers.

[99] The government has decided to abolish standards for entry into the power generation business and to introduce competition into the retail electricity market in 1998. In addition, prices for fuel were liberalized in January 1998.

[100] For example, quantitative restrictions on oranges were replaced by a tariff of 84.3%.

have lowered Korea's rate of self-sufficiency In crops to under 30%, import barriers have resulted in large gaps between the domestic and international prices of many agricultural products. The price of rice, for example, which accounts for about a third of agricultural production in Korea, was almost four times above the world price in 1995, while the ratios for some other products were even higher.

Although tariffs on manufactured goods are relatively low, there are significant non-tariff barriers to imports. Most important is the 'Import Diversification Programme', which was introduced in 1978 to reduce Korea's bilateral trade deficit with Japan by banning the imports of certain products from that country. The number of banned items was reduced from 258 in 1993 to 113 in July 1997 as part of the plan to eliminate the programme by the end of 1999. Nevertheless, it still continues to prohibit imports of major products, such as motor vehicles and televisions. Another problem in the area of trade are healthy and safety regulations that affect imports.

Significant portions of the service sector remained largely insulated from international competition until very recently. In 1997, foreign direct investment in 48 business lines (out of total of 495) was totally or partially restricted. These regulations closed significant portions of the transport, communications, finance, insurance and business service industries to foreign investment (WTO, 1996). Under the GATs (General Agreement on Trade in Services), however, Korea agreed in 1996 to take liberalization measures to encourage trade in eighty service activities.[101]

The degree of competition in Korea has increased since 1980, when the Monopoly Regulation and Fair Trade Act was established. In 1981, 88% of product markets (2,257 items) were classified as concentrated, *i.e.* markets in which the top three firms collectively account for more than half of sales.

By 1994, the number of concentrated markets had fallen to 58%. In terms of output, concentrated markets declined from 74 to 43% over the same period. In 1994, the KFTC (Korean Fair Trade Commission), which is charged with enforcing the Monopoly Regulation and Fair Trade Act was established an independent agency. It was raised to ministerial status in 1996 and enlarged.[102] During 1995 and 1996. the KFTC took almost 2,000 actions, a significant increase from the annual average of around 600 a year between 1981 and 1994. About 60% of the cases were concerned with unfair trade practices, which include predatory pricing, false advertising and refusal to sell. About three-quarters of the cases resulted only in warnings or recommendations for correction, while surcharges were imposed in 73 cases.

The government's leadership role in directing the development of the country has left Korea with a high degree of regulation. Controls on entry and exit, prices and transactions have been pervasive. In total, there are more than 10,000 regulations. While some regulations are based on law, many are enforced through internal rules and administrative guidance, leading to corruption in some cases.

In addition, a wide range of social regulations have been introduced to deal with growing concerns over safety, health and the environment. Although deregulation has received increased attention in recent years, efforts thus far have focused on reducing the burden of regulations on businesses while leaving most entry barriers in place. Of 325 industries, entry barriers remain in 205 according to a survey by the Ministry of Commerce, Industry and Energy. Even where new firms have been allowed, other regulations limit competition. In international telephone calls, for example, two competitors have entered the market, but regulations have limited the variation in their rates to a maximum of 7%.

---

[101] However, significant areas, such as postal, educational, recreational, rail, pipeline, legal, medical and dental services, were excluded from Korea's GATs commitments.

[102] Two new bureaus were created-Consumer Protection and Subcontract Policy-intended to prevent abuse of small firms in their dealings with larger firms.

Chapter IX

TECHNOLOGICAL STRUCTURE OF KOREAN MANUFACTURING SECTOR

It is generally asserted that the acceleration of economic growth in Korea was made possible by a shift in industrialization strategy from import substitution to export promotion in the early sixties and successful execution of this export-oriented strategy thereafter. For the above reasons, developing countries seem to acknowledge the Korean experience as a model to emulate at least in part, if not entirely.

This chapter examines the structural problems of the Korean economy and proposes a revised strategy based on the author's analyses of current structural problems and their causes in the Korean economy; the effects of technological change on economic growth, employment and income distribution; the determinants of international competitiveness; Schumpeter and Schumpeterian hypotheses; the speed of technological diffusion and its determinants; Korean government policy for the introduction of technology at each of the three stages of industrial development *i.e.* labor-intensive, capital-intensive and technology-intensive industrial development stage; the technology transfer model between Japan and Korea; the effects of foreign direct investment on domestic investment, economic growth, balance of payment and technical efficiency; and possible strategic alliances with the United States and Japan for technological development.[103]

1. MACROECONOMIC EFFECTS OF TECHNOLOGICAL CHANGE

A. Economic Growth

The effect of technological change on economic growth can be analyzed under the assumption that technological progress takes the type of Hicksian neutral or non-neutral. In the Hicksian neutral technological progress, the increasing rate of total factor productivity (γ) always contributes positively to economic growth by shifting a given production function upward.

M. Brown (1968)[104] proved that increase of the elasticity of substitution between factors (σ) in Hicksian non-neutral technological progress always increases economic growth rates. Change in capital intensity (δ) or labor intensity ($1-\delta$) in Hicksian non-neutral technological progress, however, affect economic growth positively or negatively depending upon the relative magnitude of change in the rate of capital to labor ($k = K/L$) and the elasticity of substitution between factors (σ).

For the analysis the production function takes the form of pure factor augmenting CES (constant elasticity substitution) production function as shown by equation (IX-1). The conditions: (IX-2)~(IX-4) are the results of M. Brown (1968).

---

[103] This chapter was heavily derived from Yang-Tack Lim, "An Econometric Study of Technological Progress, Innovation, Diffusion, Transfer and their Impacts on International Competitiveness: with respect to the Korean Manufacturing (1972~1990)", Korea Academic Association of Technological Management and Economics, the 8th Academic Conference, January 1996 and "New Technology Development Strategy and Technological Structure of Korean Manufacturing Sector," Hanyang Journal of Economic Studies Vol. 20, No. 1, Seoul: Hanyang Economic Research Institute, Hanyang University, May 1999.

[104] Murray Brown, *On the Theory and Measurement of Technological Change*, Cambridge University Press, 1968.

$$Y = A_0 e^{\gamma t}[\delta(Ke^{\phi t})^{-\rho} + (1-\delta)(Le^{\lambda t})^{-\rho}]^{-\frac{1}{\rho}} \tag{IX-1}$$

$$\frac{\partial MRTSKL}{\partial \sigma} = \frac{\delta}{(1-\delta)}\left(\frac{L}{K}\right)^{1/\sigma}\left(-\frac{1}{\sigma^2}\right)\ln\left(\frac{L}{K}\right) \tag{IX-2}$$

$$= -(MRTS_{KL}) \cdot \ln(L/K) \cdot \frac{1}{\sigma^2} \gtrless 0$$

$$\frac{\partial MRTSKL}{\partial \delta} = \left(\frac{L}{K}\right)^{1/\sigma} \cdot \frac{1}{(1-\delta)^2} > 0 \quad (\because \frac{L}{K} > 0, \quad 0 < \delta < 1) \tag{IX-3}$$

$$\frac{\partial Y}{\partial \delta} = \frac{Y}{K^{\rho}[\delta K^{-\rho} + (1-\delta)L^{-\rho}]} \cdot \left(\frac{\sigma}{\sigma - 1}\right)\left[1 - \left(\frac{\dot{L}/L}{\dot{K}/K}\right)^{\frac{\sigma-1}{\sigma}}\right] \gtrless 0 \tag{IX-4}$$

where

Y = output (measured by value-added)

MRTS = marginal rate of technical substitution between labor (L) and capital (K)

$\sigma \equiv \frac{1}{1+\rho}$ = the elasticity of substitution between the inputs (L and K)

δ = capital intensity

1-δ = labor intensity

ln = natural logarithm

B. Employment

The effect of technological change on employment can be analyzed by making use of equations (IX-5) and (IX-6). From these two equation, we can know that the effect of technological change on demand for labor depends on the relative magnitude of the increase rate of production efficiency of capital (φ) and that of production efficiency of labor (λ) and the elasticity of substitution between factors (σ). That is, only if σ<1 and φ>λ, or σ>1 and φ<λ, technological change increases demand for labor at a faster rate than demand for capital.

$$\ln(L/K) = \sigma \ln\left(\frac{r}{w}\right) - \sigma \ln\left(\frac{\delta}{1-\delta}\right) + \frac{1-\sigma}{\sigma^2} t \cdot (\varphi - \lambda) \tag{IX-5}$$

$$\frac{\partial \ln(L/K)}{\partial t} = \left(\frac{1-\sigma}{\sigma^2}\right) \cdot (\varphi - \lambda) \gtreqless 0 \tag{IX-6}$$

where

r = real rate of return on capital

w = real wage rate

φ = the increasing rate of production efficiency of capital

λ = the increasing rate of production efficiency of labor
t = time

C. Income Distribution

The effect of simultaneous changes in the increase rates (φ, λ) of production efficiency of capital and labor on the relative ratio of factor income (rK/wL) can be examined by equation (IX-7).

$$d\left(\frac{rK}{wL}\right) = \frac{\partial\left(\frac{rK}{wL}\right)}{\partial\phi}d\phi + \frac{\partial\left(\frac{rK}{wL}\right)}{\partial\lambda}d\lambda = t\cdot\left(1-\frac{1}{\sigma}\right)\frac{rK}{wL}\cdot(d\phi - d\lambda) \qquad \text{(IX-7)}$$

Thus, it is evident that change in the relative ratio of factor income (rK/wL) depends on the relative magnitude of the elasticity of substitution between factors (σ) and the increase rate of production efficiency of the two factors (φ, λ).

D. Empirical Analysis

The statistical data of variables to be used for our empirical analysis are shown in <Table IX-1>. The regression results of the estimation of purely factor augmenting CES production function are summarized in <Table IX-2> and <Table IX-3>.

<Table IX-1> The Statistic Data for Analysis

No.	Variables	Data	Sources
1	MGDP	GDP in Manufacturing Sector (Constant Price in 1985)	(a) (b) (c)
2	MEMP	Employment in Manufacturing Sector	(a) (b) (c)
3	MNKS	Net Capital Stock in Manufacturing Sector (Constant Price in 1985)	(d)
4	MKUR	The Rate of Operation in Manufacturing Sector (1985 = 100)	(a) (b) (c)
5	WPI	Wholesale Price Index (1985 = 100)	(a) (b) (c)
6	MWAGE	Average Monthly Wage in Manufacturing Sector	(a) (b) (c)

* (a): Data Base of Korea National Statistics Office
(b): Data Base of Korea Institute of Labor Research
(c): Bank of Korea, *Monthly Statistics,* various issues.
(d): Hakgil Pyo, "The Estimation of Korea's Capital Stock", the annual conference of the Korean Economic Association, 1990.

<Table IX-2> Direct Regression Results of CES Production Function :

$$Y = A_0 e^{\gamma t}[\delta(Ke^{\phi t})^{-\rho} + (1-\delta)(Le^{\lambda t})^{-\rho}]^{-\frac{1}{\rho}}$$

Period			$\ln\frac{Y}{L} = -\sigma\ln(1-\delta) + \sigma\ln\frac{W}{P} + \sigma\gamma D + (1-\sigma)\lambda t$	$\ln\left[\left(\frac{K^\rho}{Y}\right) - (1-\delta)\left(\frac{K^\rho}{Le^{\lambda t}}\right)\right] = \ln\delta - \rho\varphi t$
Entire Period	1973 ~ 1990		1.5003 -0.0766 -0.0487 0.0720 (1.921) (-0.660) (-0.295) (6.828)	8.2535 -0.0128 (16.773) (-4.256)
	for the Structural Change Period	1973 ~ 1987	-0.6996 0.2150 0.1971 0.0434 (-0.671) (1.543) (0.989) (1.568)	-5.4584 0.0002 (-4.037) (0.062)
		<Period I> 1973 ~ 1980	-0.6996 0.2150 0.1971 0.0434 (-0.671) (1.543) (0.989) (1.568)	-6.3941 0.0168 (-8.402) (0.799)
		<Period II> 1981 ~ 1987	13.1643 -1.7793 -0.6190 0.2303 (1.314) (-1.182) (-1.596) (1.616)	7.8058 0.3632 (168.313) (49.987)

- The values in parenthesis are t-values.

Table IX-3> Indirect Regression Results of CES Production Function

Period			$\ln\frac{Y}{L}=-\sigma\ln(1-\delta)+\sigma\ln\frac{w}{p}+\sigma\gamma D+(1-\sigma)\lambda t$						$\ln\left[\left(\frac{K^{\rho}}{Y}\right)-(1-\delta)\left(\frac{K^{\rho}}{Le^{\lambda t}}\right)\right]=\ln\delta-\rho\phi$			
			$\hat{\sigma}$	$\hat{\lambda}$	$\hat{\gamma}$	R^2	DW	Degree of Freedom	$\hat{\phi}$	R^2	DW	Degree of Freedom
Entire Period	1973 ~1990		0.0766	0.0780	0.9404	0.9907	2.01	15	0.0011	0.8190	2.03	17
	for the Structural Change Period	1973 ~ 1987	0.0302	0.0683	2.1948	0.9886	2.10	12	-0.00001	0.2014	2.11	14
		<Period I> 1973 ~ 1980	0.2150	0.0553	0.2020	0.9801	2.28	5	-0.0046	0.5132	1.42	7
		<Period II> 1981 ~ 1987	1.7793	-0.2956	0.1294	0.9854	2.24	4	0.8292	0.9990	2.29	6

E. Policy Implications

From the empirical analysis above, the following policy implications can be derived.

(1). During the entire period of analysis (1973~1987) the rate of increase of the productive efficiency of capital (φ) was estimated at 0.00001, and that of the productive efficiency of labor (λ) at 0.0683. The elasticity of substitution of inputs (σ) was estimated at 0.0302. Hence one can see that during this period labor was used more efficiently than capital and as capital-using technological progress (B(t)>0) occurred, the rate of increase of the productive efficiency of capital (φ) also increased.

(2). For period I (1973~1980) and period II (1981~1987) the rates of increase of the productive efficiency of capital (φ) were estimated to be -0.0046 and 0.8292 respectively and those of increase of the productive efficiency of labor (λ) were estimate to be 0.0553 and -0.2956 respectively while estimates for elasticity of input substitution (σ) were 0.2150 and 1.7793 respectively. As for technological change, there was capital-using technological progress (B(t)>0) in both the first period (1973-1980) and the second (1981~1987) which have been separated by epoch analysis.

As time passes from period I (1973~1980) to period II (1981~1987), the elasticity of input substitution (σ) increased from 0.2150 to as much as 1.7793. This means that labor was widely replaced by capital during the 1980s in relation to the above-mentioned capital-using technological progress. As shown by <Table IX-4>, in period I, it was higher than the rate of increase in labor (drastically increased from -0.46% to 82.92% while the productive efficiency of labor (λ) radically decreased from 5.53% to -29.56%. In fact, in both periods the rate of increase in capital was accelerated.

<Table IX-4> The Regression Results of CES Production Function and the Rates of Change of the Two Factors

	$\hat{\sigma}$	$\hat{\lambda}$	$\hat{\varphi}$	$\hat{\gamma}$	$\dot{K}/K$	$\dot{L}/L$
Period I (1973~1980)	0.2150	5.53%	-0.46%	20.20%	14.95%	8.94%
Period II (1981~1987)	1.7793	-29.56%	82.92%	12.94%	10.83%	4.32%

(3) The growth of the manufacturing industry in 1970s was led by the growth rate of total factor productivity (γ) and that of the productive efficiency of labor (λ). In 1980s, the growth rate of the productive efficiency of capital (φ) was the engine of growth.

(4) From the perspective of the distribution of income, it can be seen that during the period of analysis (1973~1987) the growth rate of productive efficiency of capital (φ) increased relatively faster than that of productive efficiency of labor (λ). As a result, labor (L) was widely replaced by capital (K) and simultaneously, capital input (K) increased faster than labor input (L). Consequently, the relative share of income by capital (rK) grew at a faster rate than the relative share of income by labor (wL), impairing the income distribution structure and deepening the strife that exists today between the classes.

2. Estimates of Schumpeterian Hypotheses

A. Theoretical Background

There are two hypotheses about the relationship between innovation (or technological development) and market structure (or firm size). The positive effect of monopolistic market structure (or large-sized firm) on innovation (or technological development) has been maintained by J. A. Schumpeter (1942), J. K. Galbraith (1952 and 1967), A. Kaplan and H. Villard (1958). In contrast, their negative relationship has been asserted by Adam Smith (1904), W. Fellner (1951), E. D. Dormar (1962), and K. J. Arrow (1962) among others. They argued that competitive market structure are relatively more effective for innovation.

J. A. Schumpeter (1942) suggested that economic development should be appreciated in its dynamic aspect and temporary monopoly is surely an engine of economic development but eventually disappears through the process of entry → imitation → innovation over time. That is, economic development is running through the process of "creative destruction" and policies against monopoly to promote static competition is never superior to laissez faire.

Thus, regarding innovation as the most important factor for dynamic development, J. A. Schumpeter proposed a hypothesis on the relationship between market power and innovation. The monopolistic profit, which exceeds profit under normal, competitive markets is an incentive to induce innovative activities. Since competitive market structure can not meet the necessary condition, market power is a precondition for innovation. In other words, market power eases fund raising for investment on new technology and monopolistic market concentration can more quickly to new technology.

J. K. Galbraith (1952 and 1967) insisted that R&D can be carried out only by large firms because of high costs and high risk. Both Schumpeter and Galbraith claimed R&D and innovation could be efficiently implemented by larger firms in competition because monopolistic large firms have good fund-raising ability. The proposition is that there exists economies of scale in R&D. Some studies testing this hypothesis prove that R&D input increases more rapidly than the increasing rate of firm size.

W. S. Comanor (1965) originally analyzed empirically the elasticity of R&D output to firm size. However, H. Villard (1958), J. Schmookler (1959), S. Worley (1961), D. Hamberg (1964), E. Mansfieled (1964), F. Scherer (1965) and W. S. Comamor (1967) analyzed the elasticity of firm size with respect to R&D input instead of R&D output. On the other hand, W. Fellner (1951) and H. Villard (1958) insisted that the R&D is most active under oligopolistic market structure. W. Fellner found that oligopolistic firms try to collude on price and such a market structure promotes the development of new product for product differentiation. H. Villard claimed that R&D could most likely be active under oligopolistic market structure in which the performance of R&D is embodied in the development of product and process.

R. Nelson (1959) suggested that diversification is a driving force of invention since R&D is less risky for diversified firms than for single production firms. R&D (especially basic research) is an invention activity entailing uncertainty, which can be mitigated by diversified firms who can expect higher profit on risky R&D activity.

On the contrary, Adam Smith had the opposite idea. He insisted that monopoly must be denied and market structure must developed by the invisible hand, in terms of the first fundamental theorem in welfare economics. Also, E. D. Domar (1948) and W. Fellner (1951) claimed perfect competition not only induces innovation but becomes an incentive for technological progress. K. J. Arrow (1962) suggested a theory on the effect of market structure on resource allocation for innovation activities. That is, the incentive for invention is greater under competition than under monopoly, but even under competition incentive for invention is still below socially desirable level.

So, there are two conflicting views on the effects of market structure and firm size on innovation or technological development. Yang-Taek Lim (1988 and 1989)[105] analyzed empirically the effects of firm size and degree of market concentration on innovation for the Korean manufacturing sector in connection with Schumpeterian hypothesis.

[105] Yang-Taek Lim, *A Study on the Technological Innovation of Korean Machinery Sector,* Seoul: Korea Economic Research Institute, No. 48, April 1988.
Yang-Taek Lim, *A Study on the Determinants of Industrial Concentration and Optimal Firm Size,* Seoul: Korea Economic Research Institute, No. 62, March 1989.

B. Overview of Existing Studies

Results of empirical studies on Schumpeterian hypothesis could be summarized into the aspects of market structure and firm size.

<Figure IX-1> Innovation and Invention Activities for Firm's Technological Development

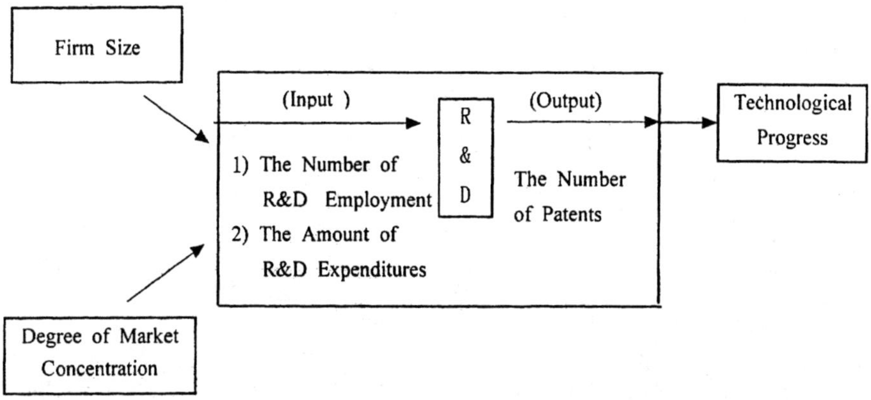

1) Market Structure and Innovation

Scherer (1983) analyzed the relationship between change in labor productivity and market share by assuming that innovation eventually increases labor productivity. He insisted that a firm with high market share can reduce production cost through technological development, and thereby increase R&D investment for the long-run profit maximization, leading to the increase of labor productivity. Rosenberg (1976) insisted that the intensity of R&D is increased by such factors as barriers to entry, advertisement and economies.

Lee and Chung (1987) analyzed the relationship between market structure and R&D for 107 firms in the Korean manufacturing sector, using the intensity of R&D (the ratio of R&D expenditures to sales) as a dependent variable and market share of firms and the concentration ratio of top 3 firms (CR3) as explanatory variables. They found that the higher the market share, the lower the intensity of R&D. That is, the more monopolistic firms are, the lower their efforts in R&D activity. In addition, the higher the CR3, the lower the intensity of R&D.

Ha and Chung (1988) analyzed the relationship between market structure and the types of R&D for 62 sample firms in the Korean manufacturing sector for 1981-84. They used the ratio of R&D expenditures to total sales and CR3 as proxy variables for technological development and market structure respectively. They found that the Schumpeter hypothesis that market governing power is proportionate to degree of R&D concentration, is not supported in their model and R&D activities in Korea are most active under corporate structure.

2) Firm Size and Innovation

Hamberg (1966) found only 3 industries in which the elasticity of the logarithm of R&D researchers with respect to firm size in terms of total employees was greater than unity among 340 firms sampled from top 500 US firms in 1960. This implies that the rate of increase of R&D researchers is higher than that of total employees.

Scherer (1965) showed that there existed an inflection point in relationship between R&D researchers and total employees. This implies that if the market concentration ratio of firms increase beyond a certain level, the number of R&D researchers is inclined to decrease, although the ratio of R&D researchers to total employees in small firms grows faster than that of total employees. In other words, to the extent the market concentration of firms reaches a certain level, the rate of R&D researcher increase is higher than that of market concentration of firms, but beyond that point this tendency is reversed.

Acs and Audretsch (1988) empirically analyzed the differences of innovation between large and small firms for 274 US industries. They used the logarithmic value of total number of innovation as a dependent variable and the market concentration ratio of top 4 firms, advertisement expenditures, capital intensity, average index of employment, total R&D expenditures and the size of industry as explanatory variables by taking their logarithmic values. Their study showed the elasticity of innovation by small firms was more than twice that of large firms, implying small firms are more active in innovation.

Kang (1992) examined which of Schumpeter's and Arrow's hypotheses was more acceptable. For the test, he selected 54 Korean industries for the period of 1983~1987. As a proxy for innovation, the intensity of R&D and labor productivity were used. He also used CR3 as a proxy for the degree of imperfect competition and monopolistic power and average index of employment as a proxy for firm size.

3) Innovation Function

The previous studies estimated the elasticity of R&D input on R&D output in a context of simple logarithmic model for inter- and intra-industry analysis. In this section, Lim (1989) estimates the production function of R&D through an inter- and intra-industry analysis with a third degree polynomial model. There are two reasons for the use of such a model.

First, the analysis of the simple logarithm model can just determine increases or decreases or constant output of R&D according to whether the estimated elasticity of output with respect to R&D input is greater than 1, less than 1 or equal to 1. However, the innovation function helps obtain the optimal level of R&D input which maximizes the average productivity of R&D input.

Second, although Schumpeter's proposition can be interpreted in terms of the elasticity of R&D output with respect to firm size being greater than 1, it is uncertain if an empirical analysis of the elasticity of R&D input with respect to firm size is a proper method to test the proposition.

Fisher and Temin (1973) concluded that the Schumpeterian's hypothesis on the effect of R&D input on R&D output can not explain Schumpeter. Kohn and Scott (1982), however, resolved the discrepancy between results of Fisher and Temin's and Schumpeter's hypotheses by introducing a production function of R&D output and its cost function. Therefore, the innovation function is very important in maintaining consistency between Schumpeter's and Schumpeterian hypotheses.

Before estimating the innovation function, it should be noted that there is a difference between the study of Kohn (1982) and Scott and Lim's study (1989). The innovation function of Kohn and Scott can be described as follows:

$$Q = G(R)$$
$$G' = \frac{dG}{dR} > 0 \qquad \text{(IX-8)}$$
$$G'' = \frac{dG'}{dR} > 0$$

where
Q = R&D output
G = Innovation function (i.e. production function of R&D)
R = R&D input (number of R&D workers in the study of Kohn and Scott)

In contrast, the innovation function of Lim (1989) is defined as follows

$$Q = \beta_1 R + \beta_2 R^2 + \beta_3 R^3 \qquad \text{(IX-9)}$$

where
Q = Number of patents as a proxy variable for R&D output
G = Number of R&D employment or the amount of R&D expenditures as a proxy variable for R&D input
β_1, β_2, β_3 = Parameters

In connection with the symbols of statistical data for the empirical study, the innovation function above can be restated as follows

$$P(t+2) = \beta_1 R \& D\ EMP_i(t) + \beta_2 (R \& D\ EMP_i(t))^2 + \beta_3 (R \& D\ EMP_i(t))^3 \quad \text{(IX-10)}$$

$$P(t+3) = \beta_1 R \& D\ EMP_i(t) + \beta_2 (R \& D\ EMP_i(t))^2 + \beta_3 (R \& D\ EMP_i(t)) \quad \text{(IX-11)}$$

$$P(t+2) = \beta_1 R \& D\ EXP_i(t) + \beta_2 (R \& D\ EXP_i(t))^2 + \beta_3 (R \& D\ EXP_i(t)) \quad \text{(IX-12)}$$

$$P(t+3) = \beta_1 R \& D\ EXP_i(t) + \beta_2 (R \& D\ EXP_i(t))^2 + \beta_3 (R \& D\ EXP_i(t)) \quad \text{(IX-13)}$$

where
P = Number of patents
R&D EMP_i = Number of R&D employees for an industry i
R&D EXP_i = Amount of R&D expenditures for an industry i
t = time

For the empirical analysis Lim (1988) made up a questionnaire and selected 797 firms (employing more than 100 workers) from the Statistics of Mining and Manufacturing Industries issued by Economic Planning Board. Among the firms, 189 firms as a sample were chosen for 1983, 207 firms for 1984 and 102 firms for 1985 for a total of 498 firms.

<Table IX-5> Sample Industries and the Number of Sample Firms

Classification	Name of Industry	The Number of Sample Firms		
		1983	1984	1985
382	Machine Manufacturing Industry (Excepting Electric)	41	45	22
3821	Engine and Turbine Manufacturing	9	6	2
3822	Agricultural Machine and Equipment Manufacturing	2	5	3
3823	Metal Processing and Woodworking Machine Manufacturing	6	5	2
3824	Machine Manufacturing for Special Industry and Equipment Manufacturing	12	11	3
3825	Machine Manufacturing for Office, Calculating, and Accounting	4	9	7
3829	Other Machine and Equipment Manufacturing	8	9	5
383	Electric and Electronic Manufacturing	99	109	58
3831	Machine for Electric Industry and Equipment Manufacturing	19	19	7
3832	Sound, Visual, and Communication Equipment Manufacturing	30	32	22
3833	Home Electronic Apparatus Manufacturing	16	10	5
3834	Electronic Tube and Other Electronic Part Manufacturing	16	34	15
3839	Unsorted Electric and Electronic Manufacturing	18	14	9
384	Transportation Equipment Manufacturing	49	53	22
3841	Shipbuilding and Repairing	9	7	5
3842	Train Equipment Manufacturing	3	4	2
3843	Automobile Manufacturing	32	37	13
3844	Motorcycle and Bicycle Manufacturing	5	5	2
3849	Unsorted Transportation Equipment Manufacturing			
Subtotal		189	207	102
Total		498		

Notes: 1) Firms with no asset item were excluded from the analysis.
2) SIC 3826 was included into SIC 3825, because the number of sample firms of SIC 3826 was so small.

3) For the consistency of the classification of industry, the sample industry with less than 4 workers like SIC 3822 was substituted with data for top 4 firms.

<Table IX-6> Sample Data for Lim's (1988) on Innovation Function

Variable	Unit	Source
1) S = Sales	10 billion won	Survey
2) E = The Number of Employment	10 thousand	Survey
3) A = Tangible Fixed Assets	10 billion won	Yearbook of Firm (Maeil Economic Daily) Yearbook of Korean Firms (Korea Headquarter of Productivity)
4) R&D EMP = The Number of R&D Employment[1]		Survey
5) Prof R&D EMP = The Number of Professional R&D Employment[2]		Survey
6) R&D EXP = The Amount of R&D Expenditure	10 billion won	Survey
7) P = Patent		Index of Applying for Patent (The Korean Association of Invention and Patent)[3]

Notes: 1) The number of special R&D employment is the number of holding Ph.D., master and bachelor's degrees.
2) Among the R&D employment, the number of holding Ph.D. degree.
3) Issued in 1985 and 1987.

In order to find a direction for policies on technological development that would boost international competitiveness, the basic characteristics of the innovative activities of enterprises must first be analyzed. The results of empirical analysis are summarized as follows.

1. When the level of innovative activity of an enterprise is expressed by the number of patents and the size of a firm by sales, employees and assets, Schumpeter's hypothesis is only confirmed by the electric & electronic industry (SIC 383). In the case of the general machinery industry (SIC 382), the transportation equipment industry (SIC 384), and the major machinery industries as a whole (SICs 382, 383 and 384), the hypothesis did not hold. This result held the same whether differences between all the sample firms of the corresponding industrial sector were analyzed or whether differences between industrial sectors were analyzed by comparing the top four sample enterprises of each sector.
2. The Schumpeterian hypothesis states that when an enterprise's level of research and development (R&D) is represented by the number of researchers, large enterprises are more active in R&D than smaller ones. This hypothesis proved both true or false depending on which variable was selected to represent the size of an enterprise; the amount of sales, the number of employees, or the amount of company assets.
3. In the case of the electric & electronic industry (SIC 383), it could be seen that an increase of market concentration is a more effective way than company expansion to develop technology by increasing the intensity of research (the ratio of professional researchers to the total number of employees).
4. In the case of R&D in the home electric appliance industrial sector (SIC 3833), the amount of input showed a positive(+) relationship with the output obtained.
5. What must be noted here is the fact that the top four enterprises of the automobile manufacturing industrial sector (SIC 3843) were able to increase their patents even by decreasing technical manpower and R&D expenditures, while the top four enterprises of the home electric appliance industrial sector (SIC 3833) were able to increase their patents at an even higher rate. The former case reflects an inefficiency in R&D system of the top four enterprises of the automobile industry. This requires a restructuring of their R&D system.

3. ESTIMATES OF THE SPEED OF TECHNOLOGY DIFFUSION AND ITS DETERMINANTS

A. Theoretical Background

Technological diffusion is a transferring process of new technology among firms, industries and the whole economy. A study on technological diffusion is used to investigate some factors in the diffusion process and to analyze how a potential user for a new technology determines usage. In technological progress, technological diffusion is as important as innovation or technology introduction. The importance of technological diffusion, for example, is well shown in a study by R. R. Nelson (1968), who explained that the productivity of American manufacturers is higher than that of the Colombian manufacturers because the speed of technological diffusion of the US is faster than that of Columbia. Thus, the technological diffusion speed can be considered as one of very important factors to determine international competitiveness of a certain country.

R. R. Nelson (1968) insisted that the productivity gap between advanced and underdeveloped countries is caused by the difference in the speed of technological diffusion. E. Mansfield (1961, 1963, 1964, 1968, 1971 and 1973) analyzed the factors to determine the speed of technological diffusion through intra and inter industry analysis for the first time.

Yang-Taek Lim (1987 a and b and 1988)[106] estimated the speed of technological diffusion among the general machinery, electric and electronic and transportation equipment industries in Korea. For the analysis, NC (numerical control) was selected because the technology is effective in promoting the industrial productivity through factory automation and thereby enhancing international competitiveness.

There are several studies which are related with the study of Lim (1987 a and b and 1988) on the speed of technological diffusion through intra and inter industry analysis such as E. Mansfield (1961, 1963, 1964, 1968, 1971 and 1973), B. Ryan and N. Gross (1943), B. Ryan (1948), J. Colcman, E. Katz, J. Menzel (1957), Z. Griliches (1987), E. Rogers (1962), R. R. Nelson (1968), F. M. Bass (1969), G. F. Ray (1969), J. S. Metcalfe (1970), A. W. Blackman (1971, 1972, 1973, 1974), J. C. Fisher and R. H. Pry(1971), R. A. Peterson, W. Rudelius, G. T. Wood (1972), L. Nabseth (1973), M. Bundgard Nielsen, P. Fiehn (1974), S. Globerman (1975), A. A. Romeo (1971, 1975), D. Sahal (1977) and A. M. Benuignati (1982).

Y. T. Lim's studies (1987 a and b and 1988) were particularly based on the studies of A. W. Blackman as well as E. Mansfield's. A. A. Blackman (1971), like Z. Griliches (1975), J. C. Fisher and R. H. Pry (1971) and E. Mansfield (1961, 1968) estimated the speed of technological diffusion with a proxy variable of market share of new technology, based on the "S" shape function of technological diffusion. Prior to the Blackman's study, E. Mansfield made the estimate with a proxy variable of the cumulated number of the firms which already adopted a new technology in the commercial jet engine market. The model of Blackman has an advantage in calculating the proxy variable of technological diffusion.

A. W. Blackman (1972) analyzed the propensity to innovate of the electric power and automobile industries. And he calculated the composite index of innovation based on sales, value added, capital investment, the ratio of new product to R&D investment, etc., then estimated the propensity to innovate for each industry. Finally, he estimated the rate of technological diffusion in the U.S. markets of shipping, automobiles, electricity and jet engine.

The following are some similarities and differences between the studies of Lim (1987 a and b and 1988), Mansfield and Blackman:

First, like Mansfield and Blackman, Lim analyzed the speed of technological diffusion speed for a given industry and then estimated the determinants based on "S" shape function of technological diffusion.

Second, like Mansfield, Lim used the cumulative number of the firms which already adopted new technology as a proxy variable of the technological diffusion speed. This contrasts with Blackman's study in which market share of new products was used as a proxy variable for the speed of technological diffusion.

---

106 Yang-Taek Lim, "A Study on Intra and Inter Industry Technological Diffusion", The Korean Society for Technology Management & Economics, Research Paper, No. 1, December 1987a.

Yang-Taek Lim, "A Study on Inter-Firms Technological Diffusion in Korean Manufacturing Industry", Korea International Academic Association December 1987b.

Yang-Taek Lim, "A Study on Technological Diffusion among Korean Machinery Sector", Korea Economic Research Institute, No. 49, April 1998.

The technology that Lim attempted to analyze was NC (numerical control) and therefore, it is difficult to survey the rate of market share all the products. Even if there is no statistical data problem, it may be more relevant for the analysis of technological diffusion to use the concerned technology rather than the market share of a product using the technology.

Lim carried out a whole survey for the analysis and chose 1,670 firms from a total of 2,051 firms registered with the Korean Association of Machine Industry Promotion excluding 140 firms in the precision machine sector and 241 firms in electric machine sector. The reasons for selecting the machinery industry for the analysis were as follows :

1. the fundamental cause of the deficit in Korea's balance of payment has resulted from the trade deficit with Japan, mainly in the machinery industry, and
2. the machinery industry furthermore satisfies the three conditions (technological progress, expansion of demand, and product diversification) for the promotion of horizontal division of labor between Japan and Korea.

NC was also selected for the analysis of the domestic technological diffusion. As previously explained, NC is closely related with the machinery industry and can greatly contribute to promoting the productivity through factory automation, thereby increasing international competitiveness. In addition, since NC has been widely spread in the Korean industries, the statistical data could be easily obtained.

The whole survey showed that 200 firms had once introduced NC. If the ratio of firms adopting NC to total was below 20% in a sample machinery industry, the corresponding industry was excluded from the analysis. As a result, 15 industrial sectors and 122 firms were selected for the analysis of the technological diffusion in Korea.

B. Empirical Analysis

1) The Intra-Industry Case

The model of technological diffusion for the intra-industry case is as follows:

$$\ln \frac{m_{ij}(t)}{n_{ij} - m_{ij}} = 1_{ij} + \phi_{ij} t \qquad \text{(IX-14)}$$

where

n_{ij} = Total number of firms which will introduce new technology j (NC) to the in industrial sector i (the machinery industry) in the long run

$m_{ij}(t)$ = The cumulated number of the firms which have adopted new technology (NC) up to time t

$$\frac{m_{ij}(t)}{n_{ij} - m_{ij}(t)} = \frac{\text{The cumulated number of the firms which have adopted new technology (NC) at time t}}{\text{The number of firms which have not introduced new technology up to time t}}$$

$$\ln \frac{m_{ij}(t)}{n_{ij} - m_{ij}(t)} = \text{The diffusion rate of new technology at time t}$$

$$\phi_{ij} = d\ln\frac{m_{ij}(t)}{n_{ij} - m_{ij}(t)}/dt, \text{ The diffusion speed of new technology at time t}$$

It seems that even though much advanced technology is introduced and new technologies are developed by a few enterprises or individuals, if they are not properly spread throughout the nation, there would be no benefit for private enterprises or inventors. From this perspective, the diffusion speed of new technologies is very important. The results of analysis by Yang-Taek Lim (1988) can be summarized:

(1) In the case of general machines, the speed of technology diffusion of large enterprises (0.3929) turned out to be slightly faster than that of smaller ones (0.1775). In the case of electric and electronic industry, it was substantially faster (0.4614 in comparison to 0.1775), and in the case of transportation industry, actually slower (0.2780 in comparison to 0.3800).

Regardless of the size of the enterprise, the diffusion speed of new technologies in the machinery industry of Korea appeared to be from as small as 1.4 to as large as 3.5 times faster than that of Canada, 0.1303. This indicates, at least in the case of the machinery industry, Korea has a larger potential to improve productivity and international competitiveness by the diffusion of new technology.

Considering the inadequate conditions for SMEs (small and medium-sized enterprises) to be technologically self-sufficient, large enterprises and smaller ones must be more encouraged to serialize their technologies to accelerate the relatively slow technological diffusion speed of SMEs. The government should promote technological serialization between large (mother) companies and SME (subsidiary) companies and establish a technical trade market like the National Central Industrial Test Center of Japan, encouraging dealers and purchasers of technical information to make active use.

2) The Inter-Industry Case

Y. T. Lim (1988)[107] estimated the determinants for the inter-industry case by applying the models of E. Mansfield (1961) and A. Romeo (1975 and 1977), but these models were statistically insignificant for the Korean machinery industry. Thus, he set up a model of the determinants of technological diffusion speed for the inter- industry case.

$$\phi_i = \beta_0 D_{1i}^{\beta 1} \cdot D_{2i}^{\beta 2} \cdot D_{3i}^{\beta 3} \cdot D_{4i}^{\beta 4} \cdot D_{5i}^{\beta 5} \cdot D_{6i}^{\beta 6} \cdot D_{7i}^{\beta 7} \cdot D_{8i}^{\beta 8} \cdot e^{ni} \qquad \text{(IX-15)}$$

or

$$\ln\phi_i = \ln\beta_0 + \beta_1 \ln D_{1i} + \beta_2 \ln D_{2i} + \beta_3 \ln D_{3i} + \beta_4 \ln D_{4i} + \beta_5 \ln D_{5i} + \beta_6 \ln D_{6i}$$
$$\beta_7 \ln D_{7i} + \beta_8 \ln D_{8i} + U_i \qquad \text{(IX-16)}$$

where

Subscript i = The Korean industrial sections (i = 1, 2, ..., 15)

U_i = Error term

ϕ_i = The diffusion speed of NC for the inter-industry case

D_1 = The ratio of exports to sales in each industry

D_2 = The ratio of average R&D expenditure to sales in each industry

D_3 = The ratio of number of engineers to that of total employment in each industry

D_4 = The ratio of number of technician to that of total employment in each industry

D_5 = The ratio of number of artisans to that of total employment in each industry

D_6 = The total number of firms belonging to each industry

D_7 = The profit rate of new technology (NC)

[107] Yang-Taek Lim, *A Study on Technological Diffusion among Korean Machinery Sector,* Korea Economic Research Institute, No. 49, April 1998.

The significant determinants of the technological diffusion speed among the industries were estimated to be company size (number of employees), the profitability of the new technology and technical manpower. Thus the size of the enterprise would not only stimulate technological innovation activities but be an effective variable in speeding up technological diffusion. For technological diffusion to be accelerated, the profitability of new technology must be guaranteed. Present systems protecting new technologies should be supplemented, or technology-promoting systems should be established and implemented but within boundaries permitted by the UR agreement.

It is also clear that much effort is necessary for the training and diffusion of technical manpower to further promote technological diffusion. However, in 1988 there were only 22.2 researchers for every 1,000 employees in Korea's manufacturing industry, which was not even half of Japan (46.8 researchers). Looking at the change in Korea's labor structure, it can be concluded that as Korean industries become more sophisticated, demand for simple technicians will decrease while the demand for expert, multi-skilled technicians will rise. Even now 51.2% of production workers in the computer business are skilled technicians, while unskilled technicians take up 24.1%. This shows that what the Korean economy actually lacks is skill rather than labor.

The trends in the lack of manpower for each industrial sector in 1988 show the following: the labor-intensive textile industry has the most workers (300,000), while the machine industry lacks the most technical manpower (lacking 42,000 technicians for every 26,000 workers). In the case of electricity, electronics, telecommunications and shipbuilding, whose total of insufficient manpower is just behind the machine industry, the areas lack a total of 1,200 technicians and 15,000 artisans.

Therefore, a labor policy that concentrates on fostering skilled technical manpower must be pursued to match demands stemming from the changes in technology and industrial structure and to cope with mass unemployment expected in the future. Such a conclusion would be supported by the following analytical results:

(1) Policy variables that should be prioritized to effectively accelerate speed came in the following order: (1) the ratio (D_5) of the number of licensed technicians to the total number of workers in an industrial sector, (2) the profit rate (D_7) of NC (new technology), (3) the ratio (D_3) of number of engineers to the total number of workers in an industrial sector, (4) the ratio (D_4) of the number of technicians to the total number of workers in an industrial sector, and (5) the ratio (D_1) of the amount of exports to the amount of production in an industrial sector.

(2) The technological diffusion speed (φ) among the industries was estimated by using the ratio of number of licensed technicians (D_5), number of engineers (D_3) and number of technicians (D_4), all to the total number of employees. The partial elasticities were estimated at 3.88324, 1.27322 and 1.01465 respectively for each variable. Thus, with all other seven variables being equal, if the ratio of number of artisans (D_5), number of engineers (D_3), and number of technicians (D_4) each increase 1%, the technological diffusion speed (φ) among the industrial sectors would increase 388%, 127% and 102% respectively. Thus, to accelerate the technological diffusion speed, a more active labor policy in science and technology should be pursued.

(3) The partial elasticity for the technological diffusion speed among the industries for the profit rate (D_7) of new technology (NC) was 3.10188, and the same variable was estimated as the variable that could accelerate the technological diffusion speed second only to the ratio of number of artisans (D_5) to the total number of workers in a field.

For international comparison, the Korea's partial elasticity for the technological diffusion speed among the industries for the profit rate (3.102) marks quite high compared to 0.864 of the US and 0.473 of Canada. Thus, when generalizing the case of NC, one can see that the profit rate of new technology is a very important determinant for the speed of technological diffusion in Korean industry.

Technological development can be promoted not only by the development of new technology but the diffusion of new or existing technology. Thus, companies are the main bodies of technological diffusion, while profit is their main decision-making factor. For this reason, to promote productivity of industries (especially the machinery industry) that grow from the diffusion of machine and automation technology, new technology-promoting systems should be enacted. Also, the present new-technology protection systems are only focussing on the development of technology, but these should also be made more practical.

(4) The partial elasticity for the technological diffusion speed (φ) among industries for the ratio of export amounts to production amounts (D_1) was 0.22708. This means that when the other seven variables are kept equal, a 1% increase in the export ratio (D_1) would increase the technological diffusion speed by

approximately 22.7%. This could be seen as reflecting that the Korean machinery industry has an export-oriented structure.

(5) The partial elasticity for the technological diffusion speed (φ) for the ratio of average R&D expenditures to sales amounts was -0.76179. This means that when the other seven variables are kept equal, a 1% increase in the ratio of R&D expenditures (D_2) would reduce the technological diffusion speed (φ) by approximately 76.2%.

The results of the analysis are contradictory to the hypothesis. However, the reason that high ratio (D_2) of R&D expenditures to sales reduce the speed of technological diffusion, *i.e.* the adoption of new technology (NC) is that most companies in Korean machinery industry have a weak financial structure. R&D, rather being a variable in the decision of whether to adopt new technology, is a variable related to companies' technological innovation activities that are intended to increase productive and managerial efficiency. This supposition could be confirmed by observing recent investigations that 92.3% of all SMEs are unable to invest in technological development, which means that the rate of companies investing is merely 7.7%. Also, the ratio of R&D to total sales amounts in 1993 turned out to be merely 0.42%.

Most companies, big or small, in Korea are suffering chronic financial problems. However, SMEs in particular do not possess sufficient securities to accommodate funds, which is why they seriously lack fund supplies. This is not only hindering production activities, but causing the companies to be passive about investing in technological development, which may have a high risk factor. What must be kept in consideration here is that financial conditions such as sales amounts, and prospects of the future are the most important decision-making factors (taking up 33.8%), when companies engaging in technological development decide the amount they will invest. The second important factor is the will of top management to invest in technology (29.4%). Similarly, companies planning on technological development will determine their investment amount according to such factors as financial conditions, prospects, and the will of top management in technological development investment.

A survey of the goals of companies to develop or plan on developing technology revealed that the improvement of quality was number one priority for companies engaging in technological development (30.9%) and also for those planning on doing so (43.3%). The second goal for technology-developing companies was adjusting to changes in demand (20.5%), and for companies with plans, it was promoting the efficiency and operation of production facilities (14.0%).

Companies engaged in technological development considered quality improvement of existing products (42.7%) as the main item of focus, followed by the development of new products (36.9%) and the improvement of the manufacturing process (13.1%). Companies with plans considered the development of new products (35.8%) most important, followed by the improvement of existing products (19.6%) and the improvement of the manufacturing process (18.1%).

Companies presently engaged in technological development are mostly making developments independently (58.5%) and by imitating other domestic and foreign innovations (11.8%). Companies presently making these developments (36.4%) and those with plans (28.2%) are both planning on making most developments independently in the future, but there is also an increasing number of companies planning to make developments by joint projects with related groups and associations by exchanging technology with other industries.

Therefore, even if SMEs in Korea are technology- conscious in the situation in which they have almost no extra fund to invest in technological development, the few companies (7.7%) that are investing 0.42% of their sales in the area are focussing mostly on the improvement of the quality of existing products. Therefore, the development of a new product, let alone the development of new manufacturing processes, materials and core components, is a luxury for most companies. One can also see that their present efforts in improving the quality of existing products are being done independently, not by technological exchanges with other industries, or by the adoption of advanced technology.

(6) The partial elasticity for the technological diffusion rate (φ) of the total amount of companies involved (D_6) came out to be "-0.89391". This means that when all other seven variables remain equal, and the number of companies increase by 1%, the technological diffusion speed (φ) would decrease approximately 89.4%. Assuming that the total amount of companies in an industry (D_6) indirectly reflect the degree of competitiveness of the companies, the fewer companies there are and the higher the relative market concentration of a few companies, the faster the technological diffusion speed (φ) among industries. Since large enterprises can be considered as having larger capacities and better conditions to invest in R&D, they would also be in a better condition to adopt new technologies.

However, although "capability" (market concentration) seems to provide a better explanation for technological diffusion rates than "necessity" (competitiveness), one must not interpret this by thinking that promoting market dominance of large conglomerates would be more effective in domestic technological diffusion than forming a competitive environment. The proper policy for adopting new technology into the nation would be to discover and support SMEs that are prospective and technology-conscious. Rather than supporting large enterprises with the "capability" to engage in R&D and adopt new technology, one should support companies that feel the "necessity" technological development but lack the "capability".

4. TECHNOLOGY GAP BETWEEN KOREA AND JAPAN

Korea has had a significant and persistent technological gap with Japan. As asserted in neo-technological trade theory, international competitiveness is primarily determined by technology gaps. Korea seeks to increase its international competitiveness and reduce its technology gap, especially *is-a -is* Japan. To do so it has committed itself to acquiring more core technology. This section considers alternative means of reducing the gap and how to best allocate resources between independent technology development and technology importation from Japan by using an econometric model of technological development transfer.

The general machinery and electrical & electronic industries were chosen for study because they have been designated by Korea as the industries that are the most basic for further Korean economic development. This section also uses the model to demonstrate the technology gap and technological transfer between Korea and Japan as they relate to the two chosen industries.

From the sensitivity analysis of the follower's technological development speed, John J. Klein and Yang-Taek Lim (1997)[108] attempted to solve the fundamental question: which is more effective to improve the technological level of the follower? Is it independent technological development or importation of advanced technologies from the leader? This study leads to the conclusion that more effective is an leader's technologies, *i.e.*, technology transfer from the leader, although it is not something the follower can achieve by its unilateral efforts.

A. The Technological Gap

Technology transfers involve two major characteristics: a dynamic (*time*) characteristic and a technology gap (*space*) characteristic. A model of technology transfer has to deal with both characteristics systematically. Few studies have done so.

Some early work attempted to address the transfer of technologies between developed and developing countries in a descriptive manner. Others used mathematical models that focused on the speed of transfer of technologies while paying little attention to the space element. Meanwhile Swan, Nesbath and Ray, and Nielson dealt with the issue by using a logistic curve.

All of these approaches had two principal shortcomings. First, the space factor in the issue (the technology gap between a technology exporter and importers) was overlooked. Second, the technological absorption ability of the importer was poorly addressed. Later studies attempted to resolve these issues. They provide the source of the methodology used here for model formulation and variable selection.

---

[108] John J. Klein and Yang-Taek Lim, "Econometric Study on the Technology Gap between Korea and Japan: the general machinery and electric & electronic industries", *Technological Forecasting and Social Change,* Vol.55, No.3, 1997.

1) The Technology Index

Yang-Taek Lim (1986 a and b, 1987, 1994, 1996 and 1997)[109] has studied on the technological development problem of a technologically less developed country in connection with technology transfer between the leader (*Japan*) and the follower (*Korea*), *i.e.* how to reduce the technology gap with Japan as one of the best means of addressing the trade Korea's technological development and technology importation from Japan.

The model for the current study is based on the three assumptions as follows:

1. the technological development functions of the two countries take the shape of a logistic growth curve,
2. the technological development process of the follower can be described by a first-order-non-homogenous-differential function developed by Baruch Raz and Isak Assa (1988)[110], and
3. following the methodology used by M.N. Shariff and A.K.M.A. Haq (1980)[111] and Yang-Taek Lim (1986 and b, 1987 and 1989), the technological level of the two countries can be measured by the complex index derived from factor analysis of some variables relating to the overall economic and social situation, the scientific and technological base and technology standing of particular industry (the general machinery and electric & electronic industries in the current study.)

Lim chose to use the following factor shown by <Table IX-7> in calculating the technology index of the general machinery and electric & electronic industries.

<Table IX-7> The Variables chosen to drive Technology Index

1) A factor relating to the overall economic and social situation (reflective of the technology gap and relative productivity of the economies studied)
   - X_1, real per capita GDP
2) Factors relating to the scientific and technological base
   - X_2, the ratio of R&D expenditures to GDP
   - X_3, R&D expenditures per researcher
   - X_4, the number of researchers per 10,000 workers
3) Factors relating to the current state of a particular industry's technological development
   - X_5, the value added by the industry
   - X_6, the volume of technology trade of the industry
   - X_7, the number of patents registered for the industry
   - X_8, the ratio of R&D expenditures to total sales of the industry

[109] Yang-Taek Lim, *A Study on Korea's Technological Dependence: with respect to Technology Transfer from Japan and Technology Diffusion in the Korean Machinery Industry,* Ministry of Technology and Science, Seoul, Korea, November 1986a.
Yang-Taek Lim, "A Model of Technology Transfer from Japan to Korea", The Korean International Economic Association, Seoul, Korea, December 1986b.
Yang-Taek Lim, "An Analysis of the Effects of Strategical Variables on the Speeds of Technological Progress and Imitation in the Korean Manufacturing Sector", The Korean Economic Association, Seoul, Korea, February 1987.
Yang-Taek Lim, "An Econometric Study on the Technology Gap between Korea and Japan: the General Machinery and Electric & Electronic Industries", the Workshop and Open Seminar on Economic Development and Technological Progress of Japan: Their Role in East Asia, Kobe, Japan, February 17~18, 1994.
Yang-Taek Lim, "An International Comparative Study of Basic Scientific Research Capacity: OECD Countries, Taiwan and Korea", *Technological Forecasting and Social Change,* Vol.52, No.1, May 1996.
John J. Klein and Yang-Taek Lim, "Econometric Study on the Technology Gap between Korea and Japan: the general machinery and electric & electronic industries", *Technological Forecasting and Social Change,* Vol.55, No.3, 1997.

[110] Raz, B. and Assa, I., "A Model of 'Coupled' Technology Transfer - A Logistic Approach", *Technological Forecasting and Social Change*, Vol. 33, 1988, pp. 257~258.

[111] Shariff, M. N., and Haq, A.K.M.A., "Evaluating the Potentials of Technical Cooperation Among Developing Countries", *Technological Forecasting and Social Change,* Vol. 16, 1980.

Since the variables used in the factor analysis are expressed in different units, the variables need to be converted to synchronize units of measurement. A statistical methodology used in converting variables with different units of measurement to those with the same unit of measurement converts the value of each variable to the probability variable concerned under the assumption that each factor forms a specific probability distribution. For example, the value of each variable can be converted to have average value of 0 and a variance of 1 under the assumption that each variable forms a normal distribution.

An index calculated in this manner possesses positive and negative values concurrently. An immediate problem of the index is that an objective evaluation is not easy. The index must be transformed so as to enable it to have positive values in a certain range. Yang-Taek Lim has originally developed a methodology for transforming an index having 0-1 value using the Z-score method. By using this methodology, the technological indices is needed for the study were derived.

The technological indexes of the two industries: general machinery, electricity and electronics of Japan and Korea during the time period of 1974~1988 in the following ways.

1. Calculating the weights of the selected variables by applying the methodology above as shown by <Table IX-8>.

<Table IX-8> The Weights Calculated by Factor-loading Matrix

Variable	General Machinery	Electricity Electronics
X_1	0.12722	0.13181
X_2	0.12851	0.12565
X_3	0.12786	0.13147
X_4	0.13197	0.13017
X_5	0.00586	0.00445
X_6	0.12587	0.12715
X_7	0.13198	0.12754
X_8	0.11916	0.10858
X_9	0.10159	0.11317

2. Transforming the value of each variable with different measurement units into the corresponding Z-scores in the normal probability distribution.
3. Computing the technology indexes with the range of $-\infty$ to $+\infty$ for each year over time(1974~1988) in the two industries of Korea and Japan respectively.
4. Transforming the above technology indexes with the range of $-\infty$ to $+\infty$ into those with that of 0 to 1 in the standard normal probability distribution.

Using the weight and Z-score of each variable, the technology index I can be calculated as follows:

$$1 = W_1Z_1 + W_2Z_2 + W_3Z_3 \qquad \text{(IX-17)}$$

where

Z_1, Z_2, Z_3 = the Z-scores of X_1, X_2, X_3, respectively, in the standard normal distribution
W_1, W_2, W_3 = the weights of X_1, X_2, X_3, respectively

$$W_1 = \frac{F_{11}^2}{F_{11}^2 + F_{21}^2 + F_{31}^2} \times Z_1$$

$$W_2 = \frac{F_{11}^2}{F_{11}^2 + F_{21}^2 + F_{31}^2} \times Z_2$$

$$W_3 = \frac{F_{11}^2}{F_{11}^2 + F_{21}^2 + F_{31}^2} \times Z_3$$

2) The Econometric Model

The technology development function for each country is derived by assuming that the function takes the form of a logistic growth curve.

$$I(t) = \frac{1}{1+e^{-(a+bt)}} \tag{IX-18}$$

where
I = technological index
a, b = parameter
t = time

The above function can be transformed into the following linear regression model.

$$Y(t) = \alpha + \beta t \tag{IX-19}$$

where

$$Y(t) = \ln\left[\frac{1}{I(t)} - 1\right]$$
$$\alpha = -a, \quad \beta = -b$$

The technological development functions of Japan and Korea can be defined :

$$I_J(t) = \frac{1}{1+e^{-(J_1+J_2t)}} \tag{IX-20}$$

$$I_K(t) = \frac{1}{1+e^{-(K_1+K_2t)}} \tag{IX-21}$$

where
J_1, K_1: a constant
J_2: the speed of Japanese technological development
K_2: the speed of Korea's technological development
t: time

Equation (21) represents Korea's technological development function when there is no technology transfer from Japan. To present one that includes technology transfer from Japan, a first-order non-homogeneous linear differential equation of the Raz-Assa model is taken, which defines the rate of change of Korea's technological development level, $dI_K(t)/dt$ as follows :

$$\frac{dI_K(t)}{dt} = g_K + \phi[I_J(t) - I_K(t)] \tag{IX-22}$$

where

$$I_J(t) = \frac{1}{1+e^{-(J_1+J_2t)}}$$

$$I_K(t) = \frac{1}{1+e^{-(K_1+K_2t)}}$$

g_K: The time rate of change of Korea's technological capacity level, *i.e.* Korea's technological development rate when there is no technology transfer from Japan

ϕ: The rate of technology transfer from Japan, *i.e.* the rate of Korea's importation of technologies from Japan[112]

$\phi[I_J(t)-I_K(t)]$: The rate of Korea's technological development contributed by Japan's technology transfer to Korea

Equation (IX-22) shows that $dI_K(t)/dt$ (the development rate of recipient when technology is transferred from an advanced country) is equivalent to g_K (the technological development rate when there is no technological transfer) combined with $[I_J(t)-I_K(t)]$.

When no technology transfer is made from Japan to Korea, Korea's technological development rate (g_K) can be obtained from the differentiation of $I_K(t)$ against the time (t):

$$\begin{aligned} g_K &= \frac{d}{dt}(I_K(t)) \\ &= \frac{d}{dt}\left[\frac{1}{1+e^{-(K_1+K_2t)}}\right] \\ &= K_2 e^{-(K_1+K_2t)}[1+e^{1(K_1+K_2t)^{-2}}] \end{aligned} \qquad \text{(IX-23)}$$

From equations (IX-21), (IX-22) and (IX-23), the following first order non- homogeneous linear differential equation can be obtained :

$$\frac{dI_K(t)}{dt} + \phi I_K(t) = R(t) \qquad \text{(IX-24)}$$

where

$$R(t) = K_2 e^{-(K_1+K_2t)}[1+e^{-(K_1+K_2t)^{-2}}] + \frac{\phi}{[1+e^{-(J_1+J_2t)}]} \qquad \text{(IX-25)}$$

If Equation (25) is solved and indefinite integrals converted to definite ones with the Gauss method to transform the outcome to match the discrete time series data for numerical computation, the following equation is obtained :

$$I_K(t) = I_{K0} e^{-\phi t + e^{-\phi t}} \cdot [K_2 \frac{t}{2}\sum_{i=1}^{N} W_i F_i(y_i) + \phi \frac{t}{2}\sum_{i=1}^{N} W_i F_2(y_i)] \qquad \text{(IX-26)}$$

where

W: a weighted value needed for an equal division into N of functions $F_1(y_i)$ and $F_2(y_i)$

$$F_1(y_i) = \frac{e^{\phi t\frac{y+1}{2}} e^{-(K_1+K_2 t\frac{y+1}{2})}}{[1+e^{-(K_1+K_2 t\frac{y+1}{2})}]^2}$$

[112] This study assumes the rate of technical transfer from Japan to be a constant. See Raz, Steinberg and Ruina (1983), Raz and Assa (1988), Blackman (1972), Fisher and Pry (1971) and Nesbath and Ray (1974). However, Shariff and Haq (1980) and Lim (1986, 1987 a and b, 1989 and 1991) assumed that the rate of technological transfer would change along with changes in the gap between technology licensor and licensee countries.

$$F_2(y_i) = \frac{e^{\phi t \frac{y+1}{2}}}{[1+e^{-(J_1+J_2 t\frac{y+1}{2})}]^2}$$

In order to measure precisely the effect of a change in the rate of import of Japanese technology on Korea's technological development, N should be maximized and the function $F_i(y_i)$ should be converted into a fraction. However, for the sake of convenience of analysis, N is set at 5 (N=5), $F_1(y_i)$ and $F_2(y_i)$ are thus divided into five, and the integrals can be numerically computed as follows :

$$I_K(t) = I_K e^{(1-\phi t+e^{-\phi t})}[K_2 \frac{t}{2}\frac{2}{5}\{F_1(-0.6)+F_1(-0.2)+F_1(0.2)+F_1(0.6)+F_1(1.0)\}$$

$$+\phi\frac{t}{2}\frac{2}{5}\{F_2(-0.6)+F_2(-0.2)+F_2(0.2)+F_2(0.6)+F_2(1.0)\}] \qquad \text{(IX-27)}$$

Equations (IX-24), (IX-25), (IX-26) and (IX-27) show the transformation of the mathematical model into an econometric model which can be tested. It should be noted that the data on the technological index I cannot be obtained directly, which is why factor analysis has to be used. If the technological index of the Japanese general machinery industry ($I_{J1}(t)$) and time (t) are substituted, and the OLS (ordinary least square) methodology applied to the statistical data, the following regression equation is obtained.

$$Y_{J1}(t)=0.06580-0.20982t$$
$$(0.449) \quad (11.772) \qquad \text{(IX-28)}$$[113]

$R^2 = 0.9142$, ( ) = t-value

The Japanese technological development function for the general machinery industries can be put in the following logistic curve :

$$I_{J1}(t)=\frac{1}{1+e^{0.06580-0.20982t}} \qquad \text{(IX-29)}$$

For the electric & electronic industry, the Japanese technological development function can be estimated in the same manner. The Japanese technological development function for the industry is estimated as shown in equation (IX-30) and the logistic function (IX-31).

$$Y_{J2}(t) = 0.31282 - 0.24236t \qquad \text{(IX-30)}$$
$$(1.620) \quad (10.324)$$

($R^2 = 0.8913$), ( ) = t-value

$$I_{J2}(t) = \frac{1}{1+e^{0.31282-0.24236t}} \qquad \text{(IX-31)}$$

Similarly, the technological development function of the Korean general machinery industry can be estimated as follows:

113 The numbers in parentheses represent the corresponding t-values. The estimated coefficients α and β are statistically significant at the 5% level.

$$Y_{K1}(t) = 2.23413 - 0.12356t \qquad \text{(IX-32)}$$
$$\qquad (21.101) \quad (9.599)$$

($R^2 = 0.8764$), ( ) = t-value

$$I_{K2}(t) = \frac{1}{1+e^{2.10758-0.11159t}} \qquad \text{(IX-33)}$$

Korea's technological development function for the electric and electronic industries has been calculated as shown in equation (IX-34) and the logistic function (IX-35).

$$Y_{K2}(t) = 2.10758 - 0.11159t \qquad \text{(IX-34)}$$
$$\qquad (23.899) \quad (10.409)$$

($R^2 = 0.8929$), ( ) = t-value

$$I_{K1}(t) = \frac{1}{1+e^{2.23413-0.12356t}} \qquad \text{(IX-35)}$$

3) Empirical Analysis

The technology gap of Korea is the difference between the technology index of Japan and that of Korea. Based upon technology function equations (28) and (34), estimates of the technology gap between Japan and Korea in the general machinery industries are provided. Similarly, based upon equations (30) and (34), estimates of the gap for the electric and electronic industries are provided.

As shown by equations (28) and (32), the technological development speed of the general machinery industry in Japan was estimated to be 0.20982, while Korea's was 0.12356. The Japanese technological levels in the general machinery industry were estimated to have stood at 0.5495 as compared to Korea's 0.1190 in 1974 and at 0.9709 in contrast to Korea's 0.4564 in 1988. The absolute magnitude of the gap between the two countries widened to 0.5145 in 1988 from 0.4305 in 1974.

In the electric & electronic industries, as shown by equations (30) and (32), Japanese technological development speed was estimated to be 0.24236 and Korea's 0.11159. The technological levels of Japan and Korea in 1974 were estimated to be 0.5127 and 0.1295 respectively, whereas in 1988 they were 0.9819 and 0.4094 each. The absolute gap between the two countries widened to 0.5725 in 1988 from 0.3832 in 1974.

B. Forecasting Potential Changes

This section estimates the effects on the technology gap of an annual doubling of the value of selected policy variables in Korea. The analysis is applied to two industries analyzed. These results for independent technological development are then compared with the potential impact of technology importation from Japan. The government policy control variables are assumed to be X_3 (R&D expenditures per researcher) and X_4 (the number of researchers per 10,000 workers).

1) The General Machinery Industry

(1) Accelerating the Speed of Independent Technological Development

The weights of the two variables: X_3 (R&D expenditures per researcher) and X_4 (the number of researchers per 10,000 workers) are calculated by using a factor- loading matrix. The technological development functions for each case were re-estimated. The following conclusions can be drawn:

1. A doubling of the selected two factors (X_3^K and X_4^K) resulted in an improvement in the technological development speed. The speed was improved to be 0.13296 for the doubling X_3^K case and 0.15073 for the doubling X_4^K case. When the yearly double increase was not given, the speed of technological development in the general machinery industry from 1974 to 1988 was estimated to be 0.12356.
2. In boosting the technological development speed of Korea's general machinery industry X_4^K (the number of researchers per 10,000 workers) was more effective than X_3^K (the R&D budget for an individual researcher). When both factors were increased, the technological development speed was accelerated the most.
3. In case of doubling annually the value of the strategic variables, the technology gaps with Japan were estimated to have widened from 0.4254 in 1974 to 0.4774 in 1988 and from 0.4167 in 1974 to 0.4459 in 1988 for X_3^K and X_{i4}^K respectively. These estimates are in contrast to the initially estimated technology gaps of 0.4305 in 1974 and 0.5145 in 1988. The Japanese speed of technological development in the general machinery industry is faster than that of the Korean industry.

Therefore, the technology gap with Japan would have widened in spite of doubling annually the value of the strategic variables in the Korean general machinery industry. However, the gap in the same case would have been relatively reduced compared to the previously estimated gap.

<Table IX-9> The Sensitivity Analysis of Korea's Technological Development Speed in the General Machinery Industry

Regression Equation case \ country		$\hat{Y} = \hat{\alpha} + \hat{\beta} t$	R^2
Equation (28)	Japan	Y = 0.06580 - 0.20982 (0.449) (11.772)	0.9146
Equation (32)	Korea	Y = 2.23413 - 0.12356 (21.101) (9.599)	0.8764
$2X_3^K$	Japan	Y = 0.05891 - 0.20400 (0.458) (13.045)	0.9290
	Korea	Y = 2.27170 - 0.13296 (19.584) (9.429)	0.8724
$2X_4^K$	Japan	Y = 0.16510 - 0.21426 (1.117) (11.927)	0.9163
	Korea	Y = 2.36108 - 0.15073 (20.187) (10.601)	0.8963

Note: 2 X_i^K implies doubling yearly the value of X_i during the given period (1974~1988).
The numbers in parentheses are t-values.

(2) Import of Technology from Japan

Assuming there is no doubling of X_3 (R&D expenditures per researcher) and X_4 (the number of researchers per 10,000 workers), but that there is an importation of Japanese technologies, the potential technology gap between Japan and Korea can be re-estimated. On the basis of the assumption that Korea's technology import rate from Japan is ϕ=0.01, Korea's technology indexes were estimated to be 0.1190 in 1974 and 0.7792 in 1988.[114] By this improvement, the gap between the two countries was reduced to 0.1917 in 1988 from 0.4305 in 1974. When the Japanese technology import rate (ϕ) is increased from 0.01 to 0.05, the local-technological level is further upgraded and the technology gap with Japan reduced additionally. Korea's technological level was estimated to be 0.8578 in 1988, reducing its gap with Japan to 0.1131 in the year as opposed to 0.4305 in 1974.[115]

---

[114] Changes in the rate of Korea's technology importation from Japan are assumed to have no effect on the Japanese technological level.

[115] The values of 0.01 and 0.05 that were chosen for (ϕ) are hypothetical and were selected for illustrative purpose. There is no way of justifying a specific value for (ϕ).

From the analysis above, it can be concluded that an increase in the rate of Korea's technology transfer from Japan is more effective in the reduction of the technology gap with Japan than an annual double increase in the strategic variables in the general machinery industry of Korea.

<Table IX-10> The Estimated Technology Gaps with Japan in the General Machinery Industry

Technological Gap with Japan	1974	1988
(1) $I_{J1}(t) - I_{K1}(t)$	0.4305	0.5145
(2) $2\ X_3^K$	0.4254*	0.4774*
(3) $2\ X_4^K$	0.4167*	0.4459*

Note: The case marked by an asterisk(*) indicates that the technological gaps with Japan were relatively reduced by doubling the annual value of the strategic variables of the Korean industry.

<Table IX-11> Comparison between Independent Technology Development and Technology Import from Japan in the Korean General Machinery Industry

1. Technological Gap with Japan in the case of increasing the rate(ϕ) of technology importation from Japan	$\phi = 0.01$		$\phi = 0.05$	
	1974	1988	1974	1988
	0.4305 = (0.5495-0.1190)	0.1917 = (0.9709-0.7792)	0.4305 = (0.5495-0.1190)	0.1131 = (0.9709-0.8578)
2. Comparison of the effects on the Technology Gap in 1988 between Independent Technology Development and Technology Import from Japan	Independent Technological Development		Increasing Technology Import form Japan	
	$2\ X_3^K \Rightarrow 0.4774$ $2\ X_4^K \Rightarrow 0.4459$		$\phi = 0.05 \Rightarrow 0.1131$ $\phi = 0.01 \Rightarrow 0.1017$	
	The actual gap in 1988 was 0.5145			

2) The Electric & Electronic Industry

(1) Accelerating the Speed of Independent Technological Development

By applying the same methodology to the case of the electric & electronic industry, the weights of the selected variables can be calculated and the technological development function for each case to be re-estimated.

1. When the selected two factor (X_3^K and X_4^K) were doubled on an annual basis, the technological development speed of the local electric & electronic industry was affected as: the speed during the period 1974~1988 had been estimated to be 0.11159. The speed was improved to be 0.11970 for the doubling X_3^K case and 0.13697 for the doubling X_4^K case.
2. As in the case of the general machinery industry, X_4^K (the number of researchers per 10,000 workers) was more effective than X_3^K (the R&D budget for an individual researcher) in accelerating the technological development speed of the industry. When both factors were boosted at the same time, the results were still more effective.
3. In case of doubling annually the value of the strategic variables (X_3^K and X_4^K), the technology gap with Japan were respectively estimated to have widened from 0.3684 in 1974 to 0.5132 in 1988 for the 2 X_4^K case and from 0.3701 in 1974 to 0.5404 in 1988 for the 2 X_3^K case. However, these estimates contrast sharply with previously estimated technology gap of 0.3832 in 1974 and 0.5725 in 1988. As in the case of the general machinery industry, the Japanese speed of technological development in the electric & electronic industry is swifter than that of the Korean industry.

Therefore, as in the general machinery industry, the technology gap with Japan would have widened in spite of doubling annually the strategic variables. Yet X_4 and X_3 turn out to be the most important factors when considering accelerating the technological development speed of both the general machinery industry and the electric & electronic industry. Also, R&D budget is probably the most important element in boosting technological development.

<Table IX-12> The Sensitivity Analysis of Korea's Technological Development Speed in the Electric & Electronic Industries

Regression Equation Case \ country		$\hat{Y} = \hat{\alpha} + \hat{\beta}\, t$	R^2
Equation (IX-30)	Japan	Y = 0.31282 - 0.24238 (1.620) (10.324)	0.8913
Equation (IX-34)	Korea	Y = 2.10758 - 0.11159 (23.899) (10.409)	0.8929
$2\ X_3^K$	Japan	Y = 0.33294 - 0.23921 (1.853) (10.951)	0.9022
	Korea	Y = 2.12771 - 0.11970 (21.199) (9.810)	0.8810
$2\ X_4^K$	Japan	Y = 0.41616 - 0.24767 (2.112) (10.340)	0.8916
	Korea	Y = 2.22465 - 0.13697 (22.549) (11.420)	0.9094

Note: $2\ X_i^K$ implies doubling yearly the value of X_i during the period 1974~1988.
The numbers in parentheses are t-values.

<Table IX-13> The Estimated Technology Gaps with Japan in the Electric & Electronic Industry

Technological Gap with Japan	1974	1988
$I_{J2}(t) - I_{K2}(t)$	0.3832	0.5725
$2\ X_3^K$	0.3701*	0.5404*
$2\ X_4^K$	0.3684*	0.5132*

Note: The case marked by an asterisk(*) indicates that the technological gaps with Japan were relatively reduced by doubling the annual value of the strategic variables of the Korean industry.

(2) Technology Importation from Japan

In this section the effects of technology imports from Japan on the technology gap between Korea and Japan are analyzed. The procedures followed are the same as those for the general machinery industry.

In the electric & electronic industry, when the rate (ϕ) of Korea's technology imports from Japan was assumed to be 0.01, Korea's technological level was estimated to be 0.1295 in 1974 and 0.7132 in 1988. By this improvement, the technology gap between Korea and Japan was reduced to 0.2687 in 1988 from 0.3832 in 1974. The results are comparable but less dramatic than in the case of the general machinery industry. If Korea increased the rate (ϕ) of importation of Japanese technology to 0.05, the technological gap of Korea's electric & electronic industry would be further reduced. The estimated local technological level of the industry would rise from 0.1295 in 1974 to 0.8128 in 1988 and the gap with Japan would drop to 0.1691 in 1988 from 0.3832 in 1974.

<Table IX-14> Comparison between Independent Technology Development and Technology Import from Japan in the Korean Electric & Electronic Industry

<table>
<tr><td rowspan="3">1. Technological gap with Japan in the case of Increasing the rate(ϕ) of Technology importation From Japan</td><td colspan="2">ϕ = 0.01</td><td colspan="2">ϕ = 0.05</td></tr>
<tr><td>1974</td><td>1988</td><td>1974</td><td>1988</td></tr>
<tr><td>0.3832 =
(0.5127-0.1295)</td><td>0.2687 =
(0.9819-0.7132)</td><td>0.3832 =
(0.5127-0.1295)</td><td>0.1691 =
(0.9819-0.8128)</td></tr>
<tr><td rowspan="3">2. Comparison of the effects on the technology gap in 1988 between 'Independent Technology Development' And 'Technology Import From Japan'</td><td colspan="2">Independent Technological Development</td><td colspan="2">Increasing Technology Import from Japan</td></tr>
<tr><td colspan="2">$2X_3^K \Rightarrow 0.5404$
$2X_3^K \Rightarrow 0.5132$</td><td colspan="2">$\phi = 0.05 \Rightarrow 0.1691$
$\phi = 0.01 \Rightarrow 0.2687$</td></tr>
<tr><td colspan="4">The actual gap in 1988 was 0.5725</td></tr>
</table>

It can be concluded that, as in the case of the general machinery industry, an increase in the rate of Korea's technology transfer from Japan is more effective in the reduction of technology gap with Japan than an annual doubling in the strategic variables X_3^K and X_4^K in the electric & electronic industry.

C. Policy Implications

This section has developed and applied a model intended to determine the most effective means of reducing the technological gap between a leader and follower country. Gap reduction is especially important for follower countries, given their relative lack of international competitiveness. In the case of Japan and Korea from 1974 to 1988, their general machinery and electric & electronic industries were considered. These industries were selected because their development was a top priority of Korean government policy in the period chosen.

Two alternative means for achieving gap reduction were considered for the two industries: 1) increasing technological development by increasing the numbers of researchers and the R&D budget; and 2) increased importation rates of technologies from industrial powers. It was found that increasing the number of researchers was relatively more important for increasing development than increasing the R&D funds available, but that it was best to increase both researchers and funds. However, most important of all would be to increase the rate of technology transfer from more developed economies.

Clearly both independent development and assimilation are important, but it appears an increased assimilation is crucial. There is a political dilemma with such a program. Increasingly, the advanced industrial nations have sought to protect what they view as their technological and intellectual properties while at the same time pressing follower countries to be less protective in the primary and secondary product areas. All of this is occurring under the auspices of the WTO. How are the follower countries to respond? The answer in economic terms are sought here. The political aspects are a matter for another study.[116]

[116] Yang-Taek Lim, *The People Perish where there is No Vision,* the Mail Economic Daily Press, September 1995

Chapter X

TECHNOLOGY TRANSFER AND THE ROLE OF FDIS FOR KOREA

1. TYPES AND CHANNELS OF TECHNOLOGY TRANSFER

<Table X-1> Types of Technology Transfer

Forms		Objectives	Characteristics	Remarks
Intra-Firm		-Technology protection -Strengthening subsidiary's competitiveness	-Monopolistic ownership of technology by parent company -Risk of weakening monopoly power of parent company	FDI Internal transaction
Inter-Firm	Market Type	-Royalty earnings -Direct technology transfer	-Technology markets -Licensing	Commercial transaction
	Non-Market Type	-Utilization of externalities	-Low degree of transfer effects -Technology transfer by contacts	Non-commercial Learning effects
	Alliance	-Utilization of complementary assets	-Cross-licensing, collaborative R&D, co-ownership of technologies -OEM, exchange of complementary assets and function by joint-venture etc.	Quasi-commercial transaction
Inter-Government		-Technology assistance -Collaborative technology development and utilization	-Political objectives -Common use of public welfare-oriented technologies -Human resource development	Non-commercial transaction

Source: Yoo Soo-hong, *Japan's Strategy for Technology Transfer to Asia and Korea's Response*, Korea Institute for International Economic Policy, 1993, p. 22.

As shown in <Table X-1>, several types and channels of international technology transfer may be considered. Technology can be transferred between two countries (bilaterally) or among many countries through international institutions (multilaterally). It can take the form of commercial or non-commercial transactions in public or private sectors. Major channels and means of technology transfer include licensing, foreign direct investment, trade of capital goods and strategic alliances. Technology transfer may take the form of intra-firm transfer, inter-firm transfer, or inter-government transfer. The main concern in the following review is technology transfer in the private sector on a commercial basis.

2. SHIFTING GOVERNMENT POLICY TOWARD AN INTRODUCTION OF FOREIGN TECHNOLOGY

A country's technological development is closely related to its industrial development. <Table X-2> shows the evolutionary stages of industrial development in Korea and its relationship with science and technology (S&T) development. The import of technology is an important vehicle for technology development, particularly in the earlier stages of development. Taking a look at the process of industrialization of Korea, which is familiar with the history of industrialization in Japan, Taiwan and Singapore, it can easily be concluded that the process is very similar among these countries with some time lags.

Technology transfer is affected by many factors such as economic environment of transferring and importing countries, strategies for industrial and technological development and incentives for transferors. In the case of Korea, these factors have changed over the periods, as shown in <Table X-2>. These will be discussed in more detail in the following review of each sub-period. The table also shows an evolutionary pattern of technology transfer, starting from a lower level of imported technologies and moving toward a more advanced one.

<Table X-2> The Development of Korean Industry and S&T

	Industry	S&T Development
1960s	-Develop import-substitution industries -Expand export-oriented light industries -Support capital goods industries	-Strengthen S&T education -Deepen scientific and technological infrastructure -Increase technology imports
1970s	-Expand heavy and chemical industries -Shift emphasis from capital import to technology introduction -Strengthen export-oriented industrial competitiveness	-Expand technical training -Improve institutional mechanism for absorbing imported technologies -Promote research applicable to industrial needs
1980s	-Promote comparative advantage of industrial structure -Expand technology-intensive industry -Encourage manpower development and improve productivity of industries	-Develop and acquire top-level scientists and engineers -Perform national R&D projects efficiently -Promote industrial and technological development
1990s	-Upgrade industrial structure by adjustment and technical innovation -Promote efficient use of human and other resources -Improve information networks	-Reinforce national R&D projects -Strengthen demand-oriented technology and development system -Internationalize R&D systems and information networks

Source: Ministry of Science and Technology, Korea, *Science and Technology in Korea,* 1994.

Like the case of industrialization, Korea's pattern of technology transfer over time is very similar to that of Japan, although Japan took a much longer period for its earlier stages which ended before World War II. A country's evolutionary pattern of technology transfer may be generalized. A country starts as an imitator of foreign technologies. As experience in utilizing technologies is accumulated and the economy develops, it achieves self-sufficiency in technology and if everything goes well, eventually it becomes a net technology exporter.

As pointed out earlier, Korea has relied heavily on foreign technology. By importing and utilizing foreign technologies and building up its technological capabilities through 'learning by doing', Korea exploited the late-comer advantage. During the early stages of industrialization, the major means of technology transfer were the import of capital goods and turnkey plants, while technology transfer through FDIs and licensing agreement was quite limited.

<Table X-3> Korean Government Policy for the Import of Technology

	1960s	1970s	1980s	1990s
Stage of Industrialization	- Import substitution and basic industries	- Heavy and chemical industries	- Technology intensive industries	- High-tech industries
Characteristics of Industry	- Labor-intensive	- Capital intensive	- Capital and technology intensive	- Technology intensive
Incentives for Foreign Technology Introduction	- Use of labor - Sales to local market	- Technology sales to heavy and chemical industries	- Increased demand for high-tech - Joint production by joint venture	- Increased demand for high tech - Strategic alliances
Technology Policy	- Control of foreign direct investment and technology imports	- R&D initiatives by government - Conditional liberalization of technology import	- Encouragement of R&D in the private sector - Liberalization of technology and capital imports	- Encouragement of R&D in private sector - Liberalization of technology and capital imports

Source: Ministry of Science and Technology, Korea.

However, one should not have the false perception that capital goods are the same as technologies. Only a portion of a capital goods embodies technology, Although the technology portion cannot be separated from capital goods and the amount cannot be measured precisely. FDI shares a similar problem of not being able to distinguish the technology portion. In the beginning of the 1980s, the Korean government liberalized its FDI policy as a way of inducing more sophisticated foreign technologies. Technology transfer through licensing agreement increased dramatically in the 1980s. Although Korea and Japan share similarities in many aspects of technology transfer, Japan has been less dependent upon capital imports than Korea for its technology transfer.

A. Development of Labor-Intensive Industries

Although Korea had a comparative advantage in cheap but skilled labor, it had neither indigenous technological capability nor sufficient domestic savings to establish and operate production facilities and plants. Instead of FDIs, loans were preferred for foreign capital, which forced Korea to earn foreign reserves for repayment and adopt an outward-looking industrialization policy. In order to minimize the cost of obtaining foreign technology and to maintain Korea's technological independence from the dominance of multinational corporations, the Korean government had very restrictive policies toward FDIs.

Technical assistance from capital suppliers and independent consultants played an important role in helping Korea's 'learning by doing'. This was possible because of the highly-trained human resources and entrepreneurship in Korea. Korea has invested heavily in human resource development since the Korean War (1950~1953). Korea's human resources became an important foundation for subsequent industrialization by enabling the rapid adoption of imported technologies and reverse engineering of foreign products.[117]

B. Development of Capital-Intensive Industries

In the 1970s, the industrial strategy shifted toward the development of heavy and chemical industries, improving the process of technological assimilation and promoting R&D to meet industrial needs. These industries included shipbuilding, iron and steel, electrical and non-electrical machinery and petrochemicals. Since these industries were still incapable of developing their R&D, the government and government-sponsored research institutes played a key role in the establishment of domestic R&D capability. These research institutes focused on the development and dissemination of industrial technology.

During this period, the government conditionally liberalized technology imports which had been under the strict controls and scrutiny. In 1970s, it was inevitable for Korea to at least partially liberalize its technology transfer and FDI policy in order to assist the development of heavy and chemical industries, which required more sophisticated foreign technologies. At the same time, the government improved institutional mechanisms for increasing indigenous technological capability.

C. Development of Technology-Intensive Industries

The decade of the 1980s was characterized by structural adjustments and technology-intensive industrial development. Excessive investment in the capital-intensive heavy and chemical industries required contractive structural adjustments in these sectors. A rapid increase in real wages and labor disputes forced firms to seek technological innovation as a solution.

Protectionism in developed countries not only forced Korea to open protected domestic markets toward major trading partners but also constrained transfers of advanced technologies. The gradual opening of domestic markets forced Korean firms to enhance their technological capabilities by importing foreign technology and R&D. Korean industries required high technologies in the areas of micro- electronics, telecommunications, bio-engineering, environment etc. These sophisticated technologies were not easy to import due to the constraints placed by advanced countries aiming to rapidly develop technology-intensive industries of their own.

---

[117] Linsu Kim and C. J. Dahlman, "Technology Policy for Industrialization", *Research Policy* Vol. 21, 1992, pp. 437-452.

Korea's S&T policy during this period has emphasized localization of key strategic technologies, development of highly capable technological manpower and promotion of private sector R&D capabilities. The special national R&D program started in 1982 is one of the most ambitious policies ever adopted by the government. The Korean government tried to induce more advanced technology through FDIs by liberalizing its foreign direct investment policy.

The 'positive list' (listing industries open to FDIs) system was replaced by the 'negative list' (listing those that were closed) system. The notification system was introduced in 1991. Domestic incentives such as more favorable tax exemptions or reductions, special free tax zones for high-tech FDIs and off-shore financing had been provided according to the revision of foreign direct investment policy. Also, Korea's intellectual property laws were revised to recognize both material and process patents and protection of IPRs (intellectual property rights) has been enforced.

<Table X-4> The Protection of IPRs

Type	Definition	Term of Protection	Relevant Office
Patent	A highly advanced Technological idea Based on the laws of Nature (major invention)	20 years from the filing date	Korean Industrial Property Office
Utility Design	A technological idea Based on the laws of Nature (minor invention)	15 years from the filing date	Korean Industrial Property Office
Industrial Design	A shape, pattern, color, or any combination of an article which produces an aesthetic impression in the sense of sight	10 years from the date of registration	Korean Industrial Property Office
Trademark	A sign, character, figure, Three dimensional shape, or any combination thereof, with its colors, which is used on goods or services in order to distinguish their identify	10 years from the date of registration (the semi-permanent if renewal is made every 10 years)	Korean Industrial Property Office
Semiconductor Chip Layout Design	-	10 years from the date of registration	Semiconductor Division of the Korean Industrial Property Office
Computer Program	-	50 years	Korea computer Program Protection Foundation
Copyright	Creative works in the Literary of artistic domain	The lifetime of the right-holder and 50 years posthumously	Copyright Division of the Ministry of Culture and Tourism

Source: The Korea Industrial Property Office

3. Trends in Technology Introduction

Reflecting the rapid economic growth of Korea, technology transfer from foreign countries continued to increase until the end of the 1980s. However, technology imports declined over three consecutive years, 1990~1992, due to a domestic recession and increased technology protectionism by developed countries. Technology imports have been increasing again since 1993, which implies that Korea is coming out of the recession and has improved its relationship with developed countries to induce more advanced technologies from them.

Korea imported most of foreign technologies from the US and Japan. The US seemed to have transferred more advanced technologies. Furthermore, the US ranked first in terms of the amount of technologies imported, whereas Japan ranked first in terms of the number of cases.

The leading sector in technology imports had been the electronics industry. The industry ranked first in terms of the amount and the number of cases since the second half of the 1980s. The electronics industry is followed by the machinery sector and chemicals. These figures roughly reflect the industrial structure and relative importance of industries in Korea.

Korean industries began actively introducing new technology from abroad in the 1980s. This was due to the increase of technology demand from policies for the heavy and chemical industries in the late 1970s, and step by step liberalization of technological introduction after 1978. 5,214 cases of technology introduction, which is 75.1% of the total amount of cases (6,944), occurred between 1981 and 1990. Much technology introduction was done by the chemical, electricity-electronics, and machinery industries, in which an independent and separate technological development is hardly possible.

From 1981 to 1990, the technology that accommodated patent rights was prevalent in order to introduce core technology that were difficult to develop independently and to reduce the time for technological development. Thus during this period, 47.0% of the technology that was introduced accommodated patent rights, 23.4% accommodated trademark rights and 11.3% were centered on trademark rights. As a result of efforts for diversification of technology introduction lines, recently technology introduction from Japan has been reducing, while introduction from the US and Europe is increasing. However, technology introduction from Japan and the US is still greatly predominant. This can be regarded as due to the predominance of technological information in the two regions and the convenience of introducing technology from them.

Before technology is introduced, independent research must be done to accumulate related basic technology. The capacity to receive the technology must also be created by understanding the main components of the technology beforehand. All of this is necessary to maximize assimilation and absorption of capacities when the contracts have been concluded and technology is being transferred. Likewise, attaining know-how and independent application and development capabilities would help maximize the effectiveness of technological introduction. However, most Korean companies are not engaging in sufficient research before they import technology. As a result, the effects of technological introduction on improvements in domestic technological capacity cannot be maximized, rather, technology that has been already been improved and developed in the advanced countries are being continuously introduced.

4. The Role of FDIs in Technology Transfer to Korea

FDIs in Korea increased steadily throughout the 1970s owing to a variety of government incentives such as a free trade zone, restrictions on labor union activities, and special favors given to heavy and chemical industries. Investments slowed down somewhat at the beginning of the 1980s but regained vitality as the enactment of the revised Foreign Capital Inducement Law and Ordinance in 1984.[118]

By the late 1980s, faced with declining export competitiveness partly due to rising production costs, the Korean government and private businesses recognized the need for high technology. External and internal pressures intertwined together to trigger Korea's adoption of a new policy direction toward further liberalization. Technological superiority became more important in enhancing international competitiveness in higher value-added industries, and foreign firms became more reluctant to share high technology with Korean firms as the technological gap narrowed.

Under these circumstances, the Korean government chose to encourage FDI in Korea, recognizing that the business activity of high-tech foreign multinational firms in local markets is an important source of technology transfer through 'learning by doing' as asserted by K. J. Arrow (1962) and R. E. Lucas (1993).

Despite the relatively minor role of FDI in Korea's economic development, there are many cases where foreign multinationals have contributed greatly to the technological improvement of Korean firms. One of the most successful episodes can be found in the Masan EPZ (Export-Processing Zone), where about 9,000 workers and technicians benefited from the opportunity for overseas training program until 1993.

[118] Approval of FDIs in Korea have been changed from a positive list system to a negative list system; restrictions on the foreign invested share ratio and remittance of foreign currency have been eased; and the investment procedures have been markedly simplified.

Subcontracting outside the Masan EPZ increased significantly, contributing to the manufacture of value-added products by foreign investors.[119] At the same time, capital inflow is an additional resource available to finance economic growth. However, it has been acknowledged that there exist inherent risks on relying excessively on external borrowings to accelerate economic growth. Without the efficient use of foreign capital, a country would never make a smooth transition from a debtor economy to a self-sustained one.

Due to inadequate domestic savings, the key question in the case of Korea has been how to efficiently use foreign capital. The Korean government intervened in order to avoid duplication of investment by channeling borrowed funds into expanding SOC (social overhead capital) including power and electricity, communication, roads and harbors, as well as strengthening major strategic industries such as iron and steel, petrochemicals and electricity-electronics.

Thus, foreign capital inflows have bolstered savings, investment, and growth, but Korea relied on foreign borrowings, whereas Singapore and Hong Kong relied on FDIs. Until the mid-1980s, most of long-term capital inflows needed for economic development was channeled through official loans, and hence the role of FDIs was not significant.

A. Econometric Analysis of FDIs in Korea

There are three major theoretical approaches to FDIs: (1) the microeconomic approach based on the perspectives of the companies concerned, (2) the macroeconomic approach based on location advantages such as labor costs and market size, and (3) the eclectic theory which takes into account both (1) and (2).

The typical example of the microeconomic approach theory is the industrial organization theory, which states that a business with monopolistic power undertakes FDIs to dominate imperfect markets. This theory has been developed by C. P. Kindleberger (1970), R. E. Caves (1971) and S. Hymer (1976). The monopolistic elements in the theory include the ability to differentiate products, marketing skills, management skills, patents, undisclosed technologies and economies of scale.

The macroeconomic approach begins with a criticism of the microeconomic approach claiming that the latter does not move beyond the framework of partial equilibrium analysis and therefore cannot identify the externalities and social cost of individual business activities on the entire national economy. The macroeconomic theory tries to explain overseas direct investments from the perspective of a macroeconomic general equilibrium analysis, arguing that based on the theory of international specialization, direct investments flow to the countries with comparative disadvantages. This theory has been developed by K. Kojima (1973, 1978, and 1982).

The eclectic theory tries to explain overseas direct investments using both the company's competitive edge and location advantages stating that an individual business makes overseas direct investments because it wants to combine its competitiveness in capital, technologies and management skills with the location advantages of other countries including labor costs and local marketing costs. This theory has been developed by J. Dunning (1981).

In connection with this matter, H. W. Singer (1950) analyzed whether FDIs in an underdeveloped country improved the welfare of underdeveloped or developed countries. The multiplier effect caused by FDIs was usually accrued to the home country (the developed country) rather than the host country (the underdeveloped country). Considering that FDIs was usually applied in the export industrial area, such an effect was enlarged when there was a big difference between the host country's productivity in the export industry and the productivity in the domestic industry. FDIs could only contribute to the welfare of the home country (the developed country), especially when that investment was made in the primary industry since terms of trade between the primary and the secondary industrial product gradually deteriorated.

Meanwhile, D. F. Burges (1978) analyzed the effect of FDIs on income redistribution of the host country (the developing country). Unlike the previous studies which concluded that the inflow of capital caused by FDIs transferred income from capital to labor due to the decline in the rate of profit in capital, he claimed that income distribution of the host country (the underdeveloped or developing country) differed according to the substitution elasticity between consumption and production.

Yang-Taek Lim (1988) proposed a new hypothesis in connection with the industrial-interdependent relationship between home country (investor) and host country (recipient) to analyze the determinants of FDIs in Korea. He has named this as the industrial interdependence relationship hypothesis. This means

[119] For a detailed discussion, see H. Byun and Y. Wang(1995).

that direct investment by home country will increase if host country has a high import dependency on the exporting products made by the home country.[120]

To analyze the determinants of FDIs in Korea based on the outstanding amount, Korea's industry as a whole and the manufacturing sector separately were analyzed for the 1970~1985 period to investigate the economic effects of FDI on Korea economy with respect to domestic investment, economic growth, trade balance, and technical efficiency as based on the outstanding amounts in balance, during the time period of 1970 1985.

The reason for the choice of 1985 as the end was that it marked the change in Korea's FDIs policy as previously mentioned.

1) Determinants of Major Countries' FDIs in Korea

The following is the summary of Yang-Taek Lim's study (1988 and 1989) on the determinants of FDIs in Korea and its macroeconomic effects[121] with respect to each of the foreign investors including the United States, Japan and Europe.

(1) Direct Investment by the United States

As hypothesized, direct investment by the United States (FDI_u) showed a positive (+) effect for the average rate of profit (π) and the growth rate of export shipment($\Delta S/S$) of the Korean manufacturing sector, while it showed a negative (-) effect for the average wage level (W) and the tax rate (t) of the host country. This coincides with the findings by N. W. Bandera and J. T. White (1968) and A. E. Scaperlanda and I. J. Mauer (1969). The Scaperlanda and Mauer model (during the 1952~1966 period) showed that the GNP of EEC nations was the only significant variables in explaining the size-of-market hypothesis. They concluded that the major determinant in American direct investments in EEC was market size.

Furthermore, not only did the direct investment by the United States showed a significantly complementary relationship with Korea's domestic investment (I), it also contributed to an improvement in Korea's trade balance. According to the above analysis of the macroeconomic effects of FDIs in Korea, it was the United States which most effectively pursued industrial and technological cooperations and settled a complementary relationship between the host country (Korea) and the home country (the US).

Such an analysis is contrary to the study by K. Kojima (1984), who analyzed the effect of the previous year's FDIs on the current year's exports. He claimed that direct investment by Japan (FDI_J) played a large role in reducing Korea's deficit in the balance of trade with Japan, whereas direct investment by the United States (FDI_U) did hardly anything to improve Korea's trade balance.

Related with the above, K. Kojima (1973, 1978, 1979 and 1982) and K. Kojima and J. Ozawa (1984) referred to FDIs in the host country's industries (labor- intensive, light industries) of comparative advantage as trade-oriented FDIs, while referring to FDIs in the host country's industries (capital-intensive and heavy and chemical industries) of comparative disadvantage as anti-trade-oriented FDIs. They claim that the trade-oriented FDIs develops the host country's comparative advantage industries while the home country specializes in the industries with comparative advantage so that both profit from international trade.

Furthermore, Kojima claimed that Japan was usually engaged in trade-oriented FDIs targeting export industries profiting both countries, whereas the United States conducted anti-trade-oriented FDIs which usually targeted the host country's domestic industry. However, it must be noted that Kojima has dismissed the current realities where a developing country's specialization in light industries brings about a subordinate relationship such as intensifying dependency on capital goods including machinery parts.

Concerning Kojima's study (1984), it should be noted that he compared FDIs in Korea with the absolute value of Korea's exports when analyzing its effects on Korea's trade balance, instead of Korea's *net* exports. The absolute value of Korea's exports is highly likely to be erroneous, especially when taking into consideration of its heavy import dependency on Japanese intermediary products, especially general machinery.

---

[120] This is in contrast to the tariff differential hypothesis by A. E. Scaperlanda and L. J. Mauer, "The Determinants of US Direct Investment in the E.E.C.", *American Economic Review,* Vol. 59, No. 4, Part I, September 1969.

[121] The theoretical background of the determinants of FDI can be found in the context of industrial organization, trade complementarity, investment selection and currency value advantage. Among the determinants of FDIs based on industrial organization are two different theories, one being the market share hypothesis by A. E. Scaperlanda and I. J. Mauer (1969) and the other being the product life cycle hypothesis by R. Vernon (1966).

Direct investments by the United States began to increase in the 1970s when public companies financed by aid money suffered serious management problems, trade deficit continued to grow and the Korean government took strong measures to attract foreign direct investments. In the middle of the decade, the US firms' direct investments in Korea stalled for a while due to the post shock of the US defeat in Vietnam and restrictions imposed by the Korean government on the foreign investment share. They began to grow rapidly in the 1980s, however, following the liberalization measures taken by the Korean government. The following is a summary of bilateral direct investments between Korea and the United States:

First, bilateral direct investments began to show a sharp increase in the second half of the 1980s; US direct investments in Korea have always exceeded Korea's investments in the US until the mid of 1980s. As the latter began to surpass the former in annual growth rate in the second half of the 1980s, the gap began to narrow rapidly. In 1980, for the first time in history, the latter (US$ 350 million) exceeded the former (US$ 320 million) in absolute terms.

Second, the gap between the two types of investments reached a peak in 1989 at US$ 1.09 billion in favor of the United States before it declined for the first time in 1990 to US$ 1 billion. As of the end of 1993, the balance of US direct investments in to Korea was about US$1 billion greater than the balance of Korea's direct investments in to the United States. The turn around in 1990 was attributed to a high domestic savings rate, exceeding the total domestic investment ratio, and an improvement in Korea's current account.

Owing to such improvements in its current account, the total overseas investment of Korea reached 4.2% of its GNP during 1986-1990, making Korea an overseas net investor country for the period. Of course, the fact that Korea became an overseas net investor during a given period does not necessarily mean that it had high degree of net direct investments (foreign direct investments abroad minus foreigners' direct investments in the country). International capital flows include a variety of short and long-term movement of financial assets and Korea, a heavily indebted country, spent a lot of money on debt repayment and accumulation of financial assets (foreign reserves).

In terms of motives, the US have sought for cheap abundant labor until the 1970s and attractive consumer markets in the 1980s. Korea's direct investments into the US were mainly to complement rather than substitute its exports to the market, the defense of its major overseas market was the primary investment motivation, to cope with US tariffs and non-tariff barriers. Of course, advanced technologies from the US were also an attraction for Korean businesses.

(2) Direct Investment by Japan

The average wage level(W) and the growth rate of domestic shipment ($\Delta S/S$) were statistically significant variables that showed negative (-) effects on the direct investment by Japan (FDI_J). The observation that the increase of shipment by Korean businesses ($\Delta S/S$) induced a decrease in the direct investment by Japan (FDI_J) coincides with the findings by the Bank of Korea (1985)[122] and J. Dunning (1981). Taking into consideration of the monopolistic nature of the Korean industry, the empirical result point to a decline in the intention of Japanese businesses to extend their business into Korea as the rate of shipment($\Delta S/S$) by Korea's big businesses increased.

Moreover, direct investment by Japan (FDI_J) showed a significantly complementary relationship with Korea's domestic investment (I), but it was estimated to have aggravated Korea's trade balance. This empirical testing result may reflect Korea's heavy dependence on the imports of intermediary products from Japan as mentioned previously.

Such an analysis coincides with case studies by S. Lall and P. Streeten (1978) and R. Cohen and J. Frieden (1981)[123]. The reason why FDIs results in a negative (-) effect on the trade balance of a host country can be explained as: first, remittances from the home country surpass the amount of original

[122] According to the analysis by the Bank of Korea, an increase in sales by Korean business showed a negative(-) effect on FDI.

[123] According to these studies, among six developing countries during the 5~7 years at the end of the 1960s, the FDIs by 159 foreign businesses showed a negative (-) effect on the trade balance of the five countries(Columbia, India, Iran, Jamaica and Malaysia), only missing Kenya. Only a handful of FDI in a host country contributed to its trade balance. Meanwhile, according to the study by R. Cohen and J. Frieden (1981), the deficit in balance of payment produced by eight foreign motor companies in Brazil in 1974 accounted for 1/8 of the total deficit. FDI also proved to have an unfavorable effect on the balance of payment in Nigeria.

investment; second, the outflow of foreign exchange is excessive due to the import of intermediary goods; thirdly, the export of many investment companies including foreign investors is stagnant.

(3) Direct Investment by Europe

The average rate of profit (π) and the average wage level (W), of the host country are statistically significant explanatory variables that showed a positive (+) effect on the direct investment by Europe (FDI_E), whereas the tax rate (t) of the host country is estimated to have a significant, negative effect on the same FDIs. Furthermore, the direct investment by Europe (FDI_E) had a significant, complementary relationship with Korea's domestic investment(I), but it also aggravated Korea's trade balance.

2) Effects of FDIs on Korea's Technical Efficiency

Following the approach of M. Blomström (1986), Yang-Taek Lim (1989) measured the yearly technical efficiency index (E) for each of 79 industrial sectors in the Korean manufacturing industry during the periods of 1978 and 1982~1986. As shown in <Table X-5>, Blomström and Lim obtained the same results except the effect of the growth rate of market size (MG). Thus, in explaining technical efficiency (E), the Herfindal index (H) representing industrial concentration showed a positive (+) effect, the rate of change in the highest level of labor productivity (ΔY+) representing technical progress showed a negative (-) effect in consistent with definition of technical efficiency (E) and the market share of foreign businesses in Korean manufacturing sector (MS) showed a positive (+) effect[124]

<Table X-5> Determinants of Technical Efficiency(E) in Mexico and Korea

	Country	Model	Constant	H	Δy^+	MG	FS	R^2	Time Period	No. of Industrial Sectors
M. Blomström (1986)	Mexico	Linear Non-Logarithm	0.6396	0.2341 (0.0675)	-0.0714 (0.0143)	-0.0044 (0.0211)	0.1866 (0.0612)	0.2891	1970 ~1975	145
		Linear logarithm	- 0.1853	0.1182 (0.0527)	-0.2293 (0.0429)	-0.0801 (-0.0569)	0.0566 (0.0190)	0.2530		
Y. T. Lim (1989)	Korea	Linear Non-Logarithm	0.2734	0.5669 (11.112)	-0.0647 (4.930)	-0.0950 (2.634)	0.2544 (2.025)	0.7030	1978, 1982 ~1986	79
		Linear logarithm	0.6135	0.3568 (7.439)	-0.4342 (5.124)	-0.0084 (0.428)	0.0018 (0.260)	0.5515		

Notes:

The number in parentheses for each explanatory variable indicates the standard error for Blomström and the t-statistic for Lim.

For the proxy variable of market growth (MG), Blomström chose the time rate of change in the number of employees (ΔL) whereas Lim chose the percentage rate of change in fixed capital (ΔK/K) of the Korean manufacturing sector.

For the proxy variable of market share (FS) of foreign businesses, Blomström chose the relative ratio of the number of employees in foreign businesses to the total number of employees in the Mexican industry (L_f/L), whereas Lim chose the relative ratio of the fixed capital of foreign businesses to the total value amount of fixed capital in the Korean manufacturing sector (K_f/K). Blomström chose all foreign businesses having more than 15% ownership by foreign investors whereas Lim chose those with more than 50% of foreign share.

From the two studies above, it can be known that industrial concentration (H) reflects economies of scale and specialization rather than the market share of big businesses in small open economies such as Mexico and Korea. This coincides with the two studies on the determinants of technical efficiency, B. Carlsson (1972) for Sweden and M. Blomström (1986) for Mexico.

It was in regard to the growth rate of market size of the host country (MG) that the two studies above showed a difference. This explanatory variable showed a negative (-) effect on technical efficiency (E) in

[124] The same result above was shown in the closed economy model and the open economy model in which an additional explanatory variable in the form of FDI was additionally introduced. It was the same regardless of the fact that the explanatory variables representing the degree of international competitiveness such as the export ratio (x), the import ratio (m) and the tax ratio (t) were additionally introduced.

Lim's study, whereas Blomström claimed that this explanatory variable hardly affects technical efficiency.[125]

Second, the market share of foreign businesses in Korea (FS) depended upon the choice of proxy variable for the explanatory variable (FS). Technical efficiency (E) of the host country was raised when the relative ratio of foreign fixed capital to domestic fixed capital (K_f/K) was selected, while it was lowered when the relative ratio of foreign shipment to domestic sales volume (S_f/S) was selected.

This result may reflect the fact that the 'learning effect' of the host country was higher with high K_f/K, and the industrial interdependence relationship between foreign and domestic businesses was intensified. On the other hand, the market share of the host country's big businesses would fall, the higher the relative ratio of foreign shipment to domestic sales volume (S_f/S); thus technical efficiency of the host country (E) due to economies of scale and specialization could fall.

Thus, technical efficiency of the host country (E) will rise in the industry where there is more FDIs with a higher ratio of foreign fixed capital to domestic fixed capital (K_f/K) and a lower ratio of foreign shipment to domestic sales volume (S_f/S); likewise, its technical efficiency would fall in the industry where there are more FDIs with a lower K_f/K and the higher S_f/S.

Third, three other explanation variables, the export ratio (x), the import ratio (m), and the tax ratio(t), were introduced to reflect the degree of international competitiveness. Among these, the import ratio (m) and the tax ratio (t) were found to be significant determinants. As the import ratio (m) increased, industrial concentration (H or CR4) decreased but the extent was minimal. However, technical efficiency (E) of the host country decreased due to the deterioration in international competitiveness when the tax ratio (t) was high; this coincides with the empirical result of B. Carlsson (1972).

Therefore, it is evident that an effective way to increase technical efficiency (E) of the host country is to lower the tax ratio (t) rather than increase the import ratio (m).

C. Summary

Analysis of FDIs in Korea showed that the direct investment from the United States (FDI_U) and that from Europe (FDI_E) had a positive effect on Korea's domestic investment, but yielded a negative effect on the growth of the Korean economy. Meanwhile, the direct investment from Japan (FDI_J) not only showed a significant and substitutional relationship with Korea's domestic investment, but also a negative effect on the growth of the Korean economy at the 1% significance level.[126]

Furthermore, it was FDI_U which most effectively pursued industrial cooperation and settled a complementary relationship between the host country and the home country. FDI_U contributed to the improvement in Korea's trade balance, while FDI_E and FDI_J deteriorated it.[127]

---

[125] The percentage rate of change in fixed capital of the host country($\Delta K/K$) and its time rate (ΔK) showed negative (-) effects in the two studies of Blomström and Lim, although statistically insignificant for $\Delta K/K$, while statistically significant at the 5% level for ΔK.

[126] Looking at other studies related with this matter, H. W. Singer (1950) analyzed whether FDIs in an underdeveloped country improved the welfare of the underdeveloped country or that of the developed country. The multiplier effect caused by FDIs was usually accrued to the home country rather than the host country, that being the underdeveloped country. Considering that FDIs was usually made in the export industrial area, such an effect was enlarged when there was a bigger difference between the host country's productivity in the export industry and the productivity in the domestic industry. FDIs could only contribute to the welfare of the home country especially when that investment was made in the primary industry since the trade conditions between the primary industrial product and the secondary industrial product gradually deteriorated.
Meanwhile, D. F. Burges (1978) analyzed the effect of FDIs on income redistribution of the host country. Unlike the previous studies which concluded that the inflow of capital caused by FDIs transferred income from capital to labor due to the decline in the rate of profit in capital, he claimed that income distribution of the host country differed according to the substitution elasticity between consumption and production.

[127] The effect of FDIs on the balance of payment of the host country was analyzed by S. Lall and P. Streeten (1978) and R. Cohen and J. Frieden (1981). According to their case studies, among six developing countries during the 5 7 years at the end of the 1960s, FDIs by 159 foreign businesses showed a negative effect on the trade balance of the five countries (Columbia, India, Iran, Jamaica, and Malaysia), only missing Kenya. Only a handful of foreign businesses that directly invested in a host country contributed to its trade balance.

Concerning technical efficiency, Yang-Taek Lim (1989)[128] analyzed that among the three variables: export ratio, import ratio, and tax ratio. The import and tax ratios found to be significant determinants of technical efficiency. Furthermore, the technical efficiency of the host country decreased due to a deterioration in international competitiveness when the tax ratio was high.[129] Therefore, it is easy to see that an effective way to increase technical efficiency in the host country is to lower the tax ratio rather than increase the import ratio.

Such an analysis is contrary to the study by K. Kojima (1975)[130] who analyzed the effect of the previous year's FDI on the current year's exports. He claimed that FDIJ played a big role in reducing Korea's deficit in trade balance with Japan, by developing Korea's comparative advantage industry (labor-intensive and light industries), while Japan specialized in its comparative advantage industry (capital-intensive and heavy-chemical industry). However, it must be noted that Kojima failed to realize that a developing country's specialization in light industry brings about a subordinate relationship which intensifies the dependency on machine parts and capital goods.[131]

Meanwhile, according to the study by Cohen and Frieden (1981), the deficit produced by eight foreign motor companies in Brazil in 1974 accounted for 1/8 of the total deficit in balance of payment. FDIs also proved to have an unfavorable effect on the balance of payment in Nigeria.

The reason why FDIs resulted in a negative effect on the trade balance of a host country can be explained as follows. First of all, the remittance from the home country surpassed the amount of original investment. Secondly, the outflow of foreign exchange was excessive due to the import of intermediary goods. Thirdly, the export of many investment companies including foreign investors was stagnant.

128 Yang-Taek Lim, "A Study on the Determinants of Efficiency in Korea", paper presented at the Annual Conference of the Korean Economic Association, Seoul, Korea, January 1989.

Yang-Taek Lim, "A Study on Technology Transfer through Foreign Direct Investment in Korea", Ministry of Science and Technology, Seoul, Korea, May 1989.

129 This coincides with the study by B. Carlsson (1972).

130 K. Kojima, "International Trade and Foreign Investment: Substitute or Complement", *Hitotsubashi Journal of Economics*, Vol. 18, No. 1, 1978.

131 Concerning the study of K. Kojima (1978), it should be noted that they compared the FDI in Korea with the absolute value of Korea's exports when analyzing its effects on Korea's trade balance, instead of the rate of change in Korea's exports and imports over time. Such a method is highly likely to be erroneous, especially when taking into consideration Korea's heavy industrial dependency on Japan.

Chapter XI

INDUSTRIAL AND TECHNOLOGICAL COLLABORATION

1. GROWING DEMAND FOR STRATEGIC COLLABORATIONS

Society in the future will be led by high-tech industries. Today's high technology has the following features.

First, the trend is that the period needed to turn technology into a product is getting faster, while new products are replacing predecessors in shorter intervals. For example, it took 33 years for the first vacuum tube, invented in 1882, to become available for common use, while it took only 5 years for the radar, invented in 1935, to come into use. Further acceleration in recent years has made even the distinction of fundamental, applied and development research difficult. Thus, time has become a very important factor in decision-making for economic actors. Potential capabilities for technological development and marketing skills, which consist of gathering and analyzing market information to be used in production and sales, are highly prized.

Second, today's high-tech development entails enormous R&D costs and risks. The development rate of high-tech products such as commercial airplanes and communication semiconductors has been accelerated. The cost for developing commercial airplanes in the 1930s was approximately US$ 3 million, while today it takes more than US$10 billion to develop and sell a new model of commercial airplane.

Third, today's high technology propagates widespread effects over industry as a whole. It dramatically changes not only those industries directly related to the high technology in question but also the production structure of existing industries. For example, the automobile industry, which is not a high-tech industry but pertains to the existing industry, has been transformed into an enterprise of a totally different nature with the application of high new materials technology and precise electronic technology.

Strategic partnerships, which have mutually compensatory use of administrative resources and functions, promotion of economies of scale, and market approach as their goals, form competitive trading relations rather than dependence dominance relations. There are mainly two reasons behind the on-going strengthening of strategic partnerships by world firms. The first is that strategic partnerships are a means of overcoming the formation of economic blocs and trade friction, securing markets, and penetrating frontier markets. The second reason is that the development costs of innovative products are more than even multi-national corporations can handle; thus the goal is to reduce the costs of high-technology development and to share the risks involved.

The reason of strategic partnerships are important to Korean firms is that the 'ability to use other firms' is becoming an increasingly important part of administrative capability. In a situation where one firm alone cannot undertake investment in a new area, it is possible to reduce time and risks by using other firms in technology development. Inter-corporate strategic alliances also play the role in preventing trade conflicts between nations. It is known that the numerous strategic alliances between America's 'Big Three' and Japanese firms acted decisively in toning down and bringing to an end the US government's attack of the Japanese automobile industry in early 1993. The American side realized that their suing the Japanese industry over dumping actions could harm inter- corporate cooperation. Complex strategic partnerships in the area of semi-conductors will also ease American-Japanese trade friction and eventually make it impossible to distinguish Japanese products from American ones in the near future.

Inter-corporate strategic alliances are mostly being drawn among firms from technologically advanced economics such as the US, Japan and the EU. Such alliances serve to prevent the entry of new firms as well as to promote economies of scale through the exchange of market and technology information. As a result, firms from developing countries left out from strategic partnerships cannot participate in high technology sectors and will eventually fall out of technological competition.

The policy implication described above should be obvious if the main characteristics of the new international technology environment are carefully examined. They include strategic technological ties among advanced countries, greater dual-technology development, a set of new "rules of the game", stronger protection for intellectual property rights and stronger enforcement of international environmental regulations.

First, strategic ties in technology are being actively sought all over the world. Current technological ties are being set up with a focus on high technology, mainly among advanced countries or between US-Japan-EU; the percentage of technological ties involving the Third World countries and developing countries compose only 2% of the total. Ultimately, strategic technological ties are being used as a means of deterring the pursuit of developing countries and promoting competition only among the advanced countries.

In the current high-tech world, however, all countries are potential competitors as well as potential partners. Cooperation takes place at the development stage rather than at the production or sales stage and much cooperation is strategic in nature. Technological ties, which are ever increasing in scope, are made in order to reduce the burden of risk and uncertainty of developing highly complex production technologies and large-scale R&D among participating countries. They seek to improve managerial efficiency and help participants acquire a joint comparative advantage.

Second, with the conclusion of the Cold War in 1989, the volume of purely military R&D is declining, dual technology for both military and civilian use is on the rise. Such a trend has become clearer with the inauguration of the Clinton Administration as the United States has seen a considerable part of its defense R&D budget, which comprises 56% of total R&D spending in dual-use projects. In 1993 the share of civilian sectors in total federal R&D budget was only 41%, but by 1998 this percentage is expected to increase to over 50%.

Third, discussions on drawing up a new set of international regulations concerning government intervention and support in technological development have taken place, mainly at the OECD. An OECD ministerial meeting has determined that the differentiated support systems for technological development among different countries are a cause of trade frictions and has begun to regulate them. The rationale for such a move by the OECD is that as the distinction between fundamental and applied research and science and technology becomes ever more blurry, it is possible that support for fundamental research and science can directly affect a firm's international competitiveness and impede fair competition and distort market structure.

Fourth, property rights for knowledge and technology are being strengthened. Current changes in the international environment show a trend towards higher patent fees and the vigorous enforcement of intellectual property rights. There is a clear trend of using permit rights as a means or objective to amend trade imbalances or promote joint research, ties or merges between corporations, especially in United States and Japan. Recently, there has been an expansion of joint permit rights of local firms or among firms of different countries on the basis of cost-and-benefit among analysis by all parties.

Last, there is a stronger global movement to restrict discharging of toxic hazards and the production of polluting-inducing products. Beginning with the 1972 Stockholm Human Environment Meeting, there have been a series of international agreements including the Vienna Agreement (1985), the Montreal Protocol (1987), the Basel Agreement (1989) and the UNCED in Rio (1992). While the above agreements on environmental protection focus on achieving international cooperation in overcoming the global crisis, they also cause conflicts between the North and the South. As for Korea, located in between advanced and developing nations, it has become more difficult to make the jump into the ranks of the developed world as did Japan, who achieved growth under lax environmental restrictions.

In the midst of the new international climate mentioned above, the author would like to present recommendations for Korea's strategic technological development in regard to strategic technology tasks, active participation in international technological ties, joint preparations for stronger intellectual property rights and the support of environmental industries.

First, it is imperative that the starting point be the identification of strategic technology tasks. Korea must seek to establish comparative advantages in a few chosen sectors since it is much too weak to compete against advanced countries in all sectors. The G7 project, started in 1992, is in line such efforts. However, there have been indications that even the 11 areas chosen for development are too diverse and investment is bound to lose focus. Because this project entails loans amounting to 5% of Korea's GDP, it is imperative that the government sharpen its investment focus and trim the figure to 2% of GDP. Of course, all this has to be done within the bounds of the UR and the OECD guidelines.

Second, Korea must actively participate in international technological ties of a strategic nature. There have been a few cases in point such as the strategic technological ties between LG and the micro-chip producers of United States and Japan but the number of Korean firms involved in technical cooperation is very small due to the fact that few domestic firms have reached the standards set by advanced countries. There must first be an atmosphere of technical cooperation among domestic firms themselves, and several firms have participated in national R&D policy projects. Because the projects have been divided up closer to divisions of the work load among participants, however, they cannot be regarded as true technological cooperation.

Third, the government and the private sector must work jointly prepare for stronger intellectual property rights. The countries most eager to enforce property rights in knowledge-related fields are United States and Japan. In the US, protection for intellectual property rights has been linked with trade sanctions in the form of Super Article 301 and Special Article 301. It is fortunate that Korea has been removed from the Priority Watch List in 1993 in recognition of her efforts in enforcing publishing rights and computer programs. Thus, gradual strengthening of administrative guidance and supervision is required as well as a systematic mechanism for conflicts with foreign agencies.

Fourth, Korea must go with the global flow in strengthening environmental policies and developing environmental technologies for an eco-friendly economy. Whereas advanced nations have set off to develop environment-friendly technology since the 60s, Korea, where environmental technology grew as an area of specialization in the late 1970s, is still at the initial stage of learning about anti-pollution equipment. Similarly, permissive standards in toxic discharges have only recently been strengthened. Technological tasks in this sector include the replacement of CFC, management of discharges, prevention of earth pollution, processing of industrial and sewage wastes, desulphurization and low-pollution combustion.

The world economic order is going through structural changes with the launch of WTO (World Trade Organization) in 1997. The major directions of the changes are market opening and globalization as defined by the Uruguay Round. Many countries have already enhanced their efforts toward international industrial collaboration based on comparative advantage.

The free competition trade order under the UR is expected to bring about many changes in Korea's machinery, electric-electronics and textile industries, but at the same time prospects are not clear. This is more so in areas where mid- term and long-term growth is expected such as factory automation, precision chemistry and aerospace because the market bases in these industries are not strong enough due to rapid technological innovation and changes in demand, and also because international specialization will be carried out fully under the UR trade order. The same are also areas where integration, systematization, formation of networks and advancement of technology are being accelerated, and under these circumstances existing managerial strategies become irrelevant.

From the demand side, the qualities sought for in consumer goods today are convenience, health and sensibility; in capital goods demand is strongest for products that offer the ease to operate and combine functionality, speed, and flexibility. There is a need for the informatization and automation of industrial production along with the creation of new industries. Thus each firm could not survive unless it strengthens its internal structure. The situation is such that each firm must seek industrial cooperation and strategic alliances as part of their business plan.

2. International Industrial Collaborations

A. The Definition

International industrial collaboration occurs in the fields of research and development, capital, technologies, production and marketing between governments or businesses to complement each other in both weak and strong areas with a view to enhancing their competitiveness. The benefits of collaboration that business partners can expect include distributional risks and financial burdens among the partners, their overcoming economic restrictions on host country and secure access to the market and reinforcement of competitiveness of the business partners as they share both tangible and intangible assets.

At the same time, collaboration enables the national economies involved to enhance their international competitiveness, correct imbalances in their trade, ease trade friction, secure stable sources of foreign technologies, promote international specialization, and secure access to new markets. The effects vary depending on the partner country. Collaborations between advanced countries usually ease trade frictions and promotes international specialization. Collaboration between a developed country and a developing country usually offers an access to the low wages and consumer market of the developing country for the developed country whereas a chance to reduce trade deficit, secure a source of advanced technologies, and market products in the developed country.

B. The Motives

The motives behind international industrial collaboration include: sharing risks and financial burdens; securing or expanding an access to an overseas market; obtaining new technologies; sharing corporate assets; realizing economies of scale; and preventing excessive competition among competitors.

The collaboration, however, is usually driven by more than two motives. In some cases, a common motive, such as advancing into a third market can be the primary motive for the partners. The motives vary depending on the areas of collaboration, the form of collaboration, the technological level of the partners and the characteristics of the partners

In case where collaboration occurs between two countries with a significant gap in technology, the leading motive for the less developed country is usually to induce technology while that for the technically advanced partner is a desire to prevent infringement of its intellectual property rights in the host country as well as to secure market access.

In the areas of relatively old technologies such as iron and steel, automobiles and traditional telecommunications equipment, advanced partners are motivated by a desire to secure access to the less developed market. In the areas of relatively new technologies such as semiconductors and genetics, companies join hands to secure access to each other's assets (usually technology).

C. Applications and Forms

Usually, collaboration occurs in five areas: capital, technology, research and development, production and marketing. Its usual form is a joint investment implemented typically in the form of a joint-venture between two parties: however, a consortium involving more than three parties is also popular for huge projects. Joint-ventures are set up between companies of different nationalities with competitive edges in either capital or management. Quite often international industrial collaboration is called international technological cooperation due to the importance of technology in such efforts. Usually, only after there is technological collaboration, does the partnership evolve into production and marketing. Technological collaboration takes the form of grants, exchanges, supports, second sourcing and transactions.

Technological collaboration is divided into vertical and horizontal cooperation: the vertical type is used by a party wanting to obtain the other party's technologies such as semiconductors, electric motors and electronics. Horizontal collaboration, meanwhile, is made to secure market access to each other's markets, for instance in the field of HDTV related businesses. Collaboration in research and development is on the rise because technical innovation is being accelerated, particularly in the fields of advanced technologies such as micro-electronics, ceramics, and biotechnology since the cycle of technologies and products has been shortened markedly.

International collaboration in the field of production is very much an international specialization in that the partners now produce their products more economically by combining their comparative edges. The collaboration can take the form of subcontracting, OEM, or joint production. OEM is the most popular form of collaboration between the firms of developed and developing countries.

Collaboration in the field of marketing usually aims to share retail networks, advance to a third market jointly, or establish a franchising relationship between the partners. It can occur separately but more often it is made along with collaboration in capital, technology or production.

Apart from the traditional pattern favored by many businesses in advanced countries, namely industrial collaboration through direct investments in developing markets, the latest trend is to form strategic alliances with a view to circumventing the various restrictions imposed on foreigners' direct investments.

Strategic alliance between companies with identical management resources is designed to distribute risks involved in the development of new products, reduce marketing costs and enhance competitiveness and management skills through an exchange of technologies, use common sales network, market jointly in a third country or undertake joint studies in the field of marketing. The alliance does not involve portfolio investment and thus the partners maintain complete independence from each other in corporate management.

3. Trends of Strategic Alliance by Korean Firms

Although the formation of strategic partnerships is popular as a globalization method, it is not common practice among Korean firms. The strategic alliances Korean firms have made with firms from advanced countries are mostly limited to the form of production consignment. Such a form of cooperation is only at the OEM level and not a strategic alliance on equal grounds. On the other hand, efforts towards increasing strategic partnerships between domestic firms or between Korean and firms from advanced countries are being carried out from several industries such as the electronics industry.

A. Strategic Partnerships Inter-Domestic Firms

It is important that Korean firms provide a common front to overcome excessive competition and to strengthen competitiveness in order to win in the competition with global companies. In 1992, LG and Samsung drew up an agreement which allowed both firms to use each other's permit technology at no cost in the three sectors of LCD, TV tubes and monitors. The two companies have thus built a framework in which they can advance into the world market by preventing duplicated investment and promoting joint technology development.

Also, the three big shipbuilding companies, Hyundai Heavy Industries, Samsung Heavy Industries, and Daewoo Shipbuilding, have participated in the form of a consortium in the tender for 5 ultra-big oil-transporting ships ordered by the National Ship Construction Company of Saudi Arabia. Hyundai and Samsung Heavy Industries have also jointly participated in the international tender of 140,000t oil-transporting ships ordered by the Indian National Shipbuilding Corporation, being each awarded construction of 2 ships. These two companies have been able to cut prices by engaging in joint development of construction plans and eliminating unproductive competition with each other.

B. Boardless Strategic Partnerships

Korea's industries have started to open their eyes to the formation of strategic partnerships with firms from advanced countries as a means of dispersing investment risks and securing dominance over markets. The form of partnerships has also become more diverse, ranging from technology alliances such as cross-licenses to learn advanced technology, to seek for capital and sales alliances.

Samsung Electronics is the most active firm in pursuing strategic partnerships starting with the semiconductor sector and expanding to information-communication and home electronics. Of Samsung's alliances, those that can be classified as joint- development projects include partnerships with America's TI, GE and Motorola and Japan's Toshiba and OKI. A joint-development partnership that Samsung had pursued was the development of 256M DRAM with Japan's NEC on in 1994. Partnerships established by Samsung towards the goal of securing markets include the undertaking of the equity participation in America's ARRAY and HMS, technological partnership with Japan's Matsushita and sales partnership with America's Hewlett Packard over RISC workstation.

Another conglomerate or *chaebol* that has performed well in the area of strategic partnerships with firms of developed countries is LG, which has drawn cooperation agreements with COMPASS in the sector of ASIC semiconductors and agreed to form a joint-development project with Qualcomm over mobile phones. To secure markets, LG's production technology and IMC's service technology have formed an alliance in order to advance into America's conversation TV market and also secured strategic alliances throughout in provision for the opening of the age of CATV. Daewoo Telecommunications has drawn cooperative contracts with America's Silicon Graphics in the field of high-speed graphic workstations.

Prospects for increased strategic partnerships in Korea are high since Korea needs to invest vast amounts of capital as R&D and installation costs in the promising areas of semiconductors, HDTV and LCD. Forming strategic alliances as the most ideal preventive measure of resolving international trade conflict is expected to accelerate in pace with globalization trends.

4. KOREA-US INDUSTRIAL COOPERATION

A. The Direction Toward a New Pacific Community

Korea and the United States have maintained close economic relations for almost a half century since the end of World War II in 1945. The US has been one of the important factors in the development of the Korean economy during the past decades; capital from the US has been the most important source of finance for Korea's economic development; the US market has been the biggest market for Korea's exports; and the US has been the primary source of technologies for Korean industries.

The author would like to emphasize that the development direction of industrial cooperation must be towards the construction of a New Pacific Community. The two countries ought to join hands to enhance their bilateral economic relations and furthermore work together to promote free trade throughout the world. The kind of economic order that prevails in this region will have a great bearing on world peace and prosperity in the 21st century and the two countries should try to forge a regional order compatible with the global one.

Under the new world trade order which has led to a tendency toward formation of blocs, now there are a greater number of possibilities for trade friction between Korea and the United States, over intellectual property rights, environmental issues, agriculture, investment services and the automobile industry. The US Trade Representative Board (USTR) designated Korea as a Priority Foreign Country for Vigilance (PFCV) in 1994. The International Trade Agency, a subdivision of the American Department of Commerce, has disclosed in its Report on US-Korea Trade Friction in January 1994 that it would use environmental issues as its frontal attack in bilateral negotiations. The United States has also made strong demands in the agricultural and automobile sectors.

It was noted above that there was quite a difference in the motives of Korea and the United States for their industrial collaboration. Now Korea and the United States need to give serious thought to the idea of establishing a strategic alliance between them for the following benefits: providing access to each other's markets; joint promotion of research and development projects; joint advance into a third market; sharing production and process technologies; enhancing economic productivity through the realization of the economics of scale sharing management skills; enhancing financial position to promote big projects; and better sourcing of raw materials.

B. Preferential Areas for Industrial Collaborations

Based on a study on the comparative advantage index and the revealed preference index to find out the most advantageous areas of industrial collaboration between Korea and the United States, the author recommends automobiles and auto parts, machine tools, computers and semi-conductors, HDTV and other electronics and aviation as optimal areas for cooperation. The following is a brief overview:

Automobiles and Auto Parts

The Korea-US Auto Parts Conference was inaugurated in Detroit in May 1989 at the request of the Department of Commerce of the US, in which Korea introduced its plan to boost imports of US auto parts. US companies could manufacture compact cars in Korea. It is true that the wage advantage has eroded somewhat in Korea but Korea has emerged as a significant market for automobiles and auto parts and as an increasingly important car exporter in the world.

Machine Tools

Korea needs to promote exports while localizing the production of crucial parts like NC, servo motors and ball screws in the long-term. Korea has little machinery technology to offer to the US However, it needs to pay much more attention to the sophisticated machinery technologies of US as a way of reducing trade deficit with Japan and mitigating excessive technical subordination to Japan. Korean firms suffer difficulties in meeting US quality standards because of excessively complicated procedures - the Korean government can try to resolve this problem through dialogue with the US government as well.

Computers

Computer technologies are now deeply incorporated into a whole range of industries, and which is why many advanced countries are reluctant to transfer their superior computer related technologies to newly industrialized countries.

Korean personal computer suppliers are equipped with an appropriate level of production technologies, but when it comes to the technologies required for the development of new products, still lag behind other market leaders and the focus remains on end products. It would be desirable to collaborate US companies such as Intel, Motorola, and MIPS on their RISC architecture and next- generation processors, and needs to set up R&D centers in the United States in the near future.

The United States has stepped up its efforts to protect its copyrights and patents overseas. Korean software companies have recently started doing business and have been assisted in the porting of Hangul, the Korean language. To avoid duplication of efforts, Korea needs to build a consortium among local suppliers, and obtain information on application and utility programs.

Electronics Telecommunication Equipment

Korea is largely dependent on OEM for its exports of electronics and telecommunication equipment to overseas (70~100% for most items). Local brands are still relatively unknown in international markets. Under the OEM format, personal computers, printers, facsimiles, hard disk drives, telephone exchanges and floppy disk drives are shipped to the US, Japan, and EU. The proportion of OEM exports, however, is declining. Local brands have now become more prominent in global markets owing to quality improvements and intensive marketing efforts.

Semiconductors

The United States has executed a large portion of its international collaboration contracts in the field of semiconductors, and thus this area needs some elaboration.

The US-Japan Semiconductor Agreement was concluded in 1986 with a view of the US taking a 20% market share in Japan by 1991. The industry is important to the US military, which maintains its strength on the basis of its advanced semiconductor technologies. The US semiconductor industry began to develop mainly for military purposes and has now become more important civilian industry. The US semiconductor industry has lost a significant portion of the memory markets to Japanese firms, although it still maintains its edges in design, ASIC and MPU.

Korea has focused on assembly production of semiconductors importing technologies from advanced countries. Lately a cross-license collaboration has been gaining popularity, whereby Korean firms can exchange technologies with businesses in developed countries. The collaboration between Korean and American firms is far from an equal partnership, the reason being the weakness of local firms in technology, capital, production facilities, marketing and management skills. Korean firms are interested in technologies relating to memory products to be used for OEM contracts. Korea has had little choice but to cooperate with the United States for core technologies in semiconductor design and manufacturing as the local semiconductor business has grown rapidly as the life cycle of semiconductors is so short that it accompanies great development risks.

From the perspective of the United States, Korea is a big semiconductor market as its telecommunications, home appliances and HDTV industries are developing rapidly. Korea is investing heavily in memory and ASIC. Korea has imported most of its high value semiconductors from Japan and thus the United States needs to intensify its collaboration with Korea if it wants to penetrate its market. While the US semiconductor industry is pursuing complementary technical alliance with Japan, it can gain more from its technical alliance with Korea by getting quality labor at relatively low prices in addition to rapidly developing production technology of memory products. Assistance for Korea in developing semiconductor technologies would be a means of holding the Japanese industry in check and achieving the common goal of securing competitiveness against Japan.

Aviation

The collaboration between Korea and the United States in the aviation industry goes back to 1978. Korean sub-contractors started shipping airplane parts to the US clients in the second half of the 1980s. Although it is now able to produce airplane bodies, Korea is far behind the US in design capability. The domestic market for large commercial jets is growing very rapidly. Demand for military jets are diverse but limited. Local firms are also weak in their ability to finance huge investment projects. The US had been cautious about collaboration with Korea in this field as the latter has an increasing trade surplus, but has activated cooperation recently as the surplus has been mitigated. Fully aware of the necessity to foster the development of the domestic industry, the Korean government has sought local production under technical guidance of aircraft companies.

The future for collaboration between Korea and the United States in the aviation industry depends on the improved technical level of Korean aviation firms, further creation of domestic demand, improved financial status of local firms and effective government strategies for negotiations with the United States. The potential areas of collaboration between the two countries in the aviation industry include sub-contracting of large US passenger planes to local firms, local production of military jets under technical guidance, joint ventures in the field of aviation electronics and direct investments by Korea into the United States.

High-Definition Television (HDTV)

The US is still ahead of Japan and Europe in HDTV development and expected to proceed smoothly according to a decision by the US Federal Telecommunications Committee. The decision has been delayed due to disagreement among the government, industry and the broadcasting stations. Even if the United States succeeds in the development of a next-generation TV, it has already lost its production base of color television sets in the 1980s and needs a partner in this regard as there is only one genuinely US color television set supplier in the United States, Zenith, which along with General Instrument and MIT research center is involved in an independent development of HDTV.

In contrast, Korea has a solid production base of color television sets and related parts, though it is weak in the basic technologies. Recently Japan has been reluctant to transfer its technologies on S-VHS and large CRT. Under the circumstances, it is really hard to create an appropriate technical environment for development of HDTV in Korea. For joint development of HDTV between Korea and the United Sates, a strategic alliance in which Korea provides its assembly and production technology for parts and equipment, and the United Sates offers related technologies is possible. To promote such an alliance effectively, the two countries can join forces in the core technologies.

5. Korea-Japan Industrial Cooperation

A. Industrial Structure and Trade Relations

The normalization of diplomatic relations between Korea and Japan in 1965 provided an impetus for cooperative relations in trade, investment and capital with Japan, which had a positive effect on Korea's rapid growth. However, due to Korea's high wages and uneasy relations between labor and capital in the 1980s, and Japan's refusal to transfer technical know-how for fear of a boomerang effect, the economic exchange between Korea and Japan has declined in almost all major areas since then. Also, due to the collapse of the so-called Japanese bubble economy, its direct investment into foreign countries began to decrease from a peak of US$ 67.5 billion in 1989, and direct investment into has also Korea dropped in the 1990s.

The reason for this decrease in economic exchange between Korea and Japan in the 1990s can be explained by the continuous depression of domestic business and Japanese expansion of trade and investment with developing countries such as China and ASEAN. Korea's balance of trade in 1994 was a deficit margin of nearly 4 times that of 1993. The factors involved in this aggravation of trade balance were: the organization of labor-intensive industry, the shift to domestic demands by the export industry, the slowing down of export due to the absence of leading sectors, the progress of free trade, and expansion of import due to high level of consumption structure.

It is quite relevant for the purposes of this section that Japan has maintained a large surplus with Korea throughout. According to a report by KIET, this adverse trade balance toward Japan will continue because a policy of export promotion by the Korean government will be quite difficult under the WTO system. It suggests that the recent scale of trade deficit toward Japan is excessive, that the import diversification system be applied in a more efficient manner, and that the import diversification system be scaled down gradually through the abolition of the indication system.

The manufacturing industries in Japan made the most of low fund-raising cost by actively pushing forward globalization and undertaking domestic industrial restructuring, but since Korea's Foreign Capital Inducement Law, which is traditionally hostile to foreign and particularly Japanese capital, had too many restrictions, Korea could not take advantage of the opportunity. The inadequate response of Korean industry to the globalization of Japanese businesses also created difficulties in its export environment as the competition between Korean businesses and ASEAN businesses of Japanese origin in Japanese markets is becoming heavier, and capital collaboration out of Japan has largely ignored Korean businesses.

The Japanese have accomplished incredible growth for more than thirty years since the 1960s through the close relationship between businesses and government, strategic cooperation among businesses, cooperation among interest groups - financial institutions, stockholders, and labor unions, loyalty and dedication of workers, and dynamic and challenging corporate strategies. However, Japan has lately been facing a challenge stemming from changes in the economic situations in and outside the country. The closed nature and exclusivity of Japanese markets are being internationally criticized. Nationally, most Japanese now want a more pleasant and relaxed style of life after a lifetime of high savings. The economic has halted to a standstill, the proportion of the elderly is increasing and a gradual increase in fund-raising costs can be expected due to financial sector restructuring. The Japanese economy is suffering greatly under such circumstances.

The Japanese recession has been going on for almost five years now, and is expected continue for another two or three years, affected overall by causes such as the decrease in internal demand due to the melt down of the bubble economy and lack of export activity due to the strong yen. Major export businesses such as electrics, electronics, automobiles and shipbuilding, have experienced grave decreases in their net profit and an increasing number of SMEs have gone bankrupt due to the worsening profitability of exports. The Japanese economy failed to recuperate in 1994 as facilities investment and individual consumption failed to pick up and stock markets failed to recover and thus the recession was perpetuated.

Nonetheless, there is no doubt that Japan, which took less than half a century for the loser in World War II to be the greatest creditor and the second largest economic unit in the world, remains the single most important economic power in Asia. Japan made such a successful turnaround by staying outside the border of the conflict region, depending on the United States for her national security, and making full use of free trade. Until the beginning of the 1970s, Japan's trade conditions were optimal. After the late 1970s, however, the barriers of protective trade have risen higher and it made Japan seek a new economic development strategy. With regards to this strategy in the 21st century, it is planning two ways of economic cooperation in the Asia-Pacific region.

The first is the V-shaped economic development where Japan stands in front of everyone else in the region with the NIEs next in line, followed by ASEAN, and other nations tagging behind. Such a plan would lead to relative development and perpetuate subordination, instead of effective international specialization or equal development.

The second, more limited system is the Sea of Japan Rim Economic Area. It would include North and South Korea, Japan, the three northeast provinces of China, and the Russian Far East. It is a huge economic area. If a mutual economic area is formed, it would be a region of vast potential and possibilities to grow.

B. Japan's Trade Frictions against Major Countries

Meanwhile, political pressure by the US to reduce its trade deficit with Japan also aggravated the situation. The high-yen trend had caused Japan's surplus balance in international payments, and Americans tried to force Japan to reduce the surplus through increased imports and adjustments in interest and foreign exchange rates. For Japan, however, the trade imbalance is not a problem that can be solved through policy adjustments, but through adjustments in its overall industrial structure. In this context, recent policies to boost consumer spending have been criticized as being inadequate in the absence of accompanying efforts at industrial financial restructuring and reduced emphasis on government intervention through budgetary policy.

Since the mid-1980s, Japan has been striving to improve competitiveness through globalization and alleviation of restrictions, to transform the economy into a domestic-demand oriented structure, and to open financial and capital markets in order to reduce trade frictions resulting from the massive account surplus and to revitalize the Japanese economy. However, since Japan's trade imbalance continued to magnify despite their efforts, America began to press bilateral open-market policies which has focused on Japan improving its domestic regulatory system, thereby actually enabling foreigners to drive right into the Japanese domestic market.

The main points of Framework Talks aimed at solving the imbalance between Japan and America are as follows: first, cooperation in macroeconomic policies such as Japan's reduction of account surplus with America and reduction of American fiscal deficit; second, cooperation in problems such as the environment, technology and human resource development; and third, governmental support, alleviation of restrictions and fulfillment of current pacts.

On the other hand, Japan's standpoint may be summarized as the following. Although the expansion of the US trade deficit with Japan stems in part from the complete heterogeneity of the Japanese culture as well as the insularity of her market, it has been caused fundamentally by the disparity in the industrial structure and competitiveness between the two nations when viewed in micro- economic sense and by the rise in the US fiscal deficit and drop in household savings rate macro-economically. The latter two factors have specifically contributed to a rise in interest rates, which in turn increases the influx of foreign capital, thereby expanding the US trade deficit once again.

Then, what is the next direction of US-Japan trade tension? It was stated in the 1994 US-Japan Summit Meeting by the Japanese Prime Minister Miyazawa that the economic cooperation between the two must be a cooperative effort based on Free Trade Principles. Meanwhile, President Clinton said the actions taken by Japan after the US-Japan trade tensions surfaced must first be investigated. After this, he proposed two ways to solve the trade deficit: structural market engagement and constraining trade of categories in which the United States can maintain competitiveness such as semiconductors, automobiles, and agricultural goods. Hence, Clinton's trade policy in relation to Japan will be determined by the extent of improvements in the balance of payments through an increase in export and recovery of Japan's domestic economy.

In contrast, Japan is expected to act on its own and take both hard and soft lines in resolving trade tension with the United States. In other words, since Japan cannot avoid being on the defensive with her trade surplus, she will check America's one-sided protective policies while outwardly showing as much cooperativeness as possible to the US to maintain the image that it is willing to aid the revitalization of the American economy and domestically improving the quality of life and fulfilling consumer needs through modernization.

For obvious reasons, the two sides have failed to achieve an agreement when the American opinion of defining Japanese market share and numerical goals confronted the Japanese assertion that such is administrative trade. Under these circumstances, the Economic Reform Committee has submitted the Hiraiwa Report, whose content included wide-range plans in the private sector. The two economic reform objectives that the report suggests in lieu of globalization are; an economic society that is transparent and open to parties in and out of the country, and building of an economic society that sympathizes with the rest of the world and is in harmony with it.

In order to achieve such goals, the report suggests that Japan must relax restrictions in the private economy, thereby promoting competition between domestic and foreign businesses, expanding imports to minimize differences in the prices of products between Japan and the other parts of the world, promote domestic consumption, revitalize the economy through expansion and creation of social overhead capital such as information communications and educational-research institutions, and link the increase in investment and decrease in savings to the shrinkage of the account surplus.

The survival tactics of Japanese companies can be summarized by the rationalization of manufacturing and management, price transfer, import expansion, reorganization of manufacturing systems and protection against currency fluctuation. That is, to overcome the double burden of industrial recession and the strong yen, Japanese companies are actually executing restructuring to counter the rise of export costs. A world-wide view of so-called 'produce at optimal location, export to optimal demand location' is also a method they are employing. Also, they are actively participating in joint research and mutual cooperation with overseas companies, something which has previously been done only internally.

For the increase of revenues and strengthening the competitiveness, Japanese enterprises are also making efforts to "return to Asia". The Asian region field production plan is aimed at escaping from the simple goal of enlarging the scale of Japanese enterprises to more efficient production. Profits would be greater than production in Japan because, above all, labor expenses are less. More and more design and development are also being done outside of Japan.

C. New Directions in Korea-Japan Industrial Collaborations

Korea and Japan have had, at a governmental level, many differences of opinion regarding the problem of Korea's trade deficit with Japan, and the decline of Japan's direct investment and technology transfer to Korea. Recently, the Japanese government has expressed positive measures for the weakening of import restrictions and increase of investment support to Korea by the Japanese enterprises. The Korean government has agreed to push forward with the alleviation of the import diversification system, which had acted as a restriction mechanism towards Japan. Both countries have agreed to the increase of investment in technology cooperation.

Japan is now actively pursuing economic cooperation with Korea. The fact remains, however, that economic exchange between Korea and Japan has declined in almost all areas such as trade, investment, and introduction of technical know-how. Still, at the industrial level, mutual technology supply and other various forms of cooperating activities between Korean-Japanese companies in such fields as semi-conductors and automobiles are being activated. Recently, continuous conferences have been held and a plan for industrial cooperation is taking concrete shape. Reasons for the renewed interest are as follows.

First, for Japan, increasing overseas production, as well as cooperation in technical and production matters with foreign companies, is unavoidable. Korea is being evaluated as an appropriate partner.

Second, from Korea's point of view, in order to solve pending problems such as the importation of Japanese technology and increase of exports to the Japanese market, it is becoming necessary to increase cooperation with Japan, rather than simply demanding cooperation from Japan.

Third, the realization is spreading throughout both countries that in order to effectively cope with the changing international political and economical environment, there must be an increase in mutual cooperation between Korea and Japan.

It cannot be denied that there has been an increase of friction between the two countries in the 1990s. However, the new Korean government announced its basic position of separating politics and economics in its relations with Japan. Japanese enterprises are increasing imports of Korean goods, and economic exchanges between the two countries are once again on the rise. The governments and enterprises have decided to make efforts to promote the transfer of government- owned technology and that of environmental protection and energy-related technology. Many leading Japanese SMEs are showing interest in investing in Korea.

The reasons that Japanese enterprises are now so eager to enter multinational projects include the bad condition of the Japanese economy, the strategies of Japanese global enterprises and the pressure of free-market trade from other developed nations. Korea was seen as the first attractive base, where a good level of technology and excellent infrastructure in electric power and communication systems could be found.

Therefore the recent industrial cooperation plan was derived from mutual necessity for the promotion of industrial restructuring in both countries, not like the one-sided request of the past. Cooperation between Korea and Japan can also be seen as necessary for the economic development of the East Asian region. A mutual existence where joint technology development and mutual profit is pursued can induce the voluntary participation of private enterprises in the pursuit of profit.

The Korean government must vitalize technology transfer to Korea by the Japanese enterprises through market mechanisms, while Japan must make efforts to strengthen the alliance and cooperation between the enterprises of the two countries across broad fields. It would also be necessary to actively induce cooperation by forming sub-economic regions to maximize geographical proximity and the mutual complementary nature of the industrial structure of the two countries.

D. Strategic Alliances

The recent trend of strategic alliances is rapidly spreading to automobile, electrical and shipbuilding industries. The method of industrial cooperation is diversifying to joint technology development, mutual supply of parts and joint marketing. Industrial cooperation between the two countries is showing an upward trend among corporate entities of all sizes. Joint technology development is being sought for the dispersion of risks. Not only can Japanese companies effectively check American and European companies and secure markets, but Korean companies can adopt high technology under conditions which are more advantageous than those of the past.

Semiconductor and Manufacturing Equipment

The semiconductor industry is the area in which the new cooperation system between Korea and Japan is most active. Samsung and NEC have decided on a strategic collaboration to reduce development risks. By combining manufacturing technology, both companies have opened a new road for cooperation in the production sector. Hyundai Electronics and Fujitsu have also decided on joint production and LG Electronics and Hitachi have agreed on a strategic alliance in the entire area of semiconductors. Technological cooperation in the semiconductor industry is also being expanded in the area of manufacturing facilities.

Home Appliances and Multi-Media

In the case of home appliances, Japanese companies are increasing orders under the OEM method to the three major electronic companies in Korea. In the area of electronics, Korean-Japanese technological cooperation is being pursued in the multi-media field in particular. To further promote and strengthen Korean-Japanese technological cooperation in these areas, Korea must heighten competitiveness in the industry of electrical-electronic machinery and tools.

Machinery and Automobiles

Daewoo Heavy Industries is taking steps to export construction machinery and automobiles to Japan. Requests for component purchases are also flooding into Samsung Heavy Industries and Ssangyong Heavy Industries.

In the automobile industry as well, Korean-Japanese industrial cooperation is being intensified at a high speed. Korean auto parts companies have become active in exporting products to Japan. It is also expected that the transfer of Japanese manufacturing sites to Korea will also become more frequent.

Shipbuilding and Construction

There have been many orders for ships from Japan and it is likely that the orders will increase. Orders for shipbuilding parts, even to SMEs are increasing as well.

Korea and Japan's cooperation in construction is becoming quite active. Korea's major contractors are working on a cooperative system with local Japanese counterparts through joint ventures and transfer of technology in order to enter the Japanese market. Daewoo, Samsung and Hyundai have agreed to cooperate with Japanese businesses by exchanging human resources.

Super-speed Information Network

The Korean Minister of Communications and the Japanese Minister of Postal Service met in Seoul in 1994 to discuss ways of cooperation in relation to the construction of a super-speed information network. The fact that both Korea and Japan have agreed to help each other in the construction of such a network for the next generation can be seen as a step further into an era of borderless exchange of information. When the two countries 21st century super-speed information network are connected, it is believed that its international competitiveness will extend to rank next to that of the US and Europe.

6. Korea-China Industrial Cooperation

A. China's High Growth and Foreign Trade

China is experiencing growth at a surprising rate since it pursued an open-door policy in 1979. Its GNP growth rate has shown a yearly average of about 9% in the past 15 years and economic growth marked the biggest in history in the open regions and coastal areas. There are prospects that China will become the world's biggest economic superpower some time in the new millennium. China's aggregate foreign trade has shown a yearly average growth of 16% from 1978 to 1992; while imports have increased 15.4%, exports have grown 16.8%. The size of China's exports was 11th in the world in 1993, already ahead of Korea, ranked two notches below. The background of such a rapid increase in foreign trade is China's open and reform policies.

In 1975 Deng Xiao Ping made the decision to concentrate on China's trade advantage in primary sector products, with the nucleus as petroleum export. After 1985, however, China went through a change in the composition of export items from raw material products to finished products and came to secure comparative advantage in labor-intensive products. Since then, her performance in international trade has been greatly improved.

The most important items in Chinese economic reforms are management of the currency exchange rate and foreign currency. China has gone through stages of liberalization in currency policies during the 1970s and 1980s. It went from a 'price-equalizing mechanism' in which profits from importing enterprises were used to counterbalance losses in exporters with the actual exchange rate differing from company to company, to the creation of an internally-settled exchange rate system to support the official exchange rate, then to a liberalized fluctuating exchange rate system. At present, the government has broken the rules of a socialist communist economy and introduced a system where foreign currency possession is permitted.

In the 1990s China has done mainly two things to promote competition and stimulate market function in the foreign trade sector. First, the government has curtailed direct aid given to trading companies suffering losses, and second, the government has expanded the functions of the exchange market. Although China has come a long way in the opening and liberalization of its economy, it still lags behind the international standards. A system of mandatory export is still being practiced in order to promote the influx of hard currency from abroad, excessive support funds are still paid to domestic trading companies and the government continues to conduct an import-management system as a trade barrier.

The investment environment in China has also improved since 1979, the year the reforms were started. China has fortified laws in the economic sector favorable to foreign investment. It has installed 5 special zones since 1980, opened 14 new coastal cities in 1984 and carried out various regional development projects. In addition, China has transferred its central inspection rights to local governments in provinces, cities and the coastal open zones.

Direct investment in China during 1992 increased 380% in comparison to the previous year in contract value and 160% in real transaction values, marking the highest increase in history. Generally, direct investment in China are 1) large in scale, 2) conducted in coastal areas and spread inwards into the continental provinces, 3) led by investments from Japan and Asian NIEs and 4) becoming increasingly focused on service sectors from manufacturing sectors.

B. Korea-China Industrial Collaborations

Korea's exports to China have increased 165% in respect to the previous year, up from 94% in 1993. China has a huge potential as an import market. On the other hand, from China's point of view, trade with Korea, its seventh largest trading partner, took up only 4.5% of its total trade. Still, in terms of the content of economic exchange and the acceleration of its growth, the importance of Korea to China is rapidly growing.

Since the late 1980s Korea's exports have undergone structural polarization according to region and item. This phenomenon consists of poor performance of exports of light industrial products to advanced countries and good performance of exports of heavy and chemical industries to developing countries. Under these circumstances, China, with a growing share of developing countries' market, has provided a breath of fresh air for Korean exports.

The author, however, maintains that China is still an unclear market for Korea and that Korea must be careful not to be too optimistic about the increase in aggregate export value. Without establishing a competitive advantage in advanced countries' markets with greater customer loyalty through a higher quality of demand, Korea will find it hard to construct a stable export basis over the long term.

1) Industrial Cooperation

At the meeting between President Young-Sam Kim and Secretary Jiang Ji Min in March 1994, four industries were selected as priority fields of cooperation: automobile, aircraft, TDX and HDTV. As an extension of the same meeting, the Minister of Foreign Affairs, the Minister of Communication, the Minister of Trade and Industry drew agreements with their Chinese correspondents towards the improvement of bilateral cooperation in the related fields.

The economic relationship between Korea and China has a dual characteristic of cooperation and competition. China endows Korea with an important role as a model of economic development. As for Korea, developing the economic relationship with China is important to ensure overseas markets, an import route of raw materials and a production base in order to raise Korea's international competitiveness.

In order to promote reciprocal cooperation, it will be desirable for the two countries to take the following measures. China should abolish or diminish the imposition of high rate of import taxes on finished products and the execution of import authentication system. Concurrently, the Korean government should abolish the regulation tax on agricultural and manufactured products.

Even though China is promoting radical reform and liberalization, there still remain many deficiencies in law that impose difficulties to companies in running local corporations. In particular, improvement of the labor management law is urgent since Korea's investments are concentrated in the labor intensive fields. Korea should exploit the huge domestic market of China, and at the same time, establish an industrial cooperation system for a better cooperative relationship. To efficiently penetrate the domestic market of China, the following strategies should be devised: first, the investigation of local markets and stamp duty of Korean goods should be promoted; second, the prerequisite of exploiting the domestic sales market of China is diversification of investing regions; and lastly, another prerequisite is diversification in the fields of cooperation.

2) Technological Cooperation

For 30 years (1949~1979), the importation of technology into China was accompanied by introduction of plants. 70~90% of the importation of technology during this period was done in the form of plant introduction. A look at importation of technology per country shows that those nations who have supplied China with technology during the period 1980~1989 are Japan, the United States and Germany. As the number of cases of technological importation increases, the number of countries that supply that technology increase as well. The mechanism behind China's strategy of economic development after 1987 was the importation of specialized equipment that would readjust production facilities, go through a process of import substitution and then foster these facilities into export industries.

China has followed 3 principles in its policies in order to maximize the effect of technology importation. First, the core of importation was put on production technology importation of software, and if necessary, facilities for essential parts. Second, priority was given to the introduction of high technology. Third, preference of support was given to sectors where foreign capital is needed for exports.

A comparison of Korea and China in terms of technology importation shows that while in Korea's case 3/4 of the cases are technology importation through joint production, China shows a higher rate of importation of comprehensive production process and facilities and the purchase of technology permits. It is also noteworthy that while Korea has for a long time depended on importation of technology from Japan and the US, China's importation is more diverse, covering countries such as England, Canada, Australia, the Netherlands and Finland.

Interaction in science and technology between Korea and China has commenced since 1990, and technological cooperation is taking on the form of Korea's 'G7 Project' and China's '863 Plan'. The author argues that Korea must play a leading role in linking China's current plan of economic development of the Yellow Sea with Korea's economic development of the West Coast, inducing the participation of North Korea.

7. KOREA-RUSSIA INDUSTRIAL COOPERATION

A. Russia's Economic Reform

Russia's reform and open door policy has two characteristics. One is that Russia has tried to realize sweeping changes by means of *perestroika* and *glasnost,* for the purpose of renovating the socialistic system and values, which have long been victims of complacency and incompetence. The other is that it has put more emphasis on reform than the open-door policy. Russia was not given an advantageous condition like China. Russia had to construct a market environment through the reform policy to provide advantageous conditions for foreign direct investments because western capital and technology are the essential elements for economic resurrection.

The Russian economic objective has been to create a regulated market economic system by introducing a market pricing mechanism and an indirect economic management method. Gorbachev's reforms made efforts to enable foreign companies to possess factories and business offices, promote decentralization of the economy, weaken government-owned and state-managed companies, promote gradual privatization and allow limited establishment of private companies.

Yeltsin's reforms can be divided into four stages. The first stage was the rapid reform period between October 1991 and December 1992 and examples include the Foreign Trade Liberalization Management Act and the Price Liberalization Management Act. The second stage involved the on-going conflicts between the conservative and radical factions within the government, and consistent implementation of policies became impossible to maintain. The third stage was when the radical powers returned and radical reforms were undertaken. The fourth stage was the promotion of moderate reform by the central conservative cabinet from January 1994 up until the present.

The privatization of state owned enterprises in Russia has also progressed rapidly. The privatization of state-owned enterprises is promoted by both State Property Management and State Property Funding. The property management committee of the concerned area, the employee group of the enterprises and tentative buyers of the enterprises make proposals for privatization. An enterprise with a final approval can be converted into a joint-stock corporation and after the property of the enterprise is sold, the property fund has the ownership of the enterprise and controls the auction of the property. Russia's privatization is enforced by agencies for Small Scale Privatization, involving small enterprises, and Large Scale Privatization, involving large enterprises.

Most recently the Russian government is showing active participation by lifting many restrictions in the process of privatization in order to enhance the inflow of foreign capital. Acquisition and Portfolio investments are ways for foreign investors to participate in privatization. Foreign investors can buy stocks from employees or managers of privatized enterprises, or through stock auction in vouchers and the second market. The difficulty lies in the fact that the stock of superior enterprises are not readily available and insolvent enterprises are not the interest of foreign investors.

Most recently, the Russian economy has faced its worst crisis since World War II. After a series of instability and constant change in reform policies, the Russian economy has gotten itself deeper into the swamp of stagnation. The continuous high inflation is also becoming a great threat. The financial situation of most companies have reached an extremely critical phase. Foreign direct investment is still not playing a significant role. The fundamental factors for Russia's critical situation is its inheritance of a distorted economy, in which its disintegration occurred more quickly than the formation of a new market economy.

B. Expected Benefits of Economic Cooperation

The necessity of Korean-Russian economic cooperation could be summarized as; first, the Russian market is not only a vast one, but because Russia has not put much importance in the light industries centered around consumer goods, Korea has early access to the Russian market since it has a comparative advantage in the area; second, Korea can use Russia as a bridgehead for advancement into the EU and East European markets; third, because Russia is abundant in natural resources, economic cooperation is necessary for the security of future resources; and lastly, because the major reason for the weakening of Korean industrial competitiveness is its technological backwardness, it must actively pursue the transfer of Russian technology to Korea.

Korea and Russia have already signed many agreements concerning economic cooperation and Korea has abolished discriminatory treatment such as tariffs, and has provided institutional conditions for foreign investment. It has also granted funds to Russia for economic cooperation.

However, economic cooperation between the two countries has withered drastically since the disintegration of the Soviet Union in late 1991. The reason for this are not only Russia's internal conditions but also the suspension since 1992 of the provision of economic cooperation funds agreed formerly with the USSR. Economic cooperation has fallen into a deadlock, but efforts are at present being made by the two countries to come to a consensus.

C. Science and Technology Cooperation

Korea and Russia are optimal partners for science and technology cooperation. Because Russia's fundamental sciences and Korea's applied sciences, Russia's advanced technology and Korea's production technology are mutually complementary. Korean-Russian science and technology cooperation will reap both sides great benefits.

The Russian side will be able to solve problems such as low productivity, low growth and inefficiency of capital distribution. The Korean side could rid itself of problems arising from Japanese and American protectionism for the adoption of advanced technology. There is no doubt that science and technology cooperation between Korea and Russia will greatly contribute to the economic, scientific and technological development of both countries.

The major economic projects between the two countries would be to adopt, improve and industrialize Russia's technology in a short period of time; to pursue labor exchange projects by promoting the mutual exchange of scientists and the transfer of technology and inviting Russian scientists for extended stays; and to exchange technological information and pursue cooperative projects by establishing technology cooperation centers in countries' major cities such as Seoul and Moscow.

Chapter XII

SOUTH KOREAN GOVERNMENT'S POLICY ON NORTH KOREA

1. KIM DAE-JUNG ADMINISTRATION

Kim Dae-jung Administration hopes to improve intra-Korean relations by promoting peace, reconciliation and cooperation. At the present stage, it is more urgent to establish durable peace and assure the peaceful coexistence of the two Koreas than to push for immediate reunification. When there is an assurance of durable peace, the Administration plans to promote reconciliation and cooperation with North Korea.

A. Three Principles of the North Korea Policy

First, no armed provocation by North Korea will be tolerated. The Administration will never tolerate any armed provocation by North Korea which would only destroy the peace. The Administration will maintain a strong security posture against North Korea to deter war and will make it clear that it will respond to any provocation. In this way, it hopes to persuade North Korea to abandon its reliance on violence.

At the same time, the Administration will continue efforts to reduce tension and build a durable peace on the Korean Peninsula, thus creating an atmosphere that would make it more difficult for North Korea to stage a military provocation.

Second, a takeover or absorption of North Korea will not be attempted. The Administration has no desire to harm North Korea nor to absorb it unilaterally. Rather than promoting the collapse of North Korea, the Administration intends to work for peaceful coexistence with the North, thus creating an atmosphere favorable to the formation of a South-North union. The union will gradually lead to peaceful unification.

Lastly, reconciliation and cooperation will be expanded. The Administration will do its best to promote reconciliation and cooperation with the North. In order to dissolve the hostility between the two Koreas accumulated since the division of the country and lay down a foundation for mutual understanding, the Administration will first promote reconciliation and cooperation in the areas where they are possible and try to reactivate the 1991 Agreement on Reconciliation, Nonaggression and Exchanges and Cooperation between the South and the North, often referred to as the Basic Agreement.

The Administration will also support North Korea's own efforts to reform itself, thus restoring the sense of national homogeneity between the two Koreas and improving the welfare of entire Korean people.

B. Guidelines for Implementing the North Korea Policy

First, simultaneous promotion of strong national security and intra-Korean cooperation. The maintenance of strong national security is a basis of an effective North Korea policy. The Administration is determined to enhance its independent capabilities to defend the nation while consolidating the ROK-US alliance and working to create a collective security structure with the countries in the Northeast Asian region.

Based on a strong national security, the Administration will be as much flexible as possible in promoting intra-Korean interaction and various cooperative efforts, thus making a substantive improvement in intra-Korean relations.

Second, promotion of peaceful coexistence and intra-Korean interaction as a top priority. The unification of the two Koreas will be a long and difficult task. At this point, the most urgent task is to remove the threat of armed provocation and achieve peaceful coexistence.

While making it clear that the road to reunification begins with the Koreas recognizing and respecting each other's system as they agreed in the Basic Agreement of 1991, the Administration will give priority to managing the national division in a peaceful manner.

Once peaceful coexistence is assured, it will do its best to improve intra- Korean relations and eventually achieve unification by expanding South- North interaction and cooperation.

Third, it is a creation of an environment conducive to reform in North Korea. It is more appropriate to try to improve intra-Korean relations by inducing gradual changes in the North than to try and contain the North in expectation that it will collapse.

The Administration does not intend to try and force North Korea to change. It will, however, try to expand its engagement with the North in support of Pyongyang's own efforts to reform.

The Administration will keep its composure even if North Korea challenges it with irrational demands and threats. Instead, it will endeavor harder to increase contacts, expand dialogue and increase cooperation with North Korea to create an atmosphere favorable for reform in the North.

Furthermore, the Administration will no longer simply provide North Korea with charity, but will promote long-term intra-Korean economic relations to achieve joint development and co-prosperity.

The two Koreas need to start working together for the joint development of an intra-Korean economic union by taking advantage of their complementary characteristics.

Fourth, adherence to the principle of self-determination and winning support from the international community. The fate of the Korean people should be determined by the South and North Koreans themselves. Nonetheless, it will require the commitment and support of the international community to end the division of the Korean Peninsula and secure regional peace.

Based on the principle that the intra-Korean issues must be resolved through direct contact between the two Koreas, the Administration will continue efforts to persuade Pyongyang to enter into a dialogue.

At the same time, the Administration will try its best through various means, including the ongoing Four-party Talks, to win the support of the international community for its efforts to create durable peace and reduce tension on the Korean Peninsula.

Lastly, public support is an important element in the successful implementation of any North Korea policy. The Administration's North Korea policy should never be made in secret nor should it be implemented through private channels.

The Administration should maintain the transparency of its decision-making process and should implement its policies with consistency and efficiency in order to win public support.

C. Directions for Implementation

The creation of peace on the Korean Peninsula is an issue of concern not only to South and North Korea but also to the international community, which is already deeply involved on the Korean Peninsula through the LWR project, the Four-party Talks and food aid to North Korea.

With a belief in self-determination, the Administration will endeavor to reactivate the Basic Agreement of 1991 through intra-Korean dialogue. At the same time, it will use the Four-party Talks as a vehicle to expand the cooperation with the neighboring countries as well as with the rest of the international community and to create a durable peace structure on the peninsula.

The Administration will also initiate a regional security forum for peace and cooperation in Northeast Asia. If, in harmony with the improvement of intra- Korean relations, North Korea wishes to expand its relations with the United States and Japan as well as with various international organizations, the Administration will provide indirect support for Pyongyang's efforts to do so, thereby helping the North to become a responsible member of the international community.

1) Reactivation of the 1991 Basic Agreement

The Agreement on Reconciliation, Nonaggression and Exchanges and Cooperation Between the South and the North to which the two Governments gave their full consent is a sacred document.

Consequently, the two Koreas need to start implementing it to improve relations. As President Kim Dae-jung said in his inaugural address, the Administration will promote intra-Korean dialogue in various fields, including making a proposal for an exchange of special envoys to reaffirm the intention and willingness of the highest authorities of the South and the North to implement the Basic Agreement of 1991.

Once intra-Korean dialogue is resumed, the two Koreas will first work on the areas where they can more readily cooperate with each other and will gradually expand their efforts to implement the Basic Agreement in other areas.

2) Separation of Business from Politics

The Administration will respect the right of private businesses to decide themselves whether to expand economic interaction with North Korea or not. Economic activities should be promoted first in the areas the North needs assistance from the South most urgently and mainly where intra-Korean cooperation would be beneficial for both Koreas.

The Administration will, thus, encourage businessmen to visit North Korea, raise the ceiling on the size of investment in North Korea by South Korean businesses, simplify the legal procedures for intra-Korean interaction and take all other necessary measures to expand interaction between the two Koreas.

3) Commitment to the LWR (Light-Water Reactor) Project

The light-water reactors are being provided to North Korea not only in return for its freeze of its own nuclear program but also as a part of a long-tern joint national development plan.

The Administration is committed to playing a central role in the KEDO (Korean Peninsula Energy Development Organization) project as it promised the international community it would do. The Administration will resolve the issue of sharing the financial burden of the project with the United States and Japan as soon as possible and complete the construction as scheduled. However, taking the current financial difficulties into account, the Administration will find a reasonable way to minimize the burden on the South Korean people.

4) Food Aids & Family Reunion

The Administration will continue to provide food aid for North Korea through international organizations in a humanitarian effort to help fellow Koreans suffering from a severe food shortage.

It will also encourage civilian organizations to provide aid to North Korea. At the same time, it will continue efforts to discuss with the North Korean authorities the possibility of government-level assistance. In addition, the Administration will assist Pyongyang's own efforts to find a more fundamental solution to the chronic food shortage.

Though more than half a century has already passed since the division of the country, approximately ten million people on both sides of the Military Demarcation Line do not know the fate of their relatives. Because many of these people are now dying of old age, the Administration has placed top priority on family reunion.

The Administration will drastically simplify the legal procedures, making it easier for senior members of the separated families to visit their relatives in the North. In addition, the Administration will promote talks between the South and North Korean Red Cross societies to help relieve the suffering of the separated families. It will also support the efforts for family reunion in third countries or at international events.

Once intra-Korean dialogue is resumed, the Administration will also work to establish a reunion and postal exchange center and visits between separated families members on both sides of the border as called for in the 1991 Basic Agreement.

2. THE LWR PROVISION TO NORTH KOREA

A. LWRs Project and Its Significance

The KEDO and North Korea cleared their first obstacle to implementing the historic North Korea-US nuclear framework agreement when they signed "The Light-Water Reactor Provision Treaty" in New York on Dec. 16, 1995. Both sides have since signed or discussed protocols on details of building LWRs in North Korea.

Unlike efforts to launch a Four-Party Peace Talk on the divided Korean Peninsula, the plan to provide the North with light-water reactors has been proceeding rather smoothly.

This is not only because the nuclear deal brings security and economic benefits to South Korea, the United States and Japan, but also because it meets diplomatic and economic interests of North Korea. North Korea has been isolated from a global trend towards democracy and free-market economy. As a result, its economy is in shambles, threatening the communist regime under Kim Jong-il. North Korea wants to improve ties with the United States and Japan by closing a deal on building the LWRs as soon as possible.

Improving relations with the United States and Japan is important for North Korea because it can bring the North security, food and other economic aids. The Geneva Accord also will help North Korea overcome its acute food shortages because it requires the United States to provide 500,000 tons of heavy oil annually to meet its energy needs until the first of the two promised reactors is completed.

The North's nuclear program has posed a serious security threat in Northeast Asia. South Korea, the United States and Japan hope to persuade North Korea to abandon its nuclear program, suspected of being used to develop atomic bombs. The three countries also hope that through the LWRs provision deal, they can guide the North's troubled communist regime to a soft landing. The North's nuclear threat is indeed of international magnitude. If unchecked, it could prompt South Korea and Japan into developing their own nuclear weapons system. That would strain the situation in Northeast Asia and endanger US-led international efforts for nuclear non-proliferation.

South Korea, the United States and Japan were also concerned about the North's bankrupt economy and near-famine food shortages. They feared that economic and social instability might trigger a sudden collapse of the North Korean government or drive the North's hard-line military to attempt reckless provocations across the border with the South.

Therefore, resolving the North's nuclear threat by providing light-water reactors is a positive way of promoting peace not only in the Korean Peninsula but worldwide.

The LWR project will increase personnel, technological and economic exchanges between North Korea and KEDO participants, especially South Korea, which is the project's leading financier. This new economic influence on North Korea may give KEDO countries a leverage in prodding the isolated country to reform and openness. South Korea is also pushing to KEDO project as the first stage in the "joint national development plan" in which to two Koreas will discuss the future of the Korean nation. For now, KEDO also is the only official contact point between the two Koreas, and South Korea hopes to use this channel to start dialogue and other exchanges with the North and to work towards peaceful reunification of the divided Korean Peninsula.

The South Korean government's eagerness to play an active role in providing the North with light water reactors also has invited criticism.

Many South Koreans, for example, noted that despite Seoul's efforts for rapprochement and economic aid, the North still refused official dialogue, maintained its anti-South propaganda and even attempted armed provocations. They question the wisdom of South Korea's participation in the light-water reactor project that may cost it at least US$3.5~4.0 billion. Some even estimates put South Korea's financial burden at US$7.0~8.0 billion. The critics also question whether the South will be able to sign an inter-Korean nuclear energy treaty with the North. They also suspect that North Korea will scheme to deny the South a central role in building the reactors.

A nuclear energy treaty with the North is needed to guarantee that the North does not divert the South's sensitive nuclear technology and equipment to military use. The problem is that the South can not sign such a treaty if the North objects because the Article 13 of the Light-Water Reactor Provision Accord stipulates that the two sides can sign it only when both of them agree.

Despite all these potential problems, however, proceeding with the LWR project seems to be the only realistic way to stop the North's suspected nuclear weapons program and steer the North towards reform and openness, and eventually towards a peaceful reunification with the South. In this context, this paper will deal mainly with three aspects of the light-water reactor project: first, how the project came into being and where it stands now; second, why the project has to be faithfully implemented, and what are its significance and expected benefits; and thirdly, what problems should be resolved in the future.

B. The Nuclear Question and Efforts to Resolve It

1) Genesis of Nuclear Question

When North Korea was developing nuclear reactors with support from the former Soviet Union, the North, at the prodding of the Soviets, joined the NPT (Nuclear Non-proliferation Treaty) in December 1985.

However, North Korea was suspected of trying to develop nuclear arms mainly because for six years it did not fulfill the treaty obligations to join the Safeguards Agreement of the IAEA (International Atomic Energy Agency) within 18 months after the signing of the NPT. The suspicion grew as the North promoted in haste the construction of a 50MW atomic reactor, a 200MW atomic reactor, reprocessing facilities and a nuclear fuel rod plant.

A 5MW laboratory reactor the North was already operating and the 50MW and 200MW reactors planned were all graphite-moderated reactors, a type which produces spent fuel from which plutonium, a raw material of nuclear arms, can be extracted.

In an effort to prevent the North from developing nuclear weapons and to maintain peace and stability on the Korean Peninsula, the government adopted with North Korea the Joint Declaration of the Denuclearization of the Korean Peninsula in December 1991, in which the South and the North agreed to verify denuclearization through mutual inspections and not to possess nuclear reprocessing facilities.

Thereafter, in January 1992, North Korea joined the IAEA's Nuclear Safeguards Agreement which they had shunned, and from in May 1992 an IAEA inspection team began looking into nuclear facilities in North Korea. However, a "grave inconsistency" from what the North initially reported to the IAEA was uncovered in six rounds of IAEA inspections.

An alleged radioactive chemical laboratory was obviously reprocessing facilities and fuel rods seemed to have been changed many times for a 5MW laboratory reactor since it went into operation in 1986. Contrary to the North Korean claim that a tiny amount of plutonium was extracted only once, there was the strong possibility that a larger amount of plutonium seemed to have been obtained on several occasions. In addition, the two facilities which the North did not report to the IAEA were possibly storage areas for spent fuel bars.

To clear such suspicions, the IAEA asked North Korea for nuclear transparency and the acceptance of special inspections, which the North rejected before announcing its intention to withdraw from the Nuclear Non-proliferation Treaty in March 1993.

2) Deadlock of Negotiations and Rising Tensions

Reacting against the ultra-hard-line stand of North Korea, the United Nations Security Council called on the North to return to the NPT, stressing that North Korea had the obligation to go through IAEA inspections. The council also urged all member countries to strive to resolve the question. In response, the United States, which had led international programs to forestall nuclear proliferation, entered talks with North Korea on the nuclear question.

In June 1993, the US and North Korea issued a joint statement saying in part that the North would tentatively withhold withdrawing from the NPT. In the following month, July 1993, the two sides supported the introduction of light- water reactors as a means of finally resolving the nuclear question, expressing the willingness to discuss the idea. North Korea, in particular, promised to have consultations with the IAEA and return to the South-North dialogue at an early date.

However, on the ground that it was in a 'unique state' because it had withheld withdrawing from the NPT, North Korea insisted it could not recognize the full IAEA competency for inspection, denying the IAEA any access to their 5MW reactor and reprocessing facilities.

Working-level contacts between the South and the North to discuss the proposed exchange of special envoys aimed at resolving the nuclear question, too, failed to register any progress due to North Korea's demand for a 'halt to nuclear war exercises' and the South's 'renouncement of an international cooperative system'. The contacts broke off before long due to unilateral moves of North Korea preceded by their threatening remarks that they would 'turn Seoul into a sea of fire'.

Consequently the IAEA convened a special governors' meeting on March 21, 1994, which urged the North to completely fulfill Nuclear Safeguards Agreement obligations. The UN Security Council, too, in its President's statement of March 31, 1994, called on North Korea to accept IAEA inspections and agree to resume the South-North dialogue.

As sanctions were discussed in earnest against North Korea while the North threatened to completely withdraw from the NPT after the nuclear question was taken to the UN Security Council, tension began to build up on the Korean Peninsula.

Under the circumstances, North Korea, in a Foreign Ministry statement on June 13, 1994, declared they were withdrawing from the IAEA, too, threatening that they would regard any sanction taken against them as a declaration of war. \

3) US-North Korea Agreed Framework and System for the Provision of LWRs

(1) The US-North Korea Geneva Agreed Framework

As the UN Security Council was discussing sanctions against North Korea and tensions were growing perilously on the Korean Peninsula, North Korea disclosed in talks with visiting former US President Jimmy Carter on June 13, 1994, the willingness to have an inter-Korean summit meeting and enter talks with the United States to resolve the nuclear issue.

Subsequently preliminary contacts took place between the South and the North to discuss an inter-Korean summit meeting while a US-North Korea meeting was held in Geneva on July 8, 1994.

The US-North Korea talks, however, were postponed indefinitely due to the sudden death of Kim Il-sung on July 8, 1994, one day after the talks. The inter- Korean summit scheduled for July 25~27 in Pyongyang was called off as well.

Though the planned summit meeting failed to take place, President Kim Young-sam, in his Liberation Day message on August 15, 1994, stated that in a move to ultimately resolve the North Korean nuclear question and promote a 'joint national development project,' the South is willing to furnish capital and know-how to the North to assist in the construction of light-water reactors and other forms of peaceful development of energy if the North ensured nuclear transparency. The President said such support could be used as an occasion to improve inter-Korean relations.

<Table XII-1> Highlights of the Agreed Framework adopted at the Geneva US-North Korea Talks

● Replacement of graphite-moderated reactors with light-water reactor power plants.
– Provision of two 1,000MW light-water reactors by a target date of 2003. – Freezing and eventual dismantling by North Korea of its graphite-moderated reactors and their related facilities. – Transfer of the spent fuel bars taken from a 5MW reactor to a third country after being duly canned for safety. – Provision of substitution energy (500,000 tons of heavy oil per year) to the North in connection with the freezing of graphite-moderated reactors.
● Improvement of US-North Korea Relations
– Easing trade and investment barriers, opening liaison offices and elevating bilateral relations to the ambassadorial level once progress is made on issues of concern to each side.
● Efforts for Denuclearization of the Korean Peninsula
– Guarantee by the United States of non-use of nuclear arms against North Korea, fulfillment of the Korean peninsula denuclearization declaration, start of South- North dialogue.
● Fulfillment of Denuclearization Obligations by North Korea
– Remaining a party to the NPT and implementation of the IAEA Safeguards Agreement. – Acceptance of IAEA special and regular inspections by North Korea of its non-frozen nuclear facilities. – Full-fledged fulfillment of the Nuclear Safeguards Agreement (including special inspections) prior to the delivery of key components of light-water reactors.

The third-round US-North Korea talks begun under the circumstances on September 23, 1994 and progressed rapidly. Finally on October 21, 1994, the Geneva Agreed Framework, the basic device of resolving the North Korean nuclear question, was adopted and signed.

The most important significance of the Geneva US-North Korea agreement was laying down the basis for the fundamental resolution of the North Korean nuclear question. Though the time of special inspections was put off until a later date than initially expected, North Korea accepted special inspections for the first time after they announced the planned withdrawal from the NPT contending that the two undeclared facilities at issue were military facilities. The road was thus paved to looking into the past nuclear activities of North Korea.

Furthermore, the freezing and ultimate dismantling of graphite-moderated reactors and other North Korean nuclear facilities served to seal from the root the possible development of nuclear arms, thereby making it possible to obtain the North's present and future nuclear transparency.

(2) South Korean Government Position toward the LWRs Project

With respect to the issue of providing LWRs to the North, the South Korean government has been adhering to the following principles and objectives:

First, the South should play a central role in the provision of light-water reactors to the North. South Korea's participation should be guaranteed in related areas such as design, production, installation and project management of the light-water reactor project let alone in the creation of an international consortium.

Second, the provision of light-water reactors to the North should always be promoted in a way that would contribute to improving inter-Korean relations. In other words, the light-water reactor project should ultimately lead to expediting the implementation of the South-North Basic Agreement and to the visible improvement of inter-Korean relations.

Third, the provision of light-water reactors should be promoted under the condition of the faithful implementation of the U.S.-North Korea Agreed Framework. For the delivery of light-water reactors, North Korea should freeze its nuclear facilities and abide by the IAEA Safeguards Agreement. In particular, North Korea should respect the provisions of the Agreed Framework such as the implementation of the Korean Peninsula denuclearization declaration and the resumption of South-North dialogue.

Fourth, the project should be promoted based on public support and consensus.

(3) Creation and Operation of KEDO

Upon the adoption of the Geneva Agreed Framework, South Korea, the United States and Japan put into motion their official consultative channel to handle issues related to the construction of light-water nuclear reactors in North Korea, holding high and working-level meetings often.

As a result, the KEDO, an international organization responsible for the finance and supply of the LWRs to be built in North Korea, was inaugurated in March 1995 under the initiatives of South Korea, the US and Japan.

The purpose of the KEDO as specified in its inaugural agreement was: first, raising and provision of funds for the project to deliver two 1,000MW Korean- standard light-water energy plants to North Korea; second, provision of substitution energy pending the completion of first of the two planned plants; and thirdly, implementation of other measures necessary for the accomplishment of the objective of the Agreed Framework.

The KEDO consists of an executive board, the highest decision maker and a secretariat. The executive board comprises three executive directors, one each from South Korea, the US and Japan, which operates only on the basis of unanimous agreement.

The secretariat is staffed with officials from the three initial member countries (South Korea, the US and Japan), whose duties include raising funds and the approval, preparation and execution of contracts. The KEDO's operating expenses are shared equally among the three countries. The director of the Planning Office of Light-Water Reactor Project represents the South Korean government as a KEDO executive director.

In addition to the three original member countries, seven countries are participating in the KEDO as general member countries. They are Finland, Canada, New Zealand, Australia, Indonesia, Chile and Argentina.

The KEDO had urged the EU to join the KEDO as part of the effort to expand the number of KEDO member nations, resulting in the EU's initialing in May 1997 of an agreement to join the KEDO. The EU is set to be an executive member and contribute 15 million ECU to the KEDO in the next five years. With the EU's entry, 15 EU member countries have come to be interested in KEDO activities, elevating the KEDO's international standing and further cementing an international cooperative system in the promotion of policies toward North Korea.

3. The Four-Party Talks

A. The Outline

1) The First Round

(1) Proposal for Four-Party Talks to Discuss a Peace Mechanism

Despite South Korea's efforts to bring about durable peace on the Korean Peninsula, North Korea, while attempting to dismantle the armistice system since April 1993, has been demanding the conclusion of a peace agreement exclusively with the US On the heels of its demand for the conclusion of an interim agreement with the US in February 1996, in particular, North Korea attempted to torpedo the Armistice Agreement in earnest, renouncing its duty to manage the Demilitarized Zone and sending armed troops into the Joint Security Area of Panmunjom.

Under the circumstances, the South Korean government began to explore multi-pronged practical measures to prevent North Korea from subverting the truce system and from launching a unilateral peace offensive toward the US.

As a result, a plan was prepared to promote a four-party meeting among South and North Korea, the direct parties to the Korean Peninsula question, and the US and China, signatory parties to the Armistice Agreement.

Finally, at the Korea-US summit meeting held in Cheju on April 16, 1996, a four-party meeting to discuss ways to bring about permanent peace on the Korean Peninsula was proposed in a joint Korea-US statement. While proposing the four-party talks, the top leaders of South Korea and the US made it clear that the question of establishing a new permanent peace mechanism should be tackled mainly by South and North Korea and there should be no separate talks between the US and North Korea with regard to peace on the Korean Peninsula.

At the four-party meeting, the South and the North of Korea, the direct parties to the peace issue, would be the main subjects of the negotiations, with the US and China supporting the talks. In other words, though South and North Korea and the US and China would simultaneously take part in the talks, the substantive negotiations would be held largely between South and North Korea while the US and China would play the role of supporting and guaranteeing the smooth sailing of the talks.

The main objective of the four-party talks is to prepare an institutional device to ensure permanent peace on the Korean Peninsula. In addition, broad-ranging issues to ease tension and promote confidence building between the two sides of Korea could also be discussed.

By offering an 'open space for negotiations', that is, broad measures to alleviate tension can be discussed without any conditions in addition to the question of instituting a peace mechanism, an effort was made to increase the chances for North Korea's acceptance of the proposal.

South-North relations would be significantly improved if the four-party talks were to take place successfully to prepare a new peace mechanism and ease tension and promote confidence building between the South and the North. At the same time, as the US and China are supposed to internationally guarantee what South and North Korea have discussed and agreed on at the four-party meeting, an effective peace regime could be prepared to contribute much to bringing about solid peace on the Korean Peninsula.

Moreover, the framework of the four-party talks could in the long run be developed into a multilateral security cooperative system, thus contributing significantly to stability in Northeast Asia region let alone peace on the Korean Peninsula.

(2) The Development Process: Joint Briefing Session, Follow-up Talks

For a while after the four-party talks were proposed, North Korea did not show any clear-cut reaction, simply saying that they were 'reviewing' the offer before they, through an unofficial channel, asked the US to concretely explain about the purport of the proposed meeting.

South Korea and the US suggested that since the proposal was the joint making of the two countries, they would explain about the talks jointly. While the two sides were still trying to iron out their differences, a North Korean submarine infiltrated into the Kangnung area of South Korea on September 18, 1996, and committed other acts of armed provocation to build up military tension on the Korean Peninsula, incurring the denunciation of the rest of the world community.

Driven to the defensive, North Korea made a public apology over the submarine incursion on December 28, 1996 and disclosed its willingness to attend a joint briefing session on the proposed four-party talks. The briefing session took place in New York on March 5, 1997 after two postponements due to the North's situation.

At the session, South Korean officials explained the background leading to making the joint proposal by Presidents Kim Young-sam and Bill Clinton on April 16, 1996. They said the objectives behind the proposal, offered without any conditions, were to discuss ways to bring about permanent peace on the Korean Peninsula and to pursue co-prosperity between South and North Korea.

The officials stressed that a durable peace mechanism on the Korean Peninsula should be prepared at the initiatives of South and North Korea, and that, to this end, tension should be eased and confidence building promoted on a priority basis between the two sides of Korea. They also suggested that the promotion of food assistance and other inter-Korean economic cooperative projects could be discussed at the four-party talks as part of efforts to ease tension and promote confidence building.

Also at the briefing session, the South Korean officials proposed that the full- dress four-party meeting should take place at a place of mutual agreement as early as possible upon the completion of the briefing session. They suggested that minister-level officials should act as chief delegates and vice-minister-level officials as deputy chief delegates and that the agenda topics of the talks should be the questions of establishing a peace mechanism on the Korean Peninsula and easing tension and promoting confidence building between the two sides of Korea. They added that if necessary, the two main topics could be sub-itemized.

The American officials present stressed that the question of bringing about permanent peace on the Korean Peninsula is a task that should always be tackled between South and North Koreas, the direct parties involved, not separately between the US and North Korea. The four-party meeting is to offer the framework for that very such inter-Korean discussion, they said.

North Korean officials reiterated Pyongyang's stand that since a non-aggression agreement had already been concluded between South and North Korea over the question of a peace regime, a peace agreement should now be concluded between the U.S. and North Korea.

On April 16, 1997, about one month after the joint briefing session took place, a follow-up meeting of the four-party talks briefing session was held in New York at the request of North Korea.

At the meeting, the South called for determining the dates of the preliminary and full-dress four-party talks. North Korea, however, rejected the idea, though they were saying they agreed in principle to holding the four-party meeting.

North Korea instead demanded that a substantial amount of food assistance be given them around the time the four-party talks open. In reaction, the South said it could not provide food prior to the opening of the four-party meeting, adding, however, that the issue of food assistance could be discussed at the four-party talks as part of efforts to ease tension and promote confidence building.

Following the plenary follow-up session on April 16, 1997 three working-level contacts and an unofficial chief delegates' meeting took place. But, North Korea refused to accept the idea of setting the objectives and times of the preliminary and full-dress meetings of the four-party talks.

The North Koreans simply urged the US to ease sanctions against the North and renounce a 'hostile stand' toward them prior to the four-party talks to improve overall US-North Korea relations. The North then delayed the opening of the four-way meeting by proposing that a 'tripartite meeting' be held first among South and North Korea and the US and then a '3+1' meeting where China would be allowed to participate in due course.

The follow-up talks ended without any progress as the North stuck to their 'guarantee for food assistance first, and preliminary four-party talks later' policy. South and North Korea and the US agreed, however, to carry on working-level contacts through diplomatic channels.

South Korea and the US ruled out the provision of any food assistance in return for the North's coming to the four-party talks. The two countries said that they would continue to positively consider the provision of emergency relief goods of a humanitarian nature in view of the difficult food situation of North Korea, adding that government-level food assistance could only be discussed in the framework of the four-party talks as part of efforts to ease tension and promote confidence building.

After the South's persistent efforts to persuade the North, telling them that acceptance of the four-party talks would be the only way to root durable peace on the Korean Peninsula and for them to surmount the present economic difficulties characterized by a serious food shortage, North Korea finally agreed to attend the preliminary meeting of the four-party talks.

At the tripartite deputy-minister-level meeting held among South and North Koreas and the US in New York on June 30, 1997, the attendees agreed to hold a preliminary meeting of the four-party talks including a Chinese delegation in New York on August 5, 1997.

2) The Second Round

According to the agreement of the first round of the Four-Party-Talks (December 9~10, 1997), the ad-hoc sub-committee for inter sessional consultations was planed to be held in middle February, 1998 at Beijing.

North Korea, however, in January 1998 notified its unilateral cancel of the subcommittee meeting to Mark Minton, Director of the Korea Desk, US State Department, through Lee Keun, Deputy Permanent Representative of the North Korea Mission to the US

North Korea, while canceling the subcommittee meeting, attempted to link the talks to the political time-schedule proposed by South Korea by insisting that since the new president of the South Korea was elected, it might be meaningless to hold the talks before the inauguration of the president.

The South Korea and the US urged that North Korea hold the subcommittee by pointing out that the South's political time-schedule had been already known during the first round talks, and the four parties had agreed in mid-February to operate the ad-hoc subcommittee regardless of the South Korean political time-schedule while expressing their regrets upon North Korea's unilateral notification of the cancellation.

As well the South Korea and the US pointed out that the unilateral notification to postpone the ad-hoc subcommittee to State Department did not abide by the practice of the 'four-party-consultation' then the notification could not be accepted, and emphasized that the North should officially explain its decision to postpone the ad-hoc subcommittee to the US and China, and suggested the North to hold a working-level conference of the four parties. North Korea and China responded to the suggestion and the working-level conference of the four parties was held on February 6, 1998 at New York.

At the working-level conference, since North Korea sustained its old position, the South Korea and the US suggested to hold a preliminary meeting at Geneva if the ad-hoc subcommittee, of which purpose was to prepare the second round Four-Party-Talks, was difficult to be held. North Korea, with China, eventually accepted the suggestion, and the preliminary meeting for the Four-Party-Talks was held on March 14, 1998 at Geneva.

As well, the working level delegates from the four parties discussed the date of the second round of the Four-Party-Talks and decided its five day schedule beginning on March 16, 1998.

The second round Four-Party-Talks began on March 16, 1998 at the international convention hall of the CICG building in Geneva, Switzerland. After a photo opportunity for the heads of delegation, the talks, closed to the public, started under the chairmanship of the Deputy Minister of the China (PRC) Ministry of Foreign Affairs.

Each party's reception and introduction were followed by keynote speeches of the heads of delegation in order of the US, South Korea, North Korea, and China. The participants were the same as the first round talks except one or two delegation members from the US and China.

The South Korean Chief Delegate Song Young-shik, the First Assistant Minister of Foreign Affairs and Trade, in his keynote speech, emphasized that Four- Party-Talks, of which purpose was to establish a peace regime on the Korean Peninsula and the South-North dialogue, of which purpose was to promote mutual prosperity through reconciliation and cooperation between the South and the North, should be progressed parallel to each other. He also pointed out that not only the present armistice regime should be fully respected, but also all the agreements between the South and the North including the South-North Basic Agreement should be truthfully implemented until a firm peace regime could be installed.

The South Korean Chief Delegate Song suggested that it would be helpful to activate the Joint Commissions, which had been agreed between the South and the North in order to implement the agreed items in the Basic Agreement including exchanges and cooperation in the economic sector aimed at the mutual interests and support.

Song, wishing that basic and substantial measures for confidence building on the Korean Peninsula could be agreed, also suggested, for the sake of effective procedure of the Four-Party-Talks, to immediately construct: Peace Regime Subcommittee; and Tension Reduction and Confidence Building Subcommittee

North Korean Chief Delegate Kim Kye-kwan, DPRK, Vice Minister of Foreign Affairs, in his keynote speech, reiterated to insist the existing position that US forces in South Korea was an obstacle to the peace regime and the withdrawal of US forces from the South and the US-North Korea peace treaty should be discussed first. He requested to decide detailed agenda before establishing the subcommittees.

Kim also insisted that US sanctions against North Korea should be eased first and expressed North Korea's discontent that the LWR project had not been progressed by the schedule.

Stanley O. Roth, US Chief Delegate and the Assistant Secretary of State Department, emphasized that the existing Armistice Treaty should be maintained for the stability of the Korean Peninsula, and that he wished to have progresses on less difficult issues through exchanges of ideas on the tension reduction and confidence building at the Four-Party-Talks in the sense that those issues could be resolved immediately whereas the issue of peace regime should be discussed for a long term period.

In the meantime, the Chinese delegation affirmed the common concept shared by the four parties that the establishment of a peace regime through the Four- Party-Talks should be necessary, but it would take a long procedure. The Chinese emphasized that the main task that the second round talks should carry were to decide the structural formality such as the subcommittees and discussion on the related issues.

The first day meeting was finished after the keynote speeches, and it was decided to have bilateral meetings next morning and convene the plenary meeting in the afternoon. Therefore, China, the chair-state, proceeded with bilateral meetings with North Korea, the US and South Korea respectively. To China, those bilateral meetings were to perceive each party's position and adjust the differences among the positions, but no other bilateral meetings among South Korea, North Korea and the US took place.

At the plenary meeting during the second day afternoon, each party presented its own position upon the keynote speeches. At the plenary meeting, South Korea emphasized that the South and the North, according to Article 5 of the South-North Basic Agreement of 1991, should take an initiative for establishing a peace regime, and that the real threat to the peace on the Korean Peninsula was not US forces in the South but North Korean military's offensive frontline deployment.

South Korean delegation also suggested, pursuing a progress in the Four Party Talks, to discuss the issue of early construction of subcommittees rather than to waste time with useless disputes caused by incessant insistence of each party's position.

North Koreans, upon the South's suggestion, restated that the withdrawal of US forces from the South should be discussed first for the sake of peace on the Korean Peninsula, and argued that construction of the subcommittees could be discussed only after the detailed agenda were determined.

The US clarified that US forces in the South had contributed to maintain peace on the Korean Peninsula and secure the regional stability, and that the forces were according to the Treaty on the Mutual Defense and Support between South Korea and the US, and then the status of the forces could not be discussed at the Four-Party-Talks.

Besides, regarding the issue of the US-North Korea Peace Treaty, the US refuted North Korea's position by pointing out that given the real concerned parties in maintaining peace on the Korean Peninsula were the South and the North, the US would not consider making the treaty between the US and North Korea.

China, meanwhile, presupposed that the differences among the four parties had been expected and suggested to develop discussions under the principle to expand common features and reduce differences. The Chinese delegation also presented several proposals related to the construction of the subcommittees, and agreed to discuss the issue of the subcommittees first at the present talks as proposed by the South Korea and the US.

The second day meeting was completed with each party's speech, and it was decided to discuss the construction of the subcommittees at the conference of heads of delegation next morning.

Throughout the third day, the conference of heads of delegation, at which the subcommittee issue was discussed, was held including the secondary head of delegation and interpreters. However, there was no progress because the differences on the number and operation of subcommittees were not resolved.

The secondary delegates' conference with three or four other attendants, was held in the morning of the fourth day (March 19, 1998). The South Korea and the US, accepting North Korea's position to a certain extent in order to make a progress in the talks, suggested to construct and operate subcommittees by proposing three work plans: confidence building measures; legal issues; and long-term arrangements

North Korea, while agreeing to construct a subcommittee for establishing a peace regime on the Korean Peninsula, raised an objection against South Korea's suggestion on the order of the work plans and insisted its demand to include the withdrawal of US forces from the South and the US-North Korea Peace Treaty in those three work plans as individual agendas.

Yet, such a demand of North Korea was opposing to the position of the South Korea and the US not to include the issue of the withdrawal of US forces as individual agendas. Therefore, the talks could not make a progress despite the North agreed to construct a single subcommittee.

During the fourth day afternoon, the delegates of the four parties made a visit to a cheese factory and ancient castles arranged by the Swiss government. Since the bus provide by the Swiss government had a conference table in it, the four heads of delegates could make discussions on the way to the cheese factory. At the bus conference, the South Korea and the US presented their position that the two subcommittees, at which the peace regime and the confidence building measures would be discussed, should be constructed during the second round Four-Party-Talks in order that substantial issues could be discussed at the third round talks.

There was no further progress since North Korea sustained its position that individual agendas be decided before constructing the subcommittees.

During fifth day (March 20, 1998) morning, the four heads of delegates had discussions, but like the day before they achieved no progress on the substantial issues such as construction of the subcommittees. Consequently, it was necessary to continue the meeting in the afternoon, but North Koreans repeatedly postponed the meeting because they did not receive an instruction from Pyongyang suggested to resume the meeting the sixth day (March 21, 1998) morning.

North Korea, at the morning session of the sixth day meeting, asserted that Payonyang's instruction ordered to sustain its position, and the second round Four-Party-Talks, which made no major progress on the substantial issues including construction of the subcommittee, were closed to adopt the Chair's Statement.

B. South Korea's Design for Maintenance of Peace

The fundamental position of South Korea for the maintenance of peace on the Korean Peninsula has been an observance of the armistice agreement as an instrument guaranteeing suspension of hostile military activities between South Korea and North Korea until the establishment of a solid state of peace on the Korean Peninsula. Following the adoption of the Basic Agreement on February 19, 1992, at the South-North high-level talks, South Korea adopted as its basic 'design' for the establishment of a solid state of peace on the Korean peninsula the creation of a peace regime mutually agreed by both South Korea and North Korea in accordance with Article 5 of the Basic Agreement that stipulates:

'The two sides shall endeavor together to transform the present state of armistice into a solid state of peace between the South and the North and shall abide by the present Military Armistice Agreement (of July 27, 1953) until such a state of peace has been realized',

This design for the creation of ever lasting peace on the peninsula also is in line with the three-phase national unification formula of South Korea which calls for reconciliation and cooperation, building of mutual confidence and establishment of a South-North commonwealth for ultimate national unification of Korea.

1) Observance of Armistice Agreement

The Armistice Agreement is an international treaty signed by the warring parties in the Korean War: the US Command, North Korea and China. Chapter I of the Basic South-North Agreement stipulates that 'The South and the North shall recognize and respect each other's system' and that 'the South and the North shall abide by the present Military Armistice Agreement until such a state has been realized'. Both sides thus recognized the basic spirit and existence of the armistice agreement.

Over 40 years have elapsed since the termination of the war but a solid state of peace has yet to be realized. In fact, over one million regular forces have been deployed on both sides of the military demarcation line and an accidental incident or hostile act is apt to touch off a major conflict at any moment. There is no denying the fact that the armistice agreement and the Military Armistice Commission established under the agreement have been very instrumental in preventing and resolving accidental incidents and hostilities in the past. In view of this, the disruption of the armistice regime without establishing more effective, alternate system will naturally pose a grave threat to the peace and security on the peninsula. This is why South Korea has been stressing the need to strictly observe the armistice agreement for peace and security on the peninsula.

2) Principle of Resolving Issue by Parties Concerned

Prior to jointly proposing with the four-party talks, South Korea maintained that military and security issues involving the Korean Peninsula should be resolved through direct negotiations between the South and the North under the basic principle that the armistice agreement needs to be maintained until after a solid state of peace is realized on the Korean Peninsula. This principle of resolving any issue directly by the parties involved also underlines the July 4, South and North Joint Statement announced in 1972 as well as the Basic Agreement adopted in 1992.

In his speech at a ceremony on August 15, 1995 commemorating the 50th Independence Day, President Kim Young-sam reaffirmed that this principle should apply for the establishment of a solid state of peace on the Korean Peninsula. He further called for a three-point formula for building a lasting peace regime on the Peninsula: first, a peace regime needs to be worked out through negotiations between the South and the North; second, such a regime needs to be supported by the other countries concerned; and third, the issues already agreed by the South and the North must be sincerely implemented.

This means that South Korea is determined to maintain the existing frameworks for the maintenance of peace on the Peninsula, frankly negotiate with North Korea for the establishment of a lasting peace regime and solicit the support of neighboring nations and nations directly concerned with peace on the peninsula for the maintenance of the peace regime. In another words, it means that South Korea, while issues involving peace on the peninsula needs to be directly resolved in principle by the South and the North, it is ready to consider a 2 plus 2 or a 2 plus 4 way talks, if necessary to solicit cooperation and support of neighboring nations in the establishment and maintenance of a solid peace regime on the peninsula.

3) The Basic Agreement and Peace Regime

South Korea has been firmly assuming the position that it is necessary to work out through negotiations with North Korea disarmament and related issues while endeavoring to build mutual trust in military affairs through the Joint Military Commission to be established in accordance with the Basic Agreement.

South and North Koreas had already agreed on a basic non-aggression principle in the Basic Agreement. Articles 9 and 10 of the agreement stipulate that the two sides shall not use force against each other and shall not undertake armed aggression against each other and that differences of views and disputes arising between the two sides shall be resolved peacefully through dialogue and negotiation. Article 11 further stipulates that the South-North demarcation line and areas for nonaggression shall be identical with the Military Demarcation Line specified in the Military Armistice Agreement and the areas that have been under the jurisdiction of each sides until the present time. It is the basic position of South Korea to endeavor to build up military confidence in accordance with Article 12 of the Basic Agreement:

> 'To implement and guarantee non-aggression, the two sides shall set up a South-North Joint Military Commission within three months of the coming into force of this Agreement. In the said Commission, the two sides shall discuss and carry out steps to build military confidence and realize arms reduction, including the mutual notification and control of major movement of military units and major military exercises, the peaceful utilization of the Demilitarized Zone, exchanges of military personnel and information, phased reduction in armaments including the elimination of weapons of mass destruction and attack capabilities and verifications thereof.'

South Korea also assumes the position that simultaneously with the implementation of these measures all the facilities and military personnel within demilitarized zone need to be gradually withdrawn in order to bring about true demilitarization of the zone and mutually promote peaceful utilization of the zone so as to pave the way for negotiation in earnest for disarmament.

It should be noted here that only through building mutual military confidence it will be possible for South and North Korea to earnestly negotiate for the elimination of weapons of mass destruction and attack capabilities. The South believes that for laying solid ground for the establishment and maintenance of a peace regime through disarmament, it is absolutely necessary to have a verification system to adequately oversee and ensure military disarmament.

It is obvious that such issues as reduction and/or withdrawal of US armed forces in South Korea and the ROK-USA mutual defense treaty belong to internal affairs of South Korea; however, it is the position of the South to resolve such issues through negotiations with the US, taking into consideration the progress in negotiations with the North on mutual disarmament and military confidence building and its influence on peace on the peninsula. This being the case, South Korea has been urging North Korea to resume South-North negotiations and to sincerely observe the Basic Agreement prior to the joint proposal for the four-party talks.

C. North Korea's Design on Peace

North Korea's design for bringing about peace on the peninsula calls for scrapping the military armistice agreement and direct negotiations with the US for the conclusion of a peace treaty without the participation of South Korea. North Korea now has no interest at all in the implementation of the Basic Agreement. In fact, North Korea has been avoiding any more dialogue with South Korea on the ground that a non-aggression accord was signed. While South Korea wants to establish a solid state of peace through faithful implementation of the Basic Agreement within the framework of the armistice agreement, North Korea has come to deny the qualification of South Korea as a party to the armistice agreement for the reason that she did not sign the agreement. North Korea now not only asserts that the conclusion of a peace treaty with the US will insure peace on the Korean Peninsula but has come to unilaterally disrupt the armistice agreement, thereby touching off serious tensions on the Peninsula.

1) North Korea's Insistence on Peace Treaty with the US

North Korea first called for the conclusion of a peace treaty with the US in a letter sent to the US Congress in March 1974 in the name of the Supreme People's Congress (3rd session, 5th assembly). The call for the peace treaty was raised for the second time in October 1980, this time in the name of the Labor Party (6th session), asserting that North Korea and the US constitute parties to the armistice agreement.

In January 1984, North Korea called for simultaneous declaration of non aggression and the conclusion of a peace treaty between the US and North Korea in its letters sent to the Seoul authorities and the US in the name of the joint standing council of its Central People's Committee and the Supreme People's Congress. It further suggested that South Korea may attend the peace parley as observer, thereby making it a three-way talks.

Following the coming into force of the Basic Agreement in February 1992, North Korea came to reason that now that an accord on non-aggression, reconciliation and cooperation between the South and the North was adopted, what remains to be done now for the establishment of a solid state of peace on the Korean Peninsula is the conclusion of a peace treaty between North Korea and the US Furthermore, in support of its argument that South Korea needs not participate in negotiations for the conclusion of a peace treaty, North Korea asserts that South Korea not only did not sign the armistice agreement but it has been a puppet of the US, lacking independence in addition to its insistence that the non-aggression accord already signed with South Korea makes it unnecessary to sign a peace treaty between South Korea and North Korea. North Korea argues in this connection that the parties to the armistice agreement were the commanders of the UN, North Korea and Chinese forces, that China has already withdrawn from Korea, and that the UN forces are substantially under the command of the US, and that, therefore, a peace treaty on the Korean Peninsula needs to be negotiated only between the US, and North Korea. In an attempt to carry through its assertion, North Korea in April 1994 unilaterally withdrew its delegates to the Military Armistice Commission in Panmunjom, cut off dialogue with South Korea and has since been demanding negotiations for the conclusion of a peace treaty directly with the US to replace the armistice agreement.

2) North Korea's Attempt to Invalidate Armistice Agreement

In an attempt to force the conclusion of a peace treaty with the US, North Korea has been maneuvering step by step to invalidate the armistice agreement since the advent of the 1990s. As a first step toward that end, North Korea substantially suspended the functions of the MAC (Military Armistice Commission) which has been serving as the sole agency for the management of the armistice agreement.

In March 1991, when the UN Command appointed a South Korean Army general as its senior delegate to the commission, North Korea began boycotting the meetings of the commission. In April 1994, North Korea announced in a statement of its foreign ministry that the armistice agreement could no longer guarantee peace and that the MAC no longer substantially exists. North Korea also said at a meeting of chief secretaries of the MAC in Panmunjom that it would withdraw all of its personnel from the MAC. In May of that year, North Korea unilaterally established the representative office of Korean People's Army in Panmunjom. In September, North Korea requested China to withdraw its delegate to the MAC and China so obliged in December of that year and thus a major mechanism of the armistice agreement was substantially invalidated

North Korea also substantially paralyzed the functions of the Neutral Nations Supervisory Commission by having two delegates of its side from Czechoslovakia and Poland withdrew from the commission. Following the demise of the Soviet bloc, Czechoslovakia came to establish diplomatic ties with South Korea. Following the separation of Czechoslovakia into Czecho and Slovakia, North Korea in April 1993 obliged Czecho to withdraw from the NNSC by refusing to recognize the qualification of Czecho to remain in the MAC in place of Czechoslovakia. In April 1994, North Korea had requested Poland to withdraw from the MAC. As Poland declined to oblige, North Korea cut off supply of food supply, electricity and water and Poland, too, had to withdraw from the MAC in February 1995.

North Korea, having succeeded in paralyzing the functions of the MAC and the NNSC, began a series of provocative military activities in the demilitarized zone, thereby aggravating tensions on the peninsula and augmenting its publicity campaign for the conclusion of a peace treaty with the US On the heels of its declaration invalidating the demilitarized zone in April 1996, North Korea repeatedly mobilized armed personnel into the northern side of the Joint Security Zone in Panmunjom for building bases for heavy fire arms, infiltrated armed soldiers into southern area of Demilitarized Zone in the central front, and on the west coast North Korea had its coast guard vessel infiltrate into south of the demarcation line - all in its maneuvers to scrap the armistice agreement.

3) US-North Korea Relations Following Geneva Accord

Following a series of provocative activities designed to make best use of its nuclear arms card, including its declaration in March 1993 to secede from the NPT, North Korea was able to open a channel of direct dialogue with the US In October 1994, a basic US-North Korea agreement was signed and through this accord North Korea had won US commitment for non-use of arms (against the North) which meant to the North, the US assurance for the security of its regime, in addition to US support for the construction of LWRs through the KEDO. Soon thereafter, the US and North Korea agreed on the establishment of a liaison office in each other's country and began negotiations for partial lifting of economic sanctions against North Korea and repatriation of the remains of US personnel missing in action during the Korean War as well as on the issue involving the North's export of missiles.

Thus, there has been marked progress in improvement of relations between the US and North Korea. In particular, seeing that North Korea's food shortage had further aggravated due to deluge in 1995, the US came to the aid of North Korea with the supply of much needed food. The US says its supply of food was part of its efforts to assure North Korea's 'soft-landing'.

At any rate, the relations between the US and North Korea have been steadily improving in a sharp contrast to almost-frozen relations between South Korea and North Korea. Under such circumstances, the situation on the Korean Peninsula including traditional ties of mutual cooperation and coordination between South Korea and the US appears to be headed for a new turning point.

Until recently, the US defined North Korea as a state of terrorists and imposed economic sanctions. However, following the adoption of the basic agreement with North Korea, the US partially eased its economic sanctions against North Korea, opened direct telephone lines with North Korea and took other measures to improve relations with North Korea. In January 1995, the State Department of the US eased sanctions against North Korea. The Treasury Department of the US in February 1995 partially lifted economic sanctions against North Korea by revising the overseas assets control regulations. In April 1995, Washington opened direct telephone lines with Pyongyang.

Having adopted so-called 'help-soft-landing policy' for North Korea in order to ensure peaceful settlement of 'the North Korean nuclear issue' and to help stabilization of North Korea, the US supplied food and cash to North Korea through government and private agencies to help prevent collapse of North Korea and/or preclude North Korea from possible provocation of hostility against South Korea due to acute food shortage. In January 1996, the US delivered US$2 million through the USAID to the WFP for North Korea. The Department of Commerce also took measures to allow delivery of such humanitarian-oriented items as relief foodstuff, health and medical care items, clothes and daily necessities to North Korea through private channels.

Furthermore, the US removed North Korea from the list of countries to which travels of American citizens are banned, thereby greatly easing restrictions of US citizens travel to North Korea, although North Korea still remains in the list of the states of terrorists.

In January 1996, the US resumed negotiations with North Korea for repatriation of the remains of US personnel missing in action during the Korean War and on again off again negotiations are likely to continue for some time over the issues involving compensations, composition of US investigation teams, etc. No tangible accords have yet been reached in US negotiations with North Korea over the issues involving North Korea's production and supply to the Middle East, and North Korea's production of biochemical arms mountable on missiles.

The US and North Korea have been negotiating for the establishment of liaison offices in each other's country in accordance with their Geneva Accord. Working-level meetings were held in Washington in December 1994 and in January 1995 in Pyongyang. In September 1995, a general accord in this respect was reached but final settlement is pending over the issue involving delivery of US diplomatic pouches through Panmunjom, etc. Nonetheless, the liaison office issue will be resolved as soon as North Korea is ready to do so in view of indications that it is being delayed due chiefly to internal situation of North Korea. Once representative offices are established in each other's country, it will greatly facilitate direct negotiations between the two countries.

D. Significance of Four-Party Talks

Ever since the conclusion of the armistice agreement in July 1953, South Korea has been upholding the principle of sincerely abiding by the armistice agreement until a solid state of peace is established on the Korean Peninsula. This principle also underlines the Basic Agreement and South Korea has been maintaining the position that the Agreement needs to be sincerely implemented so as to build mutual political and military confidence and thus ultimately bring about a solid state of peace on the Korean Peninsula. However, North Korea unilaterally declared as no longer valid the military armistice regime that has contributed for over 40 years to the maintenance of peace and security on the Korean Peninsula and renounced the armistice agreement itself, thereby disrupting the armistice system. Furthermore, North Korea unilaterally suspended the implementation of the Basic Agreement and has been demanding negotiations with the US for the conclusion of a peace treaty.

As 'cards' for pressuring the US into agreeing to its peace treaty proposal, North Korea has been utilizing issues involving its development of nuclear arms and missiles as well as the repatriation of remains of US personnel missing in action during the Korean War. On the other hand, the US, mindful of the possible collapse of North Korean regime due to acute food shortage and other causes, has come to deploy a policy designed to ensure 'soft-landing' of North Korea.

Thus relations between the US and North Korea have been improved, irrespective of almost-frozen relations between the South and the North. Thus, the principle of improving relations between the US and the North Korea in parallel and in harmony with progress in relations between the South and the North underlying the US-North Korea Geneva Accord has been rendered meaningless. Against such backdrop, on April 16, 1996 the presidents of South Korea and the US met on the Cheju island, discussed the situation and decided to jointly propose a four-party talks.

1) Re-establishment of South Korea-US Cooperative System

South Korea and the US have re-established a joint cooperative system through their proposal for a four-way talks in order to establish a solid state of peace on the Korean Peninsula. As clearly stated in their joint Cheju statement, President Clinton of the US reaffirmed the firm commitment of the US for the security of South Korea and to the ROK-US security alliance, and made it clear that he shared the position of South Korea that the current military armistice agreement needs to be maintained until after the establishment of a solid and lasting peace regime on the Peninsula.

It was thus possible to block the attempts of North Korea to sign a provisional peace treaty with the US or to hold a general-level military talks with the US It also clarified that no direct negotiations between the US and North Korea will be allowed (without the participation of South Korea) on issues involving peace on the Peninsula, thereby dealing a blow on North Korea's attempts to link the peace treaty issue with all other pending issues in negotiations with the US.

North Korea steadfastly called for negotiations with the US for the conclusion of a peace treaty in line with its basic strategy to promote direct negotiations with the US excluding South Korea - a strategy designed to maintain its current regime with US support, while disrupting traditional ties of mutual cooperation between South Korea and the US.

Such strategy in fact belies North Korea's scheme to bring about abrogation of ROK-US mutual defense treaty, withdrawal of US troops from the South, and dissolution of the UN Military Command and the South Korea-US United Command, and thus create conditions conducive to national unification under its formula. In view of this, with the four-party talks proposal, it will be possible to effectively block the ulterior motive of North Korea, as much as it sets the tone and direction of US negotiations with North Korea as coordinated with South Korea, and thus it will be possible to consolidate once again the basic framework of cooperation and coordination between South Korea and the US within which improvement in relations between the US and North Korea needs to be in parallel and in harmony with progress in negotiations between South Korea and North Korea.

It is indeed meaningful that the Cheju Joint Statement eliminated any room for confusion in coordination of issues between the US and South Korea, in US negotiations with North Korea by clearly defining that such issues involving peace and security on the Peninsula as the conclusion of a peace treaty, US forces stationed in South Korea and military disarmament cannot and should not be directly taken up between the US and North Korea without the participation of South Korea, while such issues as US humanitarian-oriented aids to North Korea including food, repatriation of remains of US personnel missing in action during the Korean War, North Korea's production and export of missiles and establishment of liaison offices in each other's country may be directly negotiated between the US and North Korea.

2) Internationalization of Korean Issues

North Korea has been contending that as much as the non-aggression accord was reached with South Korea with the conclusion of the Basic Agreement it needs only to conclude a peace treaty with the US, the other party to the armistice agreement to insure peace on Korean Peninsula. However, South Korea and the US have confirmed through their joint proposal for a four-party talks that a solid state of peace on the Korean Peninsula needs to be realized within the framework of the four-way talks participated by the US and China - signatories to the armistice agreement, with the South and the North - parties to the armistice agreement - assuming initiative.

The principle of resolving issues by parties concerned was often confirmed as the basic principle for resolving issues between the South and the North in the July 4, South-North Joint Declaration (in 1972) that upheld the principle of achieving national unification with the spirit of independence without relying on foreign powers, in the high-level South-North talks in the 1990s and finally in the Basic Agreement signed in 1992.

The issue involving the realization of a solid state of peace on the Korean Peninsula, of course, needs to be negotiated between the South and the North, the two parties directly involved. Therefore, the contention of North Korea that a peace treaty needs to be signed only with the US without South Korea betrays the fact that North Korea has no intention to bring about a lasting peace and security on the Korean Peninsula.

In consideration of the current situation marked by mounting tensions on the Korean Peninsula being fanned by North Korea in defiance of the military armistice agreement and the Basic Agreement, South Korea and the US have reached the conclusion that it is not realistically feasible to stick to the principle of resolving 'Korean issues' only by the parties directly involved.

South Korea and the US, therefore, decided to call for a four-party talks including the US and China, which are parties to the armistice agreement, so as to break through the impasse created by North Korea's refusal to have dialogue with South Korea, without unadhering the principle of resolving issues by parties directly involved.

Therefore, it may be said that the proposal for the four-party talks is quite realistic and positive approach to the establishment of a solid state of peace on the Peninsula - an international issue involving the transformation of the implementation system for the armistice agreement, which itself is an international treaty, into a solid, lasting peace system, in recognition of the current reality marked by suspension of dialogue between the South and the North.

3) Proposal for Open Dialogue

In the South Korea-US Joint Statement, President Kim Yong-sam made it clear that he was ready to unconditionally and formally meet with the representative of North Korea, and the US and South Korea jointly proposed to hold unconditionally and without delay a four-party talks including the South, the North, the US and China so as to proceed toward the establishment of a lasting state of solid peace on the Korean Peninsula.

The proposal was prompted by the need to enable North Korea, which has been unable to sincerely observe the Basic Agreement and the basic agreement between the US and North Korea, to come to the table of dialogue of the four parties to the armistice agreement to earnestly discuss the establishment of a solid state of peace on the Korean Peninsula, free of worry about possible absorption into the South or collapse of its own regime.

In fact, it was because of its fear of being absorbed into South Korea which has far greater national strength than North Korea that North Korea unilaterally suspended the South-North high-level talks and meetings of various South-North joint MACs and committees set up in accordance with the Basic Agreement.

Therefore, unless measures are adopted to remove such fears of North Korea, North Korea will find it difficult to resume such government-level meetings with South Korea. Therefore, South Korea plans to pave the way for bringing about an ever lasting solid state of peace on the Korean Peninsula through such an open negotiation channel as the four-party talks with the participation of the US and China in addition to the South and the North in consideration of the situation of North Korea.

South Korea and the US have also made it clear that it will be possible for the four-party talks to take up a broad-spectrum of agenda necessary for easing tensions on the Korean Peninsula, besides discussions of measures for building a lasting solid state of peace on the Peninsula. This means that, if necessary for peace and security on the peninsula, it will be possible to discuss any subject at the four-party talks, an open avenue for dialogue for peace and security on the Peninsula.

As has been clarified in the Basic South-North Agreement, it is necessary to proceed toward the creation of an atmosphere conducive to the creation of a regime for lasting peace and security of the Peninsula by first building political and military confidence and by realizing economic exchanges and cooperation, to be followed up with military management and disarmament and then promoting full-scale economic exchanges and cooperation, social and cultural exchanges and cooperation, and arrangement of meetings of dispersed relatives in the South and the North as well as other measures needed for improvement of relations between the South and the North.

It will be possible to effectively take up these issues within the framework of the four-party talks with the support and assurance of neighboring counties. In particular, in order to aid North Korea which has been experiencing serious economic hardships, it will be possible to promote multi-faceted economic support measures within the framework of the four-party talks such as provision of international credits and food, investment in the special economic districts of Najin-Sunbong, and North Korea's affiliation with international economic organizations in addition to South-North economic cooperation.

Chapter XIII

A New Proposal for Korea's Reunification

The early 1990s witnessed the collapse of the East-West Cold War system with the fall of the Soviet Union and East European Communist bloc and the integration of East and West Germany. In its place, liberal democracy and the market economy system have taken root as universal values while liberalization, opening and cooperation among nations for mutual peace and prosperity have become the new world trends.

The biggest assignment of all for Korea is national reunification. As far as Korea is divided, the history must be distorted. Korea has been in a sense sacrificed and a lot of energy has been spent. Since Korea's perpetual division has been a by- product of the Cold War, it is necessary to procure the support of the nations around the Korean peninsula. When the international situation is improved, the success and failure for Korea's reunification is up to national will and ability.

Unfortunately in North Korea, the suffering of the people has been increasing everyday under their failing political system. In particular, the economic gap between South and North Korea has been increasing since the 1970s and it has made North Korea impatient and desperate, resulting in terrorist tactics such as the KAL aircraft bombing (November 1987) and the Myanmar bombing (October 1983) in an attempt to assassinate ex-president, Chun Doo-Hwan. North Korea has also been pursuing a nuclear development resulting from a perception out of military and psychological inferiority.

In this situation, the most important task for Korea is peaceful reunification. Two Koreas became members of the UN (September 1991) and concluded an agreement on reconciliation, non-aggression, exchange and cooperation (December 1991). But North Korea's decision to secede from NPT brought about much antagonism to the US and South Korea.

The responsibility for reunification ultimately lies in the Korean people. Superpowers had some responsibility in the division of the Korea and the Korean War, but the international situation has changed. Reunification of Korea entails a lot of difficulties compared with the case of Germany, including threats from the ongoing nuclear problem, and North Korea's relative independence from China and Russia compared to East Germany. Korea must attempt to approach the reunification problem in concert with Japan, China and Russia.

The international scene is rapidly changing as the rules of the Cold War no longer apply and a new world order is emerging. Soon after Gorbachev's 'New Belgrade Declaration' (1988) and 'Declaration of Non-Intervention in East Europe' (1989), Eastern Europe swerved towards democratization and market economies, East and West Germany became one, then these changes in turn had a boomerang effect in leading to the dismantling of the Soviet Union. The disintegration of the cradle of leftist ideology meant that conflicts between countries would be fuelled by economic rather than political reasons, and alliances and rivalries will be formed accordingly.

However, on the Korean peninsula, North and South Korea have not yet to dismiss their Cold War stances, and alleviate their ingrained mutual distrust. As for the Koreans themselves, the question they must ask themselves at the crossroads of history is what they can do for themselves to take advantage of this opportune time in building a prosperous unified nation. The Koreas remain the world's only divided nation under the new world order framed by the 1989 Malta Conference. During their period of division the relation between North and South Korea has proceeded in the following four stages: the stage of hostility (ignited by President Seung-man Rhee refusal of an entente); the stage of goodwill competition (initiated by the signing of Joint Declarations on July 4, 1972, and the drawing of the Declaration for Peaceful Unification in June 23, 1973); the stage of efforts toward becoming 'Partners for National Prosperity' (as enacted by the Special Statement by President Roh Tae-woo on July 7, 1988); and the stage of cooperation characterized by 'Reconciliation, Non-aggression and Cooperation' (epitomized by the signing of North-South Agreement on December 13, 1991).

Further, the two Koreas joined the United Nations separately on September 17, 1991[132] and the signing of the 'Agreement for Mutual Understanding, Non-aggression, Exchange and Cooperation' by North and South policy-makers at the 5th conference of high- ranking officials.[133]

1. THREE-STAGE UNIFICATION FORMULA FOR KOREA'S UNIFICATION

'Three-Stage Unification Formula for the Creation of Korean National Community' features the basic philosophy, the principles and the process of national and unification.

A. The Unification Formula

1) The Basic Philosophy

The national community unification formula sets forth two concepts as the basis of South Korea's unification policies: one is the idea of 'liberal democracy' as the basic philosophy of unification; and the other is the construction of a 'national community' as the means of attaining unification.

It was made clear in the formula that 'liberal democracy' should be the key value which the nation should consistently pursue not only in the process of attaining unification but even after unification was realized. In other words, the formula emphasizes that unification should be achieved based on liberal democracy, an ideology that does not serve specific classes or groups but respects the liberty and well-being of all the individual members of the nation and guarantees human dignity.

As the method of promoting unification, the formula lays down the formation of a 'national community.' This means that South and North Korea, as the same nation, should form a single community and thereby move toward national unification.

The formula calls for the pursuit of a peaceful and phased unification, and the creation and development of economic, social and cultural communities through dialogue and cooperation between the South and the North. It then provides for the ultimate accomplishment of complete political unification in a single nation and state.

2) The Principles of Unification

The national community unification formula sets forth 'independence,' 'peace' and 'democracy' as the basic principles that have to be valued in the course of promoting unification.

The principle of 'independence' stresses that unification should be accomplished independently based on the nation's own efforts and national capabilities without allowing any interference by alien forces. This means that unification ought to be promoted according to the Korean people's own free will through talks between the authorities of the South and the North under the spirit of national self-determination.

The principle of 'peace' means that unification should be achieved in a peaceful manner under all circumstances, not through war or the overthrow of one side by the other. Though unification is the paramount challenge facing the nation and the most ardent wish of the Korean people, neither force of arms nor violence that would sacrifice people can ever be tolerated in attaining unification.

The principle of 'democracy' implies that unification should be attained democratically through the participation of all the Korean people on the basis of guaranteeing the freedom and rights of all the members of the nation. This means that the course of unification should follow procedures and methods based on democratic principles, and also that even after unification has been achieved, the unified society should be one in which all the members of the nation can be assured of freedom and the right to lead decent lives.

---

[132] By joining the UN separately, North and South have accepted each other as independent states. This is in accordance with Article 4 of the UN Constitution, which restricts membership to sovereign states.

[133] For comparative notes, West Germany started drafting an eastward policy in 1969; East and West Germany established the basic treaties for unification in 1972; both joined the UN in 1973.

3) The Process of Unification

The national community unification formula envisions the framework to achieve political unification peacefully by constructing a single national community step by step. Based on this, the formula lays down three stages for unification: first, 'stage of reconciliation and cooperation'; second, 'stage of Korean commonwealth'; and lastly, 'stage of realizing a single, unified nation-state.'

The first stage of 'reconciliation and cooperation' represents a stage where South and North Korea liquidate their relations of enmity and confrontation and pursue reconciliatory coexistence by promoting mutual confidence building and expanding substantial exchanges and cooperation. In other words, this is a stage where South and North Korea, while recognizing and respecting each other's systems, dispel mutual enmity and distrust through exchanges and cooperation in all walks of life such as the economy, society and culture and thereby steer inter-Korean relations in a peace-oriented direction.

The second stage of 'Korean Commonwealth' is an interim unification system under which the South and the North form a provisional alliance to institute peace and form a joint social, cultural and economic community in the course of constructing a complete unified state. At this stage, legal and institutional devices should be systematized under mutual agreement and various ways to achieve national integration could be discussed through organizations to be jointly formed. The issues of what organizations are to be created and what functions they are to perform under 'Korean Commonwealth' could be determined concretely in a South-North agreement. Basically, however, a South-North summit meeting an ministerial conference are to take place regularly while parliamentary representatives of the two sides would meet to prepare legal devices for unification such as a unified constitution.

<Table XIII-1> Comparison of the Proposed Directives for Reunification of the North and the South

	South Korea	North Korea
Category	- Three-step directive for the establishment of a single Korean National Community	- Directives for the establishment of Korea Democratic Federal Republic
Philosophy	- Free democracy (centered on the individual)	-*'Juche'* ideology (centered on social class)
Popular force	- All citizens	- Proletariat class
Principles	- Freedom-peace-democracy	- Freedom -peaceful unification - national solidarity
Prerequisites	- None	- Abolishment of national security law - Legalization of communist party activities - Withdrawal of US troops in South Korea
Unification process	- Three-step process of reconciliation cooperation →North-South coalition →completion of a unified country of 'one people, one nation' * priority on establishment of a democratic state (ethnic unification →national unification)	- Gradual completion of a federal nation * priority on the establishment of a national regime (national unification → ethnic unification)
Transitional organization and apparatus	<North-South coalition>- Summit Council - Ministers' Council - Joint Secretariat	- None
Finalizing procedure	- Democratic elections in both the North and South according to a Unification Constitution	- Political negotiation on a council format
Form of unified nation	- Unified country of 'one people, one nation, one system, one government'	- Federation of 'one people, one nation, two systems, two governments'
Future vision for the unified nation	- Advanced democracy with guarantees for freedom, welfare and human dignity	- None

Source: Yang-Taek Lim, "Economic and Military Issues in A New Proposal for the Reunification of the Two Koreas", *The Hanyang Journal of Economic Studies,* Seoul: Hanyang Economic Research Institute, March 1997.

The third stage of 'realization of a single, unified nation-state' is a stage where the two systems of the South and the North are completely integrated based on the community formed in the stage of "Korean Commonwealth" thereby resulting in the realization of a unified political community. In other words, this means the successful realization of unification into one state in one nation. At this stage, a unified government and a unified parliament would be formed in democratic elections held pursuant to the provisions of a unified constitution prepared by the parliamentary representatives of the two sides. Then the organizations and institutions of the two systems would be integrated to accomplish unification in one state in one nation. A more important task at this stage would be the pursuit of socio-cultural, economic and psychological homogeneity in addition to political unification so that all the members of the nation could participate in forming a genuinely integrated community.

B. The Three Principles for Instituting a Peace Mechanism on the Korean Peninsula

What is most important in exploring a path toward unification will be to maintain solid peace on the Korean peninsula. Without peace, there can be no unification nor any bright future for the nation.

The Korean War (1950. 6~1953. 7), came to a halt under the Military Armistice Agreement three years later. The truce agreement has been an institutional device instrumental to maintaining peace and stability on the Korean peninsula for more than 40 years.

The armistice agreement, however, is a mere military-level regime designed to suspend hostilities pending the achievement of a final peaceful resolution. This means that the Korean peninsula is still in a state of fragile peace.

This is why the South and the North agreed in the Basic Agreement between the South and the North (Article 5) that went into force in February 1992 to 'exert joint efforts to transform the present state of armistice into a solid state of peace between the South and the North and respect the Armistice Agreement until a solid state of peace is achieved'.

However, North Korea has taken one step after another to render the armistice system powerless, for instance, by forcibly evicting Czech representatives from the NNSC (Neutral Nations Supervisory Commission) in April 1993. At the same time, the North has been insisting on the conclusion of an exclusive peace agreement with the United States over the heads of South Korea on the ground that South Korea is not a signatory party to the Armistice Agreement. The attempt of North Korea to nullify the Truce Agreement has posed a serious threat to security and peace on the Korean peninsula.

Under the circumstances, a presidential message delivered on the Liberation Day August 15, 1995, laid down three principles for instituting a peace mechanism on the Korean peninsula as the basic direction for rooting peace.

First, the issue of peace regime should always be discussed and resolved between the direct parties involved, namely, South and North Korea. The responsibility for keeping peace on the Korean peninsula lies on none other than the two sides of Korea. If either of the two sides is not interested in safeguarding peace, it is impossible to build a durable peace on the Korean peninsula. Therefore, it is only proper that the issue of bringing about permanent peace should be discussed and resolved between the South and the North, the direct parties involved. It is to reflect this stark reality that the two sides agreed in the South-North Basic Agreement to jointly strive to change the present state of armistice into the state of a durable peace between the South and the North.

Second, the Basic Agreement, the Joint Declaration of the Denuclearization of the Korean Peninsula and all other inter-Korean agreements should be respected and fulfilled. To bring about permanent peace on the Korean peninsula, the first thing that needs to take place is the promotion of confidence building between the two sides. No peace can ever be attained if the two sides mutually distrust the other's intentions for peace and remain hostile to each other. Trust springs up when promises are respected. South and North Korea agreed on mutual reconciliation cooperation and the denuclearization of the Korean peninsula in talks between responsible authorities led by the prime ministers of the two sides and solemnly pledged their implementation before the nation and world. The agreements contain principles and concrete methods of realizing peace on the Korean peninsula and tasks to implement. Therefore, it is not an exaggeration to say that without the faithful implementation of the Basic Agreement and the Declaration of Denuclearization, a durable peace cannot be established on the Korean peninsula.

Third, the efficacy of a peace regime on the Korean peninsula can be better ensured when there are cooperation and support from pertinent foreign countries. Today it is a common practice for regional countries to cooperate with others and exert joint efforts among themselves to safeguard peace and stability. The situation of the Korean peninsula is not only a matter of concern to the Korean people but also directly linked to the interests of regional countries. Therefore, relevant countries are very interested in the question of firmly establishing peace on the Korean peninsula and are trying to play positive roles in this regard. In this respect, the continued participation and cooperation of neighboring countries is needed in the process of establishing a peace mechanism between South and North Korea. Participation by these countries would contribute to guaranteeing the efficacy of a peace regime on the Korean peninsula.

2. A New Model for Korea's Reunification

Yang-Taek Lim (1993, 1994, 1997, 1999) has presented a new model for Korean reunification based on the five-step approach: preparation → economic integration →social integration →political integration → military integration.[134]

A. Outline of the Existing Reunification Policies

The Government of the Republic of Korea (South) declared its 'Directives for Unification' through a so-called 'Korean National Community' made up of Koreans from both home and overseas. A summary of the major points reveals the three principles of independence, peace and democracy, which signifies the intention to achieve unification through the independent will of the people, without the use of force and by democratic means by pursuing harmony amongst all Koreans. The process of unification would aim to establish an ethnically unified nation (a unified democratic republic) with the North and South uniting under the principle of co-existence and sharing prosperity. A North-South coalition would be formed as a transitional system and would serve the purpose of pursuing co-existence and sharing prosperity, union of society and the formation of a common living environment.

Furthermore, a Joint Constitutional Committee would be formed through a summit meeting for the achievement of social, cultural and economic union with stipulations for the basic directives on unification, mutual non-aggression and the establishment of North-South coalition apparatuses. Such apparatuses would include 'North-South Summit Council' to serve as supreme decision-making authority, 'North-South Ministers' Council' for negotiation, coordination, and guarantee of execution purposes, 'North-South Peace Council' to make preparations for unification, and a "Joint Secretariat" for the handling of administrative details, while the current DMZ (demilitarized zone) would be designated as a 'peace zone' and developed into a 'City of Peace' as the logical site for various organizations and apparatuses.

The procedure of establishing a unified nation would be determined and announced by the North-South Peace Council, which according to the Constitution for Unification would follow the stages of general elections → establishment of a unified parliament and government → completion of the unified nation. The unified nation would be an ethnic union with the mandate of all Korean citizens, exist as a democratic state which guarantees freedom, human rights and the pursuit of happiness, constitute a single country, possess a bicameral system of parliament, promote the welfare of all its citizens (in the form of universal participation, guarantee of equal opportunity and freedom of ideology and expression) as its basic principle in a unified democratic republic, guarantee the security of the Korean people and maintain friendly relations with all nations to contribute to global peace.

---

[134] Yang-Taek Lim, "A New Proposal for the Korean Reunification with a Special Emphasis on the Economic Cooperation between North and South Korea as the Crucial Step", *DoSan Collected Papers,* Vol. 3, Seoul: DoSan Academy Institute, August 1993.

Yang-Taek Lim, "A New Proposal for the Korean Reunification and Economic Cooperation between North and South Korea", paper presented at the International Symposium Commemorating the 20th Anniversary of the Institute for Sino-Soviet Studies of Hanyang University, Seoul, September 1994 pp. 27~28.

Yang-Taek Lim "A New Proposal for the Reunification of the Two Koreas: Economic Issues", *Journal of Asian Economies*, Vol. 8, No. 4, 1997, pp. 547~578.

Yang-Taek Lim, "Economic and Military Issues in A New Proposal for the Reunification of the Two Koreas", *The Hanyang Journal of Economic Studies,* Hanyang Economic Research Institute, March 1997.

Yang-Taek Lim, "A New Korean Reunification Model and the Direction of Civilian Campaign for it", *DoSan Collected Papers,* Vol. 7, Seoul: DoSan Academy Institute, March 1999.

The directives for unification designate unification in the three stages, by improving existing proposals for the unification process and unified nation, but still based on the principles of independence, peace and democracy; reconciliation and cooperation → North-South coalition → completion of the unified state under the basic guideline that the process of unification should proceed in a gradual and step-by-step manner.

The first stage of reconciliation and cooperation would end the two sides' history of confrontation and their relationship of mistrust and opposition, and be a stage for the pursuit of reconciliatory co-existence by easing tensions through mutual trust and pursuing actual trade and exchange to speed up the process of reconciliation. In this preliminary stage, North and South Korea would begin to recover their national identity based on mutual trust and work towards preparing for unification in a more positive manner.

The establishment and operation of a transitional North-South coalition was designated as the second stage in order to develop systematic coexistence towards the goal of a common nation and the eventual founding of an ethnically unified country. At this stage of North-South coalition, various cooperative apparatuses would be established and operated and their legal and organizational aspects would be systematized through mutual agreement.

In the final and third stage of completing the unified state, the political systems of the North and South would be totally integrated through a systematic union in order to culminate the process of unification into a single state and a single nation. In other words, a unified government would be formed through general elections held under the Unification Constitution as peaceful reunification is finalized. Under the directives, the unified nation would have the mandate of all citizens involved and would constitute a democratic state in which individual freedom and welfare, and human dignity would be guaranteed.

On the other hand, North Korea's proposal for 'Directives for Korea Democratic Federal Republic' was set forth as a finalized version for unification at the 6th Labor Party Congress held on October 10, 1980 by specifying in detail and systematizing existing directives.[135] The North proposes the three principles of freedom, peace and ethnic integration as the logical basis and rationale behind a Korea Democratic Federation. The argument is that the most realistic and rational method for reunification under the principles of autonomy, peace and solidarity is one which grants autonomy as well as equal privileges and responsibilities to both sides by accommodating existing ideologies and systems.

As for the organization, responsibilities and function of a federal apparatus, each side should have an equal number of representatives with an appropriate number of overseas Korean residents to form a 'Supreme People's Council' or 'Resident Federal Committee' to provide guidance to local governments and oversee joint undertakings, while the name of the nation, which would pursue a neutral foreign policy, would be the Korea Democratic Federal Republic.[136] Such directives, however, have begun to show signs of change since Kim Il-sung's New Year Address in 1991.

The points of specific changes to be noted are: first, differentiation with systematic unification[137] by arguing for a federation based on 'one people, one nation, two systems, two governments'; second, elimination of possibilities for complete political unification by leaving systematic unification for posterity; third, dismissal of systematic unification as a way of 'annexing the weaker side' by taking the experience of East and West Germany; and lastly, strengthening the power of local governments.

All the points have the shared characteristic of adding and emphasizing the element of a federation. However, the North's proposal has several inherent weaknesses for it to be seriously considered as a

[135] Ibid., pp. 229-233.

[136] The 10 major policy directives of the Democratic Coryo Confederate Republic are as: independent policy making; pursuit of universal democracy and ethnic solidarity; conduct of economic cooperation and guarantee for autonomous economic development; activation of exchange in the fields of science, culture and education and united development; of science and technology, national culture and arts and education; linkage of transportation and communication networks and guarantees for unrestricted usage of related facilities; stabilization of living for the working class including laborers and farmers and systematic improvement of welfare; easing of military tension and organization of a united army for resistance to external forces; support for the privileges and welfare of Koreans resident overseas; reassessment of pre-unification external relations and coordination for the foreign activities of the two autonomous governments; and, pursuit of a peace-oriented external policy

[137] 'Systematic unification' is a terminology used by North Korea in referring to the unification of regimes proposed by the South's 'Directives for Unification', which calls for the establishment of a single democratic republic of 'one people, one nation, one system, one government' through the participation of all citizens in a democratic procedure and method, *i.e.* the establishment of a government and parliament through free elections.

proposal for unification. In particular, the so-called 'four prerequisites for independent and peaceful reunification' constitutes serious problems.

The four prerequisites of the realization of a democratic society (through the abolishment of anti-Communist and security laws), the liquidation of the South Korean regime, the withdrawal of US forces in the South, and unification based on the principles of autonomy, peaceful unification and national solidarity are all aimed at forming a favorable environment for the 'South *Chosun* People's Revolution'. In effect, they signify the disarmament of the South Korean social order. Thus, the proposal for a Korea Democratic Federation is but a cover for plans to achieve a communist unification through the establishment of a communist regime in the South. The plan simply calls for the eventual absorption of the South by the existing communist regime of the North.

B. A New Proposal of Five-Stage Reunification Model

The existing official plans and policies for the national reunification have all been products of the Cold War. They thus possess inevitable limits in accommodating the many changes in the present era of reconciliation and peaceful co-existence. North Korea's proposal is merely a 'wish list' reflecting their fears as the less-populated and less-developed side and is thus riddled with inconsistencies. South Korea's suggestions is more realistic, but seems to be inadequate for it simply has stated a present-mid stage-unification route without detailing what specific courses this route will entail.

This chapter outlines an alternative plan by improving upon South Korea's suggestions for a Korean National Community (September 11, 1989) and North Korea's plan for a Korea Democratic Federation (August 15, 1960, June 23, 1973, and October 10, 1980). Further developments such as the joint entry of North and South Korea into the membership of United Nations and mutual agreements on reconciliation, non-aggression and economic exchange and cooperation very much warrants consideration of the proposed unification plan. The strategic plan entails economic integration, social integration, political integration and military integration which is summarized in <Tables XIII-2> and <XIII-3>. A comparative review of the new approach is contrasted with official plans by the two governments in <Table XIII-4>. On the theoretical side, it borrows from D. Mitrany's functionalist theories[138], and on the practical aspects, it draws upon Yemen's example.

The functionalism of David Mitrany (1943) is built on the foundational premise that human beings achieve social unity in the process of seeking to satisfy their desires such as the pursuit of one's own livelihood and security. Similarly, widespread cross- national exchanges that arise due to the need for division or sharing of labor, information, medical knowledge and common efforts to overcome natural disasters can produce a sharp necessity for mutual cooperation. Such a process call for a political integration and develops into grassroots social movements. This is an integration spontaneously generated, through movements that work themselves upwards.[139]

According to Professor A. Etzxioni (1968), there are three elements that determine the character of unification for a nation or society.[140] The first is force that can maintain the system. This is the ability to make order prevail, guarantee security to citizens and protect the system from external forces. The second is utility to be gained from actively taking part in the establishment the community. That is, members should have an incentive to be a member such as economic interests, social status and stability. The third is a symbolic strength that enables members to feel an oneness.

When different regimes combine by force along the lines mentioned above, they form an empire. When regimes come together in pursuit of common interests, the integrated system is called a Commonwealth or Confederation. A Federal Union rests on the solidarity of the people which exercises a powerful symbolic strength on the people. From the above, it is highly recommended that the Korean unification should follow a course which starts from a national community (commonwealth) to a Confederation and eventually to a Federal Union.

[138] David Mitrany, *A Working Peace System*, London: Royal Institute of World Affairs, 1943.

[139] Yong-soon Yim, "The Logic of Approaching Unification in Stages," Myong Bong Chang ed., *Structure and Prospects of North and South Korean Politics*, Seoul: Han-ol Academy, 1992, pp. 459-483.

[140] Requoted from Yong-Soon, Yim Ibid., p.474.

<Table XIII-2> Proposed Five-Stage New Reunification Model

Stage One: **Normalization** of Relations and Promotion of Mutually Beneficial Economic Cooperation
one people, two systems, two nations, two governments

↓

Stage Two: **Economic Integration** (one mixed form of national economy, enhancing of a self-reliant national economic structures)
one people, one economic system, two social systems, two political systems, two nations, two central governments

↓

Stage Three: **Social Integration** (the construction of an advanced democratic welfare society)
one people, one economic and social system, two political systems, one confederate country, one central government with two regional governments
The name of the country: The Democratic Confederate Republic of Korea

↓

Stage Four: **Political Integration** (the enactment of the reunification constitution by the National Reunification Council)
one people, one economic, social and political system; one federal country; one central government with two regional governments
The name of the country: The Democratic Federal Republic of Korea

↓

Stage Five: **Military Integration** (establishment of a reunified nation through free general elections)
one people, one system, one country, one government
The name of the country: The Democratic Republic of Korea

Joseph S. Nye (1971)[141] lists the following four elements required for the unification of a state. First, institutional integration is vital, at least in part. Second, coordination of policies is needed. Third, willingness on both parts to accept and understand the other side is required. Last, the formation of a Community of Security in which neither side would ever use violence on the other has to be stipulated.

On the other hand, bloody conflicts of unified Yemen, where alliance of the erstwhile hostile regions was achieved over summit meetings and mutual agreements rather than one-sided absorption, suggests a great deal. North and South Yemen agreed on the basic principles of unification in the Cairo Conference of 1972 and drew up a constitution for the unified state in 1981. They were made into a single state in May of 1990.[142] At present, however, the communist Yemen People's Republic of the South, and the Yemen Arab Republic of the North which followed in Great Britain's footsteps and adapted a liberal democratic regime, have demonstrated differences in political, economic, social and cultural traditions present obstacles to unification despite a common language.

In the case of unified Yemen, a hastened unification has produced strains in the accommodation of a standardized communist regime into a plural liberal one. Administrative inefficiencies and conflicts in living styles have emerged as serious problems. Voices repressed under the communist dictatorship

141 Joseph S. Nye, *Peace in Parts: Integration and Conflict in Regional Organization*, Boston: Little Brown and Co., 1971.

142 Myong-bong Chang, "Research on the Unification Constitution of North-South Yemen," *Research on Public Law*, No. 21, 1993, pp. 113~150.

regained their freedom and various tribes spoke out with their own demands. Most seriously, a mistaken decision to put troops under separate commands led to infringements and control of Southern troops by the militarily superior to Northern ones.

Unified Yemen was not successful in dealing with the differences in living standards (at the time of unification, GNP per capita for the North and South were US$682 and US$420, respectively), nor in building a basis for trust between the two regions. Yemen did not carry out a national referendum as Germany did; its was a top-down, 'downwards unification' carried out from the top in summit conferences while Germany's was a bottom-up, upward process. As a result, bloody confrontations erupted not long after unification. On June 30, 1994, a truce was drawn between the two parties, but North Yemen has ended up occupying the Southern capital.

It must not be forgotten that South and North Korea have gone through a bitter war, and now confront each other with even more weaponry. There is also an enormous difference in their economic capabilities.

A report prepared by the central bank of South Korea on June 10, 1994 estimates North Korea's GDP for 1993 to be US$20.5 billion, showing a 4% decrease from US$21.1 billion in 1992. This sum is merely one sixteenth of South Korea's GDP for the same year. It must be taken note of that this gap is growing larger every year. In 1985, South Korea's GDP was 5.94 times of North Korea's. In 1990, it was 10.3 times as large. A comparison of economic actors on both sides in 1990 showed that there were twice as many in the South.

<Table XIII-3> A Proposal of the South-North Economic Cooperation Model

First Phase of the New Reunification Process	**Stage One :** 1) South and North Koreas' Simultaneous Admission into the UN (September 17, 1991) 2) The Reconciliation, Non-aggression, Exchanges and Cooperation Treaty (December 13, 1991) 3) The Basic Treaty needed 4) South Korea's Legislation on North-South Economic Exchange
	↓
	Stage Two: 1) Increase of Indirect Trade through Third Countries; Launching of Direct Trade under Deferred Payment Regime, Intermediary Trade and Swing System 2) Promotion of Personnel Exchanges (including separated families, industrialists and engineers)
	↓
	Stage Three: 1) Introduction of North Korea to International Financial Institutions (ADB, IBRD etc.) 2) Participation in the TRADP (Tumen River Area Development Program) 3) Opening to each other, Sea Channels, Roads, Railroads, Ports and Accompanying Facilities
	↓
Second Phase of the New Reunification Process	**Stage Four :** 1) Treaty for the South-North SEZ (Special Economic Zone) 2) Construction of Changdan SEZ Declaration of the SEZ as a Free Trade Area (no tariff and no trade restrictions) 3) Joint ventures for a Capital and Technological Cooperation under an Investment Protection Treaty · joint development of maritime and tourism resources and minerals · joint ventures in the manufacturing sector
	↓
	Stage Five : 1) Customs Union-single Market-Economic Union (free flow of personnel, capital, goods and services)- Currency Union (a single currency) 2) Economic Integration (a single mixed type economic system)-Enhancing a Self-Reliant National Economy 3) Exchange of Telecommunications and a Partial Liberalization of Movement of People across the Border

<Table XIII-4> Comparisons of the New Reunification Proposal with the Official Proposals of the South and the North

	North Korea	South Korea	New Proposal
Preconditions	- Democratization in the South; easing tensions; removal of war risks; and US renouncement of two Korea policies and its intervention in domestic affairs	None	- Mutually beneficial trade and economic cooperation
Philosophy for Unification	- Self-reliance, peace, unity of Koreans	- Self-reliance, peace, and democracy	- Unity and reconciliation of the ethnic Korean community; construction of an industrial democratic welfare society; and peace
Approaches to Unification	1. Victory thru battles on unification fronts	1. Functional unification favoring an internal collapse of the North thru a full opening	1. Political, social, and economic system based on a consensus
	2. A radical approach without intermediate steps	2. A gradual approach with intermediate political integration	2. A gradual five-step approach with intermediate economic and political steps
	3. Priority on political and military talks	3. Importance on multi-contacts in economic, social and cultural areas	3. Importance on mutually beneficial economic cooperation, promotion of a special economic zone and capital & technological cooperation
	4. Pursuit of unification through direct North-South efforts disregarding surrounding major powers	4. Awareness of changes in the environment but linkage to its proposal not strong enough	4. Positive response to changes in Northeast Asia, link between changes in the environment and unification process
	5. Emphasis on territorial integration under 'one Chosun' doctrine, emphasis on class rather than national identity	5. Pursuit of unification under the notion of an ethnic Korean community	5. The same as the proposal of South Korea
Procedures for Political Integration	Lack of details	Enactment of a reunification constitution at a North-South Council, and formulation of unification legislation and administration through free elections	Pursuit of a gradual economic, social, political and military integration based on experiences in mutual cooperation (for the final stage, the same as the proposal of South Korea)
Form of Reunified Country	Neutral federal state	Non-federal bicameral democratic republic	Non-federal bicameral democratic welfare society

Source: Yang-Taek Lim, *A New Proposal for the Korean Reunification Based on Its Economic Integration,* Seoul: Mail Economic Daily Press, November 1993.

3. Economic Integration

A. Recent Agreements

Economic cooperation between South and North Korea, is the major themes of this chapter. The author begins with looking at agreements that have been reached in the area of trade between South and North Korea.

With the legislation of the Act on South-North Exchanges and Cooperation in 1990, an institutional framework was prepared for the shipment and introduction of commodities between South and North Korea.

The Complementary Agreement on Trade Cooperation, which was concluded in 1992 for the fulfillment and execution of the South and North Korea Basic Agreement, specifically affirms to promote reconciliation and non-aggression and states the objectives and necessary procedures for trade and cooperation, given the common goals of unified and balanced development of the national economy and improvement of the Korean national welfare. To this end, it should promote trade of commodities between the two Koreas and joint investment and development of resources through intra-regional exchanges.

South and North Korea have agreed not only on the trade of goods, but also on the joint development of various natural resources, mutual cooperation in the fields of industry, agriculture, finance and tourism. The details were supposed to be agreed upon by the North and South Korea Economic Exchange and Joint Cooperation Committee in November 1992, however, North Korea's nuclear program development resulted in the cancellation of the cooperative effort.

Although direct contracts between traders in South and North Korea are permitted,[143] referral to the concerned government authorities for inspection and approval is very much recommended, because trade and economic cooperation must be conducted according to appropriate procedures. The price of traded goods will be determined by international market prices, but taking into account the specificity of price systems in socialist country like North Korea. Payments are to be made principally in settlement accounts, but other modes of payment may be possible through mutual agreement. Exchange of various data and laws relating to industrial standards and adoption of measures to protect each side's technological rights, patents and trademarks, were also agreed upon.

To support such cooperative efforts, opening up of the trade routes - water, land, air- between the two regions became on important issue. The gradual opening of sea routes between the ports in South Korea's Inchon, Pusan and Pohang and North Korea's Nampo, Wonsan, and Chungjin, land routes such as the Kyungeuson Railway by connections to Munsan and Kaesong, and air routes between Kimpo Airport in South Korea and Sunan Airport in North Korea were also agreed upon in line with the agenda of expanding cooperation and easing intra-regional military tensions with temporary transportation routes.

Furthermore, if the exchange of mail and electrical communication through Panmunjom were realized by the resumption of talks, a basis for concluding a detailed agreement on the procedures necessary for trade and cooperation would have been prepared. As stated above, a realistic legal basis for cooperation between South and North Korea has already been adopted and became effective in 1992, as per the South and North Korea Basic Agreement and the Complementary Agreement on South and North Korea Trade Cooperation. However, a follow-up agreement to implement the two agreements is not in place yet. As North Korea's nuclear crisis blocked talks in 1992, economic cooperation also suffered a setback. Therefore, trade is still being conducted mostly through third countries with only rare cases of direct business contacts.

This background information naturally leads to such fundamental questions how to optimally relate the issues - Korean reunification and economic cooperation between the two regions. There must be a rational approach to Korean reunification. The goal must be minimization of the cost of reunification. With these questions in mind, the author would like to present a new model for Korean reunification. The establishment of a special economic region between South and North Korea as an experimental site for a unified economy will be a core recommendation of this approach.

[143] This section was adopted after several disputes in the North-South Korea Exchange Cooperation Sub-Committee. It reflects the perspective of the South: due to differences in the two regimes, it is hard to rely entirely on contracts between the transaction parties.

B. Importance of Economic Integration

Stage One of the proposed approach to the Korean reunification must aim at recovering mutual trust and pursuing economic integration into a single self-reliant national economy across the peninsula. In the follow-up stage, the two sides would experiment with a post-unification economic system by creating a North-South Special Economic Zone in Changdan County at the DMZ. Through joint administration of this zone, South and North will accelerate their respective experiences in capital and technological cooperation. Indeed, it would be a learning curve toward achieving effective economic integration. A closer cooperation will be promoted through joint ventures in the manufacturing sector and joint development of mining, maritime and tourism resources.

The economic union would progress in the following order: the construction of a Special Economic Zone to be followed by the establishment of an alliance on tariffs (liberalization of trade and application of common tariff policies), the creation of a common market with complete opening of the two markets and free flow of production elements, the formation of an 'economic union' (free flow of labor, capital, goods and services across the peninsula), and the denomination of a 'currency union' (the establishment of a single currency and the central bank).

The free trade zone would be designed to allow for a free movement of goods and services between the two Koreas of the economic union through a sharp and progressive reduction and eventual elimination of all tariffs and non-tariff barriers. The creation of the zone will mark the beginning of the economic union. It follows that the economic union of South and North Korea will maintain an independent tariff and non-tariff system towards non-member countries[144]. The creation of the free trade zone will be followed by a Customs Union and the establishment of a Common Market. A customs union ensures unrestricted trade of merchandise and a single tariff system towards non-member countries; a common market ensures free flow of production elements, labor and capital.

The German Economic Union, which was a precursor to the West German absorption of the Eastern socialist economic system, defined market economy as the common economic order. Under such a Union, East Germany was required to accept the basic system of the West and to forgo its former centralized economic system. The German Economic Union put an end to the inter-German trading system (Innerdeutscher Hadel), which had gone on for some 40 years after Germany's partition under the First State Treaty and replaced it with free trade within the Union.

It is unclear whether Korean unification will take the form of absorption (as in the case of German) or unification by conference (as in the case of Yemen); chances are that it will have an element of both. It will be a Korean model with its own distinctive features. There is no doubt that a capitalist economy is more productive than a socialist one, and that North Korea will inevitably carry out Chinese-style reforms. The Korean economic union will lead to a gradual transition of the North Korean socialist economy into a capitalist one with emphasis on the role of the respective governments in providing infrastructure and welfare systems.

As is apparent in the German case, caution must be exercised in carrying out a currency union. Germany implemented the policy dictating the abolition of the East German *Ostmark* and its replacement by the West German *Deutsche Mark. Ostmarks* were made convertible into *Deutsche Marks* at a 1:1 ratio. Such an unprecedented measure was carried out since the unified government decided to overlook the functions of the market and concentrated instead on the political effects by way of strengthening national solidarity. Provision for the post-unification costs came to haunt the Germans. This measure only further weakened the competitiveness of East German products, discouraged investment and contributed to widespread adverse reactions. Indeed, there is much to learn from the German experience.

A currency union for the two Koreas must be based on a convertibility ratio which reflects the real value of the two currencies. There is hardly a case for a replication of the German model in Korea. Indeed, the Korean case does not have to adhere strictly to any predetermined model. Peoples in the two Koreas are a homogeneous people seeking reunification. In addition, the creation of a customs union presupposes the

---

144 According to the extent of elimination of tariffs, the common zone could be classified as a 'Preferential Trading Club' or a 'Free Trade Area'. The former simply reduces tariffs whereas the latter eliminates them. There is, however, a similarity in that both systems maintain an independent tariff system towards non-members.
Examples of each can be found in the 1932 British Commonwealth. Further examples of free trade areas include the Latin American Integration Association and the North American Free Trade Agreement. Because an autonomic character is assigned to free trade areas, these do not take part in the GATT as single negotiation units.

conversion of the North Korean economy into a market economy. At present, North Korea does not even have a clear-cut definition or system of tariffs and taxes. Therefore, implementation of a shared tariff system will necessarily require North Korea to acknowledge free economic activity involving individual right to personal property, and private businesses' rights to maximize profit.

Consequently, interim steps towards an economic union such as the creation of a customs union and a common market, are not necessarily applicable to the Korean case. The creation of a free trade zone along the DMZ will enable both regions to gain lessons in economic cooperation, maintaining their independent economic structures and systems of foreign relations. There will be no serious threat to the North Korean economic system. The foundation of a North-South free trading zone at Changdan County should be aggressively expedited as an institutional apparatus for mutual trade.

Beginning in 1995 after the energization of inter-Korean economic cooperation, the volume of South-North commodity exchanges has risen sharply to exceed US$250 million annually. This means that South Korea has become the third largest trading partner of North Korea after Japan and China.

In South-North commodity exchanges, the South mainly imports from the North such primary products as gold ingots, zinc ingots, steel and farm and fishery products, while the South's exports to the North mainly consist of chemical goods like polyethylene and LDPE. Processing-on-consignment projects, in which the South provides raw and secondary materials to the North, which in turn processes them and delivers processed goods to the South, have increased since 1993. Due to such projects, textile goods accounted for more than 50%.

To energize South-North commodity exchanges, there should be a switch to a direct exchange system along with the development of more items which could feasibly be exchanged so as to reduce expenses stemming from the indirect method. Institutional devices to support commodity exchanges, such as the opening of a inland transportation route should also be prepared.

C. Expansion of Processing-on-Consignment Projects

Commodity exchanges through processing-on-consignment is a method in which the South provides raw and secondary materials to the North, where they are processed before being shipped back to the South. Therefore, this is a method which can serve to deepen cooperative relations between the South and the North.

Processing on consignment between the two sides, begun in 1991, has increased sharply in amount from US$7 million in 1993 to US$25.7 million in 1994, US$46 million in 1995 and further to US$74 million in 1996. It accounted for about 25% of the total trade in 1996.

An increasing number of industries are engaged in processing-on-consignment projects with the North, taking advantage of know-how enriched through early-stage textile processing on consignment. The projects include the assembly of color television sets, automobile electric wiring and the assembly of bicycle wheels. A total of 34 industries, large and small, promoted such projects in 1996 alone.

The sharp expansion of processing-on-consignment projects was attributable to low wages in North Korea, the relatively high skill level of North Korean workers and also the belief that the promotion of such projects could help pave the way for future full-fledged investment in North Korea.

It also seems that the North prefers this method as they can earn foreign currency while only using labor without making investment, not to mention helping them to develop their underdeveloped light industries.

D. Increase in Commodity Exchange

With the legislation of the law on South-North Exchanges and Cooperation in 1990, an institutional framework was prepared for the shipment and introduction of commodities between South and North Korea. Beginning in 1995 after the energization of inter-Korean economic cooperation, the volume of South-North commodity exchanges has risen sharply exceed US$250 million annually. This means that South Korea has become the third largest trading partner of North Korea after Japan and China. In South-North commodity exchanges, the South mainly imports from the North such primary products as gold ingots, zinc ingots, steel, and farm and fishery product, while the South's exports to the North mainly consist of chemical goods like polyethylene and LDPE.

Processing-on-consignment projects, in which the South provides raw and secondary materials to the North, which in turn processes them and delivers textile goods accounted for more than 50% shipments to the North, and the ratio of materials being exported from the South to the North to the materials which are exported from the North back to the South has improved from 10 to 1 in the initial stage to 3 to 1 in 1996.

Inter-Korean commodity exchanges have been made through indirect exchanges because North Korea does not formally recognize commodity exchanges with the South yet, whereby negotiations, contracts and settlement are made through foreign commissioners in most cases. Lately, cases in which negotiations are made directly with North Korean parties while contracts and settlement are made through foreign commissioners have been increasing.

As the number of firms participating in inter-Korean commodity exchanges and the number of items exchanged have been on the increase, the scale of commodity exchanges has been swelling steadily.

E. Economic Cooperation

1) The Measures for Expanding Intra-Korean Economic Cooperation

South Korean government made, on April 30, 1998, the Measures for Expanding Intra-Korean Economic Cooperation, which can be categorized by exchanges of contact and visit, trade and cooperation project. The objectives are: to encourage the private sector to lead the economic cooperation with the North by respecting individual business' independent decisions with regard to its involvement in intra-Korean commerce; and to establish an atmosphere conducive to intra-Korean economic cooperation while preventing excessive competition and unfair trade among the participants in intra-Korean commerce.

As for exchanges of contact and visit, in general, any qualified petition to visit North Korea is now promptly approved, making it easier for CEOs of large business groups and leaders of business associations to visit the North. Multiple visit permission, which was issued to only those applicants who were with permission for cooperation project, is now issued to any applicant whose petition to visit is approved. The term of validity for permission to make contact with North Korean resident is extended from one year to three years. The number of days required in processing petitions for contact is reduced from twenty to fifteen and that for visit from thirty to twenty.

Looking at trade, while the impact of the changes on domestic market is kept at the minimum level, the number of 'categorically permitted' items is increased so that the number of the items that still require import permit is reduced from 205 to 178. The ban on export of manufacturing facilities is lifted in an effort to promote the commission-based processing trade between the two Koreas. The procedure for processing permits for import or export of materials used in cooperation project is streamlined.

With respect to cooperation projects, the ceiling on the size of investment an individual South Korean business can make in the North is completely removed. The restriction on intra-Korean investment is imposed through the adoption of a negative list of the business areas that are not allowed for joint venture. Permissions for 'cooperation partnership' and 'cooperation project' are simultaneously issued, particularly for those projects with the value of less than US$3 million.

In accordance with the government's policy of promoting economic cooperation for reconciliation and confidence building between the two Koreas, the government has approved (On January 8, 1999) cooperation partner status to Haejoo Co., Ltd. for the joint production and sales of North Korean seafood products, and on January 15, 1999, the application submitted by Hyundai Marine Co., Hyundai Engineering & Construction Co., Keumkang Development Industrial Co. to expand the scope of Mt. Kumgang project to include the developing of the area.

With this approval, a total of 41 firms have earned cooperation partnership status and a total of 15 firms have earned cooperation project status to begin their actual businesses since the enactment of the Measures for Revitalization of Intra-Korean Economic Cooperation of November 1994.

2) Current Status of Economic Cooperation between South and North Korea

(1) Trade

The South Korean government revised the Proclamation of the Procedure for Export and Import of the Goods for Intra-Korean Trade on June 19. However, despite the various efforts of the South Korean government to ease the regulations on intra-Korean commerce and simplify the legal procedure related to intra-Korean trade, the amount of intra-Korean trade, which had been steadily increasing over years, drastically decreased due to an economic recess resulted from the recent financial crisis. The volume of intra-Korean trade from January to July, 1998 showed a 45.0% decrease in comparison with the volume recorded over the same period last year.

The South Korea's major imports from the North include textile, agricultural and fishery products, ferrous metals and steel products while its major exports to the North are textile, various primary industry products and non-ferrous metal products.

<Table XIII-5> Intra-Korea Trade: January ~ July, 1997 and 1998 (unit: US$1,000)

	Jan. ~ Jul. 1997	Jan. ~ Jul. 1998	Growth Rate (%)
Import	116,405	40,248	- 65.4
Export	65,615	59,802	- 8.9
Total	182,020	100,049	- 45.0

Source: Monthly Report on Intra-Korean Interchange & Cooperation, Ministry of Unification, Korea, 1999.

(2) Economic Cooperation

Despite the announcement of 'Measures for Expansion of Intra-Korean Economic Cooperation', South Korean businesses have not been able to expand their investment in the North Korea because their investment capabilities were much weakened due to the recent financial crisis that eventually forced the South Korean government to call for an IMF bail-out.

Since the launching of the Kim Dae-jung Administration, seven applications for cooperation partnership and six for cooperation projects have been approved, bringing their total numbers to thirty seven and thirteen respectively.

In particular, owing to the Measures for Expansion of Intra-Korean Economic Cooperation which allowed CEO of large business groups to visit North Korea, Chung Ju-yung, the honorary chairman of Hyundai, was able to visit the North.

In addition, the International Corn Foundation and Doorye Foundation of Agricultural Association are currently working on an agricultural cooperation project aimed at exploring a fundamental solution to the food shortage in North Korea.

<Table-XIII-6> Permits for Cooperation Partnership Issued under the Kim Dae-jung Administration

Applicant	Project
Miheung Food *	Gathering and processing of fishery products
Ansung Development	Establishing a sesame oil factory
Doorye Foundation*	Establishing a joint plantation in the Najin-Sonbong Zone
International Corn Foundation	Experimental cultivation of corn and joint research on corn farming
Hyndai Marine, Inc., Hyundai Construction, and Kumgang Development Industry *	Mt. Kumgang tourism project
Seiwon Communication, Inc.	Agency business for the sponsorship of the N. Korean Olympic Committee for the 13th Asian Games
Korea Land, Inc.*	Development and consulting N. Korean real estate
Taeyoung Fishery / LG*	Scallop cultivation and related business
Sunghwa International Group	Establishment of Wonjong International Free Market and management of Sunghwa Department Store in Pyongyang

* denotes the applicant who is also issued the permit for cooperation project for this particular project.

Source: Same as in <Table XIII-5>

3) Joint Ventures [145]

The expansion of trade deals in low-tech processed products with North Korea will not only solve the structural adjustment problems of South Korea's light industries which currently have a vast extent of idle facilities, but also provide a building block for its future for full-scale investments in the North. To facilitate the South-North trade based on processing of raw materials into low value-added tradables, specific follow-up actions that need to be considered are: 1)permission for technical labor forces and entrepreneurs of the South to visit North Korea; 2) expansion of imports of production facilities from the South to the North; 3) launching of cooperative small-scale businesses and conglomerates; 4) institutionalization of investment risk coverages; and 5) further development of foreign export markets for commissioned products.

In January 1994 the North Korean government enacted a new joint venture Act, which newly defined prospective applicants as 'foreign corporations and individuals as well as Koreans living outside the Republic' (see table XIII-7). This can be understood as an invitation to South Korean investment, as the phrasing formerly restricted investors to 'commercial entrepreneurs from Japan and Koreans living abroad'. Article 7 of the same act promises a reduction in taxes or advantages given for the use of real property to joint ventures initiated by Koreans.

The North Korean policy on foreign investment[146] specifies the following characteristics:

First, the laws in question do not officially mention South Korea, but they do not rule out South Koreans. This is taken to mean that North Korea will permit investments by the South to a limited extent as long as they will not threaten the North Korean economic system.

Second, North Korea's readiness to open its economy can be sensed from constitutional amendments of the new foreign capital act, the promotion of Najin-Sunbong into a special zone under the direct control of the government and the expansion of its range merit with special attention.

Third, the preferential treatment of the Free Trade Area over other regions and the codification of this treatment into relevant laws indicate that Chinese-style laws of economic reform will prevail for a while.[147]

As the cases of South-North joint-ventures, we many start with the Minjok Industrial General Co., the first joint-venture between the South and the North. The Daewoo Corp. obtained a permit from the government on May 17, 1995, to engage in a cooperative project and established the Minjok Industrial General Co., the first South-North joint-venture firm, with the North Korean Samcholli General Co. on January 26, 1996.

The total amount invested in the Minjok Industrial General Co. was US$10.5 million with Daewoo's share being US$5.1 million. With its head office in Pyongyang, North Korea, the company built production plants on a plot extending about 74,000 square meters near Sinhung-dong in the Hangku District of Nampo to produce shirts, blouses, jackets and bags. The plants went into operation on August 19, 1996.

The Minjok Industrial General Co. has a board comprising six board members selected from both sides. It has about 1,300 employees with those in the production line being managed by the plant operators and those in general management including labor affairs, general affairs and accounting being managed jointly by Daewoo and the North. Currently, the plants turn out shirts, jackets, leather apparel and bags.

---

[145] For joint ventures in North Korea display the following distinctive features, see Yang-Taek Lim, "A New Proposal for the Reunification of the Two Koreas: Economic Issues", *Journal of Asian Economics,* Vol. 8, No. 4, Winter 1997.

[146] For a detailed discussion, see Yang-Taek Lim, 「TRADP and Cooperation among South and North Korea and Russia」, Seoul: The Institute for Sino-Soviet Studies Hanyang University", *Sino-Soviet Affairs,* Vol.20, No.2, Summer 1996.

[147] The Chinese Special Economic Zone and North Korea's future Free Trade Area are similar in that they share the goals of inducing foreign capital, promoting exports and acquiring high technology. However, the Special Economic Zone in China is an experimental area for economic reforms and seeks to promote the development of regional economies in all economic sectors. In addition, China has pursued a close link between the Zone and other areas.
On the contrary, North Korea has merely made the minimum legal preparation to allow the inflow of foreign capital in the Free Trade Area and is restricting investment sectors to engineering, basic facilities and tourist services. They have never intended the Area to be an experimental zone to carry out economic reforms: nor have they considered making links with other regions. Thus the North Korean Free Trade Area is a temporary resort to escape the present economic crisis by attracting foreign capital and technology; it is by no means a Chinese Special Economic Zone.
Nonetheless, China has not liked seeing her only socialist ally be the object of US-led economic reform path. To this extent China has consistently urged North Korea to adopt an open policy.

<Table XIII-7> A Chronological List of Measures for the Economic Opening of North Korea

Date of Promulgation	Name of Law
09/08/1984	Joint Operation Law (amended 01/1994)
03/07/1985	Income Tax Law on Joint Operation Firms (abolished)
03/07/1985	Income Tax Law on Foreigners (abolished)
03/25/1985	Ordinance of the Joint Operation Law (amended 10/1992)
05/17/1985	Ordinance of the Income Tax Law on Joint Operation Firms (abolished)
05/17/1985	Ordinance of the Income Tax Law on Foreigners (abolished)
12/28/1991	Cabinet Resolution on the Creation of a Free Economic and Trade Zone
04/09/1992	Article 37 of the Constitution (basis for joint operation and ventures with foreign concerns)
10/05/1992	Law on Foreigners' Investments
10/05/1992	Law on Foreigners' Firms
10/05/1992	Tax Law on Foreign Investments and Foreigners
01/31/1993	Law on Foreign Currency Control
01/31/1993	Law on the Free Economic & Trade Zone
01/31/1993	Law on the Leasing of Real Estate
10/27/1993	Law on Foreign Investment Banks
11/24/1993	Law on Foreigners' Entry into the Free Trade Zone
12/30/1993	Law on Labor Regulations in Foreign Invested Firms
01/20/1994	Operation Laws on Foreign Firms
03/ /1994	Law on Free Trade Ports

Source (rearranged by the author from): Jong-ryul Bae, "North Korean Policy on Foreign Capital and on Revitalizing Investment from Abroad", *How to Open the Era of North-South Economic Cooperation,* Unification & the Economy Research Conference, March 15, 1994. (The Sae Gae Ilbo, June 1,1994)

Major South Korean conglomerates, including Lucky-Goldstar and Samsung, have been pursuing joint investment in heavy industries in North Korea, thus crossing over the limited dimensions of industrial activities related mostly to processing in light industries. High-level executives at Lucky-Goldstar have met high-ranking North Korean officials in Beijing, China in 1994 and agreed in principle to invest capital and technology in the Kimchaek Iron Foundry, the largest of its kind in North Korea. A Lucky-Goldstar executive had already previously received a proposal for joint investment as early as 1993. They have also received an invitation to participate in Seungli Machinery, a car assembly plant in the form of a joint venture or joint management and are examining a proposal from a Chinese corporation to invest in the construction of an expressway between mainland China and Chongjin.

Samsung has also received from North Korea an investment proposal in heavy industries including social infrastructure. A Samsung official said that it has decided to accept, through China's intermediation, North Korea's proposal for investment in harbor facilities in Chungjin port. In the case that North Korea returns fully to NPT and allows inspections from IAEA, the South Korean government is likely to pursue full-scale economic cooperation, involving expansion of direct trade, incorporation of joint ventures, and broad-based support of economic development in the North by the South. Industrial ventures into North Korea by individual corporations of South Korea will be centered on light industries, progressing to successive stages of more cooperation and expansion of scales of investment.

Prospective businesses include light industries (textiles, clothing, shoes) that have to be transferred to contain increases in unit costs of production, joint ventures (foodstuffs, electric and electronic instruments, chemicals) and activities related to social infrastructure (construction, iron and steel industry). Business conglomerates are expected to assume big roles, given their resource and capabilities in manpower, capital, industrial data- base, and perhaps most importantly, risk-bearing.

F. *Changdan* County Special Economic Zone

Yang-Taek Lim (1991, 1992, 1993, 1994 and 1995) proposed the establishment and management of a SEZ in Changdan County, an area in Korea's DMZ. The opening and reform of North Korea and the reduction of reunification costs, much of it through cuts in South-North military expenditures, need to be accelerated. Exchanges between South and North Korea entail many obstacles that have to be overcome. One of the core issues will be the international recognition of economic exchange in the SEZ as intra-regional rather than inter-state, in nature. A special economic area that is non-political and non-military and transcends ideology has to be established. Changdan County is recommended as the most appropriate area.[148]

Most importantly, this plan is realistic. North Korea has plans to develop the Mount Kumkang and Mount Baekdu regions into international tourist spots; Nampo, Wonsan, and Chongjin into SEZs; and the area connecting Habsan Island at the mouth of the Tumen River, China's Hunchun and Russia's Posiet into a SEZ. North Korea, however, is going through a systematic conflict and has not been successful in inducing the inflow of foreign capital due to problems with accumulated foreign debt and international credit and internal conflicts. Establishment of the SEZ would have the following effects;

First, a joint venture in the Mount Kumkang-Wonsan tourist development could be pursued by facilitating the push for a further opening of North Korea in the future. The SEZ would be able to induce foreign capital, improve balance of payments, increase employment and GNP for North Korea. It would also be an path window to which its doors could be opened. North Korea could administer the SEZ as a foreign enclave similar to special economic zones of China; this would minimize the risk of collapse of the ruling regime in North Korea. An independent economic policy, different from that for other areas of North Korea, could be applied to the SEZ. North Korea would be able to receive South Korea's capitals and technology, plus substantive inflow of know-how without language barrier. The joint ventures with South Korea would indeed be much tangible economic aid to help North Korea overcome its economic crisis.

Second, from a nationalistic perspective, the most significant aspect of the SEZ is the initiation of economic cooperation between South and North Korea. South-North Korean economic cooperation may follow China's Xiamen SEZ (near Taiwan Strait). Complementarily of the major trade items for the two Koreas must reinforce the case for establishing the SEZ. As much as 95% of South Korea's total exports are processed manufacturing goods. For North Korea, the ratio is just 25% (of which processed minerals make up 21%). The rest of North Korea's exports are primary goods. North Korea's work force and natural resources can be made productive with South Korea's capital and advanced technology.

Third, the SEZ can be used not only as a place for economic reform and opening up of North Korea but also as an experimental laboratory of a reunified Korea, as an experimental progress from a free economic trade area to alliance in taxation, to economic community, to economic integration, to political integration, and on to one reunified nation-state of Korea.

The realistic progression of stages in economic cooperation between South and North Korea may include the facilitation and promotion of exchange activities and trade deals in processing of low-tech products, the investment ventures inclusive of construction of industrial plants, and the establishment of organic industrial structures. Currently, South and North Korea have agreed to pursue effective economic cooperation through the transfer of South Korea's light industries toward enhancing intra-Korean competitiveness. However, the absence of adequate institutional structures encompassing political relations

---

[148] The following are the reasons why Changdan County was selected as the most appropriate region to establish a North-South Korea special economic zone. The five grounds for selection are as follows: a base on the DMZ, on a region within or close to the DMZ; a region that is suitable for building a city, according to its topography; a potential place to become a transportation center when traffic between the two countries are connected and facilities laid; a region that can be the centrifugal and expediting force for the development of nearby regions, and; a satisfactory region of the basic's concept of the North-South Korea SEZ and its functions.

Following the above basis for selection, Kyodong Province region, Kanghwa District region, Changdan County and Kaepung County were chosen according to an urban engineering approach. The four regions were researched again to select the best region which fit the conditions of a North-South Korea special economic zone. The following conditions of the four regions were researched with the aid of an urban engineering specialist: natural conditions, foundation establishments, economic conditions, and socio- political conditions.

There were few differences in natural conditions. Kanghwa District ranked the best in foundation establishments. Changdan County had the optimum conditions for economic and socio-political backgrounds. Thus, it has been concluded that Changdan County has the best conditions to establish a North-South Korea SEZ.

and guarantees for investment still persist. Thus, economic cooperation continues to remain in its preliminary stages.

For North Korea, its initiatives to establish exclusive industrial plants for South Korean corporations is a welcome step. This is expected to minimize intra-Korean frictions stemming from differences in the two political and economic regimes in the South and North. Therefore, if and when the nuclear problem is resolved, closer forms of economic cooperation, involving the establishment of exclusive plants in Nampo, Haeju, Chongjin, the development of Tumen River and Mount Kumkang, joint development of natural resources and the building of social infrastructure will expectedly follow.

Taking into account South Korea's present adverse trade situation characterized by high domestic production costs, rigidities in commerce with many import regulations and deterioration of international competitiveness from the rise of newly industrializing economies of Southeast Asia and China, the Korean reunification policy should be directed towards cooperation for the utilization of natural resources and trade in processing low-tech products.

4. Social Integration

A. Current Status of Socio-Cultural Exchanges

Kim Dae-jung Administration has actively promoted intra-Korean exchanges in various socio-cultural fields, particularly in academic, cultural, religious and journalistic areas. The underlying policy in such efforts was to increase contact, to have more dialogue and to expand cooperation with North Koreans. So far, this administration has made much greater progress in this area than what was achieved over several years in the past.

Since the start of the new administration in February, 1998, six cooperation partnership permits and five cooperation project permits have been issued, bringing up the total number in each category to 10 and 8, respectively.

<TableXIII-8> Some Noteworthy Cases of Socio-Cultural Exchanges in 1998

- Visit by a Sungkyunkwan University delegation to establish sisterhood relationship and discuss academic exchanges with North Korean colleges (April 28~May 5)
- The Little Angels Arts Troupe's Performance in Pyongyang (May 2~12)
- Visit to the historic Catholic sites by the Catholic Commission for Reconciliation of the Korean Nationals (May 15~22)
- Field trip to historic sites by the Institute of Unification Culture of The Joongang Ilbo, Inc. (July 7~21)
- Visit by a the Kyunghyang Shinmun Delegation to discuss the establishment of the Korean Culture Network (August 22~29)
- Visit by a team of the Dong A Ilbo news reporters to cover the Mt. Kumgang project (August. 27~September. 5)
- Visit by a Korean Welfare Foundation delegation to discuss the construction of a pharmaceutical factory (September 11~14)

<TableXIII-9> Permits for Socio-Cultural Exchanges Approved by the Kim Dae-jung Administration

Business Name	Project	Date of Approval
Supporters Association for Yenben College of Sciences and Technology*	Establishing Najin Institute of Sciences and Technology	Jan. 9, 1998. (Jun. 5, 1998.)
Munhwa Broadcasting Corporation	Producing a TV program about scenic and historic sites in North Korea	Mar. 13, 1998
Korean Welfare Foundation*	Establishing a pharmaceutical factory and a hospital	Apr. 8, 1998 (Jun 5, 1998)
Korean Photographers Association*	Holding a South-North photo exhibition and publishing a photo book	Apr. 29, 1998 (Apr. 29, 1998)
Sports Art Co.*	Producing a video firm about scenic and historic sites	Apr. 29, 1998 (Apr. 29, 1998)
Korean Institute of the Cultural Network (The Kyunghyang Shinmun)*	Making a database of North Korean culture	May 11, 1998 (Jun. 20, 1998)
Wooinbang Communication, Co.	Producing a TV documentary on famous mountains and historic sites in North Korea	Aug. 6, 1998

* denotes the applicant who is also issued the permit for cooperation project for this particular project.
-The dates inside ( ) are dates those permits are approved.
Source: Same as in <Table XIII-5>

B. South Korean Government Policy on Exchange of Separated Families

The government has given top priority to the issue of divided families in its North Korea and unification policy, asking the North to resume official dialogue on the issue. President Kim Dae-jung, both in his inauguration address in February 1998 and in the March 1 Independence Movement Day speech, called upon the North to redress the woes of the divided families. The administration also included the divided family issue in its list of 100 Most Important Administrative Tasks. The last inter-Korean government talks took place in Beijing between April 11~17, 1998, when South Korean government offered fertilizer to the North in exchange for setting up family reunion centers. The talks, however, broke down as the North refused to agree upon establishing family reunion centers.

Since then, as official channels for inter-Korean exchanges were non-existent, the government has been committed to supporting family exchanges through a neutral third country. Recently, the government started to subsidize family reunion expenses for elderly members of the divided families, making it easier for them to contact and reunite with their North Korean relatives in a third country.

On September 25, 1998, the government opened an information center for divided families as a part of its preparation for full-scale exchanges in the future. The center, which provides a database that includes a number of files on separated families, plans to receive new entrants sometime before the end of this year. At the same time, the government is working to revise related laws to streamline the application process for visiting North Korea, particularly making it easier for elderly members of divided families to apply. In the meantime, for this purpose several tentative measures were implemented on September.

North Korea, at best, maintains lukewarm attitude about making inter-Korean government efforts to resolve the issues of separated families. However, it has recently taken a policy of benign neglect on visits and exchanges between its citizens and South Korean groups and individuals because they bring in foreign currency. Throughout many years, the North has made a number of hollow overtures, such as the announcement it made on February 15, 1998 that it would set up an Address Center within the social security agency to locate separated families and the news Radio Pyongyang reported on July 5, 1998 that letters were exchanged between the members of divided families. Naturally, these actions have not produced any real changes in their wake, strongly suggesting that the North's overtures were merely rhetorical countermeasures to the efforts of South Korean government.

C. Humanitarian Aid to North Korea

Due to a constant decrease in agricultural productivity North Korea has been short of a million to two million tons of grain every year since the mid 1980s. Therefore, North Korea's food crisis is caused by structural problems such as the inherent, inefficiency of the socialist economy and the failure of the North Korean government to improve agricultural productivity of the country. Unlike many African countries, therefore, North Korea can overcome a large part of the crisis if it works hard to do so.

Regrettably, North Korea refuses to direct its resources to overcome the crisis and wastes them on military expansion and political propaganda instead. North Korea will be able to feed its people if it saves even a small fraction of what it spends on such counter-productive activities. A simple calculation shows that if the North Korean regime saves as little as 3% of its military spending, which is as big as US$150 million in total, it will have enough money to purchase one million tons of corn from abroad.

This is why it is impossible to resolve the North Korean famine with one-time humanitarian assistance. It will require a more fundamental approach which may include technical assistance and encouragement on North Korea's self-efforts to overcome the crisis.

Despite the communist regime's hostility toward it, the South Korean Government continues efforts to provide assistance to North Korea out of compatriotic love and humanitarian concerns. So far, the government has provided food and other commodities with a total worth of US$ 273 million, including 150,000 tons of rice delivered in 1995. Meanwhile, mainly through the Red Cross channel, South Korean NGOs have provided food and commodities with a total worth of US$32 million.

Notwithstanding the financial difficulties in its domestic economy, South Korean government resumed humanitarian aid to North Korea both at the government and civilian level. The government donated 50,000 tons of corn equivalent to North Korea through the WEP (World Food Program). On the private side, the portion of shipment was delivered to the North by the end of May, 1998 as agreed at the fifth round of the Red Cross talks earlier 1998. In addition, 40,000 tons of corn and 500 head of cattle donated by a business tycoon Chung Ju-young were also handed to the North.

Along with the emergency aid, South Korean government also provided various agricultural materials including fertilizer and promoted agricultural cooperation with the North in an effort to help North Korea to find a fundamental solution to its chronic food shortage.

For the first time in almost four years, the two Koreas held a government-to- government talk in Beijing last April to discuss the fertilizer aid and other issues of common concerns. On the private side, an attempt to launch a contract farming is currently being made. South Korean government has also taken several measures to increase contact between peoples of North and South Korea and to expand private aid to North Korea. The government also permitted intra-Korean joint ventures including a food processing plant, as a way to provide assistance to North Korea.

The new measures allowed the participation of NGOs in the delivery process and their visits to North Korea for the purpose of monitoring the distribution of aids, thereby providing a greater opportunity for them to make contact with North Koreans. Restrictions on media and individual businesses are also lifted so that they can host or sponsor fundraising activities for aiding North Korea. Under the leadership of the UN, the international community, too, increased aids to North Korea this year. The international efforts were concentrated on improving North Korea's agricultural productivity. On February 12, 1991 the UN organizations disclosed their plans for the fourth round of aid to North Korea. The projected size of the aid was US$416 million, a more than twice the amount donated last year.

WFP has announced an appeal for 658,000 tons of food, while the UNDP (United Nations Development Plan) and the IFAD (International Fund for Agricultural Development) focused on improving agricultural productivity. UNDP plans to finance US$200~300 million from 1998 to 2000 for a double-cropping project which will be managed jointly with North Korea. The UN organization will also provide the North with agricultural equipment and support for reconstructing its farming system. However, the participation of the international community in providing humanitarian aids to North Korea has recently declined due to the communist regime's apparent unwillingness to reform its agricultural system.

As previously discussed, it takes both emergency aid and structural assistance to help North Korea overcome its food crisis for good. The structural assistance includes aid for agricultural development and support to enhance North Korea's ability to earn hard currency. For this reason, South Korean government will provide emergency aids to North Korea for free, while helping the regime earn hard currency by promoting intra-Korean economic cooperation based on the principle of separating politics from business.

The government's assistance will be concentrated in the area of agricultural development. It will adhere to the principle of reciprocity in providing this type of assistance.

The principle of reciprocity, however, does not require North Korea to pay back an exact amount in return. It is rather a flexible principle because all it asks for is North Korea's sincere effort to change its attitude toward South Korea in response to its assistance. South Korean government has to insist upon this principle because its assistance is paid by its taxpayers' money and the taxpayers want to see significant progress in intra-Korean relations before their money is spent. At the same time, the government should continue to work closely with international organizations to increase the transparency in distribution of aids within North Korea and to persuade North Korea to reform itself in order to overcome its economic crisis.

Private aids, on the other hand, will be promoted in a way to increase contact between the peoples of the North and the South. The opinion of private organizations and individuals should be fully respected while their actions need to be carried out in an orderly manner.

D. Academic Exchanges

Academic exchanges between the South and the North, an area which contributes to enhancing mutual understanding between the two sides and improving inter-Korean relations, have been developing steadily. The area of exchanges has become more diversified and some of these exchanges have become regularized. However, they have yet to develop into direct exchanges between the two sides of Korea. In most cases, they take place in the form of joint participation in third countries together with Korean resident scholars and organizations abroad.

Most academic exchanges take place in China, mainly due to the North's passive stance on exchanges, the experiences by ethnic Korean scholars and organizations in the Yanbian area of China in exchanges with North Korea and the geographical proximity. One exception was an international seminar held in Pyongyang in November 1993 on the issue of post-war questions involving Japan, where two South Korean scholars attended and discussed the issue of obtaining compensation for those women forced by Japan to offer sex service to frontline Japanese soldiers during World War II.

Academic exchanges so far have mainly been held in the areas of Korean studies, history, the economy, unification and national security, science and technology, language, the environment and ecology.

Inter-Korean contacts held to promote academic exchanges jumped from nine cases involving 50 persons in 1993 to 24 cases (383 persons) in 1995 and 23 cases (179 persons) in 1996. In the first six months of 1997, there were three cases (24 persons).

E. Cultural and Art Exchanges

Cultural and art exchanges between the South and the North should be realized actively not only to surmount the heterogeneity that has deepened between the two sides as a result of ideological difference and to restore national homogeneity, but also to minimize the aftermath of cultural and psychological friction likely to arise after unification.

However, it has not been possible for cultural and art exchanges between the two sides to take place actively or regularly due to passivity on the part of North Korea, differences in the perception of culture and art between South and North Korea and also to the nature of performing arts, which require a large number of persons, significant expenses and a long preparatory period. Some contacts in this area have taken place in third countries under the aegis of Korean communities abroad.

For instance, the Korean Unification Arts Exhibition was held in Tokyo and Osaka, Japan in October 1993, in which 16 South Korean artists and three North Koreans participated. Again in September 1994, the Koreana Photo Exhibition was held in Yanji, China with five photographers from South Korea and three from the North participating.

5. MILITARY INTEGRATION

This section explains the literal meaning of military integration which inevitably follows the unification process and outlines the practical aspects which should be considered in depth in the course of such integration in light of the Korean peninsula's past history of armed conflict and present state of military confrontation.

A. The Concept and Types Military Integration

Myron Weiner identifies five political meanings of integration.[149] First, he assumes the existence of ethnically and culturally diverse societies and views integration as a process by which culturally or socially separated groups are joined into a single territorial unit and a national identity is established. This process has an intimate relationship with how citizens under distinct political regimes may be merged into a single territorial and national consciousness.

Second, the meaning of integration is related with the establishment of an apparatus for objective control which subjects lower-level administrative units or regions governing distinct cultural or social groups under central national authorities. Third, integration is a matter of linking the newly formed government with its new base of subjects.

Fourth, integration implies the achievement of a minimum degree of consensus needed for the maintenance of social order Last, integration entails the ability of society to form new organizations for the achievement of new goals. In summary, integration refers to the process of uniting different functional organizations or systems operating under distinct lines of authority and merging them into a single organization or system under a united line of authority [150]

However, integration of the military functions requires emphasis on the element of systematic unification rather than the simple bringing together of integration. Accordingly, military integration is a process of merging the various functions and organizations of different military forces into a single unit as well as a process of systematic unification of military activities, which results in integration between as well as within the militaries. Such integration can not be conducted through the internal planning of the militaries involved but must be done so in a parallel manner with integration in the political, economic and social arenas

In considering the possible timing of such integration between North and South Korea, it is obvious that the methodology will be a byproduct of the political integration and will be governed by developments in the unification negotiation process One clear point is that the military integration will be among the final stages of the Korean reunification encompassing integration in political, social and military fields as it will necessarily have to follow an agreement on political unification. If it may be assumed that North-South relations will follow the stages of coexistence → cooperative coexistence → reunification, the environment for such reunification may be differentiated into one where the North undergoes drastic changes and another in which it follows a more normal path and provides a stable situation

The former scenario may again be divided into a case where a temporary governing power emerges internally and normalizes the situation on its own and one in which no such power emerges and the country is thrown into chaos; in the second case, a method for political reunification, whether it be by force or agreement, will inevitably arise and in turn determine the suitable method of military integration. As for the latter, military integration will be determined by the extent or degree of privileges and rights the South is willing to grant to its partner in negotiations, and whether a merger or absorption type of reunification will ensue.

In either case, the method of military integration will range from one based on political agreement to one which occurs hierarchically, but it is certain that it will have to be part of the many practical tasks facing the two Koreas in their quest for reunification

---

[149] Myron Weiner, "Problems in Integration and Modernization Breakdowns", Jason Finkle and Richard W Gable (eds), *Political Development and Social Change,* New York John Wiley and Sons, Inc , 1966, pp 551~553 Referred from Lee Sung-ju, "North and South Korea's Approach Based on Integration Theory", *Transitional Issues for a Separated Nation,* Institute for Social Science Research, August 1991 pp 55~56

[150] Ibid , Hong-ki Chang, Ryang Lee and Man-jong Lee, *A Study on Military Integration between North and South Korea,* Seoul Korea Institute for National Defense, 1994, p. 89.

<Table XIII-10> demonstrates the different types of military integration processes based on the examples of Vietnam, Germany and Yemen.[151] In the case of Yemen which had been classified as a case of one-to-one merger, forcible unification through absorption took place four years after the original unification by agreement

<Table XIII-10> Types of Military Integration Processes

Type	Scenario	Characteristics	Case
Forcible Unification through Absorption	War or involvement of force	– Unconditional submission and disarmament of subordinate nation – Military integration centered around dominant nation – Abolishment of the military of the subordinate nation and non-compensation for related assets	Vietnam
Unification through Consensual Absorption	Unilateral unification by agreement	– Unconditional submission and disarmament of subordinate nation – Military integration centered around dominant nation – Abolishment of the military of the subordinate nation and compensation for related assets	Germany
Unification through One-to-One Merger	Consensual merger on an even basis	– Agreement on military integration on even terms – Military integration centered around both countries involved – Military integration in which unification has lesser significance than integration – Inherent potential for future coercive conflict	Yemen

B. A Historical Perspective of the Division of Korea

The division of Korea can be traced back to the peninsula's liberation from Japan in 1945 and has continued for over half a century, causing many problems for the Korean people which are not likely to be resolved. The 38th parallel was drawn for military convenience in connection with the surrender and disarmament of Japan in the Korean peninsula, with the American and Soviet armed forces dividing and occupying the South and North portions,[152] and the two sides came to declare their independence individually as disagreement between their politicians and ideological conflict between the leftists and the rightists deepened.

During this period, political and social chaos was rampant in the South due to outbreaks of political struggle by the Communist Party whose activities had been legalized under the non-intervention policy of the US authorities, while the U.S S R. pursued indirect rule in the North through a policy of communization led by Kim Il-sung Between 1948 and 1950, North Korea incited subversive movements in the South in the form of various uprisings and riots in Cheju, Yosu and Daegu utilizing leftist powers within the South, while instigating insurgent activities in the mountain ranges through the deployment of guerrillas.

The peace propaganda of the North evident in such efforts as the "Proposal for Peace" on June 8, 1950 and "Directives for the Establishment of Inter-Parliamentary Peace Policy" on June 18, 1950 proved to be insincere as it undertook an invasion of the South on June 25, 1950 The Korean people suffered huge losses as a result of the ensuing war, but the North has not completely abandoned its hopes of forcible reunification more than 40 years after the signing of an armistice in July 1953, as it has continued to fuel hostilities between fellow Koreans through numerous acts of aggression [153]

---

[151] Ibid , Hong-ki Chang, Ryang Lee and Man-jong Lee, p 92.

[152] Respectively Deployment of Soviet forces in North Korea, August 12, 1945, deployment of American forces in South Korea, September 8, 1945, and unconditional surrender of Japan, August 14, 1945

[153] Major acts of aggressions are Kidnapping of KNA airliner (1958 2 16), Ambush on the Korean Presidential Palace (1968 1 21), Kidnapping of US Pueblo (1968 8 5), Uljin and Samchok Incidents (1968 11. 3), Panmunjom Ax Murder Incident (1976 8. 18.), Burma Aungsan Incident (1983 10 9), and 42 thousand other cases of armistices violation including espionage armed incursions · kidnapping of fishing vessels

<Table XIII-11> Ideological Conflicts between the Leftist and the Rightist after the Liberation

South Korea	
1945. 9. 6.	- Declaration of the Chosun People's Republic by Un-hyung Yeo (leftist)
1945. 9.16.	- Formation of Korean Democratic Front / declaration of support for transitional government in Shanghai by Jin-woo Song (rightist)
1946. 2.16.	- Formation of National Front for Democracy by leftists (Un-hyung Yeo, Hun-young Park, Hun Huh, etc.)
1946.10. 7.	- Formation of United Left-Right Coalition by Un-hyung Yeo and Kyu-shik Kim (Opposition to the coalition by rightists including Seung-man Rhee and Ku Kim) Opposition/support to/of the proposed entrustment of government by rightists/leftists
1948. 5.10.	- National elections held only in the South under the supervision of the UN Supervisory Committee for Korea and Formation of Constitutional Committee
1948. 8.15.	- Declaration of the establishment of the Government of Republic of Korea (a free democratic republic) (South Korea recognized as 'the sole, legitimate government' in the Korean peninsula by the 3rd General UN Council)
North Korea	
1945. 8.15.	– Establishment of the Pyongnam chapter of the People's Political Council under the supervision of the Soviet military authorities
1945. 8.17.	– Formation of a National Council by Man-shik Cho (rightist)
1945.10. 8.	– Meeting of the Transitional Committee for the five northern provinces
1945.10.	– Renaming of five northern provinces as administrative units
1946. 2. 8.	– Replacement of five northern provinces by the Transitional People's Committee for North *Chosun*
1946. 4.	– Establishment of North *Chosun* Labor Party.
1947. 2.17.	– Establishment of North *Chosun* Supreme People's Council.
1947.11.18.	– Establishment of North *Chosun* Constitutional Committee and declaration of Constitution (1948. 5. 1.)
1948. 9. 9.	– Declaration of the establishment of the Government of Democratic People's Republic of Korea
1948.10. 2.	– Recognition of North Korea by Soviet Union.

C. Present Status of North and South Korea

North Korea maintains a dictatorship based on its '*Juche* Ideology'. The basis for this political structure is the single-party system under the Labor Party. Thus, the power structure of North Korea is strictly centralized with an absolute concentration of power, and policy is determined by a single entity. The social structure, which is supported by strict supervision of citizens, has strong totalitarian, authoritarian and isolationistic characteristics which contradict the socialist principle of equality with its dual hierarchy of the governing and governed classes.[154]

<Table XIII-12> is a comparison of the political and social structures of the North and the South. The salient characteristic of the North's socialist economic system is that private property is more restricted in scope than any other communist nation. Only the state and cooperatives may own means of production (Constitution, Article 20). It is noteworthy that North Korea's economic system is intimately tied to its goals of building up military power. The bases of North Korea's economic policy is as follows.[155]

[154] Ministry for Reunification, *Korea White Paper on Reunification,* December 1994. pp. 13-17.
[155] Ibid., pp. 245~250.

<Table XIII-12> Socio-Political Structure of North and South Korea

Category	North Korea	South Korea
Political System	– Communist/socialist national system – Single party system	– Free democracy – Multiple party system
Power Structure	– Kim Jung-il dictatorship – Single ideology system	– Democratically elected president – Separation of administrative, legislative and judicial branches of power
Social System	– Totalitarian social system linking President, Party and People – Public society where all citizens are required to take part based on a national party system – Hierarchical structure with priority for party members (approximately 3 million) – Idolization of leader (Jung-il Kim) – Controlled society with supervision of citizens and communications and travel limitations	– Free society with guarantees of religion, press and assembly – Humane society with respect for individual rights – Capitalist society based on free competition – Moralistic society based on traditional conservatism
Characteristics	– Long-term rule/dictatorship of Il-Sung Kim/Jung-il Kim – Deification of Il-Sung Kim/Jung-il Kim's guidance and *Juche* ideology as religion – Social system with unilateral, controlled, dogmatic and closed characteristics – Single-ideology society	– Social system with democratic, open, diverse, creative and practical characteristics – Pluralistic practical society

First, it aims to establish an independent and socialist economy under the principle of self-sufficiency. This principle had been the single greatest obstacle to growth as it stifled specialization in areas of comparative advantage and also international cooperation through the introduction of the technologies and capital of advanced countries. As North Korea came to terms with the limitations of this policy in the 1980's, it has since realized the importance of external trade and economic cooperation and concentrated on expanding international exchanges and cooperation.

Second, heavy industries have continued to be given priority. As a result, the imbalance between wasted resources and the business areas of concentration have only deepened, thus becoming a major factor in falling productivity at plants and enterprises. Heavy industries such as machinery and tooling are integral parts of defense industries.

Third, the pursuit of both military and economic development should again be noted. In December 1962, North Korea declared its intentions of pursuing four major military directives, and has since pursued this policy after making it official in the Party Congress in 1966 in the midst of persisting small-scale conflicts with the South.

1993 was the final year of the Third Seven-Year Plan which had been initiated in April 1987. Major growth goals during this period included increasing GDP 1.7 times (annual average 7.9%), industrial production 1.9 times (annual average 9.6%), agricultural production 1.4 times (annual average 4.9%), and trade volume 3.2 times (annual average 18.1%).

However, the actual results were dismal and in the case of GDP growth, the achieved figure is estimated at around 51.8% of the target. This means that North Korea set an economic growth target of an annual average of 7.9% but real growth was actually negative 1.7%, as GDP in real terms was down 12% *vis-a-vis* the index year of 1986. Meanwhile, the per capita GNP increased slightly in nominal terms, but the living standard of citizens are estimated as having fallen about 20% in comparison to the launch of the Third Seven-Year Plan. <Table XIII-13> shows estimates of North Korea's nominal GNP.

<Table XIII-13> Estimates of North Korea's Nominal GNP

Category	1980	1985	1986	1987	1988	1989	1990	1991	1992	1993	1994	1995
GNP (US$ billions)	13.5	15.1	17.4	19.4	20.6	21.1	23.1	22.9	21.1	20.5	21.2	22.3
GNP Per Capita (US$)	758	757	853	936	980	987	1,064	1,038	943	904	923	957

Source: Ministry for Defense, Korea, *White Paper on Defense*, 1996.

On the military side, however, North Korea is now the fifth largest power in the world in quantitative terms as a result of its 1962 policy of military augmentation. As of January 1994, the standing armed forces is estimated at 1.03 million (900,000 army, 46,000 navy and 84,000 air force personnel) as the country is known to be the second most intensively militarized in the world after Israel in terms of military personnel density.[156] The characteristics of the structure of North Korea's military forces is that it remains unchanged for both war and peace-time situations. In times of war, the supreme command oversees all armed personnel including reserve forces such as the Laborer's Army, with little movement in lower-level frontline troops and only slight shuffles in the mid-level command.

Even at the present, army, navy and air force troops are deployed on the frontline areas with 200 pieces of large-caliber artillery including 170 mm and 240 mm guns, deployed at the very forefront in direct contradiction with the traditional principle of artillery as cover fire from behind the lines, in order to threaten Seoul and its metropolitan areas all the way down to Suwon. In the 1980s, however, it has been reported that North Korea has come to realize the limitations of conventional weapons and has stepped up concentrated investments in strategic weapons as missiles and biological weapons. It has already succeeded in test-firings of missiles to carry chemical and nuclear weapons for ranges over 1,000 kilometers, and is also pursuing the development of long-range artillery and medium and long-range missiles for mass-destruction purposes.

North Korea's ground forces are organized into 2 artillery and 4 mechanized armies, 10 regular armies, 18 army commands and special command centers coordinating transport, artillery and special forces functions.[157] There are also 60 infantry divisions and brigades, 25 mechanized brigades, 13 tank brigades, 24 special forces brigades and 30 artillery brigades for a total of 152 divisions and brigades. Major equipment includes over 3,800 mechanized units including 2,760 units of T-54/55/59 tanks and 800 armored vehicles including the latest model T-62 and over 12,500 pieces of artillery including 10,800 pieces of field artillery composed of 8,200 pieces of combat artillery of various calibers (76.2/100/122/130/152/160 mm) and 2,600 pieces of cover artillery (107/122/132/240 mm) and others used for the defense of strongholds and strategic positions. <Table XIII-14> shows a comparison between North and South Korea's military power.

D. Considerations for Military Integration between South and North Korea

The two Koreas, which have several common grounds for unification such as a single ethnic grouping, language and national identity, have seen a deepening of enmity due to their atrocious civil war and frequent acts of aggression by the North, resulting in an almost insurmountable ideological confrontation as the political rift between the two and their struggle for dominance in the peninsula has intensified over the years. The sharp discrepancy between the values of totalitarian socialism and free democracy and the significant gap in economic power and living standards between the two are expected to act as obstacles to reunification.

[156] Ibid., pp. 253-257.

[157] Ministry of Defense, Korea, *White Paper on Defense,* October 1994, pp. 254~255.

<Table XIII-14> North and South Korea's Military Power

Category	Sub-category	South Korea	North Korea
Manpower (in 1,000 troops)	Army	560	920
	Navy	66	47
	Air Force	54	88
	Total	690*	1,055**
Ground Forces	Armies	11	20
	Divisions	50	54
	Brigades	21	99
	Tanks	2,050 units	3,800 units
	Armed Vehicles	2,250 units	2,500 units
	Field Artillery	4,700 guns	11,800 guns
Navy	Destroyers	180	430
	Support Vessels	50	335
	Submarines	4	35***
Air Force	Tactical Fighters	530	840
	Support Crafts	160	510
	Helicopters	630	290

Note:
* Does not include reserve forces, includes marines forces.
** Marines forces included in army.
*** Includes small submarines.
Source: same as in <Table XIII-13>

Even in their militaries and their respective social statuses in the two, North Korea's state-run system and socially privileged military class differ greatly from those of the South, and disparate military systems, ideologies and equipment will present difficulties to integration. As already mentioned in this section, the method for military integration will necessarily be determined by political developments leading up to an agreement on unification and the subsequent choice of a methodology thereof, but the task is undoubtedly a practical one which must be achieved as part of North-South integration.

Furthermore, military integration can not be achieved solely through internal planning and must naturally be done so in parallel or complementary fashion with, and as a continuation of integration in the political, economic and social fields. The military is an armed but politically subordinate organization by its very nature and has a pyramid-shaped command structure which implies that it can only function properly as a single unit in terms of line of command, due to its lack of flexibility as an organization and its need for strict adherence to regulations.

As for possible problem points to consider in military integration, integration of systems, ideologies, equipment and logistics may first come to mind, but it can be asserted with a degree of certainty that the greatest challenge will be the integration of personnel, or the attainment of a common identity. Organizational restructuring, personnel management, education and training, the draft system and the management of reserve forces will all be greatly affected accordingly. Preliminary preparations should be made so that national support which will enable the sustained pursuit of directives for the alleviation of conflicts and legal systems and measures to facilitate the completion of a single, united army will be secured so that military integration may proceed in line with integration in other fields.

Chapter XIV

PROPOSAL OF A NORTHEAST ASIA PEACE CITY FOR SECURING PEACE IN KOREAN PENINSULA

The purposes of this chapter are three: first, to analyze the current security status of Northeast Asia focusing on US military strategy, and in particular, the effects of amendments to the US-Japan Defense Cooperation Treaty from the points of view of Japan, China and Korea; second, to discuss about the necessity of a collective security system in Northeast Asia; and thirdly, to propose a 'Northeast Asia Peace City' (NAPC) and its development strategy to secure and promote regional peace and cooperation.[158]

1. CURRENT STATUS OF SECURITY IN NORTHEAST ASIA

A. US Interests and Strategies in Northeast Asia

1) US Interests

The US interest in Northeast Asia can be divided into three categories: vital interest, extremely important interest, and important interest. 'Vital interest' refers to a country that cannot pursue regional hegemony and maintain democratic governmental systems in the region. As for 'extremely important interest', the US aims at preventing the introduction of weapons of mass destruction including those of a nuclear and biochemical nature should not be introduced into sensitive areas such as Taiwan Strait, the South China Sea and the Korean Peninsula while admitting China into the international community to secure and strengthen world order. 'Important interest' includes the preservation of freedom, political pluralism, progress of human rights and further liberalization of the market for free trade and investment.

Specialists in the US advocate decisive elements to secure the national interests of the United States in Northeast Asia region including a close security relationship with Japan, peaceful settlement of the intra-Korean Peninsula problem and emergence of a stable and liberal China.

Stanley Roth, an assistant secretary of the State Department in charge of East Asia and Pacific, points out the following threatening factors to the security of the region: outbreak of war on the Korean Peninsula, military conflicts over territorial disputes; hostile relationship between the US and China on the Taiwan issue; and the proliferation of weapons of mass destruction.

2). US Strategies

The key points of US military strategies are to deter the recurrence of Russia's military threats by supporting its reform, to induce enlargement of the roles and responsibilities of allied states, to hinder the emergence of hegemony by one state in the region, to prevent the proliferation of weapons of mass destruction, and to pursue selective intervention in regional, ethnic and religious disputes.

Under this basis, military strategy of the US is to maintain military intervention on a small scale and to reduce the number of US military forces to 1,400,000 with less than 100,000 stationed in Europe, while maintaining an advantage in high-tech weapons like those involving a strategic nuclear nature. The US plans to reduce its defense budget continuously, starting with US$88 billion in 1997, and increase the conversion of the war industry into non-military industries.

---

[158] The major part of this chapter was presented at the Seminar held by Institute of Developing Economies, Tokyo, Japan, on Jan. 28, 1999.

The US economic strategy in Northeast Asia is to concentrate on promoting exchanges and cooperation through regional cooperative systems such as APEC to reduce the possibility of crisis, while strengthening regional stability and maximizing its economic interests. In order to maximize such interests, the US tends to support the sustained and dynamic development of regional economies and, at the same time, pursue the abolition of trade barriers with an emphasis on inducing mainland China and Taiwan to join the WTO. The US policy toward Northeast Asian countries are summarized below.

First, with respect to China, the perpetuation of China's trade barriers and the US's trade deficit with China are problems pending between the US and China. The US State Department recognizes China's reduction in the import tariff rate from 40% in 1995 to 17% in 1997, and the improvement of the foreign exchange system in favor of foreign enterprise. However, the US also desires China to remove non-tariff barriers, increase transparency, and reduce limitations on advances into the service sector by foreign investors. In particular, the US is seeking for a solution by China's membership into the WTO in order to settle the trade deficit problem, which has been an political issue in the US.

Second, as for Japan, the US urges Japan to improve its heavily regulated structure, ease non-tariff barriers on American products, and to carry out economic policies to lead Asia to get out of the Asian crisis.

Third, toward Korea, the US has asked the Korean government to eliminate the high tariff rate, increase transparency in administrative regulations and encourages more governmental intervention in the financial sector.

Lastly, for the Taiwan and Hong Kong, even though there are still many kinds of trade barriers in Taiwan, the USTR (United States Trade Representative) reported that unfair trade barriers in Taiwan were eliminated to a great extent, and the United States generally had high marks for the free market economy of Hong Kong, except for copyright violations and infringements on trademarks.

B. US-Korea Military Alliance

The Pentagon has established a so-called 'Win-Win Strategy' which was presented to President Clinton in 1993. The direction of American policies in the Asia-Pacific region, which is directly linked to national security and prosperity of Korea is to play a role of regional balancer in achieving a long-term stability. The United States is expected to maintain some sort of a bilateral military alliance with South Korea and Japan, at the same time to pursue the establishment of an Asian multilateral security system and to induce the participation of regional nations in the PKO/PKF effort. In case the United States launches a multilateral security system, it is most imperative that Korea, the United States and Japan come to a common agreement regarding such a system.

The Korea-US alliance relationship can be divided into two parts: before and after the 1980s. Before the 1980s, the alliance was one-sided as the United States assumed the main role in the defense of Korea, and Korea took the subsidiary role. It placed 40,000 troops, practically all of UN forces stationed in Korea, and carried out its function as the administrator of the Korean cease-fire situation. Moreover, it gave more than US$12 billion of military aid. Such support, along with financial aid, has contributed to the economic and military development of Korea.

However, in the late 1980s, opinions voicing the reduction of US forces in Korea and the adjustment of their roles began to surface. It was due to changes in the world security environment such as the new détente between the United States and the former Soviet Union and the Soviet-Chinese reconciliation, the 'twin deficit' and US domestic problems, and changes in Korea itself caused by economic and military growth. Therefore, in November 1989, the American Congress and Senate decided on the Nunn-Warner Amendment to re-evaluate the function, magnitude and composition of US forces in Korea, and to demand an increase in Korean responsibility for the defense of Korea. As a result, a three-step withdrawal and defense spending cuts were planned, some of which have already taken place.

The EASI (East Areas of Inactive Asian Strategic Initiative), which was announced in April 1990, was representative of the military relationship between South Korea and the United States. Under the first stage of the said initiative, 7,000 army and air force troops were withdrawn during 1990~1992, leaving 36,000 as of the end of 1992. As for Korea's share of the costs related to their presence, a figure of US$220 million was agreed upon for 1993, up from US$150 million in 1991. The second stage (1993~1995), which had been put on hold due to the North Korean nuclear problem, is expected to be resumed shortly and the reduction of American troops continued, while Korea bears one-third of all related American costs.

Thereafter, in the third stage, the final scale of the US presence will be determined by the extent of the North Korean menace and America's role in the region. Wartime strategic control has been returned to Korea, the CFC (Combined Forces Command) dismantled, and the nature of defense costs changed to one of regional quota.

At the very present, major issues in Korea-US military cooperation include the resumption of the second stage of EASI and scale of withdrawal, relocation of American bases, the timing and method for returning strategic control, dismantling method and alternatives to the CFC, and most prominently, the nature and amount of Korea's share of costs in defense. The US Department of Defense stated in a revised report of the EASI that, 'an increase in Korea's share of defense costs is hoped for in line with its economic status'. Clearly, the United States is no longer interested in a presence for strictly military purposes or one that it can not justify from an economic standpoint.

Most significantly, even the US is showing qualitative changes in its policy toward the Korean peninsula following the end of the Cold War. Such changes became quite evident in the US-North Korea talks where the US no longer seemed to be viewing South Korea as an ally under the common bond of anti-communism, but rather tried to incorporate even North Korea within the US-led world order. Today's United States is naturally not the United States of the Cold War era. Accordingly, there is the need for a comprehensive revision of Korea's security directives. While American authorities have affirmed that reductions or withdrawal of American troops are not being considered, the possibilities of such developments can not be totally precluded according to changes in South Korea-US relations and in light of the establishment of bilateral representative offices, prospective normalization of relations and North Korea's insistence on a peace treaty with the US. At the very least, there will probably be some reductions in the American presence depending on how economic cooperation progresses.

3. The US-Japan Defense Cooperation Treaty

A. Revision of the Defense Cooperation Treaty and Its Effects

An alliance system for security between the US and Japan is the most important factor for the maintenance of *status quo* in East Asia. Even though threats of Russia have disappeared since the ending of the Cold War, now the threat of China is newly emerging. The US has judged that it should fortify the alliance system with Japan because China has become an imposing country, economically and militarily. The revision of the defense cooperation treaty between the US and Japan in June 1997 is the product of consensus, as long as it does not break the defense principle of Japan.

The US does not want to increase expenditures on the maintenance of the *status quo* in East Asia. A frequently cited example relates to the Gulf War of 1990. Though Japan spent billions of US dollars in war funds to share expenses, it did not participate in an anti-Iraq alliance with the US. It was necessary for the US to increase the role of Japan.[159]

The recent tension in Northeast Asia was caused by a nuclear threat of North Korea in 1992 and 1993.[160] In the case of an emergency in the Korean peninsula, Japan could only play a minimal role, which is one of reasons why the US was active in revising the defense cooperation treaty between the US and Japan in June 1997. Main points of the revision include the following: first, Japan's support for US military action outside its territory in an emergency is allowed, providing a stepping stone for the US's balance of power. The US could automatically intervene in a war if Japan is attacked,[161] but on the contrary, Japan is not required reciprocate, if the situation is reversed. In this manner, it is not a totally equal military alliance; Secondly, the new treaty prepares for the unstable future of North Korea and possible conflicts in Taiwan Strait.

---

[159] The new guideline was successful for the US as it concluded the dispute over the military role of Japan.

[160] In fact, the US persuaded Japan to feel the necessity of a revision of the defense cooperation treaty concluded in November 1978, which was the result of highest tension on the development of nuclear weapons by North Korea.

[161] The US did not mention the place which the new treaty covered, because it was concerned about the hostility of other nations toward Japan.

2) Japan's Rearmament

Japan has steadily expanded the scope of its military activities through a series of agreements, including the US-Japan Joint Security Treaty (September 1951) → Amendments to the Treaty (January 1960) → Signing on the US-Japan Joint Defense Guidelines (November 1978) → Enactment of the PKO (Peace-Keeping Operations) Law (June 1992) → Ratification of a New Defense Plan (November 1995), as shown by<Table XIV-1>.

If Article 9 of the Constitution, which stipulates that 'Japan may not be involved in any military action other than cases where its sovereignty is transgressed', (in accordance with the principle of 'collective sovereignty') is amended, then Japan will be free to engage not only in joint operations with the US on the Korean Peninsula, but a heavily armed Japanese army will also be able to take part in an allied war effort. This subtle trend runs counter to the efforts of the Japanese government since World War II, which has been concentrated on providing its citizens with an affluent society based on peace, and is an issue that Japan must handle in an appropriate manner.

In fact, Japan has steadily been increasing its defense budget according to its defense plan outline which began in 1976. The ceiling of the defense budget constructed in 1976 was abolished by Prime Minister Nakasone Yasuhiro in 1986. Starting from 1996, Japan reinforced tanks, ground-to-air missiles and other high-tech and quality equipment. In addition, improvement of its military organization is in progress to speed up its defense maneuvering capabilities. Also, Japan intends to introduce the US DEFCON (Defense Condition) system which classifies the readiness the nation's self-defense according to the degree of military tension involved.

<Table XIV-1> Chronology related to Constitution and Defense Treaty of Japan

1890	Japan's Meiji Constitution
1938	Japan's Enactment of Law on National Full Mobilization
Aug. 15, 1945	Japan's Defeat in World War II
Feb. 1946	Enactment of MacArthur's Constitution Draft
Nov. 3, 1946	Japan's Promulgation of Constitution
Sep. 8, 1951	Signing on the US-Japan Joint Security Treaty
1952	Enforcement of Peace Treaty (Restoration of Japan's Sovereignty)
July 1, 1954	Establishment of Self-Defense Military Foundation in the Japanese Defense Department
Dec. 1956	Japan's Joining in the United Nations
Aug. 13, 1957	Inauguration of the Constitution Research Committee of Japan
Jan. 1960	Signing on the New US-Japan Joint Security Treaty
1964	Inauguration of the Constitution Research Committee in the Japanese Cabinet
Sep. 23, 1997	Signing on the Korea - Japan Joint Security Treaty
June 1965	The US's Return of Okinawa to Japan
May 1972	Signing on the US-Japan Joint Defense Guidelines
Nov. 1978	Japan's Liberal Democratic Party, Resolution on Amendment of the Japanese Constitution for the first time
Jan. 22, 1983	Japan's Establishment of the PKO Cooperation Law
June 15, 1992	The Japanese Prime Minister Murayama states, "Self-Defense Military is Constitutional."
July 20, 1994	Japan's Adoption of the New Defense Plan Outline
Nov. 1995	Summit Talks between the US and Japan, Announcement of Joint Security Declaration
April 1996	An Interim Report of the Revision of New Joint Defense Guidelines
June 1997	Revision of the Defense Cooperation Treaty between the US and Japan

Source: Yang-Taek Lim, *Prospects for Asia in the 21st Century,* Seoul: Mail Economic Daily Press, January: 1999, p582.

With the change of national circumstances and upheaval of international politics after the Cold War, Japan was faced with the constitutional amendment instead of constitutional protection movement. The Social Democratic Party, which was the symbol of constitutional protection movement, also acknowledged the US-Japan Joint Security Treaty between the US and Japan in July 1994. The symbolic statement was that President Clinton asked Japan to be active for world peace and order. That was not a request, however, but a permission to push forward with the establishment of an independent constitution after achieving ruling party status in 1995. With strong support for the constitutional amendment, the Liberal Democratic Party logically argued that the basic military system of Japan was not based upon its constitution, but the US-Japan Joint Security Treaty, so its constitution should be revised in line with the requests of US. The reason for the revision was that Japan could not contribute to the reconcilable action of conflicts in the international community on the basis of Article Nine of the Constitution.

After the revision, Japan enlarged the scope of the use of military power through an interpretation of the constitution amendment without any revision of Article Nine, which affects Korea the most. The following are the reasons for increases in Japanese military capabilities even after the Cold War.

First, the United States has been pressuring Japan to increase her defense powers. It has been criticizing Japan for taking a 'free ride on defense' and demanded Japan to take a proper amount of responsibility fitting her economic power. The Pentagon has recently announced that the US military role in East Asia will be reduced and that it expects Japan to fill this vacuum.

Second, a 'potential Soviet threat' has been the premise of Japan's increase in defense power. Japan evaluates that the possibility of regional conflict will rise and so will the duration of such conflicts, although the Cold War is over. Japan feels that with the Chinese and Korean political situation, as well as the Cambodian conflict and other matters, the Asia-Pacific area is much more volatile than the situation in Europe. Therefore, Japan would like to keep herself armed for just in case.

Thirdly, Japan would like to participate in military activities for world peace. Lately, Japanese politicians do not argue about the unconstitutionality of the SDF any more (except for the Communists). The DLP, Komei Party, and the Democratic Socialist Party have cooperated in amending the related laws in order to enable the SDF to go abroad. Even the Socialist Party, which had formerly proposed that the SDF was unconstitutional, agreed not only to its existence, but also to PKO activities.

Of course, it is unlikely that Japan would be able to use military strength to pursue national interests and its position within the world order. Since Japan's defense policies are created on the basic framework of the Japanese-US Security Treaty, it is very hard for Japan to carry out military strategies alone. Japan will seek an economic role in the world, as it always has, but not a military one.

The present constitution prohibits the use of military power to solve the international conflicts unless Japan is invaded directly. That is the basis for the dispute over the US-Japan defense cooperation treaty regarding a potential emergency on the Korean peninsula. For now the scope of support for the US toward Japan is limited due to the constitutional limitations of Japan. The main area of support is in equipment and facilities such as airports, harbors, manpower and medical treatment. The ability of removing mines is also excluded since it can be used in military conflicts. But Japan's self-defense military would be able to engage in military practices with US forces on the Korean Peninsula without any limits. It would be also possible for Japan to participate in a war as a member of multinational forces.

D. China's Counter-measures

China has thought that the revision of the US-Japan Defense Cooperation treaty in June 1997 would be harmful to its territorial sovereignty and security interests. In addition, the revision of the treaty, which was aimed at the former Soviet Union in the Cold War era, in fact focuses more on China.

The new treaty has the characteristics of a strategic military treaty between the US and Japan, which could weaken China's status. The comparison of military power between China and Japan in 1996 is summarized in <Table XIV-2>. Japan spent four trillion eight hundred billion yens on their military budget in 1996, and appeared to be trying to expand its influence through the newly revised the US-Japan Defense Cooperation Treaty which could hinder the expansion of China's military power. With the revision, the US wants Japan to spend much more money on its defense budget and hinder the advance of China into the Asia-Pacific region.

<Table XIV-2> Comparison of Military Power between China and Japan (1996)

	China	Japan
Regular Army	2,930,000	240,000
Tanks	about 10,000	1,130
Armored Cars	4,500	730
Field Guns	14,000	850
Aviations for Military Operations	4,970	1,150
Submarines	52	16
Naval Destroyers	18	60

Source: Yang-Taek Lim, ibid., p586.

One thing to note is that one of the core contents of the new guidelines involves the security cooperation regions of the Taiwan Strait as well as the Korean Peninsula in an emergency, which could be interpreted as a threat to China and its self-concept of being one state. Taiwan is included in margins of the treaty, which could be interpreted as a challenge to China. If, for example, the US and Japan would plan a campaign in the Taiwan Strait. This prompted a Chinese official to warn that the new treaty was a bilateral defense treaty between the two countries.

In Peking, the US and China agreed on security and economic cooperation on June 29, 1998, as summarized in <Table XIV-3>. At the same time, China tried to enforce its relationship with US in order to keep the new security cooperation with Japan, meanwhile fortifying diplomatic relations with Russia in terms of a strategic alliance.

<Table XIV–3> The Agreements between the US and China on June 29, 1998

Bilateral Cooperation	Establishment of constructive strategic partnership
Nuclear Missile	Signing a treaty to cancel aiming at counterparts
Transfer of Nuclear Technology	Prohibition of supporting South Asia's ballistic missile program
Korean Peninsula	Joint efforts for peace on the Korean peninsula
Others	Drug transactions, international crime, and environmental problems

Source: Same as in <Table XIV-2>.

E. Sino-Russian Military Cooperation

It is notable that Russia and China renewed their military cooperation. Since Mikhail Gorbachev's visit to Beijing in May 1989, China and the former Soviet Union have remarkably expanded the pace, scope and level of their military relations, which include the sale of advanced aircraft and submarines, the transfer of technology and science personnel, and close defense-industrial ties. In the early 1990s not only did the Chinese People's Liberation Army capitalize on Russia's financial pinch to acquire some advanced weapon system, but also try to acquire some advanced weapons systems, and production technologies for various defense items, especially advanced aircraft. In light of their close military contacts in the first half of the 1990s, it is thus reasonable to expect that China is likely to acquire more weapons and technologies from Russia throughout the decade.[162]

F. Sino-Russia Policies on North Korea

North Korea's economic plight is a general and long-standing state of material insufficiency that has been formed by the rigidity and faults of the state running mechanism of economy. As a result, it is hard to solve the problem of insufficiency with a limited change in economic policy which North Korea is aiming at or with temporary aid from friendly countries. In light of this basic flaw which is responsible for North Korea's economic difficulties, whether North Korea will adopt reform or not is one of the most important

[162] Kim Tae-Ho, "Sino-Russian Military Cooperation in the 1990s: Issues and Prospect", *Sino-Soviet Affairs,* Vol. XX, No.1, Spring 1996.

factors in deciding the character of relations between North Korea and China. Meanwhile, when considering North Korea's political restrictive factors, it is difficult to believe that it is attempting drastic economic changes oriented towards a market economy.

As the economic plight of North Korea continues to widen, resulting in recognition of its system failure, North Korea will need China as a political and military ally and economic supporter for the survival of its system. China in its turn will hope to capitalize on the tensions on the Korean Peninsula to continue relations with North Korea for the strategic purpose of striking a balance with the US and Japan. And while the system of North Korea remains unstable, the US and Japan will want to define the role of South Korea from their corresponding points of view. Thus, chances are that political and military tensions on the Korean Peninsula will continue, and that politico-economic opportunity costs will hardly decrease.

On the other hand, the official attitude of Russia to the nuclear problem of North Korea is that an international conference with the participation of the two Koreas, the US, China, Russia and representatives of the General Secretariat of the UN and the Chairman of the IAEA, should be held.[163] This suggestion was consistently repeated by Moscow. Furthermore, Moscow proposed that this international conference could discuss the formation of a multipolar security system in Northeast Asia.

If this suggestion had been received, South Korea could have reaped the largest benefits from this scheme. At the same time, the international community could have been guaranteed security on the Korean Peninsula through an establishment non-nuclear status. On this basis, the two Koreas could have initiated dialogue, which was oriented to substantial progress in the peaceful integration of the two Koreas.

In this scenario, Russia could have gleaned large benefits next to South Korea. Even still, if there comes into being an organization for discussion on the problems of the Korean Peninsula and Northeast Asia-Pacific region, Russia can play an important role in this multilateral system, being worthy of its geographical status.

Russia was one of the most active participants in the solution of the nuclear problem of North Korea. Not having participated in the KEDO, in other words, not having provided money for the substitution of a LWR, Moscow made an attempt to sell its own reactor to North Korea at the expenses of the KEDO. Moscow failed to reach its goal, however, and in view of the fact that North Korea insisted obstinately on the reception of the Russian type reactor, it is obvious that Russia had an influence on the problems of the Korean Peninsula. Instead of selling its own type of reactor to North Korea, Russia succeeded in obtaining a tacit approval from the US in selling its atomic reactor to Iran.[164]

G. A New Relationship between China and the Two Koreas

It is also notable that the relationship of China and the two Koreas has recently changed. With the downfall of Russia and with the accomplishment of German reunification, the world has emerged into a post-capitalistic era. China also has gradually been leaning towards into capitalistic-oriented policy by succeeding the pro-capitalistic policy of socialism with Chinese characteristics.

The following three factors played important roles in shaping the previously mentioned new trend in the Northeast Asian region. Three factors can be illustrated as follows:

1. Mutual visits of Yeltsin, Jiang, Clinton and Hasimoto since 1997 had a significant impact in forming new orders in Northeast Asia region. The quartet interplay resulted in a peaceful mood in the form of the so-called Sino-Russia strategic partnership. And under the new trend in post-capitalistic era, national interests have been transformed into economic security, causing the four powers to revise their strategies from ideology oriented policy to economy oriented policy.
2. The new leadership of South Korea, China and North Korea by Kim Dae-jung, Jiang Zhe-min and Kim Jung-il, respectively, also supplied those countries with new opportunities to change their former relationships from political oriented security relations to economic oriented one. China's stable economic development, South Korea under the IMF Program and North Korea's terrible

[163] Oh Seung-yul, "Prospect for North Korea's Reform and Opening and Relations between North Korea and China", *Sino-Soviet Affairs,* Vol. XIX, No. 4, Winter 1995/6.

[164] Kang Bong-koo, "The Russia's Korean Policies (1993. 3.-1995. 6): with a Focus on the Nuclear Problem of North Korea", *Sino-Soviet Affairs,* Vol. XX, No.1, Spring 1996.

famine, ultimately have resulted in positive outcomes helping to modify their former policies toward economic oriented relationships.

3. Economic crisis in Asian regions, even in South Korea, formerly one of emerging four dragons, caused various countries seeking for the IMF bail-outs, thereby providing highly developed Western countries with the opportunity to heighten their influence toward Asian countries suffering from economic depression. China therefore, can play a unique role of leading those Asian countries out of their financial crisis by providing a model of economic revitalization.[165]

The previously-mentioned factors gave rise to quite a different shape from former international order through interplay in the Northeast Asian region. These factors will also have a deep impact throughout the Korean Peninsula. The relationship of the Korean Peninsula and China will be affected in various ways.

First of all, China's influence toward the Korean Peninsula will be stronger in terms of economic power than before. The very fact that China is enjoying economic development despite economic stagnation in Asia points to its importance in helping to stabilize hostile attitudes between South and North Korea. In particular, China's equal weighed policy toward both Koreas will help strengthen the economic relationship between them.

Second, by reconciling the US-China relations, future of the Korean Peninsula will be greatly dependent upon their relationship. And their mutual cooperation will be useful in reinforcing mitigation of North Korea's provocative activities that might result in a possibility of breaking down the *status-quo* in Korean Peninsula.

Third, the two governments of the Koreas will further deepen their tendencies of separating political matters from economic matters due to the commonality of suffering from economic difficulties. At the same time, the former antagonistic attitude based upon political conflicts, would be changed to economic competition through mutual exchange of economic benefits.

Fourth, competition between China and Japan would be accelerated in Asia region in the form of pursuiting economic hegemony. The rivalry would chiefly be developed in Southeast Asian countries, allowing them to escape from economic depression.

2. THE SIGNIFICANCE OF A COLLECTIVE SECURITY SYSTEM IN NORTHEAST ASIA[166]

A. The Necessity of Collective Security System in the Region

Looking back post-war history, fast economic development was a major cause of the collapse of the Cold War system. Following the leading success of Japan in economic development, the economic development of Korea and socialist states like China and Indochina was the cause to dismantle the Cold War system in Asia. Gorbachev's skepticism on the socialist system also had its origins in the reform and open-door policy experimented by China.

Compared with Western society, however, the Cold War system still remains evident in Asia. There are conflicts and its confrontations in the region, but fortunately, political conditions are stabilizing, and its economic development is continuing dynamic progress. Economic development resulted in the improvement of the social and political status of that region. It is hoped that East Asia will continue to contribute the world community, both economically and politically in the 21st century.

Security, the cause of threats and counter-measures to threats for regional peace, vary from nation to nation. So each state has to take appropriate action in consideration with history, politics, economy and geopolitics. In the era of the Cold War, most countries in the East Asia region had a bilateral security system with the US. Even though Russia's military threats have been reduced, the bilateral security system with the US cannot be replaced because there is still the possibility of rearmament by Japan, and rapid economic development and military enforcement of China.

---

[165] Kim Young-hwa, "Changing Relationship of South Korea-China-North Korea under the New Trend in Northeast Asian Region: Emerging of New Leaderships in the Area", *Sino-Soviet Affairs,* Vol. XXIII, No. 3, Fall 1998.

[166] This section has been heavily drawn from Yang-Taek Lim, "Proposal of 'Northeast Asia Peace City' for A Collective Security System of Northeast Asia", *Northern Policy Studies,* Seoul: Korea Association of Northern Policy Studies, No. 4, 1998, pp. 9~74.

The expansion of armaments of Asian states is a crucial issue related to distribution of invaluable economic resources and prevention of regional conflicts. A forum in Stockholm reported that arms purchased by Asian states covered one-thirds of the world arms market. Each affluent state insists on its territorial rights and has measures for the pursuit of dominance. Under these circumstances, the task of how security in the region can be achieved and maintained is a matter that leaders of East Asia must solve.

To maintain peace in East Asia, the following issues should be settled: how can bilateral confidence of states in the region be solidified? how can a stage for discussions on security be prepared?

To solve these problems, all the leaders in the region are recommended to meet frequently and discuss security matters, a code of conduct should be established, and a standing organization to coordinate and reconcile conflicts before outbreak should be formed.

When threatening events occur, it is desirable that leaders first discuss the problems and realize the necessity for harmony with the international community instead of isolating the state or imposing economic sanctions against the state.

B. Proposal of Collective Security System in Northeast Asia

1) Concept of a Collective Security

It has been frequently mentioned in history that an international organization should be established to maintain peace. For example, Emeric Cruce argued in 1623 that each country should send an ambassador to one city like Venice and make an international organization to restore world order. In seventeenth and eighteenth century, Saint Pierre argued that an establishment for peace based on a world body and promotion of exchange was necessary. He also argued that international law, currencies and calendars should be standardized. Jean Jacques Rousseau (1712~1778) criticized Saint-Pierre's argument as being naive, but after World War I, the League of Nations was established, which was later transformed into the UN (United Nations) in the wake of the World War II.

Collective security based on peace through a world body is characterized by a general collective and regional security system. The former refers to the League of Nations or the United Nations and the latter refers to the NATO (North Atlantic Treaty Organization) or the Warsaw Pact. In collective security systems, all or most countries in the world make concerted efforts to fight against wars or use military force to solve conflicts peacefully. When there are violations, signatories cooperate to counter those misdeeds.

On the other hand, regional collective security apparatuses such as the NATO and the Warsaw Pact ensure security in specific regions. At this point, regional collective security system and military alliance should be differentiated. Regional collective security system admits the authority of the UN and vows to follow the UN Charter, while a military alliance system designates a potential enemy instead of establishing relations with a world peace organization. A military alliance exists for military support. In contrast, a regional collective security system is established for total cooperation and coordination in politics, economy, technology and culture, as well as military issues. Also, a military alliance does not outlaw war, whereas a regional collective security puts an emphasis on physical counter-attack and legal criticism for illegal intrusions.

2) A Regional Security System: European Security

In April 1997, sixteen nations including the US and Russia signed the Basic Agreement on Mutual Cooperation and Security. The agreement stipulates that the NATO and Russia do not regard each other as enemies. It also includes the basic principles, institutional framework, military measures and the range and limitation of cooperation for peace. The important aspect in the agreement is the expansion of NATO. The NATO accepted the Czech Republic, Poland and Hungary as new members in 1998. As a matter of fact, security in Europe has been achieved through relative security and balance of power.

After the World War II, a new security system in Europe was created. NATO and the Warsaw Pact led the system. But Russia, who was initially an enemy of the NATO, later joined the NATO, and promised to make concerted effort to maintain security in Europe. This kind of collective security system shows new vision through political and military confidence to stave off the emergence of potential enemies.

3) Collective Security System in Northeast Asia

A security system in Northeast Asia used to be based on separate security and military alliances for balance of power as Northeast Asia may face the potential collapse of North Korea, Chinese threat and Japan's rearmament. Those trends are a contrast to that of the post-Cold War era. A European style collective security system could be argued as a institutional measure to establish security and cooperation in the Asia-Pacific region. Time would be needed, however, the NATO was launched in the August 1945 and the Warsaw Pact in May 1955. The NATO and Russia signed the Basic Agreement in May 1997.

Meanwhile, it will be more complicated for the countries in Asia-Pacific region to establish that kind of collective security system because of differing levels of economic development in this area. The US should try to play a mediator in the long run, maintaining bilateral relations including military alliance with South Korea and Japan. At the same time, Washington should lead the establishment of collective security system as a Asian security body. Also, the US should induce the countries in this area to share much more actively the burden of peace keeping forces and operations.

At this juncture, it is important to be aware of the coordination among South Korea, the US and Japan to push for a regional collective security system. It has not been determined whether bilateral alliances or a regional collective security system like the NATO should be considered.

Recently, the Pentagon released a report which stated that Washington would maintain the presence of American troops in Asia and the costs of defense would be shared with countries in which American troops were stationed. The report divided the countries in East Asia into four groups according to relationships with the US The first group contains South Korea, Australia and Japan. Washington intends to maintain staunch relations with these countries. Also, the US intends to protect allies in Asia with American troop presence. The report emphasized that Russia and China were not enemies and called upon them to prevent the proliferation of weapons of mass destruction. The report however, did categorize North Korea as an enemy. It regarded North Korea's potential intrusion into South Korea as the most threatening factor attesting East Asia's stability. The report also released a plan to neutralize North Korea's missile program.

Washington's policy objectives in Northeast Asia are based on a limited engagement policy. Through the policy, the US will establish single community in the Asia-Pacific area. This is Washington's vision on a Pacific community. In this vision, Washington and Tokyo play major roles in transforming one economic union and holding politics and economies in the area together, allowing Japan to be able to get the upper hand in politics and economy. On the other hand, the US will support this area militarily and participate in economic activities while Washington checks Japan's dominance.

3. Proposal for a 'Northeast Asia Peace City' and Its Development Plan

A. Background

Arguments for the practical use of DMZ (demilitarized zone) between North and South Korea have been proposed as: first, Felix H. Rogers, a representative for the UN side and major general of US Air Force, suggested the peaceful use of the DMZ for the first time at the Seventeenth General Meeting of the Military Armistice Commission in June 1971; Through a February 1972 statement, Foreign Minister Yong-shik Kim urged the acceptance of the maintenance of the demilitarized condition and its peaceful use as suggested by the UN side; President Tae-woo Noh suggested the construction of a peace city in DMZ in his UN General Assembly speech in October 1988; North Korea suggested the maintenance of peace in the DMZ through an Armament Reduction Proposal for Peace on the '*Chosun*' (Korean) Peninsula in May 1990; At last, South and North Korea agreed on the peaceful use of the DMZ in December 1991, which was prescribed in Article Twelve of the Basic Agreement on Reconciliation and Non-aggression and Exchange and Cooperation between North and South signed in January 1992.

B. Historical Perspectives on World 'Free Cities'

1) The Concept

The concept of a 'free city', which is similar to a 'peace city', is not new. The notion of a free city originated from four cities of Augsburg, Basel, Worms and Cologne that maintained their independence from dominance of feudal lords or emperors. These cities, in fact, belonged to the Roman Empire and took the form of a republican government. After that, free cities were differentiated into original free city and free territory. From the Middle ages, its meaning was changed into the concept of 'city state' which had aspects common to a state. In the twentieth century, a medieval concept of free city re-emerged and developed.

2) Historical Examples

Historical examples of free cities include free city of German Confederation of Krakow, Danzig, Treaty, Upper Savoy and Pays de Gex. The Vienna Congress of August 1815 ended the Austro-Prussian conflict and established the German Confederation. In the past, there were six free cities (Augsburg, Bremen, Frankurt am Main, Hamburg, Luebeck, Nurenberg) in the German Reich. These free cities continued to exist in the form of the German Confederation of Free Cities. These free cities, however, were later absorbed into parts of the German Confederation after World War I.

Free City of Krakow

According to the thirty-second article of the Paris Peace Treaty, the Congress of participating nations agreed upon the establishment of Krakow free city, which was the first systemic foundation for a free city. Originally, Krakow was one of the cities located in Vistula, Southern Poland from the fourteenth to eighteenth century. After its separation from Poland by the Vienna Congress in 1815, it was under the protection of Austria, Prussia and Russia under the name of the Republic of Krakow, free city. Later, it was incorporated into Austria.

Danzig Free City

After the first World War, Danzig free city was established as a compromise among the Allied nations. According to rules of the Versailles Peace Treaty, it was separated from Germany's dominion and returned to the dominion of allied and associated powers. Finally, Danzig free city was created as an independent city under the League of Nations. Though the city was governed by the High Commissioner of the League of Nations, it became a independent city as a self-governing district. It gradually lost its independence however, under the influence of Poland's National Socialist party in 1936. In 1939, it was formally incorporated into German territory.

Treaty Free City

On the basis of the Paris Peace Treaty, the establishment of Treaty was proposed. The permanent statute for Treaty city's independence and its territorial preservation was ensured under the Security Council of the League of Nations. For this, the Security Council played a decisive role, which led to total failure. Italy, the United States and United Kingdom met and agreed upon a memorandum with the understanding of permitting military power to occupy the city. Italy and Yugoslavia announced the Belgrade Declaration in October 1979 and they re-established Treaty free city in Sezena Fernetti for the both countries' economic development.

Upper Savoy and Gex Free Zone

Upper Savoy is located in the southern part of Switzerland and the French border. Upper Savoy had belonged to the Sardinia Empire until 1860 and Geneva developed a special relationship with its economy, politics and commerce. The relationship became closer the St. Julian Peace Treaty signed in 1603. According to the St. Julian Peace Treaty, Upper Savoy was established as a demilitarized zone and Geneva citizens could pass through the region and have commercial rights.

When Switzerland declared its neutrality in the Final Act of the Congress of Vienna in 1815, Upper Savoy also declared itself as a neutral zone to satisfy Geneva's request. On the basis of the Paris Peace Treaty in 1815 and the Turin Treaty in 1816, some part of Upper Savoy and Geneva were divided into two free zones, Pays de Gex and Upper Savoy for economic and commercial development. Through the

Versailles Peace Treaty in 1919, France and Switzerland came to an temporary agreement on completion of neutral zone. After that, in 1928, Switzerland decided to give up its entire rights to that region.

Berlin Free City

After World War II, the Soviet Union proposed the transformation of Berlin into a demilitarized free city or a independent political unit under the protection of the League of Nations. The Soviet Union, however, did not get the approval of Western allies and Germany, so the idea did not work. Up to now, the proposal was often referred to as an issue for international discussion as a political concept about free cities.

C. Basic Concept of the NAPC

First of all, the 'Northeast Asia Peace City' (hereafter NAPC) should be defined as a place in which super-national and non-ideological administrative principles are adopted, a public market in which labor, products, capitals and services can freely flow a special free city where tariff and non-tariff barriers and technological and physical barriers do not exist. In general, a city is an area which meets the concept of residence, rest, activity for employment and transportation simultaneously in a fixed region. If the NAPC is constructed under this concept, residents should belong to a fixed political system which requires complex actions of the state.

Of course, the NAPC could be built with the assumption of a state in the long term. At present, however, there is no choice but to establish the NAPC which meets only three kinds of functions; rest, activity for employment and transportation. Though residential function would be excluded, the city would still need neutrality of ideology, politics and military aspects, which are tense factors of potential conflict between South and North Korea. With the assumption of non-political exchange, the NAPC should have the characteristics of a kind of a United Nations or a neutral state run by a third-party organization which would be constituted by the United States, China, Japan and/or Russia.

The concept is different from that of a free city, a free trade zone and a free port.

First, the NAPC is distinguished from free city and free trade area. Free trade areas that admit exemption of tariff and special privileges by an international treaty are formed by a multilateral treaty. Generally, free ports are formed by a national law or an international treaty, a free city by a international treaty, especially by a bilateral treaty. The NAPC, however, would be established by a multilateral treaty and a bilateral treaty between South and North Korea.

Second, the objective of establishing a free trade area is to guarantee free trade through exemption of tariffs and special privileges. A free port is a port that grants exemption from taxation on loading, packing and exhibition, as well as exemption from tariffs on all goods. The NAPC would hypothetically dissolve enmity between the two Koreas and point to its unification by promoting each nations' economic and human exchanges.

Third, free trade generally covers whole nations, free ports just cover ports or parts of ports, and a free city is limited to some part of one nation. The NAPC, however, would be established in a part of DMZ.

At this point, it is not clear whether it would be more desirable for the two Koreas, or an international organization formed by countries with interests, to operate the city. Danzig free-city can be given as an example of a free city formed by a state and international organization. The object and contents of free cities can be divided into territorial and political purpose and economic and commercial side. The former applies to political free cities, the latter to economic free cities, while some free cities are mixed in nature. The NAPC conceptually takes the form of mixed free city. Both political and economic objectives could be pursued. For its smooth operation, economic objectives should be emphasized more than political purpose. In this regard, China's special economic zones may be considered as being similar to the NAPC, but the NAPC is distinguished from China's special economic zones by the following points.

First, while China's economic special zones were driven by China's initiative, the NAPC would be constructed and administered by several countries.

Second, China's special economic zones were established with the objectives of providing 1) an introduction window for Western capital and technology, 2) a testing ground in which China's style of socialistic system was being constructed by the fusion of the market economy system and planned economy system, and 3) making a foundation for its economic integration with Hong Kong, Macau, and Taiwan. The NAPC is a testing ground that complements South and North Korea's industrial structure with each other, a place to conduct reunion meetings, a center for development in the DMZ and a city which plays an international role for world peace.

Third, China's special economic zones have a socialistic attribute because business activities in the zones are regulated by socialistic laws. It also has a capitalistic attributes in which a capitalist can own an invested corporation. Corporations invited to invest in the NAPC would be multinational or joint corporations between South and North Korea. Laws and regulations in the district would be based on international laws agreed by both sides.

Consequently, the NAPC does not have political, ideological and military characteristics. It adheres to neutral state's attributes. It bases its administration on 'the South and North Korea Basic Treaty' and 'the Multilateral Treaty for the NAPC Development', which means that it is administered by a third-party organization established by the US, China, Japan and Russia, as well as South and North Korea.

D. DMZ as the Optimal Location[167]

1) Site Selection

First of all, site selection should be based on project purpose. A few possible areas should be examined, and the most feasible area should be selected. Standards for selection are as follows:

1. An area that is close to or on the truce line, for the purpose of perceived balance and fairness.
2. An area which has favorable conditions for construction in terms of configuration of ground and space.
3. An area that has conditions for a traffic hub.
4. An area which will be able to play a central and promotional role for development.
5. An area suitable for essential functions and basic concepts of the NAPC.

On the basis of five standards above, 1) Kyodong district, 2) Kangwha district, 3) Changdan district, and 4) Kaepung district near the truce line in Kyonggi Province were selected as candidates.

2) The Hypothetical Three Functions of the NAPC

The most important standard in selection is value. There are three kinds of hypothetical functions for the NAPC. They are, 1) the function of the international peace organization, 2) the function of peaceful use of the DMZ, and 3) the function of a special economic district.

(1) International Peace Organization

At present, Korea is the only divided country in the world and still technically at war. For some time now, the Korean peninsula has been a potentially explosive powder factory in Northeast Asia, threatening peace and stability in the region. Therefore, the NAPC can be a symbolic city for meeting and communication which can reduce tensions between South and North Korea and can also promote international peace. What is most expected of the NAPC is reunion of dispersed families and activation of trade between South and North Korea. Also, the NAPC can be used as a place for meetings for religious and scientific interchange as well.

---

[167] This part is the summary of the previous studies, as follows:

Lim, Yang-Taek, "Research on the Development Strategy of a North-South Korea Special Economic Zone and the Selection of an Appropriate Region", paper presented at the Korean Academy of Economics, February 1990.

Lim, Yang-Taek, "A Study on a North-South Korea Special Economic Zone", *Economic Studies,* Seoul: the Korea Economic Association, December 1991.

Lim, Yang-Taek, "A Study on the 3rd Reunification and Economic Cooperation Model", paper presented at the Korea Economic Association, February 1992.

Lim, Yang-Taek, "Step-by-Step Strategies for inter-Korea Economic Exchanges", *Studies on the North Korean Economy,* Vol. 3, June 1992.

Lim, Yang-Taek, "A Study on the Strategies for the Establishment of the Inter-Korea Special Economic Zone", *Economic Studies*, Seoul: the Korea Economic Association, December 1992.

Lim, Yang-Taek, "How to Utilize the DMZ for Korean Reunification", paper presented at the Ministry for Reunification, Korea, December 1995.

The two Koreas joined the UN at the same time in September 1991 and in December of the same year they agreed upon reconciliation, non-aggression, exchange and cooperation. But unfortunately, there is no permanent meeting place for communication between North and South Korea.

(2) Peaceful Use of DMZ

The DMZ is a place which can not be ideally used economically and socially due to historical military confrontations between South and North Korea. Though there are potentially reclaimable land, an environmental preservation area, and an area for potential urban construction, at present, it is only used for military objectives. It is certain, however, that the DMZ is currently a useful area in terms of peace and economy considering its size and location. So, it is necessary to open and develop some part of the DMZ that can benefit both sides substantially. That is to say, by developing it into a some area for civilian passage, a model city can be built to contribute to civilian living standards and income growth by developing it into a tourism resource.

(3) Special Economic Zone

Even though the location of the NAPC should be in the DMZ, joint investment in which Western capital is combined with labor forces and natural resources of North Korea should be actively pursued. Its management benefits can be distributed properly according to the investment rate.

The NAPC is highly likely to be successful as a SEZ. To guarantee this possibility, the use of resources and energy and all the activities for trade also should be guaranteed. In fact, it is smoother to start from economic exchange based on economic actual benefit.

3) Changdan County in Kyonggi Province

Based on the selection standards above, there are four conditions for selecting the NAPC, including natural conditions, basic facilities, economic conditions and political/social conditions. Consequently, *Kangwha* district was selected in terms of basic facilities, and *Changdan* county was selected in terms of political and social conditions. In particular, *Changdan* district is close to Panmunjom. So, if *Changdan* can be developed for the NAPC and *Panmunjom* can be established as a historic preservation place, this district would have a high potential for development as the world's free city. Hence, *Changdan* county in Korea is selected as the right place.

Detailed description of the county is as follows. Changdan county is a flat area comprised of dry and paddy fields, isolated from South Korea geographically around the *Yimjin* River which flows from North to South. It is in contact with *Panmunjom* to the North and the *Yimjin* River to the South. *Ilsan,* a new suburb of Seoul, has already been constructed as a resident city, so the NAPC and *Ilsan* could complement each other.

E. Development Plan

1) Directions

Suggestion for five development directions of the NAPC are as follows.

1. A business plan agreed upon by North and South Korea should be implemented first and gradually.
2. The short-term aspects of the business plan should be pursued first, followed by more detailed long-term plans.
3. If there is no treaty on the establishment of basic facilities in the region, facilities inside the area should be constructed respectively.
4. The construction work and establishment of basic facilities should be pursued together.
5. Facilities in the DMZ should be constructed reciprocally, and budgets should be divided by both sides based on capability.

The suggested construction plan for the NAPC is summarized by <Table XIV-4>.

<Table XIV-4> The Construction Plan for the NAPC

Stage	The Construction Plan for the NAPC
I	First, economic functions should be developed.
II	Foundations for a North-South Special Economic Zone should be formed.
III	After the completion of basic facilities in the area, a peace district should be built.
IV	After the completion of basic facilities and a peace district, the Panmunjom area should be equipped with a Korean War memorial.
V	Industrial fields in which capital, raw materials and labor will be injected should be determined.
VI	When the NAPC is successfully managed initially, foreign Corporations should be invited into the area.

Source: Yang-Taek Lim, "Proposal for a Northeast Asia Peace City to maintain Peace in Korea Peninsula", paper presented at the seminar held by Institute of Developing Economies, Tokyo, Japan, January 28, 1999.

2) Strategies

Based on the preceding development directions, the development strategies are now suggested as follows:

1. A peace district should be constructed in the DMZ, promoting a bilateral business which provides a token peace city as an international symbol of expressing practical will for peaceful co-existence of South and North Korea.
2. The regions in the NAPC will be divided into six parts from North to South, and three parts from East to West, which highlights practical efforts for sustained peace in Northeast Asia.
3. By combing the function of the NAPC and a SEZ, both functional accumulation effects can be maximized. So, urban attributes and economic aspects should be considered in the establishment and management of basic facilities.
4. It is more politically and economically useful to arrange a SEZ in the North and South Korean economic district in each administrative area.

In connection with the previously-mentioned functional roles of the NAPC, the following are suggested to build some facilities:

1. It is desirable to arrange all sorts of functions for each economic and administrative district.
2. A Korean War memorial should be constructed around the *Panmunjom* area.
3. There should be a meeting place for North and South Korea with basic facilities.
4. An intermediate area should be constructed for commercial functions in the region.
5. A peace square should be constructed in the middle and lower areas in which all kinds of facilities related with peace would exist.
6. A water park near the *Yimjin* River and a peace tower near the southern part of the river should highlight the symbol of the NAPC.
7. It would be desirable to construct a peace center in the southern part of the *Yimjin* River, which would be the location for festivals.
8. The area under the peace center above should have all kinds of research functions, where all problems related with reunification and world peace could be studied.

The *Panmunjom* area should be used as park area, a meeting square for a park, and public facilities at night. Traffic networks should include the state road that passes through the NAPC area, and the existing Seoul-Yiju railroad that passes through a peace district, because the NAPC would not have a residential function in contrast to a normal city.

F. Legislative Instruments

The success of the NAPC depends on such legislative instruments such as a 'Multilateral Treaty on the Construction and Management of the NAPC', and 'Basic Treaty between South and North Korea', and a 'Special Law on South-North Economic Exchange'.

1) Multilateral Treaty on the Construction and Management of the NAPC

The multilateral agreement should include the purpose of the NAPC, and general matters on basic developmental directions and strategies. The action programs after the construction of the NAPC in connection with its functional roles (an international peace organization, a peaceful DMZ, and a SEZ) should be manifested in the agreement. It should also include items, quantities, prices, methods of transportation, forms of trading, billing methods and exchangeable currencies etc.

The establishment of a 'Northeast Asian Economy Committee' is necessary for the stability and expansion of economic exchanges among South and North Korea and international industrial cooperation. The discretionary and judicial power should be given to the committee, and would be reasonable to have a committee reside in the NAPC. The committee should arrange all kinds of systems including investment securities and dealings with banks for financial transactions.

2) Basic Treaty between South and North Korea

It is necessary for the two Koreas to agree upon a 'Basic Treaty' for the recovery of peace and co-existence under the current tense relationship. South and North Korea have already concluded a written agreement upon reconciliation non-aggression, exchange and cooperation in December 1991. The treaty should include abandonment of any use of threat by military force according to the UN Constitution and address human rights, as the Basic Treaty agreed between West and East Germany in December 1972.[168]

3) Special Law on South and North Korean Economic Exchange

The South Korean government should establish a special law on economic exchange for the vitality of economic cooperation between North and South Korea. The basic contents of a special law are as follows.

First, the South Korean government should establish basic principles on North- South exchange to avoid confusion that may arise. It should also establish an organization to settle or coordinate all policies.

The South Korean government should accept the suggestions for trade of natural resources, agricultural produces, fully-made products and select those products which are eligible for transactions. In the long term, with increases of transactions between North and South Korea, the South Korean government should expand the variety of products in a bid to restructure the industries in both countries.

In addition, the South Korean government should ease restrictions on trade with North Korea in the fields of personnel exchanges, resources transportation, transactions, and investment, and to the various aid systems such as taxation, finance, and insurance. The mediation function of the South Korean government should be enhanced to perform effectively the economic exchanges among private firms through limitations on over-competition for approaching North Korea, and mediation of conflicts breaking out in the process of trade and investment.

G. Anticipated Effects

'The NAPC in *Changdan* County, *Kyonggi* province, South Korea can influence political and military issues in a sensitive manner. The construction of the peace city is complicated related to measures of funding ways of administration and armistice issues in the near future, and as well directly connected to the issues of economic integration between South and North Korea, and their issues of political unification in the long term.

[168] For a detailed discussion, see:
Yang-Taek Lim, *A New Proposal for the Reunification of Korea Based on Its Economic Integration,* Seoul: the Mail Economic Daily Press, November 1993.
Yang-Taek Lim, *The People Perish Where there Is No Vision,* Seoul: the Mail Economic Daily Press, September 1995.

The establishment of the NAPC should not be considered impossible at all. In fact, recent political changes are forcing North Korea to open its doors to the outside world and to reform its internal structure due to the structural contradiction of its economy. Moreover, *Pyongyang* itself needs the construction of SEZ desperately as suggested earlier. Seoul will therefore be able to propel the construction of the NAPC in order to enhance and facilitate economic cooperation of South and North Korea and industrial cooperation in the international community using UN umbrella institutes such as ESCAP, UNIDO, and UNDP.

The expected effects concerned with the three functional roles(International peace organization, Peaceful use of DMZ, and special economic zone) of the NAPC are as follows.

First of all, North Korea could utilize the NAPC as an external bridge for which its doors can be opened to, as well as the way to overcome the current economic crunch effectively through introduction of foreign capital and advanced technology.

Next, *Pyongyang* would also be able to get substantial economic aid from South Korea as well as the US China, Japan and Russia in the name of capital and technology cooperation through the NAPC. Therefore, North Korea would be able to attract foreign capital for import substitution in the sectors of key industries, automation machinery, transport machinery, and daily commodities consumed on a large scale.

South Korea in turn, could consider joint investment in the field of electricity, electronics, general machinery, automobiles, and ships for which it maintains relatively high international competitiveness at the present, and in the field of shoes and textiles currently being transplanted to other areas due to relatively low competitiveness. Therefore, South Korea could utilize the NAPC as an experimental site of a unified state. North Korea can also making considerable efforts to prepare for opening the free economic trade zone in *Najin-Sunbong* area and is mobilizing to introduce the Chinese-style opening ways of economic development through special economic zones.

What should be re-iterated here is that a SEZ in *Changdan* County is more desirable than ones in the *Chungjin*, *Najin*, *Unggi,* and *Saebyul* in North Korea. South Korea should persuade North Korea to accept the proposal for the improvement and prosperity of the national community.

In summary, *Changdan* County is a place to experiment with economic cooperation, induce industrial restructuring, experiment the fusion of political, economic, and social systems of the two nations, provide a meeting place to recover Korean homogeneity, act as a center for the nation's territorial development after realizing unification, and serve as an international peace city for world peace, particularly in Northeast Asia.

Chapter XV

GLOBALIZATION AND REGIONALIZATION IN ASIA[169]

It is generally believe that the economic center of the world is moving from the Atlantic to the Pacific, from Europe and the United States to Asia. Russia has already pronounced itself to be part of Asia, *i.e.*, 'Eurasia', the US has declared Asia to be a region of national interest and Japan has returned to focussing on the region after attempting to break away from it.

While Asian countries were attempting to adjust to the new world economic order (UR/WTO), as their efforts were reflected in the Bogor Declaration (November 1994) of the WTO and APEC and also in the Osaka Action Directive (November 1995), the Asian financial crisis broke out.

Which problem points in the economic development strategy of Asian countries have led to the recent financial crisis? If the crisis is indeed a product of erroneous strategy, then which development model is optimal? Which aspects of economic development, a primarily Western method, contradict or complement Asian traditions?

Japan, Korea, Taiwan and Thailand are all Asian nations. Why is Japan, the country with the largest trade surplus in the world currently in the throes of an economic recession? Which factors contributed to the rapid fall of Korea, the country was often cited as a successful model of economic development? How could Taiwan with similarly scarce natural resources and a relatively weak domestic market weather the financial crisis unscathed? Which factors have brought about the financial crisis in Thailand which is one of the most open economies in the continent?

Furthermore, what is a desirable direction for regional economic cooperation and joint prosperity in the region? Is the Mekong River ideal economic cooperation zone? Or is the Tumen River more optimal? Why is progress for the TRADP (Tumen River Area Development Plan) slow despite the auspices of UNDP and the profound interest of ADB, the US, China, Japan, Russia, Mongolia, the Two Koreas and Europe not to mention various conferences which have already been held toward this end? What will be a more effective directive for the TRADP which will promote international industrial cooperation in the Northeast Asia region? What directives will ensure peace while promoting industrial cooperation in a collaborative and complementary manner?

1. GLOBALIZATION IN ASIA

Since World War II, regionalism has expanded and been accelerated by the UR negotiations which led to new regional agreements or expanded existing regional agreements. In the Asia-Pacific region, there had been no organizations for economic cooperation. Regionalism has been developed in sub-regions on a small scale. Therefore, efforts to pursue economic cooperation has important meaning in the context of the WTO. It should be keep in mind that regionalism is a precondition for globalization. In other words, promoting regionalism eventually makes globalization possible.

---

[169] This chapter was heavily drawn from the author's studies as follows:

1) Yoo, Jang-hee and Lee Chang-Jae (eds.), "Northeast Asian Economic Cooperation", *Progress in Conceptualization and in Practice,* Seoul: KIEP, 1994.

2) Yang-Taek Lim, "The Role of Korea in the Asian Pacific Economic Cooperation: with special emphasis on International Strategic Alliances", paper presented at the Kuala Lumpur International Conference (May 14-19, 1996) held by American Committee on Asian Economic Studies.

3) Yang-Taek Lim, "The Role of Korea in the Asian Pacific Economic Cooperation", *Research in Asian Economic Studies,* Vol. 8, 1998.

The post-Cold War world is characterized by globalizing under the framework of political realism. Liberalism implies individual wealth maximization based on economic rationality and institutions of individual rights and liberties. States act on political rationality which takes into account power, strength and legitimacy. The realist globalization of liberalism is the sources of current dynamics of international political economy and particularly prominent in East Asia where liberalism is itself somewhat differently conceived with more emphasis on national wealth and power rather than on individual liberty and liberal democracy, where authoritarian strong states are markedly visible in managing globalization and adjusting domestic political economy, and where regional geopolitics conditions liberalize regional economies. The findings lead to the examination of the possibility of formulating a synthesis of liberalist and realist elements, both of which are empirically observable in current process of globalization. [170]

A. APEC's Bogor Declaration

The important connection to link Asia's regionalism and globalization is to abide by the Bogor Declaration of APEC (Asia-Pacific Economic Cooperation). Economic cooperation in the APEC started in 1989 in a relaxed manner but as the necessity of economic cooperation has grown, a new direction was set by the Bogor Declaration. In the second APEC summit in 1994, schedules for achieving free trade were set for advanced countries by 2010 and developing countries by 2020. In the third APEC summit in 1995, the Osaka Action plan for free trade, investment schedules were to be submitted to MAPA and executed starting from 1997.

Liberalization of Trade and Investment

Each nation agreed to strengthen the world trade system and promote the UR agreement in the Bogor Declaration. The major rules were to pursue free trade, harmonize the APEC and WTO regulations and strengthen economic cooperation. In the Osaka Summit of 1995, practical rules and general principles of the declaration were set and an action plan for free trade submitted. All nations commenced their action plans for free trade at the same time and finished their examinations and adjustments for the next meeting. Nations were to promote free trade and investment on the basis of collaborative and independent ways and the Trade and Investment Committee was to report the results.

Activation of Trade and Investment

To ensure proper methods, compliance with *The Principle of Investment in Asia-Pacific* and to deter exceptional investment, some basic principles were concluded upon with additional devices for activating trade and investment was sought.

The APEC agreement is harmonized with international standards and principles, so the standardization process started along with general statements to simplify of custom procedure and has already been harmonized with customs institutions. Earlier, an agenda was agreed upon to perform the UR agreement: compliance with TRIPs to settle the Intellectual Property System in the region; independent and unrestrictive agreements may be concluded under the WTO Agreement and share electronic networks using Internet would be perused; in 1996, the system for Asia-Pacific conflict resolution substituted the DSB (Dispute Settlement Body).

In APEC's free trade plan, some basic agreements were reached in the Osaka Summit and for specific discussion in the Philippines Summit concerning the method, control and inspection from the APEC organization. The customs agreement included investment, standardization, competition policy on government supply, alleviation of regulations and procedures for conflict settlement which are all fields of the UR Agreement.

[170] Ho-Cheol Lee, "Globalizing Liberalism and Realist Globalization in East Asia", *Korea and World Politics,* Vol. 13, No. 1, Seoul: The Institute for Far Eastern Studies Kyungnam University, 1997.

B. Osaka Action Plan

The 18 countries in the APEC submitted plans for free trade and investment to be realized by the Osaka Action Plan. The contents of the Osaka Action Plan consisted of free trade, investment and technological cooperation with advanced countries. In the field of free trade and investment, there are regulations and general principles for customs, services information-technology, protection of marine resources and the building of economic capabilities. Initial examination of results was back in 1997. In the meantime, the agricultural issue compromised the position of various countries. Thus each nation decided to deal with problems in food, energy and environment at a later time.

Execution Measures

As a result of discussions about specific procedures to promote the Osaka Action Plan, member nations decided to simplify the method of submission. At the first Manila Summit in 1996, plans were adjusted and finally selected in the eighth cabinet committee. Time frames for short-term and long-term plans were made and nations positions were mediated and submitted to the APEC Trade Minister's Conference.

Early liberalization is the means to initiate the plan for free trade and investment for advanced countries by 2010 and for developing countries by 2020. The fifth APEC summit in 1997 adopted some items as early liberalization like the environment, energy, marine industries, toys, agricultural products, jewelry, medical equipment, chemical supplies and communication industry. Therefore, each nation participated in the promotion of early liberalization, separates from the general principle in Osaka.

Japan submitted a document to congress stating that the period of tariff reduction of coal-mining products should be made earlier from January 1998 to April 1996. China cut down tariffs in the field of semiconductors from 35.9% to 23% and removed non-tariff barriers for 176 items including automobile parts, copy machines, alcoholic beverages and cosmetics. Indonesia executed a step to alleviate economic regulations with an emphasis on tariff reduction by an average of 5% on 482 items including capital goods and raw materials.

The Philippines suggested the formation of an 'APEC Economist Committee' which would enlist 450 economists to assess validity of APEC. The United States tried to suggest making the telecommunication industry, timber products and non-steel products fields for early liberalization in the Eighth Cabinet Committee (November 1996).

Evaluation and Prospects

The promotion of free trade and investment was proposed by the Osaka Summit in 1995 and each nation submitted a draft for a free trade plan which is now in practice. Therefore, the movement in the APEC was meaning if its procedure go very well under the purpose of expanding an open market but there is some possibility of conflicts during the discussions on burning issues between advanced countries and developing countries. The Asian economic crisis has made the APEC agenda of secondary importance and thus, it will be important to regain focus when the situation stabilizes.

2. Tariffs Liberalization[171]

A. Liberalization of Tariffs by APEC Member Countries

The 18 member countries of the APEC which include the United States, Japan, China, Australia and Canada, have drawn up an action plan on the lowering of tariffs as a part of plans for opening up trade and investment in the Asia-Pacific region; the plan was implemented beginning January 1997 and the progress of each member was reviewed at the Trade Ministers Meeting in May later 1997. The summary of the action plan is as follows:

The action plan for the APEC member countries in the area of tariffs is specified in the 'Osaka Directives' which were drawn up at the Third APEC Summit in November 1995 and represent part of efforts to promote trade among member nations by lowering tariffs and improving tariff systems within the region. The proposal of member countries also varied: Japan, Canada and Australia proposed in fair

[171] This section was derived from Yang-Taek Lim, "The Role of Korean in the Asian Pacific Economic Cooperation", *Research in Asian Economic Studies,* Vol. 8, 1998, pp. 69~94.

detailed list of tariff rates by industry with specification of plan for liberalization which even exceeded the levels agreed upon in the UR; the United States has displayed an active attitude towards the conclusion of bilateral and multilateral agreements in such sectors as information technology, lumber and distilled goods where it maintains competitive edge; China and Taiwan, which are pursuing entry into the WTO, have also proposed proactive liberalization plans; however, other developing countries have been passive on the matter by merely emphasizing adherence to the UR.

While it is expected that efforts will be made on the issue of the lowering of tariffs, there is a large possibility that conflicts between developing countries emphasizing adherence to UR and advanced countries trying to focus on attaining a degree of equity by amending and supplementing the existing plan will surface in the course of negotiations.

An indication of such conflict may be seen in the United States' *1997 Annual Report on Trade Barriers by Country*, which comments the Korean economy as follows:

'Korea caused a considerable detriment to exports by imposing tariffs on American barley, honey, milk powder and popcorn under operating a discriminatory system of tariffs between soju (35%) and whisky (100%) while the system of import licenses for most industrial goods has been deactivated, control tariffs are still being imposed on certain items which indirectly seek to restrain imports and protect domestic products. Custom clearance is delayed by various restrictions set forth by the Ministry of Agriculture, Ministry of Health and Welfare, and the Plant Quarantine Agency, with excessive demands for proofs of country origin.

Imports are being directly restrained through campaigns against 'excessive consumption' promoted under the guidance of the Government with special taxes being imposed in addition to tariffs on imported cars (8%) for the purpose of restricting imports thus effectively containing the entry of American cars into the market. Rice is being imported under the MMA (minimum market approach) method of the UR agreement but exports of high-quality American rice is being restricted by the Government's tight control over the entire distribution processes from import to end-user'.

The said report provides a summary of the laws, systems, policies and practices of trading partners which restrict the activities of American enterprises and their exports and is submitted annually (since 1984) to the President and Congress[172] with demands for abolition or improvements of trade barriers being based on the findings of the report and MFN (most-favored nation) status under Super 301 article being reviewed every September accordingly.

As in the 1996 report, it continues to take issue with the problems of the import and distribution of rice in Korea and Japan which have partially opened up their markets through the MMA approach under the UR and, furthermore, makes strong demands for the opening of the automotive and telecommunication sectors as well as financial markets including banks, securities and insurance firms with noting Government-led efforts to restrict 'excessive consumption' and subsidies to enterprise.

B. The Case of Korea

1) Tariff system of Korea

The world has been ushered into an era of borderless competition with the establishment of the WTO in 1995 and the Korean Government has set 'globalization' as its national goal in response to the changing trade environment while putting forth maximum efforts towards the strengthening of national competitiveness for its successful achievement. The world trade order in recent years is a mixture of multilateralism and open regionalism. Multilateralism is typified by the advent of the WTO while the EU and the NAFTA are examples of rampant regionalism with open liberalism now being actively discussed by the APEC which could grow into an apparatus for economic cooperation.

Such complex international trade order inevitably requires the globalization and liberalization of the Korean economy which will entail the gradual and long-term abolition of tariffs and trade barriers. To keep pace with such trends, the Customs Office has enacted realistic and systematic reforms such as the switch from import licenses to import registration, customs payment in arrears, abolition of the bonded warehouse

---

[172] Nine categories-this is import system, standards and license system, government purchases, export subsides, IPR (intellectual property rights) protection, service trade, foreign investment, anti-trust practices and others-are designated and identified as trade barriers in case US exports are impeded without any regard for consistency with the WTO Agreement or other international regulations.

area system and in-principle abolition of bonded transportation in order to ensure a smooth flow of goods through customs.

The minimization of distribution and supply costs, which are important cost factors in economic activity, is one of the key issue in national competitiveness and its sustainable growth. The minimization of supply costs is important not only from a 'hardware' standpoint in terms of securing social infrastructure such as roads and ports, but also from a 'software' standpoint in that systematic impediments to the flow of goods are eliminated so that supply costs may be minimized without a large investment and national competitiveness may be strengthened in a very practical manner.

Due to its characteristic as a task which has as its subjects persons and goods being moved across borders, customs administration may be construed as a trade impediment in case there are discrepancies between the relevant countries. Accordingly, overall customs administration systems which include customs systems, item classifications and customs assessment are being standardized and unified through international organizations such as the WCO (World Customs Organization) and the GATT. Due to the international nature of customs administration, major trade partners such as the US and the EU have made repeated requests for improvements in Korea's customs clearing procedure and many improvements have actually been made in recent years. In terms of the time consumed in customs clearance, an international comparison shows that Korea is one of the most time-consuming and the most expensive countries.

The Government revised the Customs Law in December 1995 to replace the import license system with an import registration system while the bonded transportation system was greatly simplified so that in the case of raw materials, usage at production facilities was immediately possible after importation (see Figure XV-1). In the case of export goods, most recognized export firms were ensured a smooth flow through exemptions from bonded transportation and inspection so that loading and shipping of goods in advance has become possible (see Figure XV-2).

The reforms on the export and import customs clearing systems enacted on July 1, 1996 include: the replacement of export and import license system with a export and import registration system; the import registration immediately after entry into port, previously only possible after storage in bonded area; the implementation of tariff payments in arrears; and the replacement of license requirements for bonded storage and transportation with a registration system.

2) Tariffs Gradually Lowered

The base tariff rate of Korea has been changed from a system of staggered rates to one where an even rate is applied with 1984 being a turning point. A base rate of 20% was applied during the 1984~1988 period, while a historical rate system with 8% as the base rate was used for the 1989~1994 period due to the abolition of the defense tax. Since then the base rate has been lowered to an average of 7.9% as of 1996, a level comparable with other advanced nations, as a low and fair tariff system is presently instituted and implemented.

According to the concerned Korean law, included in the list of flexible tariffs are anti-dumping, retaliatory, emergency, special emergency, control, offsetting, convenience, price equity, seasonal and allocation tariffs. Such flexible tariffs have been in force with 1990 as a turning point prior to which the allocation and emergency tariff systems were implemented as means of stabilizing domestic inflation and protecting domestic industries and after which the allocation tariff continued to be in force around anti-dumping, control and increased allocation tariffs for the relief of domestic enterprises from damages stemming from unfair trade practices.

To date, Korea's external cooperation in regard to tariffs has been centered around the GATT/WTO and the WCO and the bilateral cooperation with the US and Japan have also been pursued. In order to develop tariff administration which has greater international competitiveness, however, efforts to absorb the tariff systems of advanced countries into Korea's own should be stepped up through the strengthening bilateral and multilateral cooperation (see Table XV-1).

< Figure XV-1 > Procedure for Import Customs Clearance of Korea

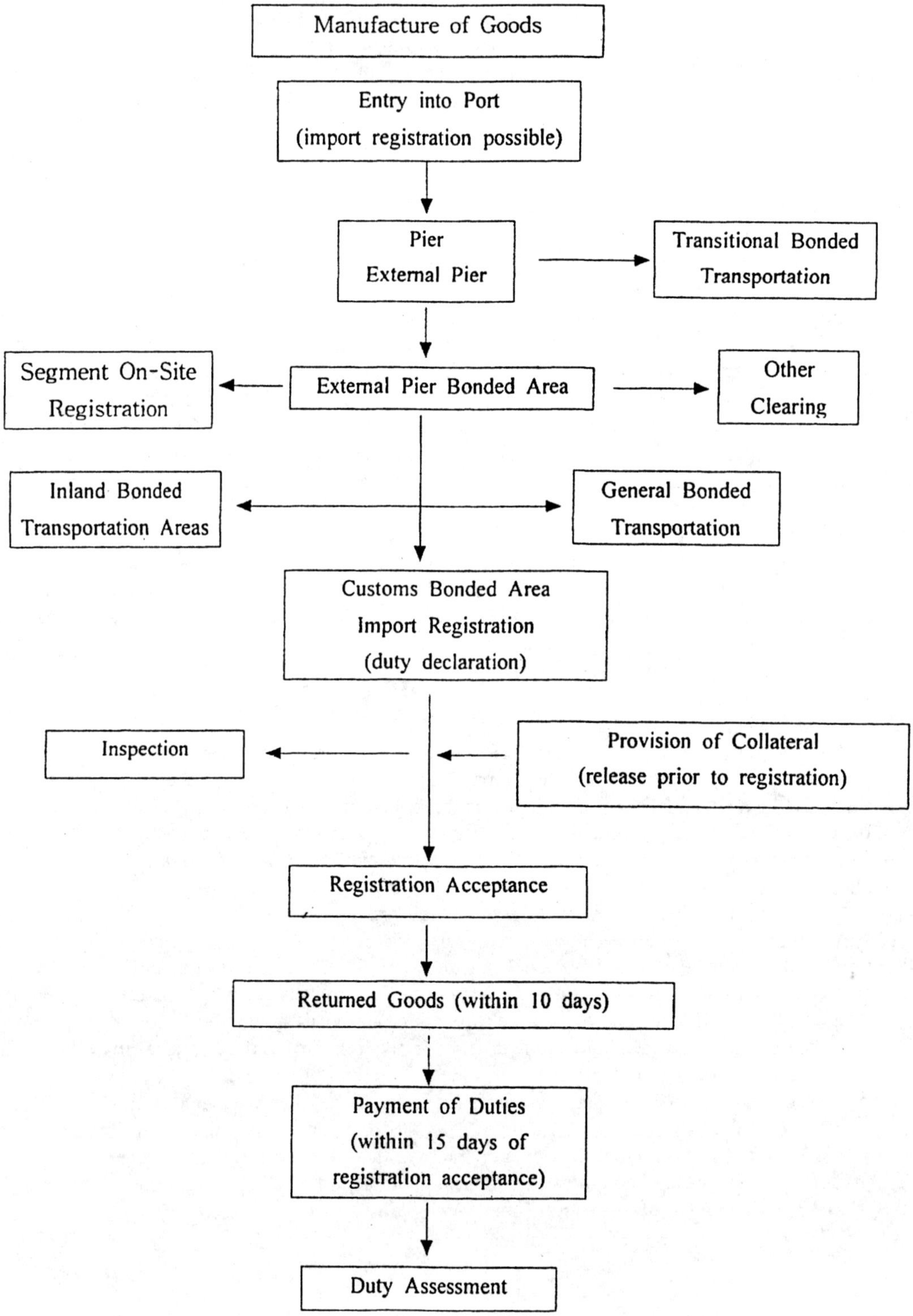

Source: Yang-Taek Lim, "The Role of Korea in the Asian Pacific Economic Cooperation", p. 89, in M. Dutta, ed., p.89, *Research in Asian Economic Studies*, Vol. 8, London & England, JAI Press Inc., 1998.

< Figure XV-2 > Procedure for Export Customs Clearance of Korea

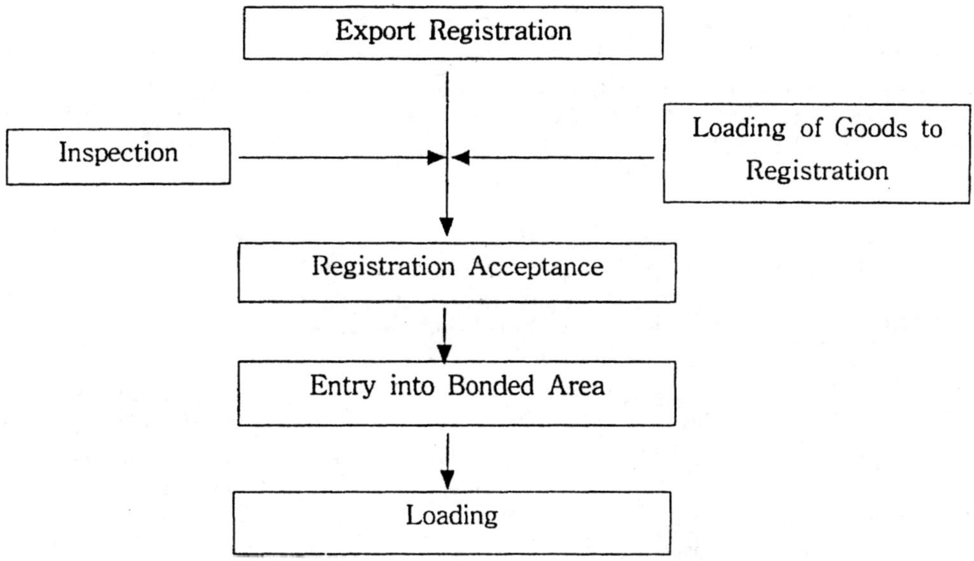

Source: Yang-Taek Lim, ibid., p.90, 1998.

<Table XV-1> Korea's Status of International Tariff Cooperation (Unit: Won)

	Category	Item	Main Items	Contents
1987. 7. 1.	Korea-USA Agricultural Goods	9	Lemon, Avocado, Cherry	Lowering of Tariffs of Agricultural Goods
1990. 7. 1.	Korea-USA Telecommunication	51	Teleprinters, Switchboards	Early (1 year) Implementation of Tariff-reduction
	Korea-USA Tariffs of Wine	20	Wine and Related Products	25% in 1991 20% in 1992
1991. 1. 1.	Korea-Hungary Tariff Agreement	31	Film, Steel, Aluminum Products	Average Tariff Rate 15.2% →10.2%
	Korea-UK Whiskey Agreement	4	Whiskey Products	40% → 30% in 1991~1993
	Korea-Malaysia	2	Palm Oil	Decrease in Tariff to Coconut Oil Level
1995. 1.	Korea-USA	129	Agricultural Products	Bilateral Agreement
		59	Automobile	Reduction from 10% to 8%
1996. 1.	Korea-EU	11	Whisky, Rum, Gin vodka, Liqueur, Brandy and other Distilled Wine Products	Reduction from 30% to 20%

Source: Yang-Taek Lim, ibid., p.91.

It also appears desirable to direct more active efforts in support of Korean enterprises which are faced with tariff barriers or other related difficulties abroad in the course of their export activities, especially since the country's economy has an export-oriented structure. Furthermore, although tariff negotiations under the WTO are still in their initial stages, the APEC is considering early and voluntary implementation of the expected results and thus Korea is now in a position where it must take a more proactive position on the matter.

3. The Prospects for APEC

After the Cold War, economic blocs which have been concentrated on a few advance countries are now being pursued by most nations who consider protectionism a major policy. Up to the present, there have been some economic blocs in Asia such as APEC, EACE (East Asia Coast Economic bloc). However, there are some smaller economic blocs like Tumen River and West Coast economic bloc in the Northeast; the South, Yangan and the China economic bloc centered around China; the triangle area with ASEAN, AFTA (Asia Free Trade Area), the Baht economic bloc and the enlarged ASEAN, and; SAARC which is centered South Asia.

There are no concrete organizations for economic cooperation in the Asia- Pacific region like the EU in Europe or NAFTA in North America. Even though Asians believe APEC could do something substantial, cooperation between countries is a problem. However, the economic cooperation in Northeast Asia has potential importance that it can share some natural resources and economic factors as well as dynamic trading conditions and scale of the region.

The future of APEC, in terms of its institutionalization, function and even nature, has been the subject of intense scholarly discussion. This study argues that institutional features of APEC influence not only the workings of the institution but also the nature and character of the institution itself. This study, adopting an institutional approach, suggests that we have to keep an eye on interactions among major members of the APEC over the issue of the APEC's institutional features, especially the openness of the institution, the size of the institution and the level of institutional authority. The future direction of the APEC will be mainly influenced by the struggle between the U.S. and the ASEAN. The role of Japan is critical in the sense that it can change the balance between two actors.[173]

As Russia has joined the APEC in 1998, it would have an important effect not only on the APEC itself but also on Korea. The major motivations of Russia's joining the APEC are as follows: First, in order to increase Russia's role and influences for overall political, economic processes in the Asia-Pacific area. Second, in order to increase Russia's international cooperation with the nations of the Asia-Pacific area in terms of mutually beneficial trade, investments and cooperation in scientific technology. Third, in order to create a favorable precondition for Russia to solve the socio-economic problems in Siberia and the Far Eastern area.[174]

Evaluating the APEC highly since activities of its member nations are fairly open and voluntary and it covers broad range of activities such as liberalization of trade and investments, econo-technological cooperation, Russia looks upon the APEC as a very efficient mechanism for actual and multilateral cooperation in this area. Russia regards energy, transportation, communications, telecommunications, investments cooperation, human resources and economic, technological cooperation as the major promising fields for multilateral cooperation through the APEC.

Russia's entry to the APEC can help to strengthen the military, political security in the Asia-Pacific area and move the center of activities of the APEC to Asia, especially North East Asia. Furthermore, it can offer a more favorable situation to the developing countries in the APEC that are more interested in technological cooperation controlling the advanced nations such as the US that intend to put priority on trade liberalization among the major objectives of the APEC.

However, despite Russia's firm declaration that it would be faithful to the basic principles of the APEC, it seems that Russia's joining the APEC has been significant only in a political aspect, not in an economic aspect so far. Thus, economically, Russia's entry to the APEC cannot have fundamental influences on the APEC for a while.

In the future, the APEC countries should make more aggressive efforts to produce favorable conditions for economic cooperation with Russia at multilateral levels through the APEC as well as to increase mutual cooperation with Russia at a bilateral level.

The beginning of the 1990s brought about drastic changes in the international environment with the disintegration of the bipolar and cold-war system. U.S. President Clinton proposed the new Pacific

[173] Hyun Seok Yoo, "A Study on the Future of APEC: An Institutional Approach", *Korea and World Politics* Vol. 14, No. 1, 1998.

[174] Jae-you Lee·Jae-young Lee, "The Background of Russia's Joining the APEC and Russian Policy toward the APEC", Survey Report 98-07, APEC Analysis Series, Korea National Committee for Pacific Economic Cooperation, July 1998.

community strategy, which aims to drive Asia-Pacific cooperation onto the path similar to European integration.

The Bogor announcement can be said to have contributed to building the concept of liberalizing export and investment for sustainable economic growth in the Asia-Pacific region. But there still remains the problem of how to put the concept into realization. Generally, if an approximate schedule can be set up on when and in how many stages to carry out the concept after agreement in principle on its realization and in consideration of the proposals by each participant country based on its own characteristics and in parallel with coordination and inspection over cooperation, it can be said to be fruitful in its own sense. But the problem lies in the possibility that the U.S. may deem this insufficient to satisfy its own intentions and may demand agreement of more-in-depth principles and more radical stage-setting, thus driving the conference up against a wall.

The Asia-Pacific cooperation has long proceeded in an ejective way and has not lost its significance because of the changes in the international environment. Only when the effectiveness for this method is respected can liberalization of trade and investment in the Asia-Pacific region be realized and can it give full play to its efficacy.[175]

A. Importance

The Asia-Pacific region, especially East Asia has recorded an unprecedented high growth rate during the past 20 years. The economic growth rate of the NIEs, the ASEAN and China far surpassed the average of other developing countries in the world from the 1970s to the 1980s. Japan also maintained over 4% of growth rate which exceeded the average growth rate of the developed countries. Thus, the high growth rate has an intimate relationship with high growth in trade.[176]

Another point worth noting is that the regional trade interdependency in the Asian Pacific economies was very high and recently has surpassed the regional trade interdependency rate of the EU. A comparison was made between the regional trade inter-dependency of the Asian-Pacific region and the EU by using the combined incomings and outgoings in intra-regional trade. The average index of intra-regional trade of the Asian-Pacific region was 1.78 while that of the EU was 1.63 and so it is clear that the region has taken giant steps toward actual economic intergration.[177]

Active investment in the Asia-Pacific region also contributed to the intensification of regional interdependence. In the Asia-Pacific region, there exist major investing countries such as the United States and Japan and major invested countries such as the ANIEs and the ASEAN. Recently, the ANIEs such as Korea and Taiwan have also taken up the role as investing nations and intra-regional investment is expected to increase even more, as China emerges as a major economy. Investment is mostly being concentrated on leading manufacturing areas and the areas related to industrial restructuring.

However, to promote high growth and regional interdependency even further in the Asia-Pacific region, conflicts of interest among the countries in the region such as trade conflict must be rationally controlled. It must be kept in mind that there are still various different alignments within the region. Economic cooperation, for example, can be divided into the NAFTA, the AFTA, the EAEC and the APEC. The first three are sub-regional in character. whereas the APEC includes the entire Asia-pacific region. This is also the reason that APEC is given the most attention as it can play the role of connecting the America and East Asia. It might more appropriate for East Asia to intensify economic cooperation in the entire Asia-Pacific region through the APEC, which would in turn be an effective safety device in checking the EC from becoming exclusive or discriminative.

The diversity of the Asia-Pacific region, which on the one hand guarantees complementary cooperation among the economies, however, also acts as a barrier to the pursuit of the closer cooperation. Therefore, the APEC has not yet been able to match the EU in unity. If the function of the APEC is strengthened, the power to check the EU could be gained; on the other hand, if economic cooperation is pursued separately in Asia and North America, effective checking of the EU could become impossible for the following reasons:

---

175 Chen Lu-zhi, "Two Methods and Ways of Asia-Pacific Economic Cooperation", *Korea and World Politics* Vol. 14, No. 1, 1998.

176 IMF, International Financial Statistics, 1992. ADB, Key Indicators of Developing Member Countries, July 1991. WEFA. World Economics Outlook, January 1992.

177 Korea Research Center of Overseas Economic Policies, *New Direction of Asian-Pacific Economic Cooperation,*. The Korean Committee of Asian-Pacific Economies, December 1993.

first, the economic size of the two regions will not be large enough for negotiating power to match that of the EU; second, if economic unification is not achieved, the EU will gain multiple counterparts for negotiation; and lastly, the EU will gain economies of scale in terms of intra-regional trade.

By reverse logic, it may be said that the unification of the EU acted as a catalyst in the formation and development of the APEC. The possibility of competition or conflict between the Asia-Pacific region and the EU will be a huge factor in the establishment of a world order of free trade.

Taking into consideration the common interests of the member nations, cooperative projects were begun at the Second Cabinet Meeting in Singapore in July 1990 with a focus on areas that have a low risk of conflict so that a positive cooperation could be achieved. As the APEC has developed, the number of participating countries has also increased with the so-called 'three China's-China, Taiwan and Hong Kong - entering simultaneously at the third cabinet meeting in Seoul in November 1991. In the process, China raised questions on the qualification of Taiwan and Hong Kong,[178] but Korea exhibited its diplomatic power as the chair nation, in mediating a compromise on the condition that Taiwan be called 'Chinese Taipei'.

B. The Development and Expected Effects of APEC

1) Major Issues

Issues that are difficult to solve by bilateral negotiations such as the opening of the Japanese market, the continuing openness of American markets, and the transfer of technology from the developed countries are expected to be discussed inside the framework of the APEC. The following is a summary of the major issues which need to be resolved if the APEC is to take form as a true economic union :

Acceleration of the UR: Other than the agricultural sector including the rice market, there are no foreseeable difficulties associated with accelerating the application of the UR agreement. Since such acceleration will not be unilateral, increased exports may be expected as the APEC members act in unison. Also, a strong stance must be taken toward requests for exceptions based on structural realignments and/or transitions to market economies, so that all APEC members including Korea may take part in this effort.

Lowering of tariffs. In the case of industrial goods. there should be little additional burden for relatively open markets like Korea which maintain relatively low rates. Lowering tariffs could also bring about further increases in exports to the ASEAN nations and China in light of the fact that the trade volume of these countries is already on the rise. It will be in the best interest of most countries to take an active stance in regard to lower tariffs and carry out gradual but swift cuts in their own tariff rates.

Liberalization of investments. Liberalization of investments will provide an opportunity for promoting the transfer of technology needed for intensive growth, so it will be desirable for non-advanced nations to take an active position on an APEC accord on investment. However, difficulties may be foreseen in the case of total liberalization so that some caution is warranted for certain restricted fields.

Development and technological cooperation. Full cooperation in the field of technology must be agreed in order to help establish a smooth cooperative relationship with developing countries while facilitating the introduction of technologies in key fields. Efforts should be made to link the responsibility for increased the ODA accompanying the OECD membership with development cooperation within the APEC, so that cooperative relationships *vis-a-vis* developing countries may be strengthened without incurring additional costs.

Strengthening of international regulations. Measures currently pursued by the APEC to prevent the abuse of anti-dumping system, strengthen competitive policies, preserve the environment, designate standards and compatibility and simplify customs clearing procedures are not only consistent with the liberalization and globalization policies but also quite desirable from the standpoint of increased exports. Countries like Korea which do not employ industry protection measures, must actively support progress in this regard and make efforts to assume a leadership role since the strengthening of such regulations should not incur much additional burden.

---

[178] While, in the process of achieving APEC, politically, China is continuously restraining Taiwan, which China is supporting Taiwan's position in the expansion of support for small and medium-sized businesses and the activation of transfer of technology. After the transition on July 1st, 1997, Hong Kong has been officially renamed as Chinese Hong Kong.

Arbitration function for disputes. Under the upcoming order of free world trade, it would be desirable to support and pursue the establishment of an arbitration board to resolve such trade disputes as anti-dumping judgements, the application of the Super Article 301 by the United States and unilateral trade measures within the framework of the APEC.

Sub-regional agreements. It will be desirable to attune any sub-regional agreement with the APEC in order to alleviate any exclusionary or discriminatory practices. In the case of Korea, an alliance must be sought with Japan and China to counter the potentially discriminatory nature of such agreements most notably the NAFTA.

2) Direction of Development

At present, the efforts of APEC to liberalize intra-regional trade have been focused on the resolution of various tasks that have been formed since the conclusion of the UR. There is a great possibility that the APEC will concentrate on the discussion of new areas that the UR did not deal with, such as environment-related trade negotiations. However, with the conclusion of the UR, the room for error in trade liberalization will be relatively narrowed, and instead, cooperative projects for strengthening intra-regional economic relations, which was the initial goal of the APEC, will become more active. Thus, as the APEC pursues expansion of trade, increased transfer of technology and development of manpower in a more concrete way, its character will become more regionalistic.

For the APEC to succeed, a cooperative environment among the Asia-Pacific countries must be formed. Real benefits from economic cooperation must be guaranteed through the pursuit of cooperative tasks including trade liberalization. If the development of the APEC is delayed, there is a great possibility that sub-regionalism in the Asia-Pacific region will intensify. In the Asia-Pacific area, besides the NAFTA and the AFTA, which are negotiations on national levels, there exist many sub-regional economic zones: the so-called 'Growth Triangle' that connects Singapore, Malaysia and parts of Indonesia; the Baht economic zone that includes Thailand, Laos, Cambodia and Vietnam; and the economic zone of the Yellow Sea that includes South and North Korea, Northeastern China and Japan.

The Growth Triangle is showing rapid growth, yet the Baht and Yellow Sea economic zones are not very active. What must be noted here is that these economic zones were not formed artificially but formed naturally from economic flow. Therefore, it would be important to steer the activation of sub-regional economic zones in the Asia-Pacific area in a positive direction to help develop economic cooperation through the growth of mutual interdependency.

There exist several issues that will determine the direction of APEC's development. However, the specific area of activity of the Trade and Investment Committee should first be set and plans for the implementation of tasks discussed. Talks that were pursued in 1994 revealed much compromise between the developing and developed countries but somewhat lacked the ability to pursue the actual liberalization of trade and investment. Also, policy cooperation will have to be discussed and eventually promoted.

The issue of establishing regulations in the APEC Summits will also have a great effect on the direction of its development. If regulations are set, policy cooperation in the OECD and G7 will be possible and the development of APEC will gather momentum. For a long-term development of APEC, it is necessary to look over the proposal of the PAFTA (Pacific-Asia Free Trade Area), presented by several prestigious groups. At present it is true that the PAFTA is against the APEC's cooperation rules preventing the formation of economic blocs. However, if the PAFTA is adopted by the APEC as its long-term vision, trade liberalization in the entire Asia-Pacific region would be accelerated.

As the structure of APEC is set and cooperative projects become more concrete, also there exist differences in opinion between the developing and developed countries are surfacing regarding APEC's overall speed of development. The developed countries, centered around the United States, mostly desire APEC to become a more concrete organization quickly, while the ASEAN countries and China wish to slow down the development of APEC. Similarly, there are differences in opinion on the selection of the major areas to be focused in trade liberalization efforts.[179] The United States is supporting overall trade liberalization, with the goal of opening Japanese markets. However, ASEAN feels that it is too early to select areas on trade liberalization and is too early to act on.

---

179 Through five cabinet meetings, the APEC achieved a great deal in the development of its organization. Taking into consideration the common interests of the member nations, plans for cooperation projects were drawn from the second cabinet meeting so that the projects would focus on areas that are low in the possibility of raising conflicts, and can readily demonstrate the achievements of cooperation.

On the other hand, Australia and New Zealand wish to make the task of opening the agricultural market top priority, while Korea and Japan, though not opposed to the opening of the industrial product markets, adamantly refuse to open the agricultural market. Conversely, the developed nations believe that technology will be naturally transferred through the expansion of foreign direct investment; on the other hand, the developing countries view the transfer of technology as a powerful tool to diminish the gap in the level of development between member nations, and to readjust their own industrial structure.

So, a cooperative organization which guaranteed the continuity and effectiveness of economic cooperation in the Asia-Pacific region is desirable for a number of reasons. At present, APEC's efforts to liberalize intra regional trade will focus in the resolution of the various tasks that have been formed since the recent conclusion of the UR. As well, through the pursuance of cooperative tasks, real benefits from economic cooperation must be guaranteed.

3) Expected Effects

The greatest expected effect of the APEC is that it will alleviate the worldwide movement toward regionalism which is at present becoming ever intense. It is expected that the APEC will maintain a non-exclusive, open regionalism. The Asia- Pacific region will share the fruits of economic cooperation with countries outside the region and thus will promote the establishment of multilateralism. Therefore, the development of the APEC will influence the opening of existing economic blocs. If the EU develops into an exclusive economic bloc, APEC could take collective opposition act as a check on the EU. Also, by leading the NAFTA members into a wider frame of economic cooperation, it could alleviate discrimination towards non-NAFTA member countries.

The success of the APEC would establish reciprocal relationships of the existing blocs inside the Asia-Pacific region and even resolve the conflicts. For example, the APEC will alleviate the protectionist tendencies of the American market which are the result of trade conflict with Japan. If there is free trade in the Asia-Pacific region, it will be easier to venture into the Japanese market and thus the United States will restrain itself from policies aimed at unfair trade practices such as Super Article 301 and 'anti-dumping' verdicts. Considering the fact that Japanese-American economic conflicts have brought about shrinking world trade, the APEC could make a huge contribution to free trade.

If the function of the APEC strengthens, the strength to check the EU would be achieved. If economic cooperation is pursued separately in Asia and North America, effective restraint of the EU would not be possible. This would be due to the limitations in negotiation power, and the EU's gain of multiple counterparts for negotiation. If the EU cannot be checked, the Asia-Pacific region will fall into a relatively disadvantageous position, and therefore the establishment of the APEC remains quite an important matter.

If the development of the APEC is delayed, there is a great possibility that sub-regionalism in the Asia-Pacific region will intensify. Several issues exist that will determine the direction of the APEC's development. A plan must be devised that will form maximum, concrete cooperative achievements in the trade and investment areas, as long as it does not raise the strong objections of the developing nations. The development of the APEC, however, will ultimately be greatly affected by the attitudes of various participating countries and the task at hand will be to bring those differing positions into harmony.

From the aspect of politics and security, the APEC will contribute to peace and stability in the region, particularly in Northeast Asia where the two Koreas are in confrontation. The collective security system which will fill the power vacuum formed from the disintegration of the bi-polar system, will clear away an anxiety in international politics, prevent wasteful arms competition and thus promote economic prosperity in the Asia-Pacific region.

Still, it would be difficult for the Asia-Pacific region to change into an united economic bloc overnight because of the diverseness of the economies of the member states, the conflicts of interests and the differences of opinion between the developed and developing countries. However, the APEC will contribute greatly to the formation of a cooperative environment in the region and the maintenance of intra-regional dynamism by the APEC will result in common prosperity for the entire region.

C. The Positions of Major Participating Countries

The development of the APEC, however, will be greatly affected by the attitudes of various participating countries. The following is a look at the positions of the major players.

1) The United States

America's overseas economic policies could be summarized as follows: first, the US will put its efforts into establishing a new order of multilateral free trade supporting the smooth inauguration of the WTO. Second, it is expected to support the strengthening of the APEC and ultimately lead the economic integration of the APEC in order to loosely tie the Chinese and Japanese economies to the American economy. Third, if America decides that the trade liberalization and the resolution of trade conflicts through organizations like the WTO or the APEC are not satisfactory, it will not hesitate to execute retaliations like the Super Article 301 or other actions by USTR.

In the early days of the APEC, the participating intentions of the United States were to check the establishment of an 'Asian economic bloc' excluding the Unite States, quicken the conclusion of the UR through APEC and possibly promote negotiating power with the EU. Therefore, in that period, the United States saw the APEC as merely a supportive tool of the UR and showed a passive attitude toward the development of APEC itself. More recently, however, it has realized that the APEC could be both an economic opportunity and important foreign policy tool. President Clinton has said that American national security depends on the country's economic power. When looking ahead into the 21st century, there would be no region more important than the Pacific Rim for the economic health and welfare of the United States. The economic systems of APEC are the main markets for American economic growth. The United States now realized its future depends on a wider, deeper and stronger participation in the Pacific Rim and greater cooperation with its APEC companions.

The responses of the East Asian countries to the NAFTA negotiations has also contributed to the US policy of putting weight on the APEC. The US was at a loss when the East Asian countries showed greater resentment of the NAFTA than expected and worried about competition between East Asia and North America as a result of the establishment of the NAFTA. This is an indication of the flip side of the coin. If the achievements of the UR are not satisfactory, it seems that the US hopes that the liberalization of intra-regional trade in the Asia- Pacific region will compensate for it. Thus, from the 'Pacific Round', the US can gain an opportunity to put market opening pressure on the East Asian countries. By the same token, as the APEC develops into a force that checks the EU, it is possible that American negotiating power with the EU can become greater.

2) Japan

Japan sees the APEC as a preferable alternative for strengthening economic ties with Asia and North America, the main markets of the country, and in coping with regional blocs such as the EU and the NAFTA. Thus, Japan is actively participating in the APEC, however, Japan is putting itself on guard against the establishment of a cooperative structure dominated by American interests and is thus advocating an open economic association. Rather than quick realization of intra-regional trade and investment, it favors a gradual economic cooperation process, starting from areas of cooperation that seem possible after considering the economic realities of the Asia-Pacific region.

3) China

China has not yet applied for membership in the WTO and so it has recognized the importance of the APEC as a stepping stone toward advancement into the international economic stage. It is focusing on attaining export markets through the APEC and in expanding the introduction of capital and technology into the country. However, like the ASEAN countries, taking into account its weak industrial competitiveness, it is opposing fast liberalization of trade and investment, and also putting itself on guard against the rapid development of the APEC into an economic cooperation framework led by the US.

4) The Six ASEAN Countries

In the case of the six countries of the ASEAN members, while they acknowledge the importance of the APEC, they are worried about the weakening of the ASEAN and are showing a tendency to oppose a quick development of economic cooperation centered around the APEC. In particular. Malaysia is showing great determination towards the EAEC, the strategy for the co-existence of Chinese and non-Chinese people in the East Asian area, thus has showed an extremely negative reaction to the movement to strengthen the APEC under the leadership of the US. Overall, the ASEAN countries are showing much interest in functional cooperative projects, such as technology training and the establishment of investment and information centers, which will promote the transfer of technology necessary for their own industrial development. However, they appear to be reluctant to liberalize trade and investment level of domestic industries and open domestic markets.

5) Canada and Australia

Canada and Australia are showing basically the same position as the US in regards to liberalization on intra-regional trade and investment. However, the two countries are showing a more positive attitude toward the provision of regulations that will suppress the dominance of the powers in the region. particularly the US. Therefore, these countries have taken up the role as intermediate powers in the region, making efforts to attain an independent position through the adjustment roles among member countries.

6) Korea

APEC, aiming at open regionalism, is not only the sole regional economic apparatus which Korea is a part of, but is rapidly emerging as an economic alternative beneficial to Korea as it unites East Asia and North America with the new world order. As a member of the Central Council, Korea has already affirmed its important status within this bloc.

As the development of the APEC progresses, opening, development and globalization of the Korean economy will be enhanced. Much of the Korean economy is already open and plans are already in place even for the areas that have not yet been opened, so there would be little additional burden from a full opening.

In regard to its political-diplomatic aspects, it is hoped for that the APEC would provide a strategic basis for Korea to secure a position as a major player in coming 21st Century Asian Pacific Era, expand its scope of influence and assume an important international political role. Given that it may play a leadership role, the APEC may be extremely useful in heightening Korea's status in the international community

Meanwhile, the APEC will serve as the optimal economic insurance policy in response to the instability of the multilateral trade system, the formation of the EU and the NAFTA and other regionalistic trends, while contributing to the formation of a stable market within the greatest economic bloc in the world. Moreover, the APEC should help provide a useful foundation from which to alleviate the unilateralism or bilateralism of advanced countries and other trade pressures at a regional level.

The promotion of regional trade should not entail any additional burdens on Korean economy as market opening policies are already being pursued in line with the OECD membership, policy talks with the US and the ongoing process of globalization. Rather, it is more likely to be an opportunity to expand into the closed markets of Japan and the ASEAN countries and foster exchanges with China. Korea is thus at a position where it should actively support an open trade format in which all member countries take part and take an active stance in regard to liberalization of FDIs.

4. The Features of Northeast Asia

There are two ways of defining Northeast Asia. First, it could be divided into six countries and nine regions such as South Korea, North Korea, Japan, China, Taiwan, Hong Kong, Macau, Mongolia and Russia. The more specific definition would only include South Korea, North Korea, Japan, the east part of China and East Russia. We shall use a more specific definition as this study concentrates on economic cooperation between countries in Northeast Asia not economic unification with other region.

Economic cooperation in the Asia-Pacific region requires the cooperation of China, Japan, the US, and North Korea. The reason is that even though these countries face different circumstances, each could get a certain amount of Population. GNP amounts to US$6.3 trillion about 25% of the whole world production. Therefore, Northeast Asia is not only big within Asia but rivals to Europe and North America in its importance. China accounts for 76% of the region's population; Japan accounts for 73% of its GDP and; China and Russia comprise 92% of the region's land area.

<Table XV-2> Major Statistics of Northeast Asian Countries

Category	South Korea	Taiwan / Hong Kong	Japan	China	Mongol	North Korea	Russia	World
Population (million)	44.5	26.2	125.0	1,190.9	2.39	23.5	148.3	5,601
Land Area (1,000 km^2)	99	37	378	9,561	1,566	121	17,075	133,478
Population Density (number/km^2)	449	708	331	124	1.5	195	9	42
GDP (billion US dollars)	376.5	375.8	4,591.0	555.2	0.823	n.a	376.6	25,223
GDP per Capita (US dollars)	8,260	14,320	34,630	530	300	n.a	2,650	4,470
Annual Average Growth Rate (1980~1994, %)	7.8	6.1	3.2	907	-3.2	n.a	-3.2	0.9

Source: Yang-Taek Lim, *Prospects for Asian Economies,* Seoul: Maeil Economic Daily Press, January. 1999, Chapter 6 (P 396).

Northeast Asia is big enough to form a regional economic zone with a population of well over 1 billion and total GDP reaching US$3.3 trillion. The countries in the region have interdependent relations in resources, technology, capital and labor. It is thus necessary to pursue joint development rather than the development of individual country.

A. Political Aspects

Northeast Asia is not only the most central area in Asia but also it is an area in which the interests of 4 powers, the United States, China, Russia and Japan, directly meet. After the end of the Cold War, global powers consider cooperation, peace and development as more important than conflicts and antagonism. However, there has been no system for ensuring peace and stability in the region.

Recently, there have been efforts by Russia and China to be a strategic companions and also by United States and Japan through a new security pact. Such alliances will cause changes in security strategy in Asia. The four powers of the regions have put into action cooperation for the purpose of mutual restraint and balance. The United States will try to restrain China's expansion while improving relations with China to restrain Russia.

After the Cold War, China adopted a multipolar strategy in opposition to unipolar control by the United States, so they have intentions of restraining the United States and also Japan. In addition, Russia has voiced their objection to the expansion of NATO and is driving forward to strengthen relations with China, Korea and Japan to accelerate domestic economic development. Japan is also trying to set new balance of power by reforming relations with Russia. The importance of Northeast Asia in the field of politics and military will be significant in that country achieving a power in the region will lead all of Asia. Thus, economic cooperation in the region should accompany political and military fields.

B. Economic Aspects

1) Rapid Economic Growth

Since 1980s, the rapid growth in Northeast Asia area has been based on international trade. Each country has developed its special industries while importing inadequate economical resources.

Japan adopted an overseas-oriented development strategy to achieve rapid growth from the 1950s until 1970s, becoming an world advanced country with an annual economic growth rate over 8%. Even though annual growth rate has slowed as the economy has stabilized, it still remains as the only advanced industrial country in the region. Developing countries have followed the history of Japan to develop themselves based on labor-intensive industries. In the case of China, it has emerged as a newly developing country with adopting such a strategy. Even though economic growth has slowed, the region has a potential energy which could make it comparable with the United States by 2020 according to the World Bank.

2) The Interdependence of Industrial Structures

The economy of the NIEs has grown continuously after the Plaza Agreement in 1985 due to the strengthening of international competitiveness. However, Japan has pursued economic restructuring after 1988, as price competitiveness weakened and trade conflicts deepened. The reform is focused on developing the domestic economy and specifically expanding investment in capital and technology. Direct investment in the ASEAN has also been accelerated cheap production costs and trade conflicts. Many countries in the ASEAN are due to driving forward for economic growth by accelerating foreign investment as well as exporting through labor-based industries. Also, economic cooperation and development planning by governments was another factor in the rapid growth.

3) Regional Trade Structure

According to economic development and industrial growth, the importance of trade structure has also grown. First, in the export structure between NIEs and the ASEAN countries, industrial products comprise a high proportion of exports. Also, the rate of exports in capital-intensive products has increased rapidly. ASEAN members have concentrated on foreign investment and export-intensive industries, so the magnitude of industrial products has expanded from furniture and rubber products to textiles, clothing and TV.

In exports, the contribution of Japan is highest, while in imports, the contribution of NIEs is growing rapidly. In the case of the ASEAN countries, NIEs contribute the greatest portion to imports and exports. It means that in the international trade of ASEAN, the importance of NIEs has become greater. The rate of export combination to other regions was over 1, while the extent of exports' concentration is relatively high compared with other regions. Especially, the NIEs' rate of export combination to Japan and China has grown rapidly.

As for the rate of trade integration, there are a lot of differences according to the political situation. Most trade integration indices formed according to trade root are being formed at over 100. In the case of the comparative advantage index in Northeast Asia regime <Table XV-3>, highly populated countries as Japan and NIEs have comparative advantage in manufacturing but comparative disadvantage in agricultural products.

<Table XV-3> Comparative Advantage Indices in Northeast Asia

	Agricultural and Marine Products	Miner and Coal Resources	Labor Based Products	Capital based Products	Technological-based Products
Japan					
1979~1984	0.14	0.09	1.09	2.55	1.30
1985~1990	0.11	0.11	0.56	1.96	1.33
1991~1995	0.09	0.16	0.51	1.60	1.44
NIEs					
1979~1984	0.70	0.35	4.03	1.08	0.65
1985~1990	0.53	0.38	2.93	1.00	0.80
1991~1995	0.47	0.43	1.84	0.92	1.88
China					
1979~1984	1.60	0.95	3.35	0.37	0.31
1985~1990	1.25	0.84	3.83	0.49	0.27
1991~1995	0.87	0.42	4.02	0.68	0.37
Russia					
1979~1984	0.52	2.58	0.07	0.26	0.37
1985~1990	0.67	4.12	0.11	0.33	0.37
1991~1995	0.81	50.6	0.12	0.24	0.26

Note: In the case of Russia, 1990 figures are for the U.S.S.R.

Source: 1) ANU, International Economic Databank.

2) Yang-Taek Lim, *Prospects for Asian Economies,* Seoul: Maeil Economic Daily Press, January 1999, Chapter 6 (P. 403).

Nowadays, Japan has comparative advantages in technological products rather than labor-based products and also NIEs have followed suit, so in 1990s, technological products have become comparative advantage industry. China lost their comparative advantage in agricultural products after the period of open door policy but that of labor-based products has increased fast instead. Russia has a comparative disadvantage in manufacturing while it has comparative advantage in mineral resources, so Russia has a possibility to export their mineral resources to Japan and NIEs, whereas imports manufacturing products from them.

Trade in an industry means not only exports of the same kinds of products but also imports between countries and is used frequently to analyze the dynamic changes and competent relations in international division of labor structure. The progress in trade of a single industry is realized due to the comparative advantage of Heckshər-Ohlin, economies of scale and technological gaps.

Here the Grubel-Lloyd index is most frequently used to analyze textiles, clothing, steel, office tools and electronics, the major export products for Korea. The horizontal division of labor structure in Korea and Japan has increased as horizontal industry are growing and specially in the field of electric-electronics goods.

However, Japan has developed technical procedures for making products and South Korea has undertaker vertical division of labor within the same industry. The relations between Korea and ASEAN are not frequently analyzed but as imports have increased in office tools and electricity and electric-electronics goods, horizontal division of labor is growing. It shows that ASEAN has develops their own industry beyond those industries of textiles and clothing.

5. Necessity for Regional Economic Cooperation and Future Development Directions

A. Necessity for Regional Economic Cooperation

Northeast Asia consists of Japan (the advanced industrial country), Korea and Taiwan, (the dynamic industrial countries), rapidly developing China, Russia and Mongolia. Because each of these countries has its own comparative advantages; Japan in capital and technology-based industries, China in labor-intensive industries, Korea and Taiwan in middle industries and Russia and Mongolia in agricultural industries, the region has high potential. Since the advent of the WTO system, regionalism continuous to grow and strong cooperation in the region is urgently needed. Also in the APEC, there were discussions of sub-regionalism and as the economic crisis which occurred in Southeast Asia in 1997 has spread, interests in economic cooperation are growing. There are several reasons why economic cooperation are being accelerated in Northeast Asia.

First, the necessity and possibilities are very high. For example, advanced and developing countries like Japan, Korea, Taiwan, Hong Kong and Singapore have affluent capital, technology and skilled manpower and China has plenty of labor and natural resources. The northern part of Russia and China have lots of natural resources and energy.

Second, because, culturally and socially, these countries are sharing many in common it is easy to invest in this region. Many companies in Hong Kong and Taiwan invest in Chinese coastal areas where culturally and socially it is very close. It eventually affects expansion and development of trade in Northeast Asia.

Third, the development policy in the region is intended at transfer of technology, capital and skilled labor force. Undeveloped countries imitate economic development strategy of advanced countries and alleviate the investment and trade system to induce needed capital and technology. Therefore, countries lacking labor move their manufacturing to overcome inadequate labor and high wage problems. In particular, the potential power of regional cooperation by dynamic economies like Korea, Japan and China is great.

However, there are many obstacles to economic cooperation in Northeast Asia: Even though the Cold War has ended, its remnants still persist; The former communist countries such as China, Russia, Mongolia and North Korea are still socialist economies or in the process of switching to market economies; and There are big gaps between countries in economic scale or level of economic development; It is hard to say that there is homogeneous cultural or racial relation in Northeast Asia despite similar cultural background.

Therefore, economic cooperation in the region should be established not only between countries but also between region and should be interpreted as the concept of all kinds of bilateral and multilateral economic cooperation.

B. Future Development Directions

Multilateral cooperation in Northeast Asia should move toward functional integration by private companies and regional centers, not toward institutional integration pursued by governments or economic groups.

1) Industrial Restructuring by Direct Investment

Economic cooperation between advanced countries like the EU and the NAFTA are aimed at generating benefits from competition as markets are unified or from economies of scale or free trade. Therefore, the best way to integrate is through free trade after all. However, in Northeast Asia, the way of cooperation would be a vertical specialization. It could get benefit all in a short period, but it could also deepen disparity in the long run.

Therefore, what is needed is cooperation toward industrial structure reform. For example, after Japan (advanced country) undertakes restructuring, Korea (developing country) follows by direct investment and China (undeveloped country) chases the developed countries as chain and eventually 3 countries would be able to achieve an economic development.

Countries in East Asia have had comparative advantage in labor-intensive industries since early industrial days. Japan in 1950s, NIEs in 1960s and 1970s and China in 1980s all entered world markets on this basis. Many countries except Japan introduced foreign capital and technology and combined with cheap labor force to strengthen export competitiveness. In the process, as capital accumulated, the level of comparative advantage became high.

Japan in 1960s and the NIEs in 1970s diverted from labor-intensive industries to heavy and chemical industries. From the 1970s, Japan developed technology- intensive industries like processing-assembling industries. This phenomenon occurred to continuous growth, economic restructuring and increased inter-dependence due the changes in comparative advantage. The advanced countries lots comparative advantages in labor-intensive industries and became to concentrate on half-processed raw materials and machinery parts production which are technology-intensive.

Trade between industries were expanded and industrialization diversifies and deepened, so eventually horizontal trade developed. As a result, catch-up effect by stages occurred and also caused mutual cooperation and competition leading to industrial cooperation and economic integration. In the meantime, during the process of catch-up, combination of industrial and export comparative advantages eventually caused unbalanced trade among region. This is a basic reason holding back continual growth in the region.

Therefore, nations in Northeast Asia should strengthen and pursue multilateral free trade zone while addressing the limitation of export strategy focused toward the US So, the role of Japan is important. Japan should serve not only as machine parts supplier but also as a market for goods. Also, China and NIEs should enlarge domestic markets to offer markets for other countries.

2) Major Target: Resource Development

China opened subterranean oil field in mid-1980s and expanded it to coal- mining, and recently even natural resources development. To cope with an food shortages, they tried to open foreign investment to agricultural development. Japan maintains a close relationship with China thanks to governmental and private sector assistance. In addition, Japan has participated in oil development through private capital. Korea is also looking to develop coal and mining resources, but it is not certain because China's delays in opening. Korea has had certain strategies in the fields of automobile, aircraft and HDTV after normalization of relations with China in 1992.

However, so far, it has concentrated on light industry products such as consumer and household electrical appliances.

The resource development of Far East Russia has been delayed due to the lack of capital, labor force, technology and market. Japan has pursued timber, coal and gas development on the condition of securing certain resources but they are at a standstill because of rigid relations between Russia and Japan. Therefore as long as there is political conflict, the joint investment by Japan or NIEs is difficult.

Korea's investment toward Russia accounts for 0.2% of total investment. In the first half of the 1997, the Netherlands (29.7%), the US (24.2%) and Switzerland (16.5%) accounted for the majority of the total amount and in the case of direct investment, the US recorded the highest amount. Investment is distributed in the fields of finance (25.6%), trade (13.8%), fuel industry (12.3%), food (11.8%), retail (5.4%), manufacturing (5.4%), timber or textile (4.7%) and others.

6. Tumen River Area Development Plan[180]

A. Development Plans for Northeast China, Far East Russia and North Korea

The TRADP (Tumen River Area Development Plan), chosen as a primary project for development in Northeast Asia, has potential to greatly influence regional economy structure and cooperation between neighboring countries as well. China is concentrating on cooperation with other countries while Russia and North Korea are forced to move to open-door policies. South Korea is trying to develop its East Coast and also to expand capital and technology exports. Japan expects to reduce the economic gap in the region by recovering its domestic economy.

[180] This section has been heavily drawn from Yang-Taek Lim, *Prospects for Asian Economies,* Seoul: Mail Economic Daily Press, January 1999, Chapter 6.

In February 1998, 'The 1998 Northeast Economic Conference' was held at Nygata, Japan. Politicians, businessmen and scholars from Japan, the two Koreas, China, Russia, Mongolia, the UN and the ADB discussed how to revitalize regional economic cooperation.

The first section, under the title of 'Northeast and Southeast Asia' discussed ways to adapt previous experience of MeKong River Development Project to the TRADP. The second section 'Improvement of Transportation System in Northeast Asia' discussed ways to improve passenger transport system for the tourism industry. This conference on the TRADP and other potential projects for cooperation provided an opportunity for multinational discussion which had been lagging due to political and economical difference.

1) Northeast China

(1) The Current Status of Three Provinces in Northeast China

Liaoning Province

Liaoning had long been the first heavy industry center under communist rule. It has not coped well with market opening because there are too many state-owned enterprises and old facilities resulting in the sluggish economic growth of Liaoning in 1980s. Recently, however, it is growing rapidly, relying on foreign technology and abundant resources. It is expected that Liaoning will play a role as a gateway to the three provinces in North East Area and will develop more rapidly if the problem of state owned enterprise is solved.

In 1994, regional gross product was 2,584 billion *yuans,* primary industries occupied 12.3%, and secondary industries 34.2%, which means tertiary industries were very important. Exports reached US$6.87 billion in 1994 which is three times that of imports. This is because Liaoning is the center of heavy industries and it has abundant mineral resources for self-supply.

Jilin Province

Though Jilin's economic level is not high, it is the biggest food production base with a natural environment suitable for agricultural development. It also has many state owned industries which have grown slowly as northeast areas. In 1994, regional gross product was 9,470 billion *yuan,* primary industries occupied 24.8%, secondary industries 46.0% and tertiary industries 29.2%. Jilin Province has emphasized those production of car, train, railway, steel alloy and carbon.

In trade, exports reached US$2.02 billion and main export items were corn, bean, iron and steel, cement, textile, ginseng, car, rice and timber. Major export markets were Hong Kong, Japan, Russia, Singapore, the US and North Korea. Main import items are steel, chemical fertilizers, car parts, raw chemicals, chrome and machinery from Germany, Japan, the US and Hong Kong.

Heilongjiang Province

Heilongjiang is a producer of oil and coal, especially Daqing oil field benefits the whole nation as a large-sized. Heilongjiang's potential has been curtailed owing to the stagnation of production. On the other hand, if resource focused investments are continuously induced, its potential could be greater than before.

(2) Special Science & Technology Zone

Harbin Province

The Harbin Province of Specialized Science & Technology Zone has favorable conditions of location, low wages and convenient transportation to Russia and Europe. It is eager to induce foreign high-tech enterprises by providing tax benefits, high quality labor and quick administrative services. At the very beginning, it was a provincial-level development, but it was escalated to a state-level development since March 1991.

The zone consists of three regions: Nangang Intensive Development Zone, Xuelu Development Zone, PingFang Development Zone and the city supposed to be rearranged in entirety by 2010. Harbin, with a population of 5.3 million, is the capital city of Heilongjiang and is a heavy-industry center with 156 fully or partially state-owned enterprises, Harbin electric industry and Harbin aircraft manufacturing firm. It enjoys abundance of high quality labor force, which is good for technology-intensive industries based on 24 institutions of higher education such as Harbin Engineering College, more than 300 science and technology research institutions and up to 70 thousand science engineers.

Changchun Province

Changchun Province of Specialized Science & Technology Zone was designated as a specialized development province by the State Council in 1991 and is one of the ten most developed provinces. It has 18 institutions of higher education and 39 science research institutions directly belonging to the state.

Shenyang Zone

In order to develop high-tech industries, the Shenyang Specialize Science & Technology Zone was designated. China expanded policies preparation of an educational-industrial complex and tax benefits. The Shenyang Zone also started from province-level development zone in 1988, but was upgraded to the status of state-designated development zone.

Its land area is 32 Km2 consisting Nanda Industrial District, 'Keji Shang Cheng' Science-Technology-Commercial District, 'Donga Science and Technology Institute' in Shenyang, and 'Huihan Industrial District' in suburban areas.

Numerous software development enterprises including some from Japan and the US have been established in this region. There is also a Chinese Robot Development Center, R&D and production information tools like IC cards, Nickel hydrogen battery and other numerical control devices.

2) Far East Russia

This area hopes to expand economic cooperation with East Asian countries, but is suffering from the Russian economic depression, lack of institutionalization and the abolition government policy favoring the Far East. It wants more autonomy in terms of dealings with foreign economies, however, the Russian government is still refusing it, due to the anxiety that economic decentralization would lead to political separation.

The Russian Far East has fairly good preconditions for building up international economic relations in the Asia-Pacific region.[181] Geographic distance from Moscow, dominance of mining and primary processing industries and rich endowment with raw materials, most of which were considered a relatively negative factor for economic growth, now seem to be on the positive side of the picture.

The Russian Far East requires a huge amount of investment resources for successful realization of its development plan. The results achieved so far fall far behind what was expected. This fact may be accounted for political instability and nearly complete abandonment of investment activities by Russian enterprises. The situation is made only worse by conflicts between federal and regional governments and among different branches of local administration. In general, the development of the Russian Far East in the near future will be determined by economic and political situations of Russia.[182]

Here is the Russian Far East to give a general picture of the region that has begun to transform itself in terms of politics, economy and society.

(1) Trends in Trade

Russia is classified by 12 economic regions. The Far East area has the largest land mass and consists of coastal area, Khavarovsk, Sahalin, Alulin, Kamchatka, Magadan and Saha Republics.

In the Far East, the Jabaical region occupies 40% of Russian land area, 7% of its population and 6% in industrial output. They have abundant hydro-power generation, rare metals such as gold, silver, tungsten, zinc, other nonferrous metals and marine products, while fossil fuel reserves are estimated of 20 billion tons.

In the East Siberia and Far East Area, there are 43% of Russia's whole coal reserves deposit, 18% of oil, 29% of natural gas and 75% of hydropower generation sources making it a prime source of energy.

Foreign trade in this area was at a high level in Russia's initial period, but since then it has steadily declined. China became its first trade partner in 1996 from the fourth in 1995. The reason for this is due to continuing depression of Russian economy to have weakened central Asia region of Russia, whereas increased trade volume with China by Sino-Russia cooperation in defense industry, at the stage that its economic cooperation with Asia-Pacific countries such as Japan and US has yet to be activated.

[181] I. D. Skorbatyuk, "The Political Changes and Situation in the Russian Far East Since the Breakdown of the Soviet Union", *Sino-Soviet Affair,* Vol. XX, No. 2, Summer 1996.

[182] Han Jong-Man, "The Russian Federal and Regional Government's Development Plans in the Russian Far East: Possibilities and Obstacles", *Sino-Soviet Affair,* Vol. XX, No. 2, Summer 1996.

(2) Long-Term Economic Development Plan

The basic objective of long term economic development plan in Far East area is minimizing obstacles in creating new economic environment, and applying soluble resources to overcome the present economic and social crisis, building a basis for growth and raising the region's living standard to the average level of Russia. Until 1998, input of 37 trillion rubles has been designated to overcome the regression of forestry and fishery, clean up poverty and ensure economic stability. By 2000, economic and social situation will be improved and by 2005 the employment will be increased and of linkage to Asia-Pacific areas improved.

The required money is supplied by budget of regional government private capital, federal budget and foreign investment (12~15%). The plan for this is that authority on controlling tariff is given to the local government, regional development fund is mobilized by using natural resources and state-warranty on foreign investment.

(3) Nahodka Free Economic Zone

Nahodka free economic zone is the main freight transportation center to go forward to the Asia-Pacific, European Part of Russia and Western Europe. So far, more than 450 corporations in the area are in the process of being established, equipped with such conditions as storage houses for consumer goods and import goods to be moved to Eastern Europe markets from Asia-Pacific countries.

The area is located in the southern east coastal region and has many kinds of abundant natural resources connecting railway to Siberian transcontinental railway, so it has the SOC to be linked with the Far East area. Owing to these favorable conditions, the area was appointed as the first free economic zone in Russia in July 1990 for the goal of inducing foreign investment and developing the Far East area.

In order to expand the investment of foreign companies, a lower limit for foreign investment was fixed; for example, the import tariff of corporations with more than US$100 million in assets or whose investment stock is more than ten million dollars is reduced for 5 years by 50%. In January 1995, 124 of incorporated enterprises and foreign invested enterprises, 19 missions and 10 branches were invested. By country, China ranked the first number invested enterprises and Japan was the first by invested amount.

3) North Korea

Special Economic Zones in North Korea can be classified into 5 zones: Najin- Sunbong Zone including Chungjin, Najin, Sunbong and Heilyung; Pyungyang- Nampo Zone including Pyungyang, Nampo and AnJun; Pakchun-Wonsan- Hamheng Zone including Wonsan, Hamheng, Hungnam and Kimcheak; Heju-Kyugsung Zone including Heju, Kyugsung Sariwon; and Abrok River Zone including Sinyiju, Gusung, Kangkye and Manpo. Of these, Najin Sunbong zone and Abrok River Zone have the possibility of economic cooperation with Northeast Asia. North Korea is especially promoting the value of the Najin Sunbong Zone.

Najin - Sunbong Zone

The area is the border of North Korea, China and Russia closed by Tumen River and is a to key point advance into Northeast Asia. Chungjin Industrial District of Najin Sungbong is the central heavy industries district in the East Sea Region that had been developed as a supply base for the Japanese army during World War II. The area is surrounded by mountains and East sea with has lots abundant natural and marine resources. There are port facilities such as Chungjin, Najin- Sunbong and also a shipyard, ironworks and chemical factories.

Pyungyang - Nampo Area

Pyungyang - Nampo Zone is similar with the Seoul region of South Korea. As the capital metropolitan area, this zone has one of high economic power and relatively well-developed infrastructure, making it a good place to invest in the short term. This place is near Seoul metropolitan area and can realize international division of labor among China, South Korea and North Korea. The weak point is that there is political sensitivity and there is no investment support like Najin Sunbong area.

Pakchun - Wonsan - Hamheung Zone

This area is by the East Sea and has a couple of rivers with no well developed harbors. Compared to Najin-Sunbong area, this area is not appropriate for trade with China and Russia as it has a bad investment environment in the short-term.

Heju - Kyesung Zone

This area is the nearest districts from South Korea. Compare to the other areas, it maintain a middle level of the industrial inland. Inland transportation such as railroads and roads are developed to a certain degree but other industrial facilities and electricity remain at a low level. The biggest problem in this area is that there are only a few industrial facilities except cement factories. If economical reunification between South Korea and North Korea is assumed, the evaluation of this area would be different, but in a short run, the area does not possess sufficient advantages.

Abrok River Zone

This area has developed mechanical products industries and is a fishing headquarter; 70% to 80% of area is mountainous, so it is famous for forestry and fishing. This area can take advantages as a border siting with China, but it is generally analyzed that investment environment such as infrastructure, SOC and market opening development is a little difficult. In the long run, this area can be used for border trade and export manufacturing complexes. Also, good hydropower system in this area can provide enough electricity for operating factories.

B. The Current Status of TRADP [183]

Northeast Asia is rapidly developing and has big potential. After relations began to improve in international environment in the middle of 1980s, the Tumen River Area became an attractive area. Exports on this area insist that it has a big interdependence in multilateral cooperation. It also has a legitimacy in efficiency and technological rationale as an economic triangle harbors located in Tumen River. Triangle is related with Pohang, Pusan, Ulsan harbor in South Korean East Sea and some harbors in Japanese Western Sea. It can also have a land bridge role to Mongolia transport routes.

<Figure XV-3> Envisaged Organizational Contour of the TRADP

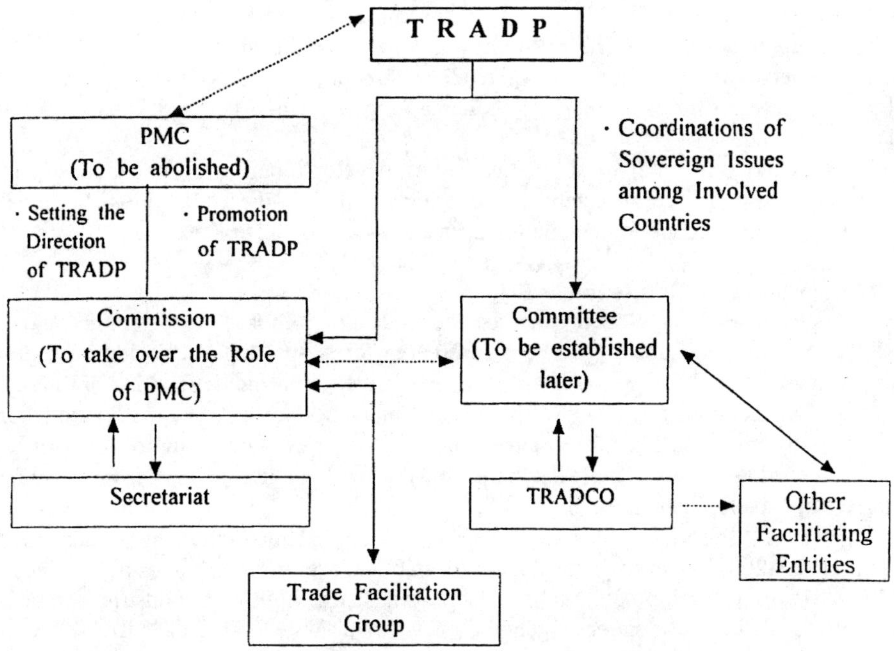

[183] For a detailed discussion, see :

1) Yang-Taek Lim, "TRADP and Cooperation among South and North Korea and Russia", paper presented at the International Conference on Socioeconomic Changes and Investment Climate in the Far East of Russia held by the Institute for Sino-Soviet. Hanyang University, April 16-17, 1996.

2) Yang-Taek Lim, *Prospects for Asian Economies,* Seoul: Mail Economic Daily Press, January 1999, Chapter 7.

If the transportation advantage is used appropriately, Tumen River Triangle could develop into a center of transportation, trade, and a new industrial area. There are also big possibilities to develop tourism, education, technology and energy.

1) Overview of the Development Plans

(1) UNDP's Plan

In September 1991, the UNDP suggested the 'TRADP Plan' to related countries. Since then, four schemes have been suggested. The first plan is that each country develop special economic zones independently. This plan would have a high availability but low efficiency. The second plan, preferred by China, is that a special economic zone be constructed on the border for improved cooperation. The third plan is that each country build a free-trade zone through joint investment and regard it as a transnational organization. The fourth plan is that infrastructure development be allotted to prevent duplication of investment. For example, Russia would develop the airport and China the industrial park. The details of the four plans would be worked out through continuing conferences according to each country's standpoint.

(2) China's Hunchun Area Development Plan

China has a plan to develop the Hunchun area as a center harbor related to Najin-Sunbong, Chungjin harbors in North Korea and Jarobino-Pociet in Russia. Also, Hunchun will be developed as an industrialized city in the middle term as an urban center in Tumen River Area. Under the strategy, China assigned the Hunchun area as an open border city in March 1992 and an economic development area in May the same year.

Thereafter many companies advanced into this area, Hunchun has developed into a big city with a population of 2.5 million. The Hunchun development plan is proceeding most actively among three countries in the border. Hunchun's main target is the build-up of capital-intensive or labor-intensive industries. The plan is divided into three steps. The first step (1990~1995) is to consolidate basic infrastructure like related railways and Fangchuan harbor.

The second step (1996~2000) is to promote networking effect through roads and harbors. The third step (2001~2010) is the final step, developing Hunchun into a center of Northeast Asian economy. As a part of this plan, China is developing Hunchun to be divided into four areas. China assigned the western part for nonferrous metal and agricultural resources development area. Also, if China cannot establish an international city in three countries' border, China has a long term plan that will build Hunchun into an international city independently.

A plan with Hunchun as a center would be pursued as: develop a harbor in the mouth of Tumen River and convert it into a free trade harbor; establish a free-trade harbor in the Hunchun at the three countries' border; and build a economic cooperating zone for China, Russia and North Korea.

(3) Russia's Vladivostok Area Development Plan

Vladivostok Special Economic Zone can be divided into Nihoka, Vladivostok, and Hatsanski. Vladivostok Special Economic Zone would be a base camp for supporting R&D, administration, finance and education. Nihoka Special Economic Zone is an extensive, land-intensive industrial area. Hatsanski Special Economic Zone can take advantage of border of China and North Korea, using the labor of North Korea and China to develop light industry or agriculture and fisheries. According to this plan Vladivostok Special Economic Zone has to be a manufacturing zone with free trade harbor. Under this assumption, they suggested a three-step development plan.

The first step (1991~1995) is a preparation step: consolidate infrastructure like roads and rail-roads. The second step (1996~2000) is an import substitution step to develop import substitution industries. The third step (2001~2010) is a development intensive step; in this step, high-tech industries are developed for domestic or export demand, but Russia has a generally negative attitude toward the TRADP.

(4) North Korea's Najin - Sunbong Development Plan

North Korea has a plan to make Najin and Sunbong areas into an important international freight relay center, import-export manufacturing center and tourism center. The target is a relay style import-export manufacturing center with a free-trade harbor under the following plan.

The first step (1993~1995): Consolidate infrastructure like harbor, roads, and rail road to develop Najin-Sunbong Zone into an international freight relay center; The second step (1996~2000).

<Table XV-4> Comparison of Three Countries' Development Plans

	China	North Korea	Russia
Basic Objectives	-Make Hunchun into a free economic trade region	-Make Najin-Sunbong into a free economic trade region	-Make Vladivostok into a free economic trade region
Form of Economic Zone	-Export manufacturing region (including free trade harbor)	-Relay-style export manufacturing region (including free trade harbor)	-Export-import manufacturing region (including free trade harbor)
Base City	-Small triangle - Hunchun, Fangchuan-Big triangle - Yanji	-Small triangle-Najin- Sunbong Big triangle- Chungjin	-Small Triangle-Jalunobi, -Big Triangle-Vladivostok
Function of Region	-International airport Jilin as industrial center, Northeast Asia center industrial city	-International freight relay base, manufacturing export base, international tourism base	-International freight relay base (to develop Jalunobi harbor)

Source: Yang-Taek Lim, *Prospects for Asian Economies,* Seoul: Maeil Economic Daily Press, January 1999, Chapter 7 (P 471).

<Table XV-5> Development Objectives of Each Country's Development Plan

	China	North Korea	Russia
Steps	**Classification of the periods of each step**		
The First Step	Developing step (1990-1995)	The first step (1993-1995)	Preparation step (1991-1995)
The Second Step	Improving step (1996-2000)	The second step (1996-2000)	Export substitution (1996-2000)
The Third Step	Leaping step (2001-1010)	The third step (2001-2010)	Development (2001-2010)
Steps	**Contents to achieve by each step**		
The First Step	-In order to construct a harbor in inland consolidate infrastructure (develop Hunchun, Fangchuan Harbor intensively)	-In order to relay international freight consolidate infrastructure (develop Najin area harbor intensively)	-Build resource-intensive manufacturing industry, -Resolve piling-up of old infrastructure
The Second Step	-Enlarge infra construction for uplift relating effect between major industries	-Extend infrastructure constructing and raising export-leading style manufacturing industry	-Foster export substitution industry
The Third Step	-Develop Northeast Asia into industrial center and build connecting Europe and Asia land and sea transporting network.	-Build multidirectional international interchange city	-Raise high-tech industries
	Focusing		
The First Step	-Regain rights to the sea through Tumen River -Build connecting rail road to Craskino -Construct Fangchuan Harbor -Establish Hunchun-Fangchuan road	-Extend Najin Sunbong and Chungjin -Build China and Russia connecting railroad and road -Establish an industrial complex in Sinheng, Dongmyung, Changpyng, Chengkye, Bakhak)	-Enlarge Jalunobi harbor -Build railroad connecting Craskino, Jalunobi and China
The Second Step	-Dredge Tuman river and extend Fangchuan Harbor -Establish Hunchun-Fangchuan road and railway	-Build highway connecting China and Russia connecting Highway -Establish an industrial complex in UngSang, Kyuankok	-Enlarge Jalunobi -Build railroad connecting Craskino, Jalunobi and China
The Third Step	-Extend Fangchuan Harbor -Reinforce North East Asia rail-way net	-Enlarge harbor -Establish an industrial complex in Huchang, Hongyi	-Enlarge Jalunobi harbor

Source: Yang-Taek Lim, *Prospects for Asian Economies,* Seoul: Maeil Economic Daily Press, January 1999, Chapter 7 (P 472).

Intensify the role as an international freight relay center and induce foreign investment in export-oriented manufacturing.

The third step (2001~2010): Develop international telecommunication city which can function to relay trade, export-related manufacturing, tourism and finance.

(5) Comparison and Evaluation

Based on the TREZ (Tumen River Economic Zone), China is trying to develop Hunchun, North Korea trying to develop Najin-Sunbong and Russia is trying to develop Jalunobi and Pociet. Based on the TREDA (Tumen River Economic Agency), China trying to develop Yanji, North Korea is trying to develop Chungjin and Russia is trying to develop Nihodka and Vladivostok.

(6) Financial Support Plans

The most difficult aspect for TRADP is fund raising, financial support plans concerned to be compared as below.

<Table XV-6> The Comparison of Three Countries' Financial Support Plans for TRADP

	China	North Korea	Russia
Level of Government Support	- Active support from central government - Strong support from local government	- Strong support from central government	- Negative support from central government - Negative support from local government, either
Legal Support	- Assign Hunchun as a opening city (1992.3) - Approve establishing Hunchun border economic cooperation district	- Assign Najin-Sunbong free economic trade zone (1991.12) - Establish a law of free economic trade zone (1993.1) - Notify various fare of free economic trade zone	- Assign Nihodka as a free economic trade zone (1990.7) - Establish a law of free economic trade zone (1990.11)
Institutional Support	N.A	- Organize foreign economic cooperation committee - Establish the authorities in free economic trade zone	N.A
The Content of Developing Plan	- Establish infrastructure construction plan in each step - Set up spatial industrial arrangement plan - Estimate partial investment scale	- Establish infrastructure construction plan in each step - Set up spatial industrial arrangement plan - Estimate investment scale	- Setting up Jalunobi harbor develop plan - Already has Hasanski development plan of UNIDO - Estimate partial investment scale

Source: Yang-Taek Lim, *Prospects for Asian Economies,* Seoul: Maeil Economic Daily Press, January 1999, Chapter 7 (P 473).

3) Basic Positions and Strategies of Participating Countries

In the TRADP, not only the role of the three related countries but also those of Korea and Japan are significant. Countries who are likely to advance into Najin-Sunbong area in North Korea are the Japan, China, Russia and European countries. Japan is interested in light industry. China is interested in road and rail road construction and service industries like hotel, restaurant and tourism, and Russia is likely to join in harbor construction. European companies would like to take part in telecommunication facilities, consulting and finance. The US is interested in selling telecommunication facilities to North Korea. U.K's private oil company 'Shell' is also interested in Najiin-Sunbong area.

China

Historical view: China has traded with Northeast countries since a long time ago, so economic cooperation between China and Northeast countries could be viewed as a part of Chinese history.

Geographical view: China has assigned and developed Round Bohai Economic Zone, Yellow Sea Economic Zone and Tumen River Special Zone Plan.

Political view: China has changed their diplomatic policy to a multidimensional one and they need political stability to maintain economic development.

Economic view: Since 1978, China has pursued development centered around the sea coastal area under the open-door and reform policy and North- east area is relatively undeveloped and there is a need to develop this area.

Although China has grown rapidly after reform and open-door policy, but foreign investment, trade and increasing revenues have been centered in Southern coastal areas such as Fujian and Canton Provinces. There were relatively small effects on Northeast and inside areas such as Jilin, Heilongjiang and inner Mongolia. Jilin and Heilongjiang provinces have a population of 60 million and have abundant resources like timber, crude oil and coal as well as produce corn, bean and rice in large quantities. So, China has a pretty active stand for Northeast area economic cooperation. China is a less developed country in terms of economy, and therefore expecting Northeast area economic cooperation to help them gain capital and technology from Korea and Japan.

Once its Northeast area is connected with East Sea and Pacific, China can expect production and exports to be active and foreign investment to increase. Thus, China has a strong desire to advance into the East Sea from the Northeast area. If China establishes a harbor in Fangchuan, not only it could be linked to the West Sea cities of Japan, but also it could advance into the Pacific. The reasons for China to try to find a way is explained as: first, even if it cost a lot, Jilin Provincial Government would like to have rights to East Sea and Tumen River at the sovereign concerns; and in the political and economic view, in case China does not have any harbors, there could be some danger if Russia or North Korea has political instability and transport route to East Sea could be shut down without warning.

Russia

Far East Russia wants to have broader 'autonomy' in terms of foreign trade relationship, but the central government is afraid of economic decentralization as a potential cause for political decentralization. Russia is urging Nihoka and Bostonichi to develop as a free trade harbor and has opened Vladivostok, the militarily protected zone in 1994. Also Russia assigned Habsan province and Pociet as a resource development area, trying to attract foreign capital. Russia consider Vladivostok and Nihoka as preferential economic development areas. In other words, they are taking negative attitude towards the Tumen River area.

Russia insists that the area's development strategy and master plan will ensure cooperation in the region.

North Korea

North Korea designated Najin-Sunbong area as a free economic trade area and Chungjin as a free trade harbor. North Korea would reap great benefit because of the TRADP in terms of inducing foreign investment, and expanding exports. These areas have the condition to expand into big harbor, railroad and roads connected to China, Russia and abundant resources.

Mongolia

Inland nation Mongolia needs to connect with the mouth of Tumen River in East Sea for trade with countries other than China and Russia. Through the TRADP, it can eliminate obstacles in transport, communication and promote exports and imports. It thus has an active attitude toward the TRADP.

South Korea

Because South Korea has poor natural resources, it is essential to secure a stable raw material supply and energy sources. Development of resources in three Northeast Provinces in China and Far East Russia will guarantee Korea a stable supply of resources. Furthermore, Korean companies are very interested in direct investment into North Korea. If multilateral cooperation in Tumen River begins, many ethnic Koreans in China can help Korean companies. There are seven major reasons why Korea wants to participate in the TRADP.

- Promoting Northeast economic area through cooperation using resources and labor in Tumen River.
- Building credit between North Korea and South Korea through investment to Najin-Sunbong free trade area.
- Enhancing North Korea's confidence about partial open-door policy which would lead to gradual openness.
- Assuring vested rights in Tumen River economic development in case of economic reunification between North Korea and South Korea.
- Reducing the cost of reunification between North Korea and South Korea.
- Ensuring Korean people's economic activity range after reunification.
- Expansion of transit trade through bridge role between Europe and Asia in 21 century.

It is very important to approach the TRADP and advancement to Najin-Sunbong free economic area in principle.

First, the UNDP multilateral cooperation and bilateral cooperation have to run hand-in-hand. It means that Korea's participation in the TRADP must be pursued through the UNDP's multilateral discussion and discussions among Korea, China, Russia and North Korea. Transparency of investment regulations and dispute resolution among involved countries must also be improved.

Second, it needs to enforce relations between the TRADP and North and South Korea's economic exchange. Even if the TRADP is not a plan for improving the two countries' economic cooperation, it would be a big influence.

Therefore, they must maintain a close relationship because TRADP economic cooperation between North and South Korea has a big interdependency. In the short and middle term, it will be ideal to focus on Najin-Sunbong Free Trade Zone.

Korea's concrete plan for approaching the TRADP is as follows: first, they have to sign investment guarantee treaty to reduce risk in Naji-Sunbong Zone; second, Korean government must allow companies in the private sector to evaluate the investment climate in an orderly fashion. If Korean companies compete with each other, it could make North Korea stand in a strategically superior position and also aggravate investment conditions; and third, Korean government must provide countermeasures against the advance of Japanese, Europe and US companies; and finally, advancement of overseas Koreans and foreign enterprises in communication, engineering and construction must be promoted.

Japan

Japan also wants to develop the Sea of Japan because it has a consensus to avoid overcrowding of industrial facilities in the Tokyo area and construct new industrial facilities in its Western area.

Although they agree with economic cooperation in Northeast Asia, there are some reasons why Japan does not want to lead it and promote it: first, Japan is afraid economic cooperation in Northeast Asia will cause friction with US; second, Japan is afraid other countries may become suspicious that Japan wants to pursue a 'Greater Northeast Asia'; and finally, Japan is afraid economic cooperation in Northeast Asia will cost it a large amount of money.

The US

The US has an affirmative attitude towards Northeast Asia regional cooperation and it has four necessary conditions: first, as an extensive open-door, economic cooperation needs to be open include their countries; second, for stability, economical cooperation in Northeast Asia needs to overcome historical factors. The area still needs the US's intervention because there still exists imbalance of power; third, in order to prosper, it has to accomplish economic growth; and finally, fourth, as a union, the cooperation must take the form of a collaboration.

4) Comparison of the TRADP with Other Regional Economic Zones

(1) Comparison with the NAFTA and APEC

The economic cooperation style which the TRADP is pursuing is different from the NAFTA and the APEC in the following senses. Whereas the latter two are the organizations for strictly economic cooperation, the TRADP is a plan which through development and investment of a certain area attempts to make area a center of transportation, which would in turn create new investment and trade and promote industrialization. This plan is not a plan which just focuses on a particular country, and furthermore, it does not require management at the national level such as international transfer of product elements.

(2) Comparison with Mekong River Development Plan

TRADP can be compared with Mekong River Development Plan in the aspects of similarities, differences, in the aspects of similarities, differences, preliminary processes and cooperation in developing infrastructure, as shown in <Table XV-7>.

<Table XV-7> Comparison of Tumen River Area Development plan with Mekong River Development Plan

		Mekong River Valley	Tumen River Valley
Similarities		(1) Business Criteria - The business to promote trade and investment at home and abroad ease regulations on the flows of freight and passenger across border, improve transportation facilities, and communication net-works) - The business to contribute to realizing and extending potential development opportunities (energy, tourism resources) - The business to solve common problems transcending borders (environmental problems) (2) Both regions have experienced war and political tension in the past and are trying to go to the market economy. (3) The objective both plan is to improve relationship between participating countries.	
Differences	**Development objective**	Target is the whole area of participating countries except Yunnan Province of China	Limited to regions in participating countries and undeveloped border areas with abundant natural resources
	Economic conditions	Forming of regional economic bloc of 6 countries though formal economic cooperation	Due to originally small economic scale and 3 or 4 main cities undergoing serious economic restructuring process, progress has been slow
Preliminary Processes		- Based on abundant labor, transforming agriculture-dependent economy into market economy and also extending trade. - After technology transfer in 1992, the participating countries received US$1.8 billions support and US$300 millions for consolidation of infrastructure.- Cooperation for businesses development - Consolidation of infrastructure for exchange of materials and human resources	- Time wasted to make basic plan and investigation, to establish formal institution such as Tumen River Development Company and to consult committee from 5 governments. - Infrastructure consolidation project which needs can not be started. - Najin-Sunbong (population 120,000) assigned as free economic trade zone but insufficient efforts to build the city. - Cities in the Chinese autonomous districts are relatively small compared to Mekong River Valley - Russia coastal area is uncompetitive due to its soaring railway fare and harbor management - - New government in Mongolia has been emphasizing development, but the effect on economic reform has been limited.
Cooperation in Developing Infrastructure		- - The transport route (railway) constructed from Yunnan in China to Laos improved credit between the two countries and an atmosphere to develop and share energy resources collectively has been formed.	- Delays in constructing border communication networks, due to legal and institutional problems.

Source: Yang-Taek Lim, *Prospects for Asian Economies,* Seoul: Maeil Economic Daily Press, January 1999, Chapter 7 (P 495).

5) Restrictions and Outlook

The brief look at the TRADP reveals both positive factors and negative factors in developing regional economic zones. As for positive factors, the region is full of energy and Western developed countries are interested in this area with the rationale for a Pan-Pacific area getting stronger in terms of economic cooperations and exchanges. On the other hand, there are several restrictions in making the region an economic zone.

First, there are political restrictions. After the Cold War, the danger of war has been reduced but the possibility of regional war has been increased. It means there are still a lot of systematic limitations and political instability because political systems of countries in this area are quite different.

Second, there are economic limitations. North-East Asian countries do not like Japan and Japan is having difficulties in its own economy. Japan should have a big economic role in this area, but in the TRADP, it is likely to play just an observer's role.

Third, there is a clash of interests among four countries, the US, Russia, China and Japan. It is true that Russia has weakened considerably but its military power is still strong and it may threaten Northeast Asia. Also, China and Japan's military power are dangerous factors. Such dangers cannot be ignored in trade or investment with China and North Korea.

Furthermore, the financial crisis of Southeast Asia, the IMF support for Korea, financial instability in Russia and slowing domestic demand and exports in China, could all influence the Northeast Asian economy, especially the TRADP. However, the biggest obstacles to the TRADP is inadequate infrastructure and insufficient funds. In order to solve these problems, it is extremely important to establish a development bank for this region but that is an issue for further discussion.

Northeast Asia is endowed with complementary factors such as natural resources, labor force, huge production infrastructure and potential markets. However, the core of the problem is that how effectively this economic complementary factors can interplay. The vertical division of labor in Asia is a result of market-driven integration of economies. However, some countries do not accept it as being desirable, because it threatens the vertical system of integration. Unlike EU, the economies in East Asia have different levels of economic openness, different phases of economic development and different political systems. Somehow, this will play an obstacle in applying the integrated economic systems. Thus, it may be better to apply the complementary industrial production system, which can maintain economic openness and still secure industrial competitiveness.

Disproportionate distribution of resources, capital and technology requires East Asian countries to pursue reciprocal benefits through joint development in resources. As the <Figure XV-1> shows that Japan and Korea have high points in capital, technology and management. Far-East Russia and inland China reserve abundant natural resources, providing an inter-dependent relationship among Northeast Asian Countries.

<Table XV-8> Analysis Inter-dependence among Northeast Asian Countries

	Oil -Gas	Coal-Mineral	Workforce	Capital	Technology	Management
Russia	VR	VR	VP	VP	S	S
China	R	VR	VR	VP	S	S
North Korea	N	R	R	VP	VP	VP
South Korea	N	S	S	R	R	R
Japan	VP	S	S	VR	VR	VR

*Notes: VR = very rich, R = rich, S = shortage, P = poor, VP = very poor, N = none

Source: Yang-Taek Lim, *Prospects for Asian Economies,* Seoul: Maeil Daily Press, January 1999, Chapter 8 (P. 499).

The regional complementary production system is a mixture of vertical and horizontal division of labor. It requires the securing of comparative advantages. It is considered that the creation of new comparative advantages through mutual development of resources and infra will be the main foundation for the formation of a regional economic bloc in the region. East Asia regions, especially the three northeast provinces of China, Far East Russia and North Korea has developed resource-dependent industries. It has comparative advantages in energy, agriculture and fisheries. Given the current and future energy supply and demand, there would be some advantages in mutual development and supply of petroleum and natural gas. Mutual development and stable supply of energy resources will be a great contribution to regional security and political stability.

Up to now, Northeast Asian countries had no comparative advantages in agriculture and fisheries over Australia and North America. However, given the overall shortage of supply in the world food market, it is considered that these countries have comparative advantages in some agricultural and marine products. Comparative advantages in the region can be increased through various factors, such as vast virgin land, infinite marine resources, cheap labor forces and reduction of distribution costs upon the construction of a Pan-Asia Transportation System.

Chapter XVI

MULTILATERAL COOPERATION IN ASIA[184]

1. ENVIRONMENTAL COOPERATION

A. Trade and Environment

The preamble to the WTO Agreement includes direct references to the objective of sustainable development and the need to protect and preserve the environment. In April 1994, trade Ministers in Marrakesh agreed to establish a WTO Committee on Trade and Environment and adopted the Marrakesh Ministerial Decision on Trade and Environment. It selected 10 items to be studied as follows.

- The relationship between the provisions of the multilateral trading system and trade measures for environmental purposes
- The relationship between domestic environmental policy and international trading measures
- The relationship between international trading measures and the requirements for products such as taxes, packing, labelling etc.
- Transparency of trade-related environmental measures.
- The relationship between the multilateral trading system and dispute settlement mechanisms.
- The problem of limitation of market access to environmental measures.
- The issue of the export of domestically prohibited goods.
- Trade in services and the environment.
- The agreement on environment-related aspects of intellectual property rights.
- The relationship with NGOs and the improvement of transparency for the distribution of documents.

The basic stand of the WTO is that trade measures under the pretext of protecting the environmental protection should be used in inevitable situations and should not be used as an alternative of environmental policy. However, some developed countries, including the US and international NGO contend that it is necessary to introduce trade regulations for the preservation of the global environment. The EU and developing countries have contended that trade measures for economic purposes should be implemented by multilateral agreements. The US, however, which will lead the next round, is in favor of unilateral trading restrictions by each country.

Developed countries argue that trade regulations are an effective means for protecting the environment and that the environmental dumping or 'free riding' policy of developing countries should be corrected to guarantee fair competition among countries. Meanwhile, developing countries argue that financial and technical support is more important than trade regulations, given the historical responsibility of developed countries regarding environmental destruction.

---

[184] For a detailed discussion, see:
1) Yang-Taek Lim, Economic Cooperation in Northeast Asia and Korea's Strategy, Seoul: Damul Publisher, March 1998.
2) Yang-Taek Lim, Prospects for Asian Economies, Seoul: Maeil Economic Daily Press, January 1999.

B. The Current Environmental Situation in Northeast Asia

Environmental problems in Northeast Asia have been grave international issues. This is attributable to the concentration of industrial countries in the region and the recent rapid development of the Chinese economy. Not enough has been done for environmental protection due to a lack of investment, technology, and indiscreet development. There has been a serious effect on exhaustion of natural resources, ecological destruction and health.

1) Air Pollution

One of the greatest areas of concern is atmospheric pollution. The main reason for this is that coal remains China's main source of energy. Dependence on coal currently exceeds 70%, which surpasses the global average of 28%, which is a large margin. Analysis has determined that 60% of atmospheric dust and 80% of sulfuric waste are derived from the combustion of coal. Areas receiving acid rain, *i.e.* rain with a pH of under 5.6, have been expanded by more than 1 million square kilometers from 1985 to 1993 from 1.75 million square kilometers to 2.8 million square kilometers. Acid rain pollution is most severe in the central part of China, where the probability of acid rain exceeds 80% during downpours. This phenomenon has been crossing the Yangtze River and extending to the northern regions. In the cities, exhaust gas is aggravating atmospheric pollution.

China's environmental agency has announced that release of sulfuric gases is expected to increase 10% per year, and failure to control it will result in the release of 35 million tons by 2000, making China surpass the US and attain the dubious distinction of becoming the world's largest releaser of greenhouse effect gases between 2010 and 2020.

2) Ocean Marine Pollution

Meanwhile, along with atmospheric pollution, the extent of marine pollution within the Northeast Asia region is also known to be severe. The marine environment of the region shows different levels in pollution according to cause. In the case of Korea's west coast, the pollution problem is becoming severe as pollutants are in flowing from China. In the case of the south coast, the amount of oil pollution has led to a high probability of incidence of oil-related pollution. In the east coast, in addition to oil pollution, there exists the danger of marine pollution resulting from nuclear waste from Russia.

The causes of pollution in the Yellow Sea are as follows. The Yellow Sea has the characteristic of being a semi-enclosed sea whose circulation of sea water is not very active and while the amount of pollutants released is rising in line with China's coastal development policy, measures to reduce pollution have been inadequate.

The deterioration of the marine life in some areas is quite serious with clam farms in Balhae Bay being depleted and 5 types of shrimps becoming extinct in Yoha. The 1995 edition of World Watch pointed out the 751 tons of annual heavy metal pollution and the release of 21,000 tons of petroleum refuse as the main causes of Yellow Sea pollution. According to a survey by the environmental protection group, the Yellow Sea ranks second only to the Black Sea as a 'sea of death'. It pointed out that there are places where the level of pollution exceeds one thousand times that of acceptable standards.

The problem lies in the fact that 40% of China's production facilities are concentrated on the coast of the Yellow Sea and the annual increase of some 3,000 km^2 of farmland results in increased disposal of pesticides and chemical fertilizers. In addition to existing factories and farmland, the formation of an industrial belt all along its coast is expected to result in an explosive acceleration of pollution.

The number of fish species living in Yellow Sea waters has been reduced to 24 at the present from 141 species 30 years ago. The reduction in this number and the destruction of marine life will inevitably lead to conflicts relating to marine resources while threatening the health and welfare of neighboring countries' residents.

The Chinese Pacific Forum Newsletter reported in March 1998 that 80% of pollutants in the Yellow Sea were derived from land activities with pollutants from ships and marine farms accounting for 15% and 5% respectively. Pollution attributable to land activities include coastal industries (paper and pulp, chemical, petroleum, food, synthetic rubber, shipbuilding, metal processing, machinery, leather and printing, etc.), sewer waste, coastal development and farming while spills resulting from petroleum exploration, shipping accidents and marine farming industries aggravated the risk of pollution.

The possibility of pollution by Russian nuclear waste in the East Sea came to attention of the international media in a March 1993 report from the Russian Federation (*the Yablokov Report*). The reported that Russia had for 30 years dumped radioactive waste into the East Sea and the coast of Ohotsk and Kamchatka. The IAEA in conjunction with Korea, China and Japan conducted two rounds of tests (March-April 1994 and August-September 1995) in the purported areas and concluded that the level of waste in these waters was fortunately negligible.

The movement of oil in the Northeast Asia region accounts for 26% (6.8 million barrels per day) of the world total with an estimated 60% (4.2 million barrels per day) going to Japan and most of the remainder going to Korea. Thus, the risk of oil spills is high in Korea's south and east coasts.

Asia region requires economic cooperation in energy, agriculture, fishing, and various other industries but at the same time bears the tremendous burden of environmental pollution which accompanies industrial development. One of the most important characteristics of environmental problems is that its goals cannot be totally achieved by the policy and efforts of one country. In order to respond effectively to pollutants which travel long distances and crosses borders such as marine pollution and acid rain, joint efforts by the perpetrating country and the victim country are required and a safe environment can only be maintained when joint efforts are made towards getting to the root cause of the problem.

The concept of an environmental community arises from this fact and it calls for regional-global frameworks for cooperation which supersede political, economic and geographic barriers. It is also for this reason that most treaties on the environment call for the establishment of cooperative apparatuses which suit countries in a region or area for the purpose or goal of worldwide environmental conservation. The cooperation between neighboring or adjacent countries is particularly crucial and regional cooperation has been taking place actively in Europe and the America in this context.

In the case of Europe, which has been a case study in success, there is a sense of 'environmental community' and policies are in place to support it ranging from the sharing of information, harmonizing of policies and declaration of joint positions in the international scene. In Northeast Asia, however, where environmental cooperation is most desperately needed due to the proximity between countries and dynamic economic growth, such efforts have been lacking due to difference in political regimes, level of economic development, recognition of environmental problems, and the priority assigned by each country to the problem.

Cooperative efforts were launched after the UNCED Conference in 1992 as countries within the region came to understand the need, the end of the Cold War and the alleviation of tension in the region, which served as a stimulus for multilateral and bilateral cooperation. Multilateral cooperation refers to participation by all the countries within the region and is being pursued in the four following types according to the principals involved.

First, government agencies within the region such as ESCAP and APEC have pursued regional cooperation within the Asia-Pacific Rim.

Second, cooperation is also being pursued in meetings between Government agencies which have as their objective the formation of cooperative organizations. Examples include the NOWAP which was formed for the preservation of the seas and the NEAREP which has as its objective, comprehensive cooperation on the environment including the atmosphere.

Third, there are also forums between respective agencies or experts in the field for the purpose of sharing information or formulating joint policies.

Fourth, bilateral cooperation includes environment treaties or agreements between governments and/or agencies with joint projects being conducted through periodic joint committees. In the case of Korea, bilateral environmental agreements have been concluded with China, Russia and Japan with joint projects being conducted by committees.

As noted above, environmental cooperation in Northeast Asia has taken on several forms but has yet to be pursued in earnest due to the lack of coordination between bilateral and multilateral arrangements and the lack of a central apparatus. The two major reasons for the inadequate level of environmental cooperation in the region are as follows: first, the basis for cooperation is weak due to the difference in the extent of economic development and political regimes; second, consensus has not been reached among countries in regard to allocation of gets and the timing and procedure for the formation of cooperative mechanisms such as a secretariat.

Given the fact that discussions on cooperation were initiated relatively later than other regions, however, prospects are that many problems will eventually be resolved through further discussions and conferences. If an organization for pro-active cooperation between government agencies is formed by Korea, China and Japan, it would be the first of its kind between the three countries and could have a positive effect on cooperation in other areas such as economy and politics.

Recently, international organizations such as the IMO (International Maritime Organization) and some developed countries such as the United States, the United Kingdom and Japan have made much effort to prevent ocean pollution by catastrophic oil spills. They have been strengthening their ability to respond to oil spills by reinforcing related laws, preparing oil pollution prevention funds and examining safety systems.

Regional organizations such as the EU and the ASEAN are raising the necessity for countermeasures for maritime safety and the environment. They are also focusing on reinforcement of international cooperation and reform of related agreements including the requirement of double-hull design for ships and regulations on oil mixture disposal. The United States, Japan and the United Kingdom are actively participating in environmental protection through international organizations and, at the same time, seeking positive measures for protection of marine environments.

This kind of international movement is due to the deepening destruction of maritime environment.

International Maritime Organization

The IMO is the United Nations' specialized agency responsible for improving maritime safety and preventing pollution from ships. It has 155 member states as of 1997. The IMO adopted a treaty known as ARPOL in 1973, which covers not only accidental and operational oil pollution but also pollution by chemicals, goods in packaged forms, sewage and garbage. The 1997 IMO Convention in London expanded regulations to all countries to limit sulfur quantity in fuel and make safety tests for ships of over 400 gross tonnage mandatory.

The purpose of the convention was to provide a global framework for international cooperation in combating major incidents or threats of marine pollution. Parties to the convention will be required to establish measures for dealing with pollution incidents, either nationally or in cooperation with other countries.

International Oil Pollution Liability and Compensation Fund

The IOPLC (International Oil Pollution Liability and Compensation) Fund was established in 1978. The main function of the fund is to provide supplementary compensation to victims who cannot obtain full compensation for damage. The IOPLC Fund had 70 member states as of 1997. After 1997, it offered more advantages to Member States, increasing compensation from 60 million SDR (Special Drawing Rights) to a maximum of some 200 million SDR, simplifying related procedures and expanding its application to exclusive economic water zones and international waters.

The EU Agreement

In November 1994, the EU decided to impose an environment recovery cost on pollution creators within the EU agreement. It then prohibited European oil companies such as BP and Royal Dutch Shell to abandon oil facilities in the sea from 1997. The ASEAN established OSPAR in 1990. It set up 11 stations including main routes such as those between Malaca and Singapore Sound. It has secured some recovery equipment such as oil fences, large oil reclaimers and oil tanks to prepare for oil incidents and has also built a related information network.

The US Oil Pollution Act

After the Exxon Valdez ran aground in Prince William Sound, Alaska in 1989, the Oil Pollution Act of 1990 was enacted. On the basis of the US Oil Pollution Act, the states changed their emergency plan to national-level countermeasures.

<Table XVI-1> Main Contents of the US Oil Pollution Act

- It makes the prevention and recovery of marine oil pollution mandatory, assigns the recovery costs and damages on the violator, imposes criminal responsibility on pollution, reinforces the structure of ships such as double hulls, and strengthens safety education on shipping interests.
- It also sets up urgent recovery plan by region, harbors and marine facilities and prepares a fund to compensate for damages due to oil pollution. It also establishes and maintains evidence of financial responsibility for ships and marine facilities.
- In the case of foreign ships, when non-double-hull ships enter port, it registers identification numbers, and observes domestic safety measures of the United States mandates.
- It established a Oil Spill Recovery Institute (May 1997) to identify and develop the best available techniques, equipment and materials for dealing with oil spills in major areas such as Gulf of Mexico and Gulf of Texas.
- It operates 3 teams for oil pollution and recovery within the Coast Guard. It makes all efforts to develop recovery technology and training and also increase recovery equipment.
- Oil companies are obliged to establish Marine Spills Response Committee, to complement insufficient recovery ability and to arrange recovery equipment, and must invest US$1 billion to build 16 recovery ships, 96 oil reclaimers and 91.4 km of oil fences. This committee also carries out simulation exercises every year.

Source: Yang-Taek Lim, *The International Cooperation in Northeast Asia and Korea's Strategy*, Seoul: Damul Publisher, March 1998.

The Japan's Measures for Oil Pollution

Japan established national measures for oil spills, which regulate the maintenance of related information networks and recovery systems and the evaluation of environmental effects and structures of wildlife. The Japanese Agency of Marine Security organized and operate 2 strike force teams for quick measures and technological support in case of oil spills. The center for marine pollution prevention stores equipment and materials to carry out prevention activities according to oil company's requests. It has also set up 99 committees on oil spill incidents around the country in cooperation with regional governments, ship owners, and shipping companies. After the oil spill of the Russian oil ship Nahotka in the Sea of Japan, the Department of Transportation directed the association of Japanese ship-owners to devise safety measures to prevent the recurrence of such incidents. From 1996, it invited Chinese and Russian officials to give lessons on marine pollution. It has also held an annual conference for international recovery experts.

The British Marine Contamination Control Unit (MCCU)

The British Department of Transportation established a 'Marine Contamination Control Unit' (MCCU) which consists of maritime experts. It also dispatched officials who are in charge of formulating the prevention plan, guiding prevention operations and training to 8 main harbors and bays. 21 oil-related companies such as BP have founded company task teams which respond to oil pollution. After the Sea Empress incident in the coast of Wales, it strengthened the organization. The United Kingdom concluded the Bonn agreement with neighboring countries such as France and Germany to prevent oil pollution at the time of the North Sea oil incident.

C. The Possibility of Energy and Food Crises Resulting from Air Pollution

1) The Possibility of Energy Crisis

The UNEP warns that if emissions of greenhouse gases continue at the current rate, the earth could warm up by 1 to 3.5 degrees by the year 2050. This rate of warming will melt the glaciers at the poles to raise the level of the earth's ocean by 15~95cm. This could lead to flooding of 80% of the Marshall Islands, 17% of Bangladesh, and 6% of the Netherlands. The rise in the ocean surface could limit living areas and decrease farming areas to expose the world to a crisis involving food shortages. So, if the structure of the current energy consumption continues, it could raise global temperature to threaten the life of human beings.

As part of international effort to respond to global warming, every country including Korea voluntarily signed and joined the 1992 Rio Treaty on Climate Change in UNEP. The treaty calls on all countries to decrease greenhouse gases such as carbon dioxide, methane and freon gas and require developed countries to reduce emissions of greenhouse gases first. Greenhouse gases are mainly emitted by fossil fuels such as oil, coal and gas which remain the main power source for industrial activity. So the direct regulation of emissions are not just regulations on the use of fossil fuels but also limitation on industrial activity.

In December 1997, the first binding international standard to reduce greenhouse gases was enacted. This was the first attempt to limit the use of fossil fuels. It is possible to say that it suggested a new principle which could restrain economic development to preserve the global environment.

Developed countries have been making an effort to reduce greenhouse gases and prepare for the possibility of decline in their industries and competitiveness. They have intensified the development of clean energy to replace fossil fuels and executed carbon taxes according to the amount of energy used. The convention in Tokyo excluded developing countries from the obligation of greenhouse gas reduction. The EU and the United States, however, strongly required developing countries to be included. The conflict between developed and developing countries has once again been an obstacle to international cooperation as countries under obligation to reduce gases.

2) The Possibility of Food Crisis

The three basic elements - soil, water and climate - for food production are deteriorating. The rate loss of soil has been very fast due to industrialization and desertification. Arable land has been decreasing by hundreds of hectares a year. As seed enhancement through genetics has reached its limits, food production has not caught up with the rate of population growth since 1990.

Water shortages are growing into international tensions. Now, 2.5 billion people in 26 countries are suffering from water shortages. It is predicted that 3 billion people will face water shortages within 30 years.

Climatic changes such as global warming and El Nino have caused drought, storm waves, heat waves and severe winters. Climate differences in a given area is more extreme now and forecasts of extreme situations in climate may happen more frequently shaking the foundation of agriculture.

D. The Relationship between Environmental Standards and International Competitiveness

Many studies about the environmental effect on trade and investment continue to show that the reinforcement of environmental standards will not have grave a influence on the flow or scale of trade and investment. It could be applied to the special situations in which an industry is responsible for relatively high costs of environmental standards. This kind of argument reveals that the hypothesis that a higher level of environmental standards narrows the gap in national competitiveness between the North and the South is reasonable.

1) The Relationship between Sustainable Development and International Competitiveness

It is predicted that in the 21st century scientific technology will develop rapidly, economic activity will become more active and populations will continue to increase. There will be limitations, however, in cleansing the earth. When pollutants are produced over a recoverable level, the destruction of the environment will be progressed rapidly. It will also lead to new threatening factors as proven by El Nino. Under such circumstances, the concept of sustainable development has been introduced to pursue a balance between nature and economic development. For strengthening competitiveness in the 21st century, this concept cannot be ignored.

Environment will act as a major factor for future competitiveness. Therefore, competitiveness without environmental issues will not be meaningful when it comes to industrial or national competitiveness. The US established 'the President's Council on Sustainable Development'under President Clinton to pursue national competitiveness under the concept of sustainable development. The EU has decided that the sustainability is the core of all R&D policy to prepare for the new age of competitiveness.

2) The Relationship between Reinforcement of Environmental Standards and International Competitiveness

International trade is the most important element in the relationship between the reinforcement and international competitiveness, which is obtained through trade policy which encourages exportation. The implementation of international competitiveness reflects the prejudice which puts more weight on advantages of producers than that of consumers. It is also a traditional concept rooted in the mercantile system.

Developing countries have received benefits to keep higher barriers for protective trade than developed countries. They were also guaranteed discretion in international trade by several international agreements.

Construction of monopolistic systems, however, to protect domestic manufacturers resulted in inefficiency and retrogression of technology. Recent trends show that they are lowering the barriers by unilateral actions, not by the multilateral agreements.

Manufacturers, especially in developing and former Communist countries, have considered it a custom and a privilege to abandon wastes in rivers, the atmosphere and empty lands. Developing countries allot only 0.3% of their GDP on pollution control costs. As a result, tremendous losses such as destruction of ecosystem and health problems occur.

These kinds of losses account for 1~2% of GDP in developed countries and 4% of GDP in developing countries. Environmental destruction brings a decline in the quality of living to people, and low production and high cost to companies.

With the exception of carbon dioxide and CFCs, most of other pollutants are not at critical levels. Nevertheless, developed countries have complained about lower environmental regulation in developing countries and unfair competition. Developing countries have allowed their companies to reduce production costs by emitting wastes without permission. Low environmental standards entail low pollution control costs.

There is some question as to whether developing countries do not include pollution control costs in their cost of production, which would necessarily be an advantage. Falling-off in environmental quality, however, will reduce national production or industrial competitiveness and increase related costs for the whole economy.

Unfortunately, models or methodologies used in debates about the relationship between reinforcement of environmental standards and competitiveness have fatal defects in reasoning. The macroeconomic model which is used to evaluate the effects of standards on economies, included only cost of pollution reduction, ignoring effects on consumers and producers by pollution and other factors. Most macroeconomists considered only costs needed in reducing the destruction of environment but ignored potential costs which were not directly related to the destruction of the environment.

Some industries require more effort to follow environmental regulations. These are pulp and paper manufactures, the oil, organic and inorganic chemical, coal, fertilizer, cement, iron, metal and the lumber industry.

According to a report from the World Bank which investigated changes in world trade, high environmental standards do not harm international competitiveness. This report showed that environment-sensitive industries of countries under strict standards have a high record of exports. It also pointed out the reason for the decline in export occupation of developed countries from 74.3% to 72.7% between 1970 and 1990 is not due to the burden of reinforcement but due to fast growth of developing countries and industrial restructuring.

Investigation of investment flows of developing countries also showed no systematic relationship between trade and environmental standards. The data on direct overseas investment proved that there was no special foundation for multinational companies moving production centers to countries with low environmental standards. For example, the United States invested 45% of direct investments in developing countries. Data shows, however, that more investment was put in developed countries rather than developing countries with the application of low environmental standards. Considering this trend of investment abroad, it would not be right to say that the reason developed countries increased their share in pollution-intensive industries was to narrow the gap of environmental regulation with developed countries.

The reorganization of pollution-intensive industries can also be explained by the hypothesis of product cycle. As an industry gets mature according to product and process planning as start, the products of key industries experience price competition, and the production is moved to countries with low costs. As a result, cost advantages come from the low cost of labor and materials. In the case of developed countries, industries with high technology and new designs maintain competitiveness. This hypothesis of product cycle clearly explains how developing countries get small profits from key industries such as chemical, metal, pulp, paper industry and other environment-sensitive industries.

E. The Direction of Environmental Cooperation in Northeast Asia

1) The Concept of Environmental Community

One of the important features of environmental issue is the fact that the goal of environmental management will not completely be reached by only one country's policies and efforts. To respond effectively to cross-border pollutants such as acid rain, joint measures of all concerned countries are needed. The environment will be preserved intact only when countries make the joint efforts to eradicate the pollutants.

Under this kind of view, the concept of an Environmental Community is introduced and the global frameworks beyond the political, economic and geographical walls are required.

This explains why most international environment protocols recommend the construction of regional and multilateral cooperation systems. The cooperation of geographically-binded countries is indispensable to solve environmental problems.

In the case of Europe, it recognized the concept of environmental community and it is now promoting the development related policies. In Northeast Asia however, regional cooperation has not been promoted actively due to different political structures, the level of economic development, the recognition of environmental issues and difference in priorities of policy.

2) The Current Status and Prospects

After the convention of the UNCED in 1992, the regional environmental cooperation in Northeast Asia was promoted according to necessity of local countries. Multilateral cooperation has been promoted by relief of tension in the region after the end of the Cold War. Current cooperation can be classified into multilateral and bilateral cooperation. Multilateral cooperation is achieved by joint participation of countries in Northeast Asia. There are 4 kinds of cooperation in progress:

First, Sub-regional cooperation in the Asia Pacific area with the existing inter-governmental organizations such as the ESCAP and the APEC.

Second, There is also a form of cooperation through regular governmental meetings for the purpose of establishing a permanent governmental conference. This includes the NOWPAP and the NEAREP.

Third, There is a kind of forum to share information and policy. It is developed as a form of cooperation between environmental bureaus and experts.

Fourth, Bilateral cooperation includes an agreement for bilateral environmental cooperation and an agreement for environmental development of each country.

In this manner, environmental cooperation in Northeast Asia has been in progress through multiple channels. It has not yet, however, gotten on track due to the lack of systematic connections and systems to promote bilateral and multilateral cooperation. There are two reasons for inactivity of environmental cooperation in Northeast Asia. First, the basic background is too weak to promote regional cooperation because of differences in the level of economic development and political structure. Second, the participating countries have not yet come to an agreement on procedure and timing. Moreover, the problems are expected to be solved gradually through related discussion and meetings.

2. ENERGY COOPERATION [185]

The joint development of energy sources in east Siberia and Far Eastern Russia would benefit all the countries in the region, simultaneously, it would achieve stable energy supply in response to the sharp increase in demand in the region, particularly in China; Korea would be able utilize it to pursue economic cooperation with North Korea and seek political stability; and Japan could reap investment income under the strategy of linking the resources of the Far East region with its technology and capital.

The speed at which energy-related investment and development in Northeast Asia is progressed will depend on the attunement of conflicting national interests, securing of sufficient export volumes and the extent of measures to protect the original investment. It is now considered appropriate timing for China, Russia, Korea and Japan to pursue realistic and specific steps such as an apparatus for multilateral cooperation.

---

[185] The contents in this section are heavily derived from Yang-Taek Lim, *Economic Cooperation in Northeast Asia and the Korea's Strategy,* Seoul: Damul Publishing House, March 1998.

A. The Current Status of Energy Supply & Demand in the Northeast Asia and Its Prospects

While the world average GDP growth rate between 1990 and 1995 was a modest 1.7% per year, Asian countries recorded an average growth rate of 8.0%, and China led the way with a 12.8% annual growth. While economic growth is expected to slow down due to the recent Asian economic crisis, it is expected that China will maintain growth of 6~8% until the early 2000s, while Japan and NIEs will achieve growth rates exceeding that of the world average based on restructuring efforts.

As a result of the high rate of economic growth, the supply of primary energy has also risen steadily and the growth in supply reached 5.9% in the Asian region during 1980~1995 compared with 1.6% for the world as a whole with a particularly high growth rate of 6.2% during the last 5 years (1990~1995) which leads to forecasts of steady growth up until 2010.

1) The Current Status of Energy Supply & Demand

The supply of energy in Asia has been declining since China became a net importer and Indonesia's output has declined due to reserve limitations, thus the region's dependence on other regions has intensified. The energy production level of Northeast Asia is well below its consumption and thus, a stable supply of energy has become a priority issue for Japan, Korea and China.

The concentration of Japan and Korea's supply line in the Middle East has been pointed out as a weakness in the energy supply of these countries. Asian countries have attempted to reduce dependence on the Middle East after experiencing the first and second oil shocks. As the export capability of China and Indonesia reached their limits, however, dependence on the Middle East oil is expected to rise to about 90% in 2010 from the current level of 70%.

Prospects are for the OPEC to account for 50% of the global supply from 37% presently, and its weight in total oil exports is expected to rise sharply from 46% to 61.8%, as member countries are expected to step up production from 80% of capacity at the present to 94% by 2010 with the decline in production and exports from non-OPEC countries.

While the possibility of a political conflict in the Gulf region is one of the risks of this concentration, the bigger problem lies in the possible changes in pricing based on the global imbalance of supply. There have been analyses concluding that the increased oil consumption in the fast-growing Asian region may be the cause of another oil crisis and the IEA has warned that crude prices may start to rise once OPEC starts producing at over 80% of capacity.

The rapid rise of energy consumption in Northeast Asia entails large energy issues in various aspects and makes close cooperation for a stable supply desirable. The undeveloped oil fields of far East Russia and natural coal resources of China are sufficient to meet the rising demand of Northeast Asia, but massive investments into energy-related infrastructure is required. Not only are direct investments for storage and power generation needed, but investments into a wide range of related areas such as infrastructure for transportation and relay/transformer stations is required.

Russia and China have been making concerted efforts to induce foreign investments into the energy sector but have been largely unsuccessful to date as the sector entails considerable risk owing to industry characteristics such as time required to reach break-even. Moreover, indiscriminate development of coal fields by China will cause far-reaching environmental problems not just for neighboring countries but eventually the world as a whole. Nuclear energy has also been developed as an environment-friendly alternative, but it, in turn, entails concerns about safety of operation.

These various problems, however, may be resolved depending on how countries in Northeast Asia integrate their complementary aspects and cooperate to maximize efficiency of energy resources and ensure stable energy supply for the region.

While there remain doubts about the possibility of constructive economic cooperation in the region due to differences in economic systems, political and military conflicts, and gaps in economic development and power, smooth energy supply within the region is not altogether unrealistic if the members focus on the basic rationale of heightening the efficiency of energy resource movements, development of areas with potential and balanced growth for the entire region.

2) Prospects for Northeast Asia

The petroleum supply situation in Asia is deteriorating due to increased petroleum import and consumption to keep pace with economic growth, increasing reliance of Middle East oil due to the slow exploration of petroleum within the region and friction between countries in regard to petroleum supply routes.

The petroleum consumption of Asia ranked second to only North America in 1995 at 16.35 million barrels a day, having surpassed Europe in 1992. The rate of increase over the past 10 years was 67.0%, far surpassing not only North America (14.2%) and Europe (11.9%) but also the world average.

Therefore, the import of crude has doubled from 4.7 millions to 9 millions barrels per day, which exceeds rises in production (24.3%) and consumption (67.0%). Crude from Middle East makes up 70% of the imports. In 1995, Japan (78.6%) and Korea (77.8%) ranked among the highest in terms of dependence on the Middle East among top 10 oil importing countries.

China, which is the largest producer of petroleum in Asia, has seen exports decline to the point where in 1993 it became a net importer. Moreover, Asia's largest exporter Indonesia has also seen domestic consumption rise by 9% per year and is expected to become a net importer within several years.

Japan, (Asia's largest consumer of oil) accounts for 8.5% and 15.6% of the global consumption and imports, and its dependence on the Middle East oil has steadily risen since 1987.

For the whole of East Asia, Japan's share of imports by the region is expected to decline to 37% in 2010 from 52% in 1994 with the weight of China (19%), Korea (18%), ASEAN (17%), and Taiwan/Hong Kong (9%) all expected to rise. Dependence on the Middle East will also be intensified with the present 70% level rising to 87% and 95% by 2000 and 2010 respectively, as the Middle East should account for 15% of global consumption and 80% of Asia's supply by 2010.

As the consumption of oil in the East Asia increases and its dependence on Middle East deepens, the main energy supply route will shift from the Middle East, North America, Europe to the Middle East, Asia, and the volume of trade between the two regions should triple by 2010. Asia's rate of consumption growth will continue to surpass its rate of production growth, leading to an unstable supply structure and as the sophistication of its industries continues with the development of petrochemical and automobile industries, consumption pressures will increase and dependence on the Middle East will have to increase.

Such dependence could make Asia susceptible to regional instability and changes in policy in the Middle East, while the need for Asian countries to secure import sources and secure transportation routes from the Middle East will be heightened. Meanwhile, as the dominance of the Middle East in the global supply is strengthened due to declining oil exploration due to stable crude prices, declines in production in non-OPEC countries and Asia's oil security environment could deteriorate even further.

B. Electric Power Market in Asia's Developing Countries

Developing Asian countries have been pursuing expansion of power plants by the use of domestic and foreign private capital and technology as a way of solving recent electric power shortages. A look at the current situation of electric power markets in Asia shows that Asia will occupy over 50% of the world's extension of equipment installations and that the supply of electric power will be three times greater than now. The demand for electric power, however, will increase by 10% a year mainly because of economic development and industrialization, thereby making the electric power shortages more severe.

As privatization and loosening of regulations takes place in the power plant construction sector, it has been forecasted that 20~40% of the planned power plants will be built by independent power producers (IPP), as power and engineering firms from advanced countries such as Sadon (US), Powergen (U.K.) and Tomen (Japan) have already made inroads in the market.

China

China planned to expand the electricity generation from 2 billion kW to 3 billion kW in 2000. It has decided on a policy which raises 25% of resources from overseas investment. Under this policy, it is planning to build private plants on a BOT (Build-Operated-Transfer) basis including a hydro-power station utilizing 250,000 kW and a steam power station using 600,000 kW.

Thailand

Thailand is planning to expand its current power capacity from 13 million kW to 25 million kW by 2006. The EGAT has decided on a plan to set up 82 million kW through private investments.

Indonesia

Indonesia has decided to expand its current 22 million kW generating capacity to 49 million kW by 2015 in 3 stages, focusing on coal, gas, and atomic energy. It has placed an order with Daelim Engineering (South Korea), to set up a coal steam-power plant with a total of 310 thousand kW in Sumatra and Sulawsei Island. It is also building a 450 thousand kW coal plant with investments in the US (Duke Power-80%) and Japan (Mitsubishi) in the central part of Java.

Vietnam

Vietnam is planning to expand its current 3.6 million kW power generation capacity to 76 million kW by 2000. It recently announced a policy to reinforce the control of the central government, which will standardize bidding procedures for the BOT and adjust the earning rate of investments with the help of capital and technology from Japanese and Australian companies, Vietnam started on the biggest coal plant.

India

India decided to expand its current 76 million kW generating capacity to 1.4 billion kW by 2002. It is now planning to set up 37 million kW generating capacity through private investment.

The Philippines

The Philippines planned to expand its current 10 million kW generating power to 20.7 million kW by 2005. It decided to set up new generating equipment by private investment. Large-sized power plants using coal and gas are now under construction.

Developing countries are participating more actively in the maintenance of the investment environment for coal and gas plants. As the importance of private investment has increased, monopolistic power industries will be changed into competitive systems. It will also create environmental issues with the increase of coal plants.

C. The Construction of Atomic Energy Plants in the Asian Region

As Asian countries such as China and Indonesia are driving to build atomic power plants to meet the surging energy demand. The IEA forecasted that the number of atomic plants in Asia would increase from the current 70 to 140 by 2010.

The expansion of atomic power plants in Asia is attributable to the surge of energy demand by accelerating economic growth. It is also caused by the fact that energy shortages have emerged as a hindrance to sustainable economic growth with the shortages in other social infrastructure such as transportation and communication. Another important cause is that atomic power has lower unit cost than fossil fuels and it is a useful energy in terms of environmental protection.

Such movements will bring about the rapid expansion of markets related to atomic energy which is of a large scale. It is also intensifying the competition among developed countries which are finding in Asia a market for construction after stagnation of atomic energy caused by the incidence at *Chernobyl.*

China

To escape from its chronic energy shortages and coal-dependent energy system, China will allocate 6% of total generating capacity to atomic energy expanding to 10 million kW in 2000, to 200 million kW in 2010 and to 400 million kW in 2020.

This trend in power plant construction makes the introduction of foreign capital and investment inevitable with the participation of America, Japan, Russia, and Canada on the rise.

Taiwan

Taiwan has a relatively a high unit price for electricity. Its main source of power supply is steam-power generation. 6 atomic power plants are currently operating and account for 23.5% of the total equipment capacity. Taiwan has planned to construct new atomic power plants since the early 1980s and finished choosing sites by 1983. The plan was cancelled, however, because of a decrease in electric power demand and public opinion against it due to the *Chernobyl* incident.

Indonesia

Indonesia started construction on the first atomic power plant on the *Muria peninsula, Java*, in 1997. It planned to invest a total of US$17.5 billion in 12 plants (7 million kw).

Others

Thailand is pushing ahead to set up 6 atomic power plants, and it will make up 20% of the total power supply by 2010. Malaysia has a plan to construct 600,000 kW in plants which will lose a total of US$1.2 billion. Vietnam has plans to build an atomic plant (US$3 billion scale) by 2012. The Philippines is preparing measures for the operation of Batan plant which was built in 1985.

D. China's Policy on the Energy Industry, Energy Supply & Demand and International Cooperation

China requires international support in trade, investment, transfer of technology, equipment sales and technological sub-contracting for the development of its energy industries. With the exception of oil exploration and development, foreign investments for the development of China's other energy resources has been inadequate and, in response, the Chinese Government has expanded the level of its market-opening and tested various forms of investment with foreign countries.

1) Policy on Energy Industry

One of the major goals of China's 9th Five-Year Plan is to attain energy efficiency in its industries with energy savings and development of new energy sources, to improve the environment and to maintain the balance of energy supply.

Towards this end, specific directives in the formulation of an energy policy such as management of energy savings, promotion of savings through incentive policies, expanded use of coal, exploration and development of petroleum, coal and natural gas, development of power industries and liberalization of transmission facilities maintenance and energy prices have all been discussed as issues.

As for oil policy, stable production will be sought in the East while emphasis will be placed on accelerating development in the West to help increase petroleum and natural gas production steadily, as part of the goal of strengthening oil-related economic capabilities.

To achieve this, China requires; expansion of crude processing capabilities to meet rising consumption; expansion of secondary processing facilities to prepare for slowdowns in demand; introduction of economic facilities as a response to increases in imports from the Middle East; and the capability to install and maintain transportation systems. Foreign investments in terms of financing and technology, however, have been difficult to come by.

2) Energy Demand & Supply

Energy Demand

It has been estimated that in China petroleum and natural gas reserves are 40 billion tons and 1.7 trillion cubic meters to account for 2.4 and 1.2% of the world total respectively, but coal reserves are also considerable at 114.5 billion tons or 11% of the world total. Production in 1995 amounted to 150 million tons of petroleum and 17 billion cubic meters of petroleum and natural gas, respectively. Production of crude, which had grown rapidly in the 1980s, has shown a considerable slowdown in growth in the 1990s despite rapid economic development.

China has met its needs by reducing exports and increasing imports as exports amounted to 20.3 million tons as compared with 22.6 million tons in imports. Export markets included Japan, the US, and Korea accounting for 64.9% of the total.

As for imports, China has traditionally imported heavily from Indonesia and other Southeast Asian nations, but has recently been diversifying its sources. In particular, dependence on the Middle East has increased and the construction of systems to import and process crude with characteristics different from those of local oil has become inevitable.

China ranks third in consumption of primary energy behind the US and Russia but 80% of the consumption is met by coal. This is because the Chinese Government decided to export crude and earn foreign currency, and switch to coal as generation fuel. But the weight of petroleum consumption has risen gradually since 1980, by 1994 it had reached 145.6 million tons.

While the forecasted growth rate of petroleum consumption is 6.10% (approximately 10 million tons) per year for the 9th Five-Year Plan, the rate of growth in petroleum production is expected to be only 1.29~1.92% (approximately 3 million tons) per year, so that by 2000, 25~55 million tons, or 29~34% of total production, will have to be imported in order to satisfy the expected consumption of 210 million tons.

<Table XVI-2> Prospects of Energy Supply and Demand in China

	Production (component ratio, %)			Consumption (component ratio, %)		
Category	**1995**	**2000**	**2010**	**1995**	**2000**	**2010**
Coal	136,100	155,000	190,000	135,447	152,000	185,000
(10,000t)	(75.5)	(75.6)	(69.4)	(75.0)	(71.7)	(64.1)
Oil	15,005	16,000	18,000	15,622	21,000	28,000
(10,000t)	(16.7)	(15.6)	(13.2)	(17.3)	(19.8)	(19.4)
Natural gas	179	250	800	179	250	800
(billion t)	(1.8)	(2.3)	(5.4)	(1.8)	(2.2)	(5.1)

Source: Same as in <Table XVI-1>.

(2) Energy Supply

As for the composition of energy production sources, coal still occupies a dominant position and forecasts call for coal production to account for 75.6% of total energy production, followed by petroleum (15.6%) and natural gas (2.3%).

Currently, China has 25 oil and natural gas production stations, pipe lines of oil transportation in Dongbei, Hebei, Huadong and the pipe network of gas in Sichuan. Its technology of energy development reached and approached the level of developed countries.

To develop the Eastern and Western areas, China is stabilizing and maintaining the production of already aged oil fields in the Eastern area and is developing new oil fields in the Western area. Although the production of the big 3 oil fields accounted for 70% in China since the late 1950, its production has gradually decreased in recent 5 years. The 45% of natural gas has produced in Sichuan.

The Daqing Oil Field, which is the biggest in China, is the general name of about 20 oil fields located in Daqing. Its current production accounts for 40% in China and once occupied 50%. China recently decided to open the new exploration and development of the Daqing Oil Field to foreign companies for the first time in history and Sunwing Energy of Canada has already been granted oil exploration. China planned to produce 5.3 million tons by 2000 and to maintain 50 million tons a year for the following 10 years.

The Shengli Oil Field, which is called the second Daqing Oil Field, is located in Shandong Province. It produced 3.35 million tons in 1990 and 3.72 million tons in 1993. Its production reduced, however, to 3.09 million tons in 1994, accounting for over 21% in China. While Shengli Oil Field saw slow production Liaohe Oil Field, which enjoyed increasing production every year, introduced the system method of construction. It has 1.5 million tons of production, accounting for 10% in China.

The marine oil fields are known to have affluent deposits. The production is not expected to surge due to payability. The production was merely 1.43 million tons in 1990. It increased, however, to 6.47 million tons in 1994 and it is under construction to increase its production to 1.5 million tons in the 2000s.

3) Current Status of International Cooperation on Energy in China

Since China first opened up to oil exploration, foreign companies have made sizable investments in this area. Over 15 countries from the US, Great Britain, France, Japan and Italy have concluded agreements to explore China's eastern and Southern seas, but results have been below expectations, yielding only moderate-sized finds. For this reason, the development of oil fields in China has failed to attract foreign investors.

In April 1985, as part of policy under the 6th Five-Year Plan to increase reliance on foreign technology and capital and to induce the interest of foreign oil exploration companies, China announced that it would open 10 southern provinces to oil exploration. These included Anhui, Fujian, Guangdong, Gujiu, Hunan, Jiangsu, Guangxi, Yunnam and Zejiang Provinces. Hainan Province was added shortly thereafter, and one joint research and 7 exploration agreements have been concluded so far with foreign companies in these 11 provinces.

As oil consumption increased rapidly with economic development, production remained slow due to lack of financial resources and limitations in technology. Further liberalization of oil exploration was undertaken in February 1993. Under the 8th Five-Year Plan, the 'Chinese Petroleum and Natural Gas Corporation' authorized joint exploration in an area encompassing 2.5 million square kilometers as 10 provinces and districts in the north were added to the 11 southern provinces. As of the end of 1995, 150,000 square kilometers have been opened under 15 joint projects with Japan accounting for 50% of the US$10 billion in foreign investments induced during the year.

More recently, China and Japan have been pursuing industrial and technological cooperation in the area of energy savings. For example, industrial energy consumption structure is being systematically improved through MITI's 'Green Support Plan', while energy-saving model projects are being pursued in conjunction with "The Agency for the Development of New Energy and Industrial Technology". Since 1993, projects undertaken have included retrieval of energy released by high-temperature ovens, and increase of efficiency at refineries. Heat retrieval from high-pressure gas and cooling systems in the steel, petroleum refining, and cement industries have been projects undertaken in Sichuan, Sandong, Shanxi and Anhui provinces, and the city of Tianjin.

A conference for cooperation on energy was held in Beijing in October 1997 to hold discussions on problems such as heightening efficiency in the energy industry and support for improved quality, where requests were made to Europe for investments. Negotiations have been held with IEA for the introduction of energy savings/storage and environmental technologies, followed by a seminar on energy saving in December 1997.

E. Russia's Policy on the Energy Industry, Energy Supply & Demand and International Cooperation

Russia has stepped up efforts to activate its resources industry. The reason therein is that there has been the need for increased exports from energy resources as the recovery of manufacturing and petrochemical sectors is expected to slow due to an extended recession along with the need to strengthen competitiveness to pursue rationalization in this field through Government support.

While the strengthening of the Government's management of resource development could act as a deterrent to foreign enterprises, it could serve as a stimulus for investment in line with Russia's recent strategy to overcome its economic crisis.

1) Policy on Energy Industry

The promotion of a resources development policy by the Russian Government, which is the result of a change in the economic environment and contrasts with the past policies of the Soviet Union, is clearly demonstrated by the 'Basic Framework for Russia's Energy Policy under New Economic Condition' announced in September 1992, and 'Basic Plan for Russian Federation's Energy Development to the Year 2010' announced in May 1995. Based on these plans, the basic direction and characteristics of resource development policy being pursued by the Russian Government is as follows:

First, the basic principles of Russia's resource development policy are; the increase of efficiency in the use of energy, formation of an environment for energy conservation, expansion of export potential for fuel and energy industries, and minimization of negative effects on the environment. Plans for the next 15 years call for the reduction on the dependence on coal, an increase in the usage of natural gas and increase in its exports of 65~71% along with increased production of high-quality petroleum products.

Laws and regulations to effectively promote improved safety of nuclear energy and maximizing of the processing and utilization of fuel and energy are being pursued while autonomy for regional local governments is being strengthened in regard to resource development. Furthermore, the Far East region has been designated as a target region for new petroleum and gas resource development as the production capacity of Siberia is declining and directives to expand investment into the Khavarovsk, Sahalin and neighboring seas for energy development is also being studied.

Second, another goal is the pursuit of large-scale resource development projects through the introduction of technology and capital from advanced countries. Policies to induce foreign investment have been expanded in order to complement the country's structural weakness of lack of capital and high-level technology, but foreign companies still have reservations about active investments due to the unfavorable economic environment.

In order to alleviate the situation and eliminate the greatest obstacle to foreign investment, the Government has concentrated its efforts on legislation of new laws such as the 'Law on the Distribution of Output' (December 1995). This law allows for exclusive exploration, transfer of exploration and development rights, recognition of shares in the output and tax breaks and guarantees of an appropriate level of profitability, all of which have been key requests by foreign enterprises in the past to the Russian Government in connection with the development of petroleum and gas.

Third, vertical integration of oil companies and privatization of the energy industries have been pursued as a means of developing the sector and ensuring stable supply.

2) Energy Supply & Demand

(1) Energy Supply

Of Russia's natural resources, energy resources make up 70% of proven reserves (petroleum 15.7%, natural gas 32.2% and coal 23.3%). Proven reserves of petroleum amount to 60~80 billion tons or 5% of the world total (of which 13 billion tons are accessible), while proven reserves of natural gas and coal reach 49 trillion cubic meters and 201.5 billion tons, making up 35% and 15% of the world total respectively.

Production in 1996 amounted to 320 million tons of petroleum (ranking third in the world), 575 billion cubic meters of natural gas (ranking first in the world) and 255 million tons of coal (ranking third in the world) but showed a decline of 1.3~3.4% over the previous year.

Production is expected to grow again, however, due to the development of petroleum and gas in East Siberia and Far East Russia. This area is of strategic interest for Russia with 43% of the country's coal reserves, 18% of its petroleum reserves, 29% of its natural gas reserves and 75% of its hydro-electric power generation. In the case of East Siberia, petroleum production is expected to increase to 24.1 and 44 million tons in 2005 and 2010 respectively, while natural gas production will reach 26 and 33 billion cubic meters in the same period. In Far East Asia, petroleum production is expected to reach 12.2 million and 29 million tons in 2005 and 2010, while natural gas production is expected to reach 30 and 43 billion cubic meters for the same years.

In 1996, petroleum and natural exports rose on a year-to-year basis by 3% to 126 million tons and 2% to 196 billion cubic meters, respectively, while coal exports decreased by 16% to 25.6 million tons. The estimated energy consumption of Russia is 900 million petroleum-equivalent tons, and energy remains a strategic industry to the extent that it accounts for 17% of GDP, 30% of investments and 46% of total exports.

The quality of oil reserves is not so high, however, and the most undeveloped oil fields have lower production and smaller reserves. The complex geographical structures and weather condition will also lead to expansion of capital expenditure for oil production.

Examination of the level of energy-related technology in Russia under the above considerations, shows that it keeps a relatively high level of technology.

The technology development, however, has been stagnant because of reduction in the governmental support. So the field of energy development is behind the advanced technology of the West. The production of machines and parts, which are suitable for the poor natural conditions in Siberia, are not enough to meet the demands.

<Table XVI-3> The Current Status of Energy Supply and Demand in Russia

	Oil(t)	Natural gas(m^3)	Coal(t)
Reserves (shares in the world)	600~800 billion (5%)	49trillion (35%)	201.5billion (15%)
Production (rank in the world)	320million (3rd)	575billion (1st)	255million (3rd)
Exports (fluctuation)	126million (3%)	196billion (2%)	255.5million (-16%)

Source: Same as in <Table XVI-1>.

(2) Energy Demand

Only 14% of oil refinery output meets the demand of current technology but the other 86% are much inferior to developed countries in durability, efficiency and ecological safety, because the refining industry stressed not quality but quantity. So, the technology of oil refining is extremely low, and the second processes are currently undeveloped or underdeveloped.

The quality of Russian oil fell far behind the international standard. 75% of the gasoline is A-76, which is a low-quality product, which among other things threatens to have a negative effect on environment. The cost of oil production and depreciation of refining equipment in Russia are so high that they need modernization and much investment.

3) Energy Resources and International Cooperation

The role of Far East Russia as a source of energy supply source will be further strengthened and the need for its development, heightened with the improvement of relations between China and Russia, the energy supply situation of Korea and Japan and China's transformation into a net importer of energy, and the world's attention, will be focussed on the possibility of a pipeline linking Far East Russia with countries in Northeast Asia.

In particular, the oil and gas fields of the Sahalin seas and the gas fields of Irkutsk and the Saha Republic have proven potential as major sources.

(1) The Oil Fields of the Sahalin Seas

The development of oil and gas fields in the Sahalin seas is being led by American and Japanese companies and has been divided into four project stages - Sahalin I, II, III and IV, with oil and gas reserves of 350 million tons and 775 billion cubic meters confirmed to date. The participating companies expect to produce petroleum by 1999 and gas by 2005 with plans to export about two-thirds of output, most of it to East Asian markets.

Japan originally proposed Sahalin-I to the Soviet Union through 'Agreement on Petroleum Development in Sahalin' as part of its policy to diversify energy sources following the experience of the First Oil Shock. Progress was slow for 20 years, however, due to the Cold War, and only recently did the project resume with the proposal by Russia to pursue Sahalin-II jointly with Western enterprises.

Sahalin-I has as its goal the development of three zones (Chaivo, Odoptu, and Dagin-skoye), where reserves of petroleum/condensate and gas have been estimated at 280 million tons and 420 billion cubic meters respectively. As for participants and their shares, Japan's Sodeco and the US's Exxon each hold 30% shares with Sahalin Sea Petroleum and Gas Development (23%) and Russia's national oil company (17%) holding the remaining portion of the US$15 billion total investment.

Sahalin-II will develop field in two zones (Lunskoye and Piltun-Astotskoye) where reserves of petroleum/condensate and gas have been estimated at 1.3 billion million tons and 400 billion cubic meters respectively. McDermott and Marathon of the US, Mitsui and Mitsubishi of Japan and Royal Dutch Shell of Great Britain the Netherlands are taking part with shares of 20%, 30%, 20%, 10%, and 20% respectively in a total investment of US$10 billion. Preliminary feasibility studies are being undertaken for Sahalin-III and Sahalin-IV and development will be take place in case economic value is proven.

This project is noteworthy in that it is the first large-scale project to be undertaken with foreign capital under the new laws enabling sharing of output and has symbolic value as cooperation between Japan and Russia in the midst of friction involving rights over the Kuril islands.

(2) The Gas Fields of Irkutsk Kovikchinsk

The development of the gas fields of Irkutsk Kovikchinsk is typical of the development of gas fields in the Far East Russia and Russia region with confirmed reserve of 870 billion cubic meters and estimated reserves of up to 1.5 trillion cubic meters. The five countries taking part in this project, Korea, Russia, China, Japan, and Mongolia held their first meeting in Moscow in December 1997 to discuss the method and timing of various issues such as survey of reserves and proposed pipeline routes and to negotiate allocation of costs. They reached the agreement that gas supplies to China would begin by 2005.

The rationale behind the development of oil and gas fields in this region is that it can alleviate the fuel shortage and atmospheric pollution in the region, as replacing oil and coal with natural gas will help reduce atmospheric pollutants by 400,000 tons annually and allow 16 million tons of coal to be exported to the Far East region. Russia plans to supply gas to Korea, China, Japan and other countries in the region by constructing a gas pipeline of 4,115 kilometers linking Irkutsk-Ulan Bator-Beijing-Sandong Peninsula-Yellow Sea. The total cost of this project will be US$10.8 billion.

In addition to the Sahalin project, the Japanese Government has shown a high degree of interest in the East Siberia pipeline and has decided not to discuss the issue of the 4 disputed islands which could be an obstacle to Japanese investment into Russia. The fact remains that due to the Sahalin project, Japan will not experience difficulties in the supply of natural gas, making the east Siberia project less than urgent; however, it is considering investment into the region with a long-term view and the Japanese Government declared its intentions to provide official support to the Irkutsk project in August 1997.

In conclusion, the Irkutsk region in east Siberia may be viewed as being ideally located in terms of transportation distance and target markets and will be able to provide all the participants of multilateral cooperation with great benefits.

(3) The Gas Fields of the Saha Republic

The Saha Republic has about 30 gas fields with combined estimated reserves of 1.7 trillion cubic meters of natural gas and 230 million tons of petroleum. Exports of gas to Korea and Japan via a pipeline through North Korea appears to be a viable project, which is probably expected to be pursued within the next 10 years. North Korea, which had been the greatest obstacle to the proposed idea, signed a document in November 1997 consenting to the passage of a pipeline within its borders, while countries and companies participating in the Irkutsk gas field project have already made long-term plans to supply Northeast Asia with gas from Saha by linking the two regions with a pipeline in case the reserves of Irkutsk prove to be insufficient.

F. Japan's Energy Cooperations with China and Russia

Japan has recently strengthened such cooperation by agreeing to joint projects for petroleum storage and use of low-pollution coal with China, while agreeing to provide technical support for resource development and efficient use of energy. Japan has a tendency to favor cooperation based on bilateral conferences rather than multilateral arrangements with the Government devising principles for resource development, energy-related security and environmental measures, while the private sector follow through with investments and technical support.

Such initiatives are based on Japan's judgement that development of new sources in the Far East region will make a great contribution to its own security and that of the region as a whole under the current situation of rising demand and environmental pollution levels in China and active development efforts in the Far East regions of Russia. In particular, efficient use of energy by the Chinese and improvements in Russia's energy equipment are reflections of the Japanese Government's determination to reduce atmospheric pollution within the region and consequently Japan's share of the cost of preventing the 'greenhouse effect'.

1) Cooperation with China

Japan and China had their first round-table meeting with both government and private sector participation in April 1998 in Beijing and agreed that the energy and environment are areas for strategic cooperation.

<Table XVI-4> Main Points of the Agreement between Japan and China on Cooperation of Energy

- Gasification and diversification of power fuel: 9 power plants including Sahalin coal thermal, Irkutsk, Konakovo, Amursk and Russia coal thermal
- Renovation of outdated thermal power plants: 2 plants in Khavarovsk and the Maritime Province of Siberia
- Energy saving: 3 refineries and steel plants including Khavarovsk refinery
- 6 other projects including maintenance of Siberian pipeline and Kamchatka geo-thermal heat plant
- In the private sector :
  - a consortium made up of the Petroleum Agency, Sumitomo and other companies are looking to take part in the construction of the Irkutsk pipeline,
  - general trading companies such as Itochu and Mitsui are involved in the Sahalin petroleum/gas development project (Sahalin-I and Sahalin-II) with American and Russian companies and hope to begin production by 1999 and 2001 and
  - Mitsui Trading plans to participate in the construction of 5 CO_2 release-restraining, energy-saving power plants (24-110 KW) by the Government of Nigegorod in Russia.

Note 1): China relies on coal for 75.5%(1996) of its primary energy requirements, while Shandong Province relies on coal thermal power for 94% of its electricity.

Source: Same as in <Table XVI-1>.

2) Cooperation with Russia

In their summit meeting (November, 1997 in Glasnoyarsk) Japan and Russia agreed to the basic principle to 'study ways of cooperating to maximize the potential of Far East/Siberia as provider of regional energy'. In a vice ministerial level meeting (January 1998 in Moscow), the Japanese proposed the joint supervision of the release of greenhouse gases through the exchange and training of personnel and dispatch of private sector manpower. In the meeting between MITI Minister Horiuchi and Premier Kirienko (July 1998 in Tokyo), a 20-point joint declaration was signed for the first time with a foreign nation towards this end.

<Table XVI-5> 20 Points for Japan-Russia Cooperation on Energy

- Both countries agree in principle to strengthen energy-related security within the region to ensure stable supply and promote efficient use of energy.
- Personnel and academic exchanges in regard to such areas as petroleum storage, utilization of natural gas, energy saving, development of alternative energy and usage of low-pollution coal are to be expanded as a response to the deepening dependence on Middle East oil and potential instability of supply.
- The basic direction for cooperation will be to complement China's resources and vast market with Japan's capital and technology, *i.e.* each country's area of comparative advantage.
- As part of efforts to clean up the environment, the Japanese Government has agreed to provide filtering devices for thermal power plants and provide specific plans during Chairman Jang's visit to Japan in September 1998.
- Nisshoiwai of Japan has agreed to expand LPG gas storage capacities within China from 200,000 tons at the present to 1.6 million tons by 2000, and Kyushu Electricity has agreed to assist Shandong Electricity in reducing pollution and greenhouse gases by improving heat efficiency at thermal power plants using coal (June 1998)[1)]*, while the Export-Import Bank of Japan has agreed to provide US$130 million in loans (July 1998) for two fusion power plants to be built in Kilin Province.

Source: Same as in <Table XVI-1>.

3. COOPERATION ON AGRICULTURAL AND MARINE PRODUCTS

The problems of world food demand and supply lie in not only the gross food production, marine products, but in some other factors like food purchasing ability, distribution network and storage capacity. Generally, developed countries have enough food production or the ability to buy food from abroad. So, they are not so worried about food shortages. Food shortage, however, is a big threat to the Northeast Asia region, which is the most overpopulated area in the world.

A. Food Supply & Demand

The world population increased to 5.7 billion in the second half of 1995. With this rate, it can be assumed that the population is expected to increase to 6.3 billion in 2000 and to 8 or 9 billion in between 2020 and 2030. In terms of absolute population growth, Asia is expected to grow by 1.6% and the population of developing countries will account for more than 83% of the world population in 2025 from 75% in 1985.

According to FAO, crop production between 1994 and 1995 was about 1,759 million tons. It decreased by 26 million tons to 1,733 tons between 1995 and 1996. The growth rate of crops in the world agriculture was 3.0% in 1960s, 2.3% in the 1970s and to 2.0% a year between 1980 and 1992.

<Table XVI-6> The Changing Trends and Prospects of World Population

Year	Population (billions)			Component ratio(%)	
	World	The Developed Countries	The Developing Countries	The Developed Countries	The Developing Countries
1985	49	12	37	24	76
1995	57	12	45	21	79
2010	69	12	57	17	83
2025	80	12	68	15	85

Source: Same as in <Table XVI-1>.

<Table XVI-7> The Trend in the World's Crop Stocks (unit: million ton, %)

	Crop Year						
Year	1990/1	1991/2	1992/3	1993/4	1994/5	1995/6	1996/7
Gross Crop Stocks	351.8	336.5	379.4	334.8	301.4	244.4	277.7
Stock to Consumption Ratio(%)	20	19	21	19	17	13.9	15.4

* 1997 figures are estimates.

Source: 1) USDA-WAOB (1996.12.12), *FAO International agriculture,* Vol. 404, Dec. 1996.
2) Same as in <Table XVI-1>.

The gap of developing countries between food production and consumption has been increasing every year. It is estimated that the import rate of the food-short countries with low income amounted to US$ 23 billion between 1994 and 1995. After all, the prices in the world agricultural products markets is expected to increase on the whole part compared to the period between 1987 and 1989. The recent instability of corn prices, for example, is very long and chronic.

The reasons can be summarized as follows: first, under the WTO, declining subsidies for farmers will make them give up agriculture, which will be followed by a decline in supply; second, the entrance of the former Communist countries into free competition brought the government purchases of agricultural foods to an end; third, as South Korea, China, India, Thailand, Indonesia, Vietnam and the Philippines, accounting for 45% the world population, have recorded 5 to 10% of high growth in economic terms, an increase in their consumption has caused export curtails or increases in imports; fourth, higher wages and the drain of manpower to other industries brought about a shortage of manpower in agriculture; the crop stock, which began to fall since the period of 1991 and 1993, has already decreased more than 15%, raising the possibility of a crop crisis; and sixth, international trade accounts for only 10% of the world gross crop production with trade accounting for 4.0%, 18.1% and 15.5% of rice, wheat, and corn during the period between 1970 and 1990.

1) Food Crisis and Necessity for Agricultural Cooperation

As droughts have spread in Asian countries including China, Indonesia and Vietnam, the slump in crop production and food shortages has deepened. The structural factors will cause 470 million tons of crop shortages in 2020. The aggravation of the food situation was caused by some structural factors such as unusual climate changes due to *El Nino*, population growth, a decline in agricultural workforce by industrialization, insufficient infrastructure and an increase in demand of feed grains by the higher standard of living. The aggravation of food situations in Asia will not lead to an immediate rise in the international crop price because world harvests expect to show a favorable tendency in 1998. However, the crop production of countries with big populations such as China and Indonesia has exposed their limitations so there are higher possibilities of serious crises in world crop markets.

China

Poor management of water utilization has depleted water resources of the main rivers and reservoirs in China. The demand of industries went on increasing and the securing of agricultural water became difficult. The water level of the *Hebei Plain*, which accounts for 40% of the gross crop production, has been in decline by 150 cm each year. This led to an decrease of crop production from 453 million tons in 1997 to 444 million tons in 1998. China is expected to import 175 million tons in 2025.

Indonesia

The crop production of Indonesia decreased as a result of *El Nino* in 1997, which caused droughts, forests fires and economic difficulties. Although Indonesia has to import 35 million tons of rice, it decided on a policy to import 15 million tons. According to government statistics, about 8 million people experienced food shortages (under 2 meals a day) as of 1998. According to the FAQ and the WFP, an additional 7 million people will face starvation.

Thailand, the Philippines and North Korea

The crop production of Thailand amounted to 25.4 million tons in 1998, a decrease of 6.6% compared to last year. Figures for the Philippines and North Korea were 15 million tons and 2.9 million tons down 2.0% and 35.6% each. While rice production of Thailand will be recovered from an decreasing tendency of last year, corn production will decrease sharply. Due to floods between 1995 and 1996, a drought in 1997 and stock shortages, North Korea is required to import 1,950,000 tons. It must depend on foreign aid, however, because of the foreign currency crisis. In the case of Vietnam, there was severe droughts around the Central plain and the southern Mekong Delta in the first quarter of 1998. This led the government to conduct a restriction on rice exports as a part of securing crop demands for domestic consumption.

2) Proposal for Food-related Cooperation in Northeast Asia

Limited farmlands made the self-sufficiency of domestic agriculture impossible in Northeast Asian countries such as Japan, South and North Korea, which are short of land. It is a foregone conclusion that this will an expanded the degree of the agricultural market openness. Under such a condition, an inflow of agricultural products through overseas development would provide more favorable conditions than imports. In addition to the price factor, the fact that the stable supply is important in controlling agricultural products will make it worth while to supply overseas produced crops for domestic markets.

Combining the rich land of China and Russia with the technology and capital of South Korea and Japan and with a cheap workforce of North Korea, stable food supply will be partially possible in the Northeast Asia.

(1) China

China, with a vast land and population of 1.2 billion, has been striving to become a great economic power through rapid economic growth since reform and opening beginning in 1979. The driving force of its economic growth has been industrial development by attracting foreign capital. As a result, it caused a relative shrinkage in the agriculture of China and it is now facing its unbalanced developments between regions and an expanding income gap between the agricultural and industrial sectors. More seriously, agricultural production has been stagnant since the 1980s because of its own limitations to increase agricultural production.

The agricultural production of China reached 400 million tons for the first time in 1984 and resulted in an oversupply. Although production has experienced a stagnation since then, it has kept the level of 430 to 450 million tons in the first half of the 1990s. The continuous growth of agricultural production led to the maintenance the balanced domestic supply and demand.

The further changes (tendency of expanding imbalance between agricultural supply and demand and the expansion of food importation) are foreseeable in its supply and demand system along the industrialization and urbanization. China has now reached the level which is required to make a new plan for food security.

(2) Russia

Agriculture in Russia is concentrated in certain areas because of weather conditions. Gross agricultural production of Russia increased by 2.1% a year during the period between 1981 and 1985, but decreased by 1.4% during the period between 1986 and 1990. Private agricultural production increased by 2.2% in 1988 and 4.2% in 1990. Private farm lands occupy less than 4% of the total sowed lands but accounts for 40% of total agricultural products. This shows the improvement direction of Russian agriculture and the potential of Russian agricultural production.

The reasons why the agricultural production decreased during the first half of 1990 include the mental alienation caused by the market economy system, recession, reduced adjustment of agricultural production and insufficient infrastructure. If Russia solves these kinds of problems, it is evident that the food consumption and crop demand will increase. It other words, Russia is required to succeed in the reform of its economy and the improvement of its domestic economy for an increase in the food consumption and crop demand. Assuming the fluctuations of crop prices in the market, it will be a great financial pressure on Russia.

(3) Japan

The food self-supply ratio of Japan is 29%, which is among the lowest in the world. Since the 1960s, imports by Japan has increased to US$59 million in 1990. The self-supply ratio has become a politically sensitive issue, particularly with respect to rice. The rice-farming area of Japan has decreased 0.4% each year during the period between 1960 and 1990. Although there were variations in fresh water due to cold-weather damage and typhoons, the yield increased to 509 kg in 1990 from 401 kg per ten hectares in 1960. The gross production, however, only rose to 1,253,9000 tons in 1960 to 1,460,3000 tons in 1990.

The self-supply of grains in Japan is also very low of 0.1%. Of 94 million tons of the world grains-importing amount, Japan accounted for 20.98% in the world crop market. Japan has prepared itself for a possible food crisis by purchasing much land in several areas in other countries to secure food supply and expand its national power.

(4) South Korea

Looking into the trend of crops in Korea, staple rice increased from 3.5million tons to 3.94 million tons in 1975 and to 5.63 million tons in 1985. It has decreased, however, to 5.06 million tons in 1994. The rice-concentrated structure of production resulted from advances in technology, changes in eating habits and economic conditions. This structure caused undesirable situations such as distorted use of farm lands and difficulties in maintaining the basic crops at a minimum level.

Moreover, rice-farming lands have rapidly decreased due to the diversion of farmlands to non-agricultural use and cultivation of other crops. The increase of fresh-water is expected to be stagnant. Because the decreasing rate of production has outpaced consumption, it is difficult to ignore the possibility of imports at levels exceeding minimum market-approach amounts. Korea is one of the largest food-importing countries in the world, with a large share in the world market. The self-supply ratio is predicated to be continuously decreased, in other words, its dependence on the international market is gradually expected to increase.

<Table XVI-8> Changes in Agricultural Production and Self-Supply in South Korea (Unit: 10 million tons, %)

Year	1965	1970	1975	1980	1985	1990	1994	1996
Total	6,524	6,937	7,654	5,324	6,990	6,635	5,774	-
Self-supply	93.9	80.5	73.1	56.0	48.4	43.1	28.5	26.7

Data sources: 1) Ministry of Agriculture & Forest, Korea, *The Main Statistics on Agriculture and Fishery*, 1995.
2) Same as in <Table XVI-1>.

(5) North Korea

Since statistics on agricultural production in North Korea is unreliable and data is too inadequate, the assumption of its situation is inevitable. There is no doubt, however, that it has been suffering from severe shortage in food supply and demand. According to the Korea Rural Economic Institute, the gross food demand is between 6 million and 6.5 million tons and the average food production is between 4.5 million and 5 million tons. In 1993, the food production was only 2.8 million or 2.9 million tons due to cold-weather damage. So it is assumed that North Korea was short of 3 million tons, which is more than 50%, supposing that the gross demand was 6 million tons. This led to a situation which temporarily stopped food distribution from September 1993.

After the transformation of the former USSR and Easter European countries, North Korea experienced severe isolation from the Communist communities. It even resumed trade with the US, a once hostile enemy. Nevertheless, the main source of food import of North Korea is still China. The portion of China amounted to 780,000 tons, accounting for 68% of the gross crop importation. It was known that 50% of this was a kind of free contribution, and the other 50% was imported at half of the international price.

<Table XVI-9> The Trend of Crop Production in North Korea

Year	1990	1991	1992	1993	1994	1995
Production (10,000 tons)	481.2	442.7	426.8	388.4	376.8	258.3
Fluctuation Ratio(%)	-12.3	-8.0	-3.6	-9.0	-3.0	-31.4

Source: 1) Ministry of Unification, Korea Trading Association, the main economic index of North Korea, 1995.
2) Same as in <Table XVI-1>.

Chapter XVIII

CONCLUSION: KOREA'S CURRENT 'FIVE CRISES' AND VISION IN THE 21ST CENTURY

In conclusion, the author would like to discuss current 'five crises' of Korea and present its vision in the 21st century. In order to propose such a development strategy to make a blueprint of Korea's future reality, a certain preliminary analysis has been inevitable. Such analysis included; externally, prospects on changes in global order; and internally, the present status of the Korean situation, its development and practical remedies for its side effects. Before such external and internal problems can be resolved, however, a national consensus must be achieved by overcoming the crisis on the Korean peninsula related to security, political, socio-cultural and economic issues.

THE PERISH OF THE KOREAN EMPIRE IN AUGUST 1910

To view Korea's vision in the 21st century, it would be meaningful to review the situation of the Korean peninsula, particularly that of one hundred years ago, during the reform period of the Korean Empire.

Daewon-kun (1863~1873) strongly pursued bold political and economic reform policies. His isolationistic and antagonistic policies against the Western powers enabled him to repel imperialistic invasion of the powers, but also hindered *Chosun* Dynasty from modernizing by delaying its emergence into international history. In contrast, Ok-Gyun Kim was infatuated with the enlightenment movement, and believed that the only way to obtain and maintain total independence was by converting *Chosun* Dynasty into an autonomous and wealthy state. He led a failed coup in 1884. It was the first attempt for political reform to have which pioneered the modernization of Korea. It became the origin of Korea's independence movement and also became a milestone for the establishment and development of Korea's modern nationalism. King *Kojong* promulgated the '14 *Hongbum* Articles', which were the first open manifestation of Korea's self-determined independence and was the basic principle for political reform.

The Sino-Japanese War (August 1894~March 1885) broke out after the *Tonghak* Rebellion (January 1894~March 1895). Japan, emerging as the victor, began to monopolize the Korean market. Exploitation by the great powers, including Russia, worsened. In 1897, the Korean Empire was established, and the new nation was called '*Daehanminkuk*'. In the early 20th century, patriotic enlightenment movements in the falling empire spread like wildfire. However, Korea's sovereignty was ultimately taken away. Japan took away military power and internal administrative authority (1907), which finally led to annexation in August 1910.

Even in the critical situation, Koreans were busy fighting themselves, which hindered modernization and, in turn, resulted in annexation and colonization by the Japanese. Specifically, the issue of transforming the feudal social system to a modern one created three different movements with their own opinions divided by social status. However, international indifference towards Japan's invasion of Korea must be noted. Korea was literally handed over to Japan after the Russo-Japanese War (February 1904~September 1905) by the First Alliance between Japan and Britain (1902), the Second Alliance between Japan and Britain (August 1905), and the Taft-Katsura Memorandum and the Treaty between Japan and the United States (July 1905). After the annexation, Japan went through three stages of colonization: the ruling by the Japanese military (1910~1919), the governing through cultural assimilation (1919~1931), and the 'squeezing' of Korea (1931~1945).

Independence finally came on August 15, 1945, but Korea was soon divided. The liberation and independence of Korea was agreed upon in the Cairo (November 1943) and Potsdam (July 1945) Conferences. The division of Korea was agreed by the United States and the Soviet Union in the Yalta Conference in February 1945. Ideas were suggested for the drawing of a military demarcation line and a trusteeship of Korea by five allied nations. Under the international situation in which the fate of Korea was being discussed, Koreans again split into pro-trusteeship and anti-trusteeship parties.

By the decision of the UN, general elections were held in the South only, and the government of the Republic of Korea was established in August 1948. This was acknowledged as the sole legitimate government in the Korean peninsula. Since then, there has been rapid economic growth through the eight Five-Year Economic Development Plans up until the present administration of President Dae-jung Kim.

KOREA'S 'FIVE CRISES' IN THE LATE 1990S

The author has called the crisis of Korea as a 'general' crisis because of its multifaceted character: the crisis is in fact an amalgamation of security, political, social, cultural and economic crisis. [186]

Security Crisis

Looking at the various changes in international political and economic order over the Korean Peninsula and the Far East, there is a high possibility that it might repeat its past sad history in the end of the *Chosun* dynasty of being pushed around by powers by the US to achieve 'Pax Americana' by Japan to once again become a political and military power of the region; by Russia to gain access to the Pacific Rim; and, by China to become an economic giant and establish regional hegemony. The two major tragedies (the colonialization of Japan in 1910 and the division in 1945) in the modern history of Korea occurred due to both internal and external reasons in changing international environments. The Korean Peninsula is still a focal point of the interests of four great powers - the United States, Japan, China and Russia - as it was in the end of the last century. The United States is expected to reduce its military presence in the region. Japan is rapidly becoming a military power. China does not seem to give up its interests in the peninsula easily. Russia is still a huge military power in the region.

The role of the US is crucial to defining the relations between Korea and the US, between Korea and Japan, between Korea and China, between Korea and Russia and between two Koreas in the peninsula. This is because just as America has a share of responsibility in the division of the Korean Peninsula into North and South, so will America's role be a big one for the peace and prosperity of the peninsula in the 21st century.

The US would be able to play a role of balancer, because the US has the key to the composition of powers such as Japan, China, Russia and the US within the East Asian region, and more broadly, in the Asia-Pacific region. However, the principle of US diplomacy and security is to prevent the re-emergence of military threat by supporting Russia in its reforms, to induce the expansion of its partners' responsibilities to prevent the emergence of regional hegemonic powers, and to perform 'selective' intervention against the threat of regional, ethnic and religious strifes.

An important issue at hand is that the US policy regarding the Korean peninsula has gone through some essential changes in the post Cold War era. As revealed in the North Korea-US meetings, the United States does not regard Korea as an absolute ally any more, and is trying to include North Korea into the world order. Thus, although American officials are stating that no reduction or withdrawal of US forces is being considered, such changes do not seem impossible. When North Korea is no longer an enemy, there is no reason for the United States to keep its forces in South Korea. Even if South Korea pays more and more of the costs to maintain US forces, the United States itself will feel the North Korean market potential. Nuclear talks with North Korea (October 21, 1994) stipulate that the United States must supply North Korea with petroleum. To this end, the United States had to change all the laws that classified North Korea as a hostile country. The justification of US forces in Korea would be come weaker if North Korea is no

[186] Yang-Taek Lim, "The Current Five Crises in Korea", *National Intellect,* Vol. 57, November 1990.
Yang-Taek Lim, "Recovery of Humanity", The Keynote Address, Humanity Recovery Council (HRC), US Chapter, Los Angeles, U.S.A., August 15, 1994.

longer considered a hostile country. It is clear that the withdrawal of American forces from Korea will result in a power vacuum, increasing the probability of war.

The North Korean nuclear problem is a very important issue concerning not only the Korean Peninsula but also world peace. North Korea has already been preparing nuclear weapons for its own survival. However, a North Korean nuclear weapon endangers the entire world. It may trigger Japan into arming itself with its own nuclear arms. India and Pakistan already went into a nuclear arms race.

In order to solve the North Korean nuclear problem, the US and North Korea held a three-step meeting in Geneva. In October 1994, it was agreed that North Korea would freeze all its nuclear facilities and later dismantle them, while the US would provide two 1,000 megawatt class LWRs (light-water reactors) and alternative energy sources, drop communications and financial restrictions, relieve trade capital investment, and aim towards future official national amity. The various restrictions against North Korea that the US government has agreed to remove following the Geneva Agreement of October 1994 have consisted of more than ten related laws and regulations. Already, the US government has removed restrictions in the three fields of foreign aid, foreign currency and communications by executive orders in November 1994.

Meanwhile, it is the well-known fact that Japan is a country of considerable military power. Its army, the SDF (Self-Defense Force), has 270 thousand troops and packs a lot of firepower. Since the end of the Cold War, moreover, Japan is raising more and more arms against the world recent trend. Japan has thirty tons of plutonium in stock regardless of the Three Principles of Denuclearization, and through the launch of the H2 Rocket in February 1994, has secured the ability to create an ICBM. Japan has the strongest navy in Northeast Asia. Her defense budget was 4.7 trillion Yen in 1992, the third largest military budget in the world. Moreover, in September 1997 has opened the doors for Japan to support US military actions behind battlefield lines in cases of emergency situations.

If Article 9 of the Constitution, which stipulates that 'Japan may not be involved in any military action other than cases where its sovereignty is transgressed' in accordance with the principle of 'collective sovereignty', is amended, then Japan may not only engage in joint operations with the US in the Korean Peninsula but a heavily armed Japanese army may also take part in an allied war effort. This subtle trend runs counter to the efforts of the Japanese government since World War II, which has been concentrated on providing its citizens with an affluent society based on peace, and is an issue that Japan must handle in an appropriate manner. When international tension rises and regional conflicts burst out somewhere however, or when US ceases to be the world police, the possibility of Japan using military power as a weapon cannot be overlooked. Japan has such a capability, and the capability is growing continuously.

Political Crisis

Korea is in a political crisis for the following reason: there seems to be no political leadership that offers a long-term vision for the nation and a blue print on how to achieve national reunification and maintain it with political compromises made by the two Koreas; and South Korea has not succeeded in democratizing its whole political system either. Its regional politics is far from being democratic and self-autonomous. It is still suffering from deep regional rivalries.

The political challenge for Koreans is thus still immense. And the author would like to emphasize the fact that Koreans seem to be losing a golden opportunity to manifest their political maturity under such relatively favorable international circumstances.

Social Crisis

Korea is undergoing a social crisis: the traditional prescription of the Korean government for the distribution of wealth has been the trickle-down effects, believing that growth will enable it to deal with the distribution issue with ease at a later stage. True, absolute poverty has shrunk. However, the gap between the have and have-nots is dangerously growing fueling the conflicts between capitalists and workers, and the urban and rural populations.

The generational gap also is becoming an acute problem in Korea too combined with the conflicts between conservatives and liberals almost to the point of an ideological confrontation in the post-Cold War era.

Cultural Crisis

Korea is in a cultural crisis. The traditional ethics of Korea have weakened while the Western cultures and their new value systems gaining popularity. The former seeks harmony based on hierarchical orders while the latter pursues reasons on the basis of horizontal orders. The fact is that traditional values are much more deeply rooted in the spirits of the general population than it seems in the first instance in any civilization. The crisis stems from the inclination to deny the traditional values. Harmony should be sought between the two different value systems.

Economic Crisis

Korea is in economic crisis, especially in the sense of the deterioration of its international competitiveness. In other worlds, Korea has failed to equip itself with quality competitiveness as opposed to price competitiveness. Korea is very poor in natural resources and international trade is its only choice. Relishing in price competitiveness, many of its corporations have not invested in R&D for many years in the past. As a result, Korea is now plagued with sluggish exports, reduced industrial investment, increasing unemployment, high inflation, growing trade deficits with Japan, trade disputes with the US and European Union. In addition, many Korean workers have lost their world-renowned hard working ethics and households have lost incentives, both physical and psychological, in savings. Most important, too many entrepreneurs are frustrated in making investments in productive areas of the national economy.

Since Korea is lacking in natural resources, export-oriented policy is the only strategy for national survival and prosperity. Though a transformation to competitiveness based on quality instead of price is being attempted to confront the international economic order and the changes in global industrial structure, Korea's international competitiveness continues to weaken as a result of neglect of technological development. Furthermore, the structural problems that Korea is facing internally were caused by excessive emphasis on the quantitative expansion through an extensive-growth policy, which failed to accomplish qualitative reform through an intensive-development strategy. Externally, elements of liberalization and globalization are pouring in without the necessary preparations to cope with them.

Korea possesses an industrial structure in which it is impossible to manufacture major products without importing essential parts and high-tech production facilities from advanced countries like Japan or Germany. Such a structure is based on what is called technological dependence on advanced nations and this is the reason for the failure in resolving structural trade deficits. Independent efforts to design and manufacture essential parts and high-tech facilities are most likely to meet with technology barriers set up by advanced countries.

Thus, the fundamental direction towards reform of the industrial structure itself is to achieve a transition of labor and capital-intensive industries into knowledge and technology-intensive industries that create high value-added. At the same time, basic materials industries in machine parts should be supported to transform the current industrial structure, which relies on imports from Japan, into a self-sufficient one. This will raise the inflow of foreign reserves and the rate of value-added.

To successfully achieve the structural transformation, the Korean industry needs to concentrate on the development of technology. Technological development is the most essential factor in the restructuring of industry and strengthening of competitiveness. In particular, under the present international circumstances in which technology protectionism is taking root, it is impossible for a country that lacks technology to achieve industrial development, export growth or environmental improvement, much less survive the fierce competition among countries.

The technology needed in the course of such rapid growth could be introduced from abroad by importing capital resources, FDI (foreign direct investment) and license agreements on technology introduction. Unfortunately, the present international environment does not readily permit a government-led or government-guided industrial development strategy. It was estimated that a technological development could be promoted by independent development, through such measures as an increase in the number of researchers and university graduates of science and engineering majors, but their effects would be less than the effect caused by increasing the transfer of technology.

Before technology is introduced, independent research must be done to accumulate related basic technology. The capacity to receive the technology must also be created by understanding the main components of the technology beforehand. All of this is necessary to maximize assimilation and absorption of capacities when the contracts have been concluded and the technology is being transferred.

KOREA'S VISION IN THE 21ST CENTURY

There are three national objectives for Korea in the 21st century: domestically, a society that guarantees the greatest happiness for the greatest majority must be created based on humanitarian principles; a reunified nation must be constructed for the people; and, Korean people must take a leading role in the coming Asia-Pacific Age.

Human Capitalism

The South Korean society has transformed itself from an agrarian society to an industrial one in a thirty-year period between 1960 to 1990. A 1990 census shows that 74.4% of the Korean people live in urban areas. Thirty years prior to that 80% of the Korean people lived in the rural area. Other demographic statistics also show that the Korean society is rapidly becoming a mature industrial society. Life expectancy has almost caught up with those of major industrialized countries, the birth rate has declined to 1.6 children per couple and the age structure of the population becomes similar to those of a mature industrialized country. Per capita income reached the level of US$5,500 in 1990, but some selected areas of the capital city demonstrate a much higher consumption level.

Several factors characterize the rapid industrialization and economic growth of Korea over the thirty years. Its initial condition was the war-destroyed economy subsisting on the US economic aid, but with the relatively good supply of educated and skilled people. An authoritarian leader with a strong motive of the national modernization emerged and began to oversee the industrialization process in the following two decades. Beginning in the early 1970s, exports were given the highest priority by the government and began to be heavily subsidized. Domestic industries were protected from the foreign competition during the 1960s and 1970s and the labor movement was suppressed by the state. Government funds as well as bank loans were channeled to a small number of successful companies, and the latter were often heavily protected even from the domestic competition by barriers to entry. This set of policies has brought about the economy that is characterized by the strong interventionist government and a group of very powerful private business firms called *chaebols*.

The democratization process which symbolically started in 1987, has challenged the fundamental structure of the Korean economy and society that had been formulated during the previous three developmental decades. Demands began to be made by the populace to change the structure of the Korean economy and the roles of the government and big business changed within broader social and economic contexts. A framework of an economic system that could meet the popular demand of the people came to be required.

In the process of rapid industrialization, the material living standard of Korean people has generally improved with economic advances. Recently, however, the economy has begun to show signs of difficulties in both the domestic and international sectors. All of sudden, a severe economic crisis has swept the Korean peninsula around November 1997. It is expected that current economic and social problems that are the unfortunate by-products of the developments strategies in the last three decades or so.

A proper cure for the present crisis is the implementation of a fundamental economic reform to resume elements of economic justice and people-centered development including the poor. In particular, a new Korean model of economic growth and social development which is conducive to the new era should be proposed. Economic policy in the future should place more emphasis on social equity rather than focusing entirely on the pursuit of economic growth. As a matter of fact, the social development of Korea has not kept pace with economic growth. in particular, social security development lags behind their economic achievements. Continuously rising income has elevated the expectations of people seeking for a higher quality of life, so the growth strategy needs to be supplemented with policy measures designed to improve the social welfare level.

Now that traditional economic policy is threatened by powerful forces in Korean society and by the Korean peoples interests, it is important to reconsider its role and functions in promoting economic welfare, human dignity, social solidarity, popular participation and empowerment. The old economic policy regime in Korea is under siege and is being recast in a new mold, simply because it is mainly focused on economic growth. A new paradigm of economic policy is required. Since the policy focus should be on the improvement of quality of life, a fundamental reform should be made by which corruption and rent-seeking would be eliminated.

The Korean economy will show a positive rate of growth in 1999. Compared to the minus 5% ~ minus 6% growth in 1998, this is a significant recovery. The unemployment rate, however, is not expected to fall because of the ongoing restructuring in the corporate sector and the M&A's in the banking industry. It will remain at the 7.5%~8% level with 1.6~1.7 million workers unemployed. With this background, the policy agenda aiming for maintaining the socioeconomic unity should focus on the following points.

First of all, the social-safety-net has to be completed in order to ensure the basic subsistence level of the unemployed and the poor. For this purpose, it is necessary to expand the coverage of unemployment benefits and social assistance. Also, the amount of benefits or the period of benefits should adjusted reflecting the reality of unemployed workers. But the most important thing is to construct a social-safety-net based on the 'work-fare' concept, not merely on the welfare concept. By this we mean that a person who wants to receive the unemployment benefits or assistance should take job training courses and eventually try to get a job.

Second, a fundamental approach to solve the unemployment problem is providing a smooth way for the unemployed to come back to the labor market and be re-employed. An indispensable component in the policy for enhancing the socioeconomic unity, therefore, should create new demand for labor and to support re-employment. Toward these ends, corporate sector must regain its competitiveness and the macroeconomy should recover from the current situation. Also the transaction costs for hiring and firing should be reduced mainly through deregulation in the related public sectors. To solve the potential mis-match problem in the labor market, the government should be more elaborate in job training programs and work out efficient mechanisms to assist personal-base job search processes.

Third, in the long run, labor and the management have to rid themselves of the old-fashioned antagonism where the relation between labor and the management often results in a 'zero-sum game'. Instead, they should design a 'positive-sum game', - that is, they need to develop productive industrial labor relations. This type of productive industrial relations will be constructed by introducing 'human capital management' that provides more incentive for employee's participation and cooperation in the management process.

Finally, in order to maintain socioeconomic unity in Korean society, it is essential to foster the middle class. However, during the 'IMF era', the middle class of Korea has suffered relatively the most among others. Many economists worry that due to the spread of unemployment and wage cuts, middle class households have substantially dwindled in 1998. To protect the middle class from economic hardships, an appropriate tax policy is needed. For example, excise tax increases should be suppressed and income tax brackets adjusted so that the (after-tax) income inequality does not widen.

The previously-described socio-economic policy should be developed further- more to reforming the Korean capitalistic structure. Korean capitalization was initiated during the colonial rule of Japanese imperialism. In contrast, British capitalism is centered around small producers and is naturally developed. Japanese capitalism is metamorphic capitalism by law and system of government.

To be more specific, British capitalism has developed in the following direction: home manual trade → factory manual trade → modern industry (ex: smithy → farming tools factory → steel enterprise), in this way enterprise is outcome. But in Japan's case, the government created the state enterprise implementing by a trade centered system, and finally established a metamorphic capitalism during the period of World War I and II. Enterprise was not made by capitalization, Capitalization was made by enterprise. Japan's enterprise is the symbol and tool of modernization. As a result, Japanese consider enterprise as a semi-government and semi-civilian in their positive view

In the case of Korea, however, enterprises had been prosperous due to the tools of colonial policy, and Corporate Law was established before national companies had taken root. Korean enterprises had become a comprador capitalist. After gaining its independence, Korean capitalism was directly connected with funding purchases from America, but by the 1960s it achieved leaping development supported by preferential aid during the period of development.

Japanese capitalism arrived about one century later than Western capitalism, but underwent all the stages: commercial capitalism → industrial capitalism → financial capitalism → monopoly capitalism → modified capitalism, and so did its enterprises.

After World War II, however, many undeveloped countries became independent and began to capitalize but could not follow in the steps of industrialized countries. The process of Korean capitalization was a procedure of subordination. After liberalization for example, aid by the US was a major part of the economy. Korean capitalization had begun with an inheritance from the Japanese colonization, at a time when most enterprises started appearing.

From the beginning, Korean capitalism and enterprises were distorted, and people came to have a negative view. After 3 years of US military administration, Korea established a government in 1948 and was to establish a national economic system through agrarian reform. Unfortunately, the country suffered the setback and devastation of the Korean War (June 1950 ~ July 1953).

The aftermath of the Korean war left agrarian reform, whose goal was agricultural democratization and industrial capitalization of agriculture capital, in ruin. Temporary property taxes were levied for provisions of war, and fair prices in grain procurement disappeared. In this manner, Korean agriculture was sacrificed for Korean capitalism.

Korean enterprises were granted monopolies in the capacity of government in- vested property. During the period of the Korean War and in the early 1950s, Korea enterprises grew rapidly through US aid and the economic stabilization policy of government. The five year economic development plan, loan capital as compensation for Korea-Japan normalization of diplomatic relations, and political- economic control by the Military junta in 1962 all helped enterprises grow rapidly. With economic development, the contradiction and complications between the traditional value system and free market system increased the need for cultural spirit and ethics in enterprises.

The corporate culture of Korea is a highly spiritual culture based on higher purpose, motivation, and challenge - a 'Can Do Culture'. This point makes Korean corporate culture different from the Japanese one. Under Confucianism, Japanese corporation culture is a horizontal one based on individualism. The Korean structure is a vertical one based on individual totalitarianism. In Japanese corporations, the separation of ownership and management, employee-centered management, and classified production have been influences of the culture. In Korea, the separation of ownership and management, headquarter-centered management, and the weak production system have been influences of the culture.

The free market concept of modern society may be characterized by individualism from an ideological standpoint, freedom from a conceptual standpoint, production from an economic standpoint, and ability from a social standpoint, which can be explained by an emphasis on achievement. Therefore, the ideals of the free market economies of Western societies are based more on reason than morality.

In contrast, traditional Korean values may be characterized by collectivism from an ideological standpoint, equality from a conceptual standpoint, distribution from an economic standpoint, and necessity from a social standpoint, which can all be summarized by a strong sense of affiliation. Therefore, traditional Korean values emphasize morality over reason as its basis.

Japan and Korea have similar Confucian cultures but different Confucian ideologies. The difference is attributable to the following differences. Korea exercised examination system, genealogy system, and master-servant relationships, whereas Japan accepted its professional consciousness and diligence to survive.

Confucianism in Korea is metaphysical idealism, while in contrast, in Japan it is physical activism. The different types of Confucianism are embodied in Korea's blood-related community spirit and Japan's village-centered community spirit, so the consciousness structure of Koreans is individualistic community while that in Japan is individualism.

In this manner not only do ideological conflicts between collectivism and individualism, conceptual conflicts between equality and freedom, economic conflicts between distribution and production, and social conflicts between need and ability exist at the base of Korean society which has adopted Western capitalism, but a morality-based sense of affiliation is at odds with achievement- oriented reason. Korean capitalism and enterprises have been growing within such a cultural environment, only to suffer or collapse during the recent economic crisis.

National Reunification

As for national reunification, there are bound to be many external variables involved, but recent changes in international and South- North Korea relations indicate a heightening of possibilities. The more important question is whether the citizens of the country can handle their given roles until these three national objectives are met. A division of roles is required before anything. The respective roles of politicians, the government, entrepreneurs, laborers, educators, the press, and other parts of society are all important.

Historically, one language and one shared socio-cultural heritage remain a strong positive factor for a unified Korean regime. The economic rationale for Korean reunification provides an articulate agenda, much beyond any and all normative idealization.

As the reunification of Germany is compared to that of Korea, it should be stressed that the former was fulfilled despite the difficulty of the Germans in resolving their problems independently. The desire for reunification runs strong among the Korean people, yet there has not been enough effort. The task of the reunification of Germany after 1945 was fully under the responsibility and claim of the four Western powers: the US, Great Britain, France, and the U.S.S.R. Militarily, West Germany was bound to NATO, and East Germany to the Warsaw Treaty. Economically, West Germany was part of the European Community, and East Germany of COMECON. Such circumstances did not make it easy for the two Germanys to act on their own accord. Thus, the reunification of Germany on October 3, 1990, was almost an achievement of what was thought to be impossible.

On the other hand, there is more flexibility in the interests of the involved international powers regarding the relationship between South and North Korea. In addition, Korea has a long history as a united nation, with same culture, language and lifestyles of the peoples of the Two Koreas. This by itself, however, does not solve the conditions that are less favorable than they were for Germany.

First of all, Korea went through a tragic civil war which deepened the rift of distrust between the South and the North.

Second, unlike the people of East Germany who were well informed of West Germany's free and prosperous living conditions, North Koreans are living in one of the world's most closed societies with little access to information about the economic prosperity in South Korea.

It follows that rational thinking from both sides is critical for the revival of trust and the resolution of conflict and hostility and for solving the problems on the Korean peninsula. It needs to be reiterated that the reunification of Germany should enable Koreans to realize the importance of building the fundamentals of a peaceful reunification, which can be done through the increase of exchange and cooperation on an economic agenda. A path to regain national homogeneity of Korea must be laid out in tangible progressive steps.

In conjunction with the cost of reunification of the Two Koreas, much has already been paid in the maintenance of the present divided status, and much is still being or yet to be paid. Net gains from the expected economic effects of reunification will far outweigh the cost. Ever since the withdrawal of the American forces from Asia following the declaration of the Guam Doctrine in the 1970s, military spending in South Korea has seen a rapid increase, accounting for 4~6% of the GNP. North Korea spends 20~25% of its GNP in defense expenditures under its present policy. In total, South and North Korea are spending about US$12 billion annually just on direct military expenditures. Furthermore, the Two Koreas are paying countless other costs of division due to ineffective use of land, military draft of the young workforce, and ideological conflicts, not to mention the pain of separated families. Reunification is not just a normative rule, but also necessary for pragmatic reasons.

The existing official plans of the two sides are both products of the Cold War and thus display inevitable limitations. Those plans simply state a present to mid-stage to unification route without presenting details. However, the author presented an alternative five-step unification plan which not only corrects their deficiencies but also copes with recent developments through a preliminary normalization of relations, which then progressively moves on to economic integration, social integration, political integration, and military integration. This author focused on an exposition of the economic issues relative to Korean re-unification. An examination of social, political and military issues involved are also important and must be independently undertaken.

North Korea is well aware of internal conflicts that may result following the execution of ambivalent policies such as the hermit policy of 'Socialism Our Way' on one hand and enactment of laws and institutions systems to attract foreign capital and technology on the other. North Korea had devised 'hyper belt-tightening' fiscal plans for the year of 1993 by minimizing investment in new facilities and concentrating instead on optimization of production in existing facilities through increased supply of energy and raw materials. It also resorted to using nuclear powers as a morale-booster for its labor and thus as a means for elevating production. However, the final results were grim. Production fell due to decline in raw material sources such as coal mines and the metalworking industry.

North Korea's economic crisis can be traced primarily to its socialist system of planned economy. In addition, much of the crisis can be attributed to the following characteristics unique to the North Korean system:

1. insistence on a closed self-sufficient economy,
2. the burden of excessive military spendings
3. lack of direction in policies,
4. unrealistic establishment of large-scale enterprises, and
5. the breakdown of the external economic relations.

In particular, estranged relations with the former Soviet Union, which had provided North Korea with continued aid for economic and technological development, has dealt the North Korean economy a big blow.

From an economic point of view, it would be desirable for North Korea to succeed in its Chinese-style economic reforms, and for the process of reunification to progress slowly and gradually. However, there is a possibility, as was the case with Germany, that South Korea would have to take charge of the North Korean economy.

Under such circumstances, it would be helpful for Korea to refer to the policies adopted by Germany in regard to the integration of currency, the process of integration of the economy, and the issue of property ownership.

First, for the integration of currency, the exchange rate should be thoroughly based on the real economic value of both currencies. Because Germany allowed the free movement of its citizens, the integration of currency and rise in wages at a 100% ratio was inevitable. For Korea, the South should find investment to the Northern regions economically profitable, matching their investment with the availability of labor forces in the North. This must not be an open invitation for a southward movement of North Korean residents, which would imbalance the process. Provision of investment subsides, various tax reductions, and massive investments of social overhead capital need to be reviewed in order to achieve this.

Second, in the process of integration of the economy, North Korea's absorption into the capitalist market economic system must be a necessary precondition, irrespective of what form of reunification may finally take place. It has been proven that the capitalist economic system is superior to that of the socialist economic system, and North Korea will have little choice but to accept reforms, as has recently been the case in China.

Third, in regard to the issue of property ownership during the process of social integration, the following course of action is recommended. The government of united Korea should not make refunds or compensation to the original owner, but rent or sell the real estate after making it the property of the state, and thus generate funds for reunification. Following Germany's policy of returning seized real estate would become a big barrier for investment in North Korea. As the legal ownership of real estate becomes unclear, there is a tendency for investors from the South to shy away from taking charge of national corporations in the North.

Finally, it must be stressed that South Koreans must make continuous efforts in the preparation for reunification. These include: the formation of a highly scientific, technological resource pool; the development of an independent economic structure; and the establishment of a developed democratic welfare society. Successes in such areas will definitely change North Korea's attitudes toward the South, and provide a basis for the cooperative pursuit of reunification. As evidenced in the discussion of the unification experiences of Germany and Yemen, many difficulties had to be overcome until a unified state was established. In the case of Germany, while it is true that there was the external development of a realignment in the international order following Gorbachev's pursuit of a new ideology and the ensuing collapse of the Soviet Union, it cannot be denied that internal factors such as the formation of a strong economic basis and the buildup of mutual trust and national identity based on continued exchanges and cooperation with East Germany finally paid off in one historic moment.

ROLE OF KOREA IN THE ASIA-PACIFIC AGE

The Age of the Atlantic is declining, while an Age of the Pacific Rim is on the rise. The Asia-Pacific area, especially the East Asian area, recorded an unprecedented high growth rate during the past twenty years. The population, resources, productivity and trade volume of the world is concentrated in this region, which accounts for 54% of world GNP, 40% of global trade volume and 36% of the earth's population. Trade with countries in this region also accounts for 68.9% of Korea's exports and 68.6% of its imports. The national interests of the US have shifted from Europe to Asia, Japan has sought a policy of 'returning to Asia' from its past 'escape from Asia', while China and Russia have also been stressing the importance of Asia - the former as the historical center of Asia, and the latter as a part of its New Pacific Strategy.

The high growth rate of exports in the region has brought about a rapid increase in trade, and as a result, interdependency in trade among the region's economies is very high, and has recently surpassed the rate of the EC. Active investment in the Asian-Pacific area has also contributed to such interdependence. Globally, the region accounts for 54% of the world's GNP, 40% of global trade volume. and 36% of its population.

International order is being reorganized into a practical one which emphasizes the economic development and prosperity of individual nations following the weakening of the East-West ideological confrontation.

In connection with one of the previously-mentioned national choices for Korea in the 21st century: Korean must take a leading role in the upcoming Asia- Pacific Age. At the same time, it must become a center for the solution and promotion of North-South problems and cooperation related to Japan, the newly industrialized countries, and the ASEAN countries which concern the region.

The national interests of such global powers as the United States, Japan, China, and Russia are also related to this region. The Korean Peninsula has historically been a bridge between the Pacific and Europe and a region where the mercantile marine powers (the US and Japan) meet the continental powers (Russia and China). Moreover, it remains one of the few regions in the world where traces of the Cold War can still be found.

The role of Korea as it faces this global historical trend is thus very significant. The role of Korea from an economic standpoint is to help alleviate the North-South problem within the Asia-pacific region, which has in it a wide range of nations at various stages of development. The technology gap between countries in this region is also large. As an intermediate nation in these respects, Korea will be able to promote the transfer of technology and movement of resources within the Rim. From an international political standpoint, Korea's role will be to help establish a peaceful harmony among the countries in the region.

The common goal of the Asia-Pacific nations is to cope together with the intensifying trend of regionalization in the world and to establish a multilateral trade order. Through regional cooperation, they are planning on working to resolve major issues such as trade imbalance, problems from investment and transfer of technology, and gaps in the development level of member countries.

For the increase of economic cooperation of the Asia-Pacific area, the role of the APEC should be emphasized because it can prevent the bisection of Asia-Pacific area into the two regions of the Americas and East Asia, and can play the role of connecting them together.

Korea has been able to uplift its political and diplomatic position through the development process of APEC, through such efforts as helping to resolve the problem of simultaneous entry of the 'three China's'. For the successful development of APEC, cooperation must be achieved in an environment where the diversity of the Asia-Pacific nations is respected, and Korea, in its capacity as a semi- developed nation, and in a unique position in terms of balance of power, can perform the role of balancing the interests of the developing and developed countries.

Through the APEC, Korea will be able to cope with the world wide trend of regionalism and accelerate the establishment of a multilateral trade order. It will be able to strengthen cooperative relations with the Asia-Pacific economies, which have strong ties. Korea should actively support and take advantage of the liberalization of intra-regional trade and investment to attract capital and induce the transfer of technology necessary for the adjustment of the industrial structure.

Korea can gain real economic profits from the APEC. The US, Japan, and the ASEAN, which comprise the most important center of Korea's overseas trade activities, all belong to the APEC. China, with which close ties are expected to be formed, will also be a member of the APEC community. The activation of the community of the APEC will contribute to an increase in Korea's exports. The strengthening of ties among the regional nations, with the APEC as the source of cooperation, will stimulate stable and continuous growth in the Asia-Pacific region, and thus provide a trade environment beneficial to Korea.

Furthermore, the political and security role of the APEC is also directly connected to Korea's national interests. Collective security would suppress possibilities of regional conflict, and contribute to political stability in the region. In the particular case of the Korean peninsula, where real threats from North Korea still exist, the APEC's political role could prove to be of critical importance.

The point worth nothing here is that among the countries in Northeast Asia, China, Korea and Japan have been historically closely tied politically, economically, racially and even culturally. Because of geographical proximity, ancient China, Korea and Japan influenced one another. Korea and Japan accepted culture from China which was culturally more advanced, and thus the three formed a cultural bloc. Korea's role was as a cultural bridge between China and Japan.

After the 19th century, the balance of power in Asia became fragile due to Japan's expansionism and China's switch to Communism. The people of China, Korea, and Japan still had some similarities in that they belonged to the same cultural regime, and Korea acted as a bridge between China and Japan and enabled the spread of Chinese culture to other areas

Last, a look at the history of these three countries shows that they are ethnically, culturally, politically, and economically closely linked. The people of these three regions have mutually migrated due to geographic proximity, and Korea and Japan assimilated the advanced culture of ancient China to form the Northeast Asia cultural zone. The formation of this zone was largely made possible by the role of Korea as a go-between.

In recent times, the balance in the region has been broken due to Japan's excessive expansion and divergence away from Asia. Exchanges with China were effectively severed for a half century due to ideological differences. The people of the three countries, however, have similar appearances and share common values based on the shared usage of Chinese characters. A big reason the three countries could share historical and cultural heritage while maintaining distinct characteristics was that Korea served as a cultural go-between and/or acted as a military buffer zone.

Despite this fact, many Japanese have contempt for Korea as a past colony. Koreans thus have reservations about Japan as 'a geographically close but distant country'. Many Chinese regard Korea as 'a marginal country which used to provide tributes', leading Koreans to think of Chinese as 'close relatives when relations are good, but very distant relatives when relations are bad'.

Also, China still leans toward China-centered ideology. This is unfortunate since it is time to cooperate to catch up with the 21st century by unifying and cooperating in many fields to help Asia prosper. In an age of globalism when countries will become interdependent. Therefore, the three countries should work together towards a common goals such as the development of technology, one of the reasons why many Asian countries have fallen behind and even become a 'colonies' to Western countries.

If China, Korea and Japan remain obsessed with the past and continue to emphasize their national pride, then they will all have difficulties in responding to the global changes of the 21st century. While the Cold War has ended, friction and conflicts due to ethnic or regional interests will continue to exist.

If the three countries of the Northeast Asia cannot exercise some unity, it will fall behind in the global community. If the three cooperate to combine their abilities and capabilities, then they will be able to lead in the global community.

In conjunction with the previously-described role of Korea in the Asia-Pacific era, the author would like to introduce a poem, 'Light of the East' of Rabindranath Tagore (1868~1941)[187] .

"In the golden age of Asia,
Korea was one of its lamp-bearers.
And that is waiting to be lighted once again
For the illumination of the East"

With Tagore, the author would like to submit that 'lamp' shall be lighted once again, depending upon the efforts of Korean people and a favorable change in the external situation.

[187] He was the first Asian to receive the Nobel prize for literature in 1913 and recited the poem (the last part of *Gitanzali*) on his third visit to Japan in 1929, according to the request of some Korean youth to visit Korea on the occasion of the tenth anniversary of the "First March Movement" against the Japanese colonialism.

If the desire of Korean people is pure and earnest, their will and efforts for its achievement should be sincere. Korean people should look back on the past with modesty and learn from it, because a close look at the past reveals the visions for the future. This is why the history of mankind is a story of endless progress.

MAJOR REFERENCES

Chang, Hong-ki, Lee, Ryang and Lee, Man-Jong, *A Study on Military Integration between North and South Korea,* Seoul: Korea Institute for National Defense, 1994.

Chang, Myong Bong, "Research on the Unification Constitution of North-South Yemen," *Research on Public Law*, No. 21, 1993.

Hong, Sung-Duk, *Source of Economic Growth in Korea (1963~1992)*, Seoul: Korea Development Institute, 1994.

Hong, Wontak, "Export Oriented Growth of Korea: A Possible Path to Advanced Economy", *International Economic Journal*, Vol. 4, NO. 2, Summer 1990.

Kim, Duk-Choong, "Korean Experience in Economic Development Planning." *Research in Asian Economic Studies*, Vol. 4A, JAI Press, Inc., 1992.

Klein, Eckart, "Free Cities", *Encyclopedia of Public International Law*, Vol. 10, 1987.

Klein, John J. and Lim, Yang-Taek, "Econometric Study on the Technology Gap between Korea and Japan: the general machinery and electric & electronic industries", *Technology Forecasting and Social Changes*, Vol. 55, No. 3, 1997.

Lim, Yang-Taek, *A Study on Korea's Technological Dependence: with respect to Technology Transfer from Japan and Technology Diffusion in the Korean Machinery Industry,* Seoul: Korea Ministry of Science and Technology, November 1986.

----------------, "A Model of Technology Transfer from Japan to Korea", The Korean International Economic Association, Seoul, Korea, December 1986.

----------------, "A Study on the Speed of Technological Diffusion in the Korean Manufacturing Sector," paper presented at Korea Academic Association of Technology and Economics, Seoul, January 1987.

----------------, "An Analysis of the Effects of Strategical Variables on the Speeds of Technological Progress and Imitation in the Korean Manufacturing Sector," paper presented at Korean Economic Association, Seoul, Korea, February 1987.

----------------, "A Study on Intra and Inter Industry Technological Diffusion", The Korean Society for Technology, Management & Economics, *Research Paper,* No. 1, December 1987.

----------------, *A Study on the Technological Innovation of Korean Machinery* Sector, Seoul: Korea Economic Research Institute, No. 48, April 1988.

----------------, *A Study on the Determinants of Industrial Concentration and Optimal Firm Size,* Seoul: Korea Economic Research Institute, No. 62, March 1989.

----------------, "An Empirical Study on the Technological Transfer from the United States to Korea," *Hanyang Journal of Economic Studies*, Vol. 10, No. 2, Seoul: Hanyang University Institute of Economic Research, 1989.

----------------, "Research on the Development Strategy of a North-South Korea Special Economic Zone and the Selection of an Appropriate Region," paper presented at Korean Academy of Economic Association, Seoul, Korea, February 1990.

----------------, "Cooperation between South Korea and the USSR, *Journal of Far Eastern Studies*, January 1991.

----------------, "Vision for the Korean Economy in the 21st Century and the Counter-measures against the possible Economic Crisis", Seoul: The FKI (Federation of the Korean Industries), January 17, 1991.

----------------, "A Study on the Economic Effect of Measurement Related Investments and the Evaluation of the Measurement Technology Level," *Hanyang Journal of Economic Studies*, Vol. 12, Seoul: Hanyang University Institute of Economic Research, 1991.

----------------, "The Causes of Korea's Economic Crisis and Its Counter-measures", Seoul: Korea Economic Daily Press, September 10, 1991.

----------------, "A Study on a North-south Korea Special Economic Zone", *Economic Studies*, Korean Academy of Economic Association, Seoul, Korea, December 1991.

----------------, "A Study on the Strategies and Anticipated Effects of Economic & logical Cooperations between South Korea and the Soviet Union", *Journal of Behavioral and Social Sciences*, Vol. 42, 1992.

----------------, "A Study on the 3rd Reunification and Economic Cooperation Proposal", paper presented at Korean Academy of Economic Association, Seoul, Korea, February 1992.

----------------, "Step-by-Step Strategies for inter-Korea Economic Exchanges", *Studies on the North Korean Economy*, Vol. 3, June 1992.

----------------, "A Study on the Strategies for the Establishment of the inter-Korea Special Economic Zone", paper presented at Korean Academy of Economic Association, Seoul, Korea, December 1992.

----------------, "A New Proposal for the Korean Reunification with a special emphasis on the Economic Cooperation between North and South Korea as the Crucial Step", *DoSan Collected Papers*, Vol. 3, Seoul: DoSan Academy Institute, August 1993.

----------------, *A New Proposal for the Reunification of Korea based on its Economic Integration,* Seoul: Mail Economic Daily Press, November 1993.

----------------, "An Econometric Study on the Technology Gap between Japan and Korea: the General Machinery and Electric & Electronic Industry", *Economic Development and Technological Progress of Japan and Korea: Their Role in East Asia,* in Proceedings of the Workshop and Seminar, Kobe, Japan, February 17~18, 1994.

----------------, "A New Proposal for the Korean Reunification and Economic Cooperation between North and South Korea", paper presented at the International Symposium Commemorating the 20th Anniversary of the Institute for Sino-Soviet Studies of Hanyang University, Seoul, Korea, September 27~28, 1994.

----------------, *The People Perish Where There Is No Vision,* Seoul: Mail Economic Daily Press, September 1995.

----------------, *Vision and Challenges for Korea in the 21st Century: Toward the Construction of a Reunited Korea,* Seoul: Mail Economic Daily Press, September 1995.

----------------, *How to Utilize DMZ for Korean Reunification,* Seoul: Korea Ministry for Reunification, December 1995.

----------------, "An Econometric Study of Technological Progress, Innovation, Diffusion, Transfer and their Impacts on International Competitiveness: with respect to the Korean Manufacturing (1972~1990)", The Korean Society for Technology, Management & Economics, the 8th Academic COnference, January 30, 1996.

----------------, "Export-led Development Strategy: the Korean Experience for India and South Asia", Paper presented at the International Conference on India's New Economic Policy held by American Committee of Asian Economics at Jawaharlal Nehru University, New Delhi, India, March 11~14, 1996.

----------------, "TRADP and Cooperation among South and North Korea and Russia," paper presented at the International Conference on Socioeconomic Changes and Investment Climate in the Far East of Russia held by The Institute for Sino-Soviet, Hanyang University, Seoul, Korea, April 16~17, 1996.

----------------, "TRADP and Cooperation among South and North Korea and Russia", *Sino-Soviet Affairs,* Vol. 20, No. 2, Seoul: Hanyang University Institute for Sino-Soviet Studies, Summer 1996.

----------------, "The Role of Korea in the Asian Pacific Economic Cooperation: with special emphasis on International Strategic Alliances", paper presented at the Kuala Lumpur, International Conference held by American Committee on Asian Economic Studies, Kuala Lumpur, Malaysia, May 14~19, 1996.

----------------, "Korea's Liberalization Policy Directives and Korea's Weakening Competitiveness", *Journal of Asian* Economics, Vol. 7, No. 4, Winter 1996.

----------------, "A New Proposal for the Reunification of the Two Koreas: Economic Issues", *Journal of Asian Economics*, Vol. 8, No. 4, 1997.

----------------, "The Role of Korea in the Asian Pacific Economic Cooperation", *Research in Asian Economic Studies*, Vol. 8, JAI Press Inc., 1998.

----------------, "The Role of Foreign Direct Investment for Korea's Economic Recovery and Future Directions in Foreign Investment Promotion Policy", paper presented at ACAES-Culalongkorn University International Conference, Bangkok, Thailand, December 16~18, 1998.

----------------, "Visions and Challenges of the Asian Economies in the 21 century", paper presented at the Institute of Developing Economies, Tokyo, Japan, January 29, 1999.

----------------, Prospects *for Asia, Seoul:* Mail Economic Daily Press, January 1999.

----------------, "New Economic Development Strategy for Korea in the 21st Century" paper presented at the 1999 Spring International Conference of Asia Pacific Economic Association (APEA), May 21, 1999.

----------------, "New Technology Development Strategy and Technological Structure of Korean Manufacturing Sector" paper presented at the Hanyang Journal of Economic Studies, Vol. 1, May 1999.

Lim, Yang-Taek, and Song, Chung-Hwan, "An International Comparative Study of Basic Scientific Research Capacity: OECD Countries, Taiwan and Korea", *Technological Forecasting and Social Change*, Vol. 52, January 1996.

Mitrany, David, *A Working Peace System,* London: Royal Institute of World Affairs, 1943.

Radelt, Steven and Sacks, Jeffrey, "Asia's Reemergence", *Foreign Affairs,* No. 4, 1998.

Schumpeter, J. A., *The Theory of Economic Development*, New York: Oxford University Press, 1961.

----------------, *Business Cycle*, New York: McGraw-Hill, 1964.

----------------, *Capitalism, Socialism Democracy*, New York: Harper & Row, Harper Colophon (ed.), 1975.

Song, Byung-Nak, The Rise of the Korean Economy, *Oxford University Press*, 1990.

Stromberg, Ronald N., "Collective Security", Alexander Deconde (ed.), *Encyclopedia of American Foreign Policy*, Vol. I, New York: Charles Scribner's Sons, 1982.

INDEX

D

E

F

G

H

I

N

O

P

Q

R

S

T

U

V

W

X

Y

Z